will upon proof made to their Agent and notice by him, deliver up the wrong doer to the United States, to be tried and punished according to its laws, and in case they willfully refuse so to do, the person injured shall be reimbursed for his loss from the annuities or other moneys due or to become due to them under this or other treaties made with the United States. And the President, on advising with the Commissioner of Indian Affairs, shall prescribe such rules and regulations for ascertaining damages under the provisions of this Article, as in his judgment may be proper, but no one sustaining loss while violating the provisions of this treaty or the laws of the United States shall be reimbursed therefor.

Article II.   The United States agrees that the following district of country to wit: viz, commencing on the east bank of the Missouri river where the forty sixth parallel of north latitude crosses the same, thence along low water mark down said east bank to a point opposite where the northern line of the State of Nebraska strikes the river, thence west across said river and along the northern line of Nebraska to the one hundred and fourth degree of longitude west from Greenwich, thence north on said meridian to a point where the forty sixth parallel of North latitude intercepts the same, thence due east along said parallel to the place of beginning, and in addition thereto all existing reservations on the East bank of said river, shall be and the same is set apart for the absolute and undisturbed use and occupation of the Indians herein named

WHERE WHITE
MEN FEAR TO TREAD

▼▼▼▼▼▼▼▼▼

WHERE WHITE MEN FEAR TO TREAD

▼▼▼▼▼▼▼▼

The Autobiography of
Russell Means

▼▼▼▼▼▼▼▼

Russell Means

with Marvin J. Wolf

St. Martin's Press ⋒ New York

Endpaper art: Original pages from the Fort Laramie Treaty, dated April 29, 1868. *(National Archive).*

Photographs in text, captions and credits:
Frontispiece: Feather Necklace, 1817–1901, Dakota patriot. *(South Dakota Historical Society)*
Part I, page 1: Russell Means's mother holds him up for his first picture, late in 1939, at Pine Ridge. *(Author's Collection)*
Part II, page 103: The first Indians return to claim Alcatraz on March 9, 1964. Russell Means's father, Walter "Hank" Means, is second from the left. Means is just behind him, his face obscured by his dad's warbonnet. *(UPI/Bettmann Archive)*
Part III, page 255: At the siege of Wounded Knee, in March 1973, Oscar Bear Runner became the worldwide symbol of Indian self-determination and sovereignty. *(UPI/Bettmann Archive)*
Part IV, page 395: Russell Means presided over his first sun dance in June 1986 at Gray Buffalo Horn, which whites call Devil's Tower, in Wyoming. *(Courtesy Gloria Means)*

Design by Richard Oriolo

Packaged by General Publishing Group, Inc., Los Angeles.

Library of Congress Cataloging-in-Publication Data

Means, Russell, 1939-
    Where white men fear to tread : the autobiography of Russell Means / Russell Means, with Marvin J. Wolf.
        p. cm.
    ISBN 0-312-13621-8
    1. Means, Russell, 1939- . 2. Oglala Indians—Biography.
3. Indians of North America—Government relations—1934-
4. American Indian Movement. I. Wolf, Marvin J. II. Title.
E99.03M386   1995
305.897'073'092—dc20
[B]   95-23289
                                                             CIP

First Edition: October 1995
10 9 8 7 6 5 4 3 2 1

This book is dedicated to the young people of every American Indian nation. I fervently hope it will inspire them to avoid dwelling on the negative aspects of their lives and to take courage from this proof that good things happen to good people when they persevere.

▼▼▼▼▼▼▼▼▼

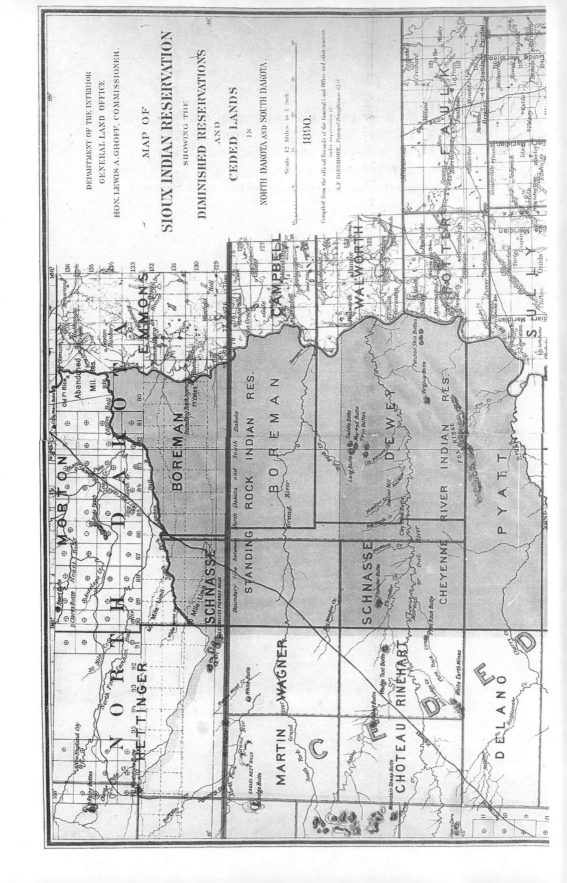

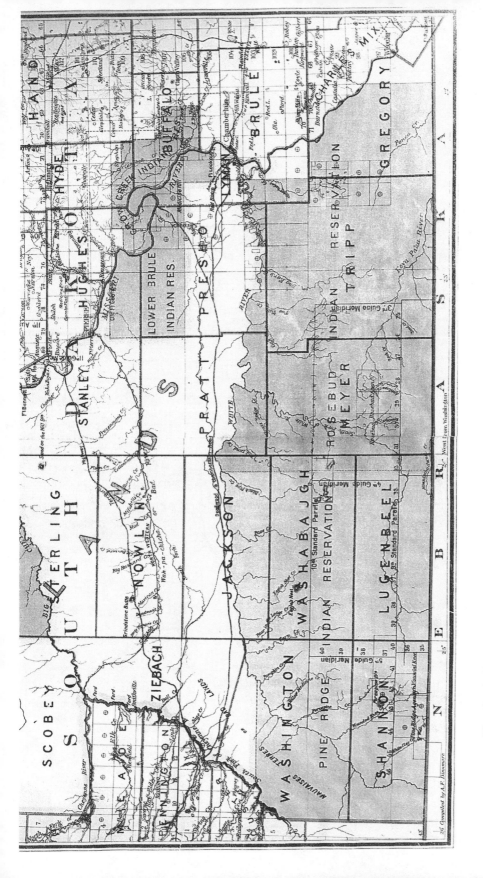

The Great Sioux Indian Reservation in 1890, when the white man had already stolen the Black Hills and much of the land reserved by the Fort Laramie Treaty of 1868. *(National Archive)*

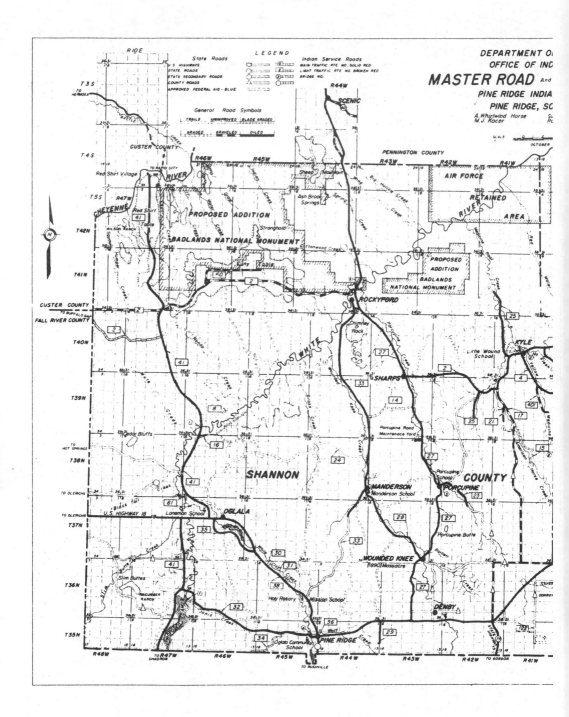

The Big Read Library

Bless Me, Ultima
by Rudolfo Anaya

Fahrenheit 451
by Ray Bradbury

My Ántonia
by Willa Cather

Love Medicine
by Louise Erdrich

The Great Gatsby
by F. Scott Fitzgerald

A Lesson Before Dying
by Ernest J. Gaines

The Maltese Falcon
by Dashiell Hammett

A Farewell to Arms
by Ernest Hemingway

Their Eyes Were Watching God
by Zora Neale Hurston

Washington Square
by Henry James

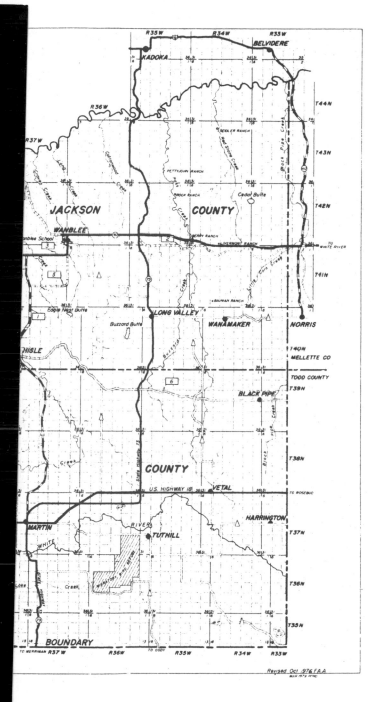

Ridge Indian Reservation as it is now.
(Courtesy U.S. Department of the Interior)

Credo of the
American Indian Movement
▼▼▼▼▼▼▼▼▼

L et me be a free man, free to travel, free to stop, free to work, free to trade where I choose, free to choose my own teachers, free to follow the religion of my fathers, free to talk, think and act for myself—and I will obey every law or submit to the penalty.

—CHIEF JOSEPH OF THE NEZ PERCÉ

Contents
▼▼▼▼▼▼▼▼▼

Acknowledgments   xvii

PART I: GENESIS 1939–1964

Prologue: Feather Necklace   3
1 *Tiyospaye*   9
2 Early Years   23
3 Vallejo   28
4 San Leandro   45
5 Winnebago   51
6 Dealing   56
7 The Irish Pup   66
8 Fatherhood and the "Hustle"   76
9 San Francisco   93

PART II: THE MAKING OF A MILITANT 1964–1973

10 A Second Name: Cío   105
11 Grandpa John and Dad   121
12 The Intertribal Car   130
13 The Rosebud   136
14 Cleveland   141
15 The American Indian Movement   149
16 Handpicked Apples   162
17 *Mayflower II*   174
18 The Sun Dance   179

19 Moses Cleaveland   191

20 Raymond Yellow Thunder   194

21 Red Ribbon Grand Juries   202

22 Schism   208

23 "Works For The People"   213

24 The Trail of Broken Treaties   222

25 Scourge of the Plains   236

26 The Path to Wounded Knee   249

PART III: OUR STRUGGLE 1973–1978

27 The Siege of Wounded Knee   257

28 Hunkering Down   274

29 White Lies   284

30 Waiting for Trial   294

31 The Trial   299

32 Political Theater   311

33 A Government of, by, and for the Liars   322

34 Ordeals by Trials   333

35 The Sioux Falls Massacre   343

36 On Trial for Murder   353

37 Sobriety   364

38 The Longest Walk   374

39 Prison   382

PART IV: REBIRTH 1978–1992

40 Black Hills Alliance   397

41 Tatuye Topa Najinwin   403

42 Yellow Thunder Camp   407

43 Catch The Bear   419

44 *Paha Sapa* Sun Dance   428

45 Fighting among Ourselves   432

46 Larry Flynt   442

47 Gloria   448

48 Nicaragua   459

49 Moonies and Libertarians   477

50 Indian Banana Republics   489

51 The "Outlaw" Navajo Government   499

52 The Movies   510

53 Good-bye, Columbus Day   518

54 Treatment   523

Epilogue   533

Appendix   545

Index   555

A c k n o w l e d g m e n t s
▼▼▼▼▼▼▼▼▼

U ntil my collaborator Marvin Wolf began to examine old newspapers and magazines to confirm dates and the spellings of names and places I hadn't thought about in decades, I believed that my recollections of the events of my life were nearly complete and almost perfect. I knew what had happened to me, and I recalled what had been said to me or by me or in my presence on every occasion I chose to describe in these pages. I also knew what I had never known or had never bothered to remember, and that was what sent Marvin to the libraries. Now I know that although my memory remains very good, age and the passage of time have sometimes played tricks on it. Therefore, although throughout this work my own recollections are the basis of all conversations quoted, many facts and figures presented here appeared in writing elsewhere first.

I am particularly indebted to the reference librarians of the Santa Monica (California) Public Library, who were extremely helpful in borrowing microfilm from libraries around the country, and in suggesting places and ways for Marvin to corroborate facts not easily located.

Attorney Larry Leventhal gave Marvin complete access to his legal files, and provided us with enormous quantities of trial transcripts and other historical documents. Attorneys Ken Tilsen and Bill Kunstler were generous with their time, and shared their individual recollections of events surrounding their roles as defense counsels for Dennis Banks and me during and after Wounded Knee. Other attorneys, including Bruce Ellison and Sid Strange, were kind enough to share their insights, anecdotes, and photos.

Librarians of the Rapid City (South Dakota) Public Library were very accommodating, as was Karen Koka of Nebraska State Historical Society. She shared articles from 1970 editions of the *Gordon* (Nebraska) *Journal* and the *Alliance* (Nebraska) *Times Herald* that their present publishers had refused to make available to Marvin. Very thorough, Karen provided even more articles than we initially requested.

LaVera Rose of South Dakota State Historical Society was especially helpful in obtaining photographs of my ancestors and copies of historical documents. Dale Connelly of the National Archives was patient and accommodating with our requests for photos taken during the Fort Laramie Treaty meetings in 1868. Fred Briggs of NBC News was generous with his time in helping me to obtain the names of those who accompanied him into Wounded Knee in 1973.

ACKNOWLEDGMENTS / xviii

Julie Wheelock swiftly transcribed well over a hundred tape-recorded interviews with commendable accuracy.

I am especially grateful to Murray Fisher, who edited the early drafts of this work, for his penetrating marginal queries which led to countless insights I had not thought to include. Murray introduced me to Quay Hays of General Publishing Group and to my coauthor Marvin Wolf, and was among the first to recognize that the scope and span of my life story might be of interest to a wide audience.

I am most indebted to Robert Weil at St. Martin's Press for his tireless patience and unflagging support. After using his own precious vacation time to edit the manuscript, he fought hard to protect the work's integrity while surmounting the many obstacles, large and small, that inevitably lie between a manuscript and a published book. I want to especially thank St. Martin's Press, from the Chairman Tom McCormack, President Sally Richardson, and Senior Vice President of Sales Michael Pratt to their wonderful staff—Director of Sales Barbara Andrews, John Crutcher, and Mark Kohut, as well as Director of Publicity John Murphy, publicist Kurt Aldag, and two more hard workers, Production Editor Mara Lurie and Assistant Editor Becky Koh. Their extremely warm welcome to their offices made me feel like I had become part of a huge family, and that I was an important part of it.

When I attended the St. Martin's Press spring sales meeting the salespersons continued the same interest and welcoming.

I feel blessed. . . . Thank you all.

Part I
▼▼▼▼▼▼▼

GENESIS

1939–1964

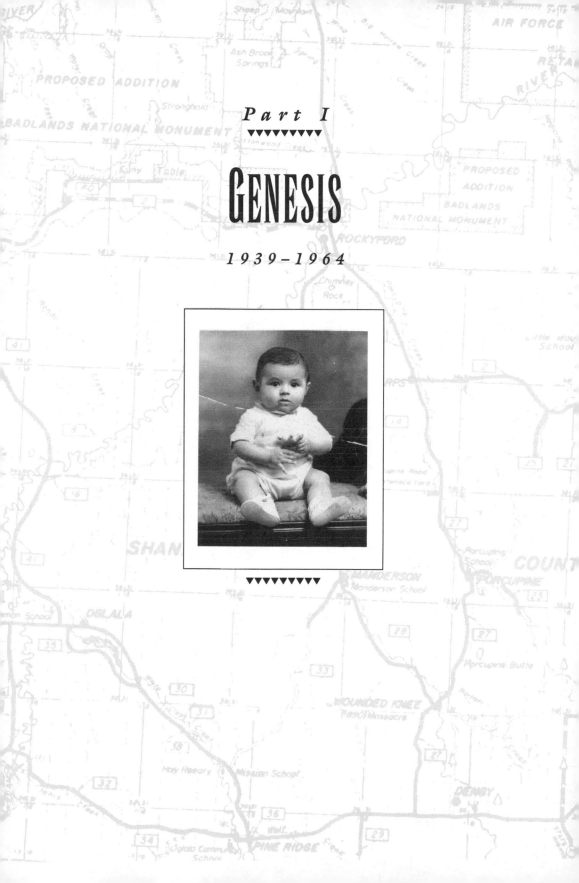

▼▼▼▼▼▼▼▼

Prologue
▼▼▼▼▼▼▼▼▼

Feather Necklace

ome with me now to Greenwood, South Dakota, where in my heart still live the carefree, wondrous days of early childhood. Slip through the rushes and cattails to the water's edge and peer south across the Missouri River to the Nebraska shore, more than a mile distant, where red sandstone bluffs, cloaked with cottonwood and box elder, rise hundreds of feet from the water.

It took a mighty river to cut this deep, wide canyon through the stone. The Missouri *was* a mighty river—until the U.S. Army Corps of Engineers dammed it at Fort Randall, twenty miles upstream, in 1956.

Above that dam today is a long lake where people swim, sail, fish, and otherwise entertain themselves. Below the dam, the river is shallow and languid. Sandbars and islands, once wiped bare by spring's annual deluge, are covered with brush and trees. Many are dotted with small homes and cabins. The river is tame now.

But when I was a boy, the Missouri ran wild and free. My mother's father told me then that in *his* grandfather's time, our people were as free as the Missouri. On a sea of rolling grassland stretching a thousand miles east to west and another thousand north to south, we roamed as we pleased, raising our children, living our lives in total harmony with nature, a sovereign people worshiping *Wakan Tanka*, the Great Mystery, who created everything and put us here to live on our Grandmother, the earth.

My own mother, Theodora Louise Feather, was raised here on the Yankton Sioux Reservation. Greenwood, a river port, was the site of an Office of Indian Affairs (later called Bureau of Indian Affairs) agency, a location selected for its convenience to white officials who preferred to make their way by canoe and steamboat through the roadless Great Plains.

Today, fewer than two dozen families remain in Greenwood, a few in modern double-wide "mobile" homes with satellite dishes in their yards, but most in old trailers or in smallish wood-frame homes. The biggest intact structure is a two-story church of red brick, with an incongruous rooftop battlement turret. The Presbyterian Church was consecrated in 1871; now it is used only for rare community meetings.

The rest of Greenwood is a jumble of abandoned, crumbling dwellings, filled-in foundations, concrete slabs with grass struggling through massive cracks, open spaces with traces of the dwellings that once stood there. The large, circular masonry government buildings—built in a style still seen on reservations because BIA bureaucrats think it suggests our council lodges of old—are nothing more than ruins, roofs long ago collapsed under the weight of winter snow. Green things grow through paneless windows and doorless doors.

Yankton is how whites say *Ihanktonwan*, which means "People of the End Village." By ancient custom, when the nations of the Seven Council Fires assembled in centuries past, their lodges were pitched in an enormous circle, open at the east end. Ihanktonwan tipis always guarded the south side of the entrance to the great encampment, a position of honor.

The grassy, gently rounded prairie hills descend almost to the river, nearly into what remains of Greenwood. Many Ihanktonwan are buried here, their graves unmarked, lost forever in a final, loving embrace with their Grandmother.

You may deny the existence of ghosts or spirits, and I will not quarrel with you. But drop your gaze to this tall grass, raise it again to the vast skies, free all your senses to explore the moment, and it is hard to walk these hills without feeling a presence, *something* that cannot be explained by Eurocentric reasoning.

On a knoll overlooking the river, rising out of chest-high buffalo grass, is a fourteen-foot gray granite obelisk. Its square base stone reads:

TO COMMEMORATE THE TREATY BETWEEN THE UNITED STATES OF AMERICA AND THE YANKTON TRIBE OF SIOUX OR DAKOTA INDIANS. CONCLUDED AT WASHINGTON D.C. APRIL 19, 1858. RATIFIED BY THE SENATE, FEBRUARY 16, 1859.

Whites inscribed this monument. What really happened was that several Ihanktonwan leaders were taken to Washington and kept there in hotel rooms for months under what amounted to house arrest. Finally, penniless, homesick, and confused by whiskey and grand promises, they agreed to cede millions of acres—their ancestral hunting grounds—to the United States, reserving in perpetuity only 430,000 acres for themselves and their descendants. In return, the "Yankton Sioux," as the federal government insists on calling them, were to be paid an annuity, during fifty years, amounting to $1.6 million.

Instead of cash, the government was to supply the equivalent in food, clothing, farm implements, livestock, and other necessities to make the transition from a hunting society to a farming nation. A U.S. agent would oversee distribution of the goods. The government also accepted responsibility for educating and providing health care to the Ihanktonwan.

The President of the United States retained the option of reducing the annuity payments or suspending them entirely if the Yankton population happened to decrease—say, after one of the dozens of smallpox epidemics induced by the President's agents after they distributed blankets infected with the smallpox virus, or if hundreds starved or froze to death because an agent had stolen their treaty goods.

The treaty also provided that payments would continue for the annuity period unless "*said Indians fail to make reasonable and satisfactory efforts to advance and improve their condition, in which case such other provisions shall be made for them as the President and Congress may judge to be suitable and proper*" [emphasis added].

Advance and improve. Other provisions. Suitable and proper. *Genocide*.

The Ihanktonwan treaty delegation was led by Padaniapapi, head of one of the seven councils, or bands, and spokesman for the Ihanktonwan Nation. Padaniapapi was born in a village on the banks of the Missouri about 1804. According to our oral tradition, on the day of his birth the village had visitors—white men with Indian guides who had paddled up the Missouri on their way west, an expedition led by Meriwether Lewis and William Clark. Padaniapapi's father, a headman, proudly displayed his newborn son to the white visitors. Lewis—or perhaps it was Clark—swaddled the infant in an American flag. Seeing him wrapped in the Stars and Stripes, Pierre Dorion, the French fur trader who acted as interpreter—and who doubtless spoke in a spirit of bonhomie—predicted that the child would become a loyal friend of the whites and a leader of his people.

It would have been better for my people if only Dorion's first prophecy had come true.

As an adult, Padaniapapi became a mesmerizing orator who, it was said, could all but hypnotize an audience. His niece, Eagle Woman, married Honoré Picotte, a wealthy French fur trader. In 1858 their son, Charles Picotte, made his own deal with white land speculator J. B. S. Todd, first cousin of Mary Todd Lincoln. Then Charles set out to get the Ihanktonwan to make a treaty with the United States. First he convinced his mother's uncle that a treaty was in the Ihanktonwan's best interests. Padaniapapi then spoke up to persuade his fellow headmen that that was so. When they arrived in Washington, Charles, the only member of the Ihanktonwan treaty delegation who could read English, thoughtfully provided barrels of whiskey to help his fellow delegates think more clearly. Making every effort at the treaty signing to accommodate the U.S. president, Picotte helpfully inscribed the marks of three headmen who had remained behind with their bands along the Missouri.

For his services as "interpreter," the United States gave Charles Picotte a 640-acre section—one square mile—of prime land. Speculator Todd helped him to develop the acreage into the town of Yankton, sixty miles east of Greenwood. Picotte became filthy rich. In public, he often lit cigars with twenty-dollar bills. He was widely admired by white settlers who flocked into South Dakota after the Yankton Treaty. Picotte, however, moved back to the reservation when he was forty-six. He gave away everything he owned to his poorer brethren, lived in the traditional manner of his Indian ancestors, and died a respected man among his mother's people.

The other side of the Greenwood monument baseplate reads:

DELEGATES WHO SIGNED TREATY OF 1858

Charles Picotte	Jumping Thunder
Mazzahetun	Numkalipa
Running Bull	Walking Elk
Standing Elk	Bad Voice Elk
Getanwokapi	Hinhanwicasa

IN MEMORY OF THE YANKTON CHIEFS WHO MADE THE TREATY OF 1858.

Struck by the Ree	Black Bear
Medicine Cow	White Swan
Crazy Bull	Frank DeLoria
Pretty Boy	Feather In The Ear

"Struck by the Ree" was what whites called Padaniapapi. When Padaniapapi was a young man, a Ree (also called Arikara or Padani) Indian had counted coup on his forehead during a skirmish.

"Feather In The Ear"—the proper translation of his name, Wiyaka Napin, is "Feather Necklace"—was one of several headmen. When the other Ihanktonwan leaders departed for Washington, he was off on a buffalo hunt. When Padaniapapi returned from Washington with the treaty, Feather Necklace was among the headmen who met him. Even though they could not read English, Feather Necklace and the others knew a sucker's deal when they heard one. They were outraged at those who had signed the treaty. In a melee between the treaty-making leaders and those who opposed it, Padaniapapi was wounded. More to the point, he was publicly humiliated.

But we are a generous and forgiving people: Padaniapapi maintained his post as spokesman. And we are an honorable people: Even though no proper council had been called to discuss the treaty, our leaders had given their word, and the Ihanktonwan felt bound by it. And we are a peace-loving nation: In 1862, after our Santee brothers in Minnesota were robbed, first of their land and then of the food and other essentials pledged by their own treaty, they were told by arrogant white agents to eat grass—or their own dung. Facing starvation, the Santees rebelled and sent messengers to ask the Ihanktonwan to join them. The Ihanktonwan held out the hand of peace, keeping to their reservation and providing refuge for people fleeing the cavalry and vigilantes who, after the uprising, tried to kill every Indian in Minnesota.

About two years after the 1858 treaty was signed, Dr. Walter Burleigh, the U.S. agent, was caught stealing many of the goods sent in payment of that year's annuity. When Burleigh locked up all the hunting ammunition and refused to discuss the incident, Feather Necklace, along with several headmen and hundreds of people, surrounded the agency building and called for Burleigh to explain his actions. He refused to come out, so the Ihanktonwan gathered incendiaries and made preparations to torch the building. Only the timely arrival of heavily armed troops from Fort Randall saved Burleigh's hide.

In 1869, Feather Necklace led a movement to force John Williamson, a Presbyterian missionary, to leave the reservation. A deeply spiritual man, Feather Necklace spoke his mind in council. If the white religion were allowed to remain on the reservation, he said, the Ihanktonwan religion, which permeated every aspect of daily life, would be in jeopardy. Thus the *tiyospayes*—extended families, the foundation of our culture—also would be in jeopardy. "Let white missionaries live here, and soon they will tell us that everything we believe is wrong," said Feather Necklace. Padaniapapi spoke eloquently on behalf of the missionary, but after everyone had had his say, the council voted to ask Williamson to leave.

Nevertheless, Padaniapapi secretly offered protection to the minister. Williamson remained; the red brick church he built still stands in Greenwood. The Presbyterians were soon followed by Episcopalians, Baptists, Catholics, and several other Christian denominations. Within four years, everything Feather Necklace had predicted had come to pass. For the next 130 years, until the very moment I write these lines, his prescient prophecy has continued to be fulfilled.

The missionaries of the various Christian denominations, each diligently trying to convert Indians to their own beliefs, disagreed over fundamentals of faith, including what the Bible really meant. But every sect wholeheartedly supported the U.S. government's draconian efforts to eradicate Ihanktonwan culture. In 1881, for example, by Office of Indian Affairs fiat, our "keeping of the spirit" and "releasing of the spirit" ceremonies were outlawed. Those rituals began and ended our traditional yearlong way of grieving for the dead, family- and community-oriented rites that nurture Indian cultural values. About six years later, the sun dance—central to our worship of *Wakan Tanka*—was banned. Within a few years, all other sacred ceremonies were forbidden.

Feather Necklace was among the hundreds who died in the smallpox epidemic—the white man's plague—that decimated the Yankton Reservation in 1901. He was eighty-three years old. By that time, the BIA had decreed that like whites, Indians must have single surnames, so on the official rolls, the names of Feather Necklace's children were shortened to Feather. His son, the first John Feather, was my mother's grandfather. The second John Feather was my own grandfather.

So you see, I come from a long line of patriots.

1
▼▼▼▼▼▼▼▼▼

Tiyospaye

Long before whites came to my ancestors' territory, which ranged for millennia from the woodlands of Wisconsin to the mountains and plains of Montana and central Canada, there thrived a grand alliance of blood and kinship called the Seven Council Fires. We called ourselves *Allies*, which translates to Lakota, Nakota, or Dakota, in the closely related dialects spoken by the nations of the Seven Council Fires. My mother, a Yankton, was a Dakota speaker; her people use a *d* sound in place of the *l* sound. When Lakota get together with Nakota or Dakota, we always tease that they speak baby talk.

Our neighbors to the east, the Ojibwa, "discovered" whites—French fur traders—in the early seventeenth century. The Ojibwa told them that the Seven Council Fires—the Teton, four Santee, and two Yankton nations—were called *Nadewisou*, literally, "cutthroats." Since French tongues had trouble wrapping themselves around Indian languages, the French called the Ojibwa "Chippewa" and chopped *Nadewisou* to its last syllable. Because English-speaking whites first heard about the Allies from the French, today the people of the Seven Council Fires are known collectively as Sioux.

The Allies are a matrilineal society. Although my father's heritage was the Oglala band of the Lakota Nation, I was raised mostly among my mother and her people, an extended family of grandparents, aunts, uncles, cousins, and in-laws.

My mother's mother, Mabel Arconge—a relative of Padaniapapi—was born in 1895. Only because my grandmother was both fortunate and brave did she escape a bitter lifetime of slavery.

It happened this way: In 1887, the U.S. Congress, ignoring hundreds of treaties with Indian nations, passed the infamous Dawes Act, now regarded as one of the most notorious pieces of legislation of the nineteenth century. Ostensibly, it was a way to make Indians into "responsible citizens" by giving each as much as 320 acres of land. Of course, it was just another attempt to separate Indians from their land, aimed at eliminating America's "Indian problem" by eliminating America's Indians.

As long as Indian land was owned by Indian nations in common, every member shared in Grandmother Earth's bounty. Despite thieving white agents who diverted our treaty provisions, we usually found enough to eat. Despite devastating lifestyle changes wrought by the near extinction of the buffalo, the Allies continued to live in extended families. Biological warfare, typified by smallpox epidemics, killed thousands of reservation Indians. White missionaries relentlessly assaulted Indian culture.

Despite all that, many aspects of our traditional life were secretly preserved and perpetuated. For about fifteen years, the Allies made good progress in adapting to life on reservations. Populations decimated by disease, massacre, and malnutrition bounded back. The Allies prospered on their reservations, raising more stock animals and harvesting more grain than their white neighbors.

That infuriated the U.S. government. Since 1824, the government of the United States has dealt with Indians through the Bureau of Indian Affairs. It was quite fittingly part of the War Department until 1849, when it was transferred to the newly organized Department of the Interior. Under either, the principal mission of the BIA, although camouflaged in lofty terms, has always been the same—to relocate and/or exterminate Indians.

Because of political considerations, BIA officials have usually preferred the slow, systematic application of cultural genocide to outright murder. When, after a few decades of reservation life, Indians began to adapt themselves to their new circumstances, Indian Affairs bureaucrats asked themselves, What the hell good is it to decimate Indian nations and cheat them out of 95 percent of their land if the survivors can still live well on what's left and still behave like Indians?

So Congress dreamed up the Dawes Act and set out to destroy the Indian nations, then take the rest of their land. One must understand that to an Indian, ownership of land is a foreign concept. The earth is our Grandmother, who provides us with everything we need to survive. How can you *own* your grandmother? How can you *sell* her? How does a piece of paper that you probably can't read prove ownership of something that can't be owned? Even if you're white, and you think you *really* own some land, try skipping property-tax payments for a few years.

Today, we have several Indian reservations, particularly in South Dakota, on which whites "own" much of the best land and which include towns where Indians are rarely seen. Martin, South Dakota, on the Pine Ridge Reservation, is a good example: Martin exists because, after the Dawes Act, when 160-acre parcels were given out, the remaining acreage, generally the best farmland—millions of acres—was opened to white homesteaders.

After Dawes, instead of living among extended families, most Indians were settled on small parcels of land. Many, however, never got legal title to this land and eventually lost it, often with the connivance of corrupt local government officials. Other Indians, without money to buy implements, livestock, and seed, leased their parcels to whites.

After most of the "free" homestead land was gone, whites swarmed onto reservations, advancing all sorts of schemes to take those parcels away from Indians. Some even married impoverished Indian women—few of whom could speak, read, or understand English—just to get the land.

A Frenchman named LaPlante came to the Cheyenne River Reservation in the 1880s, where my grandmother Mabel Arconge's parents lived. He arranged to marry both Mabel, who was still in her teens, and her older sister. LaPlante worked the girls like slaves, forcing them to tan hides by day and do beadwork by candlelight. Mabel ran off at the first chance. Some kind people smuggled her off the reservation and arranged her marriage to John Feather, my grandfather. He was living in the Choteau Creek area near Greenwood and serving as an apprentice to his older brother, a respected medicine man.

My grandparents raised most of their own food and lived in a very traditional way. They kept their allotment land for many years, leasing some to whites but retaining enough to plant acres of corn and a huge vegetable garden. They also raised livestock and several horses. John Feather was a good barber, an excellent carpenter, and a competent housepainter. Then, as a comparatively young man, he was trapped in a blizzard. Because of frostbite, he lost most of his fingers down to the first knuckle. That ended his barbering, carpentering, and painting. From then on, Grandpa John got by doing odd jobs around the community.

In summer, Grandpa John hauled barrels of water by wagon from the Missouri River to many of Greenwood's houses. In late winter, he cut thick blocks of ice from the frozen river and hauled them back to his root cellar. Before the last of the ice had melted, it was autumn, and canning season had begun.

Grandpa John was tall, and his hair was coal black to the day he died. Sometimes he seemed gruff: He was the only man I knew who could silence my mother, usually with just a look or a single word. To me, he was always kind and wise, and yet still very much a man's man. Grandpa's hands were rough and callused. I always wanted hands like that.

When Grandma Mabel helped raise her first grandchild, my cousin Darryl Powers, she often sang him the nursery rhyme that began, "Twinkle, twinkle little star . . ." All her grandchildren grew up calling her Grandma Twinkle Star.

For most of my early childhood, I spent my summers with my grandparents in Greenwood. When I was nearly four, Grandpa John took me sixteen miles from his farm to the Indian Health Service hospital in Wagner. As far as I knew then, the reason for the hospital visit was to have my tonsils out. While I was in the hospital recovering from that operation, an Indian Health Service doctor decided I should be circumcised. In those days, they burned the foreskin back: After a few days, the dead skin turned black and they trimmed it off. After that operation, I was put first in the boys' ward with two kids who had impetigo. When the boys went home, the nurses, rather than leave me all alone, put me in with the girls.

A few days later, some nurses and a doctor stood me on a stool in the middle of the girls' ward and, with all the little girls watching, cut off the burned skin around my penis. I don't remember just how I arranged it, but the next day I went in the bathroom and allowed in one girl at a time to look at my penis. First she had to give me a comic book. When the nurse came in, she was angry to discover that outside the bathroom was a long line of little girls holding comic books.

The best part of my Greenwood summers was when Grandpa John took my hand and walked with me for hours along the river or across the prairie. Afterwards, we would go down to the store. Together, we sat on the front steps while I drank icy strawberry soda and munched a bag of salty potato chips. Those were among the most wonderful moments of my life.

What Grandpa John taught me on those walks was the most important part of my childhood. As we ambled through the trees and fields, he carefully pointed out the tracks of various animals and birds, showing me how to distinguish one from another. The tracks of a dog, he said, are usually steady, because the dog is familiar with its territory and knows where it's going. A coyote or a wolf is more wary, stopping frequently to check things out. Domesticated dogs are much like domesticated humans in that their toes are closer together, explained Grandpa, but wolves or coyotes are free, so their toes are open. When we were free Indians, he said, *our* toes were spread apart.

Grandpa John told me about eagles, and he had many stories about wolves and spiders—"*Iktomi*," or Trickster, stories—that had been passed down through the generations to teach the young about life. He showed me the green things growing wild that we could eat, adding to what my grandmas had taught me about rhubarb, dill, wild turnips, and other edible plants.

From Grandpa John, I learned of our tradition that each person receives four names. The first comes at birth, the second during childhood, the third on becoming an adult, and the last as an elder. Each name is given *before* the corresponding time of life, so people have the opportunity to live up to their names. By age five or six, a child will grasp that concept, so everyone from elders down to young children seeks to live up to their names, and in that way our entire society strives to live up to its name.

Although my white name is Russell, my mother also named me Wanbli Ohitika, or Brave Eagle.

It was a good name to live up to.

Grandpa John told endless stories about young men who had opportunities to live up to their names. One day, he said, "There was a young man named Looks Twice—really, he was more like a boy—who left his village alone to hunt, hoping to bring back some meat. He wanted to prove that he was a man. It was in the springtime. He went without a bow or a lance, and he killed a deer with his knife."

"How did he kill the deer, Grandpa?" I interrupted.

"You'd better figure that out," he said. "That's what will make you a man."

He went on with the story. "While Looks Twice was gone, it rained and rained. After killing the deer and butchering it, he returned to his village—only to find that the river had risen. The gentle little creek that he had waded days earlier was swollen as wide as the Missouri. It was raging furiously, with tree limbs hurtling by. There was no way he could get across."

That was the end of the story.

I said, "What do you mean, Grandpa? How did he get back home? Did he get his meat to the village? Did he become a man?"

"You figure it out," said Grandpa.

That was his final word on the story; he never mentioned it again.

Grandpa told me many stories like that. Another went, "A long time ago people were sitting around a campfire. Pretty soon, the men witnessed the miracle of life as a woman began to grow big with child. When the woman gave birth, they watched as she took her newborn baby and fed it at her breast. The baby grew big and strong. Then the men looked at one another."

End of story.

Much later in my life, I realized Grandpa John was teaching me the Indian way of thinking, teaching me to use my imagination, to figure things out for myself, to study, and to analyze. He caused my unformed mind to frame questions—and then search out the answers. He also taught me patience. It took years to figure out some of the questions, but still more years to find the answers.

Grandpa's story about the woman giving birth haunted me until I was an adult. Now I know he was showing me the power of women, making me think about the respect due to females, about respect for the balance between male and female that is necessary in life.

But what was the meaning of the story of Looks Twice, who went to hunt alone to prove his manhood? Because it was spring, when the rains always came, he should have consulted with elders about the weather before leaving. He should have known better than to cross a river without planning a route back during a flood. In his haste to prove that he was indeed a man, he acted like a boy—impetuously. Although he stalked and killed a deer, Looks Twice failed to live up to his name.

It seems to me that the ultimate lesson in that story is how insignificant human beings are. Although we are able to kill a deer, we are nothing when compared with nature's power. It was Grandpa's gift that I would value this wisdom far more because I had found it myself.

Grandpa John also taught me to *feel* things, to instill *wisdom* instead of merely *knowledge*. In that way, during my childhood, I came to *feel* the Indians' love for our Grandmother, the earth.

In the linear, mathematical way of the Eurocentric male society that has long dominated America, that doesn't work. One is expected to *know* things, to *believe* things. Knowing and believing are all in your head—there is nothing in your heart. If you cannot *feel* that the earth is your Grandmother, then of course you will find it easy to rape her, to behave as though she is under your dominion. You will find it easy to believe that we humans are the dominant species, and to act as though the earth and everything on it are ours to do with as we please.

That is not so.

For millennia, we Indians lived as part of the earth. We were part of the prairies and the forests and the mountains. We knew every blade of grass, every plant, every tree. We knew the winds and the clouds, the rivers and the lakes. We knew every one of the creatures that fly and crawl and burrow and run and swim—all our relatives with whom we share this earth. We are part of the earth, but not the most important part.

We knew the universe and how it includes and interacts with our Grandmother. Before I was six years old, my grandparents and my mother had taught me that if all the green things that grow were taken from the earth, there could be no life. If all the four-legged creatures were taken from the earth, there could be no life. If all the winged creatures were taken from the earth, there could be no life. If all our relatives who crawl and swim and live within the earth were taken away, there could be no life. But if all the human beings were taken away, life on earth would flourish.

That is how insignificant we are.

Walking across the rolling hills or strolling along the mighty Missouri, I

listened to Grandpa John as he explained all that to me. As I grew up, I realized that the Great Mystery had given us everything we need, a heaven here on earth. For an Indian, even the desert is a paradise, with an abundance of things to eat and drink. So it is also in the forest, in the mountains, in the Arctic. Wherever there is life, the Great Mystery has provided everything required to sustain it.

Although Grandpa John was very traditional in his ways, my mother, Grandma Twinkle Star, and Great-aunt Agnes Frederick, whom we called Grandma Aggie, were fervent, devout Christians. However, they knew and showed enormous respect for Indian ways.

Grandma Twinkle Star was a storyteller, too. Although her tales were very different from Grandpa John's, they had the same purpose—to teach me the ways of our people so that I would learn to become a man. She told me about the old days, what our people had accomplished, what her father, uncles, and grandfathers had done to become men.

Once she told me about a young man who had been hunting and got into a fight with white fur trappers who sliced his stomach open. Thinking he would die soon, the trappers spoke among themselves. They supposed other villagers would soon find the hunter's body, then track them down. So, leaving the young man for dead, they set out to find the village and kill everyone in it.

But the wounded hunter refused to die. Without a horse, he had to run, clasping his belly to keep his intestines in. He knew a shortcut to the village, but as he ran, he got weaker and weaker. Despite his efforts, as he ran, his guts began to come out. There was nothing he could do: By the time he got to the village to sound a warning, his whole intestine was dragging along the ground. He died, but not before alerting the villagers, who drove off the white attackers.

Grandma Twinkle Star also told me something she had heard from her own mother and father: At the U.S. Seventh Cavalry's "sensitivity training" session along the banks of the Greasy Grass River in 1876—which whites call the Battle of the Little Bighorn—George Armstrong Custer was *not* killed in battle. He took his own life, as did many of the soldiers in his command.

It happened in this way, Grandma Twinkle Star explained. Custer was well known among the members of the Allies encamped along the Greasy Grass. They hated him, but he was not a foe worthy of respect. Custer had built his reputation among whites as an "Indian fighter," with sneak attacks on villages of women, old men, and babies. He was a butcher, not a soldier. Among the Allies and the Cheyenne and Arapaho, he was considered a dishonorable man. When he foolishly attacked what he thought were defenseless Lakota encampments near the Greasy Grass, he suddenly found himself facing armed men.

Custer must have been shocked, because he knew that unlike Europeans, Indians kept no standing armies. Before the whites came, our conflicts were brief and often almost bloodless, resembling far more a modern professional football game than the lethal annihilations of European conquest. My ancestors found honor in striking an enemy with a hand or a stick, not in killing him. This we called "counting coup."

Many of Custer's men were raw recruits, Irish or Polish immigrants with little military training. Quite a few could barely speak English. Many had been drinking. When the Lakota assembled to defend themselves and their families, many of the whites, perhaps fearing the torture or mutilation that cavalrymen had so often inflicted on Indian victims, took their own lives.

No self-respecting Lakota wanted the dishonor of killing a maggot such as Custer. (I apologize here for insulting maggots, because they, too, were put here by the Great Mystery, and so have a purpose and a role in life.) The Lakota were going to let Custer go, let him return to his people and suffer the lifetime of shame and humiliation he had earned by murdering women and children.

Dozens of women, most armed only with what they could snatch up from their tipis—tools and cooking implements—ran toward Custer, yelling and screaming for him to run away. Grandma Twinkle Star told me that Custer rode a short way, then stopped, looked back at the swarm of women, put his revolver to his head, and blew his brains out. Because no one wanted to soil his hands with Custer, the Lakota left his body where it lay.

There were no white survivors of the encounter along the Greasy Grass, no white witnesses to Custer's death. When white soldiers recovered his body a few days later, they put the best face they could on what they had found. They said Indians had so respected Custer that to spare a dying man further agony, they had administered a coup de grâce. Out of that same respect, the Lakota had not mutilated his body.

Bull!

Not until I was a grown man did I read white accounts of the Little Bighorn. Grandma Twinkle Star heard the story at the knee of her mother— who had been a child on the banks of the Greasy Grass when *her* mother snatched up a cooking tool and ran to humiliate Custer.

When I was five or six, Grandma Twinkle Star often used a strange word— *anthropologist*. At the time, I didn't know what she was talking about, but she said, more than once, "If an anthropologist comes around asking you about Indian things, don't you say anything. If they insist, then tell them lies."

When I grew up, I learned that that was because summer, on most reservations, is the swarming season for "anthros" from academia, determined

to win government grants and tenure no matter what it costs the Indians. During the last century, anthros have spent many tens of millions of dollars of government money studying "the Indians." If that money had been paid to Indian nations to invest in their future, as *hundreds* of treaties ratified by the U.S. Senate required, most of our problems—disease, unemployment, malnutrition, poor housing, alcoholism, high infant mortality—would not have existed for them to "study."

Our way of life is sacred to us. To show respect to the Great Mystery, many of our ceremonies have always been private, shared only with those who have earned the right to worship with us. That excludes most anthros, whose chief concern, aside from furthering their careers, is to put Indians under a social microscope, to reduce the people whose lives they study to objects instead of treating them as human beings.

My friend Vine Deloria Jr., a lawyer, wrote that in 1954, when Congress debated passage of a law to terminate all Indian treaty rights, no academic came forward to support our struggle against the unconscionable policy. His ancestor DeLoria is among the Ihanktonwan headmen's names listed on the treaty obelisk overlooking the Missouri at Greenwood.

I know comparatively little about my father's family tree. Walter "Hank" Means was an Oglala, a son of one of the seven bands of the Lakota Nation. His great-grandfather broke wild horses into saddle broncs for the U.S. Army. In the Lakota way of naming people, the great-grandfather's name meant something like "Trains His Horses Well," a compliment that got lost when it was mistranslated as "Mean to His Horses." When his son went off to boarding school, the name was arbitrarily shortened to Means.

On the mixed-blood side of my family, my paternal grandmother was an Allen, three-quarters white and one-quarter Oglala Lakota. My father's father, Eugene, who died before I was born, also came from a mixed-blood family. His mother was a "breed," part Crow. My great-grandmother was a full-blooded Crow. At about the turn of the century, Grandpa Gene's uncle, Gus Means, served as an interpreter for the treaty council on the Pine Ridge Reservation in western South Dakota.

My father was born in 1916 at Pine Ridge. His older brothers included Hobart, Wesley, Robert, known as Casey, and Austin. His younger brother was Quentin. Pops also had an identical twin, Johnny. Their sister, Laureen, had a twin who died at birth. Twins run in my mother's family as well: Grandpa John Feather had a twin named Buddy.

Pops was shy and quiet—exactly my opposite. He preferred to remain in the background, although his athletic prowess thrust him to the forefront. Playing guard on the Pine Ridge high school basketball team in 1936, the first year Indians were allowed to compete against whites in S.D., Pine Ridge won the state championship and Pops won a place on the all-state squad. He was also an outstanding shortstop, one of the best-known baseball players ever to come out of Pine Ridge.

Like most reservation Indians of his generation, Pops was taken from his family at age eight and sent to a boarding school hundreds of miles away. The first Indian boarding school had been established in Carlisle, Pennsylvania, in 1879. After that, for more than ninety years, tens of thousands of reservation children were snatched from their families and sent hundreds or even thousands of miles away to be raised in those schools. Because our culture is built around the extended family, boarding schools were an important part of the scheme to destroy our society by eliminating its basic social unit—a plan of cultural genocide that has succeeded brilliantly.

The Allies are matrilineal, so BIA officials insisted that all children live on their *fathers'* reservations. Reservation superintendents decided not only which school children would be sent to, but also if and when they would be allowed to return home. To make sure siblings didn't bond, the officials usually sent the children from one family to different schools, often hundreds of miles apart. If two or more siblings were sent to the same school, great efforts were made to keep them apart. Brothers and sisters were forbidden even to speak to one another. Thus my mother's sister, Auntie Faith, endured many beatings for trying to protect her baby brother from brutal matrons and teachers and from the older boys in a Minnesota boarding school.

Because they attended boarding schools, five or six generations of Indians grew up without getting to know their brothers and sisters, much less their parents, grandparents, cousins, aunts, and uncles. Most of my father's relatives, including his brothers and sister, fled the reservation to survive as families. They were "breeds," and they found it easier to live in the white man's world than to struggle under the oppression of the reservation. Even today, I have many first cousins whom I've never met, children of my father's brothers.

After Pops completed the eighth grade, his father, who worked as an interpreter on the Standing Rock Reservation in North Dakota, was transferred to Pine Ridge. Probably because his father cultivated a little influence with the superintendent, Pops was eventually allowed into Pine Ridge High School, where he could get to know his twin brother. Sometimes one or the other was allowed to come home on weekends.

My mother endured the harsh discipline of the Episcopalian Church at Saint Mary's School for Indian Girls at Springfield, South Dakota, on the Yankton Reservation. Later, she was sent to the BIA-operated high school in Rapid City, hundreds of miles from Greenwood.

Whether run by missionaries seeking to expunge all traces of Indian religion or by BIA bureaucrats with cultural genocide in mind, the boarding schools were much the same. Harsh, military-style discipline was used to break the children's spirits. Each student was assigned a number that was written on everything he or she owned or used, just as in prison. Roll calls were held several times a day, and kids were often called by their numbers instead of their names.

At my father's school, the girls dressed in middy blouses and sailor skirts, with high-top shoes and black stockings. Boys wore army uniforms with neckties, garrison caps, and lace-up leggings over brown boots.

The boarding schools were havens for pedophiles. Generations of Indian children—boys and girls—endured sadistic sexual and psychological violation from perverts, many of them priests or nuns.

I know this is so because my parents and my mother's sisters told me what happened to them. I have also spoken to hundreds of adults who described similar abuse they suffered as children in boarding schools. Senior church and BIA officials were aware of these unspeakable crimes and did nothing to stop them. In fact, school administrators went to great lengths to keep complaints of child abuse from entering official channels. Children were whipped for "making trouble" and were threatened with further beatings, death, or banishment. BIA and church authorities also intimidated parents by threatening loss of health care, welfare stipends—even the loss of their other children through forced adoption.

In the few instances when complaints were on the record, authorities whitewashed the charges and quietly transferred the offenders. This still goes on. In the 1970s, the American Indian Movement led demonstrations to protest brutal molestations at Chillicothe Indian School in Oklahoma and at Todd County High School on the Rosebud Sioux Indian Reservation in Mission, South Dakota. As recently as 1989, when a pedophile was caught white-handed, investigators learned that the BIA knew he had molested children for twenty years at no fewer than fourteen institutions.

Boarding-school discipline was harsh: Speaking any Indian language, failing to flush a toilet, neglecting the rigid dress code, even straying over a chalk line on the playground brought demerits. Every Wednesday night, demerits were cashed in for lashes. Each demerit bought a stinging stroke with a broad leather strap, administered to the bare buttocks by an older student under the watchful gaze of a matron.

I can document punishment far worse than beatings. As recently as the 1970s, boys younger than ten years were handcuffed to basement pipes and left hanging. Others were forced to kneel on sharp stones for hours, or were sprayed with water and forced to stand at attention outdoors in subfreezing weather.

Many children ran away from the schools. Those who got caught were beaten without mercy. Many were then raped. Most were locked in airless cells and held in solitary confinement, forced to subsist on bread-and-water rations, often for weeks or months. Those were the *lucky* ones.

In this century alone, thousands of Indian-boarding-school children simply vanished. Most probably died of exposure, or of hunger or thirst. Some were undoubtedly caught and murdered. To this day, neither the BIA nor any of the churches has ever accounted for those legions of missing children. I know dozens of Indian people who lost a brother, sister, aunt, uncle, or cousin in a boarding school, children who were taken away and never heard from again.

The most notorious of Indian boarding schools was the Intermountain School near Provo, Utah, run by the Mormon Church. Hundreds of Indian children, most of them Navajo, died of exposure trying to escape through the mountains. When I spoke at the University of Utah several years ago, a few Mormon people made a point of telling me how sorry and ashamed they were for what Intermountain had done to Indian children. The Mormon Church itself, however, remains silent on the subject.

In our traditional way of discipline, children were not struck. Until whites took them away, our children were never spanked or beaten. In the boarding schools, Indians were taught to abuse other Indians, a legacy of violence that is now firmly ingrained among Indians on reservations, where incest and child abuse, once unthinkable among my people, are rampant.

Through such beatings and threats, a BIA boarding school took away my father's Lakota language skills, and with them, most of his identity. He also lost much of his hearing: He was often beaten with rubber hoses, several times he was struck in the head, and one day he was rendered deaf in one ear.

After his fortunate transfer to the Pine Ridge school and because of his athletic accomplishments, Pops physically survived his ordeals and became a hero to many Indian people. Widely known on reservations throughout North Dakota and South Dakota, he certainly had his choice of the young ladies.

My mother, after high school, spent two years learning secretarial and business skills at the Haskell Institute in Lawrence, Kansas, and found a job at Pine Ridge. She became the first Indian secretary to a reservation superintendent. I'm sure she got the job only because the superintendent, Ben Rifle, was also an Indian.

Pops was attracted to my mother not only by her beauty but also by her confidence. She was as outgoing and sociable as he was shy and private. Friends introduced them soon after Mom arrived at Pine Ridge in 1936. They married the next year.

Little employment was available on reservations and what there was meant working for the government, so Pops felt fortunate to find a job as a BIA auto mechanic at Pine Ridge.

The only *good* thing Pops got from boarding school was his training in welding and automotive mechanics. He matured into a superb "car doctor," a man who could diagnose mechanical ailments by feel, putting his hand on a transmission or against an engine valve cover and letting the vibrations tell him what was wrong.

Soon after their marriage, my parents decided to start a family. I was born on November 10, 1939, at Pine Ridge. My brother Dace came along in 1941. As Dace and I began to grow up, my parents became anxious to leave the reservation: Not only was life at Pine Ridge rigorous and stultifying, but they also had developed a deep resentment of the BIA's intrusion into virtually every dimension of their lives.

Even today, BIA superintendents have totalitarian control over everyone on the reservations. They can legally force Indians to remain on the reservation or bar them from entering or taking up residence. In practice, the U.S. Bill of Rights does not apply to reservation Indians. We are *not* free to practice our religion. We are *not* free to bear arms. We have no right to be secure in our homes against unreasonable searches, and no right to an impartial jury trial. We have no right to associate freely with anyone we choose. We suffer cruel and unusual punishment all the time.

Because Indians have no rights, we therefore have to take anything and everything the government forces upon us. BIA superintendents dictate policies—rarely consistent from one reservation to the next—bred by racism, indifference, and ineptitude. Every Indian suffers the consequence—poverty, enforced by the might and power of the federal government.

On my home reservation, Pine Ridge, unemployment *today* is more than 80 percent. It wasn't much better in my parents' time. Even those with jobs were—and still are—paid wages so low that to survive, they had to eat "surplus" commodities provided by the U.S. Department of Agriculture.

Being forced to subsist on those surplus foodstuffs underpins yet another dimension of the BIA's genocidal policies—rampant alcoholism. Most of the commodity foods are cheap and filling, bean, flour, and potato products— mostly starch. Starch, of course, turns to sugar as soon as the enzymes in saliva act on it. After months and years of steadily ingesting starch, the human body becomes addicted to sugar. When a pregnant woman is forced to eat that starchy diet, the child growing in her womb also becomes physiologically addicted to sugar. The quickest way to get sugar into the body is through alcohol, since it goes directly into the bloodstream, so when such a child is born, he or she is far more likely to be an alcoholic as an adult.

A high-starch diet also encourages obesity, which brings increased susceptibility to many diseases, including diabetes. Reservation Indians in my parents' time and today suffer from diseases that are practically nonexistent in most of the rest of the country, including tuberculosis and particularly virulent forms of measles.

Indians with severe health problems have no place to go except Indian Health Service facilities. Because Indian people's chronic medical conditions grow out of a policy of genocide, the IHS clinics are deliberately maintained as substandard facilities with antiquated medical equipment and poorly trained staff members. Incredibly, Indians requiring medication are commonly given pharmaceuticals that have been removed from America's consumer-drug supplies because their shelf life has expired. They are not only ineffective, they are dangerous. That is what sick Indians get, because the IHS policy is consistent with BIA objectives.

In my parents' day, housing at Pine Ridge, as on most reservations, was terrible. Most people lived in tumbledown shacks and old log cabins because there was nothing else. Today, reservation housing looks modern, but every unit is built with substandard materials. Plumbing malfunctions routinely. Plasterboard walls crumble. Doors and windows don't open or close properly because government contractors use green lumber, which warps as it dries. In winter, icy wind blows right through the houses.

My parents didn't want their children to grow up under reservation conditions. They didn't want us to live under the BIA's thumb, and they didn't want us to experience the horror of boarding schools. When World War II began, Pops tried to join the army. Because he was deaf in one ear, the military wouldn't take him. Instead, in about the middle of 1942, my mother moved us to Vallejo, California, where my dad found work as a welder in the big navy shipyard on Mare Island.

So thanks to my mother's courage and foresight, I didn't have to grow up as a reservation Indian, cruelly trapped and systematically abused. Instead, I would grow up with many of the opportunities available to white Americans—and I would learn firsthand about American racism.

2

▼▼▼▼▼▼▼▼▼

Early Years

Vallejo's Carquinez Heights presents a breathtaking panorama of San Pablo Bay. The lucky—and mostly wealthy—people who now enjoy those vistas from their exclusive homes didn't live there in 1942, when my family moved into a small two-bedroom house at 444 Winchester. It was on the north side of an enormous low-income federal housing project.

Although racially segregated, it was an attractive place to live. Each unit was a single-story flat-roofed house, painted deep rust-red, with dark wooden skirts joining each home to its neighbors. From a distance, they looked like row after row of little wooden railroad trains. I've never seen anything like that old public housing on Carquinez Heights.

My first recollection of meeting a white person was when I was three, there in Carquinez Heights, when an older boy tried to take my tricycle away. Comparatively few white families lived on our street. On the north end of the projects lived blacks—then called coloreds or Negroes—many Mexicans, lots of Filipinos and Chinese, and one Indian family—the Meanses.

We met plenty of Indians, however. Since World War I, the U.S. military has welcomed Indian cannon fodder. Out of love for the land of our birth, higher percentages of Indians than of any other ethnic group have enlisted whenever the country was threatened. During World War II, men and women from almost every Indian nation passed through the great naval bases and army depots around San Francisco Bay. My parents welcomed all Indians at any time. Word got around, and a steady procession of young men and women, mostly in uniform, came by for a home-cooked meal of fried bread, corn on the cob, stewed rhubarb, and beef stew or perhaps roast turkey— and a few hours of fellowship. It was party time almost every weekend.

When the war ended in 1945, the enormous shipyards laid off tens of thousands of workers. We moved back to South Dakota to live with Grandma Twinkle Star. By that time, she had divorced Grandpa John and married a Yankton man, Raymond Blacksmith. One day he was describing something— it might have been a car he had seen somewhere—and he used the word *snazzy*. That was a new one to us kids. From then on, we all called him Grandpa Snazzy.

We lived in Huron, about 125 miles north of Greenwood. Huron was a farm-belt town, not very big, with grain silos, stockyards, meatpackers, and a few sawmills. We lived on the edge of town, on a hillside with a huge backyard that included an orchard. Behind our house, a narrow path descended to the James River through thickets of wild blackberries. On most evenings, after he returned from his job at the municipal power plant, Grandpa Snazzy took me down to the water. He set out half a dozen bamboo poles, each with a bobber, sinkers, and about twenty hooks baited with worms. Grandpa jammed the poles into the riverbank and left them overnight. In the morning, we went back to check the lines. Usually there were two or three dozen perch and bluegills. On deeper hooks, we often found catfish. We ate a lot of fish and blackberries when I lived in Huron.

Grandma Twinkle Star was always sewing. Mom told me Grandma worked for rich white people, reupholstering sofas and easy chairs. She went right into their homes to do that. For some reason, that really impressed me. Grandma Twinkle Star also did superb beadwork. She became widely known for her art, and wrote a book about Yankton/Sioux beadwork designs for the University of South Dakota. Whenever she showed me something she had made, Grandma pointed out that every item included a tiny, deliberate mistake. "That's the Indian way," she said, explaining that it is to show that nothing is perfect.

By ancient custom, we Indians regard the children of our mother's sisters as our sisters or brothers. *Cousins* are the children of our father's siblings and of our mother's brothers. We do not differentiate between first, second, or third cousins, or even more distant relatives. We are all, together, a single family. To offer proper respect to members of the family, they are addressed not by name but by relationship—Uncle, Auntie, Grandpa, Grandma, Cousin, Friend.

I learned more about that custom when Auntie Faith and her kids came to Grandma Twinkle Star's home for a long visit. It was a fun time. I played with my *sisters* Marilyn, Mabel Ann, and Madonna—Auntie Faith's children. Marilyn was about two years older than I. The others were younger. When we played house, I got to be the daddy. Marilyn, all dolled up in lipstick, tottered around on Auntie Faith's high heels and threw herself into the role of mommy.

Mom had taught me to read and write at age four. At five, after we got to Huron, I was enrolled in school. Because my birthday is in November and I entered first grade at five, I was always a year younger than most kids in my classes. Also, until well into my teens, I was considered small for my age. Because of those two circumstances, I spent many years having to prove that I was just as tough as my classmates.

I attended an all-white school—very few Indians then lived in South Dakota's towns. I remember a redheaded woman, a teacher, telling me, "You know, kid, you're never going to be *anything*. You're going to be just like the rest of them," meaning Indian.

Eventually, I made a few friends. One was a boy named Bobby. When his birthday came around, I wanted to give him a present, but we had no money. Grandma made a little toy drum from a Campbell's tomato soup can. My uncle painted it with Sioux designs and Grandma told me what they meant.

Not long after that, on the school playground, I stood up to a fourth-grader who picked on Bobby and me. He was an enormous kid, much bigger than I was, but I beat him up. Suddenly I was a hero in school, and had many friends to play with. In winter, I went sledding with my new friends down the hill near Grandma's house. It was a great time in my life.

Our house was on a corner of a dead-end street: Passing cars had to turn one way or another. After dark, the headlamps of those turning left swept across our front windows. On Christmas Eve, Mom told all us kids those occasional flashes of light showed that Santa Claus was making his rounds. A little later, my uncle slipped outside and tossed handfuls of coal on the peaked roof. Grandma said it was Santa's reindeer skittering across the shingles. Because Grandma's house had a stovepipe instead of a chimney, Santa was too fat to drop down it, my uncles explained. Instead, he handed our presents through the bedroom window.

So effective was that deception that to this day, my brother Dace claims that when he was three years old, he *saw* Santa Claus and his reindeer-drawn sleigh take off into the night from the snowy street in front of Grandma's house.

In Huron, I first became aware of racism. When some of the kids in my school came down with head lice, I was the first in my class to be inspected—as though *I* had infected everyone else. I burned with shame and embarrassment while the school nurse looked at my scalp through a magnifying glass. She found nothing but hair and skin. More than half my classmates—all white kids—had lice and had to have their heads scrubbed with lye. When I told my mother how I had been singled out, she was steaming.

Racism was not merely limited to the classroom. On my way to school each day, I passed a house with a little towheaded kid, perhaps a year younger than I was, sitting on the front porch as if waiting for me. When I got closer, he ran to the front gate yelling, "Nigger! Nigger!"

Well, I liked that! I didn't know what *nigger* meant. To me, it was that little kid's way of saying hello in some foreign language. When I told Grandma about it, she got hot under the collar.

"That's a dirty word," she said. "A *bad* word. If he says that again, you call him 'white trash.' "

Sure enough, the next morning as I passed by, the kid came running and yelled, "Nigger!"

I stopped and said, "You're white trash!"

His mother came out of the house, boiling mad and screaming, "Get out of here, you nigger! You dirty Indian, don't you *ever* talk to my kid like that! Now run, before I call the police!"

That scared me a little. When I told Grandma, she took me by the hand, walked over there, and talked to that woman for quite a while. I never saw that kid again. I've wondered about him for years. There were no blacks living in Huron then, and few Indians. Where did he learn hate words such as *nigger*? Who taught him?

And why?

When the school year ended in June 1946, we all returned to Greenwood and moved in with Grandma Aggie. Her husband, Henry Frederick, had gone to the spirit world some years before, leaving her alone in one of the grandest homes on the entire Yankton Reservation—surely the largest owned by an Indian. The original house had been a two-room log cabin built by Walter Arconge, Grandma Twinkle Star's grandfather, on a bluff overlooking the town of Greenwood and the Missouri River. Later generations had added a second story, extended the ground floor, and put in a porch supported by tall white pillars. By the time I went to live there, it seemed huge. Upstairs were two bedrooms and downstairs another bedroom, a living room, a large dining room, and a big kitchen.

Behind the house were an outhouse, windmill, barn, granary, woodshed, and smithy. My great-grandfather, Theodore Arconge, who had taught himself the farrier's craft, had earned a living at that smithy, shoeing horses and repairing farm implements. Among Grandma Aggie's chickens, which nested in a large coop, were several banty roosters that fought almost constantly. Dace and I loved to watch them.

Before we returned to Greenwood, Dace and I were told that Mom was going to have another baby. We really wanted a sister. By midsummer, after quite a bit of discussion, we had chosen her name—Judy. When Mom went off to the hospital to bring back our baby sister, we were so excited that we could hardly eat or sleep.

Mom came home a few days after having given birth, on August 9, to twin boys. Dace and I were devastated. She took us aside and explained that when she got to the hospital, there were no little girls left—none at all. To make up for that, Mom had picked out the two best-looking boys and brought them instead.

Well, two good-looking boys instead of one sister—that was all right. We quickly got over our disappointment. Although they are fraternal twins, Mom decided to dress them alike. Until Bill and Ted were almost three, sometimes we could hardly tell them apart.

Grandma Aggie's neighbor, Oscar Bernie, lived down the hill in a one-room shack. Like Grandpa John, he sometimes hauled barrels of water from the river and sold them around town. He had a small boat which he used to carry firewood and wild fruit—blackberries, chokecherries, plums, and grapes—which he gathered on the Nebraska side of the Missouri River. He traded them on the reservation for eggs, milk, home-baked bread, and other produce. Sometimes Oscar took Dace, me, and his own son, whom we called Skin—a kid about my age—for a ride in his boat.

Oscar kept several horses in a pasture next to Grandma's house, and allowed us to ride and play with them. Dace and I called the mare Lady. She had a new colt that summer, and sometimes we would make believe that *we* were her foals, too, dropping to all fours and crawling underneath to reach up and pull out her teats, pretending that we were baby horses feeding.

When the twins were big enough to travel, we returned to California, where the shipyards had begun to hire again. Pops went back to work at Mare Island. He was so skilled with an acetylene torch, so good at making seamless welds in thick steel, that he soon was given the most demanding work—welding submarine hulls. We returned to Carquinez Heights and moved into 465 Winchester, directly across the street from the house we had lived in during the war. Except for summers in South Dakota, when I learned more about Indian ways, I became very much a child of small towns.

3
▼▼▼▼▼▼▼▼

Vallejo

hildren raised in traditional Indian extended families were disciplined not by parents but by grandparents, aunts, and uncles, who gently but firmly corrected youngsters' behavior by talking to them. But most of what my parents had learned about discipline was in boarding school, where they had been beaten regularly, mostly by older kids, and filled with Christian notions about sparing rods and spoiling children. Although one of the reasons our family had left the reservation was to protect my brothers and me from that kind of abuse, Mom nevertheless had been conditioned to use pain and humiliation as a means of enforcing control. Thanks to the brutal traditions of boarding schools, it was the *only* way she knew.

To me, Mom seemed perpetually upset about something—dust in a corner of my room, a dirty window, a chore performed poorly or tardily, "improper" language, telling even the smallest lie, anything that interrupted her routine or disappointed her high expectations of what was correct behavior for children. Sometimes one of my brothers complained about something I did, and that was enough to set her off. Just about every day, I did something to make her angry at me. When Mom got angry, I got a strapping, often for reasons I thought were unfair.

My father never stood up for me, never told Mom not to whip me. In part, I suppose, that was because of his own experiences at boarding school. I now think that Pops deferred to Mom about that, as in almost every family matter, because he had effectually abandoned his role as head of our household.

My parents never could invite people over for a sociable drink or two because my dad, like many people raised on starchy reservation and boarding-school diets, couldn't handle alcohol. He might go six weeks or even six months between drinks, but eventually his craving for sugar proved irresistible. When Pops fell off the wagon, he drank for days until he was totally broke. Then he would come home, sleep for a while, and go back to work. He was such a fine welder that his bosses—civil service bureaucrats at the navy shipyards—tolerated his binges. Pops always had a job to return to.

Because of his drinking, he missed a lot of Christmases, birthday parties, and other family milestones. Each time Pops disappeared, Mom had to scramble around, borrowing from friends, family, and neighbors to keep food on our table and a roof over our heads. I don't remember going hungry, but I do recall more than a few suppers of ketchup soup, or sandwiches of peanut butter and Karo syrup on white bread.

I learned to appreciate food when I was growing up. To this day, when I see people in restaurants leaving uneaten food on their plates to be thrown away, I sometimes want to stand up and shout, to ask them how they can be so disrespectful to that food and to the whole chain—from the stars to Grandmother Earth to the water and the wind, everything that produces food.

Because of my father's binges, when we moved back to California, Mom knew she couldn't depend on him to bring his check home every payday. She found a secretarial job at Travis Air Force Base so we always would have at least her modest wages.

Mom often dispatched me to bring Pops home from the saloons. There I was, a little guy of eight or nine, going into those damn bars and trying to talk an inebriated man into going home. Somehow, I usually succeeded, mostly because I wouldn't go until he went with me. Sometimes he wouldn't leave, but he would give me some money to take home to Mom.

Sometimes I couldn't find Pops. On Christmas Eve, when I was ten, Mom went shopping in San Francisco and Pops agreed to stay home and watch us. Instead, he took off. When it got dark outside, I decided I had to find him and get him to come home. Since I couldn't leave Dace and the twins—they were only three—I took them along with me. We toddled off to each of the bars where Pops usually drank, but he wasn't in any of them. It was late by the time we got to the last tavern. When we found that he wasn't there, I didn't know quite what to do. We just stood around on the sidewalk, hoping he would turn up. Then a police car stopped, and we wound up at juvenile hall. Mom came and got us the next day. All these years later, I wonder what went through her mind when she came home to find an empty house.

Even when drunk, Pops was never aggressive. I can remember only one time when he slapped Mom. When Dace and I rushed to her aid, he immediately backed off. There were only three times in my whole life that he ever laid a hand on me. Once was after my first brush with the police. One Saturday after going to the movies, some older white boys talked Dace and me into climbing a fence into someone's backyard to steal seeds. There were chickens back there, and they raised a racket. The white boys fled when the owners came out, very angry. We barely made it back over the fence. The police came, and Dace and I ran up the hill with a squad car in pursuit. A giant eucalyptus grew next to a wooden picket fence, and I told Dace to hide behind the tree. I was going to crawl under the fence. We might have ditched the cops by going through a yard that led to the next street, but when I ducked behind the tree, Dace, who was only about six, kept running. The cops swooped down and caught him. I couldn't let him go by himself, so I came out and let them bust me, too.

The police drove us home. Just as we got there, Pops came up the path and saw us in the backseat of the black-and-white. He listened quietly while the cops talked to him, and when they released us, he said nothing until we were in the house. Then he said, "Okay, who wants it first?" I figured I would take my whipping and get it over with. We went into the bathroom and he locked the door. Then he started to strap me—and lost his self-control. It was the worst pounding of my childhood. My father beat me until my mother got home from work—a long time later. She heard me screaming, and she pounded on the bathroom door, yelling, "Hank, Hank, that's enough! Leave him alone!" Pops let me go only after he had exhausted himself physically and emotionally. Then, just to be fair, Mom whipped Dace. She whacked his backside twice, he screamed bloody murder, louder than I had, and that was it.

When I was about thirteen or fourteen, Mom told Pops to strap me. I don't remember exactly what I had done, but I think it wasn't much more than mouthing off. When we went into my bedroom, Pops said, "Every time I hit this pillow, scream." He hit the pillow, and I pretended to be hurt. When my mother yelled, "That's enough!" Pops whispered, "Now stay in here and pretend you're crying."

Despite everything, I found much to admire about my father, and I placed him on a very high pedestal. When I was seven or eight, I pinned his high-school sports medals to a piece of velvet. I kept them and all his trophies on my bedroom dresser well into my teen years. Pops passed along not only his genes but his interest in sports. He was also a top-notch dancer—very

smooth and effortlessly graceful, with a wonderful sense of rhythm. I was proud of his skills.

Pops was quiet, but he was a witty man who could find humor in situation. To friends and family, he seemed a lot like Will Rogers. Whene Pops cracked us up, we came away with some new insight, a lesson that carried with us long after we had forgotten the joke.

Pops never felt free to cuss around Mom, but when she was elsewhe and he was driving his car, even with us kids in it, he was far looser. If anybo honked at him he might say, "Oh, blow it out your ass." Sometimes he use words that we never heard otherwise, such as *fuck* or *shit*. We got a big kic out of hearing him cuss.

When the family returned to South Dakota every summer, we always drove. It's all interstate highway now, but in the 1940s and 1950s, we took old U.S. 40 northeast out of California, through Nevada and Utah to Laramie, Wyoming, and then drove into South Dakota. On one of those summer trips, one tire after another went flat in the last forty miles of eastern Nevada. We pulled into Wendover, Utah, just across the Nevada line, on four rims. With no money for a motel, we lived in the car for more than a week while Pops worked as a mechanic to earn money for new tires.

Our family cars were a succession of Chevies, typically from the late 1930s. Thanks to my dad's skills, they always ran perfectly. Rarely did his work on our car meet my mother's standards, however. I was always amazed when, during trips, she told him what was wrong with the car and instructed him to fix it. Pops never replied. He just nodded his head.

I thought it was very odd, for example, that Mom would tell Pops how bad the brakes were and he had gone under the car and fixed them, but they still weren't good enough for her. Then he had to fix them again. Nobody else ever complained about Pops's work. Why, I wondered, did Mom always find fault? That mystery was explained after I became a teenager. One day, after being told to fix the brakes yet again, Pops said, "Usually, when your mother first tells me to fix something, I don't do anything, but I let her think I did. Then she'll always tell me, 'Hank, you didn't do a good job. The brakes feel almost the same. I want you to fix them again.' Then I really *will* fix them. Since I've proved her right, she gets to feel that much happier. The second time's the charm."

If Mom was hard to please, if she had to have things her way, she also liked to laugh and have a good time. For years, she was an avid, knowledgeable—and very vocal—Oakland Oaks fan who often went to Pacific Coast League baseball games by herself. She was, for her time, quite a modern woman. Always very up-to-date and well organized, she had a lot of common sense. Mom also had exceptionally good taste. Although we never had much money and, as a family, never suffered from the white man's disease of lust

for possessions, Mom always managed to dress well and present a good appearance. That may explain my own taste for fine clothes.

Most of all, my mother was dedicated to her boys. Her own parents had divorced when she was an adolescent, and she was determined that her children would not grow up without a father in the house. I'm quite sure it was the only reason she stayed with my father through so many painful years of his alcoholism.

Mother took us on camping trips and on picnics, and she made sure we kept a connection to family by regularly taking us around to visit two of my father's older brothers, who lived in northern California, and her own people back in South Dakota. What we had of extended family life was due entirely to her efforts.

Within Mom's clear limits—that I always tell her where I was going and when I would return; that I was where and when I'd said I would be; that I obeyed her orders to the letter—I was permitted enormous liberty. Since I was looking out for myself and, usually, for my brother Dace, I learned early that responsibility is the price of freedom. I suspect, however, that nowadays no caring, dutiful mother would allow her children as much freedom as I had as a child.

I grew up as part of a threesome—my brother Dace, Sox, and I. Sox, who came into my life not long after my eighth birthday, was the unlikely offspring of a wandering English setter and a pampered, pedigreed Pekingese bitch. He was black, his collar ringed with white, a white blaze down his forehead and chest, a white tip to his tail—and four white socks.

Sox grew to three times his mother's size. Even when challenged by far bigger dogs, he was tough and fearless. He once got flattened in a one-sided brawl with a huge boxer, but he never backed down from any fight and he almost always won. Since Sox would also fight to protect me, he developed a fierce reputation. Rather than pick on me and take the chance of having to deal with a growling, menacing dog, many bullies passed me by.

Sox was very smart. With no training, he decided never to enter a building. If I went into a store, he would wait patiently by the door for me to come out. After I started taking the bus to school every day in junior high, though I never took Sox to the bus stop with me in the morning, he was waiting there when I returned in the afternoon.

Sox won a couple of neighborhood obedience trials, but I refused to teach him to sit up and beg or to roll over, because I thought those were demeaning tricks. Nobody should have to beg. Sox could, on command, climb a playground slide and slide down it. He answered to my whistled summons, and to no other. When I told him to stay, he wouldn't move until I was out of sight. Then he'd run home.

We went everywhere together. When I played baseball or football, Sox sat respectfully on the sidelines and watched. It was as if he knew that humans

had certain things to do and dogs weren't included. I never taught him that, he just knew it.

Most of all, Sox was my best friend. I loved him, and he loved me. Many times, I cried and held him and told him all my troubles. When I was a little kid, he was the only one who ever really listened to me.

Dace had a bike called Betsy; mine was Blackfoot. His was blue and Blackfoot was kind of rust colored, with enormous handlebars. I never saw another set of handlebars like those. We learned how to repair our own bikes, including fixing flat tires by patching inner tubes. Sometimes I borrowed Pops's wrench and turned the handlebars backwards. Or upside down. We lowered them. We raised them. We removed our fenders and rammed kids with nice new Schwinn bikes, kids whose parents worried about getting scratches in the expensive paint. Out with my friends, we'd sometimes ride as many as three or four on a bike, with a kid sitting on the seat behind me, another on the handlebars, and somebody perched on the crossbars. I never knew anyone else to do this until I went to a circus and saw Chinese acrobats. In my glorious childhood, I did many daredevil bike tricks, and we even had bicycle rodeos.

Mom bought us cap guns, but we also made our own toy weapons. We would get her paring knife or Pops's scout knife and carve swords. The ones we liked were the kind from *Arabian Nights*, curved, with a flat blade and nice handles. We didn't like those wimpy, skinny European swords. We made shields from pieces of leather or lids of peach crates. We made slingshots out of scraps of leather and slices cut from old inner tubes, and tested them on the huge windows of Carquinez Heights Elementary School, in Vallejo. Sometimes we made wooden "guns" to shoot giant rubber bands cut from old inner tubes.

When I was a little older but not quite a teen, we amused ourselves once or twice in the early evening by leaving a flaming paper sack of dog shit on someone's porch. We would knock on the door, then hide under the porch. Whoever answered the door would immediately stomp on the bag to put out the fire, and we would hold our sides, laughing.

I suppose now that if *I* had answered my doorbell and found a flaming bag left by neighborhood rowdies, or if *my* son's shiny new bike had been intentionally scratched and bent by another kid, I would call the offender a juvenile delinquent. And that's just what I was. As a bold, mischievous boy, I didn't really feel I was doing bad things. I knew only that at home, I faced oppressive rules, tight restrictions, and relentless beatings. On the streets, playgrounds, and secret places of my youth, I was free.

It would be easy to argue that I ran wild in the streets because I was too tightly controlled at home. But in truth, it's impossible to say how much my actions were shaped by my mother's arbitrary discipline and how much by my own inclinations. If mine was a dysfunctional family, that was a concept that didn't enter my mind until I was well into my adult years. When I was a boy in Vallejo, my mother was my mother, my father was my father, my family was my family—I had no others to compare them with. I remember my childhood as a time of glorious freedom—but I also remember many years of fearing to go home to face yet another beating. The contradictions continue to haunt me.

In spring, we built "coasters" out of scrap lumber, little soapbox cars with rubber buggy wheels. We raced them, lying prone and steering with a two-by-four, down the steep roads leading to Carquinez Heights. Once I sent my brother Ted down to the foot of the hill and told him to signal when the four-way intersection was clear. About halfway down, he started to scream and wave and jump up and down. I knew a car was coming, but I thought I could beat it through the stop signs. The next thing I knew, I woke up in a hospital bed. I had been in a coma for two days. Bandages were over my eyes—my first thought was that I was blind, but I healed quickly, and after several weeks, I recovered completely.

Sometimes we went hiking in the hills on the other side of Highway 40, in pastures filled with grazing cattle and sheep, and in groves of eucalyptus trees. Nothing was more fun than when Dace and I went exploring. We had a thousand adventures on our bikes, ranging widely through Carquinez Heights and Vallejo. A lot of fruit grew wild in California then, and we thought we were really something when we stole strawberries, apricots, and peaches, especially in broad daylight. We thought we were master thieves, and we would brag about it. People weren't so possessive in those days. Looking back, I realize the folks who owned that land *let* us take the fruit. They couldn't have had three or four kids in their trees or crawling through their garden without knowing about it—and yet people very rarely came out to shoo us away.

One of our favorite places to play was called "the Paths." This was a spot among the trees, on a hillside intersected by several footpaths. The paths led from the housing area down to a landing where many of the men went to catch the ferry to their jobs at the Mare Island Naval Shipyard. When I was small, Dace and I often waited at the Paths for Pops to return from work. When we saw him trudging toward us, we ran down the hill as fast as we dared. Pops always had something in his lunch pail for us—a piece of fruit, a cookie or two, maybe a candy bar.

The Paths was a great place to play cowboys and Indians. When *we* played, Dace and I, the Indians always won. Eventually, most of the kids in the neighborhood wanted to play Indians. I always assumed the character of Knife, a warrior. A kid named Johnny Buchanan always wanted to play an Apache. Bobby Loop wanted to be a Mohawk. Of course Dace and I were always Sioux. Sometimes nobody wanted to be the cavalry, so I would say, "You were an Apache last week. This time you have to be cavalry."

As an adult, I share that experience when I speak to Indian youths on reservations. Those kids have nothing comparable and don't realize that white American society still holds racist stereotypes of Indians. It goes back a long way. My childhood, in the 1940s and 1950s, was the heyday of Western movies. The heroes of most of the nine-cent horse operas shown at the Esquire Theatre's Saturday matinées were John Wayne, Randolph Scott, Roy Rogers, and Gene Autry. In almost every movie, the cavalry rode in at the end and killed all the Indians. Hundreds of kids would stomp their feet and yell "Yayyy!" when they heard the bugle, because they knew what was coming.

It made me mad, and Dace simply refused to watch movie Indians getting slaughtered. I tried to force him to look, but he hid his head behind the seats and shut his eyes. When we came out of the movie, the fight was on. We took on all comers—whites, blacks, Mexicans, Filipinos, Chinese. They would shout, "There's those Indians! Come on, you guys!" My brother and I would go back-to-back and take on all comers. Walking home, the other kids would often try to ambush us, so we took roundabout routes. Even so, they sometimes jumped us and we had to fight our way home.

With no older brothers to protect me, I grew up fighting. My special nemesis was Junior Harris, a year older and a head taller than me. His older brother, Bobby, was a nice kid who delivered newspapers. When Bobby was around, Junior would mind his manners, but when he wasn't, Junior would come after me. We fought practically every day after school. When I knew him, Junior rarely picked on other kids, because they either ran away or gave him what he wanted. I never avoided a fight with him. I was scared to death, of course, but I just wouldn't admit it. He would pound me. He would give me bloody noses and fat lips.

I don't know what became of Junior. I'd like to run into him some day. I'll bet he isn't bigger than I am now.

Whenever I came home from a fight with Junior, all beat up, I got a strapping from my mother. That hurt, both physically and in ways I wouldn't begin to understand for decades. Junior was just a big bully. He wasn't supposed to love me. But my mother was my *mother*. Although Mom gave me a lot, she tore me up a lot, too.

In those early years, my mother took Dace and me everywhere, expanding our horizons beyond the schoolyard and the streets. Once she took us to a museum to see an exhibition of paintings by a man with no arms. The artist was there, and I was astonished and impressed to watch him painting with his feet, grasping a brush between his toes. When I expressed my wonder at that, Mom took me to a tree where a bird was building a nest. "Watch the bird for a while," she said, and went home.

At that moment, I could think of nothing more boring than watching a bird, but my mother was not to be disobeyed. I watched and watched. Soon I began to understand. Here was a bird, which had no arms—let alone hands or fingers. Yet with infinite patience and unending labor, it used its beak to scavenge one twig, one blade of grass, one leaf at a time, then weave it all into a sturdy nest. Fascinated, I went back to watch that bird in that tree for days.

Aided by my mother's insightful suggestions, I came to know that there was far more to the world than Carquinez Heights. Also guided by my mother, from a very early age I read voraciously. I started with comics— Superman, Batman, the Green Hornet, Captain Marvel—all the superheroes. I graduated to library books, reading anything I could find about sports heroes—Babe Ruth, Ty Cobb, Honus Wagner, Rabbit Maranville. I also loved to read about nature and, of course, anything about Indians.

My first teacher at Carquinez Heights Elementary was Mrs. Fox. She was a little woman, fairly young and very pleasant. Soon after joining her class, I was asked to do some addition at the blackboard. I hadn't learned that yet, so I just put down gibberish. The kids made fun of me until Mrs. Fox called me up to the blackboard and told me to write my name and a sentence. Somehow she knew that although all those second-graders were still struggling with block letters, I had learned to write longhand. I wrote something and Mrs. Fox said, "See, he can *write*. None of *you* has learned that yet." That made me feel good. Mrs. Fox was a great educator who knew that it's not good for kids to be shamed. Once I knew I was as smart as my classmates, I got along much better.

My fifth-grade teacher was Mrs. McDonald. When I tried out for chorus, she said, "You can't carry a tune, and you're ruining it for everybody. You should not try to sing." Until then I'd always sung in church and really liked it, but after she ridiculed my voice in front of everybody, I never sang again. Mrs. McDonald used to make fun of my handwriting, too. I really hated her.

The summer before I started seventh grade at Franklin Junior High, we moved a mile and a half, from the mostly black north side of Carquinez Heights, to 335 Madison, on the south side, where there were no black families. One day that year I got into it with Robert Reed, a black kid. We had been rivals for years. Robert was the fastest kid in school, an outstanding athlete, but kind of a bully. We'd had pushing and shoving matches many times in grade school, but we never fought because my friend, Ellis Kinder, wouldn't let him. Ellis was bigger than me and about a year older. When we hung out to shoot marbles in the black section of Carquinez Heights, he kept a lot of bullies off me.

Ellis wasn't around when Robert and I came to blows in the gym. When a coach broke it up and took us into the office, Robert said, "He called me black." Back then, calling someone "black" was considered an insult—but I never said it. In fact, as the school's lone Indian, I was probably the last kid who would say something racist. Thinking about it now, I'm sad for Robert. The way white society treats black people, it's no surprise that young men took "black" as an epithet. No surprise that a decade later, when his generation had grown to adulthood, they set out to make "black" beautiful.

I'm happy to report that when Robert Reed grew up, he had a good career in the National Football League as a defensive back for the San Francisco Forty-Niners.

In junior high my best friends were white kids, Ronald Cowles and Larry Harrod. I was also "tight" with the Milkie boys, Ronnie, Donny, Bobby, and Timmy. Like the Milkies and my other close friends, I was very shy around girls. Dace didn't have that problem. When he entered seventh grade, two years later than I did, right away he started going with a very dark and good-looking Polynesian girl named Paulette. Once she threw a party and asked Dace to bring me along. There I was, a ninth-grader going to a seventh-grade party and feeling like an idiot because I'd never been around girls. At the party, in her parents' garage, we ate chips and ice cream and danced to records. When it got dark, they pulled down the garage door and put on the lights. When Paulette's parents went in the house to watch television, someone turned out the lights for fifteen or twenty seconds. I was standing in the dark with no idea what was going on when someone grabbed me and kissed me. It scared the hell out of me—I didn't know if it was a guy or a girl, so I pushed away and started to spit. And when I pushed, I felt breasts.

When the lights came back on, I didn't know who had kissed me, and I was very embarrassed. I thought, whoever it is hates me now. I went outside for the next "lights out," but the other kids told me I had to stay inside and play the game. The next time the lights went out, I'll be damned if I didn't get grabbed and kissed again.

That time I liked it. When the lights came back on, I was kissing Joanne Miller, the head majorette for the football team. She was as tall as I was, with nice long legs and black hair. After that, I was very much into "lights out."

Although girls continued to be a mystery, I had more confidence in myself in sports. At Franklin I went out for track and field and "C" basketball, in which the shortest guys played. Our coach was a teacher, Mr. Tosconi, a little Italian who didn't know very much about the game. I was third string, and sat way down at the end of the bench. I was pretty good at dribbling, but I didn't shoot very well.

Later, when I was older and taller, I became quite a good basketball player—but not in junior high. I fared better at classroom studies, especially English and history. One of my favorite teachers was Mrs. Tennison. I took three classes in a row from her, and I shone there, really blossomed. I loved to read, and to write book reports and read them aloud to the class. I never revealed the ending, so the other kids had to read the book to find out what happened. Mrs. Tennison loved that.

That was when my speaking skills began to develop. Once Mrs. Tennison assigned me to read *The Last of the Mohicans*. After a few pages, I decided it was a piece of shit, boring and tedious, very laborious reading. I didn't finish it. When it came time to read my book report, I stood there with an open notebook and made up a story as I went along. I had those kids spellbound as I described what the Indians did, how they sneaked through the woods. I made up one of the greatest stories that class ever heard, and I got an A.

Years later, I realized Mrs. Tennison had rewarded me for letting my imagination run wild, knowing full well I hadn't read past the first chapter. Decades later, I met another man who rewrote Cooper's classic. He got a hell of a lot more than an A for his effort—and did pretty well by me, too.

In the ninth grade, I took a course in California history. For my semester project, I wrote a report on the U.S. Navy in Vallejo. While doing research, I learned that ships at sea flew their nation's flag from the highest mast so it would be the first thing other vessels saw, even if the ship's superstructure was below the horizon. I learned that if a ship was in trouble and needed help, the crew flew that flag upside down as an international distress signal.

Beyond my success in language and history, I discovered that I was also good at math. One of my many excellent teachers at Franklin was a whiz who taught us shortcuts and made arithmetic interesting. I also had fun in astronomy and was rewarded with an A. In the ninth grade, I went after straight A's, and I let my teachers know it. When my grades came, I had three A's, but B's in gym, typing, and science.

When I wasn't in school, my mother tried to keep me busy. As the oldest child, I was always responsible for certain household chores. I can't remember being so young that I didn't wash dishes. My parents promised that when I got to high-school age, I could give up that chore. They kept that promise, much to the chagrin of Dace. By then, of course, I was responsible for much other drudgery, including gardening and lawn work.

If my parents somehow provided all the essentials, cash was always tight in our household. I did all sorts of things to earn spending money. I sold lemonade. I hawked Sunday papers door to door. I even hung out on street corners with a little pile of papers, screaming out headlines just like the boys we saw in the movies about the *Dead End* kids. I built my own little shoeshine box and went down to Vallejo's red-light district, right into the bars, and popped that rag. I went house to house with an old push lawnmower, knocking on doors, trying to get a lawn to mow. In summer, when I went back home to Greenwood, I put up storm windows or took them down. When I was eleven, I hauled heavy bales of alfalfa for fifty cents an hour on a white man's farm.

My mother always encouraged me to work hard, partly because one legacy of her boarding-school years was a strong belief in a Christian God who rewarded honest labor. She was also influenced by Grandma Twinkle Star, a Christian to her dying day. Grandpa John, however, was no churchgoer. In fact, he made jokes about Christian Indians. He told me, "Don't argue. Just do what they tell you. When you get bigger, you'll make up your mind."

My mother crammed Christianity down my throat. When I was very young, she made sure I went to Sunday school *every* week. For a time, we also had to go to Bible school, which I hated because it really cut into summer vacation. Even in summer, back in South Dakota, we went to the Episcopalian or the Presbyterian Sunday school. Each Sunday, Grandma Aggie—undoubtedly one of the first women preachers in this century—sermonized at her own tiny church in Greenwood. She and Grandma Twinkle Star experimented enthusiastically with all forms of Christianity, and made us kids come along for the ride. We went to Episcopalian, Presbyterian, and Pentecostal churches and to the Holy Rollers' tents. As a teen, I even took instruction from Jehovah's Witnesses.

Dace and I were baptized and confirmed Episcopalians in Crockett, California, across the Carquinez Straits from Vallejo. We served as acolytes, or altar boys. The priest was English, and the service was very formal and High Church. We were the only Indian family at the church in Crockett. Sometimes the white kids snickered because we couldn't afford Sunday hats. My mother made our church clothes—sport coats and suit trousers—on her old treadle sewing machine.

Pops wasn't much for church, although Mom tried and tried to make him go. Most of the time, Pops found some excuse—often a car that he had to work on. When Mom wasn't around, Pops made quite a few witticisms about church and churchgoers. I was very surprised to learn that he had been baptized sixteen times into as many different denominations. I asked him about that often, but he never would reply. Finally, when I was a teenager and Mom was out of earshot, he did answer.

"Why sixteen churches?" I asked.

"Listen, son," he said. "One of them may be right."

Although I faithfully attended the Baptist Sunday school in Vallejo, my belief in Christianity crumbled when I was in the second or third grade. I just couldn't get my little mind around the basic concepts. For example, my Sunday-school teacher said, "God knows everything. He knows how you're going to turn out—so you have to repent."

I said, "Wait a minute. If He knows I'm going to grow up and be real evil, then why should I repent *now*? I'm just going to be evil later on. If He knows how I'm going to turn out, then what's the sense of all this? Why go through it all? Why can't I just be bad?"

My teacher replied, "If you repent, you'll be saved. You'll go to heaven."

"Then why can't I just be bad all my life and repent just as I'm dying?"

"Because you never know when you're going to die. You might get run over and killed walking out of Sunday school this morning."

"Well, if I see a truck coming at me, I'll just yell out real quick, 'I repent.' "

My problem was that I couldn't believe, as Christianity teaches, that God knows how everyone will turn out. I asked, "What about the devil? I thought God was in a war with the devil. That's what we learned in Sunday school. How does God know He's going to win the contest?"

My teacher answered, "He doesn't."

I thought, well then, what's the sense of it?

As a teenager hitchhiking through South Dakota, I remember once being captured by two Mormon missionaries who offered me a ride. They pulled off on a side road and parked so they could tell me their whole story. They were well-mannered white guys who insisted that we Indians were actually the lost tribes of Israel. We had been among the chosen, but we had elected to be evil, and so our skins had turned dark. Mormons, of course, were delightfully white. If I embraced the Book of Mormon and followed their religion, they said, eventually *my* skin would become white.

I was very late getting to my destination, but at least my skin never turned white.

The summer when I was eleven, even while my child's mind was examining and rejecting Christian dogma, Grandma Twinkle Star took me to Custer, South Dakota, to a Holy Roller meeting. She didn't give me any idea what to expect. When I walked into the tent, people were going into fits, jerking around, their faces contorted, babbling gibberish. "Speaking in tongues," they call it. I thought, I'm in a nuthouse.

Grandma said, "Go repent." I walked up the aisle and somebody told me to bow my head. I knelt down and the preacher, a white guy, put his hand on my head and squeezed it as though it were a melon. It hurt. I yelled, "Don't!" The preacher cried that I was saved. It was very scary. I didn't know what that guy might do next—I thought he was going to go crazy.

I think he expected me to have a fit, too, but I just couldn't catch the spirit. When he finally let go, I was ashamed. I wanted to please my grandmother, but felt that I hadn't. The preacher announced nevertheless that I was "saved." By the time I grew up and could no longer be forced to attend Christian gatherings, I had been "saved" at least a dozen times.

The following summer I stayed with my Auntie Faith and her husband. He was a Minneconjou Lakota, so they lived at the old Cheyenne River Agency—a few years before the Army Corps of Engineers finished yet another "flood control" dam on the Missouri, and the agency went under water. Auntie Faith and her family lived at the pumphouse next to the Missouri. They had to monitor the water level and, when the tank got down so far, turn on a pump until it was full again. The tank provided running water from the Missouri to a little village of government houses. I remember being happy that Auntie Faith had an indoor toilet. We Indians got to live in the good houses as long as we pushed the buttons for the whites.

Nearly every day of that summer at the pumphouse, we ran down a path through the trees—me, Dace, and Auntie Faith's girls, Marilyn, Mabel Ann, and Madonna—and went swimming. The current here was swift and the river so nearly opaque with silt that it was impossible to see underwater. Nevertheless, we stripped off our clothes, boys and girls together, and innocently and joyously swam nude for hours.

Most of the other reservation kids swam downstream at a swimming hole near an abandoned icehouse. These were boarding-school kids, already warped by the violence they had suffered: They had been taught to tease and harass younger or smaller boys. There came a day when they went after me. Several boys forced my head underwater; finally, lungs afire, I could fight no more and surrendered to the darkness. When my body went limp, the others, scared that I'd drowned, released me to drift with the current. Some spark of life remained within me, and when my head broke the surface, I began to swim through a murky veil toward life and the shoreline. After a mighty struggle, I crawled up on the riverbank and lay exhausted, sucking in huge gulps of air.

The others came running, calling, "You all right, Russ?"

I said, "Yeah, but I'm *gasping* for air."

Now, these were reservation kids and I'd come from California, so they'd never heard that word. They laughed—and for the rest of that summer the older boys called me "Gasping." Whenever they saw me they'd all start in, pretending that they were drowning, yelling, "Ooooooh! Aaaaah! I'm *gasping* for air!" I didn't think it was funny—but I wouldn't let them see that it bothered me, so I laughed with them.

It was that summer at Cheyenne River that I became a horseman. We knew a horse rancher named Dave Summers—his Lakota name was Oeningai. His son, Melvin Iron Moccasin, was about sixteen, tall and lanky—and he could *really* ride. I loved to watch Melvin take the herd—about twenty horses—down to the river every morning and evening. He carried a long rope with a knot near the end, and used it like a bullwhip. He rode at a full gallop, cracking that rope over the horses, making a loud noise without ever hitting one.

His father had some two- and three-year-olds that had been broken to ride—but just barely. They were called "green broke." I had a great time helping Melvin and his pals get these horses used to the bit, to accept a bridle without making a big hassle out of it, to neck rein, to run when a rider hit their ribs with his heels—in other words, to finish breaking them for saddle. We had to be gentle and patient, and we also had to ride them hard every day. They were still learning, so every once in a while one would buck me off.

Along the Missouri was a wide stretch of sand we called Sandy Beach, where, recalling the Westerns I had watched as a little boy, I demonstrated the art of falling from a moving horse. The other guys thought this was something, and let me ride their horses if I'd fall off. I'd had a lot of practice at this—not always on purpose—during my summers in Greenwood. I preferred to go off the horse's side and then tumble, but sometimes I went off the back end. I also did some falls in pastures—a lot riskier than on sand, but I never worried about that.

Late in the summer of 1952, I joined hundreds of people in a pageant, part of the annual Cheyenne Fair and Rodeo Celebration at Cheyenne River Reservation. After the pageant, I noticed a *wacipi*, a dance, over at one side. When I heard the drum, I asked Auntie Faith why we didn't go over. She said, "That's where the full-bloods are." I went over by myself. The moment I heard that music, I knew: This is where I belong. It was late afternoon and the sun was very low, throwing long shadows from the dancers circling a pole. I noticed that their outfits were very different from what I usually saw at dances. Nobody had eagle feathers, only those of the hawk, owl, and pheasant. They were mostly very old men, many wearing old blue cavalry coats and Stetson hats. One elder wore a battered cavalry hat with his feathers and bells, and he carried an ax. At the end of the song, he stopped and threw the ax at the pole. It stuck—that really impressed me. Later, I asked Auntie Faith why he was dressed that way. She explained that he had captured that hat and coat from someone in the U.S. Army Cavalry.

Most of the younger Indians ignored the elders, treating the dance as if it were only for "blanket asses"—Indians who live in the past. But I identified with the elders. I had seen cowboy-and-Indian movies, I had had to defend myself over them—and suddenly here they were, real Indians, the actual people who had whipped the United States Cavalry. From that time forward, I was enthralled with elders. I began to watch them at dances, noticing the elderly couples, people born in the last century, and how they communicated without talking, relying on a gesture or a look, and sometimes a smile of gratitude or acknowledgment. They didn't have to say *please, thank you, excuse me*, but they communicated and responded. I thought, how great this is to know another person that well, to be able to communicate without talking, lovingly and respectfully. It was amazing. Sadly, all that is gone now, a lost art. I just don't see it anymore.

Not all the time I spent with my relatives was on reservations in South Dakota. Many of my father's family came to visit us in California. Sometimes they lived with us until they could get on their feet financially. One of those was my cousin Wesley "Tody" Means Jr. Even after finding work, Tody stayed at our house for a time and shared a bedroom with Dace and me. He was about fifteen years older than me, and I looked up to him like a big brother. Tody taught me a lot. Instead of a father-son talk from Pops about the birds and the bees, I got a cousin-to-cousin talk—the unvarnished truth, no beating around the bush.

When I was fourteen, my Uncle Murph—Pops's older brother, Austin Means Sr.—stayed with us for a time. He was a printer who made good money when he worked. Unfortunately, like my dad, Uncle Murph went on drinking binges. He wasn't as good a worker as Pops. He was always getting fired. Between jobs, he would live with us and, following Indian custom, work hard around the house, inside and out, improving things. When he found work, off he would go. After a while, he would go on a binge. When he was broke, he would come back to live with us.

The summer I was fourteen, my parents sent Dace and me to stay with Grandma Twinkle Star in a Christian camp outside Custer, South Dakota. My parents bought a '39 Chevy, and Uncle Murph drove us there. On the open highway, he let us drive, so we mostly did forty-five miles an hour all the way from California to South Dakota. Uncle Murph had promised my mother that he wouldn't drink, but after we got to Custer, he went into Rapid City, and the next thing we knew he was in jail. Grandma got the car, and my folks planned to come out and bring us home in late summer. In the meantime, Dace and I climbed Calamity Peak and all the heights around Custer. We designed and built traps to capture chipmunks, squirrels, and kangaroo mice without hurting them. We studied them for a little while, then released them.

The most important thing I learned in Custer was how Indians drank. In those days, Indians couldn't legally buy liquor in South Dakota. They would pay some white guy to buy them a pint or half-pint of whiskey. Getting caught with a bottle meant they would get arrested, so they would go into an alley or a park to chugalug the whole bottle. Naturally, they got drunk right away—and *then* the cops picked them up.

After Uncle Murph was busted for being drunk in Rapid City, my mother's sister's boy, Keith Powers—called Punch—came over to Custer. He was seventeen, three years older than me. He, Dace, and I couldn't take all that Holy Roller stuff Grandma was into, so we left a note on her table and hitchhiked to the Brainard Indian School, outside Hot Springs, South Dakota. Some park rangers gave us a ride all the way through Custer State Park, and from Hot Springs we walked five or six miles to Brainard. It was a Presbyterian school for Indian boys and girls. Punch had almost graduated from it the previous June. He had to return for summer school to make up a few classes before he could get his diploma.

The school authorities—staunch Christians—agreed that if we did chores around campus and went to Bible school, they would feed us. There were dozens of empty dormitory beds, but they were reserved for students whose tuition was paid. We were allowed, instead, to sleep on a pile of lumber intended for construction use in the fall. During thunderstorms, we made a lean-to from the wider boards and huddled inside.

Thus I discovered the true meaning of Christian charity.

My job was to round up the dairy cows every morning from a pasture in the mountains. Punch's job was to milk the cows. Then Dace cleaned the barn and ran the cows back outside so they could make their own way back into the mountains to graze. After breakfast, we went to Bible study, and Punch went to his classes. Then we were through for the day. In late summer, when Punch had finished his classwork, we hitchhiked back to Custer, where my parents were waiting to take us back to California. We returned to a big surprise: My mother, who had always been very careful with what little money we had, had scrimped and saved enough to make a down payment on a house. While we were in South Dakota in that summer of 1954, my parents had signed a thirty-year mortgage for eleven thousand dollars on a three-bedroom tract house in Mulford Gardens, a new development in San Leandro, just south of Oakland.

In the fall, I enrolled at San Leandro High—and almost every aspect of my life took a radical turn.

4

▼▼▼▼▼▼▼▼▼

San Leandro

San Leandro High was big and busy, with an overwhelmingly white student body. There were, of course, a few Chicanos. Back then, everyone called them Mexicans. Because I was the school's only Indian and had dark skin, I was usually treated as they were. A few poor white kids attended the school, but most of the students came from comfortable middle-class families.

So far, I had done very well in school. At the end of second grade in Vallejo, Mrs. Fox, my teacher, got together with Mrs. Woodward of the third grade and talked with my mother about my skipping third and maybe fourth grade. I remember Mom's words. She said, "Oh, my God, no! He's already too young. I started him too young in the first grade."

In one sense, my mother was absolutely right. I wasn't the social or physical peer of fourth-graders. But when those teachers recognized my academic abilities, it should have prompted my parents to take a greater interest in my schooling. It's impossible to know with certainty, but I will always believe that if my parents had cultivated my abilities, my whole life would have been very different. When I got to high school, I needed something more from them—and I didn't get it.

In fact, I got damn little. Pops's untreated alcoholism had progressed to the point that to get money for drinking, he sometimes pawned things—my brother Ted's saxophone, Mom's silverware, small appliances—whatever he could take. All too often, Pops lost the pawn tickets and then couldn't remember which hockshop he had visited. To make up for the income lost to his binges, Mom worked longer and harder, as a purchasing agent. Moving to San Leandro had forced her to transfer to Alameda Naval Air Station. She was exhausted when she got home every night, so tired she had no time for me and not much for anyone else. As much as I wanted it, no one at home showed any interest in my schoolwork by the time I started tenth grade.

I realize now that if my mother was abusive and unsupportive, it was largely because she was trying to keep a very bad marriage together, mostly for the sake of her boys. Nevertheless, without the kind of attention I needed at home, I began to bend the rules very severely in school. I tested every teacher, and easily dominated those who were wimps. Aside from that, most of the teachers at San Leandro High favored the white elite, all but ignored the dark-skinned kids, and did almost nothing to make my studies rewarding.

For the first semester of tenth grade, I took the college-prep program, including French and algebra, and got good marks. It was all *too* easy—I had no challenges. Losing interest, I found sitting in a classroom excruciating.

At fourteen, I was younger than most of my tenth-grade classmates, and still small for my age. Although I was very athletic, I couldn't really compete with kids a head taller. It became obvious to me that I wasn't going to get into the varsity lettermen's club, which, not incidentally, was pure white.

The other social elite at San Leandro High was made up of students with cars. Many drove flashy '54 or '55 Chevies, rakish customized "Deuce" coupes, souped-up or tricked-out hot rods of every description. I had no car, no money, no chance of making even the junior varsity—and so at San Leandro High, I was a social cipher, a null, a black hole. By default, just about the only kids I could pal around with were guys whom I'll call Don Miller and Richie Sharp, two poor whites who lived near my house.

Richie's parents, who were nice people, had moved to California after World War II. Don's parents, third-generation Californians, weren't very friendly, and he was just a redneck bully. I was still fairly naive and trusting. Not until I had moved away and grown up did I realize that Richie and Don, classic ne'er-do-wells, had always used me as their patsy. When I lived in San Leandro, they included me in their plans and acted as though they were my friends, and I responded with loyalty.

Most of my other friends were Chicanos, especially Richard Sanchez and Leroy Benevidez. The Chicanos were "right on." I liked the way they dressed—superstarched khakis pressed to knife-edge creases, and sweater vests. I began to emulate them, wearing my hair short and combed straight back. With my dark skin, I was a low rider without a ride. My mom was very

happy when I got past the peggers and rolled-sleeve sport-shirt look, which she called "gangster dress."

Hanging around with Mexicans, I followed some of them into the fields which then rimmed lower San Francisco Bay. It was backbreaking labor, working weekends and after school—sometimes instead of school. Aside from mowing chintzy little lawns in the housing development for next to nothing, it was about the only money I could earn. I picked cherries and dug potatoes, too, but mostly it was tomatoes. I got fifty cents a lug—a big wooden box that held almost two bushels. I had to make sure they were all *good* tomatoes, no rotten or bruised ones, and that each was green near the stem but otherwise ripe.

Most of the other pickers were braceros, legal migrants from Mexico. Man, could they work—at least three times faster than I could. I couldn't have averaged more than $1.50 an hour, but that was good money for a kid in the era before state minimum-wage laws. I was paid cash, with no deductions, at the end of each day. The braceros worked harder and made more, but they lived in squalid camps. I went home to a hot shower and clean sheets. I didn't envy them.

I wasn't the only Sioux working the California fields. Some Bureau of Indian Affairs genius had come up with a plan to send a few hundred South Dakota Indians to pick tomatoes in the Salinas Valley: The bureau would pay the growers half the pickers' wages as an incentive to hire Indians instead of undocumented workers. Of course, the damn growers put the Indians where they normally put pickers—in cesspool camps with one water faucet for the whole place, slit trenches for toilets, leaky-roofed, falling-down shacks, and filth everywhere. They were fed nothing but slop and treated like undocumented workers—with insults, tongue lashings, pushing, and shoving.

About the fourth or fifth day, a white foreman shoved the wrong Lakota and the Indian punched him out. That night, the grower sent in six or eight goons to bust the guy up—the usual tactic of intimidation. But those were not illegal immigrants, living in fear. When the goons grabbed one Indian, the whole camp rose up. The Lakota chased the goons away, then burned down the camp and started to tear up the fields. They were headed toward the grower's mansion when the police arrived. Before it was over, the Indians had started several fires and overturned a bunch of cars. The BIA immediately shipped all the Indians back to South Dakota. To cover his ass, some bureaucrat claimed that the Indians had rioted because they were drunk. I knew some of those guys, and I learned that they were not drunk—most had no money, because none had been paid. Nevertheless, one grower was quoted widely as saying, "If I ever see another Sioux Indian, it'll be too soon."

When I wasn't working, I often ditched school and went swimming or rafting in San Francisco Bay or one of the estuaries. With my young friends,

I made precarious climbs up huge, creosoted timbers to the corrugated-tin roof of a big boathouse near the Oakland airport. We climbed out on the lip, thirty or forty feet above the water, and dived in. When we got tired of that, we flipped off a nearby wharf and splashed around the bay.

When I was fifteen, I began to go to a teen club in the elementary school gym on Saturday nights and dance to records. The teachers, of course, wanted to play waltzes and that Teresa Brewer crap. We wanted hip music like Fats Domino and the Platters, so the girls—only girls had records back then—brought their 45s. When the teachers refused to let us play them, we staged a little strike outside. We said, "We're not going to dance until you play our music. If you won't play it, we'll all boycott the teen club." After maybe half an hour, the teachers relented and said we could play our music.

Right about then, Bill Haley and the Comets were a hit. His music had a different beat and parents didn't like it—but at least it wasn't *colored* music. Suddenly it was all rock and roll, it was for white kids—but we all started bopping. Bop was different from jitterbug, different from anything. For the first time, dancing was freestyle. You bopped with a partner, but you each did your own thing. The Charleston had come and gone, and then the jitterbug, but the bop stayed. It's still going on, but now it's just called dancing.

The teen club became a big part of my life. Almost every Saturday, I would get dressed up and head over there. My cousin Tody Means, a sharp dresser, lent Richie Sharp and me some sport coats. We dressed top-notch, with peggers and shirts with a loop underneath the collar so we could button it all the way to the top. I wore my hair in a ducktail.

Before going to the teen club, Richie and I would go to a liquor store and steal a half-pint of whiskey. Two drinks of that gave me courage enough to talk to girls and to dance—the only way I could do it. We would share the rest of the bottle with friends, and then go in and have a rollicking good time.

As my sixteenth birthday approached, I was spending more time with Richie and Don and less in school. My mother was all but indifferent to my grades, but she didn't like my friends, didn't like the way I dressed, didn't like where I went or the music I listened to. In fact, Mom didn't much care for almost everything about me. When she was home, she wasn't shy about telling me so.

Then came a day I will never forget. I was out in the front yard and Mom was inside the house, and we were shouting back and forth about something she thought I had done. Finally, unable to get me to confess, she said, "Get in here right this minute." It was one of her favorite sayings, a code phrase meaning the leather strap was about to descend on my backside.

That time, I said, "No."

Mom was stunned. She said it again: "You get in here right this minute."

At that moment, I realized I was as big as she was, and stronger, and if

she tried to whip me, I could take the strap away from her. I said it again: "No." I danced around, swaying on my tiptoes like a boxer, repeating it. "No. No. No." I was saying it to myself, too—No! No! No!

Boy, that felt good!

I could see Mom boiling, but there was nothing she could do. I said, "I'm leaving. Good-bye." I went off to play football with some neighborhood pals. When I went home afterward, I knew I never would have to take another beating from my mom. I was fifteen, and I was free.

Not that Mom just gave up. She kept after me, yelling at the top of her lungs, but I turned it all back on her. Poor Dace would go to his bedroom and close the door when Mom and I got into a shouting match.

Once I had declared my independence from my mother, I continued to ditch classes and drink booze. Hanging out with dropouts and misfits, I drifted deeper into crime. We weren't quite a gang, but the next thing to it—a bunch of frustrated, rebellious kids who stayed out late looking for trouble. Once we left Gordon's Drive-In in San Leandro without paying for our food. Another time, several guys and I broke into a railroad car parked behind a supermarket and stole thirteen cases of Lucky Lager beer. I had a car by then, a '48 Chevy Fleetline. A tire went flat, and I left the car in front of school. When the other kids got caught, they snitched on me, and I was nabbed with a backseat full of beer. I was arrested and taken to juvenile hall, and after sixteen or seventeen days, I appeared in court. Because it was my first time through the justice system, I got probation. Mom, of course, had a fit, but she could no longer beat me.

Later that summer, I was thrown in jail again after a friend stole his mother's 1950 Fluid Drive Buick, the kind with the front grille that looks like it has big teeth coming out of it. I was riding in it when we got caught, but the charges against me were dismissed.

After two brief trips to jail, my interest in school declined still further, but I had promised my mother I wouldn't drop out. Whenever I ditched, I wrote my own excuses. Usually I would fake my dad's handwriting, but sometimes I would have a girl with good handwriting forge my mother's. After setting a school record for cutting classes, I was suspended for two weeks. Being suspended took all the fun out of cutting classes, so to amuse myself—and make my mark—I went after a new record. Soon I had the most *two-week* suspensions in the history of San Leandro High.

American education has always seemed much like Christianity to me. It doesn't deal with reality. Aside from math, which is usually taught with logic, children mostly are taught to memorize the latest theory—a hypothesis based on what the powers that be have decided is "true" at that moment. Of course, all those theories keep changing. Even the way most subjects are taught is illogical. Why should children be isolated by age group? I think that's insane. Why are students forced to sit in rows, looking at the backs of people's heads?

America's educational system robs people of their individuality while training them to accept whatever the authorities dictate. Instead of learning to reason for themselves, children learn to obey—precisely the quality most valued by a society dependent on mass production. It's no surprise that so many children grow up to become fodder for the industrial machine. It's all they know how to do. I am a human being. Even in high school, I knew that I wanted to remain one, and that I didn't want to become part of a machine, replaced and discarded when I wore out.

Forty years ago, I could hardly have expressed such thoughts, but it wouldn't have made any difference if I had. To the authorities who ran San Leandro High, I was just a troublemaker. Eventually a truant officer came to our home, bringing with him my whole attendance record. I remember him sitting there, with the evening darkness pressing against our living-room windows as he went through each piece of paper in that file.

"Is this one of your notes?" asked the truant officer.

"No," said my mother.

"Mr. Means, is this your note?"

"No," said my father.

I left the house before the officer finished, because I knew my mother wouldn't be fit to live with for a while. I stayed away until she went to bed.

5
▼▼▼▼▼▼▼▼▼

Winnebago

After my truancy was exposed, Mom decided that my friends were leading me into trouble, and unless I got away from them, my life would be ruined beyond redemption. She arranged for me to live with my dad's brother, Quentin. He was chief clerk—quite an important position—for the Bureau of Indian Affairs agency on the Winnebago Reservation. A few weeks after my sixteenth birthday, my parents put me on a Greyhound and sent me to Winnebago, Nebraska, a small town about twenty miles south of Sioux City, Iowa.

Uncle Quentin and Aunt Phoebe had lots of children. The oldest was Michael, a very pretty girl a couple of years younger than me. There were Bertha, David, Eugene, Veronica—I can't remember all their names. I stayed at their house and enrolled in the eleventh grade at Winnebago High, which is near the reservation on the main road to Sioux City.

At San Leandro High, there were about 350 students in the tenth grade alone, most of them white. At Winnebago, I went through culture shock at finding myself in an entire school of perhaps four hundred students, three-fourths of them Indians. But the varsity athletes, the cheerleaders, the teachers' pets, the smartest and richest and most pampered kids on campus were all whites. In San Leandro, students of color were usually relegated to the back of the room or to "slow learner" or "troublemaker" classes. We didn't quite have that at Winnebago, but I was outraged that the teachers—all whites—treated the Indian majority very much as teachers had at San Leandro. And the Winnebago teachers were meaner.

Auntie Faith and her family also lived there. Marilyn, Auntie Faith's oldest, was in her first year of college at South Dakota State. She came home often to visit her fiancé, Fred "Bosco" Harden, and when she was around, it was party time. I went along with Marilyn and Bosco and began to drink with people in their late teens and early twenties. Those older guys were supergenerous, buying me drinks, inviting me to their homes to play cards. I always had a good time. Sometimes we went to North Sioux City, just over the South Dakota line, to an Indian bar that we liked. We danced, shot pool, played on a bowling machine—and drank, of course. There I was, sixteen years old but looking thirteen, with a fake ID that said I was eighteen, the legal drinking age for 3.2 beer. Most Indians look younger than their age and I was with an older crowd, so the bartenders never checked. Enforcement of liquor laws was less scrupulous in those days. You couldn't break the law, but you could bend the rules.

After the bars in South Dakota closed, we would head for Sioux City, across the line in Iowa. One bitterly cold winter night I found myself very drunk at the Cotton Club, a black after-hours joint in the lower end of town. I was there with a high-school dropout of about nineteen or twenty, a club boxer named Conrad De Cora. The entrance to the club was through an alley and upstairs. Somehow, I found myself with Conrad in that alley—I don't recall going down the stairs—and he was pounding me. The last thing I remember was falling down and Conrad stomping my head again and again.

I awoke in a snowbank. I was in a vacant lot, somewhere in Sioux City that I didn't recognize. My coat was zipped up to my neck. Blood had frozen all over it and over my jeans and shoes. My gloves and hat had disappeared, and I was colder than hell. My face was so hideously swollen that I couldn't see anything until I pried one eye open to discover that it was daylight. Holding that eye open with both hands, I staggered down the street until I found a main thoroughfare and then a mom-and-pop grocery. The proprietor chased me away. I went into another store and those people, too, made me leave. At the third store, I collapsed, and someone called the cops.

The police took me straight to a hospital. En route, they asked if I had been drinking. "Last night, not today," I mumbled, barely able to speak. I was released from the hospital a few days later, but it was another ten days before the swelling began to subside. I stayed home, out of sight. I could tell that Aunt Phoebe and Uncle Quentin were pained by my behavior, but they took pity on my condition and didn't lecture me.

While I was recuperating, Conrad came to visit and to apologize. He didn't explain what had happened or why. He just said he was sorry, and that if he hadn't been drinking he wouldn't have done it. I thought it was decent of him to come by, but I couldn't forgive him. My lips were still hugely swollen. I covered them with a scarf over my nose and mouth that made me look like a bandit. I was still squinting at the world through puffy eyes.

I felt that I had shamed myself and dishonored Uncle Quentin and Aunt Phoebe, who were leading members of the community. Very much against their often-expressed wishes, I had gone drinking. The physical effects of my ordeal were excruciating, but I felt even worse for the disgrace I had brought to my father's family. I asked Auntie Faith if I could live with her and her husband, Louis Travesie. He was head of maintenance on the Winnebago Reservation. As a young man, Uncle Louis had ridden thoroughbreds, so everyone called him Jockey. He was smallish, with thinning hair, a wiry, quiet, very stable man with an extremely dry sense of humor—a great guy who reminded me in some ways of my dad.

Uncle Jockey and Auntie Faith welcomed me into their home and proved to be very understanding. She treated me as an adult and allowed me to do virtually anything I wanted. Consequently, I didn't give Auntie Faith a rough time, nor did I shame her. But I still partied. I still drank.

I was so ashamed of the beating I had taken—and the circumstances that had led to it—that I couldn't face my classmates or teachers. I called my mother and told her I was quitting school. Mom talked to Auntie Faith, who must have told her to leave me alone. My mother said, "It's your decision." I was very surprised that she didn't put up a squawk.

Instead of going to school, I set out to make my first million. With a friend named Billy Hunter, I scavenged scrap iron on the reservation and hauled it to a junkyard for a penny a pound. I put up storm windows and took them down again. I mowed lawns and washed cars. Mostly I did farm work—steering a plow, disking fields, or riding on an alfalfa cutter behind a tractor.

Soon after my beating, Bosco, Marilyn's fiancé, had joined the navy. There was no one else to stick up for me, so I started to get into a lot of fights, especially in town. During basketball season, I walked a mile into Winnebago every evening to play at the community hall. We played a rough game, elbowing and bumping each other around the ball. As a good defensive player, my usual role was to get the other team's big scorer mad, because when somebody loses his temper he can't think right or play well. Nowadays in pro basketball, such players are called "enforcers."

Egged on by his cousins, a kid from a large and locally influential family kept trying to pick a fight with me. I wasn't looking for that, but eventually he did get me to duke it out, and I beat him up. I tangled with him twice more and beat him up both times. After that, every time I came to town I had to fight someone from his extended family. Eventually I was fighting guys too tough for me, and they beat me up. Three or four times, when I was walking alone down the gravel road from the agency to the town, a carful of guys came by. When they saw me, they stopped and everybody got out and I had to battle one of them. The same thing happened almost every time I hitchhiked up to North Sioux City. At least they never ganged up on me.

Those guys were Winnebago and I was a Lakota, an outsider with California clothes and a California mouth. The other kids wore plain jeans, but I wore peggers—very loose around the thighs but tapering to narrow cuffs. My mother never allowed me to own a pair of black peggers because that was what "hoodlums" wore. I wore salt-and-pepper peggers and white peggers and tan peggers. Nobody else on the Winnebago Reservation wore pegged pants, so they made fun of me, and pretty soon we would fight over my clothes.

Taking a lesson from that experience, I started to hang around with a big crowd of guys, including Billy Hunter and his brother Dave, and Bosco's brother, "Tomcat" Harden. Most of that bunch had been trained by a Sioux City high-school boxing coach. In those years, white farmers took some of the better Indian boys to the cow towns of Iowa and Nebraska and matched them against white guys, any size, for "smokers" and club fights. Those promoters made good money betting on their Indians against local farm-boy talent.

That winter of 1955, when I wasn't fighting on the road to town or on a basketball court, my new pals gave me boxing lessons. I put on the gloves for two-minute rounds with the champions of the small-town smoker and club circuit. We called it sparring. We had no headgear and our gloves were old, with little padding, so it meant bloody noses and big welts on my face. To me, it was fun. I got my jab going, learned some moves, and began to feel that I could handle myself.

At Winnebago, we played basketball year-round, even in summertime. Sometimes the Hunter brothers and I played at night, with just a lightbulb. We played two on two, one on one. On afternoons and weekends, even when it hit 90 degrees and 90 percent humidity, we played with shirts off, swigging ice-cold beer, rivers of sweat running from our bodies.

When I wasn't playing basketball, I got into fancy dancing. In Oklahoma and the southern Plains, they call this the war dance, although I've never learned why. In the northern Plains we refer to it as fancy dancing—freelance dancing, any style, to the drum and especially to songs. One of my party pals was Harold Rave, half Sioux and half Winnebago, a champion fancy dancer who won contests all over. I hung around the powwow grounds on a lot of spring and summer evenings. One night, some of the people who were singing around a drum asked me if I wanted to dance. They made a little ceremony and initiated me, so from then on I had the right to dance at Winnebago.

I worked quite a bit that summer, but I partied a lot, too, not in bars but up in the hills and down along the Missouri. We went swimming nearly every day and often well into the night. There was always booze around, but nobody overdid it. We just had a good time.

When August of 1956 came around, I began to think about the next year. Almost everyone I knew had plans. Some were going off to college, others had joined the service, and the rest were planning to go somewhere and get a job. I had no plans, and everybody I knew was leaving Winnebago. I knew I would be in for a hard time. There is no farm work during the winter; all the storm windows would be up by October, the lawns covered with snow by November, and I had already picked up all the available scrap iron. I called my mother and asked if I could come back. She said I could, but only if I returned to school.

It was a long, uncomfortable ride home. By the time I got off that bus in San Leandro, I was feeling the oppressive weight of failure. I was not yet seventeen, but I was nowhere in school and had no prospects of a job. I felt empty, hollow, used up.

6
▼▼▼▼▼▼▼▼

Dealing

etting home was a jolt. In the nine months I had spent in Winnebago, I had sprouted nearly six inches to become six feet tall—and I was still growing. I towered over my mother, and I was an inch and a half taller than my dad. That felt weird, because all my life I had looked up to him. Now I was looking down. It scared me. Pops was sitting in the living room when I walked into the house, and he said, "Damn, son, you grew just like a bad weed." He said it in his own way, expressing wonderment. Everyone laughed.

I didn't tell anyone at San Leandro High that I had quit school in Winnebago, and it took them a few months to get my records. By the time they found out I was still an eleventh-grader, I was taking senior classes. The principal let me finish the semester, then made a deal with me: I could take one or two senior classes, but I also had to take all those eleventh-grade classes. I was pissed off at that, so I did absolutely nothing and got F's.

I loathed school, but I still wanted to learn. I didn't want to end up with a job like my father's, coming home every night with grease under my fingernails. My mother and Grandma Twinkle Star had instilled in me the value of an education. Even one of my junior-high teachers, whom I regarded as a racist, had taught me to view education in a different way. Once when he offered to take the class on a ski trip, some kids didn't want to go. He told us, "When you're faced with anything new, accept it and value the experience. Broaden your horizons every chance you get—you'll meet people you'd never meet otherwise. All new experiences add to your overall education." All the time I was going to school—or *not* going to school—I kept a residual respect for learning.

When I got home from Winnebago, the teen club had closed. I started to hang around with Eleanor and Patty Avery, who lived in a corner house in Mulford Gardens. They were average-looking sisters, a year apart, one a brunette, the other blonde. Even though I was hanging out with girls, I still didn't have a girlfriend. I was so shy that I could hardly have a conversation with a girl. I stuttered every time I talked to one. When I had a crush on a girl, I followed her around at a distance just to stare at her. In junior high, the object of my affection had been Barbara Felker—but if she even *looked* at me, I blushed.

I was almost that shy at the Averys' parties until I met Pat Patterson, a cute redhead who was new to the neighborhood. She came up to me, kind of high from booze, and said, "How come you're so stuck up?" My mind was flashing around at a mile a minute. What does she mean? How could I be stuck up? If you only knew! Pat took me outside beside a parked car and we talked. She told me that the rap on me among the neighborhood girls was that I was stuck on myself, that I acted like I was too good to talk to them. Me, the only "darky" in the neighborhood! I thought, oh my god, I'm exactly the opposite. I just listened for a while, high and sipping wine from a little bottle, and finally I said, "I'm not stuck up, I'm just scared to death. I stutter when I talk to pretty women. It's only because I've got this burgundy that I ain't stuttering with you."

Soon, Pat and I started to date, very irregularly. Usually we just drove out by the estuary to talk. Chatting with a pretty girl was still fairly amazing to me, so those dates helped me to build self-confidence. I have many fond memories of Pat, but eventually she dropped away from our crowd.

I was still into being a juvenile delinquent, and now that I was so much bigger, I began to turn into a very bad guy. Along with two pals, I started a protection racket in high school. We sold "insurance" to students, taking their lunch money in exchange for making sure that no one—such as we— would beat them up. The other two guys got busted, but they never snitched. Word of the racket went around school in a flash. I found myself in senior math class with a bunch of lettermen, jocks, listening to them talk about what they would do if they ever caught the third guy. I said, "Yeah, man, I'd really work him over." Inside, I was laughing because they were talking about *me*. I know now that terrorizing kids was an ugly thing to do, but back then I didn't feel a bit of remorse. I quit only because I would have gotten caught.

From extortion, I moved into dope. While I was in Winnebago, my old pal, whom I'll call Alan Michaels, had gotten in with a guy I'll call Robert Davis. He was a few years older than we were, and he knew about marijuana, which we called "weed." He introduced Alan to weed, and Alan taught me how to smoke it. That was it—I went after dope like a duck after water. Forget about booze; I just wanted dope. A single joint cost a dollar, but we bought "three for two"—three joints for two bucks. We could buy about an ounce in a little matchbox, the kind with a sliding tray that held "strike anywheres," for five dollars. For twenty dollars, we could get a "lid," a tobacco tin that held five or six ounces.

We started out buying weed from a local dealer, first three for two, then a matchbox, then lids. Then we were scoring a pound. To pay for our own usage, we graduated to dealing, finding bigger dealers who gave us more dope for less money. It was an instructive exercise in the economics of the free market.

This was in 1956 and 1957, when the stereotype was that drugs were an underworld thing, that only blacks, Mexicans, motorcycle gangs, jazz musicians, and San Francisco beatniks smoked dope, and that even they sneaked around in dark basements and abandoned houses to do it. When Robert Davis, Alan Michaels, and I got into it, we smoked openly—in canoes, on picnics, when we went swimming. We laughed at the stereotype, knowing we would never get busted because no one would believe that we smoked weed openly. Few people then even knew what it smelled like. We were purely bold.

High on weed, I daydreamed about moving to North Beach in San Francisco, among beatniks who didn't care about irrelevant things such as dress codes. I could put on the colorful clothing that traditional Indians wore on social occasions, and I could wear rings, necklaces, and bracelets reflecting my heritage. I could let my hair grow and twist it into long braids, just as my ancestors had. Coming down from those marijuana highs, I wondered if I would ever really be that free.

From weed, I graduated to pills, first uppers—bennies and dexies. Dexedrine and Benzedrine weren't sold without a prescription, but Alan's mother was on a diet that required her to take Benzedrine tablets. Alan helped himself and shared with Dace and me. After more field research, we discovered that bennies were stronger and came in low-dosage, pale-blue triangular tablets or more powerful greenish capsules of five or fifteen grains.

Most local suppliers were Mexicans, but many of the bigger dealers were whites, motorcycle-gang types. The whites were pretty much out in the open, but the Mexicans were secretive and more protective of their turf. You had to be well connected in their world to get set up with anyone important. Eventually we made a big-time contact in Fremont, California, with a Mexican operator. He kept everything supersecret. I never saw his face.

In the summer of 1957, Alan and I decided to grow our own marijuana.

My mother, who always liked to pretend she had a green thumb, loved to putter around the garden. She was an executive gardener—someone had to prepare everything for her, and then she would drop in the seeds. Then I had to water and weed the garden and flower beds. She didn't pay much attention to her garden until after the planting. Several weeks before Mom started her garden, I sowed marijuana seeds in back of our house, along the west side where they would get a lot of sun. These were just starter plants. When they got to be tall enough, I planned to transplant them to someplace more remote.

That year, we had a very mild spring and Mom decided on an early start. She went prowling around the yard, then summoned me. "What the hell kind of plants are these?" she said, pointing at my marijuana. "They look like weeds." I could see she was getting ready to make me pull them out of the ground, but the sprouts were only about a foot high. They needed another six inches before I could transplant them. Thinking fast, I told her they were Mexican tomato plants that had to grow about six more inches before they flowered. In a week or so, I transplanted my little hemp crop to a field near Pleasanton, twenty miles inland—a farm town then—where it was warmer and had more sun. By midsummer, we had twenty-seven very bushy plants, ten to twelve feet tall. We knocked them down and soaked the leaves in wine, then let the plants dry before grinding them up. We sold most of that crop in matchboxes.

After that, Alan and I pulled a few jobs at drugstores—burglaries. In those days, few stores had alarms. Getting in was just a matter of forcing the back door with a tire iron. We usually scored about twenty pounds of pills and morphine, plus some watches and lighters. Two or three times, the till was open, so we took the change.

Those jobs put us in the big time, gave us the working capital to make big buys of weed and pills. To convert our stolen stockpile to cash, we found "mules" to deal for us at the high school. Until that time—at least, at San Leandro High—no lettermen, no middle-class whites were doing dope. We were pioneers, right there at the cutting edge, playing our small but vital role in the transition of America's middle class to the drug culture. Maybe I didn't turn on a whole generation, but I did my part. We started them with bennies and dexies. Kids loved them because those drugs seemed to improve their schoolwork. They could stay up all night, and talk a mile a minute.

Dace entered high school just about then. I turned him on to weed and pills, and made him a mule. He was friends with one of our other mules, who turned Dace on, too. Our mules dealt with the public, and no one knew we were the big pushers behind them.

Of course, once I got into dope, I got into experimentation. I soon discovered the best high in the world. First I dropped a fifteen-grain bennie and a five-grain dexie. Then I swallowed a quarter-size Demerol pill and washed it down with a short-neck bottle of burgundy. Finally, I smoked a big fat joint of number-one weed. That made me so cool I was walking an inch off the ground. I could rap because of the bennies and dexies and booze, but the Demerol and the weed toned things down, so I was on top of the world. That's the way it went through the twelfth grade. I had no fear of girls and women—I was so high I didn't care what they thought or said.

Most likely, I would have dropped out of school again. Even more likely, I would have spent a short, angry, useless life as a petty criminal, but about the time I got into drugs big time, in my second semester back at San Leandro, I met Miss Adele Fridhandler. She taught language skills and social studies. She was nearing thirty, very pretty with dark hair and fair skin, a tiny, delicately boned and elegantly dressed woman with a low, compelling voice. One look, and I fell in love with her.

But by then I was a rebel. Whatever a teacher told me to do, I did the opposite. My first day in Miss Fridhandler's class, she announced a quiz. No one could leave the room until it was over. Of course, while everyone was quiet and working away, I raised my hand. Miss Fridhandler wouldn't acknowledge me, so I said, "Hey! Can I get a pass to go to the bathroom?" She shook her head no, and I said, "Why not?"

"Russell, will you please be quiet? People are trying to concentrate," she said.

"Are you going to give me a pass or not?"

When Miss Fridhandler shook her head no, I stood up.

"You sit back down," she said. I stood up and walked away and she said, "You can't leave this class. Get back here. I'm calling Mr. Hunter." He was the vice-principal.

I knew the routine. After I finished in the bathroom, I went straight to the vice-principal's office. Mr. Hunter's secretary asked me what I was doing there, and I said, "I don't have a pass. The teacher will be coming here between periods."

"Have a seat," said the secretary.

Sure enough, Miss Fridhandler came in to report me, and Mr. Hunter reprimanded me and gave me demerits. I already held San Leandro High records for two-week suspensions and for cutting classes and I was out for the triple crown, so I needed to set the record for detention. In pursuit of the record, I never went to detention, so every month or so I was suspended and got another two-week "vacation."

Eventually, Miss Fridhandler became the only person at San Leandro High for whom I stayed after school. The fact that I was disobeying my own rule might have tipped her to my feelings. Whatever the reason, she took a personal interest in me. She used my attraction to her to reinvolve me in my own education, and she challenged me to succeed. She knew when I was looking down her cleavage, but she never moved or reprimanded me. Instead,

after some class assignment, Miss Fridhandler dragged me up in front of all those white kids and had me explain what I had done, and why. That made *me* the teacher. She was nourishing my self-esteem while almost every other authority figure in my life, including my mother, was telling me that I was irresponsible, no good, a failure. Miss Fridhandler even asked me to go over and help another student. I didn't know I was that smart, so that put me in a kind of heaven I had never known before. Suddenly, I loved her class. Even after she became Mrs. Levine, I still had a crush on her.

Another great teacher was Mr. Kowalski, who taught eleventh-grade English. His earlier classes were filled with honor students, eager to shine and rested from a good night's sleep. I came to him at the end of the day, drained mentally and physically and disgusted with school. That class had rows of troublemakers besides me—eight or ten tough Mexicans, and four or five members of the Spiders. That was a white sort-of motorcycle gang without motorcycles, whose members wore San Francisco Forty-Niners jackets with a spider on the back.

Mr. Kowalski, who had been a navy lieutenant during World War II, was no-nonsense. On the first day, he laid down his rules: "I'll grade you not only on the work you perform but what you put into it, what you deserve because of your effort." Somehow, he established rapport with us. He challenged us. The first six weeks of his class, I got a C. My next grade was B, and the last six-week grade was an A.

Near the end of the semester, Mr. Kowalski held an essay contest for students in all his classes. He told his other pupils that their essays would be judged competitively, but he said nothing about that to our class. Instead, he told us to write from our heart, and he would not penalize us for lack of language skills. I forget what I wrote about, but my essay won first prize, and a couple of guys in my class got ribbons and acknowledgments. It blew us all away. After that, we would have done anything for Mr. Kowalski.

Even so, most of high school was a blur because I had all that money and all that dope. I would smoke a joint before class in the morning, toke another on the way to the next, then drop a bennie and a dexie and smoke still another joint so I didn't look like a hopped-up freak.

When I started to go to doper parties, I got to know more people in drug circles. One day at Alan Michaels's, a guy was slobbering on himself, drooling like a pig. I asked what was wrong with him, and somebody said he was a heroin addict who needed a hit. Finally they brought him some heroin. I thought, God, how could he let himself do that? Is that what happens to you when you get hooked? Who wants that?

Pretty soon, the neighborhood dealers started to sell heroin. We helped cut it with powdered sugar or baking soda, then wrapped it in papers folded a special way for "dime" or "nickel" amounts—ten dollars' worth or five dollars' worth. With all that stuff around, it wasn't long before everyone was

sampling smack. They kept egging me on, so finally I said okay, I'll take a hit. I never liked a smack high. There's a point when you throw up. It's called flashing. Then you go into your high. I thought that was ridiculous. Why get sick just so you can get high?

But with all the peer pressure, soon I was injecting myself and getting sick. In a few weeks, I was hooked. Then, along with Robert Davis and a guy I'll call Sam Sjoquist, I decided I had to kick the habit. We got in Sam's car and drove to a remote spot along the bay with a beautiful view of San Mateo and San Francisco, and we went cold turkey. We stayed there all night, and it was hell—stomach cramps, vomiting, chills, and sweats. At dawn, I was still doubled over. I went home, but stayed in bed the whole next day.

I never understood why so many people get hooked, then go out and kill and rob for that damn high, since it's such an ugly thing. One day Mom found my outfit, the syringe and a little spoon that I used to melt the smack before injecting it. When she confronted me with it, I lied like hell, protesting my innocence. Mom handed it to Dad, who took me outside. I decided to tell the truth. I was doing dope, but not to worry, I had already shaken the habit. Pops just looked at me for a long time. Finally he said, "Well, I'll tell you, son. If you're really serious about getting high, then you can get yourself another needle, because I'm destroying this one." He walked away then, but his quiet words did more to chastise me than all my mother's ranting and raving. I thought about what he had said, and decided that I wasn't that serious about getting high. I never used another needle. But I didn't give up dealing.

By that time, Mom was totally fed up with San Leandro. Finding me with a heroin outfit must have been the final straw. In the fall of 1958, she put our house up for sale and moved back to Vallejo. I refused to go, so she left me there to watch the house until it was sold. Living alone, I had to figure out a way to get my diploma with the least amount of effort. Despite Mrs. Levine's attentions, I still couldn't stand school. When I began to do dope, I knew I couldn't perform in gym, so I refused to dress. Each day I didn't dress for gym took my semester grade down one notch. After a week, I had an F. To make up those failing grades, the vice-principal, in his infinite wisdom, scheduled me for three consecutive gym periods. I worked out a deal with the coaches that if I dressed for the first of those three hours, I would pass all three. I was still about twenty-five credits short of earning my diploma, but I petitioned the school officials to let me graduate anyway. I'll be damned if they didn't agree to that. I graduated from high school in January 1958.

Encouraged by Mrs. Levine, I enrolled in Oakland City College—now Merritt College—with the idea of becoming a history teacher. When I had taken ninth-grade California history in Vallejo, it hadn't even *mentioned* Indians. When I asked about them, the teacher said, "There's no history. The

California Indians were called 'digger' Indians because they lived by digging for roots." I had thought about that for years, and decided that there *had* to be a lot more to it. I wanted to find the truth about California Indians, and the truth about Kit Carson, Daniel Boone, Davy Crockett, and all those other Indian killers. Teaching history would be my ticket to that ambition, I thought. I tell myself now that it was a good thing I never became a teacher. White America wasn't ready to hear what I had to say. Having to confront institutional racism without the skills I would acquire on a different path might have driven me into an early grave.

To support myself at City College, I took a night job picking up golf balls on a driving range near the Oakland Airport.

Once back in school, I split up with Alan Michaels. I was still smoking weed, but marijuana no longer held magic for me. Every time I got high, I became paranoid. The term for a bad trip then was *bum kicked*, and so when I started looking around at people while I was smoking, they would say, "Man, you done bum kicked. What's wrong?" I would say, "No, no, I'm all right," but I would sit there thinking everybody was laughing at me. Later in my life, when I had arrived at a good self-image, I was tempted to get high again, just to see if I would get paranoid, but I'll never be *that* young and naive again.

After a while, I realized that weed was a dumb high. I thought, why not just stay straight or do booze? Now and then I still dropped an upper, but I didn't like the comedown—it made me so irritable. For several months, I more or less stepped away from dope and dealing.

In the first part of July 1958, I quit my job and, without any other income, returned to dealing. That got me back in with Alan, who by that time knew many dope people I hadn't met before. Because I was taking care of my mother's house while she was trying to sell it, I ran my dealings from there. When I had heroin to cut, a few guys came over and we put the smack into nickel and dime papers. That's what we were doing the day Mom drove up. The guys went out the back door with the dope before she came in, but I know she had very strong suspicions about what was going on. After Mom quit ranting and raving and condemning me, she said she had sold the house and I would have to move to Vallejo. I didn't want to go back, so I told her that from then on, I would make my own way. She said that was okay with her, and she left.

I didn't go back to college. Just to keep alive, I dealt marijuana and pills. As December arrived and the Christmas season was almost upon me, I realized that I missed my family. More to the point, I was getting tired of the scene in San Leandro. Faces were changing, and I didn't really fit in with the dope-dealing crowd anymore. It all ended in early December when I went to a big party in a three-story Victorian house. Hundreds of people were there, all kinds, and everyone was getting high. Suddenly the police raided the place. The house was on a dead-end street. No one could run away. Instead, people flushed thousands of dollars in dope down toilets. Others ate their drugs.

After surrounding the house, the police began to process suspects. People who were carrying dope were arrested and taken away. I was high, really high, and hanging on to a clothesline when three San Leandro cops—a captain, a lieutenant, and a sergeant—came up and threatened me. They said, "Son, we're going to get you. We can't bust you now, but we're going to get you."

I said, "Why me?"

"We know all about you, Russell Means, and we know all about your dope ring."

I couldn't believe I was hearing that. Here was the brass of the San Leandro police—and they knew my *name*. That worried me. I could feel it: Sooner or later, my number was going to come up.

I was broke, but I didn't want to go back to Vallejo with my tail between my legs. I didn't want to hurt my dad any more than I already had—and I didn't want to listen to what I was sure my mother would tell me. So I enlisted in the army. When my test scores came back, I was approved for any school the army offered. I chose Officers' Candidate School. The recruiter told me that after basic training at Fort Ord, California, I would go to Fort Benning, Georgia, for six months, and then I would be a second lieutenant. On a Friday afternoon in December, I sailed through the physical. They didn't test for drugs in those years. Except for an interview with a shrink that was required only for officer candidates, I was all set. But by the time I got to the psychologist's office, he had left for the weekend. A sergeant told me to come back Monday morning and be prepared to leave that afternoon.

All my buddies threw going-away parties for me. I stayed high the whole weekend. On Monday, I went to the recruiting station. The shrink was a middle-aged guy, very low-key. I wore my dark glasses. After all that partying, my eyes were puffy and my pupils were dilated. The first thing the shrink said was to take off my glasses. I said, "No, it's cool, man." I left them on while we talked and I said things like, "Yeah, man, that's right," and, "No, man, I don't think so."

The shrink saw right through me. He marked my papers 4-F—unsuitable for military duty. In hindsight, it was a good thing. I was so antiauthority that I'm sure I would have gone from basic training straight to the stockade, not to OCS. But I had said good-bye to all my friends. I had had my farewell parties. I couldn't stay in San Leandro and face everyone with my latest failure. I was damn near broke.

Home was the only place where I would be welcome, I realized. I got a pal to drive me to my parents' house in Vallejo. It was early in the morning on December 24 when I walked in, carrying most of what I owned in a suitcase. My mother and Dace were scurrying around, packing to go to Los Angeles to visit Auntie Faith's daughter Marilyn, who had recently given birth to a little girl. Mom invited me to come along, but I said I preferred to stay with Pops.

Although I had been up all night, I had dropped some bennies earlier and couldn't sleep. I felt restless and didn't want to hang around the house. To this day I don't know what got into me, but just as Mom and Dace were about to pull away, I ran out to the curb and said, "I'll go with you." I jumped in the car with them, and away we went.

That proved to be the most important decision of my life.

The Irish Pup

It was past midnight when we reached the Hardens' tiny apartment near downtown Los Angeles. It was Christmas. Marilyn worked as a telephone operator. Her husband, my Winnebago boxing mentor Bosco Harden, was on leave from the navy. Mom made a fuss over their new baby, Lakota Ann, and we all sat up talking for hours.

My mother had to return to work and Dace had to resume high-school classes, so they went back to Vallejo after a week. Bosco and Marilyn asked me to stay for another two weeks—until he had to report to his ship. I didn't look forward to returning to my parents' home in Vallejo and I enjoyed the Hardens' company, so I stayed.

As the new year of 1959 arrived, it occurred to me that I was fortunate to have left the dope world behind. It was true that in some ways drugs had forced me to grow up. I had met many different kinds of people, learned a great deal about human nature, and certainly dressed better when I had all that drug money. But I was realizing how stupid I had been to have wasted most of three years getting high. All these years later, looking around at how drugs have devastated an entire generation in the inner cities, I also realize how vicious and cruel it is to sell them to youngsters.

I decided to stay in Los Angeles and make something of myself. I went looking for work, determined to find a white-collar job, something with a future. To my surprise, within a week I found a position at General Petroleum, a subsidiary of Mobil Oil, in its five-story building—then one of the tallest in the city—on Flower Street, downtown. I began as a mail-room messenger, taking home a little less than two hundred dollars a month. That was more than enough to live on, and I liked the fact that I had to wear a suit and tie.

My job was to deliver the dozens of telegrams that arrived daily from all over the world to General Petroleum executives, mainly those in a fifth-floor inner sanctum. It was a suite of offices guarded by huge oak doors, a hushed place with indirect lighting, plush carpeting, and wood paneling. Because those messages contained highly confidential information, they were sealed in pink envelopes. My instructions were to deliver them to the addressees, usually the president or one of several vice-presidents, but not to their secretaries. If the executive was there, I waited until he came out to accept the telegram. If he was gone, I went into his office to put it on his desk. Those were elegant suites, each with a private washroom and luxurious leather sofas. Outside most was a veranda with a sun umbrella and patio furniture. I recall thinking to myself, someday, someday I'm going to have all that. When I got into an elevator and the beautiful secretaries coming to work looked right through me, I thought to myself, someday.

I worked hard, and soon I was promoted to mail boy, responsible for a route that covered two floors. My boss, a Chicano, had come up through the ranks. He had memorized the whole building and could sort a cartload of mail without even looking at the boxes. I watched him, committed the interoffice-box layout to memory, and soon learned how to do it almost as well. I knew I was a real mail boy when I learned how to let my cart roll slowly down the corridor while I ducked into the front end of an office—dropping incoming mail into "in" boxes, emptying "out" boxes—and emerged from the rear door just as it arrived. Very soon, I could do my two floors in nothing flat. Then I took the trouble to learn every route in the building. After only about six months with the company, I was promoted to head mail boy.

While I was delivering the mail, I zipped through offices, never stopping to chat. There were a lot of pretty girls in that building, but without booze or drugs, I was still too shy to talk to them. I often accepted invitations to parties thrown by my coworkers, but as the only Indian, I was never completely comfortable at those get-togethers. I began to look for other Indians to hang around with. In a place as big as Los Angeles, Indian people were scattered all over, so just about the only place for social interaction was a bar. Bosco had a few navy buddies who knew where to go—the Irish Pub, just west of downtown on Pico Boulevard, an Irishman's place that featured a Navajo band on weekends. We Indians called it the Irish *Pup*. I was only nineteen, but for a few bucks I got a fake ID. Soon I was going there every weekend, drinking enough to get my courage up, and dancing with girls. I was already a good dancer, but now I really cut a rug. Between sets, I bellied up to the bar and played Santa Claus, buying everybody drinks. Of course, most Indians are Joe Generous anyway, and people often bought me drinks in return. Many times, I went to the Pup almost broke and drank all night on the kindness of friends and acquaintances.

When the navy posted Bosco to a ship based in Japan, Marilyn decided she couldn't take California any longer and moved back to South Dakota. I got a room in a residential hotel near the Third Street tunnel, not far from where I worked. It was a run-down neighborhood, but I found a café where I could get three eggs, hash browns, toast, and coffee for thirty-six cents—including a penny for tax. I ate there often.

Usually the only time I saw other Indians was on weekends at the Irish Pup. Then one evening when I was walking home from work in my suit and tie, a car passed me, then braked to a halt. It was full of young men and women, some of whom I knew from the Pup. Someone asked, "What are you doing all dressed up?" They were surprised and impressed to learn that I had a suit-and-tie job. They were headed to a softball game and invited me to come along.

That's how I really got to know the Indians from Oklahoma, many of them Kiowa, but also Creek, Cherokee, Seminole, Cheyenne, Arapaho, Ponca, and so on. They were laid-back, fun-loving people who liked to joke around. They made friends easily. As I met more and more Indians, I began to ask, "How did you get here? Why did you come to LA from the reservation?" Most of them said, "Relocation." What the hell was relocation? Eventually, I learned that the Eisenhower administration had come up with yet another plan to depopulate Indian reservations. The idea was to integrate Indians into urban ghettos so that in a few generations we would intermarry and disappear into the underclass. Then the government could take the rest of our land and there would be no one left to object. I didn't quite grasp all that at the time. I understood only that reservation Indians were being offered transportation to several cities around the country, plus job training, and housing and employment assistance.

In the late 1950s and early 1960s, relocation was sending a steady stream of Indians from all around the country to Los Angeles and other cities. Most of the newcomers gravitated toward the Oklahoma Indians. Aside from my brief stay in Winnebago, that was the first time I had had a chance to become friends with Indian people from other than Sioux nations. Learning to appreciate other Indian cultures would have a profound effect on my life, but back then I knew only that I felt a strong bond of kinship with those guys from around the country. I began to hang out with them. We didn't want to spend twenty-four hours a day in a bar on weekends, we liked to get out. We went to Elysian Park to play softball.

After the games, we hung around to party. Construction had just begun on the Dodgers' new stadium in Chavez Ravine. The hill that eventually was leveled to become the stadium site was the one we called Beer Can Hill. LA cops were still somewhat human then; they pretty much left us alone. All during 1959, we went up there to sing and dance around a drum, Indian style. Some of the people who hung out in the Indian bars sponsored dances, which many folks called powwows.

In Los Angeles at that time, we Plains Indians were the most aggressive about preserving our own culture. Our dances are unique to our region, and we have our own style of singing. The Plains Indians—Sioux, Arapaho, Kiowa, Cheyenne—held all the dances. The songs and dances reflected our own culture, but we also invited other Indians. They were often lonesome and those were Indian events, so they came around. To be polite, we asked them to sit at the drum. They began to learn our songs—and that started the downfall of our Plains Indian culture.

It is our songs, not our languages, that have always been the most important part of our cultural heritage. We have songs for everything. They tell us where we came from and why, where we're going and why. Songs tell us everything we need to know to be a human being and a proud member of our nation. We never should have allowed other Indians to learn our songs. After a generation of mixing them with those of other Indian cultures, the Plains songs have been corrupted. They are *our* songs, so I resent it.

Even worse, because of "powwows," many Indian nations have all but lost the songs and dances that were unique to their nations, which are just as beautiful, if not more so, as those of the Plains. Starting in the 1950s, city-dwelling Indians have gone to powwows where they can dress up for a few hours a month to play Indian, as if that can somehow "justify" their Indian blood. The rest of the time, they are lost in the maze of white society. The powwows give them an excuse to sell out. At powwows, they dress in any style, borrowing from other Indian nations without understanding the meaning of the traditional garments, without knowing why they are worn. There is no discipline and therefore no pride. Since the powwows began, the Indian nations have become weaker year by year. They have become caricatures of their own traditions, unrecognizable as communities, as nations, almost unrecognizable as Indians.

I had no sense of that in the late 1950s. To me, the dances were camaraderie, fellowship. It never occurred to me that the Hopi sitting next to me, the Navajo across the drum, and a Santo Domingo joining in the harmony would ever forget their own melodies, or that their children would imitate—badly—Plains Indian dress at the cost of their own traditions.

Although I played basketball and softball and clung to what little Indian culture I could find in Los Angeles, I hated my life and was usually angry at myself. I didn't feel things so deeply when I was high, so the bulk of my spare time was devoted to drinking. In California, the bars close at 2:00 A.M. Sometimes after closing the Irish Pup, we would go to Santa Monica and party on the beach until the Columbine and the Ritz, skid-row saloons near Third and Main in Los Angeles, opened at 6:00. Other times, we would go to a café parking lot across the street from the Ritz and drink in our cars until the bars opened and we could go back to drinking, shooting pool, and brawling. When the Irish Pup opened at noon, we would head back there and start all over. I know many whites believe that Indians can't hold their liquor, but that's bull. Our problem is that we just don't know when to stop. I often went to jail for drinking during that time of my life, but it was only a ten-dollar fine, and I was always released the next morning.

As much as I hung around bars and socialized, I remained very self-conscious socially. Although I was almost twenty, I appeared to be maybe sixteen, tall but very skinny and rarely needing to shave. When I began to meet girls at the Irish Pup, it was usually in the company of several men in their twenties, guys who knew just what to say to them. We sat around talking to the girls and to one another, drinking beer with half-pint jugs of whiskey hidden in our boots, periodically going to the bathroom to sneak a snort. Between the booze and the camaraderie, I lost most of my inhibitions, but I was still too fearful to make the first move. It helped that girls often asked me to dance, but without the know-how or guts to pick up a girl or ask her for a date, drinking and dancing in a bar were all I could do with girls.

Then one night, a pretty Kiowa-Apache came into the Pup. In contrast to the blue jeans and plaid shirts that were our usual outfits, she was dressed very stylishly. She was in the company of several white people, all of them wearing fashionable clothes—they were slumming. She marched right up and asked *me* to dance. I couldn't believe it. We left the bar together and I spent the night with her. She was the first girl to pick me up that way. After that, it happened a lot. There were times when I went to parties, drank so much that I passed out, and woke up in the arms of a woman I couldn't even remember meeting. All that boosted my confidence. It made me start looking at myself. I began to realize that I must be fairly good-looking if so many women found me attractive. Even so, I never believed anybody who complimented me. I thought it was a lie. I have been this way all my life. I suppose it is mainly because my mother, trying to make me behave, continuously condemned me for almost everything I did or said. By the time I was a young man, I believed her. I was bad, and no girl could ever truly care for me.

I spent most of my free time in the company of other young men, imitating their behavior. One of them was Randy White Shield, a Kiowa-Apache. After we became friends, the two of us and some of our friends moved into the Kirby Hotel. One of those pals was LaVerne Reinhardt, a Lakota from the Lower Brulé Reservation in South Dakota. We called him Dad or the Old Man because he was thirty-six years old and we were all in our twenties.

We chose the Kirby because it was then the place where the BIA sent all the young single Indian girls arriving in the relocation program. We called ourselves the Kirby Cats—a pack of wolves hovering to pick off pretty Indian women.

Except for me, the Cats were all guys who could really rap down to women, especially Randy. Usually we met the Kirby girls collectively, hanging around the television set in the lobby. We steered lonely newcomers to the Irish Pup, where we would see them later, dance with them, and see what happened next.

One day as I was checking my mail in the Kirby's lobby, I saw the backside of a girl going up the stairs. She was short, a shade less than five feet, with a sensational figure and long hair falling to the middle of her back. I ran up the stairs, following her to the second floor. Sensing me behind her, she hurried to her room and closed the door. Next door was LaVerne's room. When he was there, he always kept his door open. I asked, "Who's that girl in the room next to you?" The Old Man said he didn't know her, but she had moved in a day earlier and was in school. It was October and still fairly warm out, so I hung around his doorway until she finally opened her door to get some air. Then I just strolled into her room and introduced myself.

In those days, when an Indian met another for the first time, usually the first thing they did was ask, "What tribe are you?" When I asked her, she said, "Sioux." Her voice was soft and she was very shy, like me.

"Where are you from?" I said.

"Cheyenne River."

"Oh, do you know my cousin, Madonna? We call her Donna."

"I went to school with her, we were in the same grade."

Her name was Twila Smith, and we discovered that we had much in common. She was a Minniconjou Lakota and her father, like mine, had been an automotive mechanic and had worked for the BIA on the reservation. I didn't realize it until I started to write this book, but Twila was the first girl I ever talked to and tried to get to know romantically whom I hadn't met in a bar or while I was boozing—the first one I could talk to without having had a few drinks first. At the time, however, I was just thrilled to be talking to a pretty girl who seemed to be interested in me. Aside from her sensational looks, Twila was very smart, a strong woman with a great sense of humor. Soon she was teasing me. I found that very refreshing. I had never met a girl like her. I was fascinated.

Many years went by before I learned that our meeting was not entirely an accident. Twila had seen me around, heard some of the Kirby girls talking about me, and told friends that she hoped I would call on her. She knew I was in the lobby when she made her entrance. I asked her to go out on Friday evening, when she didn't have schoolwork. Twila joined the other Kirby Cats and me at the Irish Pup, and I discovered that she was a very cute little dancer. From the moment Twila joined me on the dance floor, I knew we were going to be together. Before meeting her, I hadn't even been looking for a girlfriend. I had been happy to go out with the boys and enjoy bachelorhood. But Twila was different. She got me all worked up. That night, I shared her bed for the first time. I wanted to be with her every night, but she had homework and I respected that. We spent a little time together every day, but although we hugged and kissed, it was two or three weeks before we went to bed again.

The very first time we had made love, Twila conceived. When her pregnancy began to show, the BIA racists in Los Angeles tried to make her stay and give birth there—they were trying to depopulate the reservations. They told her that giving birth at the Cheyenne River Reservation would mean one strike against the child. Twila refused to listen. She decided to go home, where she would be among her family when the baby came. Then the BIA began to pressure her to give the baby up for adoption. Twila played the game to get train fare back to South Dakota, but she had no intention of giving up our child. When she was about six months pregnant, she took a leave of absence from Sawyer School of Business, where she was taking secretarial courses, and went home.

I had very mixed feelings about all that. I was awed by the prospect of parenthood, and I wasn't ready for it. I had begun to get over my fear of pretty girls, but I really wasn't ready to settle down with just one. I was relieved when Twila left town, because then I wasn't reminded every day of all the responsibilities of impending fatherhood. With her gone, I could continue to chase all the other pretty girls in town.

That was exactly what I did, along with the other Kirby Cats. When Bosco Harden got out of the navy, he broke up with Marilyn, moved into the Kirby, and became one of the Cats. By that time, we had begun to call him Bos. To this day, I consider him the best boxer and fighter I've ever seen in action. Unfortunately, like most Indians of our generation, he was never able to deal with his drinking problem. For years, pretty much all Bos did was get loaded and fight. It's very sad, but in my experience the old guys who fought well as young men never give it up. When Bos got older, he got beat up a lot. Cirrhosis of the liver killed him at age fifty-five.

Fights were common in Indian bars when I was a young man. Whites sometimes came to those bars, but we Indians fought only among ourselves. My generation was the first in nearly a century that was not completely shaped by boarding schools. We were far more rebellious than our parents' generation, but we were still so dominated by white culture that it never occurred to us that we could win a barroom brawl with anyone except ourselves. Most Indians sense white power the first time they see whites on an Indian reservation. They are the teachers, police, BIA administrators, priests, and nuns.

Whites are always in a position of authority over Indians. By adulthood, we had the attitude that we can't fight city hall and we damn sure can't fight the whites, because they're running it. The only one you can fight is yourself. Even today, the whole colonial syndrome continues to oppress people in Indian country. Nowadays it isn't manifested in physical fights between factions as it was in the 1960s. Instead, colonialism expresses itself in backbiting and in foulmouthed, rumormongering self-deprecation and codeprecation of our fellow Indians. Sadly, the colonized Indian today has been rendered totally impotent, and prefers pointing fingers to taking initiative—and responsibility.

In the early 1960s, the Indians I knew in Los Angeles took all their frustrations out on one another after drinking. Sometimes it was brother fighting brother, cousin fighting cousin, husband fighting wife. A lot of us, myself included, truly thought all that drinking and fighting meant we were real men having a hell of a good time. Often I got so drunk I didn't know I had been beaten until I got up the next morning with my face swollen. Other times, my friends would tell me about it. Although I woke up in an alley a few times, I never was beaten as badly as I had been that time in Sioux City.

I knew that I might get beaten badly, but I can never recall feeling fear. Thinking back over all the years that followed, all the beatings I survived, all the times I was arrested, I've never been scared. When I was little and my mother said, "Get in here," and I knew I was going to get a strapping—*that* scared me so much I would avoid going home for as long as I could. When the day came that Mom didn't scare me anymore, I had been beaten so many times I no longer feared anyone. Lately, it has come to me that when I put aside fear, I won the ultimate victory. I think most whites will never know that feeling, because Eurocentric male cultures teach people to fear the unknown. As long as you suffer fear, you cannot experience true freedom.

As much as I enjoyed my weekends, I was beginning to resent the five days when I had to be someplace, dressed just so and taking orders. Work, I had discovered, was the curse of the drinking class. But even if I stayed at General Petroleum for thirty years, I knew I still would be working in the mail room without more education. When I learned that one of those mysterious notations on my paycheck stub meant I had been paying unemployment insurance, I quit. It was August 16, 1959. I had worked for eight and a half months, and I thought it was time to kick back for a while.

Without working, I was getting twenty-seven dollars a week in unemployment. My room at the Kirby cost $10.50 a week, which left me enough to eat and party. Then I learned I could sell my blood for four dollars a pint. Officially, I could sell only one pint every six weeks, if I could pass a test which involved the speed at which my blood clotted. Someone told me that if I ate a lot of raisins the day before, I could pass the clotting test anyway. Sometimes I sold as much as four pints of blood in six weeks, going to a different clinic each time.

After I spent a few months of skimping by on unemployment and friendship, LaVerne Reinhardt, the Old Man, told me of an opening at the place where he worked, a little company in North Hollywood that manufactured swimming-pool heaters. The employees included all sorts of people—blacks, Japanese, Mexicans, French, an Englishman, and even a few Russians. I started at $1.75 an hour, a good bit more than I had made as a mail boy. The Old Man and I were at the front end of the assembly line, putting the controls together. We worked so well in tandem that we were always way ahead of the rest of the line. Sometimes after only a few hours of work, there would be stacks of assembled controls and nothing left to do. We got a few games going. The black guys were into marbles but none could beat me, so after a while I couldn't get up a game. Then we went to quick card games or shot dice, and for a time we played horseshoes, but LaVerne was so good that no one wanted to play against him.

Soon I was making enough to get a car. Not long after that, driving drunk, I ran a red light and smacked into another car, wrecking my '49 Ford. Even worse, I injured the people in the other car—two Hungarian freedom fighters, recent arrivals from Budapest. I was arrested. The judge, who was of Japanese descent, gave me a lecture about being too young to drink. I had no choice but to listen, but it was obvious that the judge didn't know a thing about being an Indian in a big city. Too young to drink? None of my friends thought so, and neither did I. I was sentenced to ten days in jail, so I called LaVerne and asked him to tell the boss I had quit. When I got out of jail, in December 1959, I went back on unemployment.

As Christmas approached, I decided to visit my mother. I put on one of my suits and caught a Greyhound to Vallejo. I spruced up at the bus station, then got a taxi. When I walked in, there was Dace, just as I had hoped. He looked me over in my suit and tie and seemed very happy for me. As far as he knew, I had flown the nest and become successful. What he thought of his big brother was important to me then.

After Christmas vacation, I borrowed my parents' new car and went back to San Leandro High. Two years had passed since I had graduated, and I wanted to see Mrs. Levine again. More, I wanted her to see *me*. I walked in wearing my best suit, really shining. A thin black fuzz decorated my upper lip, and my naturally wavy hair was combed straight back. Mrs. Levine, who had recently had a baby, was taking some time off. I was very disappointed. I got a six-pack of beer and went to see Alan Michaels. We went into his backyard, where he rolled a joint and offered me a hit, but I said no. I drank beer while he toked up. Then we went over to Sam Sjoquist's apartment. He was the guy who had introduced us to heroin, and he was still a big-time dealer. Alan, who had several joints with him, bought a bunch of pills. We were planning to go out for the evening, so I said, "Why don't you just leave all this stuff here while we go out?" Sam and his partner said, "Good idea, you never know what could happen." Alan and I climbed into my parents' car and took off. We didn't get fifty feet. Five cop cars screamed up to block the street, surrounding us. Following orders, we put up our hands, got out, and assumed the "position," with arms outstretched against the car. The San Leandro Police captain who had threatened me during the party drug raid a year earlier came up. He said, "I said we were going to get you, didn't I?"

The police searched us very thoroughly. They ripped open my pack of Lucky Strikes, made us empty our pockets—and found nothing. They tore up the car, deflating the spare tire, removing seats, hubcaps, and door panels, ransacking the trunk. They went under the hood to tear out the sidewalls, back wall and fire wall. There were no drugs at all, of course, so they finally gave up and took off, leaving behind the horrible mess that had been a car. Fortunately, Sam Sjoquist and his guys, who had been watching, lent us a car for the night and hired someone to put my mother's car back together. She never found out about the destruction.

If the cops hadn't totally ruined my day, they made me wonder why they went after Alan and me but hadn't busted Sjoquist's place, where they could have gotten all of us. I concluded that Sam or one of his guys must have set us up, because the police had rolled up dead sure that they had nailed us.

I later learned from Alan that a year earlier—just a week after I had impulsively jumped into Mom's car to go to Los Angeles for the holidays— the biggest drug bust in northern California history up to that time had gone down. Police had arrested the mysterious San Jose Mexican who had provided me with weed. They busted everybody I knew in the dope world, including Alan Michaels. They took in dozens of people I didn't know, including low riders, Hell's Angels, the white dealers we called pill poppers, and dope dealers from six other counties. Alan had gotten out of jail just a few days before I returned, and so had Sam Sjoquist. I had been incredibly lucky—or at least I thought so then. Now I know the Great Mystery had other plans for me, and they didn't include going to prison on a narcotics rap.

Fatherhood and the "Hustle"

Early in the new year, 1960, I returned to southern California and found an assembly-line job at a paint factory in south-central Los Angeles. It was terrible work, shoving empty gallon cans under the spigot of an enormous cast-iron vat that moved up and down the line on pulleys. Paint spilled if a can was a split second too late, but that line never stopped. I was very happy when I was laid off.

For a while, I collected unemployment. Then, talking to more and more Indians, I got the full scoop on relocation. One of the things I learned was that among the entitlements for those under a certain age was a job-training program that paid a living stipend plus tuition and books at a vocational school. I talked it over with Bos Harden, who was also out of work. We decided to go to our home reservations, apply for relocation to Los Angeles, and, when we returned, go to school.

I had only enough money for a train ticket to Las Vegas. From the station, I strolled over to the old Mint Casino downtown. Hoping to get lucky, I fed my entire fortune—sixteen cents—to a penny slot machine. Totally broke, I walked east out of town—and then I caught a break. An older Sioux, driving his wife and family back to South Dakota, offered me a ride. He fed me and took me all the way to Laramie, Wyoming, where I stopped to see my dad's twin, Uncle Johnny. While I was there, Pops called to say hello to his brother. Dad was heading for South Dakota and had planned to take a shortcut via Casper, Wyoming. He said he would change plans and come through Laramie to pick me up.

He was taking my twin brothers, Ted and Bill, to South Dakota. Despite her own experiences, Mom had decided that whatever might happen to them in a boarding school would have to be better than what had happened to me in a California high school. As far as she was concerned, I had headed down the wrong road and become a crook. She enrolled my brothers in the seventh grade at Bishop Hare Episcopal School in Mission, a white town on the Rosebud Reservation, east of Pine Ridge.

I told Pops I was heading back to South Dakota to get into the relocation program. He told me that Alvin Zephier, a distant relative who had been among my parents' closest friends during the first year after their marriage, ran the relocation program for the BIA at Pine Ridge.

I got to Uncle Johnsy Means's house just as the agency whistle blew, marking five o'clock, the end of the workday. Five minutes later Johnsy came home, washed his hands, and asked me to join him and his family for supper. Although he was actually my father's distant cousin, I called him uncle because he was my father's age. After I explained why I had come to Pine Ridge, Johnsy invited me to stay with his family until I could get on relocation. Uncle Johnsy and his wife were upstanding, relatively affluent people who had made careers working for the BIA.

The next day, I went over to the BIA to see Alvin Zephier, who had remained a good friend of my parents'. Even knowing that I had just come from Los Angeles, he promised to make sure I was accepted into the program and sent back there. He was doing me a big favor, because in those years, relocation applicants ostensibly were limited to three preferences among seven cities—Los Angeles, San Francisco, Denver, Chicago, Saint Louis, Dallas, and Cleveland. Rather than just send people where they wanted to go, the BIA established quotas for each city. Many Lakota preferred Denver, which was closest to the reservations, but it seemed that the quota was always filled. In general, most people were lucky if they ended up with their third choice, unless they were willing to wait—sometimes years—until the quota for a particular city opened up.

Zephier cut through all the white tape and made arrangements to get me into Los Angeles, although he said it would be more than three months before I could leave. I came to know Pine Ridge Village—then and now a depressing place. The few government buildings there seem modern, but only when compared with the rest of the reservation, where everything else is fourth-rate or worse. The housing is abominable. The town itself, besides being dry and dusty, reeks of dispirited people who have given up and accepted poverty as their lot. In 1960, nothing went on at Pine Ridge except for the work of the BIA. Even the Quakers, once a vigorous presence on the reservation, had abandoned Pine Ridge because they could see quite plainly that Christianity wasn't working for the Indians. I didn't think much about it at the time, but now I wish the rest of the churches would join the Quakers and acknowledge that Christianity serves only to further colonize Indians and rob us of dignity and self-worth. The missionaries are not likely to leave us, however. Although they came to us preaching about the meek inheriting the earth, churches have systematically taken over portions of our land. Now they hold title to much reservation acreage.

Coming from the restless energy of Los Angeles to the easygoing people of Pine Ridge was a big adjustment for me. There was no place to meet people my age except a local café, and I had to know someone before I was allowed to hang out there. I loitered at the busy intersection near the BIA offices, where people parked their cars or walked by to the BIA or the tribal government office. I hung around that corner all day for weeks, standing around with nothing to do and no one to talk to, until I met a woman I had known in Los Angeles. After finishing secretarial training there, she had got a job with the South Dakota Department of Welfare, which provided assistance to unwed mothers. I told her I was trying to meet people but didn't know where to go. She introduced me to some young men who took me to Whiteclay, an infamous village of bars and liquor stores two miles south of the state line, in Nebraska.

Then and now, it is illegal to possess alcoholic beverages on the Pine Ridge Reservation. Then and now, the BIA looked the other way at its own employees, white or Indian, who drink in the privacy of their own homes. If the BIA police or the FBI caught anyone else with booze, they were arrested, tried in tribal court, and fined or jailed. That didn't stop booze from entering the reservations, of course. There was money to be made in bootlegging, and people made it. Many bootleggers were highly situated BIA employees and tribal government officials, often aided and abetted by so-called law-enforcement types corrupted by easy money. In short, nothing much had changed since Feather Necklace's time.

None of that was on my mind when I headed down to Whiteclay. The saloons and liquor stores were owned by whites who stayed out of sight and let Indians run things. I usually went to the Jumping Eagle Inn or to a bar across the street on Friday and Saturday nights, but stayed only until about nine. By then, I knew that wherever Indians drank, we ended up fighting among ourselves. I thought it was just part of life, a macho thing inevitable in a culture in which alcohol made people belligerent and nobody backed down.

After a few weeks, I made some friends. On weekends, I often hung out with Gabby Brewer, a tough guy who got in a lot of fights at Whiteclay, and with Pedro Bissonnette, only about sixteen years old, a very smart, very likable kid. Once I became part of their circle, I was pleased to learn that they didn't argue or fight among themselves. Instead, we joked around and had fun. I didn't drink very much. I never wanted to be gassed when I got back to Uncle Johnsy's home, and I always tried to get back at a decent hour. Once I even decided to stay out all night because I was too high.

There is very little work on the reservation except for that provided by the BIA. Even most of the BIA jobs are dead ends, part-time or "temporary" positions, such as surveyor and mechanic jobs. The BIA hires people for six months, then lays them off for a day and hires them back for another six months. Pay is minimal, with no benefits, no possibility of advancement. No one can support a family on those wages, not even on a reservation. Yet the people who have those jobs are better off than most. That is why so many Indians today are economic refugees, no different than the Vietnamese boat people or the Mexicans who sneak across the border in search of decent jobs—but *we* are in our own country.

Nevertheless, as a twenty-year-old in Pine Ridge, I would have grabbed a dead-end BIA job in a Rapid City minute, if one had been available. None was, so rather than beg Uncle Johnsy for money, I scrounged around for work. Zephier steered me to a few people, all BIA employees. I cut their weeds and watered their lawns. I also did some farm work, throwing alfalfa bales up to a loft.

While at Pine Ridge, I found time to visit Eagle Butte, on the Cheyenne River Reservation. My new friends gave me a ride. I went to see Auntie Faith and Uncle Jockey—and Twila Smith. A week or so earlier, she had given birth to our baby, the prettiest little girl I ever saw, with curly black hair and creamy white skin, an infant version of Snow White. Until then, Twila and I had never seriously discussed marriage, and things were a little awkward between us. But we did agree to get in touch when we had returned to Los Angeles.

I had arrived at Pine Ridge in June, when the reservation was full of people. When school starts in September, almost everyone leaves and the village practically shuts down. Since I had been raised in a city, I found that autumn season even more depressing than summer, and I couldn't wait to get out of there. What I learned from my months at Pine Ridge was that contrary to what my parents had told me about their own generation's reservation experiences, without a job and an extended family to fall back on, Pine Ridge was a discouraging place. When I left, I felt as though I were escaping from prison, and I swore I would never go back.

Just before departing in the first week in October 1960, I suddenly came into some money—long-delayed unemployment checks totaling ninety-nine dollars, the payout on a claim I had filed in South Dakota against my California earnings. In addition, the BIA gave me twenty-four dollars for meals and expenses for the two nights I would spend on a train to Los Angeles. I had more than $120—worth about as much as a thousand dollars would be today.

Alvin Zephier drove me eighty miles to Alliance, Nebraska, the nearest place with a passenger rail station. I caught a rickety old train from there to Laramie, where I switched to a modern Zephyr that took me through Las Vegas to Los Angeles. It was a great ride, sitting in a domed lounge car and listening to the World Series on the radio. Bill Mazeroski, the Pirates' second baseman, hit a home run to win the seventh game and the series. Along with everybody in the club car, I talked about it all the way to California.

When I got to Los Angeles, nobody from the BIA was there to meet me. If I had been a typical relocation Indian, ignorant of the city, I would have been totally lost, but I knew where the BIA office was on Broadway. I decided to walk there from Union Station, a half mile or so. Passing city hall, I saw a couple of my buddies lounging under a tree on the lawn. My pocket was full of money and it was a warm October afternoon, so I invited them to join me at the Columbine for a couple of pitchers of beer. Big Ruby from Oklahoma was tending bar. The customers included several other people I knew, and everyone seemed glad I was back—and doubly glad that I had cash.

It was five minutes to five when I got to the BIA office. The bureaucrats were enraged. It was Friday, and they were about to leave for the weekend— and I was going to make them stay late. They immediately threatened to send me back to the reservation. I would come to learn that BIA officials always threatened Indians with that. They were too ignorant to realize that after a few months in a big-city ghetto or barrio, many Indians were thinking to themselves, "Yeah, send me back."

Those bureaucrats read me the riot act, and I played my role—dumb Indian. They were in such a hurry to fight the freeway home, drink beer, eat dinner, watch television, and yell at their kids that they didn't look closely at my records. I never let them know that I had grown up urban and had been around that city making a living on my own for more than a year. Instead, I said, "You didn't meet me. I got lost. Some Indians down on Main told me how to get here."

That quieted them for a bit, and they said, "Okay, we won't send you back." Alvin Zephier had told me how much subsistence money I was entitled to—enough to sustain me for four weeks, even if they couldn't find me a job or get me into school. I applied to Sawyer School of Business, but since I couldn't start until the next term, the BIA was obliged to find me a job in the meantime. I let the officials know that I was aware of my entitlements, especially the cash. I also said I needed an alarm clock, work clothing, shoes, and everything else I could think of. A white BIA man took me to a hotel near Olympic and Figueroa—a real dive—and paid a week's rent. There was a drugstore across the street where the guy could buy work clothes and a clock, but he wanted to go home. I said, "Just give me the cash. I'll buy what I need."

"You must bring in the receipts on Monday," he said.

"Sure," I said, and took the money.

It was Friday night. I decided that the alarm clock and work clothes could wait, and I headed for the Irish Pup. At the bar, I ran into an old pal, Reynold Howe. He told me Twila and Sherry, our baby, had come to Los Angeles a few weeks earlier. They were living at 1515 South Figueroa, just down the hall from his apartment. I went over and walked in on Twila. She was ironing, and very surprised—but glad—to see me. A few minutes after I arrived, Twila's door opened and in walked Bos Harden. He had been back in Los Angeles for a few weeks and was enrolled in an electronics school. He was already going with Twila's roommate, a sweet Sioux girl whose name I no longer remember. With Bos was Randy White Shield, my partner from the Kirby Cat days. Randy had recently come into big money from an oil company's settlement with his people in Oklahoma. He had lots of cash, and he had bought himself a '59 Chevy.

Twila got a baby-sitter for Sherry, and we all went out and partied. We had a great time, ending up in Inglewood at the home of a Wisconsin Winnebago named Wally Funmaker, a good singer. The next night, along with Bos and Randy and their dates, Twila and I went to the Irish Pup and did the whole scene all over again. We took the girls home and went back on Sunday to pick up where we had left off. On Monday morning I said, "I've got to get to the BIA," but someone said, "Have another drink before you go." I partied through Monday and Tuesday. I partied for five days, and I spent most of my money.

By the time I sauntered into the BIA office at midmorning Wednesday, I had my story pretty well worked out. After signing in with the receptionist with my name, tribe, enrollment number, reservation, and reason for being there, I was assigned a counselor. He was a heavyset white guy in late middle age, outraged that I hadn't shown up on Monday. He began by threatening to send me back to Pine Ridge.

I said, "Monday morning I did just what you said. I got on a bus at Olympic and Figueroa. I thought maybe it was the wrong bus, but I also thought maybe it was the right one. Before I knew it, I wound up in San Pedro. I didn't know where I was, so I asked the driver and he told me it was the end of the line. I asked him how to get back to Los Angeles, and he said to go over there and catch bus number such-and-such, so I did, but it took me to Huntington Beach. Then they told me I had to transfer, but I'd forgotten to get one. I asked directions again and took another bus and by the time I got back here on Monday, it was too late to come in.

"Then I met some friends who told me my girlfriend and my daughter were here. I went to see them yesterday, because I thought that fatherhood was more important than coming here."

The man asked, "Who is your girlfriend?" and wrote down Twila's name. He bought my story and didn't send me home. Then he asked, "Where are the receipts for the alarm clock and work clothes?" Still playing the dumb Indian, I said I had had them in my back pocket, but I was pulling out my wallet and getting on and off those buses so often that those receipts must have fallen out.

I could see that this had pissed him off, but all he said was, "Do you have an alarm clock?" I said, "Yes, sure." Then a huge fat woman came into the office to teach me how to live in Los Angeles. She began with a telephone. She grabbed my right hand and shoved my index finger into the dial of a rotary phone and "taught" me how to dial. She told me about prefixes and made me practice dialing. I was thinking that those had to be the stupidest people I had ever met, but that was my first experience with government bureaucrats. In later years, I would come to learn that they all seem like that, all the way up to White House secretaries. While the fat lady was gripping my hand and showing me how to dial, I looked at her and the counselor. With all the sincerity I could muster, I said, "What will they think of next?"

My sarcasm went unnoticed, so the fat lady gave me timetables and route maps and told me about bus transfers. In those days before the oil companies and carmakers got the state to pave everything, Los Angeles had a public-transportation grid of trolleys and electric buses. With transfers, you could go practically anywhere in Los Angeles County for a dime.

Then the BIA man asked me what kind of work I wanted. I said, "I want a white-collar job, like I had before I left." That set him back on his heels. "You've got to take what we can give you," he said. "Fine, as long as it's a white-collar job," I said. "That's what I told Mr. Alvin Zephier at Pine Ridge, and he promised me that if I came to Los Angeles, before I enrolled in school, the BIA would find me a white-collar job." I wanted an office position because I had decided I was going to a business school to become an accountant. I wanted to get rich, and the way I figured it, the fastest way was to learn all I could about money.

After the BIA's four weeks of subsistence ran out, Indians were supposed to be working or in school. Since school was out for me until the spring semester, I went to the BIA office every morning to inquire about a job. Every morning, that is, except Mondays and Fridays. The BIA people gave me a lot of flak about that, repeatedly threatening to send me back to Pine Ridge. I kept giving them excuses, mostly that I was playing dutiful father to Sherry. In fact, that was pretty much bullshit, although I was seeing Twila regularly. The BIA couldn't find me a white-collar job, and the end of the four weeks was coming up.

I moved from the flophouse hotel where I had been planted into somewhat nicer digs at 1515 South Figueroa, where I became Reynold Howe's roommate. Bos Harden also took a room there. Twila moved into an apartment near Union and Third, in the MacArthur Park area.

I wanted a job, but the BIA couldn't get me one. Finally a petty bureaucrat told me, "Until we can find you a white-collar position, you'll have to take a temporary job." I went to Los Angeles Street to load and unload freight cars in 90-degree heat. When I got my paycheck that Friday, the supervisor said, "See you Monday." It was too late to go to the BIA office, so I returned to work on Monday, worked another week, and got another paycheck. When the supervisor said, "See you next week," I said, "I quit." On Monday, I told my BIA counselor. He said, "What? You can't quit! You've got to learn to be responsible, dependable. You can't be an Indian. This isn't the reservation." He threatened again to send me back.

I said, "You told me this was a temporary job, but after two weeks it didn't look temporary to me."

After another week went by and the BIA couldn't find me a white-collar job, the guy was desperate. My allocation had expired. He told me I *had* to take another temporary job, at a small company that made aircraft parts. I became a janitor, cleaning offices at 6:00 A.M., then going into the machine shops to sweep up. After two weeks, I decided that didn't look much like a temporary job either. But that time, when I quit, I didn't go back to the BIA. I decided to find my own job. Bos was working at the data-processing headquarters for Carte Blanche, the credit card company owned by Barron Hilton. Bos told me about an opening for a sorting-machine operator in data processing. I arrived for an interview to find that more than a dozen people, mostly young men, had applied for the job. When people filled out applications in those days, they were asked to give their race—but there was never a box for American Indians. We were always told to mark "other," but I refused to do that. Instead, I always wrote in big letters, "AMERICAN INDIAN SIOUX." That's what I did that time, too.

After giving my application to the receptionist, I sat down to wait. Suddenly my name was called, way out of turn. When I entered the data-processing supervisor's office, he rose from his chair, shook my hand, and greeted me in Lakota. I replied in kind. He was from the Lower Brulé Reservation in South Dakota, son of a Lakota woman and a white man. We chatted a few minutes about people we both knew, and then he said, "You can go home now. You've got the job."

My task was to operate a sorting machine. I took punched cards, generated by accounting machines, and put them through the sorter. There was only one sorter and it was the fastest machine in that department, so I soon found myself way ahead of the accounting-machine operators. To keep my sorter running, I began to help the operators—but even so, I was always far ahead. I took cards from the sorter to a collating machine and taught myself to run it. After the collator, the cards had to go through yet another machine, and I learned how to operate it, too. Soon I knew every machine in the department, and at times, most days, I ran all of them by myself.

In short order, I had made myself practically indispensable in data processing—just as my dad had done with his welding at the naval shipyards. The supervisor liked me and understood where I was coming from, and almost anyone he might hire to take my place would know only how to run the sorter. I learned that I could often arrive late or call in sick on Mondays with no fear of getting fired.

In June 1961, I was notified of my acceptance by Sawyer School of Business. My boss arranged for me to be laid off so I could collect unemployment during the summer before school began. In September, I started accounting classes in downtown Los Angeles, the only Indian in a class of fourteen. A few weeks later, I was sitting in the Irish Pup with Don Lone Wolf, Randy White Shield, and a bunch of other guys, drinking, laughing, and having fun. At the next table, with his girlfriend, was a big, quiet Oklahoma Comanche who had been a boxing champion. Neither one drank. They usually just sat around, danced occasionally with each other, and left at about midnight. Suddenly the guy leaned forward and said, "You really think you're smart, don't you? I'd fight you if you didn't have all your buddies."

I don't know why that Comanche was pissed, but back then, I got in many fights in just that way. Maybe people didn't like me because I was having too much fun. I said, "Let's go outside." That was booze talking. I'd already drunk enough to feel good—no matter that he was much bigger than me.

"You won't bring your buddies?" said the Comanche.

"I won't even tell them. It's just you and me."

We went into the alley. He was a boxer, so I tried to box him. Boom! He hit me with a jab, then boom, boom, a combination. It dawned on me that he was a *good* boxer. I abandoned the Marquis of Queensberry rules and switched to the old reservation windmill, both arms flailing punches. Down he went, pulling me over. My left elbow smashed into the asphalt, but I was too drunk to feel much. I jumped on top and was about to whale away on his face when he said, "No fair hitting when you're down."

That stunned me. I stopped in midpunch, not quite believing an adult male would say such a thing. I hadn't heard that line since grade school. I just stared at him. As I tried to clench my left fist to hit him, I found that my arm was a rag from the elbow down. He hadn't realized I was hurt, so I said, "I'll let you go." I got up, turned around, and very deliberately walked back to the street, tucking my left hand into my pocket. I hoped he wouldn't notice that I was crippled and wouldn't try to get revenge by jumping me from behind. I felt the hairs on the back of my neck stand up, but I walked on, never looking back until I was around the corner. He didn't come after me, and I never saw him again.

I went back into the Pup, told my friends what had happened, and they took me to a hospital emergency room. I went under general anesthesia while a surgeon cut into my shattered elbow. When I left the hospital, it was in a cast. When the cast was taken off, my elbow would open only about ninety degrees to an L shape. My hand remained paralyzed, the fingers closed and thumb sticking out. The doctor said the damage was permanent. My left arm would be that way for the rest of my life, and there was absolutely nothing I could do about it.

Soon after that, I got a draft notice. I went back to the orthopedist for a letter that said I was permanently disabled. After an army doctor read that letter, he made permanent my earlier 4-F classification—unfit for military service. It was probably the best thing that happened to me in my whole life, because my arm and hand were not destined to remain as they were. Every morning, I walked from my apartment in the MacArthur Park area down Sixth Street to Union Square and then a few blocks to Sawyer School. Every morning, I used my good right hand to force open my crippled left and stick a big, thick accounting book and an equally heavy tax book between my fingers. It hurt, but I walked all the way to school like that. Later I walked back home with the books in the same position. In between, whenever I was sitting down, I took my left hand and put it on my knee, forced the fingers open and the thumb over until it was gripping my knee. In that way I kept the fingers and thumb apart for hours.

After several weeks, I noticed that my left arm could open a little farther under the weight of those books. With a few months of continued "book therapy," the arm was nearly normal. I regained much of the use of my fingers. Today, although my arm still doesn't open completely and my left hand doesn't work quite as well as the right, they look normal. During the years since all that happened, I've thought about the sequence of events many times. I'm convinced that all of it—the unlikely back-alley brawl with a previously peaceable man, the freak accident that crippled my arm, the draft notice and my subsequent 4-F status, my extraordinary recovery—shows the deliberate hand of the Great Mystery.

Again.

While I was in school and even before that, when I was working at Carte Blanche, I saw Twila frequently, often staying with her overnight. Soon after I quit my job, she told me she was pregnant again, with my child. I began to have the almost overwhelming feeling that Twila, Sherry, and the baby, soon to come, were my responsibility, that I had to claim my children and take care of them. I'm sure those feelings came from ideas and values implanted by my mother, who had always pushed me to take responsibility for my acts.

One autumn day, during the time when my elbow and hand were slowly recovering, I went to the apartment Twila shared with another young woman and asked to talk to her. We went into her bedroom and sat on the bed. Without preamble, I said, "Do you want to get married?" Twila was stunned, absolutely speechless. When, after several seconds, she didn't answer, I said, "Do you want to get married? Yes or no?"

"Of course," she said, big with a six-month fetus but glowing with joy. I've never seen anybody that happy in my life. While she ran to tell her roommate, I called my folks in Vallejo. Twila and I decided to get married on my twenty-second birthday, November 10, because it was the only time my folks could make it down. Within a few days, we got our marriage license and blood tests and went to city hall. The wedding was over so quickly and with so little ceremony that it hardly seemed that we were married. I was a little upset because for some reason my mother had excluded my dad from the wedding, forcing him to stay behind at Twila's apartment.

After the wedding, Twila and I took a little apartment on Union Street. She was working as a secretary. I was getting seventy dollars a month from the BIA while I was in school. It was barely enough to live on. Then a month before Twila was to give birth, she had to quit her job. Making ends meet was very tough.

I was at a Saturday-night Indian dance in Inglewood on February 4, 1962, when someone called to say Twila had gone into labor at Queen of Angels Hospital. Bus and trolley service was very spotty after midnight and I had no car, so it was the next morning before I made it over to see my son. We named him Walter, after my father, and Dale, after my brother. Naturally, he is always called Hank, just like Pops.

I know now that our marriage was doomed from the start. Twila and I both tried to make it work, but I was too young and ignorant, far too immature to be a husband, let alone a father. When I began to hate myself too much to bear it, I went out and got so drunk I didn't have to think. Within weeks of Hank's birth, my relationship with Twila had deteriorated to the point that we seemed more like roommates than a married couple. On Friday nights, I would ask Twila, "Where are you going this weekend?" She would tell me, then ask, "Where are you going?" We tried to avoid each other when we went out. After a few months of that, I moved out, and we just broke it off. I was very disappointed in myself, in my failure as a husband, but all I had to do to forget about it was to party—something I was very good at. When I wasn't drinking, I blamed myself for the breakup, feeling that I was probably the worst guy in the world. I can't say now that I was a *good* guy, but with hindsight, I now know that beyond mere immaturity, I had no idea of how to go about building a lasting relationship. I hated myself, hated what I was doing with my life and the many ways I had failed to measure up to my mother's high standards and my own aspirations. I was filled with a fierce anger. I could contain it when I was sober, but my rage emerged when I drank. My constant brawling was an outlet, but punching someone out or getting beaten up myself did nothing to deal with the source of my anger.

As much as I partied, I was very responsible about attending school, more so than my classmates, many of whom never returned after Christmas vacation. One by one, the others dropped out. By late February or early March, I was the last of the accounting students. At that point, the instructors gave me reading assignments and take-home tests, which I read on my own. I made a little money playing chess in Union Square, I hustled suckers around barroom pool tables, and I looked for other scams to make cash.

Sometimes on Wednesday nights, when no one I knew would show up at the Pup, I went with a Chicana prostitute and pickpocket who worked the bars. I sat in a booth with my schoolbooks and a glass of draft beer. She was in the next booth hustling some old guy. While he fondled her thigh and kissed her, she slipped out his wallet and threw it to me. I would leave and meet her later. For prostitutes or B-girls to hang around a bar, they have to cut in the establishment—if they aren't outright hired by it—so we had to give the bartender a cut before we split our share.

It was a matter of survival for me, but I remember asking the Chicana, "How can you do this—live this way?" She explained that she had a daughter in elementary school. "I've got to clothe and feed my girl," she said. "I do what I must. These men work, and if they want to put their hands all over me, they have to pay for it. I'll make sure they do."

Thirty-odd years ago, when I was a bum, I could live with myself for having teamed up with a desperate Chicana pickpocket. It wasn't pretty, however, when I rolled someone flashing a wad. I would usually get two pals, wait until the guy walked into the bathroom, then hit him very hard and quick so he wouldn't yell or put up a fight. We would take his money and run. I never carried a weapon. I recalled that once after my dad had gotten rolled, his wallet came back in the mail, so I always dropped my victim's wallet in a mailbox.

All the time I was hustling, I continued to do my schoolwork and I aced all my tests, because I loved accounting. I loved the freshly sharpened Number Three lead pencils, the twelve-column work sheets, debits and credits, amortization, profit and loss, financial statements. I loved gathering, disseminating, and analyzing information, and the final product. I loved it all. It came easy for me, even though we had no calculators or adding machines, much less a computer—everything was in the head and hand. It's kind of sad to see all that go by the boards. Today there are people calling themselves accountants who don't know a debit from a credit and can't even add. God help them if the computer breaks down!

Aside from the tests and the few times when I needed help or counseling, I never went to the school. The teachers wouldn't come in for just one student, so there was no point in my showing up. When I got my grades, they were straight A's. My BIA counselor had promised that after I completed a year of training in accounting, I would get a three-month extension to take a computer course. Just before the school year ended, one of the BIA people learned I was the only one in the class and there was no attendance record on me. He called me in to find out why I hadn't been going to school. I explained that all the other students had dropped out and there was no class to go to, but I had done all the work and had made top grades. The bureaucrat wasn't impressed. He said, "These people want our money, so they'll make sure you pass."

"That might be true," I said, "but I earned those A's." You can't finesse an accounting exam. If the numbers don't total, you're wrong and you fail. The counselor said, "Too bad we didn't catch this earlier. We'd have kicked you out of school for not going by the regulations. You must go to class every day—that's the rule."

With hindsight, it seems possible that if I hadn't asserted my rights during the previous eighteen months and demanded my entitlements from officials at every opportunity; if I hadn't taken every opportunity to jerk around and manipulate those BIA drones; if I had played the compliant, grateful Indian instead of the dumb Indian, those particular bureaucrats might not have insisted on enforcing the fine print. On the other hand, the BIA was then, and is now, overwhelmingly staffed by lazy, mindless people. They usually regard Indians as no more than annoyances who interfere with coffee breaks, lunch hours, and quitting time. Whenever they can enforce a rule that saves themselves work, they will. Moreover, behaving toward the BIA in other than the way I had was not in my nature then and is not in my nature now.

I attempted to reason with the BIA counselor, but it was like talking to a slow-brained prison guard. I was furious. Here was this program, devised by white planners in Washington and funded by Congress in good faith, and its objective was to get Indians off reservations and train them to enter the mainstream of American society. Yet a paunchy, balding, beet-red-necked, fifty-something asshole who wouldn't look me in the eye ignored my grades because he wanted to enforce a regulation so he could knock an Indian out of training. That was his chance to make sure I would be a failure.

Infuriated, I asked to see his boss. He refused to call him, but he brought in all his peers, everybody in the office. They wouldn't budge. I hadn't gone to school every day, so I didn't deserve any more training. I was out of the program, and my support stipend was terminated in June 1962. I looked for a job at which I could use my new accounting skills, but found nothing. After splitting up with Twila, I had lived with friends. Several of us had gotten together and rented a succession of cheap apartments. When my subsistence was cut off, I became homeless. I could have stayed with any of my friends, but I couldn't pay my fair share, and pride prevented me from imposing on them. I also refused to call my mother for help. I decided that since I had gotten myself into this, I would get myself out.

In those days, the homeless were called bums and treated accordingly. Many a night, I slept under cardboard or at a construction site, getting up early so the workers wouldn't find me. I spent my days trying to hustle enough money to get drunk, eat once in a while, and have fifty cents in my pocket when the bars closed at 2:00 A.M. Then I would go to an all-night theater. I learned certain ways to feel almost comfortable, resting my knees on one seat, my body on another, and my feet on a third. There was a trick to knowing how to lie there. After several nights, I learned it and got some sleep. At five in the morning, the management kicked all the bums out. I would go to a doughnut shop near Third and Main and get a cup of coffee and a doughnut for six cents. At six, the skid-row bars opened, and I started my hustle all over again. On Wednesday nights, a band played at the Irish Pup, and people I knew usually came around. Most of them would buy me a drink or something to eat. On weekends and once in a great while during the week, there would be a party, and I would be invited along. I would eat, drink, and sleep on someone's sofa or the floor. Sometimes I would go home with a woman. It wasn't that bad a life in some ways, but it was hell being without money.

Even so, I had some good times. Not long after school was out, I got my hands on a '49 Ford convertible. I cruised around in that baby, pretending that beat-up old white car was a Cadillac. One weekend, a bunch of us crazy young guys got together and drove it to San Francisco and partied there. I met a tall, beautiful girl with sharp features, a Hopi named Betty Sinquah. She was on the relocation program, working as a secretary for a big insurance company and living with two or three other girls. I was very attracted to her, but I lived in Los Angeles, and I couldn't imagine that I would ever see her again.

After returning to Los Angeles, I had little time to focus on romance. I was preoccupied with survival. There was an art to living on the street because the cops watched for what they called vagrants. You couldn't remain homeless in those days. If you were convicted of having no fixed residence, they put you in jail for ten days or more. Around skid row, the LAPD staged the dragnets they became famous for in the 1950s and 1960s. They picked up everybody on the streets, among them people with unpaid traffic or parking tickets, those who had jumped bail or were wanted on arrest warrants, and sometimes felons who had fled other states. They filled the jail for the week-end. On Monday, everyone went before a judge. I wasn't wanted for a felony or a parking ticket, so when I got picked up for "public drunkenness," I would be out on Monday morning. I was picked up about two dozen times in the three and a half years I was in Los Angeles. After I became homeless, however, I quickly became more streetwise and rarely got caught in a dragnet.

Besides hustling around barroom pool tables, I gambled on the bowling machines that were in most neighborhood saloons then. I learned that more entered into the process than the score. I had to become an amateur psychologist, learning to sense when my opponent was so far out of pocket that he would quit if he lost another game. Then I would let him win one. The dynamics of the room, including the spectators, came into play—who was rooting for me, who wanted me to lose. Sometimes it was peculiar to see a bunch of Indians—my best friends—all rooting for the white guy I was playing against. They all had their side bets, their own little hustles, and there was no telling what kind of odds they had parlayed for themselves. All that happened kind of slick and low-key, off to the side, while I worked some guy, trying to take him for all the money in his pocket. Sometimes I got outhustled. Other times, I couldn't find anyone to play for money, but I could take him for a few drinks.

Hustling pool and bowling machines wasn't bringing in enough, so I got in with some guys who went around to liquor stores and markets with a shortchange scam. We cased stores until we found one where the cashier didn't put large bills on top of the register while he made change—he put them in the cash drawer immediately. After we knew that was the normal way of handling bills in that store, my partner would take a twenty-dollar bill, write a phone number on it, and go into the store. He would buy some gum—it cost a nickel in those days—take the change, and leave. I went in immediately to buy another pack of gum, and paid with a dollar. When the cashier made change, I would say, "Hey, wait, I gave you twenty dollars."

He would usually say, "No, you gave me one dollar."

"No, no, it was a twenty. There was a phone number on it."

Then I would recite the phone number, and of course the top twenty-dollar bill in the register had that number written on it because my partner had given it to the cashier just before I came in. The clerk would usually apologize and give me $19.95. Just like that, we had doubled our money! I worked that scam over and over. There were lots of stores in Los Angeles, and in those days none had registers tied to computers that make you punch in the amount tendered before it makes change.

Once in a while one of my hustles paid off big, but whenever I got cashy, I turned into my dad—like Santa Claus, I would give my money away until it was gone. I'm still like that. Maybe I'm trying to make amends for all the things I did wrong when I was younger.

Another favorite scam, which I usually worked with Randy White Shield, was on a cafeteria. After we had sold our blood for four dollars a pint, we were ravenously hungry. Usually we'd had nothing to eat but raisins the day before. We went to a cafeteria like Clifton's, where people paid on the way out. Randy would go first and load up a tray with maybe twelve dollars' worth of food—chicken, meat loaf, baked potatoes and yams, whatever—about what fifty dollars would buy now. At the end of the food line, he got a ticket with that total, went to a table, and started eating. Then I'd come in, carrying a newspaper, and get a cup of coffee. I'd engage the woman at the cash register in a conversation. She was usually a Mexican or a black, so I'd ask if she was part Indian, and I'd say something like, "Are you sure I get free refills?" In this way she'd remember that I'd bought only coffee. Then I went to the table where Randy was eating, opened my newspaper, and started reading. When Randy had finished eating, he took out doggie bags for the leftovers, put them in a sack he'd brought with him, picked up *my* meal ticket and left, paying a dime. Meanwhile, I read and drank coffee, got a refill and drank it. Five minutes after Randy left, I'd pick up his ticket and give it to the cashier. I'd say, "Hey, what is this? What happened here?" Of course she would vouch that I had only a cup of coffee. Sometimes I'd say, "That guy must have switched receipts on me! He snookered you!" I'd pay a dime and leave. Then I'd meet Randy and we'd go to another cafeteria where I ate while he drank coffee.

I was homeless for only a few months, but I came to know skid row's secret world in the most intimate ways. Yet in my head I was never a permanent resident. Unlike most other bums, I still had hope. I knew people with money, people who would have cheerfully given me whatever they had with never a thought of repayment. I concealed my situation from family and friends out of pride. If they had known I was on the streets, many would have insisted that I stay with them. I made sure I was always clean, washing at the bus terminal. A friend let me store my luggage in his basement, and there I changed clothes or picked up clean shirts and underwear. I drifted through my skid-row, don't-give-a-damn days, knowing I would finish my education someday. I was in no hurry, not bothered that I didn't have a goal for next December—or for next week. Someday, I knew, I would do my four years in college and start on my life in a cozy house with a picket fence.

As the months went by, however, I began to realize that I didn't like my life. I tried to make myself think it was no big deal, but the lower I felt, the more I drank and partied to cover up my depression. Eventually I acknowledged to myself that I was a bum, and that station in life was my own responsibility.

Then one night I walked into the Irish Pup to find a letter addressed to me from the County of Los Angeles. The subject was child support for my two children. Twila, who was having a rough time financially, had filed for Aid to Families with Dependent Children, and that had sent the authorities after me. I had no prospects for a job. I couldn't support myself, let alone two children, so I decided it was time to leave Los Angeles.

All my possessions fit into three small suitcases and a hanging bag. Randy White Shield gave me a ride to the far end of the San Fernando Valley and dropped me on Highway 99, which leads north over the Tehachapi Mountains. Bos Harden came along for the ride. He had only a dollar, but insisted that I take it. Randy used his last money to buy gas, but he had half a pack of cigarettes, Parliaments. He gave them to me. We shook hands and said good-bye. I arranged my bags by the road so an oncoming driver couldn't see that there were so many and stood there, hoping someone would give me a ride north.

9

▼▼▼▼▼▼▼▼

San Francisco

When we were growing up, my brother Dace was the one our mother said she could always depend on—and she was forever throwing him in my face. She would say, "Why can't you be like your brother? He does his homework. He saves his money. Why can't you?" So I made sure I never did homework or saved my money. Poor Dace, of course, was caught in the middle, trying to be an obedient son but still looking up to his big brother. From the time he was three or four, already my constant companion in forays around Vallejo, I was always hustling him for something, always taking advantage of his trusting nature and the superior knowledge I had from being two years older. I used to say, "Let's trade coins. Look at this nickel, it's bigger than your dime. You can have the biggest one." Believing his big brother, he would always give me his dime in exchange for my nickel. Dace always took his time—even when he was eating. If we were each given a popsicle or a candy bar, I would gobble mine, then ask for half of his. He always gave it to me.

So on August 16, 1962, when all my options had expired and I was fleeing parental obligations and the county sheriff, I headed straight for Dace, who was living with our dad's cousins, Chalk and Belva Cottier, in their home in Mulford Gardens, San Leandro. My first hitch took me as far as Bakersfield, the second almost to Fresno. Finally, a long-haul trucker, to my amazement, went miles out of his way to drop me at a little shopping center near Mulford Gardens.

I called from a pay phone. Dace came to fetch me in his '58 Impala, a canary-yellow coupe with a Continental kit on the trunk. Dace had a good job and plenty of money. He had taken a far different path in life than the one I had chosen. After high school, he had gone to work for Standard Oil in Richmond, then married a white girl named Sandy, his sweetheart since junior high. Everyone in the family, including Mom and me, had tried to discourage him from marrying her—everyone except Pops. He never said anything about it to Dace. Exasperated, I said to him, "Dace is too young, and Sandy isn't right for him. Why aren't you with the rest of the family, trying to tell Dace not to marry her?"

My father said, "Let me tell you something. When that love bug bites you in the ass, there's not a damn thing you can do about it." That was his last word on the subject. Pops was right. I never got onto Dace again about marrying Sandy.

By the time I got back to San Leandro, he and Sandy had split up. That was partly why he was living with our cousins. I stayed there with him for a few days, until we decided that we couldn't *both* impose on the Cottiers. We moved to the San Pablo, a cheap hotel in Oakland.

As soon as we settled in, I wanted to go to San Francisco, find the Indians, and, especially, look up Betty Sinquah, the Hopi girl I had met the previous year. Dace slid behind the wheel of his Impala, and we took off. I had brought along a pint of gin and opened it in the usual manner—rapping the bottom of the bottle sharply against the heel of my hand to crack the top seal, then twisting off the cap. I took a few snorts and swallowed them, thinking nothing of it, then handed Dace the bottle. He grabbed it, then set it down between his legs. Then he looked at me, picked up the bottle, and hesitated. "Jeez," he mumbled, and I noticed he was taking deep breaths, trying to get up the courage to take a straight shot. Finally, he took a swig, a little one. I laughed, thinking, I've got a rookie here. It dawned on me that constant boozing had hardened me.

By the time we got to Betty's place, we both had a nice buzz going. She was happy to see me, totally blown away that I had turned up unannounced. We went out that night, and the more time I spent with her, the more attractive I found her. She was tall and shapely, light skinned with long hair and a straight nose. Like my mom, she was strong and self-reliant. Betty's Hopi mother had raised her as a strict Christian. Her father was a traditional Tewa, from one of the smaller Pueblo nations on the First Mesa of the Hopi Reservation, in Arizona.

Dace and I spent the weekend partying, continuing through Monday and Tuesday, as I often had done in Los Angeles. Not until Wednesday did

Dace return to his job. He was working for the Southern Pacific Railroad, in a union shop with strict rules. The company frowned on employees who failed to show up or who reported late. Because that was Dace's first infraction, however, he might not have been fired. He probably would have been put on probation or something, and there would have been a mark against his record. Nevertheless, to avoid the hassle, he just quit.

We had spent the last of Dace's money partying, and the railroad company said it would be a few days before he would get his final paycheck and vacation pay. Broke and hungry, we went to a Christian mission. Down-and-out people of all kinds were lined up for a meal, all very respectful of the charity they were about to receive. Perhaps because we were clean and neatly dressed, the people at the mission seemed happier than hell to see us. I suppose they got few converts and very few well-dressed visitors, so they seemed anxious to proselytize us. But before we could eat, we had to sit through a service. Dace and I, who had long since lost our belief in Christianity and hadn't been to church in umpteen years, suffered through it.

As soon as Dace's money came, we moved to a down-at-the-heels hotel at the edge of San Francisco's Tenderloin district. We could only afford one room, so we shared a double bed. I couldn't stand Dace's hairy legs, so we established a no-man's-land between us in the bed. Dace went on unemployment, and every Wednesday we went down to pick up his check. I was hustling drinks and a few bucks around the bars on bowling machines and I had a few other scams, but basically Dace was carrying me. After paying the room rent, he gave me an allowance, ten or fifteen bucks, and kept the rest.

I remained unemployed for my first few months in San Francisco, while Betty worked as a secretary for the Fireman's Fund, an insurance company. She had been in town for a couple of years and had a large circle of friends, all relocatees, living in different parts of the Bay Area. Her two roommates were Pueblo Indians. Betty and I dated almost every weekend. In those days, most young women took their time before going all the way with a man—and she had roommates, which made things more complicated. I courted her for weeks, taking her to movies and dancing or just hanging around the Indian Center. Late at night after the parties had died down, we loved to find some inexpensive restaurant, get a table together, and talk until sunrise. After a couple of months, when we had become very close, we became lovers, all very sweetly and naturally.

Every weekend, we went out in Dace's Impala and partied. I had even talked my brother into letting me tell Betty and everyone else we met that the Impala was *my* car. Then one night, down at the beach partying, I revved the engine too high and the bands of the automatic transmission burst. Dace still owed several hundred dollars on the car, and after quitting his job, he had missed a few payments. We just left the car there, abandoned it to the repo man who was sure to find it sooner or later. It was a nice car.

I felt badly about what had happened to it. Even today, I feel that I cost Dace that car.

Fortunately, we didn't really need a car in San Francisco. We took buses or trolleys. The Indian Center was close enough to our hotel that we could walk there every Saturday night for the dance. Afterward, we congregated in a nearby bar called Warren's. It was owned by a family of Klamath Indians from northern California. By talking to those people, I found out about an Eisenhower administration program known as termination. It had grown out of a BIA policy from the Truman years, a plan dreamed up by Dillon S. Myer, the man who had run FDR's concentration camps for American citizens of Japanese ancestry during World War II. "Termination" was designed to rid America of Indian nations by buying us out of our lands for a lump sum—paid, naturally, at 1850 prices. The owners had bought the bar with the money they had received—forty-four thousand dollars each—when the BIA had dissolved their reservation. Without its ancestral homelands, the Klamath Nation, like sixty-one others that had been terminated, was no longer recognized as a sovereign entity by the U.S. government. In effect, the government said, "Here's a little money for everything we've done to you, for everything we're doing to you now, for everything we're going to take away from you—and to hell with your heritage, to hell with your children, to hell with your future."

I wondered then how the government had convinced the Klamath elders to accept such an offer. In years to come, I learned that tribal councils often are nothing more than extensions of the BIA, rubber stamps for policies created in Washington. Termination was jammed down the Klamath's throats. When a reservation is targeted for termination, the BIA is relentless. It brings in top officials from Washington, D.C., to talk to elders and the council. Congressmen and state officials get involved. Day in and day out, everyone on the reservation is bombarded with what a good deal termination is. After months and years of that, almost everyone is worn down. If the Indians still won't go for it, the BIA terminates the reservation anyway, but with a smaller payment.

I did a lot of my drinking in Warren's, but I also went to many other bars. One afternoon, Dace and I were drinking in a bar near Betty's apartment. He started to talk about his girlfriend, Rita, an Indian from southern California whom he was living with. He was having problems with her. Jokingly, I said, "You know what—you've got to slap them every once in a while. They kind of like the caveman approach now and then." Unfortunately, my brother didn't understand that I was only joking. He got gassed, went home, and slapped Rita around. She called the cops, who threw him in jail. That happened early on a Sunday morning, while I was out partying. I didn't learn he was in jail until Monday morning. Because Dace couldn't come up with bail, he had to stay in jail until his trial. I had no income and Dace didn't want to lose his unemployment, so he asked me to pick up his unemployment check. All I had to do was tell the woman behind the counter Dace's social security number, which is almost the same as mine.

When he finally got out of jail, Dace was hot. "You told me to slap her!" he shouted. "I didn't say that," I said. "Anyway, I was just kidding around. I never thought you'd take me seriously." Dace soon forgave me. All these years later, however, I still find it painful to recall that in the name of brotherhood and don't-give-a-damn partying, I cost him a good job, a great car, and his freedom.

Not long after he got out of jail, Dace went to southern California for a while. Soon afterward, I ran into an Oklahoma Pawnee whom I knew from my Irish Pup days, Manuel Caesar, a journeyman printer. He was in San Francisco because the local union was on strike, and printing establishments were hiring scabs. Manny had got himself hired as a floorman in a shop which printed Yellow Pages directories. Desperate to keep the presses running and to stay in business, the shop was hiring anybody who said he was a printer. Manny said he could get me a job there if I told them I was a "two-thirder," a printer who is more than an apprentice but less than a journeyman. That night, he came to my hotel room and gave me a crash course in printing terminology. He also gave me the names of places where he had worked in Oklahoma, and suggested that I put them down as my own previous employment. The next day, I was hired at $3.60 an hour. That was almost two dollars an hour more than I had ever before been paid. I felt like a millionaire.

My first duty was to make forms. Manny came over to help during the day, but I knew next to nothing about printing, so I lasted only two days before I was fired. Manny said, "Hell, there are jobs all over town." He quit and found a place with a smaller house for the same wages. Then I got a job there, too. As on my first job, I had trouble operating the machine that poured molten lead into a form. Unless operated by a skilled worker, it tends to squirt hot metal all over, fouling other machines that must be cleaned, at great expense in manpower, before they will work again. Manny usually covered for me, but on the third day I had to do it myself. I goofed, and again I was out the door.

Manny went back to the Yellow Pages printer, and I went on my own to two other places. The same thing happened—after two or three days, I got fired. But by then I had had about a dozen days on the job, I knew my way around a print shop, and I was at least competent at making forms. When the strikers at the place where I worked had walked out, they had dumped out all the printer's drawers and had mixed up the different typefaces. My new bosses must have had some idea that I wasn't exactly experienced. They immediately put me to work unscrambling the drawers, sorting huge mounds of type into the correct compartments. In that way, I learned to read upside down and backwards and got to know the various typefaces. I learned the layout of the drawers, where each face went, and why. After a few days, I switched to making forms, but whenever there was slack time, we sorted type. My bosses were good to me, paid me $3.60 an hour, and seemed satisfied with my performance.

Dace was having a tough time finding work in Los Angeles, so I told my boss that he was an apprentice working in LA but he would come up if they paid his way. The company sent him a plane ticket and hired him. Then they put us both through a crash course in printing.

I was a printer for about five or six months. We were scabs, and I remember we had to cross a picket line once. I wasn't reading newspapers and didn't know what the strike was about. I was still naive in many ways, and didn't understand the union movement. All I thought when the union guys screamed at us as we crossed their picket line was, thanks to you guys, I'm making $3.60 an hour. The longer you stay on strike, the better off I am. Once when Dace and I got off work, about six union goons followed us. Approaching a part of San Francisco near downtown that was all but deserted, we knew we were going to have to get it on with these guys. We ducked into a Chinese store and used the phone to call the police. A couple of squad cars came, and the cops gave us a ride home.

What I learned about printing in the early 1960s is now all but a lost art in America. Linotype machines and floormen are gone forever, and I find that sad. I liked the work, the hustle and bustle, everybody working together to put out a printed piece of paper. Then one night Dace and I got in a fight in front of a bar. I swung at his head, but he ducked and I hit a parking meter, fracturing my right thumb. My boss couldn't hold my job open for four or five weeks until the cast came off. He laid me off, and I went back to collecting unemployment. By the time the cast came off, the strike was settled and the union printers had reclaimed their jobs.

By then, I was beginning to form an opinion about working in America. Most of my jobs were fun and there were many wonderful people among my coworkers, yet so many of them were unhappy. They couldn't wait for the whistle to blow at the end of the day. Too many of them absolutely hated what they were doing, and griped about it incessantly. Everyplace I ever worked, what most people wanted was their paychecks and the weekends off, plus holidays and vacations. Mostly they did just enough to keep from getting fired. I thought, what a weird way to live.

Eventually, I learned from my elders that traditional Indian people have never been able to accept the concept of "jobs," of forcing themselves to do something they are not happy with. Nor do Indians understand vacations. Taking time off from what you're supposed to be doing is not a lifestyle. Traditional Indians wholeheartedly accept whatever they are responsible for— and don't take time off from responsibility. When you are forced to do something you don't want to do, you must take time off to keep from going crazy—and that produces chaos. The solution, as I learned many years later, is understanding life and not fighting against it. Accepting it and embracing it and living with peace of mind—that's what life is all about, and that's what those traditional Indians have. You never hear them complain; they have nothing to complain about. What a great life! Instead of spending time in bitterness, spend it in appreciation and in thanksgiving.

A few weeks after I left the printing industry, I was leafing through the want ads and found a notice that said, "Dance instructors wanted. No experience necessary." The place was only about four blocks away, a dance studio. The owner, whom I'll call Leo Zhaun, was a middle-aged Chinese. I interviewed for the job with a young white guy who was in college, studying psychology. He was what was called a "closer," a salesman who got dance students to sign long-term contracts. I was twenty-three and had been on the streets for a few years, but in many ways I was still an innocent. I believed what he and Zhaun told me about the business, and I took the job. I received a stipend for four weeks while I studied dance. When Zhaun decided I was a qualified instructor, I worked on commission plus a base of $1.25 an hour, the minimum wage instituted by the Kennedy administration. The closer took a big chunk of all commissions because he was the one who pressured the students into signing. There were three other instructors at the studio— Perez, a Mexican; Paolinelli, an Italian; and Don Fryer, from Georgia. Fryer and I got along well.

I haven't been around the dance industry for thirty years, but I can't see how it could have changed much. Those studios play off the loneliness of old women who are desperate for companionship. Even if they are living in a home for the aged, many older women want to get out and do things on their own. There aren't many men to take them out, so they rarely get a chance to go dancing. The studio I worked for in 1963 advertised in bulletins and newspapers that old people read, offering an introductory package—eight half-hour lessons for twenty dollars. That was a good deal in those days, $2.50 a lesson to dance with young, good-looking studs who were cheerful and could carry on a nice conversation while teaching you to dance. For five dollars extra, the students could come to the Friday night party—two hours of drinks, hors d'oeuvres, dancing, and chatting with other students; all those good-looking young men asking to dance, and all of them good dancers.

We made our students spread their half-hour lessons over three weeks to ensure that they got in at least two Friday nights, because we made money from those weekend socials. By the end of the third week, when they were getting into the swing of things, it was my job to hit them with two things: Number One (and it's true), if you can walk, you can dance. Number Two, long-term membership. I tried to convince each student not just that she could dance, but that she had great potential and only needed more instruction to develop it. Then I would tell her about exhibitions coming up, and how we wanted to show her off at them. I would say we were getting along so well, and what a great place the studio was, a real family. Finally, I would get down to it: To achieve her full potential, she needed 50 to 100 hours of instruction. If I could get a student to say she was interested, I turned her over to the closer. By the time those old ladies left the studio, many had signed up for hundreds of dollars' worth of dance lessons. But instead of our introductory rate of $2.50 a half hour, it was ten dollars a lesson.

If a woman went for that, it was because she saw the studio as a social club that she had to pay to join. As far as I'm concerned, then and now, that's fine. I believe in "buyer beware," I believe in a free market, and I believe the dancing and social benefits were worth what those ladies paid—if *they* thought so. Unfortunately, that's not where things usually ended.

As a dance instructor, I never thought of my job as an issue of money. I thought of it as an issue of honest relationships. Working at the studio, I found out about gigolos. Some dance instructors seduced their elderly students, took them for all their money—sometimes tens of thousands of dollars—then dumped them and disappeared. Fortunately, most of the guys at the studio weren't that bad.

To keep the old ladies coming back, Zhaun had all sorts of gimmicks. One was the Hundred Hour Club on Wednesday nights, for women who had more than 100 hours of instruction. We took them to the very finest places in San Francisco, including the Fairmont Hotel and the Top of the Mark. From 9:00 to 10:30 P.M., they danced to the best bands in the ritziest nightclubs. The package included only two cocktails. Don Fryer and I would get half-pints—gin for me, whiskey for him—and down them just before we showed up for the evening. We had to be gassed to go to the best places in the city to dance with elderly women. People stared at me, a slim twenty-three-year-old darky, dancing cheek to cheek with a chubby old granny. I felt their eyes on me, and it wasn't a good feeling.

The gigolo among our little group was a guy I'll call Paolinelli, then about twenty-six, a very slick guy. He got involved romantically with some of the old ladies, the richer ones. Soon he was sporting around town in a Corvette, spending lots of money.

Apart from being around gigolos, which turned my stomach, being a dance instructor was a great experience. The best thing about it was that I didn't have to go to work until 6:00 P.M. and was usually done by 9:00. In three hours, I made more than I could have gotten on unemployment. It wasn't as good as a regular job, but the money was adequate, and I could party every night after work. I love to dance, especially Latin dances, the mambo, the rumba, the merengue, and the tango.

Soon after I joined the studio, I moved in with Betty. Because she knew I wasn't the least interested in romancing my elderly students, she was very proud of me. She was a good dancer, too. We went to the Indian Center on

Saturday nights. I would lead and she would follow, gliding around that floor, turning heads. It was great.

There came a day when one of the closers quit. Leo soon became very picky and demanding, keeping after us to produce more and more money. He kept dreaming up new promotional ideas to push to our students. He kept pressuring us to romance those old women and make them want to come back. He never came out and said so, but we knew he really wanted us to play the gigolo game so he could get money out of it. He had many private meetings with Paolinelli, who told us later that Leo was angry with him because he wouldn't share the wealth he took from the old women.

Not long after that, Paolinelli quit, then Perez. The old women drifted away. The family spirit was gone. Finally, after about a year as a dance instructor, I quit. Fryer left the same day. Maybe I could have found another job at a different studio, but I wanted more money than dance studios paid. To make a clean break of it, I quit going to dancing bars and returned to the Indians at Warren's.

The only job I could find was as a janitor at the Cow Palace, the big convention center near the bay. When the Ringling Brothers and Barnum & Bailey Circus came to the Cow Palace, my detail was cleaning up after the elephants. I found myself one day wearing hip boots and standing damn near knee-deep in elephant dung. I shoveled and shoveled, and suddenly I stopped and took a look at myself. What the hell was I doing? I was shoveling elephant shit! Aloud I said, "Elephant shit to this!" I threw down my shovel, walked to the office, and quit. When I went back to pick up my check, one of the foremen said, "Would you be interested in being night watchman?"

"Here?" I answered.

"Yes. It's more money," he answered.

That's all it took. I accepted the job. I worked Wednesday through Sunday. After about three or four weeks, I found that I didn't mind the work, but I didn't much care for working weekends. One Friday night—Saturday morning, really, after the bars had closed at two—when I knew most of my friends were partying at the beach, I decided to borrow one of the dozens of State of California cars parked in the government motor pool. Each had a key in it and I had keys to the gates, so it was very simple. I got myself a case of beer, then headed down to the beach. A party was going full blast when I pulled in, and I had a great old time until almost daylight. I drove back to the Cow Palace, parked the car in its space, and passed out. I woke before 8:00 A.M. and went into the office, where the supervisor said, "Where have you been?"

"I've been here," I lied.

"No, you haven't. We've got the tape," he said. Thus I learned that when a watchman clocks in at each station by turning a key, it punches a tape, leaving a record that he has made his rounds and the time when he passed each station. I was fired on the spot. At least they never found out that I had borrowed a car.

I went back on unemployment, twenty-seven dollars a week. I was once again adrift, feeling like a failure, hating myself—and Betty was pregnant, although she was still working. We moved into an apartment in the Tenderloin, newly redecorated and refurbished. Late one night, there was a knock at the door—my dad, just in from South Dakota. My mother had kicked him out, and he was having a rough time. Not only had his marriage ended, but a year earlier, while I was in Los Angeles, he had slashed his wrists in a suicide attempt. Fortunately, someone found him before he bled to death, but his wrist tendons had been severed. He had lost the fine motor skills that had made him a superb welder. He was barely getting by on a small Social Security disability pension.

It was the first week of March 1964. Pops told me his cousin, Chalk Cottier, who was on the board of directors of the San Francisco Indian Center, had called to ask him to join a demonstration the next day.

"Do you want to go along?" he said. "We're taking over Alcatraz."

Part II

The Making of a Militant

1964–1973

▼▼▼▼▼▼▼▼

1 0
▼▼▼▼▼▼▼▼▼

A Second Name: C'io

When the U.S. government—its cavalry troops defeated several times by Red Cloud's freedom fighters—begged the Lakota for a peace treaty in 1868, the document presented to Indian leaders and later ratified by the U.S. Senate gave the Sioux the right to claim any federal facility or real estate for which the government had ended appropriations. Sitting in my San Francisco living room in 1964, Pops explained it all, adding that the federal government had recently closed the prison on Alcatraz Island and ended its appropriations. Before it was turned into a national park or something, he and Chalk Cottier and a few other Sioux, in the name of the Lakota Nation, were going to claim the island for all American Indians. As a Lakota, I was invited to come along. Until that March evening, I had never had the slightest clue that my quiet, easygoing father might have harbored the principles or the spirit to boldly and publicly seize Indian land back from white America, to stand up for Indian rights—or even to step into the spotlight that was sure to follow him. It made me proud to be his son, and to be a Lakota.

The next morning, we went to the Indian Center near Sixteenth and Mission, where Chalk briefed us. He had arranged for lawyers to accompany our occupation force, and had chartered a boat to get everyone to the island.

Among those present were some of my relatives, members of the Brown family of Pine Ridge. They lent me a dance outfit to wear during the occupation. En route to our boat at Fisherman's Wharf, we held a press conference, where Chalk and the lawyers explained the legal basis of our claim to Alcatraz. When a reporter said that the law allowing Indians to claim unappropriated land had been repealed, our lawyer agreed that it had—but that the Sioux, and the Sioux alone, were exempt from that repeal.

On Alcatraz, we put up a tipi and began a celebration of singing and dancing. I danced for a while. Then, getting into the spirit of things, I ran around laying claim to various parts of the island, just as the many whites who had come to our land had claimed our rivers, forests, hills, and meadows. For a few exhilarating hours, I felt a freedom that I had never experienced, as though Alcatraz were mine.

Then boatloads of U.S. marshals arrived, spoiling for a fight. First they tried to get rough with members of the press, shoving them around, but the reporters and photographers and television people brushed the marshals aside. A reporter said, "Either arrest me or keep your hands off me, or my paper will sue the hell out of you and your agency!" The marshals backed off, then regrouped. They said, "Only Indians can stay. The press must leave. If you refuse to go, we'll arrest you." The reporters chewed on that ultimatum for a bit, then decided to leave. One of them said, "We're sorry for you guys. We know what's going to happen when we're not here to record it." Our lawyers, reluctant to take a beating, advised us to leave and let them pursue our claim in the courts. So Chalk and the other leaders decided to go back to the mainland. We returned to the Indian Center to wait for early editions of the next day's papers. One of the headlines said, "Wacky Sioux Raid Alcatraz." Pops's picture was splashed all over the front pages, signing our claim to Alcatraz on a drumhead. He called me over and held up all the newspapers and said, "How's that for twenty-four hours?" I was amazed by all the print and television coverage. It was my first inkling of what direct action can accomplish, even though the media—and the authorities—missed the point completely and treated our claim as though it were nothing more than a publicity stunt.

Looking back, I'm not surprised. White America has always trivialized Indian people. That was my first experience at such treatment by the *San Francisco Chronicle* and the *Examiner*, and it pissed me off. Our treaty wasn't "wacky," it was the law of the land. Even though we had brought attorneys from the Indian Center to explain the issues involved, whites didn't want to hear about Indians asserting their legal rights—so we became "wacky" Sioux. The lawyers filed suit to press our claim on Alcatraz, but eventually the case was thrown out. There was no legal basis for the judge's refusal to hear the suit, but in those days there was so much racism that no one cared. It would be five more years before another group of Indians took over Alcatraz—and then the white man knew we were serious.

I was increasingly disenchanted with my life and with living in San Francisco. I began to worry more and more about providing for the child that was growing inside Betty. Once again, I got down on myself. I couldn't get a job, I had no skills, I was no good. I could have gone back to dance instruction, but I didn't want to. That part of my life was over. Since the printers' strike had been settled, nothing was available there either. I might have gone looking for an apprenticeship and hoped nobody found out I had been a scab, but I really didn't want to be a printer. I didn't want to spend years looking forward to nothing but a paycheck and the weekend. I couldn't bear the idea of coming home every night with ink under my fingernails—not even for ten dollars an hour.

All the same, it galled me that far from supporting Betty, I was mostly living off her earnings. She had planned to return home to the Hopi Reservation to have our baby, but I couldn't wait until then to leave San Francisco. Then one night in June 1964, out partying, I met the Kelly brothers, who are related to me. They were from Pine Ridge and had a car. Even though I had grown up mostly in California, that reservation will always be a living link to my people and to our ancestors' way of life. We were all homesick. When they said they were leaving, I decided to go along, not knowing what else to do, even though I was deserting Betty when she needed me most. When I told her I was going, she pleaded with me to stay. I said, "I've got to go somewhere and find a job."

For several months, my mother had been living in Rapid City and working at Ellsworth Air Force Base, not far from Pine Ridge. The Kelly brothers took me to her home. But I couldn't find work in Rapid City, so I began to hitchhike around South Dakota. I went to Pierre, Sioux Falls, Vermillion, Huron, and just about every city in between. Eventually I covered almost the whole state, but no one offered me a job. Finally, I made my way to Sturgis, in the Black Hills, where I found a big construction project at Fort Meade, an old cavalry post. E. F. English Construction of Hutchinson, Kansas, had the contract to tear down the old stables and build an addition to the veterans' hospital. The company needed someone to supervise bookkeeping and run its field office. Because I had been trained in accounting, the bosses hired me as office manager. The project had just begun, so there was only one employee under me. Once I was aboard, the company began to hire construction workers and more office help. Less than three weeks after I was hired, however, the chief engineer, a good guy, called me in. He was from Kansas, where there isn't as much prejudice against Indians. He said, "I'm getting pressure from the powers-that-be at the hospital and in the town of Sturgis who don't want an Indian bossing whites." The U.S. Civil Rights Act had been enacted that year, but most white South Dakotans didn't care. "I've run into prejudice toward blacks, but never in my whole life have I experienced anything like this," he told me. "I'm going to have to lay you off and hire a white man. I'll give you a good recommendation and do whatever I can so you can collect unemployment." He let me finish the week.

I was far beyond anger. South Dakota was my home, but going back as far as my first-grade experiences in Huron, I had encountered racial discrimination—and there was nothing subtle about it. Until that moment, I hadn't realized that whites couldn't work for an Indian. That's the way it was—and still is—except on reservations, where BIA Indians in supervisory jobs are acceptable. Whites see them as "their" Indians, meaning, they know their place.

Fortunately, I had worked enough in California that I could still draw unemployment of twenty-seven dollars a week. For a little while, that got me by. I kept in touch with Betty, who had moved back home with her parents. The birth of our daughter was imminent, so I decided to join Betty on the Hopi Reservation, in northeastern Arizona. At that time, Auntie Faith was married to a Navajo and working at Greasewood Boarding School on the Navajo Reservation, near Holbrook, Arizona—only about fifty miles from where Betty's parents lived. My mother was driving down to visit Auntie Faith and she invited me to go along.

That wasn't my first trip to Hopi land. The Christmas after I went to San Francisco, in 1962, I had gone there to meet Betty's family. On that visit, to honor her parents' beliefs, we stayed in separate rooms when we were in their home. Betty's father was a Tewa, one of the smaller Pueblo Indian nations. Long ago, the Hopi gave the Tewa the eastern half of First Mesa, one of three mesas on the Hopi Reservation. Betty's family, the Sinquahs, lived in Walpi, a picturesque old village on the west side of First Mesa. All Betty's sisters and brothers were still in school. Both parents worked at the BIA boarding school, her father as a janitor and her mother as a dormitory matron. In time, their oldest son would grow up to finish college and become superintendent of that school—a great American success story for the BIA.

Although Betty's father is very traditional in his ways, her mother was a Christian. Nevertheless, they accommodated each other's beliefs very well. On Christmas Eve, Betty's mother had asked me to go Christmas caroling with her and some people from her church. It would have been rude to refuse, so I accepted—the only time in my life I ever went caroling. Betty's mother talked to me, shared her beliefs, tried to make another convert. I'm sure my caroling made Betty happy, but as I wandered among the homes of those white government workers, led by Christian missionaries, I was secretly thinking, throw up, throw up, throw up. I couldn't make myself ill enough to leave, so I had to stick it out.

I felt far more at home with Betty's father. He took me to spend a night of prayer and meditation in a kiva, an underground ceremonial chamber on the mesa. In the gray hour before dawn, holy men handed out prayer feathers that the Hopi people keep for an entire year. Some pin them to their clothing, others hang them in their trucks or cars or next to their beds as a reminder to say daily prayers of thanksgiving.

As a guest of Betty's family, I was also privileged to attend some of the Hopi dances, my first introduction to the Hopi people's deep wells of spiritual strength. I was very impressed by what whites call "mudheads," a poor translation that gives no inkling of the religious significance of the men who wear mud masks. Mudheads are clown princes, teachers, and disciplinarians who help people to understand and revere their traditions. In fact, such clowns are universal among Indian people. In the Plains Indian culture, the clowns were part of a society by invitation only, a brotherhood schooled in all the fundamentals and intricacies of traditional life. One or two clowns, usually just one, attend each dance. With laughter and teasing, they teach us about our foibles and weaknesses, gently chastising us when necessary.

It is the same among the Pueblo nations. Once, I was on First Mesa for a Hopi dance when it began to rain. A young Hopi woman, who apparently had just returned home after living in Phoenix, opened her umbrella. A mudhead crept up to her, snatched it away, snapped it in half, then lectured her. "You've been away too long and have forgotten that we are Hopi and always thankful for rain," he said. "Remember that rain is a sacred blessing. You don't have to hide from it or cover up from it." I really liked that. I, too, was raised to understand that rain brings cleansing and refreshment to our Grandmother, the earth. In the arid Southwest, people are always grateful for water, but all Indians know it is holy, that it is where life began. We knew about evolution long before Darwin.

During that Christmas of 1962 on my first visit to Hopi land, I fell in love with the Hopi and the Tewa, who are great and generous people. My family-to-be said nothing to me about my relationship with Betty and treated me as Indians traditionally treat all guests, with respect and honor. After I went caroling, however, Betty's mother and her Christian pals thought they had a new recruit. They blubbered over me, literally pawing me in ecstasy at the thought of a brand-new Christian. I never told Betty how badly I felt about all that. I just went along with it.

When Betty's parents offered to take us to Phoenix, where we could catch a bus to San Francisco, they asked me to drive their car. On the way, I got a ten-dollar speeding ticket. Her father said they would take care of it, so not only did I embarrass myself, I cost them a day's pay. Once we were on the bus, Betty told me that her parents vehemently opposed our marriage and wanted us to break up immediately. It had nothing to do with me personally. It was because I'm not a Hopi or a Tewa. Marriage outside any Indian nation is taboo. I asked Betty how she felt about it. She said, "I love you."

I also loved Betty very much, but we should have listened to the wisdom of our elders. What Betty's family knew is exactly what all our relatives on this earth teach us: Golden eagles don't mate with bald eagles, deer don't mate with antelope, gray wolves don't mate with red wolves. Just look at domesticated animals, at mongrel dogs, and mixed-breed horses, and you'll know the Great Mystery didn't intend them to be that way. We weakened the species and introduced disease by mixing what should be kept separate. Among humans, intermarriage weakens the respect people have for them-selves and for their traditions. It undermines clarity of spirit and mind.

I was young. Betty and I disregarded the Sinquahs' wishes, and we stayed together. Now, two years later, with the first of our children about to arrive, I returned with my mother to Hopi land. Betty's family treated Mom warmly and took her to some of their traditional dances, where she enjoyed herself.

On September 10, Betty gave birth to a beautiful little girl whom we named Michele Bridget. With her birth, our need for cash was greater than ever. I didn't have a job. In those days, the Navajo invited people from other Indian nations and paid them to dance at the annual Navajo Tribal Fair at Window Rock, Arizona, capital of the Navajo Nation. I borrowed a dancing outfit and moccasins from some local BIA Indians and some beadwork from a couple of Plains Indians who worked in the Hopi agency, then hitchhiked seventy-five miles to Window Rock. There I met up with Bill Iron Cloud, several members of the Lonehill family, and Timmy Hale, all Sioux who had come to dance at the fair. They graciously invited me to join them, and I danced for several days for audiences consisting mostly of Navajo people. Before leaving Window Rock, I met a guy from Albuquerque named Sonny Tuttle who said he was an Oglala Lakota. He told me the New Mexico State Fair was the following week, and invited me to join his group of dancers there in Albuquerque. Eager to make some money, I agreed.

After returning to Betty for a few days, I hitchhiked to Albuquerque. Sonny and some Indian people who belonged to the New Mexico Indian Council had put up a little village of two Sioux tipis, an Apache wickiup, a Navajo hogan, a dance stage, and booths. I was at the fair for ten days, appearing in several shows daily, wearing another makeshift outfit borrowed from Sonny and others. Besides the Sioux, there were Apaches, a few guys from Oklahoma, dancers from most of the Pueblo nations, some Kiowas, and other Plains Indians. They did the buffalo, eagle, butterfly and crown dances.

Even offstage, we were treated as curiosities. Tourists came around and looked inside our tipis. The fact that those were our homes never bothered them. They untied the door, opened the flap, and barged right in, touching our things, poking through our bedrolls, inspecting everything. It boggles the mind that tourists feel they have a God-given right to intrude anywhere. One day just before we went on, I was standing in front of a tipi with a couple of other guys. We were in dancing outfits; my arms were folded across my chest in a stereotypical pose. Three elderly white ladies looked me up and down as though I were a statue. It was an infuriating, hateful, racist moment that conjured up the image of wrought-iron hitching posts, caricatures of foppish black stable hands, that used to decorate whites' front yards—pure trash that meant the same thing as a wooden Indian in front of a smoke shop. You seldom see those hitching-post boys in yards anymore, but cigar-store Indians are all over Utah and Arizona and many other places. While all that was whirling through my head, the tourists began to touch our beadwork, our feather bustles, our clothes. One even raised my breechcloth to peer beneath it. I wore swim trunks, but I would have given part of my little finger to have been naked underneath just then.

In that humiliating moment, I came to realize how white people look upon us: We're not real human beings, we don't exist, we have no cares, no rights, no sensibilities. We're tourist attractions. To this very day, women—never men—come up to me when I'm wearing braid ties and grab my braids. Until the Black Power movement of the 1960s, white women used to grab little black kids and rub their heads. They don't do that anymore, but when they see an Indian with braid ties, they still march right up and give them a yank. That's a violation of my person, and I have learned a way to stop it. When a woman grabs my braid and says, "Oh, how cute!" I grab her breast and say, "Oh, how cute!" She never touches me again.

Even worse than debasing myself by dancing for tourists at the state fair, the performances were another step on the road to cultural genocide for Plains Indians. The fancy dancing that I specialized in began in this century, in the 1930s. It grew out of the freestyle dances of the traditional clown and the seasonal grass dance, which honors the stars that control the water, which governs the grass. Grass, of course, was sustenance to the buffalo, which were everything to my people and all Plains Indians. Grass was our friend, and it gave us much all year long. This dance acknowledges the power of grass, all that it gives, where it comes from. It explains how the insect and grass worlds interact. When I was younger, I often saw it performed as it had been for centuries, with the dancers waving gracefully like long sheaves of grass in the prairie wind. It was beautiful.

Our ancestors made dancing outfits from bunches of grass fastened around knees, ankles, arms, chest, and waist. In time, they started to sew some of the grass to pieces of cloth that were easier to wear. When the missionaries came, they forced all the men to be fully clothed in trousers and long-sleeved shirts, so dancers sewed fringes on their garments where once they had simply worn the grass. Then they began to substitute yarn for grass—why, I'll never know. Now the grass dance has evolved into a competition. Instead of grass, people wear yarn of different colors. It's not the grass dance anymore, it's a meaningless rainbow yarn dance, and I'm embarrassed whenever I see it.

There were many grass-dance songs in the old days, which taught each generation what it needed to know. They are hardly sung anymore and many have been lost or will be soon, when all who knew them have passed on to the spirit world. Today, they sing fancy-dance and contest songs without words, just rhythm, and do the yarn dance. We've evolved to a caricature of what we once were.

Some people lament the loss of those old songs, including whites who have figured a way to make money out of it. One of them, for example, was Judith Fein, a white woman from Los Angeles. She hung around Indians near Santa Fe for a year and made money from writing a book in which she says the songs should be preserved. But as Fools Crow, the Lakota's most revered holy man, often said, most Indians don't deserve to retain them. You have to *live* a way of life that has value and principles and freedom—a responsible life governed by spirituality. Then you deserve your culture, including its songs, and you deserve to know the secrets of your heritage. Nobody is going to pass down such sacred knowledge to a Judith Fein or even to a Russell Means. They will pass on to us the knowledge that we deserve.

That wisdom came to me only later. In the 1960s, I was like everyone else, prostituting my culture for money at the New Mexico State Fair. When the fair closed in September, I called Betty to say I was going to stay in Albuquerque and look for a job. Sonny Tuttle invited me to stay with him in a converted garage he had rented from Preston Monongye and his Apache wife. Preston was a master silversmith whose fine artistry was expressed in traditional Hopi jewelry.

Dancing was just a sideline for Sonny. He made his living as a BIA biologist, traveling to several nearby reservations to monitor the conditions of their grazing ranges. Sonny was funny, a great guy. Every night when he came home from work, he locked his bedroom door while he cleaned up. I wondered about that until one night that winter when I came home unexpectedly and glanced through an open bathroom door. There was Sonny, with soap lathering his chest and stomach, shaving. Most Indians don't have hairy chests, so if he's Sioux, then I'm Norwegian. I teased him about it, and now I think I should have given him a nickname, such as Soapy or Hairy.

When my mother heard that I was dancing in a makeshift borrowed outfit, she bought a fancy-dance outfit from one of our relatives, an older guy, and sent it to me. It was blue; the beadwork included a little bit of black and yellow, but was mostly red and white. It had a fringed, beaded cape, and the front apron was decorated with a pair of crossed American flags. Through his BIA connection, Sonny had access to dead eagles. He gave me a bunch of eagle feathers and showed me how to make a bustle with them. There was a certain way to fix the feathers, with the longest ones sticking out from the top so they moved in the wind like wings. The style then was to wear tights, so under my outfit I wore red tights and a red T-shirt.

I sometimes went along with Sonny on his range surveys. Visiting different pueblos in New Mexico, I got to know some of the Pueblo people well, particularly those of the Laguna, Santo Domingo, San Felipe, Isleta, and Jemez Pueblos. When I wasn't traveling with Sonny, I kept looking for a job, but with no success. I had some unemployment benefits left. To supplement the trickle of cash, I spent weekends dancing in shopping centers and other places around Albuquerque. Few Indians lived in Albuquerque then, so our audiences were mostly tourists. We assembled a little troupe—Sonny, Preston's son, a Kiowa singer named Ralph Zotigh, and me. We didn't earn a lot of money, but it was all cash.

As soon as I could, I sent for Betty and Michele. We moved into a nice little adobe house on Griegos Road. It had a natural-wood floor covered by Early American–style rugs, and a big backyard with fruit trees. The place was filthy. I made a deal with the owner, a white lady, to clean and paint. She bought paint and cleaning supplies, and gave us a month's free rent. I started a lawn—the only time I've ever had one—but Albuquerque's soil is so sandy, our yard was never much more than clumps of dirt pierced by scraggly green blades.

I suppose Betty could have looked for secretarial work, but I wanted her to stay home to take care of the baby. I believe it's essential—and natural—for a child to be close to its mother, especially during the first five years of life. We really didn't need the money. Between unemployment and dancing, we were getting along all right. We didn't have a car, and that was tough, but there wasn't much to do anyway except spend time with our friends. Ralph Zotigh and his wife took us on weekend drives. In our conversations, they explained many things about the Indian world. Sonny Tuttle took us all over, to different pueblos.

Parenthood, however, was increasingly expensive, and I decided I did need to find work. I was receptive in the spring of 1965 when Judge Yazie of the Navajo tribal court asked me to join a dance group headed for Hershey, Pennsylvania. I found an older fellow, a southern Cheyenne, to sing for me. We joined the troupe, which included a friend from the New Mexico State Fair, Muggy Monatachee, a Comanche. There were also Navajo dancers, buffalo, deer and ribbon dancers, dancers from each of the Pueblo nations of the Rio Grande, and a group from the southern Plains. Several people flew to Hershey, and it took two buses to haul the rest of us and all our gear.

When we weren't performing, we toured the Hershey chocolate plant, where we were given all the chocolate we could eat. We also went to an amusement park and tried the roller coaster and other rides. What interested me most was in the nearby town of Carlisle—the BIA's first boarding school, now the Army War College. Just walking around it made me angry. This was where whites had first chopped the hair off thousands of Indian children and forced them to wear military-style uniforms. Now the War College included a museum, a tourist attraction exploiting the memory of its student athletes, among them the incomparable Jim Thorpe, from Oklahoma. I thought, how *white* of them!

One evening I was hanging around with dancers from the Laguna Pueblo. They talked about how much they missed the desert, where the wind blew sand in their faces. They wished aloud for some rocks they could lie on. It took me aback. I thought, my God, here's grass and trees, what more could anyone want? Then I realized that those people felt about their home exactly as I felt about mine.

The dance event in Hershey was a flop, and our only good crowd was on Saturday afternoon. We were booked through Sunday, but the white promoters skipped out on Saturday night, taking all the cash. There was no money to pay anyone, so the bus drivers left, stranding all of us, including families with young children.

Our Cheyenne singer called the BIA in Washington, D.C. To my surprise, the BIA sent people to help, hired buses, and sent most of our troupe back home. The BIA also chose a few of us to go to Washington, D.C., including me. I flew first class—my first time on a plane. The BIA put us up in a fancy hotel and gave us a tour of Washington. All we had to do was give affidavits about what the promoters had promised and what they had done. That was my first *good* experience with the BIA. I didn't know then that it would also be my last.

Since the promoters had skipped out, I never saw even a dime for my dancing in Hershey. When my unemployment ran out in the spring of 1965, we could no longer afford the eighty-dollar monthly rent on our little adobe. Betty found us a couple of rooms in the back of someone's house, a murky place that didn't get much light. I couldn't stand it there, and I felt embarrassed that my family lived like tramps. My dad came to visit, and we went out to get gassed. When we talked about the lack of work in Albuquerque, Pops said, "There's good money in dancing up around Rapid City." So in June 1965, we decided to go home. Pops and I bought bus tickets to Rapid City—and Betty had a fit. She thought I was deserting her again. I said I had had it with Albuquerque. I was going up there to get a job, and then I would bring her and Michele up. I packed a suitcase and grabbed my dancing outfit.

I moved in with Mom in Rapid City. She told me that my sister Madonna, Auntie Faith's girl, was living with Conrad De Cora and they had just had a little baby girl, Dawn. Conrad was the Winnebago who had beaten me up and left me to die in a Sioux City snowbank. In the years since I'd last seen him, he'd turned himself into the navy and served time for desertion. Since he was family now, I forgave him. But one night we got into an argument in a bar and went into the alley to settle it. I whipped his ass—but when he went down, I didn't stomp him as he had me.

Soon afterward I began hanging around with the Fast Horse family. Their matriarch, Lizzie Fast Horse, was in her fifties then, and she had a big family, sons and daughters from elementary-school age up to their early thirties. Lizzie, who still lives in Rapid City, is a strong, feisty woman, one of those beautiful older people who really know who they are. I became almost part of her family. The Fast Horses lived mostly on state welfare—Aid to Families with Dependent Children (AFDC)—but Lizzie sometimes worked, as did some of her kids. They stuck together: Whatever they did, it all went for the family.

Four-day *wacipi*—dances—were held every Thursday at reservations in South Dakota. I didn't have a car, but my friends the Fast Horse family went to almost all the *wacipi*, so I usually piled in with them. I began to win prizes for fancy dancing, taking home twenty-five to one hundred dollars for each contest. My brothers Ted and Bill were enrolled at Black Hills State College in Spearfish, several miles north of Rapid City. When school was out for the summer, Ted joined Mom and me. He was a good dancer, so I made him a feather bustle and Auntie Faith sewed him an outfit. When we entered fancy-dance competitions together, he usually came in second and I took first.

As the summer tourist season began, the Fast Horses began to get contracts to dance at various tourist places. Besides several Fast Horses, Ted and I were joined by Sonny Larvie, a champion fancy dancer. Then Madonna and Conrad found a Lebanese-American named Jim Abourezk, owner of a restaurant and bar, who agreed to let us dance in front of his place. It was a good restaurant in a tourist trap of a town near Rapid City called Rockerville, where people staged "gunfights" with blanks and reenacted all kinds of "frontier" crap for tourists. Abourezk, a dark-haired man of average height, was going to law school in Vermillion, South Dakota. One of his classmates was pudgy, towheaded Bill Janklow. When school was out for the summer, Jim hired Bill to tend bar. Both of them were talkers, very friendly guys.

They put up a couple of canvas tipis outside Abourezk's place. Madonna, wearing a buckskin dress, sat demurely holding her infant daughter strapped to an Indian cradleboard. Conrad, wearing a headband and an Indian vest, beat on a drum and sang while Ted and I danced. Busloads of tourists came to that restaurant daily, joined by many others in cars. We developed a nice little pitch. Ted and I were "working our way through college," and Dawn, the little baby, "needed care," blah, blah, blah. Conrad was as good as any carny at barking out that hustle. We put out a little bucket for donations. Abourezk let us keep all we got, and gave us free meals. We worked four hours a day, Monday through Wednesday, the slowest part of the week in that town. We each made at least twenty dollars a day—top-notch wages at a time when you could rent a nice little house in Rapid City for eighty dollars a month.

There was only one drawback: Just as in Albuquerque, I loathed myself when I danced for tourists. I knew the joy of dancing and I knew the songs—and they are *not* about hustling tourists. The songs are about beauty and tradition and respect and love—all the good things our culture has enjoyed for eons. We dance for our ancestors, and as long as the songs go on, we are once again free Indians. The tourists know nothing of all that. They think it's quaint and primitive to chant and beat a tom-tom. They never realize that the rhythm is the heartbeat of our nation, the pulse of our entire existence on earth—or that our songs were handed down from one generation to the next for centuries. Dancing for tourists, I came to know exactly how prostitutes feel when they sell their bodies. When my culture is violated, so is everything that I am, everything I care about. Sometimes in my dancing for tourists I made fun of their stupidity in ways they could never understand.

That summer of 1965 in Rapid City was the first time in my life that I had money every day of the week. I had to sell my soul to get it, but by August I had saved enough to bring Betty and Michele up on the bus. I knew I couldn't support my family with dancing after the summer tourists evaporated, and I still needed to complete my education. I applied for a scholarship at Iowa Technical College, in Ottumwa, in the southern part of the state.

Entire clans turned out for the *wacipi*, hundreds of people of every age, most of them camping out in military-style tents in the surrounding countryside. Near the dance area, people put up booths to sell food, beverages, and handicrafts. The entire community worked year-round to raise prize money for dancers and to pay singers and drummers.

They worked so hard because the *wacipi* were in essence our cotillion ball, our block party—the year's major social event, the place where people did their socializing and made their connections. The dance area was a cleared circle about 100 feet in diameter with its east end, "the east door," left open. Everyone entered and left by it, moving around the circle, never across it, moving as the sun does, from east to south. Even if your seat was way over on the north side, you went all the way around, never breaking the circle, but completing it to remember and honor the cycle of life. For the same reasons, our ancestors' tipis were pitched in circles, each clan's perimeter with an east door, and every tipi door facing east. In those peaceful, beautiful days when my people still knew what we were doing at our dances, spectators, dancers, and singers alike entered a dancing bower from the east door.

All those customs are gone now, along with the understanding of why we did such things. Today it's all backwards and upside down. For example, in the early 1950s, when I was a boy, old men carried the U.S. flag around the dance circle. Our people had captured that flag in battle, so we were honoring the courage of our ancestors. Slowly, that became perverted. Now, marching the U.S. flag around the circle is to honor military veterans and the U.S. government—to honor our oppressors! It is the same with the drum.

People hit it now as though they are beating somebody they hate. It was never that way in my youth, when we didn't use amplifiers, and the drum was never louder than the singers. We heard clear, strong voices plainly singing our vividly beautiful songs.

The dance arena was a bower of pines cut and trimmed to make tall posts. They were put into the ground in two concentric rows around the dance area. Cross poles were laid between the posts, and brush was piled atop for shade. In those days, we always had a center pole, symbolizing the tree of life. Usually there were lightbulbs on it. Sometimes, if the community was poor or if it was hard to get electricity far out in the countryside, the bulbs were small and dim. Even without much light, we sang and danced late into the night.

Arriving at each *wacipi*, usually on Thursday, we heard the starting songs. I always called them "calling songs" because it seemed they were calling me—come, dance and be free. Ted and I were always the first dancers to arrive and the last to leave. We hung on through the last notes of the quitting songs. Singers from all the drums gathered around one drum to sing while the women came out and the last dancers danced through the east door—just as the drums had entered to begin the day.

Traditional dance outfits included bustles of hawk feathers worn at the waist. In those days, fancy dancers wore a single bustle at the rear of the waist, usually made from eagle feathers. Others were of long pheasant plumes, sometimes with turkey feathers mixed in. Every detail of the beadwork on dancing outfits, even those of fancy dancers, meant something. Even the manner and the sequence used to put on each garment had meaning. Dressing the exact same way every time was observing a small but important ritual.

Up and down this hemisphere, the essence of traditional Indian dress is simple elegance. More and bigger never meant better—but that's the way it is now, because of the influence of the urban-raised generation, part-time Indians who have taken up the so-called powwow. Ignorant of their traditions, they feel no responsibility to turn away people who aren't qualified to attend religious ceremonies, or to make sure that everyone dresses right, acts right, and *is* right. Since people can now dress any way they want, they overdress, white-man style. Some grab anything and stick it on their bodies or shirts with glue. Beadwork, scarves, and fringes hang all over the place, everywhere and anywhere. Feather bustles are bigger and brighter—and represent nothing except that their wearers have sold out the white way.

The dancers now paint their faces in grotesque colors and grotesque ways to make them look exactly how the white man wants them to look—like wild savages. When I was young, each *tiyospaye*—extended family—and the brotherhoods that are part of them, awarded their adult men the right to paint or mark their faces. All colors are sacred to Indians, and each has a meaning. The meanings are similar, but not always identical, in each Indian nation.

Different nations have different priority colors, according to the nature of their environment. For example, among the Lakota, pink means medicine. Each spring, when plants bud, if the inside of the bud is pinkish, that plant has medicinal powers. Blue represents the universe. To my people, black represents the thunderclouds that bring the lightning and thunder spirits, which bring us the rain, which purifies, cleanses, and refreshes our Grandmother and all her children, including us. So black means cleanliness and purity. Red represents energy, strength, and endurance, because when blood is coursing through your veins, you feel energized. Yellow represents the morning star and the dawn of a new day, when you can start again by not repeating the mistakes of yesterday. White represents the south, source of the warm winds. Brown represents the living races of people. When you mix black, red, yellow, and white, the four colors of the human race, you get brown, the color of our Grandmother, the earth. Purple stands for the sunset and the wind that travels in a circle. Green, of course, represents plant life. The Great Mystery is able to recognize your face when it has holy paint on it.

The face paint granted to a man by the *tiyospaye* was his to keep for life. With this privilege came an obligation. A man took his place in our culture as a provider and a protector. By the time I became a young adult, the *tiyospaye* on my dad's side had splintered and gone off in all directions. Most of my uncles, trying to survive, had taken the white man's path. My cousins, the Meanses who live near Allen, South Dakota, were Christianized. No one ever gave me the right to paint my face, so I have never done so.

In my youth, we began each fancy-dance contest with a warm-up song, then a slow song, followed by a medium-speed song and then a fast one. The songs today are much faster because of the southern Plains Indians' influence. When I was young, we heard the slow, beautiful Lakota melodies. Dancers carried whistles of wood or bone. To show appreciation for the song and the singers, any dancer could blow his whistle four times at a certain time in a song. Then the singers would continue until they came again to the point when a dancer might whistle for the song go on. Sometimes you would get caught up in a song and other dancers would join in and whistle it on and on until the dance seemed to last forever. You were transported into another world. As the song continued, you *became* a bird.

Those whistles honored our winged brothers, the ultimate source of song. Among the Lakota the wingeds, who are two-leggeds like us, are held very close. We worked together to defeat the four-leggeds so that we two-leggeds could be the dominant species on earth. The whistle is blown four times because among Indians, four is a most sacred number. It honors the four points of the universe, the four winds, the four directions, the four ages of the earth, the four ages of human beings, the four seasons, the four quarters of the moon.

If the singers were good enough, a song might go on for twenty or thirty minutes. Sometimes a dancer whistled at the wrong time or lost track of how many times he had blown his whistle. Then he had to give something of value, whatever he could, to the singers. If the singers miscounted or failed to honor a whistle blown four times, they were obliged to give money or goods to the whistler. Back then, there were few other rules for dancers except that when each contest song ended, dancers had to stop on time. If they didn't, they were disqualified. Most dancers had so much respect for their own dancing and for their knowledge of songs that if they stopped too soon or too late, they would walk off. I've done that a few times myself, because if people saw me make a mistake, they knew it. Certainly I didn't fool myself, so I did the honorable thing.

The summer sun takes a long time to set on the Great Plains. When it was low in the sky, after the day's dancing had ended but before the night dances began, the "doorway" singers came around. Back when we were a free people, these roving singers went from tipi to tipi, singing at each doorway. In my day, they went from campsite to campsite, singing whatever people wanted, often including honor songs for someone in the family or a visitor to the camp. Everyone sang traditional Lakota songs, the familiar ones known to the entire nation and those peculiar to each band or to a specific clan, songs usually heard only on another reservation or in a different part of your own. You don't hear them anymore. As night settled on the encampment, the old songs echoed through the prairie stillness from every quarter. It was wonderful. Singers in those days were honored men. People were generous with them, inviting them to sit down and eat, and giving them blankets, clothing, money, food, and other valuables. The singers' wives or girlfriends came along to help sing and carry their gifts. Later, some of those items were sold. Many singers subsisted through the summer in that way and were able to go from one *wacipi* to another.

When I was dancing in the summers of the 1950s and 1960s, each dancer had his own style, distinctly different from all others. We made up our own steps, always within the song's rhythm, always keeping time with the drum. Our dance judges were always singers, people who knew the songs.

The best champion dancer of the early 1960s was Timothy Hale, a Minniconjou from Cheyenne River. To this day, he is the greatest fancy dancer I have ever seen. Many of his steps came from the grass dance. He got very low, shimmied his shoulders, and kept his head constantly moving—and yet he was always smooth and intricate. Other top dancers those years were Sylvester Rubideaux, Sonny Larvie, Uris Blue Arm, Ted, and me. When we all competed together, people went wild. Indians didn't applaud in those days. It was quiet when we went up to get our awards; silence was a sign of respect.

The Eagle Butte Fair and Rodeo on the Cheyenne River Indian Reservation was the last celebration of summer for South Dakota Indians in those days. Winning the fancy-dance contest at that event was considered very prestigious. For a Lakota, it was almost like taking the singles cup at Wimbledon or the U.S. Open golf trophy at Augusta. All the fancy-dance champs turned out at Eagle Butte, and there were some sensational performances. When the dancing was over, the judges called out third place, and it was Ted. When Uris Blue Arm took second, I figured Timmy Hale had to be first. I just about died when they called my number. It was a great honor.

Later that summer of 1965, I went to Greenwood, where my mother's sister, Aunt Evelyn, gave me my second name. I was no longer Wanbli Ohitika, Brave Eagle. I was known instead as Cío, our name for the bird that has a beautiful mating dance. Whites call it the prairie chicken. The name was bestowed in a small ceremony with a special song for the occasion—and therefore a dance—and the traditional giveaway, with presents to all.

Soon after Betty and Michele had arrived in Rapid City, I was accepted by Iowa Tech in Ottumwa. My mother bought us a dark green '49 Chevy Fleetline, which we loaded with our possessions. The trunk overflowed with clothing and our television set, so I had to tie down the lid. By the time everything was loaded in and on that car, we looked more like the television Clampetts of Beverly Hills than an Indian family headed for Iowa.

Looking forward to the calm and enlightening life of a college student, I had no clue that when I returned to South Dakota, my heart would be broken.

Grandpa John and Dad

I liked Ottumwa. We were the only Indians in town, but people were very friendly to us. One day soon after we arrived, Betty and I went to the drugstore. As we approached the entrance, a white man arriving at the same time opened the door for us. Wow! I told Betty to go on inside, and I waited on the sidewalk until another white man came. I went for the door just as he did, and the same thing happened. He held the door for me. I did that a few more times, just to get the feel of it. Each time, a white man opened the door for me. After living in Rapid City, South Dakota, it was a brand-new experience to have white people treat me like that.

My scholarship at Iowa Tech included a weekly stipend of thirty-five dollars for living expenses—not much for a family of three, but we got by. We found a small second-floor apartment with living-, dining-, and bed-rooms. We had our own tiny kitchen, but shared a bathroom with a couple living in the apartment across the hall. It was only ten dollars a week, fully furnished. Our landlords, who lived downstairs, were nice people.

Michele was rapidly developing into a cute little girl with a mind of her own. Before she was two years old, however, she began to have seizures, very scary episodes that included uncontrollable shaking and loss of control over her bodily functions. A doctor diagnosed epilepsy and prescribed powerful drugs. They controlled the seizures, or most of them, but they also changed Michele's personality. Once a calm and sunny child, she became moody and irritable when she began to take those drugs, and she couldn't concentrate for more than a few minutes. Her teeth, once perfectly white, turned yellow.

Betty soon discovered that she was expecting another child, the following June. Because of Michele's problems and the other strains on our relationship—including my drinking—we were having difficulties. Betty, still a staunch Christian, thought that if I began to go to church with her it might strengthen our relationship. She also wanted to have Michele baptized, and for me to be part of that process. Since I, too, felt a spiritual void in my life, I agreed to try church again to see if it would help.

Since I had been an Episcopalian acolyte as a boy and knew the most about that particular brand of Christianity, we went to see the local Episcopalian priest. For a while, I liked what he had to say. Then, in conversation, the priest said, "God knows how you're going to turn out." I had had trouble with that concept when I was in elementary school, so we got into a long discussion. Finally, I recall saying something like, "I can't accept it. If the fates of human beings are nothing but a way of keeping score in a contest between God and the devil, then it's the most asinine game I've ever heard of. People suffer, babies die, and folks get sick or are born crippled—and for what? A game between two beings out there in nowhere land? That's bullshit." I told Betty I was sorry, but I was not going back to church. That was my last foray into Christianity.

At Iowa Tech, I majored in accounting and computer programming, but I also took English and speech. The speech class included speed-reading techniques. At the beginning of the semester, we were tested. I gave it all I had. When our reading rates came back, I was the fastest in the class. That was puzzling to me: My classmates included some very sharp people, including a National Guard officer. Near the end of the semester, we were tested again. My reading speed was still tops, but I hadn't improved as much as most of my classmates had. I got a grade of C, but people who read slower than I got A's because they had improved so much. Then I realized that my classmates, who knew they would be graded on their degree of improvement, had deliberately slowed down on the first test. They didn't need to cheat, but when an opportunity to better their grade without working hard presented itself, they took it. To me, it was a message about white man's ethics—cheat whenever you get a chance.

My first talk in that class was based on a book called *America's Concentration Camps*, about Indian reservations. I gave an impassioned speech, and the class members' reactions were overwhelming. They all wanted to know more about Indians. I continued my reading, and gave several more lectures on related subjects. I knocked myself out in that class, and when I did that, I usually got A's. When semester grades came, however, the teacher gave me a C. I went to him and complained. He said, "You moved around too much and didn't provide a stationary subject for people to focus on. You moved your hands too much; you're supposed to grip the lectern and use gestures only to make specific points. You had terrible eye contact with your audience." Some years later, in Cleveland, Ohio, when I got my first thousand-dollar speaking fee, I wanted to take that check, go find that professor, and make him eat it.

None of the players on the Iowa Tech basketball team was taller than six feet five inches, so I went out for the squad and made it. Along with a black guy named Curtis who, like me, was about six feet three, I played defense. Just before the season started, the coach quit, in a squabble over money or something. At twenty-six, I was a few years older than the other players, so the school officials asked me to coach the team—without pay, of course, because I was also a player and had to remain an amateur. I gladly accepted. It was a makeshift squad. Curtis and I played guard. Because the others had limited skills, we had few plays. With only eight players, there was no depth to our bench, but playing was fun. We finished the year winning six games and losing about twenty. Midway through the season, Pops came to stay with Betty and me. He had been a high-school basketball all-American, so I wanted to impress him. He came to only one game. I cut loose and went all out, scoring twenty-five points to lead the team.

After my dad came, I started to hang out with him. Pops was receiving his shipyard pension checks. He could see that Betty and I needed help, so he bought us groceries and other things. He kind of liked the town, too, because good people were there. My father was only forty-nine, but his health was deteriorating, probably because he had abused alcohol for so many years. He had come through a minor stroke the year before, and he suffered terribly from hemorrhoids. With Pops helping financially and in other ways around our apartment, the rest of the school year passed quickly. I was in a class of superachievers, and the competition kept me on my toes. Except for speech, I aced all my classes. As spring came, Betty got bigger and bigger. We talked about where our new baby would be born. We had already decided that all our kids would be born on a reservation. When we had been on relocation, we had seen how important it was to have a connection with the land, so we decided that Betty would go back to the Hopi Reservation to give birth. Since Betty didn't yet know how to drive, she and Michele took the train.

When Betty returned to her parents' home on the Hopi Reservation, she went to see a medicine man named Richard Yowytewa. After talking to her about Michele, he told her to bring Michele to his home, along with some clothes and cooking utensils. "You'll never see them again," said Yowytewa, without saying why. Michele stayed with him for four days and four nights. She returned to Betty wrapped in a new blanket—and cured of epilepsy. All Yowytewa told Betty was that he had removed "a large snake from Michele's stomach." Perhaps that matter-of-fact statement was merely a metaphor for some spiritual process that I'm not worthy to understand. I know Western medicine has no cure for epilepsy. I don't understand the Hopi way, but I do know that my daughter never had another epileptic seizure, and since the day she went to stay with Yowytewa, she has taken no more of the prescription drugs the white doctors had given her.

By the time school was out, our tired old car had finally stopped running—for good. Pops and I caught the bus to Arizona to join Betty on the Hopi Reservation while we waited for the new baby. My father-in-law, Dennis Sinquah, took Pops and me to his family's desert garden plot, where we helped him plant and weed. I still marvel that for centuries, a mile above sea level in the sandy soil of northern Arizona, the Hopi have grown corn, beans, melons, squash, and other vegetables with absolutely no irrigation. Of course, botanists have known for decades about the durable, hardy, drought-resistant Hopi corn, and have used it to make hybrids widely used by modern agribusiness. Such hybrid corn is almost as tasteless as a cigar-store Indian—that's why Europeans use it only as animal feed. I find it incredible that Americans eat that hybrid corn, but I suppose there is no accounting for taste.

The Sinquahs planted in the traditional way—one seed for the crow, one seed for the earth and all our relatives who live in the soil, one for the Great Mystery and the four winds, and one seed to grow. My dad and I learned to cultivate the Hopi way, by hand. To deal with the big cutworms that are attracted to gardens, we sifted through the sand around each plant with our bare hands. When we found a worm, we pulled it out and squeezed it, just as we did with caterpillars and sow bugs or anything else that would eat the plant. Before leaving for the fields, Dennis had led us in a little ceremony to pray for those worms, caterpillars, and other creatures we were about to send to the Great Beyond.

I still don't know how the Hopi water their crops, except that they depend on the Great Mystery. That is why they pray—and why they are successful. The Hopi, like all traditional societies, know how to live with Grandmother Earth the way she wants us to live. They know that the earth and the stars determine what the water will do, that all three together ordain what they will do for the green things. The green things determine what will become of all other living things, including, at the bottom of the food chain, human beings. It's a very logical, commonsense approach. You don't argue with life, you don't try to master life, you don't try to manipulate life. You *live* with life. In that way, you don't need psychiatrists, psychologists, or counselors, Tibetan monks, Mormon missionaries, Catholic priests, "New Age" crystal readers, or Scientologists with "E-meters." If you're perfectly happy with life, you don't argue with it, so you don't need jails or loony bins or locks and keys.

Living with the Sinquahs, I discovered that although white people describe this as desert, a barren place, to an Indian living in traditional ways, it's the Garden of Eden. I learned how much sustenance was available from nature, and it blew me away. There I was, digging in the desert, planting seeds in the sand, then watching the plants grow and flower and yield food. It was awesome.

The only thing wrong on the Hopi Reservation was that the BIA forced the people to send their children to boarding schools in Phoenix or Albuquerque or Nevada or Riverside, California. The only alternative was to bus their kids a couple of hours each day to schools in Winslow, Arizona, then, as now, a racist town. I saw the results of the violence-worshiping boarding-school experience in Betty and in her brothers and sisters. They had been taught, as my mother had, that disciplining children requires brutality.

Pops and I worked around the Sinquahs' home and garden until my new son was born on June 17, 1966—my mother's fiftieth birthday. Long before, I had made a deal with Betty. She got to name our daughters and I would name our sons. I called him Scott, but her family also wanted to give him their clan's magnificent name, Sinquah, and I agreed because it's so beautiful.

While waiting for Scott Sinquah Means to grow old enough to travel, I enjoyed life among the peaceful Hopi. When I lived there, one policeman covered the entire reservation. He was an amiable three-hundred-pounder who was unable to find a job, so the Hopi elders let him be the cop: There was also a makeshift jail in the BIA agency. Everyone joked about it. The Hopi had plenty of order, but the BIA didn't see any law, so they built a jail and hired a cop. He drew a paycheck for sitting around day after day with nothing to do. On hot afternoons, I often saw him relaxing in the shade near his patrol car, a '49 Chevy. He must have dozed off now and then, because there was no crime on Hopi land.

I didn't think much about it at the time, but now that I've traveled over much of the world, I know you can gauge how "civilized" an Indian reservation or native village has become by the number of jails it has and how many indigenous people can be talked into becoming policemen. The best measure of Western civilization is not mathematics or anything that goes with it, not agriculture or political systems or theology or philosophy. "Civilization" to the Western mind is police and jails: They signify law and order.

It has always cracked me up to see where whites build their homes. Indians don't build in gullies, creek bottoms, or floodplains—that's where the refuse of life settles, from gnat crap to bird shit. It's where the water that collects all that defecation runs, and where most insects breed. When you invade the insect world, it will make sure you're uncomfortable. So, of course, the BIA put the Hopi agency in a deep gully.

The Hopi have always lived high above the insects on towering mesas. White anthros like to believe that the Hopi lived up there because they feared other Indians. Believe me, before the whites came, the Hopi had no enemies.

Just think—the Hopi have lived on mesas for centuries, while their gardens, hunting grounds, and water supplies were on the desert floor. Would they leave their entire livelihood at the mercy of enemies who had only to lay siege and wait for them to die of thirst or starvation? Hardly. The Hopi live on mesas, then and now, for spiritual reasons.

Pops and I came to love the spirituality and warmth of the Hopi people, but we didn't want to overstay our welcome. When Scott was a few weeks old, big enough to travel, it was time for Betty, our children, and me to go. My dad took off for South Dakota. In July, we went down to Phoenix and rented a small house on an unpaved barrio street off Grand Avenue.

I applied for a scholarship at Arizona State University, in Tempe, but until school started, I needed a job. I found one immediately at Transamerica Title Insurance, which hired me as a computer operator for an IBM 1401, already an obsolete machine. As soon as the data-processing supervisor learned that I could also program, he added that to my duties. It was good pay, and that summer I had a great life. I could have stayed on and worked full-time at night, but I didn't want to go to school all day and work at night. In September, the State of Arizona approved my scholarship and I enrolled in the computer-sciences program, where I learned a little about programming languages COBOL and FORTRAN. More important, I was soon working on the IBM 360, then the top-of-the-line mainframe computer.

Since we couldn't afford a phone, I wrote to my mother and brothers instead. In late autumn, I learned that my dad was back at Pine Ridge, living in the Felix Cohen Old Age Home. It had been built in the late 1950s, when our culture was still very strong on the reservation, and so it was an utter failure. Lakota families wouldn't let their elders go there. We took care of our own, and anyway, our old people refused to be farmed out. Unfortunately, that was no longer the case, just as in white society. In 1966, the Felix Cohen Home was a sort of rooming house where my dad, then fifty-one, paid rent. When I learned it was an old-age home, I couldn't let him stay there. I wrote, demanding that he come to live with Betty and me.

The previous year, while Betty, Michele, and I were heading to Iowa Tech, my Uncle Murph Means had suffered a massive stroke which left him little more than a vegetable, unable to move anything except his eyes. After his own stroke, my dad's right side was temporarily paralyzed. He was told to take a drug that would thin his blood and reduce the risk of blood clots that could lead to another stroke. After Uncle Murph's stroke, Pops refused to take his medicine. When he came to live with us in Phoenix, I was always on him to take his pills, but he said, "I'm not going to end up like my brother. When it's my time to go, it's my time to go." With that philosophy, Pops wouldn't see a doctor and wouldn't take his medication. Long before that, I had often heard him say, "I want to go with a smile on my face, a woman in my arms, and a bottle of whiskey by my bed."

We gave Pops one of our bedrooms, while Betty and I and the kids made do in the other. He settled in with us and became part of our household, helping out around the house, occasionally baby-sitting, and contributing some of his pension money to help buy groceries and such.

Pops arrived on December 1. Until shortly after the new year of 1967, he didn't drink. Then one night he went out and came home gassed, carrying a six-pack. I didn't like it when he was drinking, so I gave him a mean look that meant "go to bed." He looked at me and said, "Russ, I know you'll handle everything." Then he went to bed. I knew Pops would wake up the next morning hung over. I wanted to tease him about getting drunk, so I told Betty, "I'm going to hide that beer." We put it in the bottom of the refrigerator and covered it with all sorts of stuff. When he looked for it, I was going to pretend I didn't know where it was, and let him hunt awhile.

Even when he was drinking, even when he stayed out till the small hours of morning, my father was always an early riser, rarely staying in bed past six. When I got up at about nine the next morning—it was Sunday, January 7— and Pops wasn't already moving around the house, I was a little alarmed because it was so unusual.

Michele, inquisitive as only a two-year-old can be, knew that going into Pops's room without knocking first was a big no-no. Nevertheless, that morning she had quietly opened his door and climbed onto the bed to sit beside him. I started into the room after her, but one glance told me everything. I froze at the door. I don't know how I knew, but I did. Just to make sure, I touched his arm. It was cold. In hushed tones, I told Michele, "Everything will be all right. Grandpa has left us." She was too little to understand. "There's Grandpa," she said, pointing.

I picked Michele up and carried her in the other room. I told Betty, "He's dead." She said, "No!" and ran in to check him. Betty came back and burst into tears. I put Michele in her arms and went to call my mother. I walked down the block to a phone booth on Grand Street. Mom was living in Ventura, California, with Ted and Dace. When she answered, I just said, "Mom, Pops is dead."

"Oh, Russell," she said. I could hear her crying. After a moment, she said, "Your Grandpa John died yesterday." I had lost my father, and Grandpa John Feather, who had walked with me along the untamed Missouri when I was a little boy, who had bought me sweet strawberry soda to wash down salty potato chips at the Greenwood store, the stern but kindly man who had taught me what it meant to be an Indian and to be a man.

Shocked that my always strong mother was so devastated by the two deaths, I gave her my love and sympathy. If I could hardly bear the thought of never again seeing my wise and strong grandfather, much less could I contemplate the loss of my father. He had gone to the spirit world before telling me all the things I would need to know, and before I could tell him how much he had meant to me. I knew that if I allowed myself to feel anything, I would be so overcome by emptiness that I couldn't function. There was much to do, so I forced myself to think about other matters.

The police and an ambulance came to take my father's body to the county morgue. We learned that he had died from coronary thrombosis, a blood clot in his heart. Years before, he had told me how and where he wanted to be buried. I kept myself busy for hours, making arrangements to get his body back to South Dakota on a train.

We had little money and no warm winter clothing for Michelle and Scott, so they stayed in Phoenix with Betty. Ted and Dace drove over from California in Ted's Volkswagen and picked me up to go to Pine Ridge. Meanwhile, Mom flew back to South Dakota to make arrangements for her father's burial at Greenwood. I couldn't bring myself to go to Grandpa John's funeral, the day before my father's. I just couldn't put myself through such an emotional wringer—and then trust that I would make it through my dad's funeral without collapsing.

People from all over the United States, everyplace my dad had ever lived, sent flowers. A lot of friends came to his funeral, but besides Mom, my brothers, and me, only Uncle Casey and Uncle Johnny, Pops's twin brother, were there to represent the Means family. When Uncle Casey arrived, he took over from my mother and made final arrangements at the Episcopalian Church in Martin, where all the Menses of my father's generation had been baptized. It was a completely Episcopalian ceremony, which still makes me angry, but I was powerless to change things.

The burial was in a private cemetery southwest of Martin, in the lower part of Bennett County, on land that the Means and Carlo families had owned before white men got hold of it. In accordance with his wishes, my father was buried next to his mother.

Of all the Means brothers, only my father had remained Indian all the way. In the last summer of his life, he had gotten a dance outfit and returned to the traditional dances and songs of his forefathers. Many of my father's cousins had gone to other reservations, to the Northern Cheyenne and the Arapaho. All Pops's brothers except Uncle Quentin had taken the white man's path, passing in a world that seemed to have no place for Indians. My father had often said he wanted Indians to sing over his grave, but when I told that to my uncles, they got an Indian chorus from the Episcopalian Church to sing hymns in Lakota. I knew that was probably enough to set Pops spinning in his coffin.

I still miss my dad. He died too young. He had a good way of looking at life, even though he wasn't always there when I needed him. Most of all, I'll never forget his saying, "If anything bad happens to you, it's your own damn fault." As a little kid, when I tripped and skinned a knee, I knew I couldn't go to him for sympathy. I had to take responsibility for my own actions. When I got beat up, it wasn't the bully's fault, it was mine, because I should know how to take care of myself. I passed that teaching on to all my own kids, but with one positive addition. If you learn from an experience, that's good—so nothing *bad* happened to you.

Mom and my brothers had cried after Dad's death, but I hadn't been able to let myself go. Uncle Casey, like most of my dad's brothers, was quiet, respectful, and undemonstrative, but as the casket was carried to the grave, I saw tears rolling down his cheeks. I lost control, throwing myself on the coffin as if I could somehow bring Dad back. My uncles had to drag me off. They took me back to Martin, where Uncle Johnny had some booze in his hotel room. We had a few drinks, and I tried to pretend it all hadn't happened.

12

▼▼▼▼▼▼▼▼▼

The Intertribal Car

In February 1967, about a month after Pops died, my mother sent me fifteen hundred dollars, a fourth of what was left from his insurance after she had paid for his funeral and for transferring his body back to South Dakota. Each of my brothers got the same amount. I used the money to buy a year-old white 1966 Plymouth, a dealer's demo car. Finally, we could go shopping anywhere, and I was no longer dependent on the bus to go back and forth to Arizona State University.

I found my classes challenging, so I applied myself and aced every course. Even so, I had plenty of time to socialize. Phoenix's Indian community was the friendliest I had ever been in. I started to hang around the only Indian bar in town, and before long I had made new friends. One of them was Lucky Salway, a Pine Ridge Lakota and a tough rodeo cowboy. Along with Lucky and another new friend, Roy Track, I joined an all-Indian basketball team, the Phoenix Chiefs. I had many good times playing basketball that winter.

Drinking or traveling around for basketball, Lucky and I often talked about rodeo. In the northern Plains, it is pretty much a summer thing, but it's damn near a year-round sport in the Southwest. When I had been with my brothers just after our dad died, I learned that Ted, who had begun to enter rodeo events, had promised to teach Dace rodeo riding during the coming season. Dace and I had always been in some kind of unspoken competition. He had kissed a girl before I did, lost his virginity before I did—he had even ridden on an airplane before I did. I made up my mind that this time, I would beat Dace and take up rodeo first.

I went with Lucky to the rodeo at the Salt River Reservation in Arizona, where he talked me into signing up for the bareback-bronc and bull-riding events. Lucky got me a bareback rig and set me down on my first rodeo bronc. Those animals were top-grade professional rodeo stock. To this day, the horse I drew that day was the rankest I have ever ridden. He came out of the chute like an explosion on four legs. I flopped over on one side and then I was upside down, clinging to the rigging. When I finally had to let go, I landed on my head, with my whole weight jamming my neck. I was lucky I didn't break it. I didn't really know how to ride rodeo style, and I failed to keep my right elbow tight to my body and my wrists in my lap. That horse did a number on me. I had internal bleeding from my crotch all the way down to my right knee, and in the underside of my right arm. My leg and arm turned black and blue.

Most of the Indian rodeo cowboys I met competed only in local and regional events, but many were good enough to have done well on the professional rodeo circuit. Long after my own bronc-riding days were over, I became very close to Leon Grant, an Omaha champion. He won events at New York's Madison Square Garden, Chicago's Soldier Field, the Cow Palace in San Francisco, the Calgary Stampede, and lots of other big-time venues. White racists judge professional rodeo, and if you're an Indian, you have to be twice as good as a white just to start even. There are several Indian riders now who, if they were white, would be ranked in the top fifteen.

After I got out of school in June, I didn't know what I could do to earn a living. Betty was busy around the house with the kids; it was starting to get hot again, and my scholarship's meager stipend had ended with the school term. I hadn't had a job while I was in school, so I had no unemployment to fall back on. After looking hard in the Phoenix job market, I could find no suitable position, nothing that would use my accounting and computer skills, nothing that would support a family of four. Once again, as I had in Albuquerque, San Francisco, and Los Angeles, I started to get down on myself, feeling that I was no good, a loser.

Since my only role model for husband and father was my dad, at times like that I usually got drunk, just as he had. When I wanted to disappear for a few days and go drinking, I picked a fight with Betty. By that time, she didn't panic when I dropped out of sight for a few days. Our kids never saw me drunk, but from reappraising my own childhood, I know now how very much they missed me.

One day, depressed and anxious about my continuing failure to find work, I went drinking with Chris Clay, a tall, lanky guy I knew from my time in Winnebago. He was also down because he couldn't find a job. We got a little gassed, and Chris said, "Let's take off and go up to Flagstaff and find a job." Chris had only a dollar, and I had three. The gas tank was a quarter full. It was long before dawn, after all the bars had closed, and we had drunk enough to feel no pain. I said, "Let's go," and we took off. We spent our little money on gas. By daylight, we had driven the winding mountain roads until we were several miles south of Flagstaff. We were almost out of gas, so I pulled into a Union 76 station. Rolling out my brand-new spare tire and wheel, I hocked them in exchange for a tank of gas. When we got to Flagstaff at about seven or eight in the morning, the bars were open. Chris knew where the Indians hung around, and we went to one of those bars, where we met a Hopi guy and a Navajo guy. We joined them, drinking and having fun, telling jokes and laughing at theirs.

At some point the Navajo said, "I know where there's a squaw dance— north of Winslow on the Navajo Reservation." Then the Hopi said, "I've got some money, and we can buy a case of booze and bootleg it, triple our money." We got a case of beer, some gin and whiskey, a "ring o' red" (a hunk of bologna), a loaf of bread, and some chips. The Navajo and the Hopi had been traveling and they had some luggage, so we put it all in the trunk of my Plymouth and headed for Winslow. We got there by afternoon, when it was already hot. We headed over to the Indian bar to wet our whistles. Outside, staggering and getting pushed around, was Tim Curley, a Crow from Montana. He had lost his boots and was barefoot and falling-down drunk. I knew Tim from rodeo events. He had been a bull-riding champ, but drink was getting the best of him, as it had gotten and still does get a lot of Indians. We forced him into the car with us, took him to a gas station, and cleaned him up. The Navajo had an extra pair of boots, and he gave them to Tim.

That evening, we went to a liquor store and bought a case of wine— twenty-four pints. Then we headed for the squaw dance way out in the middle of nowhere, south of Greasewood. Everybody had a great time there. We sold two bottles of wine as soon as we got there, but we were soon so happy-go-lucky drunk that we began to give it away. When we ran out of gin and whiskey, we started in on the remaining wine. When we awoke in the morning, sick and hung over, sweating in the heat, we realized that we had taken in only about one-fifth of what the wine had cost.

We kicked our own butts for a while, and then it struck me that we had, in one car, a Sioux, a Winnebago, a Crow, a Navajo, and a Hopi. From that moment on, the five of us were the "Intertribal Car," an Indian version of five musketeers—one for all, and all for one. Tim said he knew some Crow people in Albuquerque, and I knew Sonny Tuttle. "Let's go there and sell our blood and party," I said. We drove to Albuquerque, where Tim got a few dollars from one of his relatives, I got some money from Sonny Tuttle, and we continued to party. I had left Phoenix two nights earlier and Betty had no idea where I had gone, but I didn't worry about it much.

We each sold our blood for ten dollars a pint, except Chris Clay, who was chicken. With that forty dollars and what we had gotten from Sonny and from Tim's relative, plus what little money that the Navajo still had, we had nearly a hundred dollars. Then we heard about a ranch in Colorado that was hiring, and we decided to go there. Maybe we would work for a week, then head out. Or maybe we would work there all summer. We got another ring o' red, a loaf of bread, some chips, a case of beer, some gin and wine, and took the old highway north to the dude ranch. It was in the mountains near Colorado Springs.

That ranch held a little amateur rodeo for about ninety minutes every day. It was really just for the guests to enjoy, so it was mostly riding events. Dude guests don't like to see cute little calves roped and jerked off their feet by big old mean cowboys. We didn't want to spend money for rodeo entry fees, so the ranch people agreed to give five dollars apiece for each event we entered. That was the only time in my life I ever tried bulldogging—and I missed the steer. I knew I had no hope of catching him, but I went for him anyway because those rodeo arenas are plowed dirt and pretty soft if you know how to fall. I just took a dive. I didn't know anything about saddle-bronc riding either, so I rode a bull and a bareback bronc. I collected fifteen dollars for the afternoon, and everyone else got at least ten.

We were "cashy" again, with enough for gas, food, and booze. We headed up to Denver, where we thought we might find work. I knew a cowboy from Rapid City, Sidney Whitesell, an Indian dancer who was going to college there. When we got to Sidney's place, he said he was serious about school and didn't want to party until the weekend. He directed us to a bar around the corner from the Brown Hotel. The bar was a rough, tough, frontier place with B-girls drinking colored water at premium whiskey prices, bought by horny guys who thought they were going to get laid but were only going to get screwed. We were just a bunch of rowdy cowboys with our hats on, drinking and dancing with the B-girls to jukebox music. Chris Clay was so naturally funny that we all played off him, making us look funny too. We had a rollicking good time. Because there were five of us, nobody hassled us.

By the time we had blown our money, one of the B-girls had come to like us, especially me. Nothing sexual happened, but she let us all stay at her place, sleeping on the floor in her dive of an apartment. Although it had been only about four days since we got blood money in Albuquerque, the next day we munched on raisins, then sold our blood again. Even Chris gave in that time, although he almost fainted. We were having too good a time to leave Denver, so we drank up all our cash again. Then we talked about making money by hustling in a gay bar next door, about selling ourselves for a blow job. Tim and the Navajo agreed to try. Chris and the Hopi said, "No way," and I said, "I ain't going to do it either. I'll panhandle."

Right about then, as we were all walking down to the bus depot to clean up, I called someone. I've forgotten if it was my mother or a neighbor in Phoenix. I wanted to send a message to Betty about where I was and that I was okay. Betty was used to my erratic, alcoholic, irresponsible behavior, but she didn't like it or tolerate it. I always had to face reality when I got home, just as my dad had. Sometimes I would return home to a shouting match, and sometimes she wouldn't say a word. There were times when I came back drunk on a crying jag and Betty would mother me until the next day, when I was sober but hung over, and then she would let me have it. When she did give me a piece of her mind, I would sit silent, beating myself up, agreeing with her that I was a no-good lousy father, husband, and human being. On that day in Denver, as on other days when I had been drinking, I wasn't exactly in a rush to go home and hear what Betty had to say. Believe it or not, I was still hoping to find work.

Chris went off to panhandle on Broadway, but I couldn't bring myself to beg for money. Instead, I went back to the B-girl bar, arriving just in time to see Tim come out of the gay bar with a guy and get in a car. My pal the B-girl bought me a draft beer that I could nurse for an hour or two. When the Hopi came back from panhandling, we hustled him a beer, too. Looking out the window, we saw the Navajo leave the gay bar with a guy. They got in a car and drove off. After a while, the Navajo returned—with money. Tim also came back with cash. When Chris returned, he had some money from panhandling. Suddenly Sid Whitesell walked in, and after a while he laid ten or fifteen dollars on me. We held a quick meeting of the Intertribal Car and decided that we should have left when we had sold our blood. It was time to get the hell out of Denver.

Dace, Ted, and Bill were all working on the Rosebud Reservation in South Dakota, so we decided to head there. One more time, we got a ring o' red, loaf o' bread, chips, beer, gin, and whiskey. On Friday night, we pulled into Mission, a white town surrounded by the Rosebud Reservation. We went to Irish's, a beer joint with a pool table, where we found my brothers and several old friends. We partied the whole weekend.

I woke up Sunday morning in Dace's room. Something was very wrong. Every time I turned my head, I became nauseated. The room was swimming, I couldn't focus my eyes, and I couldn't stand on my own. I had suffered many a hangover, but this was very different. Dace and Ted took me to the Indian Health Service hospital. At first, the white admissions clerk wouldn't let me in. She kept saying I was drunk. She probably thought so because my brothers were carrying me, one under each arm.

I was trying to concentrate on keeping my head still. I couldn't move my head or stand up straight or talk, much less defend myself. Eventually my brothers got angry and started to yell and swear at the IHS people, telling them to call the cops if they wanted. Finally they admitted me, but offered no medical attention. There was a physician on call over the weekend, but not until Monday did a doctor come to examine me. When he finally came, his examination was superficial. He didn't even bother with X rays. His diagnosis was that I had been in a barroom fight and had been hit on the head, so I was suffering from a concussion.

I had been in a lot of barroom fights, but not that time. All I could do was lie there—trying not to move my head and trigger overwhelming nausea for two more days. On Wednesday, the fourth day of my misery, an eye, ear, nose, and throat specialist from Omaha came through on his regular monthly rounds. After examining me, he became visibly angry. He told a nurse to put me in a wheelchair and wheel me to a tiny office. He then summoned all the IHS doctors. When everyone had squeezed in, he pulled down an ear chart, the kind you see in junior-high biology classes. He was boiling mad as he proceeded to tell them that I had an infection in my inner ear. He said if those idiots had listened to what I had said, if they had examined me when I came in, they would have known that. He said, "With a single dose of antibiotics, you could have cured that infection. You didn't do that, and so he's now deaf in his left ear, and will be for the rest of his life."

1 3

▼▼▼▼▼▼▼▼▼

The Rosebud

T he infection that had attacked my inner ear in that summer of 1967 was
so far advanced that it affected my balance. After antibiotics knocked out
the infection, I had to learn to walk all over again. It was tough—although the nausea had passed, my head still swam. Sometimes it felt as
though it weren't even connected to my body. If I forgot to keep tension in
the neck muscles holding my head up, it flopped to one side. Until I learned
to walk again, the IHS people gave me a walker, the kind of tubular metal
thing I had seen only in old-age homes. If I hadn't been so sick, I would
have been mad enough to kill the doctors who had allowed that to happen.

Lying in bed the following Friday afternoon, I had a visit from Sonny
Waln. He ran the Community Action Program of the Office of Economic
Opportunity, the Johnson administration's antipoverty program, on the Rosebud Reservation. My brother Bill had spoken with him that day. When Sonny
mentioned that he was looking for an accountant, Bill told him about me.
Sonny interviewed and hired me on the spot. "The doctor says you'll have
to stay in here at least another ten days," he said.

"Bullshit," I replied. "I'll be in to work Monday." I was. I couldn't
drive for a while, but I got help from the Intertribal Car guys. Soon, however,

my Navajo pal and Tim went to work running stock on a ranch. The Hopi found some kind of temporary, menial job. Chris Clay struck out, even though he looked hard around the Rosebud. Finally, he took off for Sioux City. Later that summer I heard, to my sorrow, that one night, drinking, he had climbed a water tower or something and had fallen to his death.

I missed the partying and easy camaraderie of the Intertribal Car, but I also enjoyed learning my new job as director of management information systems. For weeks, I staggered around, trying to cope with my balance problems, but I went to work every day at the CAP office in the old BIA boarding school east of Mission. I soon discovered that the OEO was the best thing ever to hit Indian reservations. It was overwhelmingly successful everywhere I visited. Community health representatives brought medical care to long-ignored elderly and handicapped people, and worked with young mothers to improve the health of their babies. The Legal Aid program was a tremendous boost. For the first time, people in remote communities began to feel that they could get something done, that someone with authority would listen to their problems and help them fight for their rights in tribal, federal, and state courts. Legal Aid lawyers also actively defended the rights of Indians accused of criminal acts. Those OEO programs and others that helped communities form and manage their own organizations, to find solutions to their own problems inspired hope. After generations of despair, Indians began to feel that they could shape their destinies by administering their own affairs. And as I got to know the Rosebud elders at that time, I came to love and admire their way of handling things.

My first task at OEO was to design financial and personnel reporting systems. I'm proud to say that the OEO used those systems for years, until it got computers. Every other Friday, CAP representatives from all the Rosebud communities came in to pick up their paychecks and attend an orientation meeting. I usually spoke at those meetings. As I began to learn my job and meet more coworkers, I had a really good time. When my responsibilities became routine, I was given additional duties that included reaching out to the communities. I often drove to different parts of the reservation.

Once I had collected a few paychecks, I sent for Betty and the kids. We moved into a trailer house south of Mission on Highway 83. One of the first people I met in my new job was Bill Janklow, the bartender at Jim Abourezk's restaurant in Rockerville where I had danced for tourists in the summer of 1965. Abourezk had recently been elected to the U.S. House of Representatives as a Democrat. Janklow, who had graduated from law school the previous summer, had become a Legal Aid attorney on the Rosebud.

Janklow had already won some important lawsuits, including one against white businessmen who had been trying to repossess property held by Indians living on the reservation. On behalf of his Indian clients, Janklow had won a decision affirming that Indians on reservations were not subject to state laws. He was in the midst of another suit that would also affirm the sovereignty of the Rosebud Sioux.

One of the reasons Janklow was so enthusiastic was because of his up-bringing in Flandreau, South Dakota, a tiny farm town near the Minnesota border, a few miles from the quarry at Pipestone, Minnesota. For centuries, my mother's people, the Ihanktonwan, found at Pipestone the red stone from which the bowls of sacred pipes are carved. Even today, the Ihanktonwan continue to work that quarry. The half of South Dakota east of the Missouri, unlike the part west of there, is very segregated. Janklow grew up in what is called "East River" without knowing anything about Indians or prejudices against them. When he came to the Rosebud, he was flabbergasted by the flagrant racism he saw.

When I started to work at OEO, Janklow told me all the things he was trying to do. He was determined to make big changes. He helped set up a better tribal court system. In the next few years, Legal Aid did an excellent job, not only in strengthening tribal sovereignty but also in enhancing the power of the individual on the reservation. Legal Aid helped people so much that the Congress, prodded by the BIA, pulled the teeth out of the program rather than lose their arbitrary power over every dimension of an Indian's life.

In 1967, Janklow and the other young Legal Aid lawyers under his leadership were still eager beavers, working hard to overcome a century of neglect and racism. Janklow and I took an immediate liking to each other. He lived at the old boarding school, near my office, and sometimes invited other Indians and me to his place. His wife, Mary, was a pretty blonde. His young son, Russell, looked just like Bill. Once in a great while I went out with Bill, and he sometimes eyed Indian girls, but it never went any further than that. Even if Bill were looking for more, because of colonization, boarding-school life, and the white cops and FBI agents on the reservations, Indian women were deathly afraid of white guys.

As early as 1967, Janklow was among the people who had helped to uncover and publicize the fact that quite a few Indian families were living in abandoned car bodies during the bitterly cold Great Plains winters, and that countless reservation Indians suffered from severe malnutrition. Those children had sticklike arms, sunken chests, and distended bellies—kids in the America of 1967 who looked like the children in those gut-wrenching photos from Biafra later, and like the television pictures from Somalia in the 1990s.

That winter, volunteers from the CAP program, including the Legal Aid lawyers, bagged up candies and peanuts and food baskets to pass out to Indian families on Christmas Eve. Bill dressed up like Santa Claus. Along with another lawyer, we went out to deliver some of the gifts. We had just gotten on the road when a blizzard hit, but we continued through the fiercely blowing snow, driving through the whole night to visit remote communities.

We couldn't always drive all the way to the houses, so we walked, pushing through deep snowdrifts. In Grass Mountain and other places, we visited people living in shacks so tumbledown that snow leaked through the roofs. We saw homes where people had spread waxed paper all over their bedding and clothes to try to keep them dry. Some of the women and old men broke down and cried when we arrived. No one had ever before brought them anything for Christmas. Since joining Legal Aid, Bill had been in a few such homes, but that was the first time he and the other lawyers had really been hit in the face by such misery.

Some of the children had never heard of Santa Claus. Indian children are told about *jiji* men, bad spirits. When Bill appeared in his red suit and false whiskers, they shrank from him, thinking he was a *jiji*. He explained that he was Santa, and asked them to sit on his knee. Of course, they wouldn't do it. Then the parents and grandparents, who were happy to have the gifts and food we brought, told their kids that Bill wasn't a *jiji*, he was a good white man. After the kids got over their initial fright, it was wonderful to see them react to Bill in his Santa suit. It was a beautiful, heartrending learning experience for all the volunteers, white and Indian.

A couple of our vehicles got stuck that night, but when cold daylight came on Christmas Day, we had finished all our deliveries. We went to a bar for a few drinks. When Bill walked in, still dressed as Santa Claus, he cracked me up. Later, he ingratiated himself with the Indian community, especially many of the elders, by learning to speak a little Lakota. To this day, there are Rosebud Sioux who have stood, and will stand, by him through thick and thin. Years later, when Bill was elected governor of South Dakota, they all got jobs.

When I knew Bill in 1967 and 1968, I considered him a good human being and a close friend. He was the first of many who tried to convince me to go to law school. I'm glad I didn't, but he made me think about it. Late in 1969, we happened to find ourselves in Washington, D.C., at the same time. We went to Congress and watched Jim Abourezk from the House of Representatives visitors' gallery. I asked, "Are you still friends with Jim?" Bill said, "Oh, sure. You don't let politics get in between friendships." I thought that was a great statement. I wish he could have lived up to it, because my memories of Bill remain positive. He was young and full of fight then, but I would come to wish that I had known that he was also very ambitious. In time, it was ambition rather than politics that would get in the way of friendship.

Besides hanging around with Bill Janklow, I renewed my passion for rodeo. For two years, I entered bareback and bull-riding events, but I got bucked off almost every time. Near the end of the 1968 rodeo season, I was bucked off a Scottish Highlander bull. The bullfighter clown, whose job it was to keep the bull from trampling or goring riders, had gone off somewhere. I was prone in the sawdust, so I lifted one leg, hoping my spur would catch the bull's face. Instead, he hooked my right buttock with a horn, and I sailed ten feet through the air like a rag doll. Then he came after me again. At the last instant, a Lakota cowboy named Jim Calumb jumped off the fence and threw a body slam into the bull. Then a couple of other cowboys ran up and distracted him until I got over the fence. My wound wasn't serious, but I had trouble sitting down for a few weeks. That was the end of my rodeo season.

I had worse problems than not making it as a rodeo rider—my CAP job. The system began to corrupt itself. There were opportunities for abuse, so people found them and used them. It took me a while to learn how bureaucrats operate. I didn't know I was supposed to pad my expense account. I was actually logging the *correct* mileage. Most of the others claimed mileage even when someone else drove, and they routinely increased the distances they drove, to get more money from the government. Some people abused per diem—reimbursement for government-connected travel expenses. One of the reasons I had been hired was to establish systems that were more accountable, but I wasn't prepared for the politics-as-usual mentality among civil servants. I learned that whenever anything in Indian country is successful, as with all colonized peoples, everybody wants to get in on it and then remove those who preceded them and put their own people in. Sure enough, that's what happened in the Rosebud's OEO program.

After rumors began to circulate that I was drinking on the job, my boss, Sonny Waln, fired me. I don't know for sure who started that talk, but it was absolutely untrue. I had partied too long and missed a few workdays now and then, but otherwise I did *all* my drinking on my own time. I fought the dismissal. Because I hadn't been accorded due process, I was reinstated. Then I quit. By then I was getting tired of drinking. I had two beautiful kids, and I wanted my marriage to work. Betty and I talked it over and decided to go on the relocation program. I applied for Cleveland, figuring it was about as far away from Indians as we could get. There was no Indian center in Cleveland, and no Indian bars—and that, we thought, would improve our family life.

In the middle of July 1968, we packed our belongings into our blue '62 Chevy and headed for Cleveland in what Betty and I hoped would be a fresh start. Our lives *were* about to change, but as we drove toward Ohio, we had no inkling of how profound those changes would be—or what they would do to our marriage.

14
▼▼▼▼▼▼▼▼▼

Cleveland

We pulled into Cleveland in the late afternoon of a hot July day. By the time we found the federal building and the BIA, signed in, and filled out the paperwork, it was past quitting time. Almost everybody except our counselor, who assigned a flunky to guide us to a hotel near downtown, had gone home. I had never been to Cleveland before, but one look at Euclid Avenue and I knew I was on skid row, the meanest section of the red-light district. The hotel was crumbling and seedy. Our room was in the basement, the filthiest part. I was filled with revulsion, but it was too late to do anything until morning. The hotel staff put us in one dimly lit room, with threadbare carpet, worn sheets, rat droppings in the corners, cracked bathroom fixtures— a traveler's nightmare.

Later, I learned that several other Indian families lived in that basement, including a Choctaw couple from Mississippi with seven or eight kids. They had stayed in two rat-infested rooms for three years, mostly because they could speak only a little broken English and the father's minimum-wage factory job paid so little they couldn't afford better.

When I went to the store that first night to get some food for my family, the hookers hanging out in front of the hotel gave me the once-over. When I returned, I saw one bringing her john inside. What really got me was when

Michele, then four, said, "Daddy, why are those men kissing?" Before I could think of an answer, she said she had just seen two men kissing each other in the corridor. That was enough for me. One way or another, we were moving out in the morning.

At sunrise, Betty and I bundled everything back into our car and drove to the federal building, where I told my BIA counselor that we were not staying another minute in that sewer. When I demanded that she find my family suitable lodging, she said, "You're going to have to stay there." She insisted it was the only place where incoming relocatees could go for temporary lodging. This was 1968; a few years earlier, I might have accepted that, but I was no longer so naive. I said, "Show me the budget—how much money is allocated for this program and for each family in it?" The counselor refused, although I kept after her. Finally she agreed to tell me how much had been earmarked for my family. It was the same as when I had gone on relocation in 1960—allowances for temporary lodging, rent, furniture, and clothing, plus work clothes for me. It seemed like more than enough to put us up in a decent hotel. I again demanded that the BIA find us one until we could find an apartment. The woman passed the buck to her boss, a white guy. I told him what I wanted and why. Visibly angry, I said, "If I don't get some action, I'm going to let somebody know about the whorehouse you put us in."

I was bluffing—I had no idea whom to report it to—but my threat scared him into action. Unlike those folks from Mississippi, we possessed the verbal skills needed to demand a change. We moved into a clean, modern hotel in Lakewood, one of Cleveland's best neighborhoods. It was an exclusive place with a swimming pool, wall-to-wall carpeting, and a view of Lake Erie. Our room cost the BIA about thirty-five dollars a night—seven or eight times what it had paid for our basement hovel on skid row.

Surprised and happy, I asked to be shown some apartments, but the BIA counselor still didn't catch on. She took us first to a black ghetto and then to a white slum where the stench of urine permeated the rooms. It was all I could do to keep my breakfast down. In the best of those dives, the window shades were cracked and torn, patched and taped, and there was no bathroom door, only a makeshift curtain. After three or four such places, I said, "We're not going to live in a neighborhood like this."

"Anything else is too expensive," said our counselor. "Let *me* worry about that!" I snapped. "I'll be the one who pays the rent, and I want to live in suburbia." Finally she took us to a horseshoe-shaped apartment house near Fairview Park. I said, "Right there! That's where we want to live."

"Oh, no, that looks too expensive," said the BIA woman. I insisted, and we went in and found ourselves a great apartment with a view of the park. After paying the first and last month's rent, the counselor said, "Your rent allowance was supposed to last four months—you just spent it on two."

"All I need is a job," I said, "and you're supposed to help me find it, so what are you worried about?" Next, I demanded my furniture allowance, but again I had to fight. "Just get some mattresses and wait until you have a job and a paycheck, and then you should buy some things on time and build up your credit," she said. "We don't want credit," I replied. "We want furniture." Reluctantly, the BIA gave us the money—less than two hundred dollars, but enough for what we required.

In a week, we had spent our entire relocation allowance, but we had everything we needed to reestablish ourselves—exactly as Congress had intended relocation to work. The BIA officials had fought us over every penny, as though it were *their* money and we ought to live like the Choctaw family in a skid-row hellhole. I know now that very few Indians insisted on their relocation entitlements as firmly as I did. I also know that when they got screwed out of their money, as most did, the funds saved meant awards and promotions for BIA supervisors. That money, instead of going to help poor Indians live decently, was turned back to the government.

Once we were settled into our new apartment, I demanded that the BIA help me find a white-collar job. As I had expected, they couldn't. Because I had a data-processing background, I went to an employment agency specializing in that field. The people who ran the place hired me on the spot. My job was placing people into the huge industrial corporations and banks with headquarters in Cleveland. On my first day, I was shown a list of companies that had quotas for Jews and blacks. I couldn't believe what I was hearing, but I kept my mouth shut. My boss explained that *this* corporation will hire this many Jews and *that* one will take so many "niggers," as he put it. I was puzzled. At a time when those big companies were crying for people trained in computers, they accepted fewer Jews than African-Americans, and some of the biggest firms would take no Jews at all.

As it happened, my first two clients were a young blond guy, who had just graduated from a prestigious Ivy League college with straight A's in math, and his pretty wife. Their name was Goldstein. Later that day, a black guy came in with his wife and their small baby. He was a C-average math graduate from an all-black Southern college. I placed him in a downtown bank on my first call. I tried to place the Goldsteins, but every personnel director I spoke to told me their quota was filled. Of course they never actually put it that way. They said, "We're not hiring today, call back tomorrow with a black or a white." That blew me away. I didn't know that kind of prejudice existed, and I couldn't understand why whites hated Jews. I thought about it a lot, sitting at my desk. The more I considered it, the more it bothered me. No one who saw those people walking down the street could tell if they were Catholic or Episcopalian or Jewish. I never did place the Goldsteins. After two weeks on the job, when my first paycheck came, I decided I couldn't blind myself to such racism anymore, so I quit.

We talked it over, and Betty decided she would go back to work. She soon found a job as a secretary for the Cleveland Housing Authority. Because I had worked for the Office of Economic Opportunity on the Rosebud Reservation, I decided to look for work in one of the OEO programs in downtown Cleveland. By the end of August, I had found a spot as an accountant—actually little more than a glorified payroll clerk—at the Council for Economic Opportunity. It was run by African-Americans, but the head of my department was white, a retired army colonel. He was old and crusty, but spineless. Under him were two Orthodox Jewish guys who took off early every Friday so they could get home before sundown. Aside from one black guy and me, everyone else in the department was female. My computer training was of little use. All we had to work with was adding machines and old-fashioned Comptometers, the kind with dozens of multicolored keys.

After Betty and I had settled into our jobs, we were hungry to meet other Indian people. We started to go to Chicago on weekends with our kids, for dances at the Chicago Indian Center. I won a couple of dance contests there. Then we heard about a dance at a school in Cleveland. When we got there, I found that the audience was all white. Some Indian singers who had come there on relocation were sitting around teaching their songs to whites, but I thought more Indians might show up later. I had brought my dancing outfit, and I wanted to dance, so I got dressed—but still no Indians showed up. As it turned out, it wasn't an Indian dance at all, it was an event for white hobbyists. When the dancing started, they announced a fancy-dance contest, and I entered, of course. I was a champion, a very good dancer. The judges, all whites, gave first prize to a white guy. Years later, he became the head of Lakota studies at Black Hills State College, in South Dakota.

That was my first experience with "wanna-bes." Since then, I've learned that the whole phenomenon—whites trying to emulate Indian cultural trappings—is the latest pathetic phase of a rebellion against spiritual bankruptcy. In the 1960s many whites, led by the Beatles, traipsed off to India to see the Maharishi. They wore Nehru jackets and played the sitar and gave up meat and recited mantras, but it didn't make them happy. They tried Zen Buddhism, but that didn't work either, so they switched to Taoism. What I find curious about the wanna-bes is that they appropriate what they think they need to satisfy their desires of the moment, but they never really commit themselves. In the end, they are never fulfilled, so they try something else—Hare Krishna, Scientology, Branch Davidian—the cult of the month. Now when I see wanna-bes, my first reaction is to reach out to them, poor things, to pet them and say that if they will just pay attention to who they are, they will be all right. My second reaction is to say, "You want to be an Indian? All right, great. Come on, let's go!" My third and abiding reaction is that I know they won't stick it out, so I just walk away.

After attending the hobbyists' dance, I went looking for someplace—

anyplace except a bar—where Indians congregated in Cleveland. I soon discovered that there was nothing but a few bars where Indians hung out. I finally went to one, even though Betty and I had chosen Cleveland because we hoped it would get me away from drinking. By then, I had recognized that going on benders for days at a time got in the way of having a family. I cut back my drinking even after I found Club 77 on Detroit Avenue.

I learned that Cleveland, which never had many Indians and for that reason had been the least popular relocation city, had fallen far short of BIA quotas. The BIA began to ship in Indians from all over the United States. Also arriving in Cleveland around then were Mohawk and Six Nations people—whom whites sometimes call Iroquois—including many Canadians. They were mostly ironworkers who had come to Cleveland to build the new skyscrapers going up downtown. Standoffish, they rarely mixed with other Indians, preferring their own bars on the east side.

At Club 77 I became friends with Sarge Old Horn, a Crow from Montana. He was a couple of years younger than me, kind of stocky, about five feet ten, but very quick and a former all-state basketball player. Sarge was a barber, married to a Sioux from the Fort Peck Reservation in Montana. They had four little girls and another baby on the way. He liked to joke around and have fun, and he really liked women—any kind of woman, as long as she was alive.

We often commiserated that the Indians in Cleveland had no place to go except that bar. One night when it was very slow at Club 77, one of us said, over a beer, "We ought to start our own Indian center." By then we had met quite a few Indians, including Cheyenne, Arapaho, Seminole, Kiowa, and Navajo people—enough for a good nucleus. Sarge and I and the rest of us wanted a center that would help Indian people with the problems we often experience in the urban environment. Hardly any Indians lived on skid row for long, but many were underemployed and many more were stranded, unable to get back to their homes. Our teenagers also needed someplace where they could stay out of trouble, and where they could retain their attachments to their traditional cultures.

The next week, Sarge and I talked our idea over with some friends, including Irma Yellow Eagle and her family, all from the Rosebud. We all agreed that we needed an Indian center, but where could we go? Irma, an Episcopalian and a member of the oldest church in Cleveland, introduced Sarge and me to the priest there, but he didn't immediately offer us anything. We got a mailing list from the BIA. Our little ad hoc committee of four or five people met around my kitchen table to handwrite meeting notices, fold them into envelopes, lick stamps, and mail them out. In April 1969, we elected a board of directors and I got an OEO lawyer to incorporate us as a nonprofit organization. We were officially the Cleveland American Indian Center, but we still had no real place to meet, not even an office.

When summer came, I returned to Pine Ridge to visit family and friends. Many of them had come back home to attend the sun dance, the most important annual event in our traditional religion. Sarge Old Horn stopped by for a few days to look around before going on to the Crow Indian Reservation in Montana. His people have their own sun dance, which they got from the Shoshone. Our Nakota brethren in Canada hold one, but at that time the only sun dance for the Lakota Nation in the United States was at Pine Ridge. It was then less a spiritual event than a big fair, with a carnival, social dancing, a softball tournament, rodeo, and food booths all around. Sun dancing went on only from sunup until noon.

I didn't participate in the dance except as a spectator, but I met an older fellow, Pete Catches, who began to tell me what the dance had once meant to our culture and what it still meant to him—why he danced. Enthralled, I soaked up everything he told me. After I listened to Pete and watched him dance, the sun dance seized my imagination and inspired me to explore my Lakota heritage with renewed fervor.

When I returned to Cleveland, Sarge and I had a few more meetings with the Episcopalian priest. Finally he offered us a big room in the church basement to use as an office for our Indian center. He said we could use his auditorium whenever it wasn't booked for church events.

For months, we had been trying to organize members of the Indian community, even those such as the Withorne family who had their own social organization for Friday night bowling, Sunday softball games, and summer picnics. Most of those people were breeds, skilled workers or office people who had gone on relocation to integrate with white society, and who wanted nothing to do with anything identifiably Indian. Brought together by blood or skin color or common experience, they wanted to do only white things. More power to them, we said. In the long run, those of us who wished to remain Indians, on the reservations and in the cities, have been better off without them.

The late 1960s were turbulent times in Cleveland. On the east side were blacks struggling for civil rights to make up for several centuries of exploitation and bigotry. The west side, in those days, was where all the white ethnic Europeans lived, mostly Irish and hillbillies who tended to be of Scottish or English ancestry. Cleveland was a very polarized town. The civil-rights movement was in full bloom, the antiwar movement was still strong, and the hippies were smoking dope and spreading their message of peace and love. The steelworkers hated the hippies, and the unions hated the blacks and all other people of color.

Now here came us Indians, organizing community groups on the west side. We made an alliance with a Puerto Rican council. I met constantly with community groups, mostly white but a few black, all trying to get political power. Then Carl Stokes, whose brother Lewis was in the U.S. House of

Representatives, was elected mayor, the first black to run a major U.S. city. The faces at city hall changed forever. Sarge and other community activists and I went to see Mayor Stokes. After that, we got along with city hall. We also established positive relationships with the police commissioner. Sarge and I spent a lot of time in each other's company, constantly discussing our culture and what it meant to us. He was active in the Native American Church and knew much about the sacrament called peyote: Through our discussions, I gained tremendous respect for his church and its peyote prayers. Sarge was also a fountain of knowledge about many other cultural traditions, partly because, unlike many Indian nations, the Crow people have pretty much kept their extended-family units together.

Through Sarge, I came to admire the Crow people. When I was growing up, I had always been taught that they were our traditional enemies. For generations, the descendants of Sioux living farther east were taught by white missionaries and schoolteachers that the Chippewa, as whites call the Ojibwa, were their enemies—just as the Ojibwa were taught that Sioux were *their* enemies. I'm still amazed at how all of this white disinformation filled our heads. The truth is that the correct translation of Indian words usually rendered in English as *enemy* is *aggressor*. We had no word for *enemy*.

When we weren't out meeting people in the community or at city hall, Sarge and I worked to make our fledgling Indian Center into a viable enterprise. We heard about the National Urban Indian Council, with headquarters in Chicago. We wrote to its leader, Jess Sixkiller, and asked him to come to Cleveland to give us organizational advice and to show us how to write grant proposals. Jess was an Oklahoma Cherokee, a former lieutenant in the Chicago police force and a good man. In the autumn of 1969, after Mayor Stokes had helped establish the Cleveland Fund to provide seed money for local communities, Sarge and I decided to get some of that money for our center. We set up a meeting with the mayor, and Jess came to help us. We met in one of those dark, dignified City Hall chambers paneled in old wood. When we walked in, Jess marched to the head of the table, took out a tape recorder, turned it on, and said, "Now, let's start the meeting." The look on those officials' faces was priceless. We walked out of there with the promise of a grant of five thousand dollars. You could have bought two new Chevrolets with that in those days, and had money left over.

Jess had been going around the country for more than a year, trying to get Indian centers and urban Indian groups to join together in one big national organization. He and his people decided to have what they called a National Urban Indian Organization (NUIO) conference in San Francisco in October. When Jess sent me a round-trip ticket, I took a couple of days off work and flew out. Waiting for the meeting to begin, I stood near the ballroom talking to people. In those days, my hair was down to my shoulders and very wavy. I wore stylish "mod" suits with bell-bottom trousers, colorful shirts, ascots, and cream-colored loafers. Some guys walked by. I couldn't help noticing the way they were dressed and their haircuts—parted on one side and combed into waves falling across the other side, the way Indian boarding-school students had once been forced to wear their hair. They wore beaded belts, sashes, chokers, moccasins, headbands, and lots of Indian jewelry. I thought, what are they trying to prove? There I was, in the swing of things, accepted by the white man, wearing his stylish clothes. Those guys looked ridiculous, all dressed up like Indians. I asked somebody, "Who are those guys?"

"They're from the American Indian Movement in Minneapolis," he answered.

When the conference started, those guys from Minneapolis got up and condemned the National Urban Indian Organization. Jess Sixkiller responded with a defense of his goals. I was on his side, so I gave an impassioned extemporaneous speech in defense of the organization, my first public address outside a classroom. I described how Jess had come to Cleveland and what he had done to help the Indian community there.

Among the last speakers were two of the guys from AIM, Dennis Banks and Clyde Bellecourt. Banks said, "You have one of two choices—either radically change your organization, or we'll destroy it. Tomorrow, we're going to come back and tell you how to change it." With that, they left.

When Banks and AIM returned in the morning, they had an angry war of words with most of the other people. Members of Jess's group argued that their organization was doing good work, so there was no reason to change it. The AIM guys said, "Maybe you're doing good work, but you're not accountable to anyone for the money you raise and spend. You have no constituency." Jess's people said, "The national organization is our constituency."

"No," replied the AIM guys. "Your constituency has to be the community. You just popped up and started the organization, got a Ford Foundation grant and all that, and you're traveling all over the country talking to Indian groups—but you're not accountable to anyone. You called this convention to find a constituency, but you still don't have one." Finally, the AIM guys said that if NUIO would move its headquarters to Minneapolis, where AIM could monitor its activities, they wouldn't destroy it. Nobody wanted to move to Minneapolis, so Banks, Bellecourt, and the rest reiterated their threat to destroy NUIO. They walked out looking disgusted.

Until that San Francisco meeting, I had never heard of AIM and didn't care much what they had to say. I was more intent on a good time back in my old stomping grounds. Anxious to look up some old friends and enjoy myself, I went out and partied, putting AIM out of my mind completely.

15

▼▼▼▼▼▼▼▼▼

The American Indian Movement

B ack home, I met with the other directors of the Cleveland American Indian Center and reported what I had seen and heard in San Francisco. We were sympathetic to Jess Sixkiller and his organization, but we were far more concerned with our own situation in Cleveland. Whatever might happen to the NUIO and no matter what those wild AIM guys from Minneapolis might try, there was little *we* could do about either. Our first priority was to open our office so we could begin to work on behalf of our own Indian community. Since we had been promised five thousand dollars from the Cleveland Fund, we discussed how best to use that money and get our center operating. Finally, we agreed to open our office on January 2, 1970.

Several weeks later, the phone on my desk at the Council for Economic Opportunity rang, and Dennis Banks was on the line. Although I had seen and heard him in San Francisco, we had never spoken. I was surprised when he said, "We're going to Detroit to confront the National Council of Churches at their triennial convention. We'd like your support."

"Why me?" I said. "I was against you guys."

"Because you're a good speaker and we need your help."

I said, "Sure, I'll go." I didn't even think about it. I told my boss I needed a day off, and about a week later I caught a plane to Detroit. A whole slew of AIM guys, including Banks and Clyde Bellecourt, were at the airport to meet me, all looking very Indian in their beads and moccasins. I must have looked like a gangster in my brand-new shoes, black suit, violet shirt, and white tie. I thought, what have I gotten myself into? After introducing themselves, they gave me some literature, including a pamphlet explaining the American Indian Movement, other handouts, and their list of challenges for the National Council of Churches.

Thousands of churchmen and churchwomen, including many ministers, were meeting at Detroit's newest and classiest hotel, the Ponchartrain. On the way there, I glanced over the AIM pamphlet. A quotation on its front page, from Chief Joseph of the Nez Percé, jumped out at me:

Let me be a free man, free to travel, free to stop, free to work, free to trade where I choose, free to choose my own teachers, free to follow the religion of my fathers, free to talk, think and act for myself—and I will obey every law or submit to the penalty.

Those words nailed me. Although I couldn't yet articulate it, from that moment, I was for AIM with all my heart and soul.

AIM had prepared a list of challenges to the churches. One was about money they raised in the name of Indian people—millions that went into their general funds, to be spent mostly on things that didn't benefit Indians. From the AIM literature, I learned that to inspire sympathy for their collection efforts, churches and church schools with no connection to Indian communities sometimes used old photos depicting "starving Indians." I later met an Indian woman in her twenties who had come across such a Catholic Church solicitation, and recognized the ragged and dirty child in the fifty-year-old picture as her own mother. There were plenty of needy people on reservations, of course, but the churches couldn't easily get photos of them without exposing their own hypocrisy and greed. Their ads talked about feeding Indians and giving us baseball uniforms and sports equipment, but all most churches ever gave to reservation Indians were piles of used clothing, usually just dumped on the open ground.

AIM demanded that money raised in the name of Indians be put into funds expressly for Indian people, and that all boards controlling those funds have Indian majorities and Indian chairmen. Another demand was that each church create an Indian desk responsible to an Indian committee. I didn't know it then, but AIM had already forced one of the Lutheran synods in Minnesota to make just such changes. Sprinkled among many serious challenges were a few whimsical items. Among them were that the churches support AIM in an effort to change the name of the anti-Indian American Red Cross to the American *White* Cross, and change the name of the Salvation

Army to the Salvation Band and Choir, because although they are truly an army of beggars, Indians have had enough of armies and don't need more on our reservations or in our communities. Later, when I got to know him, I realized that was Dennis Banks's sly brand of humor, slipped in to startle the churchmen.

We had a long list of serious challenges, but presenting them publicly wasn't easy. The National Council of Churches tried to pull a BIA-type bureaucratic shuffle on us. Each time we went into a small room and gave our presentation, those pious churchmen said, "Yes, of course you should be able to speak, and we'll see if we can get you up there on the podium, but first you'll have to go see this other committee."

We played that game for a few hours, until Clyde Bellecourt had heard enough. He is a few years older than me, a big, dark, ruggedly handsome Ojibwa. He had done a little boxing, and more than a little time—twelve years in prison. In 1968, he, Dennis Banks, and George Mitchell had founded AIM, and that freed Clyde from the cycle of despair, violence, and jail. I liked the way Clyde carried himself. He took confrontation politics to the very edge. People sensed an aura of danger surrounding him. When Clyde asserted himself, they backed off.

When we realized they were shuffling us from one committee to the next in the hope that we would just give up and go away, Clyde finally said, "Bullshit," and took action. It was the middle of a plenary session and thousands of people were in the enormous hotel auditorium. He walked up to the podium, grabbed the microphone, and said, "I'm not leaving, and I'm not letting go of this microphone until you listen." Someone in the control booth shut off the mike, but Clyde has a booming voice. As he shouted, the auditorium grew quiet. Then people on the floor began to clamor for the microphone to be turned back on. After a few minutes, it was.

Clyde and Dennis began by charging the churches and their ministers with gross violations of the Ten Commandments: "You say, 'Thou Shalt Not Steal'—unless you're stealing Indian land. You preach, 'Thou Shalt Not Lie"—unless it's an Indian treaty—and 'Thou Shalt Not Kill'—unless you kill an Indian. And 'Thou Shalt Honor thy Father and thy Mother'—except you Indians, *your* fathers and mothers are savages." Then Clyde, joined by Dennis, went down AIM's list of challenges.

After listening to the AIM filibuster, the National Council of Churches— which then included more than thirty mainline denominations, including the United Church of Christ, Methodists, Episcopalians, Presbyterians, and Quakers—voted a formal resolution accepting AIM's demands. In the months that followed, virtually all the mainline churches created Indian desks with Indian-led committees to control the funds. During the next years, the council funneled millions of dollars to Christian Indian community groups, churches, and other organizations. With that support, Indian people in many of the church hierarchies found their backbones and began to advance some of their own ideas and programs.

To this day, however, AIM has never received credit for that achievement, not even so much as a single thank-you. Many Christian Indians, after reaching positions of authority in church hierarchies, turned on AIM. Worse, in the 1980s, the National Council of Churches and other denominations backed away from all the commitments they had made to AIM in 1969. Now, Christian churches are again begging for money around the world in the name of Indian children and Indian people on reservations, but they put most of that money in their own pockets. AIM was never set up to be a watchdog, however. In 1969, when Clyde, Dennis, and the others confronted the churches, they still believed that true Christians would not lie. At the time, I thought so, too. Now I realize, as my ancestors discovered in each generation after the white men came, that they have *always* lied.

I was an outsider, so I said very little to anyone. I just absorbed everything I saw and heard. One thing that blew me away was that after seizing the microphone and confronting the rank and file, AIM's most productive work with clergymen was done in saloons. We plotted strategy, extracted commitments, and planned actions with priests, pastors, and lay church leaders over drinks in a bar. They were the same people who regularly mounted their pulpits to sermonize about the evils of alcohol.

During that week in December 1969, I was impressed with AIM's sense of purpose. The leaders had clear goals and had researched their subject for facts and statistics to back up their assertions. They had brought along a Lutheran minister, Paul Bow, and a lawyer. They knew they were right, so they would do whatever it took to get their point across.

Later on the day when Clyde had seized the microphone, I approached Dennis Banks. He is a well-built, slender man a few inches shorter than I am, and eight years older. Like Clyde, he had done time—two years for burglary. Clyde can seem menacing, but Dennis practically glows with charisma. I asked him, "How do I join AIM?" He said, "You just did."

I was very excited by what I had seen and heard. For the first time in my life, I felt truly empowered. However, I had asked for only one day off and was scheduled to fly back to Cleveland the next day. I called my boss and said, "There's a lot of floor work, and I need to stay another day." My boss said that was no problem, since I had vacation time coming. When the next morning rolled around, I was so exhilarated by the excitement of direct action that I didn't want to leave. Again I called my boss, and he gave me still another day off.

I hadn't expected to stay overnight, so I had little money and no fresh clothes. Because I was doing so much standing and walking, my new shoes were giving me blisters. Some of the churchmen treated us royally, giving me money to buy new clothes and shoes. On the third day, Dennis and almost everyone else had to return to Minneapolis. Dennis asked Clyde and me to remain for the rest of the week and make sure everything the National Council of Churches had promised was done. I called my boss yet again, then moved with Clyde into a suite at the Ponchartrain provided by one of the Methodist churches. They also gave us carte blanche on room service, so we ordered whiskey, gin, beer, and hors d'oeuvres. We threw a party.

After the party, I got to thinking. If Dennis and Clyde could work for their people every day to reverse centuries of oppression and racial injustice, so could I. During the twenty minutes it took to fly from Detroit to Cleveland, I wrote out my resignation from the Council for Economic Opportunity. It said that starting January 1, 1970, I was leaving to work full-time on behalf of the Indian community. On Monday, I went to the director's office and presented my resignation. A little later that day, he called me in for a meeting with some of his top staff members. I said, "Unless you pay my salary for a month after I resign, I will get the Puerto Ricans to join the Indians and we'll demonstrate against you." The associate director said, "We really want to work with the Indians, so when you get out there, come to us for anything you need. We'll be glad to fund your salary for a month after you leave." They probably laughed at me after I left, because they got off so cheaply. I'm quite sure now that I could have gotten them to pay my salary for a *year*, even without threatening a demonstration.

A week in Detroit with AIM had changed my whole outlook. It had crystallized thoughts and feelings and desires long buried within my psyche. As a teenager in San Leandro, I had fantasized about going to San Francisco to live among the North Beach beatniks, where I could let my hair grow long and live as an Indian should. Now here was a way to be a *real* Indian, and AIM had shown it to me. No longer would I be content to "work within the system." Never again would I seek personal approval from white society on white terms. Instead, like Clyde and Dennis and the others in AIM, I would get in the white man's face until he gave me and my people our just due. With that decision, my whole existence suddenly came into focus. For the first time, I knew the purpose of my life and the path I must follow to fulfill it. At the age of thirty I became a full-time Indian.

My main contact at Saint John's Episcopal Church in Cleveland wasn't a priest, although he eventually would become one. I usually dealt with the deacon, a former truck driver. When I told him I had quit my accounting job and was now executive director of the Cleveland American Indian Center, he gave us the use of a big room in the rectory basement next to the Head Start school. Upstairs were living quarters, a very large kitchen—many community groups met in it—and an auditorium where we could hold dances and social meetings.

I started to work on January 2, 1970. The five thousand dollars promised from the Cleveland Fund wasn't due until March. We went into operation on faith that the community and the Great Mystery would somehow provide what was needed. I had some experience in the nonprofit sector, but there was no one around to tell me how to do things—so I usually made it up as I went along.

The center's first board of directors, myself among them, had agreed that Indian people are smart and capable and should be paid what they are worth. Accordingly, we set the executive director's salary at ten thousand dollars a year, far more than I had been making as an accountant with CEO. Now that I was on the job, one of my first priorities was to go out and find that money. With the deacon's help, I submitted a proposal to the Episcopal Diocese of Cleveland. They responded with our first grant, sixteen hundred dollars for administrative costs. They promised it for February, just in time to cover my first paycheck. Betty, who had lived with great uncertainty since I quit my CEO job, was happy about that—at least for a little while.

Later, Betty became uneasy that I had quit a steady job to accept a position in which it was far from clear that I would ever see a regular paycheck. She was upset that I hadn't talked it over with her first. Mostly, she was angry because the Indian Center wasn't an eight-to-five job. I was in the office all day, but in the evenings, instead of going home, I often had to go to meetings. I was trying to get the Indian community organized, and it was important that I become better known among Cleveland's activist leadership. I had to attend Puerto Rican meetings, I had to go to east-side African-American community events, I had to visit the Polish, Ukrainian, and Russian neighborhoods and the hillbilly area. I wasn't home much, and when I was, it was often so late that the kids were in bed. Betty and I argued about my hours, but I wasn't out carousing, I was working. I felt that she didn't understand what I was doing. I thought she should be really proud of me, and she wasn't—quite the contrary.

Feeling unappreciated, after most workdays I went to a bar and spent an hour or two moping around, drinking beer, and mulling over not only my home life, but also ugly rumors that I had created the new center for myself and was using the grant money for my salary. The gossip was so unfair, so depressing. One evening, it was as though a lightbulb flicked on in my head. I thought, I *know* those folks who are talking about me behind my back, and they are all good people. We laughed and joked and did things together. When I visited their homes, I was treated with courtesy. As soon as I sat down, I was offered something to eat and drink. Suddenly I realized that as long as they were doing Indian things, they were wonderful—but when they had to deal with the non-Indian world, things became chaotic and confusing for them. Some took on all the negatives of the dominant society and forgot how to act like human beings. As I stood around that bar on Detroit Avenue drinking beer and shooting pool, those thoughts crystallized. I realized that the Indian people I knew were essentially beautiful, and whatever they said in their unhappiness should have no effect on me. I put all my negativity aside. From that moment, I have ignored what others say about me and have focused on what I need to do for my people. With that burden lifted from me, my life as an activist really began.

I also recalled something a Crow man had said to me when I decided to join AIM: "You must realize that you're making yourself a target." That proved to be profound and prophetic. Because I was a target, right there in the bar I made a vow that no matter what temptation should cross my path, I would not get involved intimately with women from Cleveland's Indian community. I was married, and I didn't need that headache.

Soon after our center began to operate, I established, as a separate entity but based at the center, Cleveland AIM—CLAIM. It was the first chapter outside Minneapolis. We put out bumper stickers and buttons with slogans such as, "Custer Died for Your Sins," "Indian and Proud," and "Custer Had It Coming . . . and So Do Some Others!" CLAIM was a distinct organization, but most of what we did was inspired by AIM and modeled on what it was doing in Minneapolis.

Long before recognition of such racism became fashionable in America, we sued the Cleveland Indians baseball team over its mascot, "Chief Wahoo." We pointed out, among other things, that if the team were called, say, "the Blacks" or "the Jews" and had a mascot dressed as a grotesque ethnic stereotype come to life, there would be rioting in the streets. After I went on the *Today* show and Joe Garagiola asked me why we had gone after Chief Wahoo, I got hate mail from all over. That is the only time that has happened during my career as an activist. I didn't care, because our lawsuit inspired Indians from coast to coast. Students at Dartmouth and Stanford demonstrated against teams named "Indians." Both universities caved in and changed the names.

At that time, many churches were giving grants, acting like the Christians they claimed to be and funding bequests *in toto*, trusting everyone to spend the money in accordance with the proposal. These days, churches act exactly like the government—tightfisted, overbearing, and distrustful, doling out money in quarterly installments and shaming grantees by coming in to inspect their books. After our first grant from the Episcopal Diocese, others started to roll in from local and national sources. To help the Indian Center's secretary, Marie, we hired Lucille Gray Fox, a Gros Ventre from North Dakota, as my second secretary. I had stopped cutting my hair on July 4, 1968—my own personal independence day. In October 1969, after San Francisco's Indians took up the fight my father had started in 1964 by reclaiming Alcatraz Island, I became the first man in AIM to wear braids. My new secretary, bless her, volunteered to braid my hair every morning.

I asked Sarge Old Horn to quit barbering and come to work with me. I said it was going to be like being ranch hands or fruit pickers: For a while we'd be cashy and then we'd be broke. Sarge had a profession and five young daughters, but he was dedicated to helping our people. He accepted the risk. His wife, a very beautiful, light-complected Sioux from the Fort Peck Indian Reservation in Montana, had a job and that helped. Unfortunately, my prediction turned out to be true. Once I didn't get paid for six months. I always made sure the secretaries got paid, but there came a time when all the professional staff—Sarge, who became deputy executive director; Herb Johnson, our accountant; and me—went unpaid for four months. Our families survived on our wives' salaries and groceries from the center's food program. When the money finally came in, we got our back pay in one lump.

I don't remember what our first program was, but as soon as word got around that we were open, Indians started coming in with their problems. We plunged into social work and referrals, helping people to collect pensions and Social Security benefits, and getting their paperwork started for food stamps and Aid to Families with Dependent Children. By the time I left Cleveland in 1973, the center operated twenty-four hours a day, seven days a week, and offered twenty-six ongoing programs. One that I'm very proud of was our burial program. When a member of an Indian's extended family dies, the loss to us feels no different than if it were our mother or father or brother or sister. We established a fund to help people get back home for family burials—the only such program in America at that time.

We also had cultural programs, including Indian singing. We started a used-clothing operation, scholarships, tutoring, job training. We had youth excursions and other programs for children and teenagers. Our community education project sent the center's staff members to speak to elementary- and high-school students about who and what we were. We worked closely with the Cleveland police; every time an Indian was arrested, the police alerted us. We had employment and housing programs, a medical clinic, and a Legal Aid service. We sponsored potlucks and community dinners. We gave away groceries, and if people were down on their luck and needed something to eat, we gave them a ticket that could be exchanged at local restaurants for a meal.

In 1969, while I was still working for CEO, my daughter Michele, then a kindergartner, had come home from school just before Columbus Day and said, "Daddy, where were the Indians before Columbus discovered America?" That slapped me in the face. I already knew that when Indian children are bombarded with historical lies and stereotypes, they begin to lose their self-esteem. That was confirmed by studies in the 1960s that discovered most Indian students do better than the national average until the fourth grade, when racist lies and stereotypes cause them to fall far behind their non-Indian peers. I had explained that Columbus didn't "discover" America, that Indians discovered *him* when he was lost, saved him and his men from scurvy, and nursed them back to health. In gratitude, he stole our land and enslaved and murdered us. I went to Michele's school the next day and told the class the *real* Columbus story. It went over so well that I was invited back to talk to other classes.

We got the Cleveland Public School District to cooperate with us in reviewing and revising its American Indian curriculum. As soon as we could, the center started an alternative school, in the basement of a local library, for kindergarten through grade six. We taught those kids what *really* happened in American history. We also worked with the Cleveland Public Library— second only to New York City's—to upgrade its collections of books, periodicals, and recordings so patrons would have access to the truth about American history. We meant the whole truth, not just the white man's truth. We then placed John Fletcher, a Piegan Indian, in this job, and he coordinated the program.

In January 1970, still struggling with funding, I took a few days to attend a gathering in Denver, the National Indian Conference on Alcoholism and Drug Abuse. Clyde Bellecourt and Dennis Banks were in from Minneapolis, and Clyde introduced me to his older brother, Vernon. He lived in Denver and was married to a white woman. A fast-talking type, Vernon made his living styling and hustling women's wigs.

That was only my second national Indian conference, but I was beginning to recognize faces. Before long, I discovered there is a group of Indians who love traveling around the country to attend those meetings. A lot of them are reservation people, midlevel tribal government managers and such. When they travel, the taxpayers pick up their expenses, including per diem money. Most of those conferees take in only a workshop or two in early afternoon, then retire to the bar. After a few years, we in AIM realized that at any event we attended, no matter what it was about, we always saw the same people. I know some who started with the Office of Equal Opportunity conferences in the 1960s, conferenced hard through the '70s and '80s, and are still conferencing vigorously in the '90s. Some AIM guys, wanting to think that those Indians didn't sacrifice their livers for nothing, called them "all-conference" Indians, like champion athletes who are chosen as all-conference players. We even talked about giving out pins and trophies to those people who have dedicated three or four decades of their lives to attending conferences.

Because so many people at the National Indian Conference on Alcohol and Drug Abuse were on per diem, everybody went out to spend that money. Morning workshops were 80 percent empty; everyone was sleeping off the previous night. At noon, they stopped in the bar for a little hair of the dog, a wake-up to fortify them for a couple of early afternoon workshops. When the three-o'clock meetings let out, it was party time. The irony escaped me at the time, but along with almost everyone else in attendance, I got as high and as drunk as I've ever been. Maybe I did learn something about drug and alcohol abuse!

That night, I saw some of the all-conference types, men and women, who had passed out in hotel hospitality suites. I saw women carried through corridors with their skirts up over their hips, their panty hose and everything else showing. Nobody molested them. Their pals were merely carrying out the disabled who had drunk so much they couldn't swallow any more; they were moving them to rooms with beds so the party could continue.

I didn't go to many all-Indian conferences after that one, and I didn't do much serious partying after I got back to Cleveland. By spring, we were fairly solvent and I could turn my attention to matters beyond the immediate survival of the center. A few months earlier, the movie *A Man Called Horse*, starring Richard Harris, had been released. Its depiction of Indians as cruel savages was totally false, historically inaccurate, and highly racist. Dennis Banks called for a national demonstration against it. Groups in New York, Cleveland, Chicago, Minneapolis, Denver, and Seattle demonstrated simultaneously at theaters. About a dozen people picketed in Cleveland and generated media coverage. As far as we were concerned, it was a huge success. But the New York City demonstration was ignored, and the national media didn't cover the story. In 1970, nobody was interested in Indians.

After we got things going at the Indian Center, we wanted the BIA to leave town. We were providing almost all the services that it was supposed to be doing, and many that it never did. Hundreds of people had been stranded when their relocation grants ran out——people who never found decent jobs or received training. We started a reverse relocation program, helping families that wanted to return to their reservations by making arrangements and paying their way. In fact, that was our most successful program. I still bump into people from Cleveland who come up to say "thank you" for getting them back home to Oklahoma, Arizona, New Mexico, or the Dakotas.

A few weeks after our demonstration against *A Man Called Horse*, AIM coordinated joint sit-in demonstrations at BIA offices in seven cities across the country. We ridiculed the bureau's oppressive, suppressive, and repressive policies that robbed Indian people not just of their money but also of their dignity. We wanted people around the country to know that the BIA was filled largely with incompetents who were wasting tax dollars, and if those people couldn't be replaced, the BIA should be abolished. The Cleveland press was so thankful that someone besides blacks was demonstrating that it paid a lot of attention to us. Again, there was no national coverage.

That was just the beginning of AIM's emergence on the national scene. Steve Fast Thunder, his mother, and their whole family had started the Native American Committee, an Indian youth group in Chicago. NAC members usually wore red berets, so that's how I always think of them. In late winter, Steve called Dennis and Clyde and asked for AIM's help in exposing government hypocrisy at the annual National Conference of Welfare Workers, to be held in Chicago that year. The keynote speaker was to be U.S. Senator George McGovern of South Dakota.

So many thousands of people attended that the events were scattered among five downtown hotels. I brought a couple of guys with me from Cleveland, including about twenty young people from NAC. One of the NAC people, a young woman, told us about the BIA booth in the basement of the convention center. It was filled with rosy pictures of Indian reservations—clean, well-fed children, nice homes, development projects, all to show how much the BIA was doing for Indians. We went en masse to look at it. Naturally, a white guy was running the booth. We confronted him with all the statistics about deprivation on reservations. At that time, life expectancy for reservation Indians was two years *less* than that for Guatemalan Indians—and it still is—but the Indians of Guatemala are now oppressed by a genocidal government that massacres them a village at a time, causing two million to become refugees in Mexico. We took over the booth and put up our own pictures—personal photos provided by people in the Chicago Indian community. Next, we marked up all the BIA pamphlets to correct the lies, and left people to man the booth and explain the BIA's lies to visitors.

The rest of us went to confront the leaders of the U.S. welfare establishment. We took a page from Dennis Banks, who, the previous year, had led AIM's attack on the Minnesota welfare convention. He had taken a five-pound sack of government-surplus commodity flour—exactly what thousands of reservation Indians are expected to live on most of the time—and burst it on the lectern, dusting everyone on the dais.

We marched in while George McGovern was speaking. Our signs read, "George Custer McGovern Protects BIA," "George Custer McGovern Ignores Article VI of the U.S. Constitution"—it protects treaties—and "George Custer McGovern Represents the Most Racist State in the Union, South Dakota." We prayed silently in front of him. McGovern looked down from the dais and tried to make a joke, but almost nobody laughed. People applauded us, but because we hadn't said anything, no one bothered us. Then I shouted, "Indians don't want welfare! It's dehumanizing and degrading, and the way you welfare workers treat Indian people is stereotypical and racist! We're not going to stand for it anymore—we don't want any more of your damn commodities! We don't want your smelly old, cast-off clothing anymore! If you do-gooders *really* want to help Indians, then whatever you do must be substantial! It has to be meaningful! Whatever that might be, from now on, Indians are going to control the whole process!"

Meanwhile, our people from the NAC opened cardboard boxes and threw the contents at people in the audience—used shorts, used panty hose, mismatched tennis shoes, pre–World War II apparel dug out of musty attics, ugly worn-out clothing of all descriptions. It was exactly what we get from whites who come to reservations with truckloads of the stuff, dump it in parking lots, and leave as fast as they came. Now we were giving some of that crap back, and it felt good. Because Senator McGovern was there, AIM finally got national media exposure. My son Scott's picture, with me holding him, made national television and the wire services.

A few months later, Dennis called and asked me to bring some people and join him at the Ojibwa Reservation in Sault Sainte Marie, Michigan. Every spring, the Catholic Church held a pageant there to honor the Jesuit who had brought godliness to the heathens. Dennis and Clyde decided it was time for AIM to enlighten their brethren. For that particular show, the church paid a little money to a bunch of local Ojibwa to join the celebration. Playing the role of their heathen ancestors, they put on a big, joyous welcome as the "priest" arrived to save the primitives. It was all bullshit, of course, but staged with the ritual pomp and pageantry that the church has always been so good at.

We went backstage where the Ojibwa were dressing, and Clyde delivered our rap. I learned so much just listening to him and Dennis speaking in those first few years. Always belligerent and militant about Indian pride, Clyde was an imposing figure. One must understand that in those years, few Indians had any pride in their origins. "Educated" Indians were the worst. Probably 99.9 percent of them were ashamed to be Indians. Loaded with self-hatred, they dressed in all the white man's accoutrements and referred to Indians who revered and pursued their traditional culture as "blanket asses."

Clyde didn't attack the Ojibwa. He just gave them a little straight history, and he knew what he was talking about. Clyde's forte in those early years was challenging Christians. On that occasion, as he often did, he told what Christianity had done to us, and he gave examples. "They tell us, 'Thou shalt not steal,' yet the Catholic Church owns more land on Indian reservations than any other single entity." He talked about how in this century and the last, various Christian churches lobbied Congress, and bartered deals between denominations to allocate sections of Indian lands where they could accompany the U.S. Army and save the souls of the redskins whom the army didn't kill. They divvied us up! Clyde's punch line was, "The missionaries came with the Bible in one hand and the sword in the other. They had the book and we had the land. Now we've got the book—and they've got our land."

I got up and talked about colonialism—what it means and where it comes from. I said, "We've got to stop shaming ourselves. That day is over now. We're not going to do this anymore, it's demeaning." Those were reservation Indians who had no jobs, and what little money they got came from that once-a-year pageant event. They had been thoroughly brainwashed for years, and now here comes Clyde with just one speech. They knew he spoke the truth. They said, "You're right, we'll join you." What a lot of guts that took, what a sacrifice it was! It was a magical moment. They all walked out, and that ended the pageant. As far as I know, it was never staged again.

That was AIM's first overt action on a reservation, and probably the first time in more than eighty years that a substantial number of Indians had stood up to whites. We had already had some publicity in Minneapolis and elsewhere when we demonstrated against *A Man Called Horse* and held our BIA sit-ins. Now the BIA put out the word to "their" Indians that we were militants, troublemakers who endangered everything the Indian "Establishment" had worked so hard and long to achieve.

What had it achieved? It certainly wasn't economic opportunity for Indians. The government's own statistics admitted 40 percent unemployment, but that was conservative. On some reservations, it was higher. Per capita income for Indians was the lowest of any group in the country. The Establishment hadn't achieved good health among Indians, either. Thousands of Indians died every year from measles, diphtheria, tuberculosis, cholera, dengue—diseases almost unknown in white America. Our infant-mortality rates were higher than in any country in the hemisphere, including Haiti. Housing was wretched also. Many reservation people were without adequate shelter.

What the BIA *had* achieved was the creation of a slightly privileged class of colonial administrators, hang-around-the-fort Indians. To live a little better than the rest of their people, they would do literally anything the BIA told them to do. The BIA was right about one thing: AIM *was* a threat—to the BIA. We were never a threat to our own people. But as the government sought to discredit us, AIM and its leaders were bad-mouthed throughout the Indian world.

For different reasons, I was getting bad-mouthed in my own home. By the middle of 1970, it had became practically unbearable. Betty totally resented the fact that my job kept me away from home so much. We were speaking to each other less and less. Usually, our only communication was her telling me what a sorry husband and father I was. I would reply that I was only doing what I felt I had to do. That would generally be the end of the conversation.

Betty worked at the housing authority, near Lake Erie. One drizzly day, I dropped in on her there. She came outside and we stood by a tree, talking. I had felt it coming for months, but that was when we made it official. Our marriage was over. I walked away and, never looking back, went through a dark underpass and straight to my office. AIM and the Cleveland American Indian Center were now my whole life. I had no other place to go, so I started sleeping on my office floor.

16
▼▼▼▼▼▼▼▼

Handpicked Apples

After AIM's visit to Sault Sainte Marie, Michigan, in 1970, things began to move fast. Several weeks later, I went to Minneapolis to help protest an annual festival that ostensibly celebrated the region's lakes by parading floats, some of which featured grotesque caricatures of Indians. AIM had stationed people to hold up signs and placards as the floats passed, but we also had a surprise planned. We borrowed horses and stashed them on a side street along the parade route. Six of us stripped to our waists and painted ourselves with lipstick and black paint. We put feathers in our hair or wore red berets, and a few of us carried authentic shields and lances. As the parade came toward us, we galloped hard at it, yelling and whooping. Our shouts and the clattering hooves, amplified as they bounced off the buildings along the narrow side street, must have sounded like a hundred riders. The parade and everyone watching it scattered, screaming. Indians on horseback! The Great Sioux Uprising all over again! The police didn't know what to do, so that was the end of the event. In the years that followed, the whites who put on that festival paid attention to the desire of the Minneapolis Indian community to be represented respectably.

The local cops hated and feared AIM, of course. One of the first things AIM did in Minneapolis was to fight police brutality. Until recently, Minneapolis was the only major city in America with an identifiable Indian ghetto. Indians comprised about 10 percent of the city's population, but, according to *Time* magazine, represented almost 90 percent of its jail inmates. When I first visited the AIM office, I saw a wall display of police victims—dozens of pictures of Indian men and women. Many showed hands swollen like balloons after having suffered for hours in severely tight handcuffs. Others showed scalps missing huge clumps of hair, yanked out by cops. Faces were beaten black and blue, mouths battered and teeth broken, backs lacerated, legs scarred by welts. More than one picture of Clyde Bellecourt was in that display.

AIM had begun by calling press conferences about police brutality in the Indian ghetto, and soon it had attracted formidable backing. With a grant from some churches, Dennis and Clyde formed the AIM Patrol. In the ghetto, there is no chance that police will respond quickly to reports of an alleged crime. When the AIM Patrol, monitoring police radio, heard a dispatcher say Indians were raising hell somewhere, members of the patrol, wearing red vests, would get there before the cops arrived. Using nonviolent methods—usually—they would quell the disturbance and remove those causing it. The patrol also photographed arrests, which acted as a deterrent to police brutality. The patrol got word to all Indians arrested that they did not have to plead guilty and were entitled to a jury trial and a lawyer appointed at public expense. After the patrol was established, no Indians were arrested in Minneapolis for twenty-two consecutive weekends. After six months, the Indian inmate population of the Minneapolis and Hennepin County jails went down to 10 percent of the total. *Time* magazine wrote about it many years before neighborhood-watch programs, before the Guardian Angels or the Fruit of Islam. It was one of AIM's first recognized successes.

It didn't make everyone in Minneapolis happy. Although the AIM Patrol saved tax money and freed law enforcement to handle real crimes, the embarrassed Minneapolis police went after Clyde with a vengeance. In twelve months during 1969 and 1970, they arrested him more than fifty times for nearly every alleged minor infraction imaginable. They included traffic offenses, parking offenses, loitering, public drunkenness, resisting arrest, assault on a police officer, suspicion of this or that. All were bullshit, of course, and all the charges were thrown out. Clyde was a former convict, a repeat criminal, so the cops always had an excuse to watch him—or work him over. Clyde was belligerent and would never knuckle under. He kept his head up even when they hit him across the face with blackjacks. He went through more than a year of hell, but he never broke. He is an amazing guy, so proud of being an Indian, of knowing who he is—and letting everybody see it.

One night when I was riding with Clyde in his Ford, the cops pulled us over, jerked him out of the car, and started to pound him. I rolled down my window and yelled, "What the fuck do you think you're doing? Goddamn pigs, leave him alone!" They pulled me out and began to pound me, too. Clyde told me to shut up, that the cops would have their fun and then quit. After they did, they took us in on charges of reckless driving, threatening a police officer, resisting arrest, and assault on a police officer. In those days, if a lawyer came to jail and vouched for you, you would be released without bail. Larry Leventhal, a young lawyer who became my good friend and later handled several very important cases for me, got us out. A judge later dismissed all charges.

It was hard enough struggling against racist white authorities, but by that time, AIM and its supporters realized that our struggle for Indian dignity and self-determination couldn't succeed unless we also exposed and deposed our own sellouts. Those were the Indians we sometimes called "apples"— red on the outside but white inside. The biggest apples were "elected" tribal officials who, for the most part, were ashamed to be Indians. Most were handpicked by the BIA because they would keep their tribal governments operating as rubber stamps for BIA policies. They were voted in because—as BIA's careerists surely know—most reservation Indians, when asked to vote only for unacceptable candidates, refuse to participate in such bogus proceedings. That leaves the way clear for a comparative few political cronies, friends, and relatives of the BIA's candidate—people who get jobs and other rewards if their man wins office—to vote in the BIA's stooges.

In May of 1970, AIM decided to confront those apples at the midyear convention of the National Congress of American Indians, in Kansas City, Missouri. Founded in 1944, it is the oldest national American Indian organization. Its membership includes reservations—the nations that whites insist on calling tribes—and other Indian organizations and individuals. Clyde, Dennis, George Mitchell, and the others from Minneapolis had their hands full at home, but I brought an AIM contingent from Cleveland. We were joined by young Native American Committee Red Berets from Chicago and by some Kansas Potawatomi, a few people from the Sac and Fox Nation, and people from small nations in Washington and California.

We were all disgusted with the NCAI. It was supposed to lobby government as an advocate for Indian people. However, it was really nothing more than a way to kiss up to senators, congressmen, and especially the powerful administrators who control day-to-day activities in government agencies. One especially egregious example of NCAI ass-kissing had occurred in 1964, when the U.S. Army Corps of Engineers stole ten thousand acres of Seneca land in upstate New York and flooded it behind the Kinzua dam. Every expert study proved that taking the land was the most costly and least efficient option. Any of several other sites would have been more cost-effective and ecologically sensible. That exercise in eminent domain also violated the eighteenth-century Seneca treaty with the United States. Locating the dam elsewhere would have meant flooding land that whites owned, their ancestors having stolen it from Seneca and other Six Nations people. That would never do! Despite the outcry from Indian people around the country, NCAI refused to take *any* position about the dam. Against legal precedent and environmental, financial, scientific, and even common sense, the army took the land. From then on, most Indians knew that the NCAI was a sham, a tame bear that danced for the amusement of government bureaucrats.

About a thousand all-conference Indian delegates, many accompanied by spouses and nonvoting staff members, attended the NCAI convention in Kansas City. The keynote speaker was a Baltimore mobster and extortionist named Spiro Agnew, then Vice President of the United States. AIM and its supporters had no voice at the convention, so Dennis and Clyde suggested that we call a press conference. Some Potawatomi women had brought documentation about NCAI's ineffectuality. We used that in our attack, laying out the facts of how NCAI had sold out to the government. We named the principal sellouts, including several men since deceased, along with Robert Jim, Chairman of the Yakima Nation; Roger Jordain, Chairman of the Red Lake, Minnesota, Ojibwa; and Wendell Chino of the Mescalero Apache. Chino has been Chairman since the 1950s. As I write this, he is *still* Chairman, having lasted longer in office than Franklin Roosevelt, Franco, Chiang Kai-shek, Tito, Castro, or any other national leader.

Because Agnew was speaking, the national press covered the convention. In those days, when dissent was widely reported, it was unusual to hear about Indians standing up against anything. That was why the 1969 occupation of Alcatraz had made such a splash. Now there we were, young Indians attacking Establishment Indians, and we got a lot of ink and airtime around the country. That was when I first realized that the white media love it when Indians fight Indians. We could get practically any kind of coverage we wanted.

Because of all that exposure, Bob Jim decided to answer us. Speaking in a packed ballroom at the convention center, he condemned urban Indians, and specifically AIM, for being after "their" money in Congress. He said they wanted to protect "their" money—taxpayers' money!—from us. He held up one of our bumper stickers, "AIM for Sovereignty." He couldn't even pronounce it correctly. He said, "Here's what we think of AIM and their sove-rain-itty," and he cut up our bumper sticker with scissors. He got a wild ovation from hundreds of tribal officials, every last one of whom was there at taxpayer expense.

Then the NCAI's executive director asked me to speak. It was eerily silent as I mounted the dais and approached the microphone. I looked out at a sea of faces. Here were hundreds of Indians looking down their noses at others who had been forced into relocation—including many of their own relatives—because they, the tribal councils, couldn't provide the economic sustenance necessary to keep them at home. Now those sellouts condemned urban Indians because they thought we wanted a piece of their meager pie. History had shown that little, if any, of the federal money spent on reservations helped Indians who honored their culture by following traditional ways. Instead, it rewarded those who were ashamed of their heritage. Federal money bought patronage, created all-conference Indians, and perpetuated the reign of those who danced to the BIA's tune. Somewhere in that room, staring at me in scorn, were the Pine Ridge council members who, with 90 percent of their people living in dirt-floored huts without plumbing, had spent tribal money to build a jetliner-sized airstrip so Washington-based officials wouldn't have to drive two hours from Rapid City. Glancing around that room full of sellouts, I thought, I don't have anything to say to these people—I don't want to be a part of them. That's what I said, short and sweet. I told them *why* we were urban Indians, and that one of our axioms was to refuse all federal money.

They gave me a standing ovation! As I walked off, people were slapping me on the back and congratulating me on a great speech. I kept thinking, phonies! They just told me they don't want me or any of my kind because we live in cities, and now they're slapping me on the back because I told them we don't want their money. Bob Jim would tell another convention a couple of years later, "I heard Russell Means stand up before NCAI and say, 'We urban Indians don't want the money,' and I believed Russell Means then and I believe him now."

Sure enough, a few years later, Bob Jim and the tribal chairmen who had cheered when he cut up AIM's bumper sticker had learned how to pronounce *sovereignty* correctly. Some could even spell it, because by then they were starting to use that word to get themselves reelected. Of course, like any government official, they were afraid of the sovereignty of the individual. In only four years, they would pervert that word to mean its exact opposite. Not knowing what was coming. I returned to Cleveland feeling that I had accomplished something, that I had helped get AIM national exposure, that I had told those sellouts what we thought of them.

I spent the summer of 1970 in South Dakota with my brother Ted, campaigning for Jim Abourezk, who was running for the U.S. House of Representatives. He rented us a white Plymouth and paid us two hundred dollars a week in cash to go from one reservation to the next, dancing at the weekend *wacipi* and talking him up.

In September, AIM held its second annual wild rice festival, which included an Indian dance, and I went to Minneapolis to dance and party. The AIM leaders didn't want anything to happen that might provide a pretext for police to intervene, so they had laid down the law—no drinking, and no drunks allowed during the dance. When Dennis Banks showed up gassed on Friday night, AIM security guards wouldn't let him in, even when he shouted,

"Do you know who I am?" The guards answered, "Yes, sorry. You're the one who said no drunks."

After he sobered up, Dennis called a meeting and told us that Lizzie Fast Horse, whom I knew from my summer of dancing in South Dakota, and Muriel Waukazo, another elder, were organizing a protest at Mount Rushmore to assert the Lakota claim to the Black Hills under the 1868 treaty. They wanted AIM's help. Dennis got a church grant to charter a bus and pay trip expenses. When we boarded the bus on Sunday night, the first stop was a liquor store. Dennis bought a shopping cart full of booze. We partied all the way to Rapid City, a fourteen-hour ride. We got off the bus to be greeted by several elders, a little sheepish because we were so obviously hung over.

We drove to Mount Rushmore, where we were joined by several people from the United Indians of America, which had headquarters in northern California, led by Lehman "Lee" Brightman. Half Lakota, a doctoral candidate at Berkeley, Lee was considered one of the young lions of the Indian world. The United Tribes of Alcatraz, which had been formed to maintain possession of that island, was represented by John Trudell, a smallish, graceful Santee Sioux, and a few others.

We sent someone into the park grounds to reconnoiter. He returned to tell us that the whites who ran the concessions were selling prints depicting the 1890 massacre at Wounded Knee, South Dakota. One print showed a mass grave stacked high with Indian bodies, and cavalrymen standing around looking proud. Even today, whites sell those cards. I've seen them in Montana and in Vancouver, British Columbia. It's sick and demented, but whites continue to buy them. We wrecked the display, confiscated the prints, and yelled at the tourists, "Look! Look at these! Think of the Jews at Dachau and Auschwitz. If the park sold pictures of their remains, would you buy them?"

We demanded a meeting with Wallace McCaw, the park superintendent. We told him that Indians should have all the concessions, because the Black Hills are our hallowed ground and Rushmore was a sacred mountain before the sculptor Gutzon Borglum desecrated it with four white men's faces—a project commissioned by the State of South Dakota. We demanded to speak in the half-shell amphitheater where the park service gives presentations about the sculpted heads. Lee Brightman got up and talked about each of the four presidents portrayed on the mountain. I really went to school on his speech. Lee explained that George Washington had become famous as an Indian killer during the French and Indian War. He had risen quickly through the militia ranks by butchering Indian communities and burning the homes. The father of his country massacred men, women, and children. It had taken dozens of such My Lai massacres for George Washington to became a hero. During the Revolutionary War, when his troops were starving at Valley Forge, everyone seems to have forgotten that they all would have died if the Seneca hadn't fed and clothed them. When Washington crossed the Delaware on Christmas Day 1776, an Indian woman was in the bow of his boat to guide him across—not at all the way it appears in the famous painting by Thomas Sully.

Then Lee spoke of Thomas Jefferson, who more than once had proposed the annihilation of the Indian race to "cleanse" the Americas. Later, through my own research, I came to admire Jefferson for having been against large government and suspicious of Christianity. It was, however, Jefferson who wrote the Declaration of Independence, which as every American schoolchild should know, includes the phrase "the merciless Indian savages, whose known rule of warfare is an undistinguished destruction of all ages, sexes, and conditions." Or maybe schools don't teach that part of the declaration.

Next, Lee spoke about Abraham Lincoln who, two days before issuing the Emancipation Proclamation, signed an order to execute thirty-eight Indians for the so-called Great Sioux Uprising in Minnesota. Lincoln apparently didn't care that those men had been chosen at random, without a hearing, much less a trial. He never investigated the reasons for the rebellion. The Santee Sioux had been starving because U.S. government agents had stolen their treaty annuity money. Those same white thieves made sure the Santee leaders were hanged in the Minnesota town of Mankato, to cover up the whites' own crimes and to appease white settlers—the customers for goods stolen from the Sioux.

Finally, Lee spoke about Teddy Roosevelt, the biggest thief ever to occupy the White House. Roosevelt violated scores of treaties, and illegally nationalized more Indian land than any president, before or since. He called his booty "national parks" and "national forests" to cement the thefts into law. Roosevelt, too, believed that we ignorant savages should have been exterminated because we had no right to land that we didn't know how to use "properly." He represented the epitome of Manifest Destiny, the doctrine popularized by Jefferson. It claimed, in essence, that God had intended all of North America for European men.

Listening to Lee fired me up. I decided we had to do something about those four faces that defiled our sacred mountain. The elders wanted to discuss it. The old Lakota ladies wanted to bring up the 1868 Fort Laramie Treaty that acknowledged Lakota ownership of the Black Hills forever. But by then, the sun had set and it was twilight. If we were going to do something, it had to be soon. Suddenly John Trudell, the man from the Alcatraz group, and a young, longhaired Nez Percé guy from Idaho, said, "Screw it, let's take over the mountain." We had no weapons, no food or water, no camping gear, no flashlights, but everyone caught the spirit. John, the Nez Percé, and I melted into the night and headed up the mountain. Most of the other young people followed.

The Forest Service rangers were beside themselves. They came after us, rounding people up and hauling them down. By the time they got to the three of us, we were on the summit, behind the stone faces. We edged down a path, with me leading and John bringing up the rear, until I came to a ledge. Below me, the mountain fell away hundreds of feet into total darkness. I said, "Let's turn around and go back." Suddenly we were bathed in the glare of a spotlight. Someone yelled, "Freeze! We've got you covered!" A ranger stepped out. He held a shotgun, and it was pointed at me.

John said, "Go ahead, shoot! You can't get all three of us." I said, "Wait a minute! Don't shoot!" I knew that if anybody got shot, I would be the one. After a long moment, it became apparent that the ranger didn't really want to shoot. We stood around on the ledge while he kept asking, "Are you coming down?" We kept saying, "Nope."

One of those guys had a walkie-talkie, and he radioed back, "We got the three ringleaders." Finally, one of the lawmen said, "You're coming down with us, or you're going off the ledge. Choose."

"We're not coming until you promise that we'll go to jail."

They looked at one another, not believing what they had heard. The one with the walkie-talkie called down to his boss, "You're not going to believe this one. These Indians *want* to be arrested." I wondered then, and do now, if they had ever watched television or read newspapers—hadn't they heard about protests?

When the rangers finally got everyone down—about thirty people—they began to discuss among themselves what they ought to do with us. They asked if we all wanted to be arrested, and we said we did. That didn't satisfy them. I think they had no way of transporting so many prisoners. While those discussions were in progress, John whispered to me, "I'm not going to sit around and get arrested. I'm going back up the mountain." He slipped away into the trees.

I told the Nez Percé I was going back up, too, and quietly the word went around. I crawled away. One by one, more of our guys followed. There weren't enough rangers to watch us all, and they were exhausted from chasing us all night. They just threw up their hands, and everyone else split. We crawled all over that mountain until daybreak, when we found a little sunken glade behind Roosevelt's head. It was a place of great beauty with enough flat, open space for several people to camp. We decided to stay there, and the park rangers didn't try to stop us. Indian people brought tents and camping gear from Rapid City and established a supply system to bring us food and water, usually twice a day.

I soon discovered that between the heads of Roosevelt and Lincoln was a ledge about six feet square, reached by crawling through a little tunnel. From that point, the whole Park Service facility at the foot of mountain is visible, but no one down there could see me on the ledge. I could holler from there and be heard plainly in the amphitheater below. The mountain's massive slope amplified my voice.

That ledge became my favorite spot. The main reason we were occupying the mountain was because of the 1868 treaty, which the U.S. government had broken only eight years after signing. Every evening as darkness descended, I crawled out on my ledge to yell: **"Listen, my children, HONOR THY FATHER AND MOTHER . . . THOU SHALT NOT STEAL."** I went down all of the Ten Commandments, then added an eleventh: **"THOU SHALT HONOR THY TREATIES. I forgot that one in my last message."** Even in daylight, my voice echoing out of the mountain was very spooky to people below. At night, with those enormous faces dramatically lit by searchlights, it was positively scary. Some tourists, especially older ones, freaked out. I did my routine two or three times a night.

After a week or so, an NBC television reporter and his crew came puffing up to the top of the mountain and interviewed Lee Brightman. Thus, our demonstration made national television. One afternoon after that, I climbed over to the top of George Washington's head, opened my fly, and peed on him. I had hoped he would have permanent yellow-stained tears, but the park staff whitewashes those heads every year. I've since shared this personal protest with several members of the media, but every time it was reported it was as though my act was trite or inconsequential—or maybe just nasty or infantile. I mention it here to make the point that what I did symbolizes how most Indians feel about the faces chiseled out of our holy land.

When I first climbed Mount Rushmore, I had thought I was afraid of heights, and I made it a goal to conquer that fear. After a little while, I realized I wasn't actually afraid. Soon, I was walking casually atop huge boulders beside a drop of five hundred feet and thinking nothing about it. It was just part of living up there. As it turned out, occupying Mount Rushmore was fun. Some folks fell in love up there, and a few babies were made on that mountain. The women proved to be the strongest and most determined of our group. They stayed until well into December, when fierce winter storms finally drove them off. I had to leave after only three or four weeks to return to my responsibilities in Cleveland.

One of the volunteers at the Cleveland Indian Center was a tall, slender, pretty young Jewish woman who was studying art at Case Western Reserve University. I'll call her Sally. Married then to a young doctor, she was very liberal, a well-meaning, good-hearted woman. At first, she just wanted to work with children on Saturday afternoons. Soon, she volunteered to help out wherever she saw a need—sorting clothes, sweeping the floor, or doing secretarial duties. She quickly made herself an integral part of our operation and came to serve as my ad hoc assistant. She started to go to evening meetings with me. Afterward, we sometimes talked for hours.

As much as she wanted to know about Indians, I was curious about Jews. Sally said she was a Zionist, so we often spoke about Israel and the history of her people. I knew about the discrimination Jews suffered. Many people around the world treated them as nonwhites. Then and now, I'm amazed that Jews even *want* to be considered whites, but maybe it's because they think they will escape persecution by taking on the trappings of their oppressors. Unfortunately, the inevitable result of that approach is that they themselves become oppressors. Because of that and other parallels, it seemed to Sally and me that the Jewish experience was much like the American Indians', so we had lots to talk about.

One night, chatting in a parked car in Edgewater Park, we kissed—just once. She immediately felt guilty. I thought, what am I doing, fooling around with a married woman, with a non-Indian? I chalked it up to loneliness. Betty was gone, and I had stayed away from all women whenever I was anywhere near Cleveland. But as much as we fought it, Sally and I were very attracted to each other. As our talks continued, we started to share our hopes and desires and our innermost feelings. All that led to more kisses. Pretty soon, we were involved, and Sally decided to leave her husband.

One thing that made our relationship different from any of my previous ones was Sally's circle of friends, mostly couples whom she knew from her marriage—her husband's crowd. Once she invited me to a backyard barbecue in Shaker Heights, one of the wealthier communities in America. Our hosts and all the other guests were doctors or nurses and their spouses. All they talked about was medicine and real estate. I found nothing interesting in those conversations. My real estate is always being threatened with rape and theft by white society. The medical discussions, of course, were highly technical and therefore totally incomprehensible to a man who spent most of his time trying to beg a few hundred bucks to keep some poor Indian family from having to sleep on a Cleveland street. What I needed at that party was another accountant. We could have exchanged views on the latest trends in amortization schemes and tax shelters.

To get away from the babble, I wandered around, passing near an open kitchen window. Through it I heard Sally, inside, begging the other women to go outside and change the subject so I could be included in the conversation. Sure enough, they came out. After some whispering around, somebody looked at me and asked how long the Indians had been in Cleveland. "As far as I know, the baseball team has been here since before the turn of the century," I said. "If you're talking about real Indians, we've been here from the time the earth was formed, or soon thereafter."

To my amazement, those learned doctors began to say things such as, "I've never visited an Indian reservation, but I've always wanted to." "I just love nature," somebody's wife said. "You should see all the potted plants in my house. I take care of them, and I talk to them and water them faithfully, and I feed them plant food." I think they meant well, but in trying to include me in their conversations, they went far past the ridiculous. They asked questions such as, "How many gods do you have? Do you keep track of them all—can you name them all?" and, "Do you really do the rain dance? Why?"

That day, I realized that most whites don't measure Indians as fellow human beings. Their scale of measurement goes out the window, and they assume that we have no common experiences and no concept of what life is all about. It's sad that such people are incapable of building a relationship with or getting to know anything or anyone but their own kind. If they can't establish a relationship with an Indian, what chance do they have with other living things? No wonder the earth is raped, no wonder the air is fouled, no wonder there is filth everywhere, no wonder there is disease.

One weekend, a month or so later, Sally took me to a beach in a rural area near Pennsylvania. On our way back to Cleveland, we passed an antique shop and she asked to stop. She poked around for a bit, picking up pieces she thought were "cute" and showing them to me. Almost everything in the place was similar to items that people on reservations still use in their daily lives. They have had such kitchen utensils, tools, furniture, and other objects in their families for generations. Disgusted, I went outside. When Sally came out, I told her, "You were in there admiring exorbitantly priced items, but stuff just like that is still used by my people because they're too poor to replace them. I find that insulting and elitist—part of a world with no concept of reality." Sally, who always tried to please me, said she was sorry. I said, "You don't have to apologize. It's your world—this is part of how you were brought up. You've got to understand there are people in my world that can't share in your excesses—and I'm one of them."

After that day at the antique shop, Sally and I began to drift apart. It was very evident to her that I was totally consumed with the well-being and future of my people, and that I was quickly becoming alienated from urban life. At the same time, Indian people in Cleveland, for dysfunctional and for practical reasons, had made it plain to both of us that they didn't like the fact that we were together. Nevertheless, Sally wanted to marry me—and a part of me wanted to marry her. I knew it was impossible. I couldn't see her living on a reservation for the rest of her life. I couldn't envision her conversing with Indian women in their languages.

One afternoon while we were sitting in Sally's Volkswagen, she said she would do anything to make me happy. I said that even so, it would never work out. I walked away with tears rolling down my cheeks and a lump in my throat, feeling her pleading stare burning into my back. Not looking at her was one of the hardest things I ever had to do, but I knew that if I turned to meet her gaze, I would go back to her. When I had walked out of sight, I felt as though something had been ripped from the back of my head—a strange and terrible sensation.

*　　*　　*

In November, I went back to Minneapolis, where I had been invited by Will Antell, an Ojibwa educator who headed the National Indian Education Association, to moderate a workshop panel at the University of Minnesota for the group's second annual conference. My speakers were Lee Brightman, John Trudell, Dennis, and Clyde. Officially, our topic was "activism."

In those days, few Indians were proud of their heritage. All the NIEA Indians were trying their best to be facsimile whites in fancy hairdos and designer knockoffs. The keynote speaker was Dr. Alfonso Ortiz, a Santa Clara Pueblo and an anthropologist. He wore a three-piece, cream-colored suit with matching loafers and looked like he had just stepped off a boat from Panama.

We remained quiet as Ortiz spoke—but his eyes kept darting furtively around the room at AIM guys in long hair, ribbon shirts, beadwork, and Indian jewelry. Before long, it was apparent that no one was listening. When he finished, we started to beat a drum and sing a traditional melody. People in the room seethed with anger and impatience—they acted as though they were ashamed of us. My mother was there; suddenly she got up and started to dance. Never have I been prouder of her. After several moments, a few older people joined in. Then still more got up. Soon almost everyone was dancing, mingling with AIM, enjoying themselves, socializing in the manner of our ancestors.

Far more important than these personal experiences was the historic groundwork laid during the early 1970s. That was the period following Alcatraz, which had inspired Indian imaginations and brought young Indian militants together by making them realize they could call on other Indians for help. It was a time when there was a stream of national publicity about AIM's activities, the first examples in this century of Indians speaking up and standing up for themselves, of showing pride in their heritage by wearing distinctive everyday dress. We had shown that we were willing to take any risk, make any sacrifice, because we knew we had to win. People were aroused. Activism bloomed all over the country. An army missile site near Chicago was taken over by Wisconsin Indians who put up a tipi village. The Indian nations of Washington had been struggling to retain treaty fishing rights since the early 1960s and were being arrested, clubbed, maimed, beaten, shot at—even assassinated—by police and game wardens. Those nations joined with other nations to seize and reclaim Fort Lawton, an abandoned army base near Seattle. The "successful" established Indians around the country wanted to know about that phenomenon. They wanted to see and hear those young Indians who were standing up. I knew this was our time. Indians were breaking out everywhere; we were on the verge of something big, it was all going to happen soon—and I was part of it.

17
▼▼▼▼▼▼▼▼▼

Mayflower II

Soon after I returned to Cleveland in the fall of 1970, Betty went back to her home on the Hopi Reservation. I drove to the airport to say good-bye to her and our kids, and it was not a happy moment. Michele was six, a first-grader, and we had a very special relationship. She had taken it very hard when Betty and I broke up. I had told her then that I had to go away to work and her mother and I just couldn't get along, that we fought too much and it wasn't good for anyone. Kids don't care to hear that—they always try to blame themselves. Once again, at the airport, I tried to tell Michele that it wasn't her fault. No matter where she lived or wherever I might be, she would always be my daughter and I would always love her. For the next few years, every time I saw Michele we had a long talk. Poor Scott was only four when our family broke up, and he didn't understand. He was just a wide-eyed baby with piercing black eyes that looked right into my soul.

The only good thing that came out of my family's departure was that after nine months of sleeping on my office floor, I had a real place to live again. I moved into the apartment they had vacated. There was so much for me to do in the community that I had little time to be lonely.

Nor did AIM activities slow down. On our trip to Mount Rushmore, Clyde Bellecourt had made contact with Leonard Crow Dog, a holy man, a leader of the Native American Church, and the great-grandson of Crow Dog. In 1861, when Spotted Tail was chosen to lead the Brulé Lakota in the battles to save their lands and their way of life from the armies of the United States, his cousin Crow Dog had promised to kill him if he disgraced his nation's name. Crow Dog and many other Lakota believed that in yielding the sacred Black Hills to the treachery and armed might of the United States, and by taking inappropriate privileges and perquisites later, Spotted Tail had indeed disgraced his people. So in 1891, Crow Dog fulfilled his vow to kill Spotted Tail. A white court sentenced Crow Dog to death, but the Supreme Court overturned the decision in a ruling that affirmed Lakota sovereignty. Leonard Crow Dog and his family lived in Crow Dog's Paradise, the green, idyllic spot on the Rosebud Reservation to which his ancestor had been exiled by Brulé elders after having killed Spotted Tail. Leonard offered himself as AIM's spiritual adviser.

Clyde was also a good friend of Eddie Benton Banai. After winning parole from Stillwater State Prison in Minnesota, Eddie had become one of AIM's earliest members. He was taking instruction to become an Ojibwa medicine man. After learning more about different dimensions of Indian spirituality from Eddie and Leonard, Clyde suggested that AIM membership and its activities on behalf of Indians should include a spiritual component. Everyone immediately agreed. It was the right thing to do.

AIM was very proud of its heritage. We had buttons made that said "Indian Power," "Indian Pride," and "Red Power." Because my own dress was particularly distinctive, it inspired a running joke. At that time, I usually wore turquoise jewelry, beadwork, a bone choker, braids wrapped in ermine skins, and a vest covered with buttons. Whenever Dennis Bowen, youth director at the Indian Center, or my brother Ted knew I was flying somewhere, they would have me paged at every airport I passed through—*"Russell Means, of the American Indian Movement, please use the white courtesy telephone."* They did that partly to spread AIM's name, but also to have a little fun with me. I was usually the only Indian in the entire airport, and dressed the way I was, heads swiveled and people stared when my page was announced.

About the time of the Mount Rushmore occupation, AIM had decided on a policy: We would be advocates for any Indian man or woman, any Indian family, any Indian community, or any Indian nation. All they had to do was call us, and we would respond. But we would not go anywhere unless we were invited. Right after my overflowing National Indian Education Association workshop on activism, AIM was approached by some Boston-area Indians and by the Wampanoag people who lived near Martha's Vineyard and the original Plymouth Colony. They asked us to join them in a demonstration at the reconstructed Plimoth Plantation. Some Boston-area Indians had raised money to put on a conference, and they offered to pay our transportation. We were joined at Plymouth by John Trudell and some of his guys from Alcatraz, and by Floyd Westerman, known to his people as Red Crow, who had headed the youth workshop at the drug and alcohol conference in Denver.

When we met with the Wampanoag people, they told us that in researching the history of Thanksgiving, they had confirmed the oral history passed down through their generations. Most Americans know that Massasoit, chief of the Wampanoag, had welcomed the so-called Pilgrim Fathers—and the seldom mentioned Pilgrim Mothers—to the shores where his people had lived for millennia. The Wampanoag taught the European colonists how to live in our hemisphere by showing them what wild foods they could gather, how, where, and what crops to plant, and how to harvest, dry, and preserve them.

The Wampanoag now wanted to remind white America of what had happened after Massasoit's death. He was succeeded by his son, Metacomet, whom the colonists called "King" Philip. In 1675–1676, to show "gratitude" for what Massasoit's people had done for their fathers and grandfathers, the Pilgrims manufactured an incident as a pretext to justify disarming the Wampanoag. The whites went after the Wampanoag with guns, swords, cannons, and torches. Most, including Metacomet, were butchered. His wife and son were sold into slavery in the West Indies. His body was hideously drawn and quartered. For twenty-five years afterward, Metacomet's skull was displayed on a pike above the whites' village. The real legacy of the Pilgrim Fathers is treachery.

Most Americans today believe that Thanksgiving celebrates a bountiful harvest, but that is not so. By 1970, the Wampanoag had turned up a copy of a Thanksgiving proclamation made by the governor of the colony. The text revealed the ugly truth: After a colonial militia had returned from murdering the men, women, and children of an Indian village, the governor proclaimed a holiday and feast to give thanks for the massacre. He also encouraged other colonies to do likewise—in other words, every autumn after the crops are in, go kill Indians and celebrate your murders with a feast.

The Wampanoag we met at Plymouth came from everywhere in Massachusetts. Like many other eastern nations, theirs had been all but wiped out. The survivors found refuge in other Indian nations that had not yet succumbed to European diseases or to violence. The Wampanoag went into hiding or joined the Six Nations or found homes among the Delaware or Shawnee nations, to name a few. Some also sought refuge in one of the two hundred eastern-seaboard nations that were later exterminated. Nothing remains of those nations but their names, and even some of those have been lost. Other Wampanoag, who couldn't reach another Indian nation, survived by intermarriage with black slaves or freedmen. It is hard to imagine a life so terrible that people would choose instead, with all their progeny, to become slaves, but that is exactly what some Indians did.

In November 1970, their descendants returned to Plymouth to publicize the true story of Thanksgiving and, along with about two hundred other Indians from around the country, to observe a national day of Indian mourning. Whites usually celebrate Thanksgiving with a costume parade in the Plimoth Plantation, a re-creation of the original Pilgrim village. Because 1970 marked the 350th anniversary of the colony's establishment, a new replica of the *Mayflower* was bobbing at a wharf near Plymouth Rock. Carrying signs, beating drums, and singing Indian songs, we marched three or four miles on that brisk autumn day to the Plimoth Plantation, stopping all traffic as we moved down the highway. After about forty minutes, we arrived at the village dining hall, where a turkey dinner was waiting.

Dennis Banks and a few other people had driven in and were waiting for us. The white organizers, dressed in Pilgrim outfits, invited us to join them at what was clearly a Thanksgiving gourmet's delight. In the middle of the welcoming speech by the "Pilgrim Fathers," Dennis suddenly stood up at the head of the table, yelled, "We're not going to eat this shit!" and upended the table. The rest of us started to yell and turn over the other tables. I was hungry after that long walk. While everyone stumbled around in shock, while the white women were screaming and people were trying to get to the door and we Indians were hollering and whooping, I ripped off a turkey leg and stuck it under my coat.

It was clear that nobody was going to get much to eat, so we headed to Plymouth Rock. Some of our people were spitting on the rock and others were throwing trash at it. Dozens of cops with bullhorns threatened us with arrest if we went inside the enclosure surrounding the rock.

Dennis came up and said, "While the police are here, let's go take over the *Mayflower*." We told a few key guys what we were doing, and then went over to the wharf. High-school volunteers were taking admission tickets and guiding visitors around the ship. We got in line with the tourists, but AIM never bought a ticket to anything. We told those teens we were going aboard, and they said, "Yes, sir. Yes, sir." We took the regular tour, looking at the layout and at mannequins costumed like Captain John Smith of Jamestown, Miles Standish, and all the others who had sailed from England to steal Indian land. By the time we returned topside, more Indians were streaming aboard. White tourists, visibly nervous, quickly left the ship.

When all our people were aboard, Dennis stood up and said, "This ship is ours. Get rid of the gangplank." Some of the guys tore it off. Then someone said, "Get the flags," and some guys climbed the mast and rigging. They took down all the flags and used them to wrap around themselves. Someone yelled, "Let's throw the dummies overboard!" We started to chuck mannequins into the water. Then some of our guys said, "Let's torch it!" Dennis yelled, "No, no, no! Not yet! Not when everybody's on here!" I suppose he was worried that someone would get hurt or that too many people would be arrested. By then the police had arrived to negotiate with us. They said, "Please don't destroy anything else, and we'll let you all go." After a while, Dennis agreed and told us to go ashore.

I was still fired up. I had done my homework on the Plymouth Colony, but more important, in the time I had been there, I had spoken at length with Slow Turtle and other Wampanoag who knew their history. As we were leaving the *Mayflower II*, I realized that the truth about Thanksgiving illuminates an important dimension of Eurocentric culture: The white man doesn't know how to say thank you, and he never gives away anything just for the pleasure of giving it away. Instead, he always expects something in return. I wanted to share that insight with everyone. Just as that thought came into my head, I recalled what a Crow man had said soon after I had joined AIM: "Always speak from the heart and nothing can go wrong."

I looked around for a place to speak. Near the ship was a huge statue of Massasoit welcoming the Pilgrims. I stood on its base and gave the most impassioned speech I had ever delivered. I described the generosity and peacefulness and beauty of the Wampanoag. I told how they had welcomed the Pilgrims, how they saw them through two winters when otherwise the whites would have starved to death. I added that 350 years ago, all we would have had to do throughout our hemisphere was let the whites forage for themselves and they wouldn't have made it, because they didn't know what to eat. They didn't even know how to go about finding out. I said our culture is about having patience and building relationships with life itself, is about becoming part of life, which allows us to *live with* nature rather than *conquer* nature. The white man's culture is all about trial and error. A society that advances itself through trial and error guarantees that sooner or later someone will get hurt—usually sooner *and* later. As I spoke, I realized that virtually everyone was so interested in what I had to say that they were hanging on every word. It was one of the first times I realized that people would listen to me.

That evening, most of us partied at some of the Plymouth motels. When I got up in the morning, I learned that Trudell and a few of our Indian brothers had slipped off and lathered Plymouth Rock in red paint. That and our activities of the previous day brought AIM more national exposure. We had served notice that Indians no longer would accept placidly whatever white America handed out. Suddenly, Indian people everywhere knew about us and dared to hope again.

18

▼▼▼▼▼▼▼▼▼

The Sun Dance

After our success at Plymouth Rock, I was totally enamored with AIM. With much contemplation and soul-searching, I decided that the organization deserved nothing less than my complete sobriety. By the winter of 1970–1971, I had stopped drinking. But whenever a guy jumps on that wagon, he wants everyone else to quit too, so I quickly became holier-than-thou on the subject of booze.

My first opportunity to discuss sobriety with AIM's leadership came in the early spring of 1971, when the Ojibwa of the Lac Court Oreilles Reservation asked for our help. Their northern Wisconsin lands included the headwaters of the Chippewa Flowage, source of the Chippewa River, a tributary of the Mississippi. The issue was the Ojibwa treaty area. The Northern States Power Company had built an earthen dam there for water-usage control and downstream hydroelectric-generation plants. The treaty entitled the Ojibwa to part of the water and electricity, but the power company refused to give them any. The Ojibwa needed a way to present their case in the media. By showing that Northern States Power was a greedy bunch of profiteers, the Ojibwa could mobilize public opinion in their favor and force the company to offer them a fair settlement.

AIM took over the dam and threatened to open it up. We were willing to be arrested. We thought the police might try to kick us out, so we intimated to the media that we were armed. We never actually said we had weapons, just that we would fight back. Probably because of that threat, U.S. marshals and the FBI kept their distance. The local police didn't know what to do with us, but as long as we were merely camped there and didn't bother the dam itself, they let us alone. We didn't get arrested, but our protest made news and generated local and national support for the Ojibwa. Even more important, AIM found them Larry Leventhal, the lawyer who helped win their points in court.

One evening, standing at the edge of the dam, I shared my new thoughts about alcohol with several AIM members. Among them was Clyde's brother, Vernon, the wig stylist, who had come from Denver with his non-Indian wife and kids. He said he wanted to be part of the Indian movement. Vernon agreed with me about drinking, but said it was okay to smoke marijuana because it comes from our sacred Grandmother.

Vernon didn't know he was talking to a guy who had been on the most intimate terms with weed. "That's a good excuse to get high," I replied, "but using dope instead of booze is just substituting one high for another. It reminds me of when I was fifteen and went to a peyote meeting in Winnebago. All the town drunks were there. I wondered why then, but of course, it was only because they could get high. If marijuana was intended for this part of the world, then it would be growing around here naturally."

Vernon went into a long rap about how much safer it was to smoke marijuana than to drink alcohol. That riled me. "There's one strange difference between an alcoholic and a dope addict," I said. "An alcoholic doesn't talk about it, or he denies that he even has a problem. He damn sure doesn't try to justify getting gassed—but a doper tries to convince you that what he's doing is right. There's a reason why it's called *dope*." We talked more about that, but in the end, Vernon won the debate in his own mind and kept on doping.

That night on the dam, I told Dennis Banks about something else that had been on my mind. AIM now had chapters in Minneapolis, Saint Paul, and Cleveland, and in Kansas. People in Denver wanted to start one and so did a bunch of guys in Ann Arbor, Michigan. Our movement was starting to spread around the country. We were the vanguard of the Indian-rights fight. People were falling in love with the idea that we were independent advocates, the only ones who would go wherever Indian people needed us. I said we ought to have a convention and organize AIM as a national entity.

Dennis agreed, and we decided to get together later that spring in Saint Paul. We had no money for a hotel, so Eddie Benton Banai helped to line up a kind of Boy Scout camp on a lake in Saint Paul. We held our meetings and workshops there. AIM people paid their own way—no taxpayers financed our gathering. Even so, there was good representation for a first conference. We had about a hundred members, including groups from Rapid City, Denver, Cleveland, Minneapolis, Kansas, Wisconsin, Michigan, and Chicago. We also drew many all-conference Indians, including observers from the National Congress of American Indians and the National Indian Education Association. When they found that we had no bar or hospitality suites, and that they had to bring their own campers or sleep in dorms with the rest of us, they stuck around for only a couple of hours a day.

We put up a purification lodge, an *inipi*—commonly but erroneously referred to as a "sweat lodge"—and cleansed ourselves before conducting business. As the only newly sober AIM member, I pushed through a resolution to our national manifesto: "AIM advocates no alcohol or drugs." We decided this meant that what AIM members did in their personal lives was their own business, but as long as they were doing AIM's business or representing it, there would be no drinking or doping. Then Vernon led a group that persuaded a majority to chop *drugs* from the wording of the manifesto.

We discussed electing a national leader. I said, "AIM is really a loose confederation of chapters, each with its own programs and its own agenda. Instead of having a chairman or president like white people would, we should do things the Indian way. The job should be to coordinate national events among all the chapters so that on nationwide matters, we can all support each other. Why not call this position the national coordinator?"

Everybody liked that idea, and of course Dennis and Clyde were the obvious first choices for the job. They were, however, busy overseeing Minneapolis AIM programs such as court advocacy, in which mothers monitored and reported on racism in the Minneapolis juvenile-court system. Their Legal Justice Center—not just for Indians, but for all poor people in their urban area—got lawyers to represent them *pro bono*. AIM Minneapolis had a curriculum program that worked with schools to get rid of racist textbooks. AIM had so much going in Minneapolis that neither Clyde nor Dennis could commit himself to additional national responsibilities. When AIM elected its first national coordinator, the members chose me. Vernon Bellecourt finished second in the balloting. But right after the election, he sent Rod Skenadone over to ask me to step down and name Vernon as national coordinator. Rod told me I should do this—speaking for Vernon—because the Denver chapter was just getting started and needed that kind of important position to enhance its status, while I already had a well-established chapter.

I had never heard of such a thing. Then I realized that Vernon, who until recently had been content to tread the white man's path, was jealous of me. His brother Clyde, who had busted his balls for years to help the cause, was recognized as a leader. Now Vernon wanted to be one, too. I said, "No."

Rod said, "Why not?"

"Because a lot of people here have faith in me."

We both knew that I had won by only a few votes, but many people did believe in me. I wanted to be part of something far bigger than myself. I thought I had something to contribute. Because I was so in love with AIM that I believed all the rhetoric and thought we could do no wrong, I made an enemy. At the time, however, I wasn't aware how much anger and jealousy were part of Vernon's character, so I thought nothing more of it.

By the time of that first national convention, the BIA was condemning AIM members throughout Indian country as militants. In response, we decided that our policy would be to emphasize that Indian people should return home to their reservations. To set the example for everyone else, we leaders would return to our reservations. We would get involved in Indian ceremonies to find out more about who we are, what we are, why we are, and where we are going.

I was already planning to return to South Dakota for the annual sun dance when the Oglala elders asked us to go back on Mount Rushmore in June 1971. On the way, we stopped on the Rosebud Reservation at Crow Dog's Paradise. It really is a paradise—little houses along a creek, surrounded by pines, cottonwoods, and lush green plants of every kind. We were there to see Leonard Crow Dog, who lived with his father Henry, a renowned medicine man. He could call eagles to him. I've seen pictures of him sitting on the ground surrounded by them.

We had come to hold a *yuwipi* ceremony before returning to Mount Rushmore. AIM had asked for the ceremony because we were going again into the *Paha Sapa*, the holy land of the Lakota, to possess it and to renew our ownership claims as guaranteed by the Fort Laramie Treaty of 1868. In a *yuwipi* ceremony, the holy man's body is bound tightly and put under a blanket. During the ceremony, the spirits release him, signifying that they have heard our prayers. All people present pray for whatever reasons brought them. Whoever had asked for the ceremony "gives away"—makes a gift of tobacco or something valuable to the medicine man. After the *yuwipi*, Leonard asked, "Which of you doesn't drink?" I alone raised my hand. He gave me tobacco ties and an altar to take to the mountain.

All plants are sacred, but like sage and other medicinal plants, tobacco has special meaning. When lit, it signifies the molten fire that is the center of our Grandmother, the earth. Fire is cleansing. The ashes and smoke produced by burning sacred tobacco carry our messages to the Great Mystery and dissipate them among the four winds. Tobacco, too, is cleansing. Western science doesn't realize that pure tobacco, smoked in a good way on a ritual occasion, cleanses the lungs and helps the respiratory system. It is soothing and allows you to relax. In this century, as we Indians became familiar with cloth, we learned to make tobacco ties, small bundles of tobacco tied with strips of colored cloth. They carry our message. We are alerting all of nature that we are surviving, that we still maintain our traditions, that we understand

and continue to be part of all that is natural. Whatever else the holy man wishes to add to that message is signified by the colored ties around the tobacco bundles. The colors are selected in recognition of the different reasons why each color is sacred. Sometimes they are all white, sometimes black, red, and white, sometimes black and red, sometimes yellow. That time, setting out for our holy land, Leonard selected ties of all four sacred colors— black for cleanliness and purity, red for energy, yellow for the new start promised by the dawn of each new day, and white for the south, source of the warm wind.

That year, we didn't have a bus and there weren't many people attending from Rapid City—only about two dozen of us in all, including the AIM Minneapolis people. It was June 6, 1971. When we reached the top of the mountain, I erected the altar as Leonard had instructed me. Park Service rangers were waiting for us and warned us not to set up a camp. We had brought baseball bats to defend ourselves, so the rangers knew that if they came up, they were in for a fight. Soon they called in the National Guard to surround the mountain.

Rangers came partway up the mountain to negotiate with us, and for a while it was just like in the movies. I knew the mountain very well from the previous year. Whenever they hollered for me or one of the others, we would slip down silently, traveling on the rocks in tennis shoes. I loved to suddenly appear, *poof!* from behind a bush or atop a rock three feet away to say, "Yes?" The rangers were startled every time. They looked at me as though they were thinking, damn, these sneaky Indians sneaked up on us again.

They wanted us off the mountain, but we said, "We won't come down unless you honor the 1868 Fort Laramie Treaty." Talk about a naive demand! Sure, all those white ranchers, miners, real-estate speculators, land developers, and owners of souvenir stands, restaurants, gift shops, and motels—thousands of whites who lived in little towns—were going to leave the Black Hills just so we would come down off Mount Rushmore! But we had come to make a point. That was *our* mountain. The white man's treaty had affirmed our ownership, and the white man's law had promised to guarantee equal protection to all Americans.

When the Park Service people came up a second time, they said they weren't going to fool around anymore. They knew we had baseball bats, but the National Guard was coming to remove us, period. If we made trouble, we could get killed. We said, "It's up to you. Whatever you want those boys in uniform to do, go ahead. It's *their* lives." Since we knew they would love any excuse to use their guns, we tossed all our bats down a deep hole after the Park Service people left.

Then an argument started. Some guys said, "We'll get arrested and go to prison, or they'll just shoot us—we should get off now." My brother Ted, our cousin Mitchell Zephier, and I said we were going to stay and get arrested. My sister Madonna, Clyde's wife Peggy, and most of the other women said, "We're staying." Vernon talked his brother George into leaving with him. At first, Clyde said he, too, was going, but when Peggy said, "You're going to leave me up here?" he decided to stay.

Charlie, oldest of the Bellecourt brothers, also remained. He was only forty-six, but he had lived a very rough life. He drank a lot, and looked far older. What little hair he had left was white. Charlie had always been poor. He had been in and out of jails his whole life and had always been treated like dirt. He was a tough old buzzard, but down deep a great guy. He wasn't in the American Indian Movement, but he had come along with us because he was tired of being beaten down, of never fighting for his rights. He had decided that at least once in his life, he was going to make a stand, and this was the time and place to do it. Vernon tried to persuade him to take off, but Charlie said, "Hell, no! I came up with these boys, I'm going down with these boys. I'm going to stay here and get arrested and I'm going to jail with them." He made us younger people feel proud. That was the only time I met Charlie. A few years later, he moved on to the spirit world.

Vernon led his people down the mountain. He mingled with the crowd of tourists watching the National Guard soldiers moving up the mountain to remove us. The rest of us got inside our altar, surrounded by a circle of sacred tobacco ties. We sat there listening to the cops and soldiers struggling up toward us. Some of us prayed.

We heard the cops and soldiers chattering as they climbed:

"Isn't there an easier way to get up there?"

"Shut up."

"Are we close to the top?"

"Shut up."

"You see anybody?"

"Shut up."

We heard what sounded like a herd of idiots—labored breathing and muttered curses, uniforms and gear catching on the brush, rocks, and gravel displaced by awkward boots peppering those below. Finally I saw the top of a park ranger's hat slowly rising from behind a big rock, first the crown, then the brim and a forehead and eyebrows, and finally a pair of eyes. Anybody could have blown off the top half of that man's head before he got a look at him—or flipped a pebble at his hat and scared him shitless. Finally the cops stood up with their shotguns and acted macho. A few minutes later, the guardsmen came up, and oh, my god, were *they* macho!

Some of those guys were visibly disappointed. They had come up with their assault rifles cocked and aimed at us from the shoulder, eyes staring down their sights, shouting, "All right, down on the ground!" We sat silently and looked at them. Walking on tiptoe, as though we might explode, it took those soldiers almost forever to get to us. When the first guardsman finally touched an Indian, they all grabbed us and started to throw men and women around, kicking and dragging us across the ground. Others jumped into the altar and ripped it apart, arguing and fighting among themselves for souvenirs.

Clyde had had the most experience dealing with police, so I followed his lead. It hurt when the guardsmen poked and punched us with their rifle muzzles and billy clubs, but we didn't say a word. The cops said, "You're going to walk down," and handcuffed us behind our backs. Only Charlie, who was in no shape to take another beating, cooperated. When they prodded the rest of us to go, we went limp. They kicked us a couple of times, then said, "This won't work." They changed the handcuffs so that our hands were in front, and said, "We'll drag you down." They shoved billy clubs between our cuffed arms and a policeman took each end of it and dragged us, face up, down the mountain. The trouble was that there wasn't a path. The way down—normally about a ten-minute jaunt—includes huge boulders that must be climbed or jumped. We said nothing and we did nothing to help our captors as they dragged us over rocks and twigs, anything they could find to rip us up.

It was hard work. Soon the cops and soldiers were sweating and bringing in more manpower so they could change off. I noticed that some of the police were highway patrolmen, others were park police, and still others were from different state agencies, plus the guardsmen, of course. The cops tried to maim Ted by hanging him from a billy club under his jaw. When he started to turn blue, they dropped him headfirst about five feet down a cliff. After Ted had almost got his breath back, they started to drag him again.

About that time, the little helicopter that tourists rent for five-minute flights around the mountain began to circle us. If I had been able to see inside its cockpit, I would have noticed Vernon Bellecourt, who had spent a few bucks to see how the other half lived—or died. By the time the cops had dragged us about halfway down, they were almost totally worn out. One of their honchos came up and gave us the "good cop" routine. We remained silent, and they continued to drag us. Then they decided to carry the women, who were lighter. That gave the cops a chance to fondle their bodies. The women immediately told them to quit. The bosses said, "You women are going to walk down or face getting felt wherever our hands go." They didn't want white men feeling them up, so they decided to walk.

About two-thirds of the way down, the cops stopped to rest again and to plead with us. So far, we hadn't said a word or even changed the expressions on our faces, but we were tired and pretty well beat up. Ted was having a tough time. His Adam's apple was almost crushed. Clyde was so tough that I didn't worry much about him, but I could see that Mitch Zephier was bruised and very stressed out. I stood up and said, "Okay, we'll walk down."

At the old Rapid City jail, which had been built in the 1920s, they lined us up—Ted, Clyde, and Charlie, and me, all in handcuffs—while newspaper photographers took pictures of us. It was like a scene from an old Western—the renegade desperadoes captured by the posse.

We were charged with trespassing, and we demanded jury trials. In our defense, we cited the 1868 treaty, which affirmed that the Black Hills were our holy land. We couldn't be trespassing on our own sacred mountain. Because of that issue, the federal district judge, Andrew Bogue—who owned property in the Black Hills—recused himself. The feds didn't want to transfer our cases to another judge. It would have meant burdening themselves with the prosecution of misdemeanors hundreds of miles away, so all the charges were dismissed. We were from out of state, so the authorities probably thought they never would see us again. Once again, the Great Mystery was at work. South Dakota's federal judges would rue the day we were arrested on Mount Rushmore.

So would Rapid City. Lizzie Fast Horse must have had a dark premonition: As we were dragged off the sacred mountain that has been defiled by the white man's idolatry, Lizzie began to shake her head and mutter, "The white man doesn't know what he's doing." A year later—nearly to the day—I would understand what she meant.

After I got out of the Rapid City jail, I began to prepare myself to participate in my first sun dance at Pine Ridge, on the first weekend of August. Until my ancestor Feather Necklace's time, the sun dance had been one of the most important annual events for the Allies. As with so many of our spiritual observances, Christian missionaries forced the BIA to ban it in 1881. Our right to the sun dance was restored in the 1950s, but with so many restrictions that the ceremony was reduced to a mere shadow of what it had once been. Throughout the seven decades when participating in the sun dance meant going to prison, a few Lakota secretly conducted the holy rituals in remote parts of their reservations. They selected open places where winds would disperse the sounds of singing and drums. They guarded the locations with outriders on horseback to make sure no government agents or missionaries found them. In that way, the Lakota preserved knowledge of the ancient rituals.

In 1971, the only sun dance legally allowed to the Lakota in the United States was little more than a sideshow at a seasonal carnival that included a softball tournament, rodeo, food stands, and "powwows." By strict BIA fiat, the sun dance began at sunup and ended at noon each day.

My fascination with the sun dance went back to childhood. All my life, I had heard different things about it—that it was torture and suffering, that only the toughest men could endure it. Two years earlier, while watching the dance as a spectator, I had overhead a medicine man named Pete Catches talking to a white woman, explaining why he danced. It opened my eyes, gave me a new slant. It made clear the connection between the sun dance and the way traditional elders could communicate with their spouses without speech.

Pete explained why he participated in the sun dance—to seek balance between the female and the male; to try to understand, through sacrifice and ordeal, the experience of giving birth, the ultimate human act of creation. He spoke about how he prepared during the whole year for each sun dance. To get his mind and body ready, he worked hard to make himself strong, continuing to work long past quitting time, standing up when he was tired and ached to sit, going without water when he was thirsty. Throughout the year, he fasted and prayed to get himself ready spiritually. At each change of the seasons, Pete acknowledged with prayer the power of nature's perpetual cycle. He rose very early every day to greet the morning star, thus acknowledging the universe and its power. Pete said many more things about how he used the entire year to look forward and prepare himself for the sun dance. He said more than I remember now. I stood, silent, listening, totally enraptured by the concept of the sun dance.

I had long yearned to feel like my ancestors, to find out more about the vital business of balance. It was part of being an Indian. I knew the sun dance could give me some insights, and now that I was sober, I was determined to participate in one. The day before the dance, Mary Menard, who lived on the Rosebud Reservation, lent me her blue shawl to use as a skirt for the sun dance. When I rose the next morning in the darkness before dawn, I wrapped it around my waist and fastened it with a safety pin.

I knew very little about what to do, but I did know that dancing was supposed to begin at sunup. I found my way to the purification lodge, but no one was stirring yet. I went to some bleachers on the west side of the dance area and noticed that there was trash everywhere, and a guy had passed out in the bleachers. I sat a little away from him, looking east. Suddenly I heard someone coming. When he got closer, I discovered that he was an older man from California, a white who had been adopted by the Red Cloud family. He showed me how to make crown, wrist, and ankle bands from sage. Traditionally, Lakota sun dancers have always worn on their chests medallions depicting the sunflower, with beads or porcupine quills or a painting of one. The blossom bends to follow the sun all day, always looking into it, just as sun dancers do. I didn't have a sunflower, so the old man lent me his. I was grateful to have the correct things to honor my ancestors.

After a while, the other dancers drifted in. The dance grounds were enclosed by an arbor with the opening in the sacred circle to the east, as always. There were eight of us, including four old men and Buddy Red Bow, a young man in his teens. Before we could start, a Catholic priest, the biggest drunk on the reservation—a remarkable achievement—showed up. Without even removing his shoes, as is customary on the dance circle's hallowed ground, he started to carry a sacred pipe around the perimeter so our sun dance could begin with the church's blessing. I was stunned, not quite believing what I was seeing. Ed McGaw, who had grown up in a Catholic boarding school and was decorated for heroism while flying Marine jets in Vietnam, said, "This is bullshit—our sun dance has nothing to do with Catholicism! We can't let him do this." He and I stopped the half-pickled priest's desecration of our holy rites.

When we danced, I wore no clothing but the borrowed skirt. Buddy and some of the older men wore moccasins, but I knew the traditional dancer was barefoot. I had seen how Pete Catches danced in previous years, so I patterned myself on him. To this day, that is how I dance—each of my steps keeping time with the drumbeat and kicking my knees high all day long, or as long as I can. That first day, I met old George Eagle Elk, who had danced in about twenty-eight sun dances. He was from the Rosebud Reservation, a Brulé who told me many things—what was expected of me and how to prepare for the dance, and what natural medicines I could use.

At noon on Thursday, the first day, we stopped, following the BIA's strict orders. Since I had no place to camp and no tent, I returned to my car. All sorts of festive events were going on all around me, but I was there to dance. Following our ancient custom, I neither ate nor drank. That night, I slept fitfully beneath my car. There was more room to stretch out than there would have been inside it. I was awakened several times by the sound of people, including many of my own relatives, partying after the *wacipi* ended at two in the morning. It didn't really get quiet until about three.

I rose before five, when the sun came up, and danced for a second day. That night, as I sat at a drum helping the singers, I noticed some of the sun dancers still dancing. I thought, boy, those guys are really tough! They have fasted and danced, and here they are, dancing all night long!

Each day as I danced, I prayed, concentrating as hard as I could on my prayers. My prayers were never for myself. I was taught that everyone else was praying for me, so my responsibility was to pray for them. I offered prayers of thanksgiving for everything I could think of. Two years later, my brother Bill, during a break in our first sun dance together, asked, "Russ, what do you pray for after you've prayed for everything? I've even prayed for my spare tire." My lips were cracking, my mouth was as parched as cotton, my throat felt like sandpaper—and I doubled over with laughter. It was so damn *Indian* to pray for a spare tire! In our poverty, we depend on such things. I remember opening my car trunk many times, never knowing whether the spare was going to be flat, too, but hoping hard that it was still inflated. When I could breathe again, I told Bill, "Start over, play the record again." That's what I did, looking for gaps I might have missed in my prayers and then filling them in. I became consumed by prayer. Almost before I knew it, the song was over. We were supposed to sing twenty-one songs before the medicine man called for a rest, but because of the BIA's many constraints, there wasn't time enough for all of them.

On Saturday, the third day, we could dance only until 11:00 A.M. because the parade from Pine Ridge Village ended by going around the sacred circle. The tribe charged tourists if they wanted to take pictures, so I saw several movie cameras. My great-uncle, Matthew King, whom I thought of as my grandpa, was the public-address announcer who explained to the spectators, which included many white people, the truth about the sun dance. When it came to some of the more important dimensions of the sun dance, George Eagle Elk sometimes expanded on Uncle Matthew's commentary. They said essentially the same things, but each had his own inimitably beautiful and poetic way of saying it. Although I was long past exhaustion and was light-headed from my fast, it bolstered my spirits and made me feel better to hear them. During a break in the dancing, Ed McGaw got up and gave a great talk. Later, Frank Fools Crow, the most renowned Lakota holy man, who was in charge of the ceremonies and knew I was fasting, asked me, too, to speak. It's a very high honor to be chosen to speak at any sun dance, and especially at my first.

After we quit dancing that day, I saw some of the sun dancers drinking and going up to the stands. Several AIM members, who had come to watch the dance and knew I was fasting, teased me, swilling liquids in front of me and offering me things to drink. I didn't mind that too much, but near the end of that third day, I learned that all of the other sun dancers had been drinking and eating all along. I was disappointed in them, but I was there to dance and all that outside stuff didn't matter. I was learning and experiencing being an Indian. That's what was important to me.

That evening, Fools Crow invited me to his camp. When his wife, Kate, offered me food, he waved her away, explaining that I was the lone sun dancer observing the fast. Later, when the doorway singers stopped by on their rounds, Fools Crow asked them for an honors song. To my astonishment, he adopted me as his grandson! Afterward, he gave away some of his most prized possessions to the singers, including a bone choker and other ceremonial items he plucked from his clothes.

On the fourth day, we pierced. Grandpa Fools Crow, who was born about 1890, had spent much of his life fighting for the right for the Lakota to sun dance and pray in our traditional ways. Even though he would never admit to speaking or understanding English, he had gone to Washington, D.C., and lobbied the BIA in the 1940s and 1950s. Finally in the late '50s, he persuaded the BIA to give permission to start the sun dance again, but during the Eisenhower administration, everything had to be done in a harness that "simulated" piercing. The sacred buffalo skull that was dragged around the circle was attached to a harness instead of to skewers of chokecherry wood embedded in a dancer's back. Dancers who hung from a tree didn't pierce. Instead, they put on a harness and pretended they were pierced. When Fools Crow finally won the right to pierce—and only he had permission—a government doctor accompanied him to ensure that he didn't pierce too deeply. Fools Crow had me lie on a buffalo skin. With a razor blade, he pierced the fleshy part of my chest very lightly on one side and inserted a stick from a chokecherry bush. A rope tied to the sacred tree in the center of the circle was fastened to the stick. Moving to the beat of the drum and praying, I approached the tree four times with the other dancers. After the last time, I pulled away, tightening the rope until the stick pulled out, tearing my flesh. It was painful, but as mothers say when describing childbirth, it was a pure and holy moment, more spiritually fulfilling than agonizing. It helped me feel what all men owe all women, the hallowed relationship between female and male that balances the universe.

Afterward, we stood in line while people came into the sacred circle to shake our hands. The elders told me not to take anything cold before I drank something warm. Kate Fools Crow brought me potato soup. All the young people, the whites and even the educated Indians, gave me firm handshakes and said, "Congratulations," or, "Well done," as though I were being rewarded for some kind of macho thing. But all the old women and many of the old men, who could speak little or no English, came to us weeping. They all said, "*Pilamiya*," which means "thank you." At that moment, I grasped what the sun dance was all about. It wasn't for the pride and glory of the dancers—it was for the people. Only those old Indians knew that.

19
▼▼▼▼▼▼▼▼

Moses Cleaveland

My brother Ted had come to the sun dance, but like almost everyone else, he just partied. In fact, he drank right through Sunday and passed out in the backseat of my Buick. I could have awakened him or dragged him out, but I had a better idea. The only job he had been able to find was working for the BIA, and just before the sun dance, I had seen him putting fertilizer on a Rosebud Reservation ball field. I thought, how unfortunate for my brother, but spreading shit around is the ultimate statement about the BIA. I had told Ted then, "I've got to get you out of here." When I found him unconscious in my car, I drove him back to Cleveland. He didn't know he had been shanghaied until early Monday. He woke up as we passed under a huge green sign on the interstate at the Sioux City cutoff.

I made Ted director of manpower at the Cleveland American Indian Center. Months later, my sister Madonna, her husband Sylvester Smells, a Montana Crow, and her two children, who had been living in Minneapolis, moved to Cleveland. Madonna and Sylvester also went to work for me.

Everything we tried to do to help our people, not only in Cleveland but throughout Indian country, was undercut or made more difficult by the BIA. When Richard Nixon appointed Louis Bruce—half Seneca, half Dakota, but raised Seneca—as the new commissioner of Indian affairs, we thought things would change for the better. They got worse. The reason, we discovered, was an assistant commissioner named John O. Crow, who undercut whatever Bruce tried to do. I called for an AIM action in Washington. We wanted to put Crow under citizen's arrest.

I took Dennis Bowen and a few other guys from Cleveland AIM, and the week before Thanksgiving, we went to Washington to join Indians from all over the country. About thirty or forty men and women walked down to the BIA building. In those days, we always announced in advance the date and time of our protests. The press showed up to greet us, along with the General Services Administration police. The fight was on! Reinforcements rushed in from everywhere to overwhelm and arrest about two dozen of us. We ended up in the D.C. lockup.

When we got to court, the BIA was represented by Ernie Stevens, a great guy and one of the young lions Commissioner Bruce brought in to turn the BIA around. Ernie refused to press charges, and when he asked the judge to let us go, he did. Even if we hadn't dragged John O. Crow out of his office, we accomplished what we had wanted: We called attention to his hidden agenda. Within months, he was forced to retire.

Back in Cleveland, most of the city was getting ready for the biggest birthday party in its history, the 175th anniversary of the city's founding by Moses Cleaveland, who had surveyed the land next to Lake Erie and laid out its first town plan. Nearly everyone in town got excited when it was announced that Bob Hope, who had spent his youth in Cleveland, would make a speech and serve as grand marshal of a parade. It would begin at the edge of the Cuyahoga River and end at the parklike town square.

By then, the Cleveland American Indian Center was well known around the city, and we expected an invitation to the Indian community to participate in the festivities. We never got one. We weren't about to *ask* to participate, but we felt very insulted at being left out. Finally, late on the afternoon before the celebration, somebody on the anniversary commission realized that their scheduled re-creation of the arrival of Moses Cleaveland, which featured a civic leader wearing a period costume and sailing up the Cuyahoga River to come ashore and read a proclamation, needed one more thing—Indians to meet, greet, and dance for him. At four in the afternoon, someone at the commission telephoned Dennis Bowen. Bowen and I shared an office. When he got that call, he put his hand over the mouthpiece and said, "You're not going to believe this, but they want to know if we'll come down to where 'Moses Cleaveland' is going to land and *dance* for them tomorrow." I said, "Tell them we'll be there."

We would be there, all right!

Bowen and I, the rest of the center's staff, and much of Cleveland's Indian youth group stayed up most of the night, painting signs and strategizing. In the morning, Bowen and his teens turned out in red berets. We assembled along the river, keeping our signs under cover until the boat carry-ing "Cleaveland" was about to dock. Then we pulled the signs out: "Go Home, Illegal Immigrant," "Liar!," "Polluter!," "Stay Away, We Don't Want Your Disease," "White Men Don't Keep Treaties," and many others. Every time that boat came in, Bowen and I shoved it back into the river. We shouted, "We might be 175 years late, but this time he ain't landing!" The police were there, but they didn't know what to do. The shore was lined with news reporters, photographers, and television camera crews. They went wild. As the word spread, other reporters came running. The city wanted to get on with its celebration, so several officials begged us to let the boat land. "What do you want?" they said.

I said, "We want to be the first three speakers after the parade." They were desperate to get on with the celebration, so the commissioners said, "Okay, but please, just let the boat land." When the guy playing Cleaveland finally got off the boat in his colonial-style hat, he unrolled an old parchment scroll with a proclamation and began to read a flowery, benevolent speech addressed to the Indians. When he said, "We come in peace and we want to deal fairly and justly with you," Bowen lost it. About twenty-five years old then, well over six feet tall, and built like a fullback, he ran up and, with both hands, grabbed the tall, skinny, red-faced, elderly white guy by the neck and started to throttle him, shouting, "You liar! You never keep your treaties!" That poor guy—he'd probably never seen an Indian before. I know he really wanted to be sincere; that was his role. As Bowen shook him, the three-cornered hat danced all over his head, an event captured by a CBS News camera. The story also made the front page of the *Wall Street Journal*.

Then we marched to where the parade was scheduled to end, at a big band shell in the middle of the town square. Bob Hope refused to come there, much less speak. The Indians had upstaged him, so he just left town. A crowd of more than five thousand people had gathered. I spoke first for about fifteen minutes. Sarge Old Horn went another fifteen. When Dennis Bowen started in, he didn't quit for an hour and a half. Our speeches were very well received, in part because the white Establishment had no answer for us when we said we hadn't been invited to participate in the celebration until the last minute, and then were asked arrogantly to come and dance for them. The blacks in the audience loved it. It was only a few years after the riots in East Cleveland, so in a way, we were speaking for them, too. The local press lapped up all this because the only other speaker who stuck around was Mayor Carl Stokes. By the time he started in, most of the crowd had gone home.

20
▼▼▼▼▼▼▼▼▼

Raymond Yellow Thunder

The early 1970s were the days when Indians were forming local and national organizations for almost everything—the American Indian Press Association, the National Indian Association of Students, the National Association for Indian Nurses, even a national Indian pilots' group. New ones were popping up every month, it seemed. Not all of them were as lucky as the Cleveland American Indian Center. Just as Dennis and Clyde had predicted in 1969, Jess Sixkiller's group, the National Urban Indian Council, had faded away for lack of a constituency. As relocation continued and more and more Indians traded the stultifying poverty of reservations for the appalling squalor of urban ghettos, the Nixon administration proceeded to gut and fillet the few remaining OEO programs. The dire needs of many thousands of urban Indians became even more pressing. To find new and better ways to help them, a coalition of urban Indian groups invited me to be among those attending a conference in Omaha, Nebraska, in late February 1972.

Just before I left for the meeting, I heard from Birgil Kills Straight. He called to tell me about the shocking death of a Pine Ridge man named Raymond Yellow Thunder in Gordon, Nebraska, a little town below the South Dakota border. Yellow Thunder, who was forty-seven, was a farm worker.

Through years of hard work and dependability, he had earned the respect of many white farmers and ranchers. Birgil said the Gordon authorities claimed that Yellow Thunder had died of "exposure" on the front seat of a panel truck in a used-car lot. In that part of the country, anytime a dead Indian turns up, white authorities say he died of exposure; then they bury him as quickly as possible. Yellow Thunder's sisters weren't going for it. They knew something terrible had happened to him: Just before the coffin was sealed, the sisters glimpsed the body, and it appeared to have been mutilated, Birgil said.

The weekly *Gordon Journal* had reported in its February 23 issue—three days after the body was discovered—that after an autopsy indicated "evidence of foul play," the county attorney had filed manslaughter and false-imprisonment charges and had issued arrest warrants for four white men. Birgil said Yellow Thunder's older sisters had become suspicious of a cover-up when authorities refused to let them see the autopsy report. The sisters had turned to their tribal council for help, and when they got none, they went to the BIA and then to the FBI. They had even tried to hire a private attorney, but nobody would do anything for them. I told Birgil that I was headed to Omaha for a conference that most of the AIM members would attend. I invited him to send somebody down to tell us everything the family knew about Yellow Thunder's death.

We met with Severt Young Bear, a relative of Yellow Thunder's, in an Omaha hotel room. In his own special brand of fractured English, Severt told us how, after his aunts had spoken to authorities in Sheridan County, Nebraska, county sheriff's deputies and Gordon police had arrested Leslie D. Hare and Melvin P. Hare. They were the twenty-something sons of Dean Hare, a breeder of registered rodeo stock and one of the wealthiest, most influential ranchers and businessmen in that part of the state. Also arrested in Yellow Thunder's death were Bernard Lutter, Robert Bayliss, and his girlfriend, Jannette Thompson. Lutter was charged with manslaughter, and Bayliss and Thompson were charged only with false imprisonment. All five were released on bond. Yellow Thunder's family felt that second-degree manslaughter charges were ridiculous—the Hares and Lutter should have been charged with murder—but there had not been a proper investigation of Yellow Thunder's death, and no one would open one.

On their own, however, the family members had pieced together a partial picture of what had happened. On the frigid night of February 12, 1972, Yellow Thunder had been walking down a Gordon street, minding his own business, when the four white men and Thompson came by in a car. Killing Indians remains a favorite sport in that part of the country, where even today, liquored-up white cowboys display their manhood by hunting down and stomping homeless Indians to death. The Gordon cowboys stopped to taunt and abuse Yellow Thunder, beat him severely on the face and head, removed his trousers and underpants, and locked him in the trunk of their car. After driving around town for a few hours, the young thugs pulled into the gravel parking lot of the American Legion post. They took Yellow Thunder inside the log-cabin-style building and forced him to dance—still naked from the waist down—for the amusement of about two hundred people at the legion's regular Saturday night dance. A few days later, his body was found by some little boys who, while playing in a used-car lot, opened a truck door.

Severt Young Bear asked AIM to come to Gordon to help Yellow Thunder's family get justice. We chartered a bus, loaded the overflow into several cars, and headed toward Pine Ridge, stopping at the Winnebago Reservation. We called ahead to invite people to a meeting, at which we explained what had happened and invited the Winnebago people to join us in a demonstration in Gordon. Many did.

At Pine Ridge, we met with tribal officials, including Gerald One Feather, the lame-duck tribal president, and president-elect Dick Wilson. Wilson had hair past his shoulders—hardly a trivial matter. In those days, only a few traditional Indian men and "militants" such as AIM members wore long hair. Wilson told us he was behind AIM "110 percent," would support our efforts in Gordon, and once he was inaugurated, we would be welcome to come to see him. That was the last time I saw Dick with long hair.

AIM called a community meeting in Billy Mills Hall. We explained why we had come to Pine Ridge and why we would be going into Gordon—to demand justice for the killers of Raymond Yellow Thunder, to expose white racism, and to serve notice that Indians would no longer accept whatever the white man handed out when it included degradation and murder. People rallied behind us, many asking to join our caravan. On March 1, we held a press conference and announced that we were going to Gordon on March 6.

Many of the white farmers who founded and built Gordon and neighboring towns in the 1880s had sustained themselves through years of crop failures by plowing up Indian graves and selling the bones. These brought high prices from eastern manufacturers who turned them into pipe bowls, buttons, collar stays, corselets, and the fancy carved combs that modish white women wore in their hair. Since it is inconceivable that they would have dug up their own ancestors' bones and sold them, it is plain that those white people regarded Indians as less than human. Things hadn't changed much by 1972. Indians who lived in Gordon came up to tell us about the kinds of racially motivated atrocities inflicted on them. As cops in many of those border towns still do, Gordon police often forced young Indian girls into their cars, took them into the countryside, and raped them. The girls were told that if they dared to open their mouths about it, they would be arrested and taken to jail. At other times, police had even raped Indian girls right in the

Gordon jail, the Indian people told us. They named a cop who had become notorious for that.

Besides occasionally killing us for recreation, ordinary white citizens of Gordon found hundreds of humiliating ways to discriminate against Indians for fun and profit. Merchants routinely jacked up prices for Indian customers. Landlords refused to rent decent housing to Indian families, and charged outrageous rents for filthy, tumbledown shacks and hovels. Indians were often refused attention by local hospitals and clinics. Many employers refused to hire Indian workers, or offered wages far lower than they paid whites. The schools used racist textbooks that fostered ugly stereotypes about Indians.

After our press conference, Gordon officials met with us in the Pine Ridge tribal offices, and begged us to stay away. "We can settle this without you all coming down," they said. About the Yellow Thunder case, they said, "Everything has been done that could be done." We told them, "Bullshit. We're coming. Get ready." The night before we went into Gordon, we heard that the National Guard, highway patrol, and local police had sent men to protect the city. We were warned that there might also be white vigilantes.

While getting ready that night, I recalled a paper I had written in the ninth grade, which discussed the international distress signal: a ship's national ensign flown upside down. I recall telling the group, "When a ship is in trouble, they fly their national flag upside down to show that they need help. Now we, the Indian nations, are in distress. Let's round up all the U.S. flags we can find around Pine Ridge, and tomorrow, when we go into Gordon, let's fly them all upside down." That caught on. To this day, AIM flies the U.S. and Canadian flags upside down.

Our caravan left early in the morning with more than one hundred cars plus our bus—about five hundred people in all—with dozens of inverted American flags flying from car antennae and from poles sticking out windows. From Pine Ridge, it is seventeen miles east on U.S. 18 to the Gordon cutoff, three miles to the state line, and then another dozen south to Gordon on Nebraska 27. The two-lane blacktop dips and rises through grassy, treeless sand hills intercut with dry, meandering streambeds. The country is almost empty except for a few farm buildings sitting well back from the road. The town begins at the top of a steep hill and descends a half mile to a saloon-studded business district through large, wooded lots dotted with smallish Victorian houses. On the day we arrived, American flags flew in front of many Gordon homes. We sent people to pull them down, and we wrapped ourselves in them.

Word of our arrival flashed through town like wildfire. People left half-eaten breakfasts on kitchen tables, and abandoned their homes with doors wide open, as though their ancestors' worst nightmares had come true—a horde of bloodthirsty savages was invading their town. Rather than allow themselves to be scalped or raped, hundreds drove in panic into the wintry countryside. I'm sure that's why to this day my name is a curse on the lips of most Gordon citizens.

Some of Gordon's Indian people had parked an old flatbed truck trailer in a vacant lot near the center of town. We stopped our caravan there, set up a portable microphone, and turned the trailer into a stage for a rally. The National Guard had been placed on standby alert. Dozens of state troopers, county sheriff's deputies, and local police were in town, but they kept their distance. Several AIM people made speeches and fired up the crowd.

We wanted to meet with city officials to discuss the Yellow Thunder case and our other concerns. The mayor responded with an invitation to meet "just four" of us in the basement of city hall. "This is an insult," we said when we got down there. "Why aren't you meeting with us up in the mayor's office? Why are we in a basement?" When they didn't invite us upstairs, we flooded the basement with people and took over the whole building. There was nothing they could have done except shoot us—all unarmed and defenseless people—in front of half a dozen television crews.

As more and more people came into the basement, we squeezed all the city officials into a corner. When I snatched the chief of police's hat off his head, he got so scared that he said, "Oh, g-g-g-go ahead, Mister Muh-Muh-Muh-Means, feh-feh-feh-feel freh—freh-freh-free." Still wearing the hat and with a flag draped around my shoulders, I went outside for an interview with a CBS television reporter. We took over the city hall for two days, scandalizing the town by wearing and sleeping on American flags.

On our second day in Gordon, Dennis, Clyde, and I, along with other AIM representatives, met with Mayor Bruce Moore, Police Chief Robert Case, County Attorney Michael V. Smith, and Clive Short, the personal emissary of Nebraska governor J. J. Exon. AIM's leaders had developed a negotiating strategy based on our experience on the streets of America's big cities—the good cop/bad cop routine. When we dealt with bureaucrats and politicians, Clyde and Dennis would be the angry shouters. Later, I would come in as a soft-spoken nice guy. Lacking street savvy, political hacks and appointed officials would always be so relieved to deal with an obviously educated Indian that they would give us almost anything we wanted.

We demanded that the people who had killed Yellow Thunder be charged with murder and kidnapping, and that the county attorney seek the death penalty. We told the officials that we had permission from Yellow Thunder's sisters to have his body exhumed, and we demanded that it be examined by AIM's pathologist. We demanded that the cover-up of Yellow Thunder's murder be investigated by a federal grand jury, by Congress, and by the U.S. Department of Justice. We also demanded that the town fire a local cop whom several Indian women had charged as their rapist.

Smith, the county attorney, agreed to suspend him, turn over a copy of the coroner's report, attend AIM's autopsy, and join us in asking for investigations. He insisted that charges against the Hares and Bayliss would remain second-degree manslaughter and false imprisonment unless his investigation could develop evidence of murder. He also told us that several days earlier, police had questioned Jannette Thompson and Bernard Lutter. Both had agreed to testify against the others.

Gordon's schools got a lot of federal money through various programs, supposedly for educating Indian students. It had all been diverted to the benefit of white kids. We said that must come to a halt. We demanded that Indians be appointed to administer those funds and to review school curricula to eliminate racist texts and lessons. We also demanded that Indians be represented on the local police force, school board, city council, and chamber of commerce and have equal voting rights and whatever else might be needed for equal treatment. Gordon officials agreed to everything.

Our most important agreement was to create a biracial committee that consisted of local Indian people along with the chief of police, mayor, school superintendent, and hospital administrator. The committee would monitor racism in Gordon, making sure fair and accurate coverage of Indians was included in the local newspaper.

With a grant from the Native American Rights Fund, AIM arranged to have another pathologist examine Yellow Thunder's exhumed remains. So controversial and highly publicized was the case that nowhere in Nebraska or South Dakota could we find a doctor willing to do that. Eventually, we persuaded Dr. George I. Ogura, chief pathologist for the Denver coroner's office, to fly to Rapid City and examine the body. Along with him came NARF attorneys Bruce Greene and John Echohawk, a young, longhaired Pawnee who had been raised as a Mormon in Farmington, New Mexico.

Both attorneys were present, along with members of the victim's family, during the postmortem. The first pathologist's report said the cause of Yellow Thunder's death was a subdural hematoma—bleeding in the brain—caused by a blunt instrument such as a fist, boot, or tire iron, and death had occurred within two days of the injury. Every contemporary newspaper and wire-service account that reported the results of the second autopsy said it revealed nothing that the earlier procedure hadn't, but they were wrong. Newspaper stories also erroneously claimed that Dr. Jesse Samuels had performed the second autopsy, but he was merely a consultant to Dr. Ogura. Wire reports quoted Echohawk as saying he was satisfied that neither necropsy showed evidence of torture or mutilation—but the victim's family told me otherwise. They said they had seen discolored areas that appeared to be cigarette burns on Yellow Thunder's chest, stomach area, and thighs. Knowing the sensitivities of Yellow Thunder's shy and gentle sisters, I wondered if they said *thighs* because they couldn't bring themselves to say *genitals*.

As AIM's occupation of Gordon and the story of Yellow Thunder's humiliation at the American Legion dance made regional and national headlines, television crews began to swarm through town. Faced with the most damning incident in the community's eighty-seven-year history, the redneck Establishment went to extraordinary lengths to cast doubt and to explain away the facts. The *Gordon Journal,* like most small-town papers, survives on advertising from local merchants—among them several people who had attended the legion dance that night. The paper ran front-page stories and breast-beating editorials quoting whites who claimed to have attended the dance. The articles said that far from having been forced to dance, Yellow Thunder, naked from the waist down, had simply been shoved into the building through an outside door, and legionnaires had quickly gotten up from booths and tables to shield him from view. The articles also claimed that the incident lasted no more than thirty or forty seconds, and Yellow Thunder had been escorted outside immediately afterward. They claimed nobody had even attempted to interview any of the people who had witnessed the incident, and out-of-town reporters had simply embellished rumor and reported it as fact.

I heard the ugly truth from eyewitnesses, a couple of young white men who were decently ashamed that they had been at the dance and had done nothing to help Yellow Thunder. They came to city hall to tell us what they knew. Yellow Thunder had been forced to prance and shuffle for the amusement of the whites. The Gordon rednecks who tried to peddle their "it-never-happened" line of swill were simply perpetuating a local tradition inaugurated by their ancestors—the settlers who had taken possession of northern Nebraska's sandhill country in the 1880s, land stolen from the original Lakota reservation.

In 1890, those settlers had fed outrageous lies and half-baked rumors to newspapermen who then flocked to Pine Ridge to report on "Sioux unrest." The locals worked the reporters, feeding them whatever they wanted to hear so they would stick around to buy the town's goods and services at inflated prices. The rumors invented and spread in that way created hysteria about a wholly fictional "Sioux uprising" that brought thousands of federal troops, some from as far east as Chicago. The presence of all those armed soldiers and the continued outpouring of incredible rumors generated by rapacious merchants in Gordon and nearby towns led directly to the massacre of more than three hundred Indian people at Wounded Knee. Given that history, already familiar to Pine Ridge residents, the *Journal's* attempts to whitewash the Yellow Thunder affair were predictable and ridiculous.

After the Gordon city council gave in to our demands, AIM members and our supporters drove back to Pine Ridge in triumph. We felt that with so much publicity, the authorities would be obliged to make sure the killers of Raymond Yellow Thunder would at least get long prison sentences. Around Pine Ridge, everyone in AIM was treated as a hero. We were invited to address a packed house in Billy Mills Hall. It was an electric moment. I could feel pride and excitement and hope in the air and I was thrilled to realize that every person in the room—just about everybody who lived in Pine Ridge Village—was ready to join AIM and start to stand up for their rights.

21
▼▼▼▼▼▼▼▼▼

Red Ribbon
Grand Juries

Early in that spring of 1972, I joined an AIM contingent at Pine Ridge that caravaned to Denver and stayed a few days. We tried to boost our local membership and credibility by giving talks about what we had accomplished in Gordon, Nebraska. When I returned to Pine Ridge, I learned that there had been trouble at the Wounded Knee trading post, a store owned by Clive Gildersleeve and his son-in-law, Jim Czywczynski. Indian people who lived there didn't like the fact that the Gildersleeves, along with the Catholic Church, had turned the mass grave of Big Foot and the three hundred other victims massacred there in 1890 into a tourist attraction. Several cars caravaned from Pine Ridge for a demonstration and a confrontation with the owners. Newspapers reported some minor property damage to the trading post. BIA police were called. Most of those participating in the incident were locals who had become brave the first time they had someone to back them up, but the press reported that AIM was responsible. That made many Pine Ridge people angry at us.

White commercial exploitation of the mass grave provided a genuine reason for protest, but Indian people who lived near Wounded Knee and elsewhere on the reservation had long harbored a smoldering resentment toward the Gildersleeves and other whites who ran reservation trading posts.

For generations, white traders had ruthlessly abused Indian customers. Nowhere on Pine Ridge was there a grocery, drug, clothing, hardware, or convenience store. Whatever people needed, if it could be found at all, was at a trading post. Because that setup is so obviously tailor-made for profiteering, Congress requires whites who do business with Indians on or near reservations to obtain licenses from the Department of the Interior, with license fees going into a fund to benefit Indians. In theory, any kind of serious misconduct by a storekeeper could result in loss or suspension of his license, thus endangering his livelihood. The BIA has virtually failed to enforce that law since it was passed early in this century. The Gildersleeve family, among many others, had taken full advantage. They ran their trading post like the company store in a coal miners' town, abusing customers and treating them like retarded stepchildren.

The Gildersleeves inflated prices outrageously while encouraging customers to buy on credit, so nearly everybody in the community was in perpetual debt to the trading post. Many Indian people lived on welfare, Social Security, unemployment, or pensions, but the Gildersleeves wouldn't allow them to cash their checks. Instead, a white storekeeper would literally hang onto the check with two hands while an Indian endorsed it, then keep the proceeds, deducting a finance charge and applying the balance to the customer's account. Even Indians who *didn't* owe money couldn't cash checks: The Gildersleeves turned them away or forced them to buy goods equal to the value of the check. Indian people therefore never had cash and couldn't shop elsewhere, even when they had an opportunity to visit another part of the reservation or a border town.

Those practices were common on reservations. They became widely known in the late 1960s after publication of *My Brother's Keeper—The Indian in White America*, a book edited by Edward S. Cahn, which described many of the abuses committed by whites against Indians. The government was well aware that traders on Indian reservations held their communities in virtual economic bondage, but still the BIA did nothing to enforce congressionally mandated licensing.

AIM remained at Pine Ridge in force for five or six days while looking into some of the programs the so-called tribal government had at the reservation. We found that we had almost unconditional support from the old people, especially the traditional ones. We also had wide support and admiration from the younger generation, those in their teens, twenties, and early thirties, who loved what we stood for. People between youth and old age, those in their forties and fifties—the generation that had endured the boarding-school ordeal—had a very different view of AIM. Like all colonized people, their livelihoods and identities depended on the federal government, either from menial BIA jobs or through the puppet tribal government. For those people, jeopardizing their relationship with the feds meant putting their entire lives at risk, so they were suspicious of AIM and antagonistic toward our goals.

After our experience at Gordon, Dennis Banks had another brainstorm. Taking his suggestion, we decided to stay in South Dakota and caravan from reservation to reservation, holding public meetings to expose evidence of government abuse. Thanks mostly to AIM's 1969 challenges to the National Council of Churches in Detroit, mainstream churches had become responsive to community organizations and willing to fund certain projects, even on an emergency basis. That was how AIM usually got money to send out caravans. We also found that many Indian people would chip in.

Dennis dubbed our investigations the "Red Ribbon Grand Jury Hearing" Several people from the Community Relations Service of the U.S. Department of Justice joined us. The CRS ostensibly functioned as arbitrators between dissenters and government authorities, trying to prevent violence and working to facilitate negotiated settlements. The ones who came with us to the South Dakota reservations were great human beings, wonderful people whose continuing presence served temporarily to restore a bit of our faith in America's justice system. That restoration was, of course, a big mistake. It was also thoroughly Indian, and I make no apologies for it.

The first Red Ribbon Grand Jury was held at Pine Ridge where, as everywhere else, we took complaints in affidavit form. Then we drove east to the Rosebud Reservation, and held hearings in a hall lent by the Catholic Youth Organization. As we went along, we picked up more followers. Our caravan grew from about a dozen cars to more than fifty, plus several filled with newspaper reporters and camera crews. Heading east from the Rosebud to the Yankton Reservation, we held hearings at the Marty Mission, an enormous school complex run by the Catholic Church, a few miles north of Greenwood. It includes nearly the whole town of Marty. Next, we went to the Crow Creek Reservation on the Missouri River, then to Eagle Butte on the Cheyenne River Reservation. We finished in an auditorium in McLaughlin, a white town in the South Dakota portion of the Standing Rock Reservation.

Leonard Crow Dog opened each meeting with a pipe ceremony, which amazed many Indian spectators in those months of the rebirth of Indian spirituality. We sat in a circle on the floor and passed the pipe, as Indians always have. I was surprised at how many people my age and older didn't know how to hold the pipe or pray with it. Leonard usually had to instruct people, even many who were in their forties.

After the pipe ceremony, Dennis would open the proceedings with a talk; then I would speak. Both of us touched on the same points—Indian people should be proud of who they are, they should not be afraid, and they should come forward to tell their stories. Those pep talks were necessary because in 1972, Indian people in general—and those on reservations especially—were so beaten down by white authority that most feared to voice any complaints. When we started the hearings, our talks were long. It was hard to instill courage in those people. But as word of our hearings preceded us through Indian country, our talks got shorter and shorter. By the time we got to McLaughlin, neither Dennis nor I had to say more than a few sentences. We learned that the key to getting people to open up was to ask a few older women to start things off. Those grandmas feared nothing. As people came forward with complaints, several stenographers took down testimony in longhand. At some places, we were able to borrow a typewriter.

Most of the problems were about land. Even today, it is still the biggest problem on reservations. A common complaint was about ancestral property lost to scams aided and abetted—sometimes instigated—by BIA officials. Many reservation people had inherited land from parents or siblings, but often that meant a single parcel might have several owners, all relatives. Typically, all but one of those owners had been relocated to a city while the remaining one, usually a full-blood, lived on the land. The BIA often approached one of the city dwellers with an offer from some white rancher. For a pittance, a white got title. Sellers had been told that they were selling only their own fraction. Without warning, the owner living on the land was told that it had been sold and he must leave immediately. The law then was, and is now, that before land could be sold, buyers had to get the permission of *every* owner. If those occupying the land protested, however, the BIA either ignored them or claimed that all that was needed was the permission of a *majority* of owners. BIA officials often threatened people. If they didn't vacate the land immediately, they would lose their Social Security payments or their commodities food, or the state would take their children away. We heard those stories over and over, differing only in small details, at every reservation.

Along with a stream of horror stories about how trading-post proprietors were keeping whole communities in economic bondage, we heard many complaints about housing, especially from elders and traditional people. Most lived in dilapidated one-room shacks. For example, Charlie Red Cloud, grandson of the chief who forced the United States to beg his nation for peace in 1868, was to the BIA "the hereditary honorary chief" of the Lakota. Every time some big shot came out from Washington, Charlie Red Cloud was invited to put on his ceremonial clothing and a warbonnet and walk three miles to the BIA agency to shake the white man's hand.

In any other country, visiting "dignitaries" would travel to their host's official residence to pay their respects, but the BIA's Pine Ridge minions never took visitors to Red Cloud's dirt-floor hovel. He had to carry every drop of his drinking water from a well more than a mile away. When it rained, the roof leaked. Winter blizzards drove snow through the cracks between boards. Less than a hundred yards away, within clear sight—and smell—was a sewage pond overflowing with shit. Red Cloud, like Grandpa Fools Crow and Frank

Kills The Enemy and all the other respected elders who lived in the same miserable circumstances, was a man of such pride and integrity that he refused to beg the BIA for a better place to live.

After land and housing, the most common complaint of the Indian people was the cold, impersonal treatment that U.S. bureaucrats have made infamous. They have devised all sorts of dehumanizing ways to keep Indians in their places. Several people told horrific stories of relatives dying in hospital waiting rooms because they were forced to wait in line. Some went in suffering severe chest pains, had cardiac arrest, and died unattended in Indian Health Service waiting rooms. Others told of women going through miscarriages and bleeding to death while waiting to be seen by doctors and nurses who insisted on dealing on a first-come-first-served basis in cases of skinned knees, broken fingers, even common colds. This still happens today, although not as often.

Many Indians told us they could barely exist on welfare and wanted to work for their livings. Their only kinds of jobs available were as seasonal farm laborers. Even though their meager wages were paid in cash, those honest people reported the income. The BIA and the state deducted that amount from their welfare checks. No matter how hard they worked, they could never get more than survival wages. It was small wonder that with no financial incentive to work, many gave up and turned to drink. Hearing their stories, what touched our hearts and enraged our souls was that the white man relied on Indians' honesty to screw them. The whites even deducted the few dollars a month that some people got from mineral-lease payments. The Indians could never get ahead, never save any money, never break out of hand-to-mouth poverty and dependency.

Wherever we went, we also heard how viciously Indians were treated by their own people in tribal courts and jails. Again and again, we heard stories of helpless and harmless drunks brought in by the BIA's Indian police to be beaten bloody—not just one cop beating them, but often two or three at a time. On the Standing Rock Reservation, we heard testimony from a Hunkpaka Lakota grandmother, Mrs. Taken Alive, about how local white police had broken her arms, then arrested her for resisting arrest. That kind of thing had happened to me. While visiting the Rosebud Fair in 1971, Ted and I were worked over by a gang of BIA cops in a bar. Unconscious from the start, neither of us could recall the beating. A pal, Jimmy Claremont, said that when those thugs with badges found me on a barstool, they grabbed me by the hair and started to pound me. He said it was so bad that he stood there crying because he was powerless to help us.

Everywhere along our route, we heard bloodcurdling stories from young women and girls who had been raped by Indian men, then raped again by FBI agents or police supposedly investigating the crime. Victims said they

ABOVE: Crow Dog, the Brulé Lakota leader who fulfilled his vow and killed Spotted Tail for having failed his people by selling out to the white man. Crow Dog's great-great-grandson became AIM's spiritual adviser. *(South Dakota Historical Society)*

RIGHT: Red Cloud was the masterful political leader and military strategist who forced the United States to leave his territory. *(South Dakota Historical Society)*

RIGHT: Struck by the Ree, or Padaniapapi, a Dakota leader and headman and a relative of mine, made peace with the white man in 1858. *(South Dakota Historical Society)*

BOTTOM: General William Tecumseh Sherman led a contingent of military and civilian officials to Fort Laramie in July 1868. Having been defeated by Red Cloud and his defenders, Sherman agreed to every condition demanded by my ancestors and received nothing in return from the treaty signed at Fort Laramie. *(South Dakota Historical Society)*

ABOVE: Taken in October 1956, when I was sixteen, this was my senior class picture at San Leandro High School, in California. *(Author's collection)*

LEFT: Adele Fridhandler Levine was my high school social-sciences teacher in San Leandro, California. She changed my life and helped to steer me away from a troubled path. *(Courtesy Adele Levine)*

LEFT: My dad with (*left to right*) Bill, Ted, and Dace in Mission, South Dakota, in about 1961. (*Courtesy Lakota Harden*)

BOTTOM: Grandma Aggie—Agnes Frederick—was a grandniece of Struck by the Ree. This photo was taken in August 1963. (*South Dakota Historical Society*)

ABOVE: This is how Twila Smith looked at the Cheyenne River Reservation in January 1960, just before she went to Los Angeles on the relocation program. *(Courtesy Sherry Means and Twila Smith)*

RIGHT: Family friend Bill Memberto with *(left to right)* Grandma Twinkle Star (Mable Arconge), my mother, and Auntie Faith, in February 1965. *(Courtesy Lakota Harden)*

TOP: Betty, Sherry, Scott, and I in Cleveland, 1969. *(Courtesy Betty Sinquah Means Thunderhawk)*

BOTTOM: Peggy Phelps Means and I. *(Courtesy Peggy Phelps Means)*

OPPOSITE TOP: My daughter Veronica Renville at age sixteen. *(Author's collection)*

OPPOSITE BOTTOM: My daughter Sherry graduated with two B.A. degrees from the University of Minnesota in 1988. *(Courtesy Sherry Means)*

OPPOSITE RIGHT: My youngest daughter, Tatuye Topa Najinwin, was named for my late mother. Her name means Woman Who Stands Strong in the Four Winds. This is how she looked in 1994, at age fourteen, when she won the first of several South Dakota beauty contests and a National Science Foundation award. *(Author's collection)*

TOP: Tatanka, Nataanii Nez, and I at Chinle, Arizona, in November 1994. *(Author's collection)*

LEFT: Scott, with his chest covered with scars from his participation in several sun dances, as he appeared in 1994. *(Courtesy Scott Sinquah Means)*

OPPOSITE TOP: With my eldest son, Hank, in July 1994. *(Photo by Marvin J. Wolf)*

OPPOSITE BOTTOM: Gloria, Tatanka, and I at Porcupine, South Dakota, on the Pine Ridge Reservation, in 1986. *(Author's collection)*

OPPOSITE: When I joined an AIM march at Plymouth, Massachusetts, on Thanksgiving Day 1970, I didn't know I was going to give one of the best speeches of my life from the base of the statue of Massasoit. *(AP/Wide World)*

ABOVE: AIM seized BIA headquarters in Washington in November 1972 and held it for a week. We physically destroyed it and took tons of documents—and absolutely no one missed the BIA for six weeks. Can there be clearer proof that the BIA isn't needed? *(UPI/Bettmann Archive)*

OPPOSITE: When the Trail of Broken Treaties caravans came together in Minneapolis, in 1972, Hank Adams wrote the "Twenty Points" that we sought to present to the White House. A dozen years later, he accompanied me to Nicaragua. *(UPI/Bettmann Archive)*

BELOW: The week before the 1972 presidential election, more than 100 Indian people of all ages went to Washington to demand that the United States honor its Indian treaties. When the bureaucrats made us wait all day in the BIA auditorium but refused to work with us, we took over the building. *(UPI/Bettmann Archive)*

TOP: Dozens of Indian people went to Custer, South Dakota, to demand justice for the white killer of Wesley Bad Heart Bull, but the authorities refused to negotiate with us and sent riot police to attack unarmed men, women, and children.
(UPI/Bettmann Archive)

RIGHT: Carter Camp attended the AIM convention in July 1973, and on behalf of AIM, barred federal and state inspectors from our campsite.
(UPI/Bettmann Archive)

When I ran for president of the Oglala Sioux tribe in January 1974, Dennis Banks *(standing)* helped to tally the votes. I won—but Dick Wilson stole the election by stuffing ballot boxes. By the time I proved this two years later, the election of Al Trimble made my victory moot. *(UPI/Bettmann Archive)*

Andy Warhol created a series of
images of me in 1976. This one
was in a Los Angeles gallery
when I visited there with Peggy.
*(Photo by Linda Dietrick, courtesy
Peggy Phelps Means)*

William Kunstler *(center)* was
one of the attorneys who represented Dennis Banks *(right)* and
me at several trials in the 1970s.
(Courtesy Peggy Phelps Means)

were told to strip at hospitals and forced to submit while FBI agents fondled them or enjoyed a leisurely look at their private parts.

Day after day, I heard such stories, an unending river of horror. It came to me, long before the end of the Red Ribbon Grand Jury trail, that conditions were so extreme for Indian people that we were barely hanging on—our very survival was in doubt. I also heard that we were tired of that, very tired, and wanted to break out. We wanted to live. We wanted our children to aspire to lives of dignity. We wanted to be valued as human beings.

Hearing firsthand accounts of the most outrageous and shameful things I had ever heard enraged me. For a time, I had a death wish. I dreamed of going insane, taking an automatic weapon, and indiscriminately killing white people to make them feel the same fear and powerlessness they had inflicted on Indians. That was crazy thinking, but during those weeks I often voiced such thoughts. I wasn't the only one. We were all outraged by what we saw and heard. Dennis made several fiery speeches, inflaming every Indian in the audience until they were ready to get up right then and fight whites.

Fortunately, we all remained linked to our culture. Deep down, I felt that none of us could ever grab an assault rifle and start to kill people. I didn't think I could have worked myself into the state of mind that would have permitted me to shoot everyone in sight. We had our elders as living examples of how to endure a century of indignities without abandoning the humanity of our heritage. We shared the conviction that what goes around comes around; that we must each understand and embrace time and immortality; that we will survive and even prosper only as long as we maintain respect for our traditions.

Such notions didn't crystallize for me in those years, but our culture has always taught patience and optimism. AIM had its own axiom: When we chose to fight, *we* would pick the time and the battlefield. Because we knew we were right, we took heart in the justness of our cause and proceeded straight ahead in whatever we did without fear, certain that nothing bad could befall us.

2 2

▼▼▼▼▼▼▼▼▼

Schism

There was one bit of unfinished business from our Red Ribbon Grand Juries. We needed to ensure that the dozens of devastating affidavits we had collected would be used to help put an end to the abuses they documented. When I asked Dennis Banks what he had done with all that information, he said, "Oh, I turned it over to the Justice Department."

"Did you keep copies?"

"No."

I bit my tongue. "Who did you give all that stuff to?"

"Community Relations Service."

When I said I couldn't understand the logic of that decision, Dennis replied that the justice officials had promised to look over the material, make copies, and return the originals to us. They never did. What a surprise! A few years later, when I inquired at the Justice Department during the Nixon administration, I was told that our material had been "lost." I know the Indians' innate faith in the goodness of human nature and our belief in the spoken word have always been our Achilles heel, but I never want us to lose the simple beauty of believing in human beings and their promises. I continue to hope that someday—and it will not come without struggle—all those promises will be honored, and we will treasure our faith and the kind of people who have it.

Ted and I stuck around Pine Ridge for Dick Wilson's inauguration as president of the Oglala Lakota. I was surprised when he showed up in a crew cut. I thought, how sad—if only he would stick with his pride. Ben Black Elk, son of the famous holy man Black Elk, gave a talk just before Dick took the oath of office. I'll always remember Ben's words. He said, "It's time for us to quit being *Sioux*, a word that comes from another Indian nation and means 'cutthroat.' For too long, we've been acting like cutthroats toward one another. Now it's time for us to be Lakota, which means 'people together,' or allies. From this administration on, we should no longer be Sioux but become Lakota." Sadly, almost no one heard his talk, and the point of Ben's speech was lost to the Oglala under Dick Wilson's regime.

After a pipe ceremony concluded Wilson's inauguration, those in attendance were invited to the school cafeteria for a catered buffet. Everybody who was allegedly anybody in the Pine Ridge Establishment was there—people who had BIA supervisory jobs or who worked at the hospital or for the tribal council. I thought it curious that except for Ben Black Elk and his family, almost no full-bloods were present. I asked around and someone said, "Oh, they're down at the old gym." I decided that was where I wanted to be, so I left the buffet and walked over there. It was the first part of April and still cold outside, but a long line of shivering people stretched around the gym, people waiting to get food. I got behind the last person. When I finally got inside, I saw that in contrast to the expensive meal served at the cafeteria, the full-bloods were eating watery meat stew cooked in big outdoor vats, and bread fried in skillets over a trench fire. The building was so small that few of those old people could stay inside to eat. They ate outside in the cold; the few with vehicles sat in them.

It was such blatant segregation that it made me sick. Of course, everybody around that old gym knew what was going on. They mentioned it, they felt it. I'm sure the only people on the reservation who didn't realize something was very wrong were the ones who had come to wallow in Wilson's inaugural feed in the warmth and comfort of the cafeteria. That's usually the case with racists. They do what's natural to them, never thinking of the consequences to those they oppress. I had a vague premonition that what I had seen was an omen, an indication of how Wilson would treat people now that he held power over them.

After the inauguration, I went back to Cleveland for a time, and then to AIM's second annual convention at the Leech Lake Reservation, on Dennis Banks's reservation. In contrast to the adulation AIM leaders had received from people at Pine Ridge after returning from Gordon, the Leech Lake Ojibwa—they still called themselves Chippewa—held poor opinions of Dennis and Clyde. They believed all the negative accounts that had been published about Dennis and Clyde and about AIM in Minnesota newspapers. Clyde was constantly getting arrested and he and Dennis had served prison time; so the press mercilessly repeated that they were ex-cons, as if that somehow tainted everything they did, no matter how right they were, no matter how much they accomplished in trying to liberate their people. My heart went out to Dennis as he endured a cold reception from his own people. We wound up holding our meetings in a youth camp on a reservation lake, on land the tribe had leased to outsiders. They gave us electricity, but no hot water or heat, and early spring is mighty chilly in Minnesota.

Many South Dakota Indians, especially older ones, came to the gathering wanting to be part of AIM, to join those whom they now regarded as heroes. They caravaned to Minnesota on their own, about fifty or sixty from Pine Ridge alone. All told, our gathering attracted about 150 people. Among the Pine Ridge contingent were Wallace Chips and his son, Godfrey, who was in his early twenties. Both were medicine men who lived at Wanbli, South Dakota, which appears on white men's maps as Wanblee. During the Red Ribbon Grand Juries, Dennis had begun to consult them. Vernon and Clyde Bellecourt and I preferred to consult Leonard Crow Dog. When they all came together at Leech Lake, I was surprised and alarmed at the hostility and antagonism that I sensed among those medicine men.

Early in the convention, Godfrey invited us to a *yuwipi* ceremony. Those ceremonies are held in total darkness, a practice going back to the era when the white man outlawed our religion and made the practice of our prayer ceremonies punishable by imprisonment. Soldiers and later vigilantes or BIA Indian police patrolled our reservations day and night, looking for any sign that indicated we might be practicing our traditional ways, so we began to hold the *yuwipi* at night without lights. The ceremony is very involved and includes preparations before the lights go out. When they come back on, the rite is over except for a small ending ritual. Afterward, everybody drinks holy water and then usually shares a meal.

We arrived at the *yuwipi* hosted by Godfrey and found the place set with dishes for the feast afterward. Oddly, Leonard told everybody who supported him to sit close by. Then he told us quietly that when it got completely black, we were to cover our faces with our hands. He didn't say why, but a few seconds after lights-out, a cup or plate—something—came flying through the darkness and hit my knuckles hard enough to drive my hands into my face. In the blackness to my right, a woman screamed. The ceremony proceeded, but from time to time I heard more dishes shattering against the wall. A few times I heard a dull *conk* like the sound of someone being hit on the head, usually followed by a scream. In the dark, I heard Godfrey speaking in Lakota and his interpreters translating into English that "the spirits were angry" because there was "bad medicine" present. People were wishing bad things, so the spirits were fighting back and throwing dishes.

Sure they were!

When the prayer ceremony—actually, the dish-throwing ceremony—was over and the lights came back on, what was going on was obvious to everyone because all the crockery had been thrown in one direction, toward Leonard and his supporters. I saw that the woman who had screamed was a beautiful Osage girl with a wonderful, luminous complexion. Now her cheeks were bloodied with three scratches on each side—it looked as though someone with long, sharp fingernails had raked them. She was sobbing along with several other women who had been hit on the head with cups. Leonard and everyone who supported him stood up and left, and Godfrey Chips said, "The spirits were right. See—all the evil is leaving." Most of the people who got hurt were those who hadn't listened to Leonard or protected their faces. I was amazed that he knew what was going to happen before it did.

Leaving the *yuwipi*, I was stunned. I had been raised to revere elders. I thought they could do no wrong, that they lived lives of wisdom—and yet here were men from my own reservation, Wallace Chips and his son, defiling a holy ceremony to carry out a personal vendetta against a professional rival. Even worse, when we were alone, Leonard began to condemn the Chipses. Confused and devastated, I wouldn't respond. My mind raced, thoughts crowding in one against another. I wanted to say, "Why are you doing this? I don't understand. I thought you were supposed to have patience and wisdom and respect. My god—you're fighting a spiritual turf war! You're yielding to envy and jealousy. You're no better than Christians. Even worse, by fighting among ourselves, we help the white man to destroy us."

After that *yuwipi*, I was so listless that I even walked with a stoop. I couldn't go into the purification lodge. I couldn't do anything. I didn't have an answer to anything. But I was AIM's national coordinator, so I had to hold myself together to run the general meeting.

The next day, as everyone packed into the hall, rumors went around that Dennis was pissed off at those who still supported Leonard, and that Dennis's supporters had taken all the guns. Sure enough, he and some of the guys from Kansas and Oklahoma took over one side of the room, many of them carrying rifles. When I got up to talk, Dennis said, loud enough for everyone to hear, "You'd better choose your words very carefully." He said it in such a way that no one could doubt the meaning of what he had left unsaid: "*Or else.*" I found this deeply saddening. I was seeing that AIM had come down to issues of personalities and control, and the split was out in the open. Dennis, a Ponca named Carter Camp, and their supporters were backed by some Oglala people from Rapid City and Sisseton, South Dakota, who also favored the Chipses. On the west side of the room were those who favored Leonard, led by the Bellecourts. Clyde took the lead, backed by Vernon, in trading barbs with Dennis. From the center aisle in front of the room, I launched into a talk on unity. In an emotional, cracking voice, almost crying at times, I expressed my frustration and displeasure. I told everyone what I thought AIM stood for and that there was no place in it for backstabbing, infighting, or bickering.

Dennis responded by publicly condemning Leonard because he drank. It seemed that Dennis was anointing Godfrey and Wallace Chips as AIM's spiritual leaders. Leonard rose to his feet and replied emotionally. Tears rolling down his cheeks, he said, "I live my life the way I've been taught."

Soon after we had met, Leonard had told me that he was *Heyoka*. He said it only once, but traditional people expect others to listen. Such is their reverence for the spoken word that they don't anticipate repeating themselves. Nor do traditional people usually explain themselves. They expect others to use their brain and figure things out. When Leonard said he was *Heyoka*, I understood. It is an ancient tradition, a teaching mechanism among my people. *Heyoka* live contrary lives, doing everything they are not supposed to do. In my grandfather's time, they even walked backwards or rode their horses by mounting and facing to the rear. They obtain things in reverse order, and purify themselves while facing west instead of east. As much as possible, *Heyoka* conduct their whole lives contrary to the way people are supposed to live. Like the childhood stories Grandpa John had told me about the Trickster, *Heyoka* are backwards for positive reasons—to teach others that life can be contrary, and to show by example what others should avoid.

On this occasion, however, Leonard never mentioned that he was *Heyoka*, that his drinking was an integral part of the backwards life he had chosen. He didn't explain anything. He didn't apologize. Then Vernon rose to condemn Dennis. "You'd better watch your mouth," growled Dennis, bristling. As tension and barely restrained fury seethed through the room, I intervened again. We were headed toward open violence. I couldn't let that happen. I called for an adjournment.

During the next hours and days, I slid into a deep depression. AIM had changed my life, filled me with hope, given me the courage to quit drinking. I thought AIM could do no wrong, that we were perfect, the answer for dispossessed, disenfranchised, disrespected, and discouraged Indians everywhere. We were following the dictates of our ancestors. Now the feud between self-described "holy men" had laid bare our human frailties, our weaknesses, and our petty jealousies. If everything I had believed about AIM was a lie, if all our toil, risk, and sacrifice meant nothing, if reaffirming our connection to the ancient traditions was meaningless, then what would become of our people? I felt the blackness crushing my soul until it was hard to breathe like a free man.

"Works for the People"

AIM's takeover of Gordon, Nebraska, had focused media attention in that county on the Yellow Thunder case, and as a result, the trial of the Hare brothers a few months later was moved to Alliance, in neighboring Box Butte County. AIM wanted to go there in force to demonstrate its commitment to seeing justice done, but the split in the leadership made it imperative to separate our feuding factions temporarily. We decided to split into two caravans, with Dennis and his followers going west from Leech Lake through northern South Dakota and then through Pine Ridge. I drove through Minneapolis and then to Winnebago with the Bellecourts and their supporters.

We stopped in Winnebago to encourage people there to rally behind our cause. We went to private homes throughout the town and cleaned things up, removing fallen branches and dead trees from yards, trimming trees, and hauling away trash from streets. When we left town, several carsful of Indian people joined our caravan. Swinging north to Yankton, we picked up some Zephiers, then continued west through the Rosebud to pick up even more supporters. Finally we arrived in Alliance, Nebraska.

We met with a white preacher, a good man who worked with and helped the Indians in Alliance, and he told us their complaints. Then we met with the town fathers. As hundreds of Indians converged on Alliance, the town leaders agreed to some of our demands. They closed all bars and liquor stores during the trial, assured us that police would protect Indians while they were in town, established a community-relations council, let us use Bowers Field as a place to camp, and gave us a meeting place in the city auditorium. They balked, however, at donating money to help us buy food; the chamber of commerce turned us down flat.

The trial was close to my heart because Raymond Yellow Thunder was of my father's generation. He came from Pine Ridge, and he had many friends in common with my parents. I felt very bad for his family, which was represented in Alliance by two of his older sisters. Still showing animosity from the Leech Lake incident, Dennis Banks, Carter Camp, the Bellecourts, and other AIM leaders papered over our differences to present a united front as we met to plan our activities in Alliance.

West of the city is a big electricity-distribution complex that controls most of the city's power. I proposed that we shoot it up. I wanted to put Alliance in the dark, serving notice that we weren't leaving without justice for the Yellow Thunder family. Dennis and several others were against my proposal, fearing that we would all be arrested or that vigilantes would come out in force to pick off our women and children. There was no consensus, so my idea was voted down.

None of us believed that an all-white jury would convict the Hare brothers—or any white man—for killing an Indian in any racist western Nebraska community, so we developed a plan to deal with that eventuality. When the jury came in with "not guilty," I was going to assault the judge—no weapons, just my fists and feet. Other people chose their targets until we had everyone covered, including the prosecutor and all twelve members of the jury. We were going to kick ass until we all got dragged off to jail.

While that planning went on, tension from the Leech Lake incident was building steadily within AIM. One evening during the trial, visiting a church meeting hall that doubled as the Alliance Indian center, Dennis and I walked in to find several of the toughest, most dedicated AIM members, mostly guys from Oklahoma, pointing guns at Vernon. Apparently there had been an argument of some kind, and Vernon had said the wrong thing. He was pleading for his life. It looked as if they were going to shoot him at any moment. I didn't know what to say—I was stunned, speechless. Dennis defused the situation, but the whole thing made me feel sick inside. I was seeing AIM, and all that I had believed it to be, crumble before my eyes.

Somehow, we managed to focus on what had brought us to Alliance. When the trial started, we alerted the media that something heavy was going to happen when the verdicts were read, and we issued a statement that said, in part:

The American Indian Movement will take any and all steps to insure justice for our people. WE ARE PREPARED TO DIE FOR THESE BELIEFS AND, AS IN ANY WAR, WE ARE PREPARED TO TAKE THE OFFENSE TO INSURE OUR PEOPLE MAXIMUM PROTECTION.

The *Alliance Times Herald* printed much of our statement. Testimony in the Hares' trial lasted eight days and ended at about three on a Friday afternoon. Just six hours later, the jurors sent word that they had reached a decision. Fearing the worst, we packed as many AIM members into the courtroom as we could.

From my aisle seat, I looked over the courtroom and planned my route. The moment the not-guilty verdicts were read, I would vault the low railing, leap to one side of the judicial bench before the bailiffs could react, and take the judge down before he could escape through a side door.

Anxiety gripped the room in a steel vise as the jury foreman read the verdict—they were guilty of false imprisonment, guilty of manslaughter. A collective sigh fanned the courtroom, everyone exhaling at once. The judge continued bond so that the Hares could file appeals, and postponed sentencing until probation reports could be prepared.

We were overjoyed. It seemed that we had gotten what we came for. We thought the Hares would be sent away for years. We had no way of knowing that months later, at the end of August, the judge would fine each brother a paltry five hundred dollars on the false-imprisonment charge; Leslie Hare would be sentenced to just six years in prison and Melvin only two. Both would be treated with kid gloves, and put into protective custody to keep them away from the brutal "lifers" who ran things inside the Nebraska State Penitentiary. Killing Indians is still not widely disparaged in Nebraska, so Leslie would be paroled after just two years and Melvin after only ten months. Lutter subsequently pleaded guilty to unlawful imprisonment; the other charges against Lutter, Bayliss, and Thompson were dropped.

All that was far in the unseen future. After the verdicts came in, we headed back to Mission, South Dakota, on the Rosebud, and I started to drink again. I believed then that if AIM was less than the perfection I had imagined it to be, I didn't need to be perfect either. When I got to the Rosebud, I disappeared—from AIM and everything else—and went off the wagon. I drank in Mission's bars and in friends' homes. I bought booze in liquor stores and went out in the countryside to drink. I drove to Nebraska on Sundays and drank beer in border towns. On weekdays, I hit saloons in the counties surrounding the reservation. All that was because I was feeling disillusioned with AIM.

I couldn't handle the thought that AIM members could be petty, jealous, and spiteful. I wanted to get away from all that. While outwardly laughing and drinking and having a good old time, inside I was crushed and dying.

Everything I had lived for had come crashing down around me. I drank for two weeks, although it seemed much longer. Many people in AIM wondered where I was or if something bad had happened to me.

I might have gone on drinking many weeks longer, but a natural disaster forced me to sober up and start to deal with reality. On the morning of June 9, 1972, to the surprise of local weather forecasters, enormous dark clouds formed over the Black Hills. There were only a few sprinkles in Rapid City, but bolts of angry lightning creased the skies above our sacred *Paha Sapa,* and great curtains of cleansing water washed every hillside. In a little more than two hours, fourteen inches of rain drenched the watershed above Rapid City, creating a lake behind the earthen dam on the west end of Rapid Creek, which runs through the middle of town. Just after dark the dam burst, sending walls of muddy water surging from every draw and gulley. By the time the great flood had subsided late the next day, at least 260 people were dead or missing, and property damage in Rapid City amounted to $60 million. In the Black Hills, the federal government fixed losses at $105 million—precisely the amount we Lakota had refused to accept a few years earlier in settlement of our claim. The unprecedented catastrophe occurred almost exactly a year after Clyde and I, among others, had been dragged off Mount Rushmore. Lizzie Fast Horse and other elders who had predicted that the white man would pay for defiling our sacred mountain did not think it was a coincidence.

AIM was the first organization of any type to respond to the disaster. While the waters raged, my brother Ted and dozens of AIM members from Rapid City were helping survivors. They saved the lives and salvaged the property of whites and Indians. We even rescued some Red Cross workers and National Guardsmen. We never got any credit for helping. There was never a word in the *Rapid City Journal* about our hard work, or even about the guys who had risked their lives to pull people out of the water.

After Nixon had appointed Louis Bruce as commissioner of Indian affairs, he brought in his new team. The guy who got us out of jail in D.C. when we tried to arrest John O. Crow—Ernie Stevens, a Wisconsin Oneida and former head of the Los Angeles Indian Center—became head of economic development. Lee Cook, a Minnesota Ojibwa who later became president of the National Congress of American Indians, ran Indian education. Sandy McNab, a Micmac from Maine, was in charge of transportation. There were others very friendly to AIM and very dedicated to change. At Bruce's direction, AIM was provided with free office space and telephone service in the BIA building in Washington. Dennis established our national headquarters there. I knew Ernie Stevens from my basketball days in Los Angeles, so I went to D.C. and met with him and the others.

*   *   *

The era of the 1960s and early 1970s, in terms of social promise and progress, was an exciting time in America. All kinds of people were organizing in dissent and talking euphorically—if prematurely—about liberty, one of the few times such a profound movement had arisen in America since the Revolution. These new visionaries attempted to release themselves from the authoritarianism that had pervaded the country in the 1950s. Its roots went back to the early nineteenth century and the rise of big business. Many young white women were trying to become "liberated," and there was, of course, "free love." It was the best of times, but it was also the most dangerous. I once observed an antiwar demonstration at Case Western Reserve University, a Cleveland school largely for rich white kids. When I saw mounted police running down students, and cops attacking demonstrators with fire hoses and dogs, beating unarmed kids and dragging them off to jail, I knew the government didn't care how rich you were. As far as Nixon's America was concerned, once people were labeled "antisocial," they were a menace and had to be rubbed out.

The day after that demonstration, somebody, maybe some Case chemistry students, blew the head off a campus replica of Rodin's *The Thinker*—one of only four in the world. They left a sign hanging from where the neck had been: "I sat here thinking about the Vietnam War . . . and it blew my mind." I thought, how fantastic what youth could conceive and accomplish! Responsibility for that explosive act of defiance was never fixed, but the Weather Underground, a group of mostly upper-middle-class students who bombed government buildings to protest the war in Vietnam, issued a public denial that it had done the deed. That started us thinking. AIM decided to get in touch with every other dissident group we could find. We established contact with the Weather Underground, the Black Panthers, the Young Lords, a Puerto Rican freedom movement, a militant Chicano organization known as the Brown Berets, and the National Lawyers Guild, a small group of mostly young, mostly Jewish revolutionaries. Those contacts, reported by informers, led the Nixon administration to label AIM covertly as one of America's top "terrorist" groups.

That was also the era of the Youth International Party, known as Yippies. They were another breed entirely—wild, anti-Establishment revolutionaries who had come together with the so-called Chicago Seven in 1968 to disrupt the Democratic National Convention in Chicago, and had got beaten bloody in a police riot. They were arrested and tried on all sorts of outrageous charges. Everyone thought of them as crazed, dope-smoking hippies—they actually ran a pig for president—but mostly, Yippies wanted to disrupt things and turn government upside down. They established a loose connection with AIM. I wish the Yippies were still around. They were a massive storehouse of everything we needed, including information. It was unbelievable what information they had.

Virtually every federal department and bureau, down to the most obscure little backwater bureaucracy, had its own telephone credit-card number. Somehow the, Yippies got hold of them—*all* of them. You would think if you ripped off information like that, you would pass it clandestinely. The Yippies handed out numbers like confetti, literally offering them to people on the street, saying, "Here's a couple of credit-card numbers, feel free to make some gratis phone calls." Soon, even people in Canada were using U.S. government credit cards. The Yippies did a good job of disrupting the government. I'll always believe that the reason Nixon ran up so much debt that year wasn't because of the Vietnam War; it was the Yippies and their phone calls! They offered AIM any numbers we wanted, so we chose the FBI's credit cards because, we said, FBI meant "full-blooded Indian."

In those days, before everybody in government and industry had a computer on his desk, it took the feds months to correct that snafu. Meanwhile, everyone in AIM had free access to long-distance phoning. We got a lot of work done. In the process of making those calls—always believing in the justness of our cause and never thinking that our movement was trying to do anything that would invite savage retaliation—we provided FBI officials with what they supposed was a complete list of every contact, every supporter, every friend and relative that AIM and its members had. They investigated for years to ascertain who was who, never knowing that we and the Yippies had also made thousands of bogus calls to numbers chosen at random from telephone books around the country.

When we crisscrossed South Dakota during the Red Ribbon Grand Juries, I began to think, *here* is where the war is happening, here on the reservations, not in the cities, here where my land and my culture are, where my people live. Even though we were doing a good job at the Cleveland American Indian Center and at similar places in other cities, it was clear that Indian people on reservations were suffering the most and needed help most urgently. I resolved to go back to Cleveland and stay just long enough to resign. That decision solved another problem for me. By that time, mid-1972, I had been gone so much on AIM business that even my strongest supporters in Cleveland were annoyed with me. I began to feel that it was time to make a choice between AIM and the Indian Center. I chose home and AIM.

Dace was still living on the Rosebud, working as a BIA surveyor in a dead-end job that was abolished and renewed every six months. Steady, dependable, and conscientious, Dace was probably the best surveyor in the department, but he never got a raise from GS-3 entry-level wages. Because he was a "temporary" employee, he got no benefits either. At about the time I returned to South Dakota, Dace's marriage was rapidly deteriorating, and he had met Paula, whom he later married.

When I returned to Pine Ridge, I found virtually no housing available.

Even today, more than twenty years later, there still isn't any. I went back home to find overcrowding so severe that as many as thirteen people were living in one small cabin—or rather, sleeping in it and then getting out in the morning because there was no place to stay unless everyone carefully lay down in his or her allotted place and didn't move. No wonder there were people living in abandoned car bodies! It's the same on all reservations. There is no place for the younger people. They must either leave or accept total dependency on the BIA.

When I couldn't find anywhere to live, Severt Young Bear offered to let me stay in an old log cabin near his home in Porcupine. His family cleaned it up so I could move in. On the other side of a nearby creek was an old empty house. Eventually I got it into livable condition and moved in.

After moving back to Pine Ridge, I made contact with the Legal Aid office there. Gary Thomas, a young Texan, headed the office. He and Mario Gonzalez, who was fresh out of law school and clerking while he studied to pass the South Dakota bar exam, let me use their phone and establish an ad hoc AIM office there.

Without any steady income, I lived by my wits. Every once in a while, I would get a paid speaking engagement, or somebody would have me give a talk and would pick up my expenses. Everyone I knew and a lot of people I didn't know were chipping in and helping out. To this day, I don't quite understand how I got by, except that my people took care of me, as they still do. For a while, I had a car that I had brought from Cleveland. One night while it was parked outside my brother Dace's house, some hang-around-the-fort Indians in a pickup came along and deliberately smashed it up.

I was in and out of the Legal Aid office nearly every day, meeting many people who came there looking for help. One was a very elderly lady who lived alone in an old log cabin down by the creek in Pine Ridge Village. She had no glass in her windows—they had all been broken out. For more than five years, she had been trying to get the glass replaced. In desperation, she came to the Legal Aid office. When I went to her place and saw the cardboard she had tacked up, I knew it would never keep out the winter cold. I took her to see a white BIA social worker, a big, fat fifty-something woman who had been at Pine Ridge practically her whole adult life. She barely listened to my request that she help this Lakota grandmother. She turned us down flat and treated us like dirt. "I told you we don't have the money!" she snapped.

I went back to Legal Aid and called Sandy McNab in Washington and told him about the situation. Then I called Lee Cook and Ernie Stevens and told them the same thing. I don't know who came through for us, but the next day a BIA truck was down by the creek and that obese social worker was there, dripping sweat and swinging a hammer. She had been ordered to install those windows herself. She hated my guts, but after that, if I brought her someone with a problem, she would do whatever we asked. As word went around the reservation that I had connections in D.C., I soon had a bigger clientele than Mario and Gary did. We got many things done for the people of Pine Ridge. The officials I knew in the BIA were responsive. When I didn't know whom to call or couldn't get the right person, I would ask Dennis, and he always knew just whom to go to.

As long as we didn't talk about spiritual things—and we made it a point not to—there was little friction between Dennis and me. I occasionally went to Washington and visited the AIM office. It was great fun watching, and suggesting what memos Dennis should write to the commissioner. He also lobbied the federal agencies and both houses of Congress on Indian legislation, and quickly learned that wading through the bureaucracy was for dummies. AIM's policy of starting at the top and moving down expedited our work. To this day, I believe that's the way to deal with the white world.

We learned how to handle the bureaucrats who control the money. We went in first thing in the morning, at about 9:10, before the head of the particular department could find time to relax with his first cup of coffee or his first drink of the day. He was usually still hung over from the night before and was very impatient. When we would start to snow him with facts and figures and statistics he didn't want to hear, he would say, "Yeah, sure, whatever you want," and sign off on our project. In that way, Dennis was able to get a few reservation programs funded, get various agencies to ease up on land-use restrictions, and get them to funnel a little money to certain schools and reservation highway repairs. If he had waited until after 10:00 A.M. to make his pitches, it would have been a different story. By then everyone had had his first drink and turned into a full-fledged asshole.

Within a few months, however, it was obvious that despite many tiny accomplishments, things weren't changing at all for most Indian people. Dennis began to realize that the conspiracy against Indians always centers on land. It was easy to talk about upgrading services and maybe to get some slight improvement in the BIA's responsiveness on one reservation or another, but never for more than a month or a week. There was no way to get Congress or a federal agency to change policies on anything related to our land. That subject was closed.

Dennis found an impenetrable wall protecting secrets that he wasn't supposed to know even existed. His frustration was so obvious that whenever I saw or called him, I teased, "I don't know how you can stand it up here at the brick wall." When you pound your head against a wall trying to get something done, one of two things happens: Either you pound so long your brains turn to mush, or you realize it hurts and back off. When Dennis couldn't stand it anymore, he moved to Minneapolis and then to Pine Ridge.

No matter how little was accomplished in Washington, my presence and the small things I was able to do around the reservation were appreciated, especially by the elders. At Porcupine on the weekend of the Fourth of July, I received my third name. Among my people, I would now be known as Oyate Wacinyapi, "Works for the People." To celebrate the event, there was a ceremony with dancing, songs, and a giveaway, when I presented gifts to everyone attending. I was pleased to see Dennis there, because we were sort of at odds and had been staying away from each other.

Some older ladies, staunch AIM supporters from Wanbli, in the north-eastern part of the reservation, came to my naming celebration just to warn me. They had recently attended another religious event, at which Wallace Chips had predicted that I would be killed soon. I hardly knew the Chipses and had not even spoken to them since returning to Pine Ridge, but I vividly recalled the flying dishes of the Leech Lake *yuwipi*. I knew they were ambitious people who would go to great lengths to justify their black-magic mumbo jumbo. I had to believe that someone might try to kill me.

I sought out Alfonso Good Shield, a medicine man in Porcupine, and told him about the prediction. I had never met a holy man like him before nor have I since. All his medicine came from the daytime, so he did not practice *yuwipi*. Alfonso took me behind a hill above Porcupine and sat on the ground with his back to me, praying in Lakota. For a moment, my attention wandered. I watched a spider crawling nearby. With his back still turned, he said, "Pay attention! Concentrate." That blew me away.

When he had finished the ceremony, Alfonso told me to remove my shirt and stand up. After I did so, he walked completely around me once. Quite suddenly, he bent down and began to suck hard at a spot just above my left kidney. For a minute or two, he alternately sucked and spat something onto the ground. Alfonso stopped as abruptly as he had started, and told me to sit down and put my shirt on. When I had done so, he said, "That's where you are going to be shot. But you'll be all right."

24
▼▼▼▼▼▼▼▼▼

The Trail of
Broken Treaties

Before the white man came, we Indians had no chiefs. We had leaders, of course, men and women chosen by consensus for their wisdom and courage. The idea of a pyramidal hierarchy with a single person at the top was European. When whites first demanded to speak to a "chief," my ancestors didn't quite know how to respond. They pushed somebody out in front as spokesman—not necessarily the brightest or the bravest guy around, just someone willing to talk to the strangers and find out what they wanted in our country. But as far as the whites were concerned, he was our monarch, a sort of petty king, and therefore entitled to special privileges. That didn't always serve our best interests, but we have been stuck with chiefs ever since, and we try to make the best of it. Our chiefs don't rule. When important issues arise, they meet, discuss, seek consensus among themselves, and then tell the people what they think ought to happen.

Other leaders who represent their communities and who consult with the elders and among themselves are called headmen. After my naming ceremony, I was asked to a house in Porcupine, where the seven chiefs met to select new headmen. Conferring among themselves, they honored Birgil Kills Straight, Severt Young Bear, Ed Fills The Pipe, John Attack Him, and me with a ceremony that confirmed us as headmen. I was greatly honored to be chosen at so young an age. I went off to the sun dance feeling even more determined to serve my people.

After the sun dance, feeling very spiritual and free, I joined an AIM leadership meeting in Moccasin Park, south of Pine Ridge. The animosity between Clyde and Dennis surfaced again, this time in a shouting match. I was so disappointed about that kind of negativity that I resigned as national coordinator. There was no talk of electing a replacement, so that left AIM without someone to coordinate the activities of its different chapters. It didn't seem to make much of a difference, since each had always pretty much done its own thing and asked for help only when it was needed.

I wanted to go to the annual Rosebud Fair on the last weekend in August, but I had business elsewhere and couldn't. Dennis Banks was there, along with Robert Burnett, former chairman of the Rosebud Sioux. They organized an informal meeting that was attended by dozens of Indian people from reservations and cities around the country. We had heard nothing from the Department of Justice's Community Relations Service about the affidavits that AIM's Red Ribbon Grand Juries had gathered the previous spring, so they decided at the meeting it was time to dramatize the condition of America's Indians and to shame the federal government into doing something meaningful. Out of those discussions came the idea to take as many Indian people as we could to Washington, D.C., and air our complaints at the BIA. Detailed planning was deferred until a meeting in Denver three weeks later. I was invited to that gathering.

I drove over with my cousin Dennis, son of my dad's twin brother, Johnny. On the way, we each resolved to quit drinking, at least until the trip to Washington was over. Denver had been chosen as the meeting site because it was home to several other Indian organizations that we had invited to join us, but no one except Burnett and AIM members showed up. About eight of us met in a hotel suite for discussions that lasted two days. By the time we adjourned, we had agreed to call our planned trip the "Trail of Broken Treaties," focusing attention on the two hundred years of lies and empty promises our people had received from the United States. We decided to start caravans from Los Angeles, San Francisco, and Seattle, stopping to pick up more supporters and converging in Minneapolis/Saint Paul. From there, we would go to Washington in one big caravan. Dennis Banks was to organize a group leaving from San Francisco, visit Indian country in central California, Nevada, and Utah, then meet me in South Dakota. George Martin, from California was to leave from Los Angeles and recruit from there and Arizona, New Mexico, and Oklahoma.

My job was to lead the caravan leaving from Seattle, which would stop in Washington and Montana on our way to South Dakota. Since the 1950s, the Indian nations of the Northwest had been involved in a struggle over fishing rights. The treaties they had made with the United States in the 1850s had ceded vast tracts of Indian land. Fish—especially salmon—was as vital to their livelihoods as the buffalo had been to my ancestors, so the treaties forever reserved to Indians the right to fish taken from the rivers and lakes of Washington and Oregon. As the white man built hydroelectric dams and raped our Grandmother the earth with toxic pollution and overfishing, the salmon, which once had seemed an inexhaustible resource, became scarce.

Instead of changing their greedy ways and cleaning up their filth, Washington and Oregon officials, under pressure from white commercial and sport fishermen, began to arrest Indians who fished without licenses or who violated state laws in conflict with treaty rights. Indians who continued to assert fishing rights were assaulted by cops and game wardens. The most notable confrontations came at Frank's Landing, at the mouth of the Nisqually River near Puget Sound. The conflict had gotten national publicity in the 1960s when actor Marlon Brando came to show his support for the treaty rights of the Puyallup, Tulalip, Nisqually, and Yakima Indians.

Members of the Survival of American Indians Association, especially its brilliant president, Hank Adams, had led the struggle for fishing rights. The members were receptive to the idea of joining us in a caravan to Washington, D.C. Hank was about my age, a midsized fellow with a slight build, a part Dakota from the Fort Peck Reservation, in Montana. He lived near Olympia, Washington, and had married a woman from one of the Washington state Indian nations. Author and lawyer Vine Deloria Jr. calls Hank one of the greatest Indians of this century.

Hank sent his right-hand man, Sid Mills, to meet me at the Seattle airport. Sid is about five years younger than me, a Yakima/Cherokee and a highly decorated Vietnam veteran. He took me to Frank's Landing, where we held a press conference to announce the Trail of Broken Treaties. Our journey, we explained, would forge a trail across the whole country, through the lands that had been stolen from us by 371 solemn agreements, each ratified by Congress and proclaimed by the president as the law of the land. The United States had yet to live up to any of them, so we were going to confront the people responsible for Indian affairs in this country and ask them when they were going to start.

We departed downtown Seattle with four cars, including a green van. When we got to the summit of a pass through the Cascade Range above the city, we pulled off into a roadside park. We had brought two big sheets of plywood and on them we painted signs, red against a white background—"Trail of Broken Treaties, United States." It showed the three caravan routes, where they would converge, and our route into Washington. Hanging one on each side of the van, we let the paint dry as we drove across the state to Spokane. We held another press conference in the Yakima Indian community. Many of those impoverished people contributed small sums of money, and another car with three or four people joined us. Several others, who had things to take care of before they could leave town, promised to catch up with us before we got to Washington. Most of them did.

I rode in the lead van with Sid and the others from the Survival of American Indians Association. We used walkie-talkies to stay in touch with several Indian auto mechanics who brought up the rear. Whenever a car broke down—which was constantly—we got it off the road and found rides for its passengers while the mechanics fixed it. We traveled slowly and stayed together.

We had to raise money for gas and food as we went along. At each place we spoke, people came forward to donate cash or something we needed. We met with local church groups, Indian organizations, and Indian nations to see what they could give us. People called ahead to folks they knew and asked them to put us up for a night. We slept in church basements and often dined on little more than fried bread or rice or beans, but somehow the Great Mystery always provided. By the time we reached Montana, we had more than a dozen cars and a bus—more than eighty people.

We "overnighted" at an Indian girls' school in Missoula. After we spoke there and at the Indian center, many students from the University of Montana joined us. Quite a few other people came with us or said they would meet us farther along the trail. We stopped at Butte, and at Montana State University in Bozeman, and at Eastern Montana University in Billings. At each place, college kids joined up. Those young people were very adventurous, like most their age. Being among so many AIM supporters made them even bolder. When our caravans stopped for gas or to do some "AIM shopping," local residents sat up and took notice. Unlike most Indians of that day, we were rough-looking types with long hair and braids, wearing vests festooned with buttons, and red berets or bandannas. We were always polite, but most white people assumed we were terrorists and stood back. I was always amazed that they wouldn't lift a phone to call the cops while our guys came out of their stores with new jeans, shirts, gloves, axes, candy, soft drinks, chips— even coin boxes from soda-pop coolers. Everything that wasn't nailed down went into someone's jacket or pants pocket. We did that with clear consciences: We were repossessing, in another form, that which had been taken from us. As Clyde often said—and it took a lot of balls to say that to white men in those days—"We're the landlords of this country, and we're here to collect our overdue rent."

When we arrived at the Crow Indian Reservation, southeast of Billings, the tribal leader officially welcomed us. We stayed in a gymnasium in the tribal headquarters complex. One of the young guys who came with us from Seattle was a sculptor who had brought welding equipment and a piece of steel plate. At the Crow reservation he made a plaque to honor the defenders of the Lakota and Cheyenne Nations who had fought in what whites call the Battle of the Little Bighorn, in that Montana valley where Custer got his "sensitivity training" in 1876. The Crows got excited about that. Several Crow scouts, including Curley, White Man Runs Him, Hairy Moccasin, Goes Ahead, Half Yellow Face, and White Swan, had been with Custer, but had left before the battle when they realized it was suicidal to stay. The sculptor included their names on the plaque. Some Crow people found a mason to build cement forms, and others volunteered to help us put the plaque on a column.

The next morning, we got cement and water, took the plaque, and, with almost twenty cars, drove to what was then called the Custer Battlefield Monument. I'm pretty sure it's the only memorial the National Park Service ever built for a loser; there isn't even one for Robert E. Lee. The Park Service superintendent, a middle-aged white man, came out to meet us, and we told him what we were going to do. Almost in tears, he begged us not to put up our monument, promising that he would ask the National Park Service to build an appropriate memorial commemorating the Indian dead and their valiant stand. There were so many Indians present that he couldn't have stopped us from putting up our marker, but he seemed sincere, so we took pity on him and left.

Until then, AIM had been little more than rhetoric. We had taken over a few small towns and public buildings; we had collected some "back rent" from merchants; but we had yet to break even a window and had been arrested for nothing other than sit-in demonstrations. Even so, we were known as "militants." We tried to make the Trail of Broken Treaties an all-Indian project. After leaving the West Coast, AIM became a minority among those involved in or supporting the project, but we had a tough time getting the pan-Indian aspect of the caravan across. We had planned the event, and of all the other participating groups, only the Survival of American Indians Association continued to identify itself separately from us. Nevertheless, until we reached eastern Montana, we had complete cooperation everywhere. Each state's highway patrol and police agencies received us with open arms.

Nonetheless, as we moved across the country, the BIA circulated an internal memo warning that we were an AIM caravan out to stir up trouble. We found that out as we left Crow country for the adjacent Northern Cheyenne Reservation and a BIA school in the town of Busby, Montana. We had called ahead, and school officials gave us permission to speak to the children. But Busby's principal must have read the BIA memo: When we arrived, he barred us from classrooms and other buildings, including dorms.

It was, however, a big campus with many low structures housing junior-high and high-school students—without fences. We pulled into an open area on the grounds and announced on our loudspeaker that we were going to give a talk right there. Within minutes, Indian kids began to climb out of classroom windows. One high schooler with more guts than sense got hold of a BB gun and held his teacher at bay until all the kids got out, then followed them. At least two-thirds of the student body swarmed into the sunlight to hear our speeches. The kids loved it. Some of the older ones wanted to go with us to Washington, but we couldn't take people younger than eighteen unless they were escorted by a parent or had written consent naming a specific guardian. Nevertheless, long before we got to D.C., some of the adults in our caravan were appointed guardians of youngsters. Eventually, we had people of all ages, from babes in arms and mothers-to-be to elders well into their eighties.

We stopped at the far edge of the Northern Cheyenne Reservation, in Ashland, Montana, at the infamous Saint Labra Catholic School for Indian Children, one of the world's most proficient beggars. For decades, the school had solicited contributions for the Catholic Church, one of the richest institutions in the world, by using direct-mail campaigns. The school offered pseudo-Indian trinkets made by students' slave labor in exchange for donations. Those were the people AIM had helped to expose at the welfare workers' convention in Chicago a few years earlier, the ones using fifty-year-old photos of reservation children to milk money from well-meaning contributors, but never giving a dime to Indians. We had picked up a few more carloads of people at the Crow and Cheyenne Reservations, and so, with more than a hundred people, we were a formidable caravan when we pulled into the Saint Labra school. The Christian fathers being what they were, they wrote us a check for one thousand dollars in lieu of letting us speak to their kids. That was ten times what the impoverished Crows and Northern Cheyenne could afford. We knew exactly how the school had got that money, so we were happy to take it for an all-Indian cause.

Our next stop was Pine Ridge Village, where at the junction of Highway 18, we met Dennis Banks with six or eight cars, just rolling in from San Francisco. By that time, we had raised a few thousand dollars, Dennis a few hundred. We merged into a single caravan and turned all the money over to Robert Free, a short, light-skinned man from one of the New Mexico Pueblo nations, who managed our funds along the rest of the trail. At the Rosebud, we did more recruiting, starting with a meeting in the Catholic Youth Organization building.

By the time we rolled into the state fairgrounds at Saint Paul, Minnesota, we numbered more than three hundred. Dennis and the other AIM leaders left the caravan to attend to other matters. Until Dennis rejoined us in Washington, D.C., I became AIM's representative on the trail. During our stay at the fairgrounds, more Indians joined us, including people from Oklahoma and Kansas. We broke up into workshops to tackle our major concerns—the federal courts, tribal government, treaties, international law, land rights, fishing and hunting rights, all the issues facing Indian people. As each of our concerns was voiced, the workshop moderator wrote down suggested solutions. Those filled a file cabinet, which we gave to Hank Adams. I learned then that he is a genius at analyzing problems and interpreting the Indian outlook vis-à-vis the Eurocentric male worldview. Hank shut himself in a motel room for forty-eight hours and produced a twenty-point document summarizing our key issues.

A SUMMARY OF THE TWENTY POINTS

1. Restoration of Constitutional Treaty-Making Authority: This would force federal recognition of each Indian nation's sovereignty.

2. Establishment of a Treaty Commission to Make New Treaties: Reestablishes all existing treaties, affirms a national commitment to the future of Indian people, and ensures that all Indians are governed by treaty relations without exception.

3. An Address to the American People and Joint Sessions of Congress: This would allow us to state our political and cultural cases to the whole nation on television.

4. Commission to Review Treaty Commitments and Violations: Treaty-based lawsuits had cost Indian people more than $40 million in the last decade alone, yet Indian people remain virtual prisoners in the nation's courtrooms, being forced constantly to define our rights. There is less need for more attorney assistance than for an institution of protections that reduce violations and minimize the possibilities for attacks on Indian rights.

5. Resubmission of Unratified Treaties to the Senate: Many nations, especially those in California, have made treaties that were never ratified. Treaty status should be formalized for every nation.

6. All Indians To Be Governed by Treaty Relations: Covers any exceptions to points 1, 2, and 5.

7. Mandatory Relief against Treaty Violations: Federal courts to automatically issue injunctions against non-Indians who violate treaties, eliminating costly legal delays.

8. Judicial Recognition of Indian Right to Interpret Treaties: A new law requiring the U.S. Supreme Court to hear Indian appeals arising from treaty violations.

9. Creation of Congressional Joint Committee on Reconstruction of Indian Relations: Reconfiguration of all committees dealing with Indian affairs into a single entity.

10. Land Reform and Restoration of a 110-million-acre Native

Land Base: Termination of all Indian land leases, reversion of all non-Indian titles to land on reservations, consolidation of all reservation natural resources under local Indian control.

11. Restoration of Rights to Indians Terminated by Enrollment and Revocation of Prohibition Against "Dual Benefits": An end to minimum standards of "tribal blood" for citizenship in any Indian nation, which serves to keep people with mixed Indian ancestors from claiming either heritage.

12. Repeal of State Laws Enacted under Public Law 280: Eliminates all state powers over Indians, thereby ending disputes over jurisdiction and sovereignty.

13. Resume Federal Protective Jurisdiction over Offenses against Indians: Since state and local courts have rarely been able to convict non-Indians of crimes against Indians, Indian grand juries should have the power to indict violators, who will then be tried in federal courts.

14. Abolition of the Bureau of Indian Affairs: The BIA is so much a prisoner of its past that it can never be expected to meet the needs of Indians. Better to start over with an organization designed to meet requirements of new treaties.

15. Creation of an Office of Federal Indian Relations and Community Reconstruction: With one thousand employees or fewer, this agency would report directly to the president and preserve equality between Indian nations and the federal government.

16. Priorities and Purpose of the Proposed New Office: The previous agency would address the breakdown in the constitutionally prescribed relationship between the United States and the Indian nations.

17. Indian Commerce and Tax Immunities: Eliminate constant struggles between Indian nations and the states over taxation by removing states' authority for taxation on reservations.

18. Protection of Indian Religious Freedom and Cultural Integrity: Legal protection must be extended to Indian religious expression, and existing statutes do not do this.

19. National Referendums, Local Options, and Forms of Indian Organization: An appeal to restrict the number of Indian organizations and to consolidate leadership at every level.

20. Health, Housing, Employment, Economic Development,

and Education: Increased funding, better management, and local control.

We intended to present the document to the bureaucrats and lawmakers who made Indian policy in Washington, and to press them to commit to a timetable that spelled out when each of the twenty points would be implemented.

From the Twin Cities we went to Milwaukee, picked up more people, and went south around Lake Michigan to Indianapolis. With Indian country mostly behind us, our caravan started to pick up speed. Highway patrol cars shepherded us through each state on the interstates. We rolled into Washington, D.C., with more than a thousand people in cars and school buses in the autumn chill of early November 1972. We drove through darkened streets to a large church in the city's black ghetto and bedded down in the basement, exhausted but thrilled with anticipation. In the morning, we would demand justice for Indian people everywhere.

There were hundreds of rats in that church basement, more than a few of which were the size of a small dog. Bold and hungry, they stalked past sleeping mothers to bite infants, and burrowed into baggage to steal small food items. After a restless, fearful night, we returned to our cars to find that many of them had been burglarized. Several people, including elders, had lost ceremonial clothing, priceless garments that had been in their families for generations. At daylight, Clyde Bellecourt said, "This is bullshit. We're not letting our children stay here any longer. We're going to go down and confront the BIA, *make* them meet with us."

We got back into our buses and cars and motored to the BIA building on the Mall, not far from the present site of the Vietnam Veterans' Memorial. Surrounding the BIA building with our vehicles, we demanded that officials find us a decent place to stay. The brass sent a junior "gofer" down to tell us that since we hadn't been invited and had come on our own initiative, we would have to fend for ourselves. When representatives from Indian organizations with headquarters in D.C. came to the BIA building, the bureaucrats sent us down the street to an armory and said we could stay there. Although we had money enough to buy groceries for a few days, there was no place to cook meals and nowhere to eat them. Even worse, there were no showers, and the toilet facilities were very limited. We told the BIA's flunky that the armory was unacceptable.

He told us to go to the BIA auditorium, and we packed in there. We wanted to meet with the authorities and explain the purpose of the Trail of Broken Treaties and why we were in Washington, but they kept stalling, never refusing to speak with us but never agreeing to meet. A few minutes before closing time on Friday, November 3, 1972—four days before the national election—some midlevel honchos came in, accompanied by Government

Services Administration police, and said, "It's five o'clock. You all have to clear out now."

Nobody moved until Clyde stood up and bellowed, "We're not moving! This is our home! We're staying here!" I got up and yelled, "This is no longer the BIA building! This is now the American Indian embassy." People cheered. Others yelled, "Take it over! Let's go!" Spontaneously and with no thought of consequences, we took control, barricading the doors with furniture and finding chains and other things to keep them closed.

We let the officials and most of the bureau's rank-and-file employees leave. Several decided to join us. When a few young Indians began to break into a cigarette machine, they were stopped by our own security people, who fanned out through the halls to secure everything. We put out the word: "No stealing or breaking in. Leave the desks and the offices alone." That's when we found a young GSA cop, a Latino, hiding in a secretarial room. Scared half to death, he had drawn and cocked his revolver and was keeping everybody at bay. I went in and said, "Look, I don't have a gun. We have no quarrel with you. You can leave anytime. Just walk out the door." He said, "I'm going out the window," and climbed down a fire escape.

The next evening we were joined by Commissioner of Indian Affairs Louis Bruce and some of his key young executives, including Ernie Stevens, Lee Cook, and Sandy McNab. They must have known that it would cost them their jobs, at the very least. We also welcomed LaDonna Harris, the half-Comanche wife of a senator from Oklahoma. Then and now, she heads Americans for Indian Opportunity. They came to show that the Trail of Broken Treaties had wide support from Indians everywhere, and that our intentions were honorable. The public support of Commissioner Bruce sent political shock waves through Washington. He was acting against the express wishes of his boss, the assistant secretary of the interior, a rock-ribbed Southern conservative named Harrison Loesch.

Bruce and his people offered repeatedly to set up a meeting with Interior Department officials. At first, we turned him down, because we didn't want to negotiate with a jerk such as Loesch. On Sunday night, however, after being guaranteed safe conduct, we decided to try a different approach, and went to the Interior Department building. When we got into Loesch's office, filled with big overstuffed leather chairs and all sorts of mementos, Clyde didn't even bother trying to talk with the man. He simply told Loesch to get out. A short, stocky, balding, red-faced guy in his mid-fifties with a purple-veined prizefighter's nose, Loesch was choking on his own rage.

The other Interior Department guys said, "Here's our best offer—vacate the BIA property, and then we'll talk." Naturally, we told them to go to hell. We also assured them that everything was safe inside the BIA building. If they wanted to come in with the media to see for themselves, we would arrange a tour. The Interior people held their position for a couple of hours, and then the meeting ended. I had walked out after thirty minutes because I could see it was going nowhere. Back in the BIA auditorium, where people were singing and dancing, I told them exactly what was going on, as we always did. On Monday morning, we were presented with our first threat. The GSA police said they were coming in to eject us. Most of those cops were African-Americans. The few whites remained on horseback behind those who were going to storm the building. We put empty filing cabinets on the fire escapes so nobody could climb up. We barricaded all windows and doors so that the only way in was through the front door. There, we would make our stand.

Some lawyers who had volunteered to help us arrived with an injunction, and the cops backed off. We used the lull that followed to get a few of our oldest people to donated facilities where they could be safe and comfortable. We found places for anyone else who wanted to leave—no more than a few people. Nixon was out of town on election eve campaigning against Senator George McGovern, but on Monday night, after we had rejected negotiations with the Interior Department for several days, some White House aides invited our leaders in to talk. I refused to go, preferring to remain with my people and find ways to boost morale. I won't visit the White House until I can go as a free man, not as a hostage in my own country, over which the federal government has total control.

That afternoon the cops, armed with a court order for us to vacate, threatened again to come in. Again, we readied ourselves for the attack. At the last minute, our lawyers got a restraining order, but we had no warning that a legal maneuver was in the works. On Thursday, for the third time, the ranks of the GSA cops were reinforced by police from several other government agencies who massed on the grassy area across from the BIA, waiting only for the order. I asked one black officer, "Are you really going to attack this time?"

He said, "Yeah, we'll be coming."

"Isn't it obvious to you that black people are going to do all the dirty work here while the white man stands back?"

"Sure. It's very obvious. But we've got to follow orders, just like always. I'll tell you one thing: I pity the first man through that door," he added.

The third attack, like the two before it, fizzled. The Nixon administration probably didn't want blood spilled on television in America's living rooms quite so soon after the election. But neither could Nixon allow himself to seem weak. By Friday, the seventh day of our takeover, he returned to town in triumph, savoring his election victory. Busloads of cops and other uniformed mercenaries pulled up to the BIA building. Once again, they pulled on gas masks and face shields and formed ranks. We became convinced that there was now no turning back. We knew that Nixon didn't want us to occupy that building and continue to paralyze the BIA for a second week. By six, it would be dark, making it hard for television crews to film everything. We figured the police would come then. I thought of the traditional song our ancestors had sung on similar occasions, "It Is a Good Day To Die." I decided that our cause was everything. If it came down to it, that *was* a good day to die. While our elders and pregnant women huddled in the basement and tension rose steadily, we told ourselves that although we had no weapons but Molotov cocktails and homemade clubs, we would make those pigs pay dearly for our lives. We hung a sign inside the auditorium door, facing the front entrance: WHEN YOU WANT TO BUILD ANEW, YOU HAVE TO DESTROY THE OLD.

At 4:00 P.M., we met in the commissioner's third-floor corner office, filled with overstuffed leather chairs and an enormous desk, all very plush. In the room were representatives of all Indian groups involved in taking over the building. Sitting behind the commissioner's desk was Hank Adams. He and his people were adamant that we demolish the building rather than surrender, but most of AIM was against it because it would be counterproductive strategically and from a public-relations perspective. We had maintained firm discipline so far, and we wanted to leave that way. We also knew that we alone would take the heat for any vandalism. Clyde said, "If we destroy this building, it's going to be AIM they come after." Our debate went on, with Hank continuing to assert that we should smash the building. We were moving toward consensus on that, but Clyde and Vernon, backed by Dennis, still argued strenuously against destruction. I leaned toward Hank's position, but I was with AIM. We hadn't discussed it among ourselves and I didn't want to publicly disagree with other leaders, so I said nothing. Suddenly Hank got out of his chair, pulled out a pocketknife, and said, "I've always wanted to do this." As he cut the leather chair to shreds, Sid Mills and a couple of other Survival of American Indians guys followed suit, slicing up the leather couches. People began to pull books from library shelves and break furniture and anything else that came to hand. Disgusted, Clyde left the room. Vernon trailed him out the door. I stayed a while to watch.

At about five o'clock, the White House called. We sent a team there for a last-ditch negotiating effort. All our talks had ended with the politicians refusing to give an inch until we were out of the building, so we had very low expectations. Before the team members left, they understood that if we didn't hear from them by six, we would torch the building. Meanwhile, wholesale destruction and looting continued. There was much beautiful, valuable stuff in those offices, and most of it was taken. People, including some of the leaders, "repossessed" paintings, pottery, jewelry, rugs—many of them artifacts that had been plundered from Indians in the last two centuries. I'm sure some of it was private property, but nobody knew what belonged to the bureau and what belonged to the bureaucrats, so we took it all. I decided not to take anything. If the police were going to arrest us, I didn't want theft to be one of the charges. I hadn't joined AIM to enrich myself.

People started to destroy bathrooms, then offices, and then the whole building. After a few minutes, I remembered something that Lee Cook, the deputy BIA commissioner in charge of education, had suggested earlier. "If I were to take the documents, I would take the financial, land, health, law-enforcement, and tribal-council records," he said. I hollered, "Wait, wait! Let's not burn the files! Let's take them! Start getting them together!" My sister Madonna and I put together teams to go through each floor and collect the kinds of documents Lee had suggested. As the six o'clock deadline drew near, we piled all sorts of other records on the floor for fuel, soaking them in gasoline from Molotov cocktails we had stashed on the roof. When the attic and the floors below were spread with gasoline-soaked papers, we assigned men with matches to each floor. We planned to light them all, starting at the top, clearing people off each level just before torching it.

Across the street, the police were ready, with gas masks, flak vests, and riot shields in place. As we feverishly taped windows to prevent them from being shattered by tear-gas canisters, cops blocked off the streets on all four sides of the building. Along with several other men and women, I went out in front of the building and walked back and forth on the sidewalk, taunting the black cops and calling them "house niggers." "Why are you going to kill for the white man?" I shouted. "We're ready for you inside. Do you know what Indians do to buffalo soldiers? Do you know the tortures? Who's going to be the first nigger through the door?" I was trying to play with their heads, but I got no response.

My job was to ensure that everyone was cleared off each floor before the fire was lit. Just before six, I went inside and up to the stairway between the third floor and the attic. Above me was our fire starter. In his left hand, he held a book of matches with the cover closed. The thumb and forefinger of his right hand grasped the stem of a paper match, its head resting on the top end of the striker. All he had to do was pull that match a half inch toward him, then flip it onto the floor—and the whole attic would go up in flames.

At exactly six, just as I was about to give the word, Vernon Bellecourt came running up to the foot of the stairs below, yelling, "Stop! Please stop, please!" Almost hysterical, he tried to persuade me not to torch the building. He said, "At least don't do it until the negotiators get back." I agreed to wait a little while. At about four minutes past six, one of our negotiators phoned and the word was passed upstairs to me: "Don't do anything, the team's on its way back. We've got a settlement." If that call had come even two minutes later or if Vernon hadn't come running just when he did, the building would have gone up and everyone involved would have been hunted down from then to doomsday. I would *still* be in prison—if I was alive.

The deal that had been struck was that the White House would "consider" our "Twenty Points" and would give us an answer within thirty days. We would have a police escort out of town, and money to pay for sending our elders and pregnant women back home by air and for the rest of us to drive back home. If we were out of the building by six the next morning, no one would be prosecuted. That night, we rented two U-Haul trucks and backed them up to the entrance. With a crowd of people standing around to block the feds' view, we spirited three thousand pounds of BIA documents out of the building. We told the cops the trucks were carrying our bedrolls.

That last night, we let the media in to see the destruction. We held a press conference and said that we knew what they were going to report, but we wanted to tell our side of the story anyway. Of course, they never told our side; they focused on the damage to the building. Later that night, Caspar Weinberger and Leonard Garment, who then were lawyers serving as Nixon's "special assistants," came down to give us the money we had demanded for departure expenses. Weinberger handed us a brown paper sack filled with $66,650 in cash. I still have no idea how Robert Free, who was in charge of AIM's finances on the Trail of Broken Treaties, came up with that figure. When a government negotiator said they would have trouble coming up with that much cash on a Friday night, one of his colleagues suggested tapping CREEP, the Committee to Re-elect the President. A few years later, when the details of the Watergate scandal became public, everyone in the country would learn that CREEP money included illegal campaign contributions. Perhaps the negotiators acted on the suggestion because the campaign had safes bursting with cash. If so, this was no donation: After we left town, the White House would have undoubtedly reimbursed CREEP. We later learned the money was charged to the Indian antipoverty program, money allocated by Congress to help the poorest people in the country.

We left Washington the next morning in jubilation. We had come, a thousand Indians from dozens of nations, but one people in spirit, bearing the sacred pipe, to tell the white man we had heard enough of his lies. We had taken over the alleged nerve center of the BIA for seven days and had trashed it so thoroughly that it would be more than six weeks before operations could resume—and no one missed it! We had confiscated tons of documents, had been paid to leave town—and no one had been arrested. I felt the growing force of our convictions and knew that spiritual power was our greatest strength.

2 5

▼▼▼▼▼▼▼▼▼

Scourge of the Plains

eaving Washington in November 1972, we split into two groups. My caravan headed west. We planned to stop along the way and explain to Indians and others what had really happened in Washington. From what we had seen and read in the media, we knew the truth had yet to be told. Dennis led another caravan, with most of the documents, to the Tuscarora people in North Carolina. Other records went north, to New York and Boston. Through the efforts of Hank Adams and Dennis Banks, those BIA files found their way to syndicated columnist Jack Anderson. For more than a year, he wrote exposé after exposé about BIA corruption. John Trudell, Vernon Bellecourt, and hippies from the Hog Farm commune in Vermont went to New York City to work with singer-actor Harry Belafonte and others. They planned to turn the movie footage that had been shot about the occupation into a documentary, but that never came to fruition.

As we had expected, AIM alone was blamed for everything that had happened to the BIA building. Dick Wilson, president of Pine Ridge, told the U.S. Justice Department, "Russell Means is from this reservation, he's with AIM, and he's probably coming back here. Last year, they went down to Gordon, Nebraska, and took over the town, so I expect them to attack the BIA building here. I want some money to beef up my police force so I can protect my people." In his own way, Wilson was already protecting his people. After taking office, he put his brother Jim on the payroll. Wilson also hired his wife and other family members.

Then Wilson wanted to buy the loyalty of more people than his own family could provide. The Law Enforcement Assistance Administration, a Nixon-era program to turn America's police departments into paramilitary organizations with tanks and other heavy weapons, gave Wilson millions of dollars, all channeled through a highway-safety program. Wilson used the money to hire goon squads. With hundreds of armed men, he began to act like Haiti's Duvalier or Nicaragua's Somoza. Wilson became a tin-pot dictator who sought to exterminate all political dissent on the reservation, especially in Pine Ridge Village. Anyone whom Wilson or his henchmen thought opposed them was beaten up, often along with their families. Car windows were smashed or tires slashed. Threats and intimidation were used to extort money. People were thrown in jail on the most ridiculous charges.

In response to the terror and violence, honest people formed the Oglala Sioux Civil Rights Organization, headed by Vernon Long, with Pedro Bissonnette as vice president. Wilson seized on the emergence of OSCRO to intensify his campaign of repression, telling the feds that he faced an imminent threat. An eighty-man paramilitary team from the U.S. Marshals' Special Operations Group was dispatched to Pine Ridge.

I didn't learn about most of that for several weeks because I stuck with the caravan. As we moved west, we stopped to give talks about our "Twenty Points" and our week in Washington. We drove through Minnesota to South Dakota, dropping people off along the way. Winter had fallen on the Great Plains. Many of our people, especially the guys from Washington state, California, and Arizona, had no overcoats or warm sweaters and were in ragged tennis shoes. We were also running out of money. By the time we reached Pierre, South Dakota, we had about eight vehicles left in our caravan. When we learned that representatives of the United Sioux Tribes were meeting there, we stopped to ask for their help. UST is the umbrella organization for all nine Sioux reservations in the state. They offered us a place to stay for one night in a dorm at the old boarding school. When we asked for gasoline and expense money, they acted as if they were pissed off and didn't want us there. The bureaucrats suggested that we make our pitch that night at the conference banquet. Those tribal chairmen, vice chairmen, and council members were all dining on U.S. government per diem, but we had to invite ourselves in. Dallas Chief Eagle, a UST official from the Rosebud, and a few others who hadn't sold out their Indian brothers and sisters invited us in to eat.

Most of the other distinguished people seemed more than a little upset. A ragtag bunch of militants, fresh from a week in Washington, D.C., where we had embarrassed the whole Indian community by trashing the BIA building, was crashing the party and getting a free meal. Outside, it was snowing and thermometers were heading for zero, but inside it was even cooler. We were among our own people, but it felt as though we were invading some strange redneck territory.

Then Dallas got up from his table. "What's happened to us?" he said. "These people are our defenders! They've just returned from battle—and they won. Look at them, they have no winter clothing, and it's freezing outside! In the old days, we would be saluting them for their courage. We would be having a feast for *them*, not for us. We should be proud of them and treat them like the heroes they are." Dallas went on in that vein for five minutes, a terrific speech that made all the tribal big shots look very small and made us party crashers feel larger than life. When he finished, almost everyone donated generously for our people. Except for a few hardnoses, the UST folks treated us with warmth and friendship.

From Pierre, we headed for Denver, where Vernon Bellecourt threw a big party and we had another leadership meeting. Then we decided to go to Tempe, a suburb of Phoenix, where a group of Christian clergymen was meeting. We wanted to take along as many Indian people as we could get, so on the way, we stopped in Hopi country. The whole reservation knew AIM was coming. The BIA temporarily closed its agency, and the superintendent and other top officials left town. The Hopi people joked about it. They said, "You should come more often." I took Michele, Scott, and Betty up on the mesa and we held a pipe ceremony. After all I had been through since last seeing my children, I was so overcome that I cried. My poor kids were glad to see me, but they didn't know what was going on.

From the Hopi Reservation our little caravan drove to Tempe, where we raised money at a miniconvention of ministers from around the country. We had been dropping people off as we moved across the country, so our caravan was down to only four or five cars by the time we rolled into Los Angeles. We checked into a Hollywood landmark, the Holiday Inn, and took two top-floor suites. After a party started, I went downstairs to make a quiet phone call. I returned to find an LAPD SWAT team, with all my guys on the floor. It turned out that some local Indians had joined us. They had to prove they were as tough as AIM, and they started to trash the place. That was always a danger whenever we allowed non-AIM Indians to party with us. Many would decide they had to be "militants" and prove their manhood by becoming destructive. The LAPD, of course, doesn't mess around. When its head brass heard AIM was involved, it came up with a SWAT team, hauled the guys responsible for the vandalism to jail, and told the rest of us to get out of town. We went two miles, to West Hollywood, then county territory, and partied with some Indian students from UCLA.

Los Angeles was the end of the Trail of Broken Treaties for me. I hustled up a few speaking engagements and convinced a church leader I knew in Washington, D.C., to spring for my plane fare back to South Dakota. Before

I left town, I went to Santa Ana, about thirty miles southeast of Los Angeles, where Twila was living with Sherry and Hank. It was the first time I had seen them in a long time. It was rather awkward all around, but I had never forgotten my kids and it meant a lot to me to spend even a little time with them. Sherry was thirteen, and so gloriously beautiful that I couldn't believe she was actually my daughter. She had gotten into some little scrape with the law, so I went with her and Twila to talk to her probation officer.

When I returned to Pine Ridge, I moved into another old house in Porcupine. At about Thanksgiving time, Wilson issued an illegal executive order prohibiting "all AIM activities" on the reservation. Dennis was served with a restraining order from a tribal judge. When Dennis refused to leave, he was arrested and escorted off the reservation. After goons arrested me for allegedly having violated Wilson's ban on AIM activities, I moved to the Rosebud.

About a month later, one of my former Porcupine neighbors, Edgar Bear Runner, an idealistic young man with a mind of his own and a very enthusiastic AIM supporter, told me about an upcoming conference in Scottsbluff, Nebraska. Many Chicanos were in that area. Before wheat became the big money crop in the 1950s, that part of the Great Plains used to be mostly sugar-beet and potato country. Most of the crops were picked by migrant workers, principally Mexicans, but also many Indians. They were men with a strong work ethic and a traditional value system whose seasonal wages were enough to support their families on Pine Ridge. Indians and Mexicans worked side by side in the fields; we Lakota thought of Mexicans as just another kind of Indian people who spoke a different language. Most migrant workers went home after the fall harvest, but some Mexicans and Lakotas settled in at Scottsbluff. They lived mostly in their own barrios on the edges of town, particularly along the banks of the North Platte. The white majority in Scottsbluff didn't care much for dark-skinned people, and police did whatever it took to keep those second-class citizens subservient.

In the second week of January 1973, Dace and I drove from South Dakota to a little community hall in a Scottsbluff barrio. A local Chicano group, the New Congress for Community Development, was hosting a conference there to find ways to deal with police brutality and racial discrimination. A lot of other AIM people and supporters were there, including the Red Bears and a family of Scottsbluff Lakota. The police, especially the new chief, James Teal, just hired from LAPD and out to prove that he was the right man for the job, didn't like the conference.

Teal's cops harassed people. They stopped cars driven by dark-skinned people and questioned the occupants. They surrounded the meeting hall with squad cars, claiming to have an arrest warrant for a Chicano whom they said was inside. They demanded that we let them search the hall, but refused to show us a warrant, and the guy wasn't even around. That kind of bullshit went on constantly in Scottsbluff, but when we refused to let them in, more police surrounded the hall, claiming to have information that AIM had hidden weapons inside. We weren't that stupid, and neither were our Chicano brothers. Instead of bringing guns into the hall, they were stashed around the barrio. If the police had tried to force their way in, they would have found those guns at their backs. Fortunately, when we refused to let them into our meeting place, the cops backed off. After a while, they left.

With the conference nearly over, we went to a motel across the river in Gering for a party. Afterward, we crossed back into Scottsbluff to another motel, next to a bar. Almost as soon as we arrived, a string of police cars sped up. When the cops began to harass Indians and Chicanos, I went outside to see what was wrong. The officers claimed that shots had been fired and wanted to search everyone and see if any of our guns had been fired recently. We didn't have any guns! I told them about our constitutional rights and that they had no reasonable cause to search us. I became belligerent. I said, "What about all the rednecks who drive pickups with rifles hanging right in the back windows? Why don't you stop them and check their weapons, see if they've been fired? Why are you picking on us? We're just having a good time."

That was too much Indian lip for them, so they knocked me down, handcuffed me, searched me, threw me in a car, and took me to jail. I had to get out of the backseat with my arms cuffed behind me. When no one would help me, I stumbled and fell to one knee, then got up, and was taken inside to be booked. Before they would remove my handcuffs, I was searched again. Then I surrendered my personal property and was fingerprinted and forced to pose for a mug shot. After being searched a third time, I was thrown into a cell. It was fairly big, with open floor space in the center and about six bunks, all empty. I was tired and went to sleep, but soon afterward I was awakened by someone shouting, "Wake up!" I had been curled up. My back was toward the speaker. When I looked over my left shoulder, I saw five or six cops in flak jackets. They were all pointing shotguns at me.

One of them said, "Go ahead, make a move for it." I looked down. On the floor was a .22-caliber revolver. Another cop said, "Go ahead, try for it! You're a tough guy. You're a militant." They taunted me with all kinds of names. Between the booze I had had earlier and the lateness of the hour, I was too sleepy to bother with them, so I just rolled over on my good left ear and closed my eyes. Those guys came into the cell like gangbusters, threw me off the bunk, spread-eagled me on the floor, stepped on my arms, and searched me again.

Then they hauled me to an interrogation room with a tape recorder and one-way mirror—the whole gestapo setup. "Where did you get the gun?" At first, I couldn't take them seriously. I said, "Come on, you guys, what is this?" They were relentless, demanding over and over, "Tell us where you got the gun!" I never should have said what I did—it was used against me later—but in a spirit of whimsy appropriate to their ridiculous charade, I said, "Well, the Great Mystery has always smiled on me, so the Great Mystery must have placed that in there for me." Humor was very low on the job-qualifications list for police officers, and they didn't get it.

"Tell us about this great mystery guy," they said.

The cops kept questioning me until I got into a whole long rap about the Great Mystery. I said, "Oh, the Great Mystery—he goes by a lot of names, or maybe *she* does—I don't know. Some call him *God*, others say Jehovah, and he's also known by various and sundry other names, including Allah." Exasperated, they finally returned me to the cell. Before I could get back to sleep, I was taken out again to be recharged and rebooked on another felony count—illegal possession of a weapon. The next day, I was arraigned for disorderly conduct, resisting arrest, illegal possession of a gun, and two counts of felony assault on police officers. The officers testified under oath that as I got out of the police car with my hands cuffed behind me, I had lunged at one cop with my right shoulder, then at the other with my left. They said they had to subdue me. A judge set bail for twenty-five thousand dollars and bound me over for trial on three felonies.

I wasn't the only one from the Scottsbluff conference who was put behind bars. Several conference leaders were taken into custody. My brother Dace was arrested for parking illegally in an alley by the community hall, and was held in lieu of one-hundred-dollar bond. My brother Ted was charged with assaulting an officer. He had tried to stop the cop from grabbing his wife and forcing her and the child in her arms out of a building. Even Leonard Crow Dog got arrested for allegedly driving without a valid license. Within a day or so, we all got help from lawyers from the Mexican-American Legal Defense and Educational Fund—Francisco "Kiko" Martinez, Ken Padilla, and Federico Peña, now U.S. Secretary of Transportation. Young and militant, those patriots were hassled widely and constantly by law enforcement because they were always fighting for people's civil rights. They raised bond money for all of us.

After everybody was back on the street, I had an idea—give the police a dose of their own medicine. The arresting officers' names were on my booking papers, so we looked up their addresses. I took four AIM cars to one of their houses—in broad daylight, of course. With an empty camera, I made a pretense of snapping pictures of windows and doors. Then we drove to the other officer's house, where I did the same thing. When we headed back, six or seven squad cars, with sirens wailing and red lights flashing, barreled past us toward the house we had just visited. Those cops never realized who we were. I wonder how long they kept watch, how many times they and their families jumped out of their beds at night at every loud noise in the neighborhood. It served them right.

Along with our Chicano brothers, we picketed the jail. Later, we met with county commissioners to demand changes in the sheriff's office. All we got was double-talk. We filed a federal lawsuit against the sheriff, the chairman of the county board of commissioners, the county attorney, Scottsbluff's police chief and mayor, and the head of the Nebraska Highway Patrol. We asked for $200,000 in damages and an injunction against further violation of our rights to free speech, travel and assembly, due process, and equal protection of the law.

After ten days of constant confrontations, AIM left Scottsbluff in a caravan. Police and National Guard helicopters shadowed us all the way to the South Dakota line. When I arrived in Rapid City, I learned that Dick Wilson had recently issued an illegal order prohibiting me from attending meetings of any kind on Pine Ridge. I couldn't go to a birthday party or join a Boy Scout hike without risking arrest. Nixon's White House, far from considering our "Twenty Points," announced that no dialogue could begin until AIM returned all the documents and artifacts taken from the BIA building.

Sure!

We brought the AIM caravan to Rapid City to help motivate the city's white Establishment to deal with the community's rampant racism. We stayed in a two-story dormitory at the Mother Butler Center, a defunct alcohol-rehabilitation halfway house run by Jesuits. Because of the help AIM had provided to victims of the flood in June, the priest in charge invited us to stay as long as we liked. He also gave us the use of a big Quonset hut, with a kitchen and auditorium, as a temporary headquarters and meeting room.

Rapid City's racism was most obvious in notorious downtown juke joints and dives on a stretch of Main Street. Redneck cowboys beat up Indians just about every night of the week, but rarely was anyone arrested except Indians. The city jail was full of our people, so we went down there and demonstrated. On another day, we took over the downtown business district with a caravan that snaked back and forth along the streets, honking our horns and yelling out car windows. We also had a few pickup trucks with people singing around drums. It was our own impromptu parade to remind all of Rapid City's redneck citizens that we were *not* going to leave their town until they made some changes.

AIM also wanted to do something about racist employment practices in Rapid City. Many retailers did a lot of business with Indians, but refused to hire any. Among them were several lumberyards without a single Indian on their payrolls. One morning, we got a call from the white owners of those companies, asking to meet with us. Dennis and a few guys went down to learn that those businessmen had found a few Coca-Cola bottles lying on stacks of two-by-fours. The bottles were filled with gasoline and stoppered with rags. I never learned how they got there, but everyone in AIM understood that white men dream of painted savages coming out of the night, yelling and screaming, burning and pillaging. When Dennis arrived, the lumbermen told him, "We can take a hint. What do you want?" He said, "Since you make so much money from government contracts on the reservations, we think it would be appropriate if you hired some Indians." They agreed to do so.

While we had been in Nebraska, we had heard about the stabbing of an Indian named Wesley Bad Heart Bull in Buffalo Gap, South Dakota. A mile off Highway 79 on the east side of the Black Hills, between Rapid City and the Nebraska line, Buffalo Gap is right out of a Clint Eastwood movie. A few hundred people live in tired, weather-beaten wooden houses on streets of mud or dust—depending on the season—with corrals for steers and sheep at roundup or shearing time. The center of town features a falling-down two-story hotel, a couple of tiny churches, and two saloons. Most of the action in town is across from the post office at the Stockman's Bar and Café, a low-slung corner building decorated with sheets of knotty plywood.

Wesley Bad Heart Bull, with his mother and wife, had chanced a rutted, unpaved road from the western part of Pine Ridge to buy a few drinks at Stockman's. He had hardly wet his whistle when he ran into a white man named Darld Schmitz. The Black Hills newspapers would later describe him as a "businessman," but Schmitz made his drinking money pumping gasoline, wiping dipsticks, and scrubbing windshields in a gas station. He was known around Custer County as "Mad Dog." Earlier that night, according to one white guy who was present, he'd told his redneck pals that he was "going to kill him an Indian."

Schmitz insulted Wesley until he agreed to go outside. There several cronies surrounded Wesley while Schmitz stabbed him seven times. According to one eyewitness, Wesley's mother, Sarah, was forced to watch the murder. After his arrest, Schmitz claimed he had been forced to kill that savage Indian in self-defense when Wesley threatened him with a chain. "Mad Dog" was charged with involuntary manslaughter.

That was outrageous. AIM announced that it was going into Custer on February 6 to meet with the deputy state's attorney about filing murder charges. We had two caravans from Rapid City, about thirty cars with almost a hundred people, including women, children, and elders. Dennis led one out Mount Rushmore Road and through the hills to Custer. I took the other south to Hermosa and then west through Custer State Park. Custer is a small Black Hills town that has a few sawmills but mostly milks tourists with its tacky motels, gift shops, souvenir stores, and family-style eateries. Back from the business district, dark pines shield small, neat houses, many with pseudo-Victorian facades. The red brick courthouse in the center of town was built in the 1880s. A rusty cannon and nineteenth-century farm implements littered the front lawn of the courthouse behind a white picket fence.

It was snowing heavily as our caravans converged at the courthouse. Riot-equipped state troopers, local police, and sheriff's deputies were deployed along Mount Rushmore Road. Word of our arrival went around town like wildfire—"Indian trouble!" White men broke out their guns, made their women and children safe, and prepared for the worst. We got everybody out of the cars and held a little rally. When we started up the front steps of the courthouse, we found our way blocked by deputies who said only four people would be allowed inside—Dennis, Leonard Crow Dog, David Hill, a Choctaw who had a black belt in karate, and me. We presented evidence developed by our own investigation. Despite the frontier mind-set that brands as traitors any whites who dare to testify against their own race when the victim is an Indian, we found a few people who would attest that Schmitz had boasted about finding an Indian to kill only hours before he did just that. We asked the prosecutor to raise the charge for that cold-blooded act from manslaughter to first-degree murder.

The prosecutor adamantly refused to up the ante against "Mad Dog." Once a charge had been filed, the system didn't allow him to change it to a more severe allegation for the same offense, he told us. That was plain bullshit. We all knew plenty of Indian people who had been reindicted for far more serious crimes when it was politically expedient to do so. We said, "The truth is, you can do anything you want to do about this."

I glanced out the courthouse window and saw that blowing snow had driven everybody in the caravan to shelter. It didn't look much like a demonstration to me, so David and I went outside and started to pound on car hoods, yelling "Come on, everybody, let's get out of these cars!" We mounted the courthouse steps, and I told our people what had been said inside. I made an angry speech about Schmitz. Then I told David, "Let's go back inside." After I reentered the building, the sheriff stood in the doorway with a couple of deputies and refused to allow David back in.

At that moment, Sarah Bad Heart Bull, Wesley's mother, headed up the sidewalk for the front door. A cop stopped her. While she mouthed off to him, I grabbed a deputy by the back of his collar and threw him on the ground while David slipped into the building. A few moments later, the trooper clubbed Sarah over the head, ripped off her clothes, and started to beat her. That was the signal for the other troopers to riot. Highway patrolmen in helmets, masks, and flak jackets under big winter coats began to swing riot batons. Their first targets were women. The troopers tore off the women's clothes to fondle their breasts, then clubbed them.

Dennis and Leonard went out an office window, leaving David and me to face a swarm of troopers who suddenly came rushing from hiding places in the basement and on the second floor. A few people, including my twin brothers, came through the front doors to help. For several furious minutes, we fought back every wave the police sent against us. David went wild with his karate, feet and arms flying, a dervish in constant motion laying out cops. We were outnumbered at least ten to one inside, but for a few frenzied moments, David had those guys backed up.

While I was punching away in very tight quarters, fending off two or three uniformed cops who tried to club me, a man in civilian clothes—apparently an important guy—kept pushing closer to me, trying to score some licks of his own. My fingernails were very long. As a cop pressed against me, I reached around his head with both hands, raked the big shot's cheeks and gouged his eyes, drawing blood. I took the helmet off the cop in front of me and saw David fighting off four or five troopers. He was putting up a hell of a struggle, while I was backed against the wall in a corner opposite the door. I thought that if I charged, those behind me would follow. I rallied myself and pushed forward, but just then tear-gas canisters came flying into the building. Everyone but David and I ran outside. My brother Bill got clubbed on the head and went down on all fours. Ted tried to help him, but as everyone rushed out, they stepped on Bill's back.

I thought, ah, shit! It was just David and I. In seconds, I was clubbed to the floor. The cops twisted my left arm behind me, then deliberately smashed the elbow with their batons, hurting my arm, the same one I had injured in Los Angeles years earlier. I was absolutely useless. As I writhed in pain, the cops dragged me out by one braid, laughing behind their gas masks. They cuffed my arms behind my back and forced me to sit on the porch steps as clouds of tear gas rolled out of the building. My lungs were afire, but I was determined not to let those pigs see I was hurting. I wasn't going to ask them for mercy. I wasn't going to give them the slightest satisfaction. I sat on a step with my feet on the one below, and tried hard to look as if it were just a lazy afternoon and I had nothing better to do than sit there in a burning, stinging fog.

It was pure torture.

Finally someone said, "That's enough, get him down here." David was already in handcuffs, and they made him lie face down in the snow. The cops, along with local vigilantes toting rifles and shotguns, formed a circle and began to shove me from one to the other. "This is Russell Means! We got Russell Means!" they shouted proudly, passing me around the ring like a trophy. Each man punched me in the gut or on the arm, taunting me— "What's wrong with your arm?"—to scream or beg them to stop. Finally, some redneck grabbed my collar with both hands and said to one of the cops—he called him by his first name—"Let me take him home. I'll put him in my basement, and I tell you, when I get through with him in the morning, he won't be no leader. Let me just have him one night. He'll still be alive when I bring him back."

The tear gas had filled my throat with thick phlegm. I got up a big, green, sickening wad and spat it right in his face. He punched me, of course, but it was worth it to know that he would have nightmares about that gob in his eyes. When he kept beating me, the cops pulled him off. David and I were thrown into a panel truck that served as a paddy wagon, and were hauled off to jail in Rapid City. After we left town, the city hall and the chamber of commerce building caught fire—probably from the police tear-gas canisters—and burned down.

Dennis and Crow Dog had escaped a beating, but they hadn't been idle. Dennis flagged down a passing gasoline tank truck, threw the driver out, and drove it away. Medicine men are supposed to avoid violence, so Crow Dog, a quick thinker, went to the gas station across the street where, we had been told, Schmitz worked. In the midst of riot and fire, he waved our cars in and stood there with a gas hose, filling up Indian cars. He was worried about our people getting home.

The next morning, we were put back into the paddy wagon and returned to Custer for arraignment. I was charged with three or four felonies. The prosecutor was the man whose face I had raked with my fingernails. His face was all scabbed up. He looked at me, his features a mask of hatred. I thought, no matter what happens to me, every morning for the rest of your life as you stand in front of your mirror to shave, you'll remember Russell Means.

After our arraignment, the judge set my bond at thirty-five thousand dollars and police took us back to the Rapid City jail. The night before, my AIM brothers had burned up the phone lines from coast to coast. A lot of good Christians kicked in to come up with our bond money. I was out of jail the same day, just in time to see national television coverage of what people were now calling the "Custer courthouse riot." Pictures of bloodied policemen fired up Indians around the country. In the next few days, Indians of all ages from Minnesota, North Dakota, Montana, Oklahoma, and Nebraska arrived in Rapid City.

We heard reports that Indians were being systematically mistreated at the city jail in Hot Springs, a small town in the south of the Black Hills, so we sent a caravan down there to talk to the sheriff. To attract tourist dollars, the town has been maintained to look like a John Wayne movie set—false-front buildings, wood-slat sidewalks, hitching posts, all that stuff. When our caravan drove into town, the sheriff, a tall, skinny guy, acted as if he were in Northfield, Minnesota, on September 7, 1876—the day the James gang met its match. Vigilantes were on every rooftop and behind every building, all armed to the teeth and each hoping to get himself an Indian. The sheriff wouldn't talk to us. It seemed as if he just grunted for a living. With all those guns pointed at us, the only thing we could do was turn around and go back to Rapid City.

About the time Wesley Bad Heart Bull died, a twenty-two-year-old man named Harold Withorne Jr.—I had known his parents when we lived in Cleveland—was arrested for the rape and murder of Harriet Milo, a fifty-four-year-old white woman, in Sturgis, South Dakota. The victim's blood-alcohol level was well into the legally drunk range, and no physical evidence connected Harold with the crime. But he was an Indian—reason enough to hold him for more than thirty days in the Meade County jail without a preliminary hearing—a violation of due process and the right to a speedy trial guaranteed by the U.S. Constitution. Under community pressure to solve the murder, Sturgis police had used that time to locate "witnesses." In exchange for having petty crimes against them excused, they testified that Harold had confessed. He was charged with rape and first-degree murder.

On February 12, 1973, an AIM caravan of about a hundred people went to Sturgis—a city of five thousand people about twenty-seven miles northwest of Rapid City—to demand that Harold be allowed to post bond and that the county appoint an Indian attorney to prosecute him. A low, sprawling collection of small clapboard homes on broad, tree-studded streets, Sturgis is yet another Black Hills town that keeps the frontier spirit alive by persecuting Indians. It is named for the colonel commanding the U.S. Seventh Cavalry who, in 1876, was sent on detached service so George Armstrong Custer could take temporary command. Custer's political patrons, grooming him for a run at the presidency, needed to get Sturgis out of the way so Custer could cover himself with glory by murdering more redskins.

Robed Ku Klux Klansmen had moved openly around Sturgis as recently as the 1920s. When we arrived, Sturgis was an armed camp—everyone we saw was carrying at least a side arm. The governor had sent in about 120 state troopers and had local National Guard units on standby. Dozens of deputized vigilantes had seized parking lots near the courthouse, forcing us to park far away. But we had learned from the fracas in Custer and the armed vigilantes in Hot Springs: This time we were better organized. When we rolled into town, we broke into teams, each with a specific responsibility. One group of women brought in explosives and incendiaries, and scouted out target houses around town. If police attacked us again, we would burn the whole city.

Another squad surrounded a fire truck that had been positioned in front of the courthouse. We were not going to allow the firemen to use hoses on us in subzero weather. If trouble started, our people would immediately take out that truck. When we asked the firemen to move it, they said, "We've got to stay here; it's orders." But the mere act of encircling that expensive piece of equipment scared the hell out of the fire chief. He knew it would be a rusting hulk if he didn't do something quickly, so he came outside. "We've just got the fire truck here for emergencies, and not to use on any human beings," he begged. "Please leave it alone. It's the only one we've got." We said that if he really wanted to keep that truck, he had better move it. He did just that.

We put a few spokesmen out front, including Rod Skenadone and me. Highway patrolmen in full riot gear lined up shoulder to shoulder in front of us. Our anger was growing. The white men could see that this time, we weren't fooling around. We were ready to die, all of us. When we spoke to our people, the authorities listening knew how serious we were, and that the results of our meeting with city officials would determine AIM's response. It was getting closer and closer to out-and-out war. We were ready. Besides explosives, almost everyone except the leaders was packing a gun. I was un-armed because I expected to be arrested, and didn't want to give redneck judges a real reason to put me behind bars.

Instead of meeting us in pitched battle, the Sturgis authorities acted very humanely. They invited us to come in and talk and brought hot coffee to the demonstrators remaining outside. I must give them credit. They put out the fuse, and though they didn't know it, they saved their town.

We met with Harold and his mother. He was tall, very slim, a good-looking young man and a fine athlete. We assured him that we would get him a good lawyer, but he was dejected when we left. It seemed that every-thing was stacked against him, and indeed it was. Harold was denied bail. Two months later—when virtually every AIM leader was tied up—he copped a plea, and a judge sentenced him to life imprisonment without parole.

At about the same time—at the height of anti-Indian hysteria in South Dakota—"Mad Dog" Schmitz went on trial in Custer. Although he admitted having killed Wesley Bad Heart Bull, an all-white jury found him not guilty of manslaughter.

26

▼▼▼▼▼▼▼▼▼

The Path to
Wounded Knee

All the time we were at the Mother Butler Center in Rapid City in early
1973, Pedro Bissonnette and other leaders of the Oglala Sioux Civil
Rights Organization at Pine Ridge had been telling us about the terrible
beatings and intimidation inflicted by Dick Wilson's goons. We didn't know
why Wilson had turned against his people, but many on the reservation and
in AIM thought he had been bought off by white ranchers. They were rich,
politically powerful men who paid next to nothing to lease vast areas of the
reservation for grazing. The tribal council, at least theoretically, could have
ended that cozy arrangement. That theory, however, never quite explained
why Wilson got so much support from the feds. Many years later, I finally
learned the truth through the Freedom of Information Act and Ward Churchill, who investigated the matter for years.

The seemingly arid and empty lands that were turned into Indian reservations contain more than half of all known U.S. uranium reserves, about
a quarter of U.S. low-sulphur coal, 20 percent of U.S. oil and natural gas,
and large quantities of copper and other important metals. If Indian nations
were allowed to control those resources, the government would have to deal
with us on the basis of equality. The United States could be forced to pay
for two hundred years of lies and swindles as the price of access. Or we might

decide that we don't want to rape our Grandmother, the earth, by digging up minerals to sell to *anyone*.

On Pine Ridge, the government desperately wanted to maintain control of the Sheep Mountain Gunnery Range, an area amounting to about an eighth of the reservation. During World War II, the land had been "lent" to what became the U.S. Defense Department. It was supposed to revert to tribal control after the war. While prospecting it secretly, the feds discovered large deposits of uranium and molybdenum, essential to making high-strength steel alloys. After Wilson became tribal president, he agreed to the permanent transfer of the gunnery range to the feds. In return, he received their unrestricted support. Giving away Sheep Mountain violated our treaty. Wilson, on orders from his white masters, knew that traditional Lakota people would never permit the transfer. Because those people and AIM supported each other, he set out to destroy AIM and to crush all resistance.

Nixon's Justice Department had another reason to aid and abet Wilson's efforts to destroy AIM—COINTELPRO (Counterintelligence Program), a secret agenda based on the ridiculous assumption that all organized American dissidents were supported by or linked to Soviet-bloc sponsors. The program dated to the Eisenhower administration and the height of the "Red Scare" in the 1950s. Congress had ordered the FBI to end it in 1971, and J. Edgar Hoover had reported that it was discontinued. That was a lie. In the Nixon administration, COINTEL was directed against "radical dissidents" such as the Black Panthers, the Young Lords, the Weather Underground—and AIM. COINTEL had an overt strategy—arrest members of radical organizations on any pretext, and force them to spend all their time and energy raising bail, finding lawyers, and appearing in court. FBI informers infiltrated AIM to fabricate evidence that could be used to bring charges. AIM members, especially leaders, were arrested on any excuse. COINTEL also had a *covert* strategy: If police riots, malicious prosecution, and astronomical bond fees don't neutralize dissidents, kill them. That is what happened in Chicago to several Black Panthers, along with innocent women and babies.

In February 1973, however, COINTEL was still secret. Nobody in AIM knew that we as a group had been marked for elimination. What we did know was that the people of Pine Ridge had asked for our help. Because that is my home, AIM assigned me to assess the situation. Because of our actions in Gordon after the killing of Raymond Yellow Thunder, AIM had made a lot of friends around the reservation. Many of them later became goons who turned over for Wilson because he controlled jobs and money. I found that sad, but understandable. The hang-around-the-fort Indian always knows which side of his bread is buttered.

The Oglala Sioux Civil Rights Organization asked the tribal council for help during Wilson's reign of terror, bringing in a petition with the signatures of more people than had voted to elect him the preceding year. Under the leadership of councilmen Birgil Kills Straight, Severt Young Bear, and Hobart Keith, articles of impeachment were drawn up. Along with a couple of hundred other Oglala people, I attended the proceedings in Billy Mills Hall. It was one of the most curious meetings I have ever attended. Wilson, backed by BIA Superintendent Stanley Lyman, presided over his own trial! Council meetings in those days were conducted in Lakota, even though Wilson required an interpreter. The hearing was held in English, allowing him to silence most of the traditionals. Wilson isolated Birgil, Severt, and Hobart and wouldn't let them speak. Everyone trying to introduce evidence against him was ruled out of order. One of his supporters on the council moved to dismiss the impeachment. Another immediately seconded it. Then Wilson quickly called for a vote and dismissed the charges against himself.

That was such an outrageous abuse of power that I couldn't believe he would get away with it. But when I went along with Severt Young Bear and Edgar Bear Runner to the FBI's Rapid City office and asked them to intervene, the Bureau's officers said, "We have no jurisdiction." They suggested we try the U.S. Attorney. We asked him to act, but he said, "It's up to the Oglala Sioux tribe." As a last resort, we contacted BIA headquarters, but nobody there would listen either. I wasn't surprised that my name opened no doors in a building I had recently helped to take over.

In early February 1973, eighty U.S. marshals of the paramilitary Special Operations Group, armed with automatic weapons and backed by armored personnel carriers and helicopters, surrounded the BIA agency in Pine Ridge and fortified the building. Only people approved by Wilson could enter. Severt Young Bear, Edgar Bear Runner, Pedro Bissonnette, Vern Long, and I met with the marshal in charge, Wayne Colburn. We explained that we were representing a civil rights organization, and that I was there from AIM as an arbitrator who had been asked to intercede on AIM's behalf. Colburn said his mission was to protect the BIA from AIM or from any assault, since there were "a lot of important records" inside that the BIA didn't want destroyed, as others had been in Washington. We explained that his men were intimidating people who had important personal business to conduct in the agency, but Colburn didn't want to hear it. He said, "If you guys try to get tough, we'll just shut you down. We'll take care of you."

While we were seeking justice from the white man's law, Gladys Bissonnette, Ellen Moves Camp, Agnes Lamont, and many other upstanding Pine Ridge women demonstrated outside the BIA building. They demanded that Wilson be impeached and that the marshals, who had no jurisdiction on Pine Ridge, leave at once. The women were ignored. Once again, all the gates of officialdom were slammed in our faces.

If the feds considered Wilson the supreme Oglala authority on the reservation, that was never true in the traditional community. Most of those people boycotted all BIA-sponsored elections. They understood that whoever engineered the most votes from his extended family in the reservation's eight electoral districts would win the election and the title, but the support of the white man only. To the traditionals, the real power on Pine Ridge—the supreme spiritual leaders and therefore the moral authorities—lay with our eight traditional chiefs and holy men, all born in the last century. They embodied our culture and our aspiration to sovereignty. Frank Fools Crow, Charlie Red Cloud, Pete Catches, Matthew King, Weasel Bear, and the others were the legitimate heirs to leadership of the only nation that had ever forced the United States to beg for peace—the Lakota under Red Cloud's leadership.

For the first time in living memory, seven of those elderly leaders—the other was too ill to travel—gathered at a log-cabin community center in Calico, just north of Pine Ridge Village, to hear the complaints of their people. I spent two days and two nights at Calico listening to the litany of horror: Women and girls had been raped by goons, men jailed, whole families beaten by Wilson's police, money and valuables extorted at gunpoint, and homes firebombed by night riders. Tribal officials had ignored all official complaints. I went back to Rapid City and reported to everyone at the Mother Butler Center what I had seen and heard on Pine Ridge. We had a meeting of all members in the basement of that halfway house. Then the leaders held a second meeting. After hours of discussion, we couldn't come to any satisfactory agreement. Most of the AIM people at Mother Butler had been away from home since October and wanted to return to their homes. Finally, Dennis and three or four carloads of people who were headed to Arizona and then to Oklahoma agreed to attend another meeting at Calico before making up their minds.

On the afternoon of February 27, twenty-one AIM members, including some of the toughest guys in our organization, drove down to Calico in six cars. We joined about three hundred Oglala Lakota, mostly older women, who were packed into the meeting hall. One person after another got up to give testimony about the loss of civil rights under Wilson's dictatorship. After hours of that, the chiefs went downstairs to deliberate. When they returned, they had agreed that something had to be done quickly, but hadn't decided what it should be. They asked to talk to AIM members in private.

We all went across the highway to Holy Rosary Catholic Church. More than 160 churches were on the Pine Ridge Reservation, but that parish owned eighteen square miles of our land, more than any of the others. The pastor, Father Paul Steinmetz, perhaps afraid that Wilson's mostly Christian goons wouldn't like it, refused our request to help feed the people gathered in the community center. He did, however, let us meet in the church basement.

At one end of the room sat our seven chiefs, men of immense dignity who had earned the respect of all traditional Oglala. The others in the basement were Gladys Bissonnette, Pedro Bissonnette—a nephew by marriage—Ellen Moves Camp, Severt Young Bear, Edgar Bear Runner, Vern Long,

Dennis Banks, and me. The two women spoke first. They said it was up to the chiefs to lead our nation and to protect the people. They went down the list of responsibilities which tradition reserved for our leaders. They asked, "Where are our *men* today? Where are our *defenders?* Why is it mostly women and older men who are marching? When will decisions be made?" Gladys and Ellen spoke movingly about how the Lakota used to be—proud and democratic. The people's welfare always came first. Then each of the men spoke, including me. Dennis had the last word. We all agreed: Things could not continue as they were. If we didn't stand up now for our treaty, we would never be able to do so. Our people were ready to die, if necessary, to end the abuse.

By then, we all knew that the BIA's two-story red-brick building had been fortified with sandbagged bunkers and .50-caliber machine guns that could spit more than six bullets a second, each weighing more than half a pound. Bullets a half inch in diameter, and capable of hitting somebody more than a mile away with enough velocity to tear off an arm, turn a torso into a mass of red jelly, or literally explode a head. That building, the seat of the BIA's power on Pine Ridge, represented Wilson's oppression. He couldn't have lasted an hour without BIA backing. We all thought the chiefs would ask us to demonstrate in front of the BIA building, and we were ready to do it—even though we knew the whites were ready for us and would have liked nothing better than a chance to mow us down.

In my mind's eye, I still see the chiefs sitting in that basement. Their clothing was old and worn, their faces lined with a lifetime of struggle—but their eyes burned bright with righteous wisdom. Finally, Grandpa Fools Crow, speaking for all of them, said, "Go to Wounded Knee. There, you will be protected." No one had to ask what he meant. It was suicidal to go to the BIA building. Wounded Knee would always remain the haunting symbol of the white man's murderous treachery and of our nation's stoic grief. At Wounded Knee, on ground consecrated with the blood of our ancestors, we would make our stand. At Wounded Knee, as nowhere else, the spirits of Big Foot and his martyred people would protect us.

Part III

OUR STRUGGLE

1973–1978

▼▼▼▼▼▼▼▼▼

The Siege of
Wounded Knee

When the chiefs had filed out of the church after the historic meeting at Pine Ridge in February 1973, those of us in the basement spoke among ourselves. We agreed that if we told everyone we were going to take over Wounded Knee, some people might panic and some wouldn't go. We were also concerned that among the hundreds in and around the meeting hall, there might be a few with ears hired by the goons or the feds. Because the road to Porcupine ran through Wounded Knee, I suggested that we announce we were moving the meeting to Porcupine, where there was more room. It was twenty-five miles to Wounded Knee: Once we got through Pine Ridge Village, where marshals surrounded the BIA building, there was little chance that they could get ahead of us on that two-lane blacktop.

I called over a couple of carloads of AIM's best defenders and told them in a low voice, "We're going to take over Wounded Knee and make a stand there. We need you to hurry there right now and secure the guns and ammo at the trading post. The rest of us will come later." They were all veterans of the Trail of Broken Treaties, of Scottsbluff, Custer, Rapid City, Sturgis, and Hot Springs. Just as I did, they felt frustration and righteous anger building inside them. We knew we had to follow a path through whatever the Great

Mystery might put before us. None of those patriots asked me a single question. They just got in their cars and drove into the night.

It was about 6:00 P.M. and bitterly cold that February evening, with a little snow on the ground. The sky glowed with stars as we started to line up the caravan. Pedro Bissonnette had a police scanner in his old Cadillac and could monitor the BIA radio. As the last carload, we were still in Calico when the vanguard reached Pine Ridge. We could hear marshals calling to each other on their two-ways. I remember their saying: "They're coming!" Moments later, the radio crackled again: "They're approaching the hospital. They're at the hospital now. . . . There's a line of them—we've got a report of over eighty cars . . . up to ninety now. . . . They're coming down the hill. . . . They're at the creek . . . at the jail . . . they've reached the intersection. They're turning east! . . . They're continuing east! . . . They're not stopping! . . . They're driving right by! . . . They're not stopping!"

Hearing all those marshals and realizing they were heavily armed, I suddenly felt naked. I had no gun, and neither did Pedro. I remembered that my friend, Legal Aid lawyer Gary Thomas, had a .30-30 lever-action rifle, so we decided to stop at his house and borrow it. By the time we caught up with the caravan, the first cars had arrived at Wounded Knee. As we topped a rise overlooking the valley where the Wounded Knee creek meanders, I saw a long line of cars crawling bumper to bumper down the blacktop. More were parked all around the Gildersleeves' store. We went around the cars on the shoulder. As we passed the store, I saw people ransacking it and the museum. Angry and worried, I rushed inside. The advance party had secured the ammunition and weapons, but carloads of people who arrived afterward were ripping off groceries and everything else in sight. Others were carrying stuff away from the museum. Everyone was celebrating, ransacking, and looting. Even Pedro got caught up in it. He mounted a glass counter, wearing a big old headdress from the museum and waving a handgun. He was small and wiry, but that glass wasn't made to hold anyone. The top broke, and he fell through into the display case.

I shouted, "Stop! Take this stuff back!" Soon, other AIM leaders were trying to stop the looting. I thought, shit! The feds will be coming soon to attack, and we'll be sitting here breaking glass and carrying stuff away. We had no time to waste. I grabbed Pedro, some AIM guys, and others I knew from the reservation. I said, "We must get ready to defend this place. The highest point around is the church. Let's get up there and secure that hilltop."

We jumped into several cars and drove up to the church. *Hill* is too grand a word for that height. It was more of a gentle mound above rolling, wooded land intercut with stream beds, all of it surrounded by much higher ground. I told everyone to park the cars all around the church with the front ends facing out. "When they attack, we can throw on our headlights," I said. "They'll be blinded, and we can fire from behind our cars."

The Church of the Sacred Heart was locked. Everything I knew about breaking down doors came from the Western movies of my youth. I grabbed my borrowed .30-30, went around to the back door, and slammed it with the gun butt. It was just like in the movies—except that the stock splintered and fell off. Now I had a rifle with no stock. Somebody got a tire iron, slid one end into the crack in the door, and twisted. The door popped open. Inside, we turned on the lights, yelling and looking for the Jesuit priest, Father Paul Manhart. We found him in black trousers and long woolen underwear, napping in the choir loft. Half befuddled with sleep, he said, "What's wrong?" I sent someone to tie his hands behind his back. He was too stunned to protest. We took over the building and used the area with pews as our meeting hall. In the basement, we found a cookstove, sink, tables, and chairs.

Of all those who came to Wounded Knee that night, less than two dozen were AIM members. Nevertheless, because we were the most disciplined and organized, everyone looked to us to lead the way. After the hill was secured and our puny defenses were ready, I sent for Dennis and the rest of the leaders to tell them that our headquarters would be the church, at least for the time being. It would also be our last line of defense.

Most of the men came to a meeting at which, among other things, I asked Vietnam vets or anybody who had military service to come forward. Stan Holder, who had served three tours in Vietnam as a Green Beret, was put in charge of our security force. My brother Bill had been a paratrooper and many others had served in the military, so they headed squads of people who had no such training. We had brought few weapons, but several hunting rifles and other guns were at the trading post. We passed those out. Stan made sure everyone who got a weapon knew how to use it—and would. Early in the evening, we heard gunshots and sent patrols out to reconnoiter, but they found nothing.

The people who owned the trading post, the Gildersleeves and their son-in-law's family, were in their respective houses. We asked them all to move into the largest house, which belonged to the elder Gildersleeves, and they agreed. We posted guards at the store to save what was left of its goods—which was considerable—for the people who lived in the community.

I returned to the church and met with the OSCRO people, including Vern Long and Pedro. Because that was our land, Pedro and I decided to draw up a list of demands and present them to the FBI officials when they showed up.

We wanted to know as soon as possible when they arrived, so we established manned roadblocks on the bridge over Wounded Knee Creek and on both highways leading north, to keep anybody from driving in on us. We sent patrols out to screen the surrounding hills. Blacktopped Highway 33 ran northwest to Manderson, and Highway 27 went northeast to Porcupine and south to Highway 18, which connected to Pine Ridge. A gravel lane called Denby Road ran east through the hills to Batesland, a tiny Shannon County town. We used the phone in the trading post to call the media in Minneapolis, Cleveland, and elsewhere about what we had done and why.

With everything more or less under control, things quieted down. Except for those on guard, everyone tried to get some sleep. Looking for a place to lay my head, I went toward a little trailer house across from the trading post and museum near the Gildersleeve home. I saw people coming out of the museum with blankets filled with loot. I stopped them and had them return the stuff. I found a back bedroom in the trailer, and closed my eyes for two or three hours. With my mind racing a mile a minute, I could barely sleep. I got up before dawn and walked in the calm half-light. I could see my breath. The air was only a few degrees above zero.

Someone came rushing up to say we were on network radio news. The announcer said we had taken white hostages, but one man had managed to escape. What had really happened was that when our advance guard came in to seize the trading post, Jim Czywczynski, Clive Gildersleeve's son-in-law, abandoned his wife and small children—including one in diapers—jumped into his pickup, and drove off. So that chickenshit had invented an "escape" story! The radio also said the U.S. Marshal's Special Operations Group was in charge of several federal agencies, including the FBI, and was surrounding us, sealing off Wounded Knee. Visitors to Pine Ridge were cautioned to proceed "at their own risk."

When I heard that broadcast, my first thought was, my God, what have we gotten ourselves into now? I went outside to be alone and think, but Severt Young Bear and Edgar Bear Runner came out with me. I said to them, "We probably won't get out of this alive." Edgar nodded his head. "Yeah, I know," he said. "Like our ancestors," added Severt. It was a sobering moment. The three of us stood in the cold looking into the misty eastern sky, waiting for the sun to come up, each lost in his own thoughts.

I thought of my kids, Sherry and Hank and Michele and Scott, and how they would never get a chance to know me. I offered a little prayer of hope that my death would make life easier for them, and that whatever happened, things would somehow get better for my people. I believed that we would have to stay there until we died—and at that moment I had no faith that the feds would even listen to us. I thought that as soon as they could assemble their forces, they would attack.

A few minutes after sunup, a pair of F4 Phantom jets raced low across the valley of Wounded Knee, trailing thick ribbons of dark smoke. After skimming low over our heads, going south, they banked sharply, then leveled off and came directly at us. They were so low I could read their markings and could see dark, streamlined bulges tucked under swept-back wings. They looked like napalm canisters.

I thought it was all over for us.

Dennis pulled out his revolver. In a last act of defiance, he fired once at the jets. The shot was all but drowned out by the incredibly loud roar of their engines.

We should have combed our hair and smiled, for we found out later that those were only reconnaissance planes. The dark shapes under the wings were cameras. We had just had our pictures taken!

Soon the FBI called on the trading-post phone. Joseph H. Trimbach, from Minneapolis, special agent in charge, wanted to meet with us. We told him to come to our roadblock on the Pine Ridge Road. We decided to let him wait in the cold for us instead of the other way around, so when he arrived, the roadblock guards signaled and I walked down there with OSCRO's officers, including Vern Long and Pedro. One look told me Trimbach was definitely out of the running that year for FBI poster boy. His eyes were rimmed in red and his jaw was covered with an eight-in-the-morning shadow, like a five-o'clock shadow but darker. A limp tie dangled loosely from his neck. His white shirt was in the terminal stages of ring-around-the-collar. And he was crabby.

I don't know what Trimbach was expecting, but most of our demands were for actions that the U.S. government had already agreed to in 1868— to enforce the provisions of the Fort Laramie Treaty by returning our sacred Black Hills and reestablishing an independent Oglala Nation. We further demanded that Senator Edward Kennedy's subcommittee on administrative practices and procedures immediately investigate the BIA and the Department of the Interior for the way they had handled things on Pine Ridge. We called for Senator J. William Fulbright's Foreign Affairs Committee to investigate U.S. compliance with all 371 treaties it had signed with Indian nations. In particular, we wanted them to confirm that the United States had violated every one of the treaties. Because Dick Wilson and his followers were nothing more than puppets, we demanded that the Oglala be permitted to choose their own officials without BIA interference.

Trimbach read our list of demands and stared at us in disbelief. "This is it? You can't be serious," he said. "You people have to lay down your arms and give yourselves up or we are going to have to come in."

We all smiled. "Take this to your chief," I said. As we walked away, Trimbach yelled, "Who do you think you are? You're in a fishbowl. Don't you understand? We can wipe you out!"

When I got back to the trading post, the Indian people who lived around Wounded Knee and had been ripped off for years by the Gildersleeves started to come in. They filled their cars with gas and loaded up on groceries, hardware, dry goods—all free. All of them seemed to feel they had to get something. I saw a kid about ten years old riding away on his bicycle with a hunter's trophy, the mounted head of a mountain goat, teetering on the handlebars. By midday, the place was picked clean. We rounded up brooms and mops and tidied the inside of the store.

All around the country, the headline news was that a bunch of savages—radical, militant Indians—was holding white hostages. A reporter named Walter Fisk had accompanied us from Calico the first night, but it was days before his reports were published. CBS had the first broadcast network crew to arrive. After trying the road from Pine Ridge and being turned back by the feds, they rented a carryall with four-wheel drive and came overland. A wire-service photographer got into the trading post when it was still filled with trash, and his pictures were distributed worldwide. Naturally, none were published showing how the store looked after we cleaned it up.

Those pictures stimulated press interest around the world. Reporters from everywhere converged on Pine Ridge. The smartest of them realized they couldn't rely on what the government was saying about us. Media types with cameras came in through our lines in the hills, among them a UPI reporter. He was among the last of the newsies to arrive, and he was exceptionally nosy. He horned in on everything, trying so hard to be buddy-buddy that he made a nuisance of himself. We figured him for a fed posing as a reporter, but his credentials were genuine, so we let him stay.

As local people came in to the trading post, several told us that the Gildersleeves had a huge stock of government commodities, foodstuffs that the Department of Agriculture provided free to the poorest of the poor, including rice, beans, lard, flour, sugar, fruit juices, instant mashed potatoes, and dried eggs. When we looked in their houses and in the post office—run by the Gildersleeves—we found commodities everywhere, in clothes closets, under beds, in basements, even in postal storage bins. It was unbelievable: There were several tons of the stuff. The only way those whites could have gotten their hands on such quantities was from impoverished Indians who paid debts to the trading post with their only food because, as we had learned during the Red Ribbon Grand Juries, it was the only way they could get cash. The Gildersleeves held the Indians' checks ransom in the post office for debts owed to the store. Possession of those goods was a federal crime, but for years those white bloodsuckers had been black-marketing them to ranchers, double-dipping profit from both ends. It made me sick to think about all the Indian children who went hungry because those whites illegally hoarded and sold tons of food.

We also found that the Gildersleeves didn't have a valid federal license to operate the trading post. We boxed up all the records and smuggled them out of Wounded Knee. Feeling sure the feds would charge us with mail theft, violation of postal regulations, and everything else they could dream up, we wanted a way to bring to light all the Gildersleeves' illegal acts. We also boxed up records from the store and the museum and sent them out for safekeeping. As it turned out, although we demolished a U.S. post office and could at least have been accused of destroying government property, no one at Wounded Knee was ever charged with postal violations. I'll always believe it was because the government didn't want all the illegalities committed in that post office to become public during a trial.

Long-oppressed locals looting the trading post to put food on their tables didn't bother me, but I felt that the contents of the museum belonged to all Lakota people, to all Indians. Despite my efforts to stop them, however, people carried off almost everything in the museum. I have learned since that much of it was apparel that had been dug out of the mass graves of victims of the 1890 Wounded Knee massacre. Other items, such as pipes, had been bought for a trifle from poor reservation Indians after the massacre, when they were too scared to refuse their oppressors. When cavalrymen went around pointing at things they wanted for souvenirs, the Indians gave them up instead of risking getting shot or raped over a trinket. I've heard that some items from the museum remain in the possession of descendants of victims, and that some were sold. The vast majority of those artifacts, however, were put back into the earth they came from, without being wrapped or placed in a coffin, so they would deteriorate and disappear, never to be robbed again. Pottery was smashed to smithereens so it could never be reappropriated.

One of the most racist items in the museum was a book dating to the nineteenth century. It was a record of the delivery of live cattle to individual people on Pine Ridge. The cavalry captain in charge had made up names for the Indians who received that beef—the ugliest, sickest, nastiest names anyone could imagine—"Shits In His Food," "She Comes Nine Times," "Fucks His Daughter," and "Maggot Dick," to recall a few. When I first had seen that vile book in 1967, I got so mad I had to leave. When we took over in 1973, we burned it.

On that first day, we put up a large tipi. We also built a small purification lodge. Because it was Crow Dog's and he was *Heyoka*, it faced west. We framed it with red willow. It was a low hut, entered on hands and knees, that represents the womb of our sacred Grandmother. Only about a dozen people could sit around the fire pit in the center where the sacred stones were placed after they were heated. When the willows were covered with blankets and tarps and the door was closed, it was completely dark inside. Then water was poured over the stones to make steam. Crow Dog led us in thanksgiving and other ceremonies, and that began our spiritual healing, which continued throughout the siege. Purification-lodge ceremonies went on almost constantly, and for several consecutive nights he held *yuwipi* meetings.

On the afternoon of the first day, February 28, we held our first mass meeting. Everyone came except the guards at each of the bunkers we had begun to build as defensive positions at each roadblock. The leaders told everyone, in the bluntest terms, what we were up against—the same thing our ancestors had faced in 1890. We were brutally honest about the resources and firepower being brought in against us. According to radio reports, thousands of armed troops were converging on Pine Ridge. We told our people that anyone who wanted to leave was free to go at any time. Almost everyone gave some kind of talk, fiery speeches and heartrending speeches and very beautiful speeches. The essence of them all was that we had chosen that time and place to stand up for our 1868 treaty—and that it was our last chance. Just before dark, we all went to the mass grave in the cemetery behind the church. Shivering in the cold, Crow Dog presided over a sacred pipe ceremony.

Several white families lived in and around Wounded Knee. Besides three generations of Gildersleeves and Czywczynskis—who occupied four houses and a trailer—there were three families of missionaries living in well-kept, well-heated homes with running water and basements stocked with canned goods. The missionaries all left at the start of the siege, so some of our people bunked in their homes. We turned a second church complex, very new and nicely built, into a meeting hall. A third, built at about the turn of the century, was a small, humble place that kept a few of us out of the cold. Dennis took refuge in one of the Gildersleeve homes. I found a place to sleep in their trailer house, which I shared with about half a dozen of our security guys.

By the night of the first day, the feds had begun to show up, first on the hill southwest of Wounded Knee. They established roadblocks out of our sight on the highway to Porcupine, in the hills south toward Pine Ridge, on the Denby Road, and to the north on the Manderson Road. When they didn't attack immediately, we hunkered down for what we were beginning to realize might be a long siege. After dozens of our cars had taken free fill-ups, we decided to conserve our remaining gasoline and put a lock on the pumps.

After a few days the weather turned unseasonably warm. Soon we were going around outside without jackets. Stan Holder's defenders scrounged around to find tools and materials to build bunkers. We found a few picks and shovels, but the earth was frozen solid two feet deep and it was hard digging. Once they broke through the frozen part with picks and shovels, the guys went to work with golf clubs from a missionary's house. It wasn't easy digging with a four iron, but there weren't enough shovels to go around.

We gathered all the food we could find, and recruited volunteers to lead supply runs through the hills in and out of Wounded Knee. The most awesome of them was Oscar Bear Runner, a tough, wiry little World War II vet in his fifties. Almost every night he trekked to and from Porcupine, bringing in people and supplies. That was an eight-mile ride down the highway, but Oscar's route led through forested hills. He was a miracle worker, carrying a heavy rucksack on a journey of at least ten miles each way. Many times he left at dark and made *two* trips, walking all night without a break to finish just before dawn.

Initially, everyone in AIM regarded Wounded Knee as an Oglala fight. We had come to lend our discipline, organizational expertise, and experience in confronting the white man. The women, led by Gladys Bissonnette and Ellen Moves Camp, met constantly with AIM's leaders and OSCRO's officers. As both an Oglala and an AIM member, I went back and forth between the groups. Because I wore both hats, I became the obvious person for everyone to come to with questions, complaints, or suggestions. During the first week, at least, I knew of no secrets in Wounded Knee. We held at least two general meetings daily, in late morning and early evening, to keep everyone informed and to maintain morale.

At that time, we had about 350 people at Wounded Knee, but fewer than a hundred men. Among them was my sun-dance idol, Pete Catches. Even though he had just come through surgery and had an open wound that needed constant care, he felt he had to stay with us. We also had some children and teenagers, but the vast majority of our people were women—well over two hundred of them.

Most Indian women in those years, like Gladys and Ellen, were strong, and they were also innately wise. Taking the glory was not on their agenda. Understanding the female-male balance, they felt no need to be anointed publicly with leadership. They also knew that whoever was up front usually ended up getting shot at or going to prison, so their contributions were usually behind the scenes, functioning as an informal network of advisers and keeping everyone informed and motivated. They knew a woman's role is *different* than a man's—not better or worse—and they didn't try to become something they weren't. By respecting that natural balance, women helped move us all along toward our common goals. That insight first occurred to me at Wounded Knee. I began to realize that my grandparents' generation, raised by people who were born free, was not contaminated by the white man's schools. They knew how to be one with their mates and how to show respect for one another. If our older women knew and respected their role, Indian men of my generation didn't. We had been robbed of our heritage through the brutality experienced by our parents and passed on to us all.

But for ten weeks, surrounded by all the might of the U.S. government, we, too, were free—and inside the Knee, nobody had time to worry about gender roles. Following the lead of strong, traditional women who knew what nature expected of them, everyone came to respect the balance between the sexes. The oldest of our women was Sally Hat, a traditional Oglala of nearly eighty who made her headquarters in the church's basement kitchen. She was an extraordinary woman, a natural teacher. Often we talked far into the night, and Sally told me all sorts of little things about our culture that no one would ever think to ask. She explained the meanings of certain Lakota words—not as the white man translates them, but what they *really* meant. Sally told me that the Lakota translators whom the U.S. Army had relied on in the last century were liars and the worst sort of men, and their language skills were very poor. Extending her forearm with a sweeping motion to embrace all of Pine Ridge, she said, "They were just like all the young people you find on this reservation now—they didn't know how to talk Lakota and they didn't know how to talk English."

Sally worked in the kitchen all day, then talked far into the night. It seemed as if she never slept, but then I would come to the church early in the morning and people would say, "Sally's sleeping." A hush would descend over her kitchen. That church is now long gone; all that remains is a filled-in foundation. In all the years that followed the siege, whenever I visited Wounded Knee, I went to peer down into that dirt-filled basement. Sometimes I believe I can still see Sally around her stove, some bit of sewing in her hand, talking, teaching, passing on the wisdom of past generations.

We released Father Manhart from his bonds once he was assured of our intentions, but from the start, the national media sensationalized the FBI's claim that we were holding white "hostages"—Manhart, the Gildersleeves, and the Czywczynskis. Our leaders, at least, began to worry that we would get nailed for kidnapping. At first those fears were unspoken. Every time the media or the feds talked about "hostages," we all looked at one another, knowing that once *we* said we held "hostages," it would be the final nail in our coffins. Everyone refrained from using the "*h*" word, and continued to tell the Gildersleeves that whenever they wanted to leave, all they had to do was tell us. We were very forthright with them and didn't try to lie about what we had found in their store and the post office, but we also explained that our war wasn't with *them*. We never came right out and said in so many words that we were willing to keep silent about their crimes, but I'm sure they understood that we were treating them well and they had nothing to gain—and much to lose—by claiming to be held against their will.

As the media continued to trumpet "hostage" stories, South Dakota Senators Jim Abourezk and George McGovern contacted us. They asked to see for themselves how the "hostages" were being treated. We had nothing to hide, so we invited them both in on March 2. They were accompanied by a small army of camera crews, foreign press, and wire-service reporters. We negotiated the terms of their visit in front of cameras. All we asked was that the senators accept armed guards for their own safety. Then we all packed into one of the Gildersleeve houses for another meeting to tell the world why we were in Wounded Knee. When the senators said they wanted to see the "hostages," we reminded them again that we held none. They said they wanted to see the Gildersleeves, the Czywczynskis, and Father Manhart, and we said, "Of course."

Abourezk said, "Can we see them with the news media present?" We hadn't discussed that possibility among ourselves, so I looked at Dennis and Clyde, and everyone looked at one another. Then we shrugged. We weren't afraid of the truth. "Sure," we said, knowing that this was our big moment, that things had become deadly serious: One word from a white, and we were all kidnappers. We packed into the living room of the largest house, the senators, a few Oglala and AIM leaders, and a swarm of newsies. Lights, camera, action—this was for all the marbles. The Gildersleeves sat before a battery of movie and still cameras and tape recorders. McGovern came right out with it. "Are you hostages?" he asked.

Agnes Gildersleeve, then in her seventies, was indignant. "Of course we're not hostages!" she said. "These Indians are here and they have legitimate grievances. You people—it's all *your* fault. If you people had done something about their problems, they wouldn't be here today. We're here not only to protect our property, but also because we want to help save the Indians, and we know you're ready to massacre them."

We knew this was bullshit, of course, but we didn't care. Knowing the whole scene was going to be on national television, we looked at one another, grins all but swallowing our faces. The spirits haunting Wounded Knee must have worked hard for that moment. Both senators sat in amazement, repeating, "You mean you're not hostages?" They went around the room, the cameras following, as one by one all the people, including Father Manhart and a teenage girl, were asked if they were being held against their will. Each said no. Then the senators went around the room again and asked everybody if they wanted to stay or go. Again, everyone said, "I want to stay." Then a reporter asked if we would allow anyone to leave who wanted to. We said, "You can take them out right now in front of the cameras." As I recall, the teenager and her father decided to leave then.

What none of us knew then was that for several days, since we had taken over Wounded Knee, a little miracle had been going on in that house. The wonder-worker was Eddie Whitewater, a Winnebago in his late thirties. He was in charge of the guard we had posted over the Gildersleeves, a necessary precaution because so many Indian people living in that area had suffered from the Gildersleeves' predatory ways at the store or post office. Although the family was free to go anywhere, we had asked them to accept an armed escort for their own protection. They had been quick to see the wisdom of that.

We had given the job of supervising their guards to Eddie in the belief that he would allow no conversation whatsoever. For some reason, he began to talk to the Gildersleeves. Soon he was pouring out his heart about why he had joined AIM, why he had come to Wounded Knee, and everything that was going on. Those people, who had spent most of their lives on a reservation but had never taken the time to listen to what an Indian really thought or felt, quickly came to admire Eddie. He convinced them of the righteousness of our cause, and that whole family came to love him. Because he stayed with them through the night, they all slept soundly, feeling secure in his presence. When he took a few hours to sleep, they asked for him constantly.

The senators left, satisfied that no white people were in danger from us. We were elated. Things couldn't have worked better if we had written a script. As it was, we all wanted to kiss Eddie. Instead, we took the heavy guard away from the Gildersleeves' house and left Eddie only. Within a few days, however, things around Wounded Knee became far more dangerous. As supplies, especially food, got low, the Gildersleeves, Czywczynskis, and Manhart decided they wanted to leave. We helped them pack their clothes and personal things, and they drove off.

After Abourezk and McGovern left, the FBI said it wanted to negotiate. A group of women headed by Gladys and Ellen told the agents we wouldn't talk to Marshal Wayne Colburn or Special Agent Joseph Trimbach or anybody like them. There could be no negotiations, the women said, unless we were speaking to top-level people from Washington who had real authority. They asked to speak with one of Nixon's personal representatives, either Bob Haldeman, John Ehrlichman, Charles Colson, or another top assistant.

That was the end of "negotiations" until March 4, when Ralph Erickson, a Justice Department negotiator, arrived from Washington. He sent us a message that said, in effect, that because nothing serious had happened yet, the government would go easy on us if we all gave up now.

Apparently anticipating our quick surrender, the feds allowed more press to come in the next day, March 5. The networks rented big motor homes and came back in with whole teams of people—lighting, electrical, and sound men, cameramen, reporters, and a producer. ABC, then still the runt brother of network news, moved almost its entire Chicago bureau to set up camp in Rapid City, Pine Ridge, and Wounded Knee. Like most of the other newsmen, they were all veterans of Vietnam—all great guys. When we watched the nightly news, some of those cameramen and reporters, who had risked their lives to smuggle film through the feds' perimeter, got very pissed off because the lead Wounded Knee story was usually narrated by a reporter outside talking about what was going on inside.

After the media, the feds allowed the first of what would be several volunteer medical teams to come in. Most of them were Chicanos, including a group sent by the Crusade for Justice, a Denver group run by Corky Gonzales. Because they supported us at Wounded Knee, they were made to suffer at home. Riot police assaulted their headquarters a couple of times. People known to sympathize with them were harassed by the police. Louis Martinez was mysteriously murdered, and many other AIM sympathizers were thrown in jail by the feds or the Denver police—not only during the Wounded Knee occupation but also afterward.

On March 6, a young guy named Bill Zimmerman flew in a planeload of medical supplies. He landed on the highway near the trading post—an act of tremendous courage. He had painted over his aircraft numbers so the feds couldn't trace him. After Zimmerman showed that it could be done, Rocky Madrid, a Chicano medic, flew another small plane in. He swooped low over the trees, dodging a hail of FBI machine-gun fire to bring medical supplies. The marksmen continued to shoot at him while he unloaded, taxied down the Pine Ridge highway to turn around, and took off. A few days later, Rocky walked back in through the woods.

On March 6, our leaders called a meeting in the hilltop church to share the feds' "proposal" with everyone. With Crow Dog and me standing beside him on the pulpit, Dennis read the letter, then held up the paper it was written on. "This is what we think of their offer," he said. He lit a match to it. As the flames devoured the paper, everybody went wild, and the church rocked with our cheers.

After dark, between little firefights that went on most of the night, about forty people slipped in to reinforce us. Among them was comedian Dick Gregory, who put on a little show, lifting everyone's morale. Nixon had just abolished the gold standard backing the dollar, which led to its international devaluation. Dick cracked us up by saying what had *really* knocked the dollar down was the world's realization that we Indians hadn't been conquered and were trying to take back our land. He told jokes about white people on television and how, to judge by the commercials, they are all in terrible shape. On television, only whites have body odor, skin blemishes, colds, and coughs. Only whites are so fat they need girdles. We were in stitches. Dick risked his life to make us laugh, and I, for one, will always be grateful.

Other visitors, escorted through the roadblocks by marshals, included the Reverend Ralph Abernathy of the Southern Christian Leadership Conference and the Reverend John Adams of the National Council of Churches. They came to see what they could do to help resolve the crisis. We also met with the U.S. Justice Department's Community Relations Service.

Dick Wilson's goons had not been idle while most of AIM was in Wounded Knee. Wilson himself threatened to kill Gary Thomas, the Legal Aid lawyer, unless he left the reservation at once. The Pine Ridge home of AIM member Aaron DeSersa was firebombed and burned to the ground. On March 7, the day after we rejected the Justice Department's "offer," Wilson threatened to attack us with nine hundred men.

Instead of launching an assault, however, the feds decided on March 8 that they wanted to talk again. They wouldn't come into Wounded Knee and we wouldn't go out, so we set up a tipi in no-man's-land—a hilltop between and in full view of our respective roadblocks on the Pine Ridge Road. Our delegation was headed by Gladys, Ellen, Pedro, Crow Dog, and his assistant, Wallace Black Elk. Ralph Erickson, the Justice Department's emissary from Washington, knew how to bargain. He said, "The U.S. Government does not negotiate with a gun to its head." Instead of an opening offer, he handed us an ultimatum: If we didn't leave by a certain time the next day, they were coming in, supported by helicopter gunships, tanks, artillery, and fast movers from the Tactical Air Force, to take us out. As darkness fell, we could hear armored personnel carriers moving into position all around us.

We had shotguns, a few pistols, and some hunting rifles. Even with hundreds of women and children present, the feds from the start had shown little restraint with their overwhelming firepower. Air Force Phantom jets roared overhead night and day. Before the siege was over, the feds would have expended more than $5 million worth of ammo. They fired small arms and automatic weapons, including .50 calibers, into our area every night. Sometimes we shot back, and firefights went on until well after daylight. Mostly, the feds shot at shadows or at noises. On many nights, the feds let Wilson's goons and white vigilantes creep through the woods to snipe at us or stir things up. If they couldn't find an easy target, they would take a few random shots, then run away when the firefight started.

The feds surrounding us represented several agencies. There was so much bureaucratic infighting between the FBI and the marshals that Nixon soon put the Pentagon in charge. Every night, Wounded Knee was illuminated with flares fired from heavy mortars miles away. Their shells exploded high overhead, dropping blazing flares that dangled beneath tiny parachutes, producing harsh, oscillating light that cast weird shadows. Whenever a flare popped overhead, everyone outside either hit the ground or froze in position until it came down. Often, those incendiaries started brush or grass fires where they landed. In a matter of days, everything around Wounded Knee was burned black. Talk about stupidity—the feds made it easier for us to get supplies and people in and out. Instead of forcing us to go across snow-covered ground where we would be easy to spot at night, we could walk through blackened areas, where we were practically invisible.

Probably because media people were present, there was no attack. Two days later, on March 10, the feds announced that they were taking down their roadblocks. Everyone was ecstatic. That afternoon Dennis made a big victory speech in the community hall, and everybody celebrated. People were jumping up and down, some firing their guns in jubilation. I was very worried, and I almost panicked. I got up on a table and asked people to please quiet down. When I could be heard, I said, "Look, it isn't over. Don't leave, because if you do they'll arrest you." Many of the Oglala people said they felt they needed to go home and check on their wives and husbands and children. I kept saying, "Wait! They're going to arrest you all! They'll put you in jail with a high bond and grill you. They will go back on their word." Few people would listen. I tried again. "I'm not leaving!" I shouted. "Anyone who leaves will be arrested!"

Finally, the leaders agreed that we had to stay—but it was too late. People were already leaving, among them Pete Catches. He wanted to stay, but his wound had become infected. When the roadblocks came down, his family came in after him. Grandpa Fools Crow went out so he could become the main spokesman of the traditional people to the feds. He was a sly old fox who could speak and understand English but always pretended that he couldn't—even to Thomas Mails, coauthor of his 1979 autobiography.

People were streaming out of Wounded Knee, but the next day even more began to pour in. They were men and women who had driven night and day from every corner of America, mostly from other Indian nations, but also a few whites, Asians, and blacks. In this impromptu changing of the guard were several people from the Rosebud, replacing about the same number who had returned to their Rosebud homes. Altogether, about 200 Oglala went home, but in their place came about 150 other Indians. Most of the whites and some Indians were from Vietnam Veterans Against the War, including guys in wheelchairs who had been crippled or had lost limbs. Many adopted nicknames such as White Bob, Honky Killer, and Hillbilly—a great guy but a strange dude who looked, sounded, and dressed like the television character Jed Clampett come to life. I never learned his real name.

We held a meeting in a big tipi to talk about sovereignty and the 1868 treaty. Many responsible, traditional people attended, including former Pine Ridge tribal president Gerald One Feather and most of our chiefs and holy men. We agreed that we would stand up for our treaty and declare Wounded Knee the Independent Oglala Nation. We would start to build our nation and would defend its territory militarily. In late afternoon as the meeting wound down, reports began to filter back. People leaving the area were being arrested. We sent out new patrols and learned that the feds had taken down their roadblocks to allow traffic to move, but marshals in APCs were monitoring traffic and taking down license numbers.

We still hadn't forced the government to enter into real negotiations about our treaty. Without a confrontation to focus public attention on Wounded Knee, the government could ignore us. The war would be over, and we would lose. I decided to try to start a firefight so the marshals would put the roadblocks back up and we could continue the battle. I joined a patrol that moved north toward Porcupine. As we hiked across an open hillside northwest of the church, marshals in foxholes, bunkers, and an APC opened up with M-16s. We dropped to the ground and returned fire. As Webster Poor Bear raised his rifle to his cheek, a bullet struck his hand. If he hadn't been holding the stock, the bullet would have smashed his face. A moment later, a Lakota named Milo Goings was wounded, ironically, in the knee. I aimed my battered, borrowed .30-30 and fired a shot, then another and a third, jacking a fresh round into the chamber with the lever each time. The fourth time I squeezed the trigger, I heard a dull click—out of ammo. I couldn't believe it. Within seconds, everybody else ran out, too. The marshals started to pour it on. We lay on our bellies in a shallow fold in the ground, arms flat at our sides or around our heads, with little clods of dirt kicking up all around us where bullets struck. I've never hugged Grandmother Earth as tightly before or since.

As bullets rained down on us, a man from another of our patrols, Bernard Escamilla, a Nebraska Chicano, came along a fence to the top of a low rise, hollering, "Quit shooting! You're causing fire to come down on us!"

"You dumb shit, can't you tell *they're* shooting at *us?*" I yelled. "What do you mean, quit firing? They're firing at anything that moves!"

We were out in the open, completely exposed. Finally there was a brief lull in the action. A convertible driven by someone—I remember him as Clyde Bellecourt, but I could be wrong—came zooming up to us. We threw Milo on the floor in back. As the car turned around, the marshals cut loose again, but Clyde zipped back down the hill and out of range.

A van that belonged to one of our guys pulled up near a cluster of three or four guys long enough for them to jump in. I was with a half-dozen people several yards farther down the slope. If I was going to do any open-field running, it wasn't going to be *toward* the feds or parallel to them. While the van lurched and bumped down the hill with bullets ricocheting all around it, the rest of my patrol got up and ran. We zigged and we zagged and we sprinted, with single shots and bursts of automatic fire snapping and hissing around our ears. I could *feel* some of those rounds whiz by—the heat and the shock wave. I ran the two hundred longest yards of my life toward some empty houses that offered cover. It was an eerie feeling, expecting a slug with my name on it. I ran with my back muscles knotted in anticipation. I ran until my lungs were afire and my heart threatened to burst.

When we reached the safety of the cabins, we were all so winded that none of us could say a word. I couldn't believe we had made it. It was a miracle that only two men had been hit, and superficially at that, the first casualties in Wounded Knee. Rocky Madrid, the medic, came over to help out. Suddenly Black Horse, a guy from Canada, came driving in. He had been in a firefight, too. "I think I just shot an FBI agent," he said, upset. A bunch of guys started to rag him:

"What the fuck did you do that for?"

"Goddamn it, what's wrong with you?"

"What are you trying to do—get us all killed?"

After a few minutes of that, I remember Dennis saying, "Wait a minute! This man's a hero. We should be celebrating. We should be congratulating him. We should give him an honor. He defended our nation and lived to talk about it." Everyone was quiet. There were sheepish looks all around. Our struggle to force a serious discussion of our treaty rights would continue.

2 8

▼▼▼▼▼▼▼▼▼

Hunkering Down

When the roadblocks went back up on March 12, most of us prepared again to die. Crow Dog mixed a special red paint made from grinding certain rocks, and offered to mark every man among us who was willing to fight to the death. Quite a few guys said no, thanks. Just before sundown even more people, myself among them, gathered around a bonfire near the mass grave of Big Foot and the other victims of the 1890 Wounded Knee Massacre. Each of us accepted a single line daubed across the cheeks and the bridge of the nose, just below the eyes. William Kunstler, one of our attorneys, joined us as we circled the grave marker. He put his hand on it, and Crow Dog said, "The spirits will welcome you." To this day, Kunstler recalls with awe that he felt the huge block of stone move beneath his fingers. Several other people also reported the same experience.

We let the media film that rite, and the reporters went into a feeding frenzy. That was exactly how they wanted to show Indians, circling a blazing fire, chanting and singing and putting on paint. Later, reporters and commentators who had not been at Wounded Knee said we had staged that for the cameras. Nonsense! We "staged" it for ourselves, the way a Catholic stages Mass or a Jew stages Yom Kippur or a Muslim stages a pilgrimage to

Mecca. Of course it was dramatic and solemn. We were all pledging to die for our beliefs.

After proclaiming the Independent Oglala Nation, we put someone in charge of citizenship. Passports were issued to everyone. On one side was a copy of our 1868 treaty, on the other our own personal data—in Lakota.

With the roadblocks back up, food became a paramount concern. Thousands of cattle, most belonging to white ranchers, were grazing on leased Indian land on Pine Ridge. To find some of them, Edgar Bear Runner, Pedro, and I borrowed horses from some Indian people living in the area and rode north into the woods. After wading across a creek through freezing water belly-high to our mounts, we came across a small herd of cows that damn near asked us to take them back for dinner. We herded them back to the creek, where some changed their minds and ran back the way they had come. Edgar was riding rear guard. For some reason, he jumped off his horse and started to wave his arms, jumping up and down, trying to stop them. They ran right by him, of course, and spooked his mare. We had to chase after her. We teased him about that all the way back to Wounded Knee.

On March 13, Dick Wilson rammed a resolution through the Pine Ridge tribal executive committee to bar anyone who wasn't Oglala from entering the reservation. Obviously, the feds weren't going to leave, so that illegal "law" was intended only to make criminal the presence of our supporters from Indian nations around the country. That same day, Harlington Wood, an assistant secretary in the Civil Rights Division of the Department of Justice, flew through a blizzard to reopen negotiations. He told us that if he couldn't take substantial concessions back to Washington, we would have to deal with someone else. He visited a couple of times, but just about all he said was that the government wouldn't negotiate until we surrendered.

The next day, a federal grand jury handed down thirty-one indictments for conspiracy, burglary, civil disorder, and other felony complaints. Much of the AIM and OSCRO leadership was charged. Two days later, more than five thousand people marched in Denver to show support for us. At about the same time, marshals raided the Porcupine community center, perhaps hoping to find some of our supporters. On March 17, Wood presented us with a surrender plan, his "best offer."

To make the point that we had no choice, after the "proposal" was delivered, the feds spent three hours spraying thousands of rounds at us. Rocky Madrid took an M-16 bullet in the belly. Normally, an M-16 bullet tumbles on impact, tearing huge wounds in the body. After striking Rocky, this bullet turned ninety degrees and traveled just below his skin for about four inches. At our little makeshift hospital in what had been the elder Gildersleeves' home, Crow Dog treated Rocky. As everyone watched, he used a scalpel to make a tiny incision over the bullet, then pulled it out with his fingers. A little antiseptic, a few stitches, and Rocky was almost as good as new. The television crewmen, who had seen the horrific wounds made by M-16s in Vietnam, couldn't believe it.

We presented Wood's surrender offer at a mass meeting. Our people decided that we of the Independent Oglala Nation wouldn't negotiate with a gun to our heads, either. The siege would continue until the government was ready to talk about honoring our treaty. The next day, Oglala people outside Wounded Knee presented Department of the Interior officials with a petition bearing more than 1,400 hundred signatures, calling for a referendum on the tribal constitution that allowed Dick Wilson to rule Pine Ridge through fear and intimidation.

At about that time, a copy of a letter written by Senator McGovern to the U.S. Attorney General was smuggled to us. McGovern was the man who had run for president on the Democratic ticket in 1972, and who for years had led the peace movement in condemning the United States for attacking Vietnamese villages and killing civilians. This time, however, the men, women, and children were in his own backyard. Such is the hatred whites harbor for Indians that the essence of McGovern's letter to Nixon's chief law-enforcement officer was a suggestion that the feds drive us out.

While all that was going on, Wilson was spouting a fountain of garbage. He told the media that the Indians occupying Wounded Knee were tools of a Communist plot designed to destabilize the U.S. government. He claimed that other AIM leaders and I had visited Hanoi and were receiving support from Russia and China, and that only he stood between America and our monstrous alien conspiracy.

The Wilson I knew was hardly so creative. I can't even imagine who fed him such nonsense. Clearly, it was part of the feds' strategy to get the American public to believe Wounded Knee was about radicals and Commies breaking the law. That strategy had always worked for the FBI. Whenever it wanted to crush someone, it accused him of being a Red. The FBI must have known from the first day, when we presented our demands to Trimbach, that Wounded Knee was about our treaty rights—about the Fort Laramie document that affirmed Oglala sovereignty. We were risking our lives not only for the right to elect our own officials, but also to choose our own system of government, which for us does not involve the electoral process. Eurocentric males can't comprehend it, but majority rule guarantees minority suffering. The human, intelligent way—the Oglala Lakota and Indian way—is to rule by consensus. *That* is true democracy.

Wilson screamed so long and so often about Commie plots that the media started to play up that angle. I doubt that many people believed or cared about the supposed Red connection, however, because the Harris Polls showed that most of the country sympathized with us. In fact, only 13 percent of Americans were against us. More people were aware of what Wounded

Knee was about than knew who Spiro Agnew was—and he had been Vice President for four years.

But if almost everybody *knew* about us, comparatively few whites cared enough to get involved. We in the Knee were pretty much on our own in the fight of our lives. A lot of Indian people came and went—more than a thousand by the time the siege ended—but this is Oglala country, Lakota country. It doesn't mean nearly as much to an Indian who lives in Oklahoma or Florida or New York or Washington. Some came and showed support and helped, then went home. They used Wounded Knee to advance their own causes in their parts of the country. The Oklahoma Indians, for example, staged a local, miniature version of Wounded Knee, seizing some government real estate, turning it into an armed camp, and issuing demands. The nations in Washington, still struggling for fishing rights, took advantage of our notoriety to reinforce the message that they were, as always, ready to protect themselves by any means necessary.

What Wounded Knee told the world was that John Wayne hadn't killed us all. Essentially, the rest of the planet had believed that except for a few people sitting along highways peddling pottery, there were no more Indians. Suddenly billions of people knew we were still alive, still resisting.

By the time Harlington Wood showed up to deliver his latest ultimatum, the feds had cut off all electricity and telephone service to Wounded Knee. When they wanted to talk to us, they opened the phone line to the trading post. Courtesy of Vietnam Veterans Against the War, however, we had our own tactical communications. They brought us not only expertise but also reliable, sophisticated radio equipment, enough to equip all our bunkers. Most of our vehicles had departed after the roadblocks were taken down, but we still had a few, including a van and a white Volkswagen. While our gasoline lasted, we used them to charge the batteries that powered our radios. We turned the museum into security headquarters. From it, we monitored the feds' radio nets. They listened to ours, too, of course.

Since we were all constantly under the government's guns, we had to stage a distraction whenever we wanted to move around. The van, which we called our APC, would roll out and start firing. The feds would retreat to bunkers or button up in their APCs. Meanwhile, we would run like hell. Sometimes at night we sent our noisy white Volkswagen toward a roadblock. The feds could see and hear it moving. While the guy riding shotgun fired a few times to make them think we were attacking, we ran through the dark in a different direction.

After the second day, we all thought in terms of staying at Wounded Knee for a long time. We tried to make ourselves as comfortable as circumstances permitted, working on our bunkers constantly, enlarging them, digging them deeper, reinforcing the walls. We found woodstoves to warm them.

Many of us had grown up in drafty shacks, so we knew how to live small; our bunkers were homelike. The feds, however, hoped that each day there would be their last. They had kerosene heaters and lanterns, but they were too lazy to put roofs on their bunkers. Most had no side walls. When it snowed, they were miserable. Many sipped whiskey to keep from freezing.

We took every opportunity to remind them just how uncomfortable they were. One way we did that was with a woman we came to call "Wounded Knee Winona." I've forgotten her real name. She was from one of the Washington nations, and was only about five feet tall, with a sensational hourglass figure and a lovely face with very high cheekbones. She was a tough cookie who feared nothing. At daybreak after a wicked firefight, Winona got on a bullhorn and, in the tradition of Tokyo Rose and Hanoi Hanna, purred, "Hi, you federal marshals out there, how are you doing on this cold, cold morning? I'm down in our bunker and we've got a woodstove, so we're nice and cozy. We don't have any clothes on. Come on down and get warm with us. I'd sure like to meet you." She went on like that for half an hour. It was great. Wounded Knee is in a bowl of hills; her voice could be heard for miles. It was colder than hell, but we went outside just to listen and to laugh at her jokes. The feds were not amused. We heard them on the radio, calling her every vile name they could think of.

A few nights later, I was hanging out in security headquarters, monitoring the feds as they made periodic communications checks or chatted back and forth on their radios. They patrolled the wooded areas between roadblocks with jeeps equipped with searchlights and machine guns. One of those units called Roadblock One and said, "Do you see those Indians out there?"

"What Indians?"

"There's four of them . . . on horseback. They're carrying shields and spears or bows and arrows."

"No, we don't see them."

At first, that was intriguing—weird, really. I would have known if we had anybody out on horseback, but we didn't. We damn sure had no shields, bows, or spears.

Suddenly, another roadblock chimed in. "Yeah, we see 'em."

I saw nothing. Neither did anyone else inside Wounded Knee. We had nobody in that area. Then I realized that the apparition, four horsemen in traditional Lakota battle gear, could only be the benign spirits of those who protected us from the white man's fury.

After Harlington Wood returned to Washington empty-handed, a higher-ranking Justice Department official, Kent Frizell, arrived. The government's sense of the negotiations was that they had sent their underlings to negotiate with Indian underlings. In reality, their underlings were dealing with the real sovereigns of the Independent Oglala Nation—the people themselves, and principally the women. They, in their wisdom, said no to everything the feds proposed. The FBI, the marshals, the BIA—none of them could get to first base with the Oglala negotiators. The feds couldn't answer the questions they raised and couldn't deal with any of the demands. We had to educate the government about our treaty rights and about Indians. When we had seized the BIA building in Washington, we negotiated with the White House. Now we demanded to do so again. As far we were concerned, having our treaty rights meant all or nothing. We *had* to have them, because our lives weren't worth much without them.

Eventually, the feds begged for someone different to negotiate with. We never replaced anyone; we just added people such as Carter Camp, one of AIM's leaders in Kansas. Later, I joined the negotiations. In response, the Justice Department came back with higher-ranking people to deal with us. At the conclusion of each day's negotiation, we held a meeting, attended by almost everyone except those on guard. Crow Dog, Gladys, Ellen, Carter, and I reported to the people what had gone on that day.

The feds promised nothing except varying degrees of leniency if we surrendered. I couldn't imagine we would ever do that. Thinking I would die at Wounded Knee, I wanted to see my family one last time. Before phone service was cut off, I had called Twila and Betty and asked them to bring our kids. Twila didn't. She had remarried, and I imagine her husband wasn't too happy about letting her go into a war zone. Betty said she was coming. I didn't know it then, but after driving from Arizona, she was turned away at several roadblocks and eventually made her way to the Rosebud. When I didn't hear from her, I figured that I would never see my kids again.

Led by Oren Lyons, a delegation of about a dozen people from the Six Nations arrived on March 19. These people of the Iroquois Confederation are the only Indians to reject formally U.S. citizenship as inconsistent with sovereignty. They were permitted through the roadblocks as nonpartisan observers. Once inside, however, one old guy named Papaneau said, "Bullshit, I ain't no observer, I know what side I'm on," and grabbed a gun. The other delegates provided much useful advice as we began to set up and structure the Independent Oglala Nation.

The constant shooting was hard on everyone, including the Vietnam veterans. I liked to sit in the security building and listen to those guys bullshit and joke around. One night I got talking with one of them, an Indian from another reservation, about his home. When the shooting began again, he started to cry. He said, "Those fuckers are still firing at me, and look—this is what I gave to this fucking country!" He was in a wheelchair, swaddled in a blanket. When he lifted it, I saw that both his legs were gone.

On another night, one of the vets said, "Over in 'Nam, I went on lots of operations where we'd surround a village just like this one, down in a little bowl, and pour fire in. I never thought I'd be on the receiving end. Why'd you guys pick *this* place?" That was my chance to explain about the spirits and about *yuwipi* ceremonies and our purification lodge.

Most of our Vietnam vets did much more than sit around bunkers. They helped us carry the fight to the enemy, several times sneaking up on one of the APCs, which were tracked vehicles with little visibility when buttoned up. When it got cold out, the feds were too lazy or stupid or scared to protect the APCs with infantry. There was no chance that our shotguns and hunting rifles would pierce armor plate, but the sound of bullets clanging off the hull scared the hell out of everyone inside. We could have immobilized an APC anytime by jamming a big tree limb or rock between the wheels that drive the tracks. If we had wanted to kill the occupants, we might easily have tossed a Molotov cocktail inside or captured the guys and dragged them away. We could have done anything we wanted with those vehicles—and the feds kind of knew it. They didn't get too cocky with them.

We also practiced the fine art of deception. The feds never knew how many men we had. While talks went on, Dennis sometimes ran a couple of "platoons" through a close-order drill within sight of the negotiating tipi. One moonlit night, he took a party of folks into an open area near the Denby Road junction. They spread out and dug dozens of small holes, carefully placing pieces of cardboard that resembled antitank mines, then "camouflaged" the ground around each one. To the end, the feds believed we had a minefield.

Compared to the feds, our firepower was pitiful. To discourage them from just driving in with their APCs, we planted and cultivated the impression that we had heavy weapons. We had one smuggled AK-47, the standard Soviet-bloc assault rifle of that era, perhaps brought in by a Vietnam vet, and never had more than fifty rounds of ammo for it. That weapon makes a distinctive sound on full automatic. On a couple of dark nights, one of our men dashed from bunker to bunker with it, ripping off a burst or two from each. Whenever we fired the AK, the feds' guns would go silent. They had a lot of respect for it.

Somebody found a short length of belted .50-caliber rounds. It was mildewed and corroded, so we cleaned it up and polished the brass shell casings. We weighted two dark-green ammo cans with rocks and had twelve inches or so of the .50 calibers hanging out of each. Two men carrying these "blundered" into our daily press conference. "Hey, where do we put these?" said one. As photographers snapped dozens of pictures, I pretended to be pissed off and shooed the guy away. The media duly reported that the defenders of Wounded Knee had heavy machine guns, the kind that could turn an APC into Swiss cheese. A few nights later, at a time when we had almost no ammunition left except shotgun shells, our guys in the Denby and California bunkers fired off dozens of rounds as fast as they could—*boom boom boom*

boom boom boom! On the radio we heard the Feds saying, "Yeah, they got that fifty opened up now."

That worked so well that we tried it again, dummying up a length of stovepipe and assorted hardware to look like a bazooka or an RPG, the Soviet-made equivalent. We laid it in a corner of the security building, partly covered with a blanket, and sent a man to invite a reporter to see me up there. When he came in, I jumped up, made a show of sending a couple of guys to screen off the suspicious-looking gear in the corner and told the newsie to leave. Then I loudly chewed the defender's butt for bringing him inside. Within hours the feds "knew" that we had acquired antitank guns.

Food became more important as time went on. Our human packtrains ran at capacity just bringing in ammunition and medical supplies. We would have gone hungry if not for dozens of cows that wandered in from white ranchers' leased grazing lands. The newspeople, however, ate well. Couriers brought food and took film out. Almost every night before suppertime I dropped in on the crew of one of the network vans. We would shoot the bull, and lo and behold, they would invite me to eat with them. On Monday, I might join NBC correspondent Fred Briggs, producer Ted Elbert, and cam-eramen Randi Birch or Charlie Ray for a delicious concoction by soundman and former chef Aaron Holden. On Tuesday, I would be the guest of CBS producer Phil O'Connor and correspondent Jeff Williams. On Wednesday, I would share a meal with ABC correspondents Irv Chapman or Herbert Ka-plow and producer Aram Boyajian. Then I would go back to NBC. I couldn't be quite so obvious as to go back every four days, so I sometimes mooched food from the Community Relations Service guys—Justice Department em-ployees who went back and forth through the roadblocks as part of the ne-gotiations. They smuggled boxes of C-rations in to us.

One of our regular visitors was John Adams, a tall, very erect, white Methodist minister from the National Council of Churches. Adams had worked in the civil-rights movement, and had been on a first-name basis with Martin Luther King. His chief passion was trying to get rid of the death penalty. He is the only true Christian I ever met, including my grandmothers. I never met a finer human being. He was inside the Knee constantly, listening to people, taking messages back and forth, going around with a notepad to take down lists of things he could smuggle in to us. One night in the trading post, I watched him talk to Clyde for a long time, filling a page with notes. I wondered, what the hell is Clyde doing? Finally, John came over and said, "I'm going in now. Do you want me to bring you anything?"

"First, tell me what you were talking to Clyde about."

"Oh, he gave me a list of all the things he needed," said John. I glanced at it: lettuce, tomatoes, cucumbers, celery, olives—salad ingredients! I guess all Clyde really wanted out of Wounded Knee was a decent meal! My cowboy boots were worn out, so I asked John to bring me a new pair, and he did.

When Wounded Knee burst into the headlines, we attracted the attention of some of the best lawyers in America, including Mark Lane, William Kunstler, and Ken Tilsen. They dropped everything and came to Rapid City to offer support and advice from the moment of their arrival, on March 22. The three of them, and AIM's young friend from Minneapolis, Larry Leventhal, along with Ramon Roubideaux, Doug Hall, and several other attorneys, formed the Wounded Knee Legal Defense/Offense Committee, commonly called "Wikledoc" (WKLD/OC). Three days later, WKLD/OC got Andrew Bogue, the federal judge for western South Dakota, to issue a court order to allow food and medicine to be brought in to Wounded Knee. The government appealed his order and got it overturned. WKLD/OC filed a writ of mandamus asking Bogue to order the government to allow humanitarian assistance for Wounded Knee. Although he had a reputation as an excellent jurist and, like all federal judges, held a lifetime appointment, Bogue turned his coat and refused to issue another writ. Political pressure had come down from Washington and from South Dakota's reigning rednecks.

Then the feds told the media inside the Knee that they could no longer guarantee their safety. The press then left. That scared hell out of us. We were convinced that only the presence of all those network cameras had kept the FBI from wiping us out. White ranchers throughout the region were organizing to attack us; the FBI tolerated their death squads roaming our reservations. However, when they heard, on March 12, that a group called South Dakotans for Civil Liberties was threatening to get an aircraft to bomb Wounded Knee, they warned it off. Some of this gang's members later joined such well-armed, highly organized, and well-financed white-supremacist organizations as the Order and Posse Comitatus. They try hard to appear as lunatic-fringe kooks, but they are some of the most dangerous people in America.

Exactly a month into the siege—the night after the press left—the feds initiated one of the fiercest firefights of the struggle. Fifty-caliber tracer rounds rained on Wounded Knee, skipping off the highway to ricochet high into the sky. The only casualty that night was a U.S. marshal named Lloyd Grim who was struck by a rifle bullet and seriously wounded. The feds, reinforced by BIA police from reservations around the country, clamped down hard on Pine Ridge. They raided our houses, arrested our supporters, and intensified their efforts to cut off our supplies. For some reason, Vernon Bellecourt was at Crow Dog's Paradise telling everyone there to stay away from Wounded Knee. The situation became so critical that Dennis and I decided to smuggle ourselves out and go to the Rosebud, where we had more friends, to try to enlist support.

It was a hundred miles to Crow Dog's Paradise, on the Rosebud. With four escorts, we set out after dark on March 26 for Manderson, about eight miles north by the road but half again that far through the hills. By dawn we had passed the last fed roadblock, but snow was on the ground and we had to cross open cornfields. We had no way of knowing who was watching from the woods. If we got caught in the open by goons or feds, we were all dead meat. One by one we ran across the field to the cover of some trees near a creek. Moving up the stream, we saw a house with wood smoke curling from its stovepipe. We had no idea whose home it was, so we squatted down to watch. After a time, the door opened and a teenage boy came out and stared right at us. Then he waved to us to come in. It looked like a trap, but with the creek at our back and little cover, we would get hit if we tried to run. We each took a big gulp of cold air, cocked our rifles, and went in.

The Great Mystery had guided us to Dave Flying Hawk's place—the first stop on the "underground railroad" out of Wounded Knee, and the last going in. The house was full of people from the West Coast, all going in to Wounded Knee as soon as it got dark again. As poverty stricken as any people on the reservation, the Flying Hawks gave us a meal. They were Indians, and anyone who came to their door would get fed. They risked everything they had to help us; if they had been caught, the feds would have taken away their lease money, their welfare payments, their commodities—anything they had—and jailed the adults and put the kids in foster homes. The Flying Hawks and hundreds like them were willing nevertheless to take the risk because of the goons and the BIA police. Wilson's terrorism had turned most of his people against him. Even those who minded their own business weren't safe. Any Indian with long hair—even women—risked being removed from car or home, taken into the countryside, and beaten with clubs, boots, or gun butts. Some were shot. Many disappeared, never to be seen again. Homes and cars were firebombed. Even livestock was butchered.

The Flying Hawks put us in their car, but they had only enough gasoline to take us to the DeSersa place, on the other side of Manderson. Those were Black Elk Clan people, staunch AIM supporters whose sons were all inside the Knee. They arranged for a car to take Dennis and me to the Rosebud. Our four escorts then went back to the Knee. Dennis and I crowded into the backseat, but when we stopped for gas in Wanbli, near the eastern edge of Pine Ridge, several goons came up. Our long hair was tucked into stocking caps and we wore dark glasses, but our faces had been on television almost nightly for nearly a month. As goons peered into our car, I slowly edged my hand toward a .30-30 hidden under some clothes. Maybe goons didn't watch television. Maybe they were drunk. Maybe it was our stocking caps. Or all three. Whatever the reason, after a quick glance, they lost all interest in us.

29

▼▼▼▼▼▼▼▼▼

White Lies

We arrived at Crow Dog's Paradise to find about five hundred people waiting for us. We went first into the purification lodge, where Grandpa Henry, Leonard Crow Dog's father, led us in a ceremony. After eating, Dennis and I gave talks about what was going on inside Wounded Knee, about our treaty, our reasons for making the stand, and our determination to continue. We talked about the kinds of support we needed—most critically, medical supplies and ammunition. I was introduced to a priest from Saint Francis Catholic Mission Boarding School, a community on the Rosebud that everybody referred to as "Sin City" because it swarmed with bootleggers and dope dealers. The priest, who shall go nameless, was planning to help bring ammunition and guns into Wounded Knee, and we discussed ways for him to do it.

Before leaving the Rosebud, I was reunited briefly with Michele and Scott. After having been turned away from the roadblocks around Wounded Knee, Betty had found her way to the Crow Dogs'. Michele was nine and just getting into her gawky years. She had some idea what was going on in Wounded Knee, but I wasn't able to say what was in my heart. I feared that I would never see her again. I held her in my arms for a long moment and we both tried hard not to cry. Scott was six and didn't understand the situation at all. He just looked at me in wonderment through his huge, dark eyes. I wanted to tell him how much I missed him, but the words never came. It was a bittersweet moment. I still thought I would never leave the Knee alive, but at least I had had a chance to see my kids one last time. I told them to always be good to their mother and to pray along with their ancestors—and that I loved them more than life itself.

Soon after our return to Wounded Knee, Crow Dog announced that he was going to have a ghost dance. In the white man's history books, Wounded Knee is forever linked to the so-called "Ghost Dance craze" that "swept across Indian Country." Even Dee Brown got it wrong in *Bury My Heart at Wounded Knee* when he repeated the myth that the Sioux had embraced the teachings of the "Paiute Messiah Wovoka, who had founded the religion of the Ghost Dance" and had begun to hold dances to bring back the buffalo and restore the dead. Whites are taught that followers of the Ghost Dance "religion" believed bullets would bounce off their ghost shirts, also believed they would become invincible supermen, and were getting ready to attack settlers, so the cavalry was dispatched to end that threat at Pine Ridge. The lie continues, asserting that when the troops encountered Big Foot's band, which had left the Standing Rock Reservation in North Dakota, they were attacked. This is bullshit—U.S. military propaganda lies to excuse the mass murder of Paiute, Shoshone, Nez Percé, and Sioux people.

What really happened was that in 1890, the Lakota sent Kicking Bear and Short Bull west to what is now Nevada, to learn about Wovoka, a great Paiute medicine man, and the Ghost Dance. They returned to report that the Paiutes were doing a good thing. Wovoka taught his people that they must continue to live and think and act like Indians. No matter what the white man did to them, no matter what they were forced to endure on their reservations, if they remained true to themselves and the ways of their ancestors, eventually everything good would happen for them. That's what AIM believes also: Remain true to who you are, and you will find peace of mind. The living proof of that is found in the wonderfully fulfilled and spiritual lives of Fools Crow and other Lakota elders, as well as those among the Miccosukee, the Navajo, the Hopi, and all the other nations who still follow traditional ways.

What really happened was that Big Foot and his band were camped out on the Standing Rock Reservation when two Indian men who had been accused of raping an older white woman came to ask for his protection. By the standards of our culture, he couldn't turn them away. Then Sitting Bull was killed by Indian police, and the cavalry stepped up patrolling and brought in reinforcements. Big Foot realized that if Sitting Bull, who had done so much for his people, could be killed, then nobody was safe. Because Big Foot was sheltering fugitives, he worried that the white soldiers would come after him next. He decided to head for Pine Ridge and ask for Red Cloud's protection, because Red Cloud was cooperating with the U.S. government. Big Foot was about two miles south of Porcupine when the Seventh Cavalry caught up with him. They disarmed his men and took everyone to Wounded Knee. A scuffle broke out the next day while the troops were searching their Indian captives for weapons. The cavalry started to shoot—and didn't stop until every Indian in sight was dead.

When we began our own ghost dance at Wounded Knee, Crow Dog explained that he wanted us all to acknowledge the spirits present there, to call out to them to help and protect us. The night before, the women had made dancing skirts and shirts for us. We began at sunup. It was clear but cold, with much snow on the ground. Crow Dog assured us that although we danced barefoot, no one would be harmed. Men and women together, we danced until noon. As in the sun dance, we went through a cycle of songs, then started over. The dancing, singing, and suffering were familiar. Through prayer, the time flew by. Everyone's feet became numb and swollen, but we didn't realize it until we had finished and headed back to the trading post. Suddenly, walking was weird—I could feel nothing below my ankles. Crow Dog was ready. He had buckets of snow brought in to massage our frozen feet as he prayed. Not one dancer was injured. The power of Crow Dog's medicine in those years was awesome. He is an astonishing man.

One dark, moonless night, we packed into the purification lodge. An intense firefight raged outside, but we were so involved in singing and praying that we didn't hear it. We finished our ceremony during a lull in the shooting. When we opened the flap, people rushed over, thinking that everyone inside was dead or wounded. They told us the feds had been shooting at the fire pit next to the lodge. We looked for bullet holes. Crow Dog said, "Look at this," pointing to an expended .223-caliber slug—like those fired by an M-16—on the ground near the lodge. Circling the hut, we found three or four more. When daylight came, we found still others imbedded in the lodge itself, in blankets draped over the framework. It was almost the same at our tipi—no holes in it, but slugs lying atop the snow all the way around. I still find that amazing.

Kent Frizell, a top Justice Department official, had once been the Kansas attorney general, but he was also a real cowboy who had grown up on a ranch. After sparring with him for days, we focused on ten demands, but Frizell needed his bosses—Attorney General John Mitchell and the felons-in-waiting at the Nixon White House—to think he was a tough negotiator. He wouldn't accede to all ten, and we wouldn't back off, so Frizell rewrote our list to consolidate it into what looked like only six demands. We agreed, because it still gave us everything we asked—congressional hearings into the status of our treaty, an investigation of the wholesale violations of Oglala civil rights, and a meeting at the White House.

The night before signing the agreement, we held a mass meeting at the trading post to select our White House delegation. Four is the most sacred of numbers, so we wanted to send that many people. We decided that our emissaries should include a lawyer, a spiritual adviser, an Oglala elder, and a member of the Wounded Knee leadership. As our lawyer, we chose Ramon Roubideaux, a full-blood and my mother's relative. The eldest Oglala traditionalist present was Tom Bad Cob, then in his eighties; he agreed to represent us. Naturally, we asked Crow Dog to be our spiritual representative. That left only someone from the leadership. Several names were suggested, but there was no consensus. Wounded Knee was my home and I didn't want to leave—and I certainly didn't want to submit to arrest. That was part of the agreement, even though our lawyers had assured us that everyone would be promptly bonded and allowed to go to the White House. When my name came up, the people unanimously agreed. I couldn't refuse the honor. I was almost overwhelmed to think that they had so much faith in me. When I said I would go, I was all choked up with emotion.

The next day we held a signing ceremony in front of the tipi, witnessed by the press. Then Crow Dog and Bad Cob were driven to Rapid City while I submitted to arrest. I had always wanted to travel by helicopter, but not until I became one of the FBI's ten most wanted did I finally get my free ride. Before I was allowed aboard, the marshals cuffed my hands behind my back with plastic handcuffs. When I objected, they said it was standard procedure. That's how all government idiots avoid having to act like human beings. They say it's procedure and that they must follow regulations.

When we landed in Rapid City, I was the last off the helicopter. As I hit the tarmac, I handed the handcuffs to a marshal at the door. His face fell and his eyes bugged out. When they put the cuffs on, I was allowed to keep my hands in front. After booking in the county jail, I was placed in a cell by myself. I guess they didn't want me to contaminate the other prisoners with un-American thoughts on freedom and self-determination. WKLD/OC lawyers brought in Stan Adelstein, a Jewish liberal Republican and one of the richest men in the state. It was our first meeting. He stared at me as though trying to decide what kind of person I was. I can't blame him; he was being asked to put up thirty-five thousand dollars for my bond. All he said was, "You're not going on the run, are you? You're not going to skip to Cuba or anyplace." I said, "This is my country. No white man is going to run me out of it." He said, "That's good enough for me."

I was released, but Judge Bogue put several restrictions on me. I couldn't return to Wounded Knee, drink alcohol, or even go in a bar; I couldn't hang around with felons, carry a firearm, or commit another crime. It was like parole, except I had yet to be tried, much less convicted.

After a visit to WKLD/OC's offices, I went to AIM's headquarters and slept. After a few hours, Herb Powless, an AIM leader from Wisconsin, woke me and took me with three other guys to a Rapid City motel room to see a white guy from Arizona. Herb said only that it was about buying guns. I wasn't interested, but I agreed to go along because I wanted to hear what the guy had to say. He gave us a pie-in-the-sky pitch about a shipment of M-16s and AK-47s coming into Arizona from Mexico, and he offered to provide us with grenades and plastic explosives—anything we needed. I listened to him, thinking, this is too good to be true—the guy's got to be a fed. We said, "Oh, bullshit!" and left the room.

In the morning, I joined Bad Cob, Roubideaux, and Crow Dog at the airport and we flew to D.C. first class. The next day, we went to the American Arbitration Association building. From there, we were supposed to go to the White House. What the feds had wanted all along, of course, was for our people in Wounded Knee to give up. We told them that the last time we did that—at Wounded Knee in 1890—our ancestors had been massacred. We had resolved that that would not happen again, and had told Frizell that we wouldn't give up our arms until *after* our White House meeting had produced tangible results.

One of the conditions under which I had surrendered was that the feds would turn the trading post's phone back on. Dennis and I had worked out a code. What I said and how I said it would tell him whether to stand down the weapons or not. I had called the night before to say in code that we hadn't been to the White House yet. At the American Arbitration Association, the feds said that since our people wouldn't give up their arms, the White House refused to meet with us. I told them, "That wasn't our deal—that's bullshit." Reporters and cameramen were following us around, so we called a press conference on the spot. I said, "I submitted to arrest to come here and deal honestly with the government to settle our grievances—but these people aren't honorable. The White House flat out lied to us."

I hung around Washington for a couple of days, but since I couldn't go back to Wounded Knee, WKLD/OC told me to raise money for our cause by speaking at universities. I was invited to Oklahoma, where some Indians had seized a place near Stillwater and were demanding that the government live up to their treaty. Police and state troopers had avoided direct confrontation, although they professed to worry because the Indians were armed.

On the way to Stillwater, I stopped to speak at the University of Kansas, in Lawrence. More than a thousand people packed in to hear me. Before another speech at Oklahoma State University, in Stillwater, I joined an AIM press conference at the airport in Tulsa. After we gave our prepared statements, a UPI reporter said, "If you win at Wounded Knee, what will you do next?" That was such an obviously stupid question that I answered facetiously, "We're going to militarily take over western South Dakota. That happens also to be within the 1868 Fort Laramie Treaty area." Everybody cracked up, so I thought they all understood I was trying to give an amusing reply to something that never should have been asked. Wrong! My jest was printed from coast to coast, and scared the bejesus out of a lot of otherwise rational people, especially in the northern Plains states.

After that speech, I was taken to the Indians' armed camp, where everyone was drinking. I joined in. Still drinking, they drove me to Stillwater on back roads. As I sat in the middle of the front seat, an Indian in the back pulled out a gun, thumbed back the hammer, and put it to my head. He said, "You really think you're some cool guy, don't you? You just think you're some hot shit, right?" I was within a heartbeat or an involuntary flinch or a bump in the road of having my brains blown through the windshield—but I was just drunk enough not to care. I said, "I'll tell you what I know. I'm an Oglala Lakota patriot and I'm a leader of the American Indian Movement— and if you don't like that, either pull the fucking trigger right now, or stop the car and let's take it outside." One of the guys in the car, Sam English, now a painter of world renown, talked the guy into giving up the gun. We pulled up to a bar in some small town and left him there. Afterward, I thought, what a stupid way to die. I made sure not to drink around any more self-destructive Indians.

I made a speech the next week from an outdoor mike on the UCLA campus in Los Angeles. At Wounded Knee, it was colder than hell and snowing, and those guys had put their lives on the line—but many in my audience of students paid no attention to my message. They lay on the lawn, soaking in the warm California sun and chattering, so I cut myself off in midspeech and walked off. As I was leaving, a reporter came up to say, "We got word that Judge Bogue is going to revoke your bond unless you publicly apologize for your remark."

"What remark?" I replied.

"About militarily taking over western South Dakota."

"Publicly apologize? That's bullshit!" I growled, walking off. When the story ran, it quoted me as saying, "The judge is full of bullshit." The next day, I appeared at a scheduled press conference at the Los Angeles Indian Center and got word that the feds were coming to bust me because Bogue had revoked my bond. I had a plane ticket for Rapid City, so I decided to turn myself in there. I sneaked out and got in the backseat of a Volkswagen bug owned by a married couple I had just met. On the freeway headed for the airport, we were stopped by six carloads of LAPD cops. They surrounded our car, a dozen officers kneeling and pointing handguns at us.

"Come out with your hands on your head!" they barked. I tried, but an adult cannot execute that maneuver from a Volkswagen's backseat, so I pushed the seat forward and started to get out. As they screamed, "Put your hands over your head!" I heard a chorus of metallic clicks—cops cocking weapons. As I got out and stood, hands down, a cop slugged me on the head with his baton. When I went down to one knee, he grabbed me by the back of my collar and threw me against the car. "Spread 'em!" he shrieked, kicking my legs and clubbing me in the back.

At that moment, two carloads of FBI agents screeched up. The agents poured out, waving their IDs while racing toward us full speed and shouting, "Stop! Stop!" They were obviously afraid the cops were going to do something irreversible that might ultimately embarrass the Nixon administration. They said, "We're taking this man," and bundled me into their car.

They took me to a jail near downtown Los Angeles. After stripping for delousing and suffering the indignity of having a rubber-gloved finger poked up my anus to discover any contraband I might be carrying, I was locked into a maximum-security isolation cell. The next day, I had a visitor. On the other side of the Plexiglas window was a white-haired old Indian. Behind him was a young Indian man, probably still in his teens. I don't know their names and I've never seen them before or since. The old guy said, "You're the reincarnation of Crazy Horse. I'm saying my prayers for you. Don't worry, you'll be all right. Is there anything we can get for you?" He left me twenty dollars for candy. I couldn't help recalling that I was then about the same age as Crazy Horse at the time of his murder in 1877 by a BIA goon named Little Big Man. According to one story, Crazy Horse's bones and heart are buried at Wounded Knee.

I stayed in that jail only a day and a night. Then, handcuffed, chained, and escorted by three marshals, I was driven to the Western Airlines tarmac. We got right on the plane, and I was seated in the last row with marshals on either side. Others were across the aisle and in front—five or six in all. When we changed planes in Denver, one asked if I wanted a coat over the cuffs to hide them. "Hell, no," I said. "I'm a political prisoner." As we walked through the airport I held my fists up to show the cuffs and people clapped and yelled.

We got on another Western plane and flew to Sioux Falls, South Dakota. I was surprised. The marshals said, "We don't want you in Rapid City." I wound up in a Minnehaha County jail cellblock with three "Banditos" bikers who were awaiting trial for murder, and a couple of Indian guys. I stayed there for six weeks, leaving my cell only for meals and to go to a dayroom where we could play cards and watch television. I got no exercise. My only regular visitor was Carol Clark, daughter of a white man and an Osage woman. She was rich because her mother had "headrights"—royalties from oil wells on Osage land. Carol became my conduit to WKLD/OC, flying back and forth to Rapid City to talk with the lawyers. When it came to getting me out of jail, they stalled her with all sorts of excuses. I bought them until Carol dropped in on a WKLD/OC meeting and heard one of the lawyers say that the longer I stayed in jail, the better it would be for everyone. Although he has denied ever having said that, this lawyer is a lifelong leftist.

He believed that if I were AIM's martyr, everyone would rally around, making it easier for us to raise money, and simpler to point out the federal government's continued oppression.

But no one had asked *me* about that. When Carol told me what was going on, I got very angry. I sent word that I wanted out, no matter what. Since WKLD/OC wouldn't help, Carol did. She knew a lot of people, and she set about stringing them together to raise the eighty thousand dollars I needed for bond. I've forgotten most of their names, but one was actor Mike Farrell, then starring in the hit television series *M*A*S*H*. He contributed eight thousand dollars.

Before Carol could raise all the money, however, federal marshals came without warning one morning after breakfast, took me to the airport, and put me on a private plane. When we were airborne, they told me I was going to Scottsbluff, Nebraska, for a preliminary hearing on the counts I had been charged with after the Chicano-Indian conference. It was all bullshit, false accusations, of course, but now I was to have my day in court for disturbing the peace, resisting arrest, illegal possession of an unregistered gun, and two counts of assaulting police officers. A marshal said, "Your attorneys have been notified and will be there."

The purpose of the "prelim" was to establish that the state had sufficient evidence to take me to trial. The defendant doesn't get to introduce evidence—only prosecution witnesses testify—and a smart lawyer will ask nothing on cross-examination which could reveal his defense strategy. I sat and listened as two cops said that I must have concealed a long-barreled revolver between my legs, because they didn't find it when they searched me at the scene or when they searched me before, and again after, booking at the police station. Somehow, it hadn't fallen out while I was allegedly assaulting them as I got out of a squad car with my hands cuffed behind my back. After I was in the cell, they said, I must have taken that gun from between my legs and put it in my back pocket. Then while I moved around in my sleep, it fell out and somehow rolled to the middle of the cell.

I didn't think it was particularly unusual for two cops to be so unconvincing. But I found it incredible that the judge nevertheless bound me over for trial on all charges. I was taken from the court to the airport and was returned to Sioux Falls. Within a few days, Carol had lined up the rest of my bond on the Wounded Knee charges. After forty-three days behind bars, I was free—for the moment.

While I was still in jail, the siege continued. Before I was released, two people were dead and our resistance at Wounded Knee had ended. Because churches were traditional sanctuaries, we had put our older people there when the shooting started. Those Christian marshals and Christian FBI agents and Christian soldiers had no respect for their own spiritual roots, let alone ours. They fired on every single building at Wounded Knee, even those with a cross atop them. Every church was riddled. On April 25, a .50-caliber bullet came into the church near Denby Road, ricocheted around inside, and nailed Frank Clearwater in the head. He was a Cherokee, forty-seven years old, who had arrived with his wife only a few days earlier. He is buried at Crow Dog's Paradise.

Buddy Lamont, a Vietnam vet and one of Stan Holder's best men, had served with AIM at the Custer courthouse and was among the first people into the Knee. His mother, Agnes, was one of the demonstrators who formed OSCRO. His niece, Kamook, was married to Dennis Banks. Buddy was proud to serve at Wounded Knee. His grandmother, at age twelve, had survived the 1890 massacre in which her aunt and uncle had perished. Buddy's great-grandmother had been at the Greasy Grass with Crazy Horse.

Buddy was killed on April 26 by a fed sniper who violated a cease-fire to shoot from ambush. Buddy's family, all but destitute, had to borrow eighteen hundred dollars to ransom his body back after the BIA sent it to a coroner in Rushville, Nebraska. Buddy is buried in the hilltop cemetery, near Big Foot and the other massacre victims. Until the sacred four winds no longer blow across our Grandmother Earth, every Lakota child should know and revere his name as they do Crazy Horse, Red Cloud, and Big Foot.

Buddy's death, which saddened everyone, convinced Grandpa Fools Crow and the other elders that there had been enough death. Since we were too few to fight and too many to die, Fools Crow asked the Wounded Knee leaders to try to find a peaceful resolution. On May 2, a Department of the Interior negotiator stated for the record, "I do have the authority to insure that the Government of the United States, and probably Congress, will discuss anything with your chiefs, anything and everything you want to discuss about the 1868 Treaty. . . . I have authority to tell you that any and all criminal violations against you by any outsiders will be prosecuted. I do have the authority to tell you that members of the tribal government will be prosecuted."

On May 4, the White House promised that if our defenders laid down their arms, top-level representatives would meet with "the headmen and chiefs of the Teton Sioux"—another white term for the Lakota—during the third week in May "for the purpose of examining the problems concerning the 1868 Treaty." That was what we had been demanding all along, so the elders agreed. The siege ended on May 8, after seventy-one days.

According to the agreement, no one would be jailed. Instead, people would be "processed." The marshals would take names and addresses and, if there were outstanding charges, they also would take fingerprints and mug shots. Then everybody would be released. Hardly twenty minutes after the stand-down, the feds broke that agreement. Sacred medicine bags and ceremonial clothing were confiscated from Crow Dog and Black Elk. Like everyone else still inside the Knee, they were handcuffed and dragged off to a

Rapid City jail. The feds thought they were going to get the whole leadership, but the prize—Dennis—was gone. Along with several other people, he had sneaked out the night before, and remained a fugitive for several months.

Before allowing the press back into Wounded Knee, the feds pulled what I'm sure they thought was a great public-relations stunt. They trashed all the homes, then showed them to the media and said that was what AIM and the Oglala people had done. I thought that was lower than low. The missionaries and all the longtime residents of the area became homeless. Most of them had to move out of the community, and some of them blamed us.

Hundreds of Oglala people came on May 17 to Grandpa Fools Crow's place in Kyle, in the northeastern part of the Pine Ridge Reservation, to meet the promised White House delegation and to discuss our treaty. Those emissaries from Washington, however, had no official standing and no authority to offer anything. After hours of evasions, the white men left, promising to come back in two weeks with answers. The Oglala people returned on May 31, the day the white delegates had said they would come back, but nobody from Washington, D.C., showed up. Instead, Leonard Garment, the same Nixon henchman who had rejected the "Twenty Points" from the Trail of Broken Treaties, sent an insulting note. It said, in part, "The days of treaty making with the American Indians ended in 1871; . . . only Congress can rescind or change in any way statutes enacted since 1871. . . ."

Once again, we Indians had accepted the white man's promises—just as our ancestors had. Once again, the government of the United States of America had lied.

30
▼▼▼▼▼▼▼▼

Waiting for Trial

Of the hundreds of people arrested in 1973 because of Wounded Knee, the government had decided that the ringleaders were Dennis Banks, Vernon Bellecourt, Clyde Bellecourt, Pedro Bissonnette, Leonard Crow Dog, Carter Camp, Stan Holder, and me. Our bonds were set at an astronomical $135,000 each, the equivalent of about $1 million in 1990s money. Somehow, WKLD/OC raised it. Even though the government had tricked the defenders of Wounded Knee into surrendering with lies and promises never intended to be kept, everyone who had been in the Knee—and even more who only claimed they had—was a hero in Indian country. For the first time in generations, we had stood up to the white man. A few hungry people with shotguns and hunting rifles had taken everything the U.S. government dished out for seventy-one days—and most of us had lived to tell about it.

As spring turned to summer on the northern Plains, Indian people renewed their bonds with their ancestors and Grandmother Earth, with singing and dancing and weekend *wacipi* social gatherings. Veterans of the Knee and AIM members from around the country were welcomed with even more warmth than usual. That summer, we roamed the Dakotas, camping together on reservations or wherever a *wacipi* was held. Our AIM camp was easy to find. We always flew the American flag upside down, to the consternation of law-enforcement agents and many Indians, particularly middle-aged veterans of World War II who didn't seem to understand.

When I wasn't dancing at *wacipis*, I partied. AIM and its supporters included a lot of cocky guys who often went in groups of five or ten to redneck cowboy joints to drink and shoot pool, daring somebody to start something. Sometimes they did. We weren't looking for trouble, but we never ran from it. We also partied in private homes. One day a bunch of us were at Sidney Ear's house, about halfway between Highway 18 and the Rosebud, when the long-simmering feud between the Bellecourts and the Camps boiled over. The antagonism went back to the time in Alliance, Nebraska, when several AIM guys had pointed guns at Vernon Bellecourt. I didn't know it at the time, but that was because of Vernon's big mouth and bellicose, I-give-the-orders attitude. That was bad enough, but it also was apparent that he was unwilling to do most of the things he commanded others to do. The best example of his courage is that while most AIM leaders were inside the Knee, Vernon took a trip to Italy, supporting us with a telegram congratulating us on the good coverage we were getting in the media!

At the house near Rosebud, Clyde went outside to argue with Craig Camp, Carter's younger brother. When Carter followed to back him up, Craig pulled a gun. I was sitting at the doorway and happened to lean outside just then and see Carter off to one side, aiming his gun through a small tree. Without warning, he shot Clyde in the gut. Clyde doubled over, holding his stomach, and ran past me into the house, his eyes very big. He said nothing, but continued through the living room, hallway, kitchen, and then out the back door. I yelled, "He's shot!" We ran to get him just as he collapsed.

Carter and his friends took off as we drove Clyde to an Indian Health Service hospital three or four miles down the road, in Rosebud. We took him to the emergency room. I told the doctor, "If he dies, *you* die." "We can't do anything with a gunshot wound here," he replied, and called a medevac helicopter to take Clyde to a hospital in Winner, South Dakota.

Winner was another virulently racist border town that had been part of the Rosebud reservation before the area was opened illegally to white homesteaders. We got back in our cars—about thirty of us, most packing side arms—and sped over to Winner. Later, the local police turned up with warrants for Vernon and me. Months after our arrest during the Custer courthouse police riot, a grand jury had handed down indictments on additional charges. I had eight felony counts against me for the courthouse fracas, and my bail had been upped to fifty thousand dollars.

We told the cops, "Wait until Clyde gets out of the operating room and we find out his condition. Then we'll go with you." Outgunned and not about to mess with us in a hospital, they agreed. A couple of hours later,

Clyde was wheeled into a recovery room in stable condition. Vernon and I submitted to arrest, waited in the Winner jail until we were transported to Custer, and were released on bond raised by WKLD/OC.

In the meantime, one of our attorneys, Mark Lane, had convinced Carter Camp to turn himself in. I later learned that he had shot Clyde because he didn't want Craig to shoot him and get in trouble with the law. At the time, I didn't know whether to laugh or cry. Now I see Carter's brand of logic operating around the world—in Bosnia, Somalia, the West Bank, Northern Ireland. When a Sioux Falls grand jury opened an investigation into the shooting, of those present at the Ear house only Clyde and I were called to testify. Clyde had served twelve years in prison and would do nothing to put another Indian behind bars. Moreover, most people in AIM admired Carter, and his leadership had been important during the siege of Wounded Knee. When we met in Sioux Falls, Clyde told me, "I won't testify against him." I said, "You're the one who got shot, so I'll go along with you."

Meanwhile, Dick Wilson's reign of terror on Pine Ridge had continued. After media attention focused on his death-squad goons, Wilson began to call his bullies "Guardians of the Oglala Nation," to justify *GOON* as a descriptive acronym. By any name, they ran rampant, caravaning through outlying districts, carloads of brutal drunks armed to the teeth and itching to cause trouble. But the BIA police were even worse. People were beaten to death in the countryside. Others were taken to jail to be stomped or pounded on. Some just disappeared. To this day, none of them has been found and nobody has accounted for them.

Because of the situation on Pine Ridge, the sun dance was called off that year. Instead, in the second week of August, we held one at Crow Dog's place on the Rosebud. People came from all over, including renowned medicine men from many other reservations, among them Fools Crow and John Fire Lame Deer. My brother Bill came; this was his first sun dance. Although the Pine Ridge event always had a rodeo, carnival, softball, drinking and partying, and half days of sun dancing, we went to Crow Dog's place only to dance. We began at sunup and quit on the first day in early evening, a couple of hours before sundown—my first experience at dancing all day. As in previous years, our eyes and bodies followed the sun across the sky, as we prayed all the while. When we took a break, I sat while singers smoked sacred pipes and came to help us pray. After the pipes were returned to their places, we danced again.

When we stopped, Crow Dog told everybody to get into pickup trucks, and he drove us to the creek. We all went in, swimming and splashing. I had had nothing to eat or drink all day, and although I tried mightily, I couldn't hold out with all that water around. Like everyone else, I drank from the creek. Soon another car came with oranges, juice, and lemonade. I was astonished. It was the sun dancers' equivalent of a rabbi bringing ham sandwiches to synagogue on Yom Kippur. I had to keep reminding myself that Crow Dog was *Heyoka* and lived his life backwards. For the rest of the sun dance, although we danced until sundown, I ate nothing for four days and nights and drank only after quitting at the end of each day.

In previous years, almost everyone except Pete Catches had pierced on only one side. He had explained to me that piercing twice represents the female/male balance, something we need to recognize always. He was my sun-dance idol, so I followed his lead. When we queued to pierce on the fourth day, Crow Dog put me first in line. When he came with paint to circle where I wanted to be pierced, I fingered two places. Almost everyone did the same. From that moment on, it became customary for each person to pierce both sides.

I spent a lot of time that summer working on my legal defense with Mark Lane, Bill Kunstler, Ken Tilsen, Larry Leventhal, and the other lawyers in the WKLD/OC headquarters in Rapid City. One day Mark and other WKLD/OC people noticed that several men in business suits had moved into an apartment house next door. Mark went there with everybody else, threw open the door, and exposed them. The "suits" were FBI agents who had bugged the WKLD/OC offices. They were breaking the very laws they had sworn to uphold. Our lawyers went to Judge Bogue and got a restraining order to prohibit the FBI from installing bugs or tapping our phones.

With many federal complaints hanging over my head, my immediate concern was preparing for the Wounded Knee trial. The feds would try to convict Dennis and me of thirteen felonies each. Although I faced a dozen other felony counts in South Dakota and Nebraska with possible sentences of 330 years *plus* life, I hardly worried about them. Looking back on it now—I certainly didn't realize it then—I was already thinking like an elder.

Starting with my years in Cleveland when Sarge Old Horn and I had discussed Indian spirituality, and later through conversations with the older people I met on reservations, my confidence in spiritual power had deepened steadily. During Wounded Knee, I had become "personal" with the Great Mystery, and had developed communication and felt very close to the spirit world. We Indians do not teach that there is only one god. We know that *everything* has power, including the most inanimate, inconsequential things. Stones have power. A blade of grass has power. Trees and clouds and all our relatives in the insect and animal world have power. We believe we must respect that power by acknowledging its presence. By honoring the power of the spirits in that way, it becomes *our* power as well. It protects us.

By the summer of 1974, I realized that acknowledging that wisdom allows me to know when I am right. As long as I don't abuse the power of any living being, any inanimate object, the wind, Grandmother Earth, or the universe, don't abuse *any* power but respect it, those powers—or spirits or gods, or God—will watch over me. I *know* prayer works—all prayer—and with that knowledge, I have no fear. With such realizations, my life became easy to live. I wasn't worried about going to prison for our stands at Scottsbluff or Custer or even Wounded Knee. I knew the spirits were watching out for me and for what was right. I put my faith in the Great Mystery and in my lawyers and never doubted that they too were guided by the same force, whether they were aware of it or not.

31
▼▼▼▼▼▼▼▼▼

The Trial

Wounded Knee was never about criminal activities. It was, from the first, a *political* matter. Did the Fort Laramie Treaty mean what it said? Did the U.S. Constitution mean anything?

Officially, it was the United States versus Russell Means and Dennis Banks. The charges included felonies, ranging from burglary and larceny of the Wounded Knee trading post to three counts of assault with a dangerous weapon and wounding an FBI agent, interfering with law-enforcement officials in the performance of official duties, arson, possession of "unregistered Molotov cocktails," conspiracy, and auto theft. If our attorneys had tried to defend us by responding to those as ordinary criminal matters, it is likely that the feds, with virtually unlimited resources, would have put Dennis and me away for many years.

Our strategy, however, was to turn the proceedings into a political trial. Our first critical issue was to force a change of venue. Anybody with eyes and ears knew anti-Indian racism in South Dakota was at least as widespread and deep-seated as it had been before and after Wounded Knee I in 1890. The federal court with jurisdiction over western South Dakota was run by that staunch conservative, Judge Andrew Bogue. When AIM had led demonstrations in South Dakota and Nebraska, he had condemned us publicly.

In June 1971, when I was among those arrested for trespassing and dragged off Mount Rushmore, we had cited the Fort Laramie Treaty as the basis of our defense. Bogue owned property in the Black Hills, so he properly recused himself from the case. WKLD/OC now used that recusal to keep him from hearing any case involving AIM defendants. The government transferred our trial to what was then the only other federal court in South Dakota, at Sioux Falls.

Marginally less anti-Indian than the west, eastern South Dakota still remained a hotbed of racism. To prove that, WKLD/OC asked the National Jury Project—a nonpartisan, nonprofit foundation based in New York, which worked to find fair juries for indigent people—to survey South Dakota. The group demonstrated that no Indian could get a fair trial anywhere in the state, much less an AIM leader. Our case was transferred to Saint Paul, Minnesota, to the court of Judge Alfred Nichol, an opinionated Democrat. It wasn't the best possible venue. Saint Paul draws much of its juror pool from farm country, where people tend to be far more conservative than in Minneapolis. Moving from Sioux Falls to Saint Paul was only jumping from the fire into the frying pan.

In October 1973, lawyers for both sides began to argue pretrial motions. In December, WKLD/OC's attorneys succeeded in getting one charge dismissed—arson of a motor vehicle. We lost an important round, however, when Judge Nichol ruled against appointing Dennis and me as cocounsels. That was a blow to our strategy. In a political trial, the minutiae of the case are generally much less important to jurors than their perceptions of the justice of the defendant's cause. Even though we were represented by several other lawyers, having the status of cocounsels would have permitted us to speak without having to mount the witness stand. We had planned to turn the courtroom into a guerrilla theater. While cross-examining witnesses, we could make statements to bring out issues that the rules of evidence would otherwise preclude.

After partying on the Rosebud through most of the weeks before the trial, I drove to Saint Paul with Lillian Little Hawk in her car late one night in early January through a blizzard. An interracial group called I-CARE, funded by Indian Family Services, had been active there for months. It established a receiving facility for visiting Indians and helped find them living accommodations. Through the efforts of I-CARE, the manager of a Holiday Inn offered complimentary rooms to Curtis Bald Eagle, who had been assigned as my bodyguard, and me.

The night before jury selection began, I had some business to attend to—Carter Camp. Although his charges for shooting Clyde had been dropped when he refused to testify, Carter had been held in the Sioux Falls jail, in lieu of fifty thousand dollars bond, on Wounded Knee charges. After Carter had spent four months without a trial, WKLD/OC convinced Judge

Nichol to issue a writ of habeas corpus because Carter's right to a speedy trial had been violated. Released on token bond, he came to Saint Paul to observe our trial. AIM leaders thought we ought to present a united front in public. I acceded to the suggestion that we welcome Carter back with a ceremony at the University of Minnesota, but not everyone agreed, and a heated argument ensued.

The discord was exacerbated by a controversy about WKLD/OC funds. Among others, Vernon Bellecourt and Michael Haney had access to that money. There were recurring reports that not everything that came in was properly accounted for. I couldn't stomach that petty infighting. Rather than be part of it, I announced my resignation from AIM the day before the trial was to begin. Saint Paul was jammed with reporters covering the trial, so my resignation made national news. Early the next evening, I went to a WKLD/OC meeting attended by practically everyone connected with our case, including most AIM leaders. Crow Dog said, "To resign from the American Indian Movement is like resigning from Grandmother Earth. It's impossible." He sat down, and everybody looked at me. Feeling very small and foolish, I said, "Can't you guys take a joke?" Everybody cracked up—and that was the end of my quitting.

Courtroom proceedings began with jury selection on January 8, 1974. I spent the night before at a party in Minneapolis. I didn't know taxi service in the southside Indian ghetto was horrible, so next morning when I called a cab to take me to Saint Paul, it never came. Eventually, WKLD/OC sent someone after me. I was two hours late, and Judge Nichol was not amused. He chewed my butt in front of the press and threatened to revoke my bond.

Finally he calmed down and we got started. Jury Project research had revealed a lot of bigotry against Indians in Saint Paul, so Nichol granted our motion for individual voir dire. That meant our lawyers could question each potential juror about his ability to be impartial. We got lists of names and addresses the day before each batch was to be questioned. Our investigators tried hurriedly to discover politics and biases by interviewing the potential jurors' neighbors or employers. Every evening, we went through the lists, flagging names of people we thought were prejudiced and questioning them as they went through voir dire. We could ask that anyone be excused for cause, but we had a limited number of peremptory challenges, by which we could reject people without stating a reason. After we had accepted someone, the Jury Project people conducted a more thorough investigation, trying to get a better picture of the person's attitudes and inclinations.

Dennis and I also had Phillip Deere to help us. He was an Oklahoma Muscogee medicine man. His technique was to say each name before dropping a pinch of tobacco into a glass of water. If it went in a certain direction after hitting the center, the person was acceptable. If it went the other way, he was not. Usually, Deere confirmed our investigators' recommendations, but not for a black Saint Paul woman whom our lawyers, Legal Aid workers, and Jury Project investigators wanted on the jury. When the tobacco went the wrong way, Dennis and I were adamant: She was not going to be on the jury, even if it meant using one of our few peremptories. Furious, Mark Lane stomped out of the room. Ken Tilsen rolled his eyes, and Bill Kunstler applied all his powers of brotherly persuasion. Larry Leventhal shrugged his shoulders but didn't comment. The Jury Project people, who had given us thousands of man-hours, couldn't believe it. I could tell they all wanted to say, "We can't run a case on goddamn witchcraft." They never used those words, but they said it every which way except straight out.

We also had two psychologists studying body language to help decide whether to keep or strike potential jurors. That black woman's body language was nebulous; the shrinks couldn't read it. After our lawyers questioned her, they asked us again to let her serve on the jury. We refused, and she was excused on a peremptory challenge. Everyone was pissed at us, but within a few days, Jury Project investigators—no doubt anxious to show how foolish we were to depend on Phillip—brought in a raft of information. The black woman was a reactionary, known widely in her neighborhood as intolerant, and a very strict law-and-order person. Our team learned a good lesson. Not every minority is a liberal. Maybe a few also learned not to scoff at our beliefs or to condemn something because it didn't square with Eurocentric logic.

Phillip couldn't be with us on the day a young union worker went through voir dire. Dennis and I both disliked him, and the attorneys agreed. Another potential juror, a blond, crew-cut Young Republican, worried us. Rather than waste a peremptory challenge, we tried to disqualify them for cause. The judge wasn't going to let us win every time. Both of them got on the jury. So did an elderly white woman named Therese Cherrier. She scared us all because she looked so unhappy. We also lost several people we really wanted to be on the jury.

There were no Indians in the jurors' pool, so we challenged its racial composition. Our lawyers were very thorough about objecting to everything they could possibly think of. Nearly every objection was overruled, but that was expected. We had to get our challenges on record so we could use them as the basis for an appeal if necessary.

Marlon Brando came by the courtroom during jury selection and later held a press conference. He told reporters, "I've come to back the great people who made a stand at Wounded Knee." During the siege, he had donated twenty-five thousand dollars to WKLD/OC, and had refused to accept his Oscar for *The Godfather* to protest the way American movies portray Indians. Later in the week, Harry Belafonte came and he, too, held a press conference, to condemn the government for trying us.

Just because I was involved in a proceeding that might end in the loss of my liberty didn't mean all I did was go to court—far from it. The trial would take more than eight months to complete, but there were many days when court was not in session, including two weeks when Judge Nichol flew off to attend judicial conferences in Florida and Hawaii. We also got a few recesses when one of our lawyers was obliged to be someplace else. Once, Bill Kunstler had to return to New York to fight a disbarment attempt caused by contempt citations from Judge Julius Hoffman during the trial of the Chicago Seven. Bill had represented several of those arrested in the police riot at the 1968 Democratic National Convention.

Sometimes Dennis and I left town. After San Francisco newspaper mogul Randolph Hearst's daughter Patty was snatched by the Symbionese Liberation Army, Hearst agreed to pay a ransom of $2 million worth of food to Bay Area poor people. That day, February 18, Dennis jumped on a plane and flew to California. Many impoverished Indians were in the area, and we wanted to make sure they got a share of that food. The next day, Dennis called to ask me to join him.

In those days, when I flew anywhere into Indian country, AIM sent dozens of defenders for security purposes. Every time I got off a plane, the airport would reverberate from the AIM drum and the hallways were lined with guys in red berets, headbands, and vests with an assortment of buttons proclaiming, "Indian and Proud," "Indian Power," "Custer Died for Your Sins," and so forth. They would sing the AIM song and it was always a dramatic moment. Dennis had arranged that kind of reception for me in San Francisco, and all the media came out. It was like a circus.

Dennis said representatives of literally hundreds of organizations, some legitimate but many no more than con men, were flocking to San Francisco to get a piece of the ransom. They had come up with really wild ideas for that food money. We came up with our own concise plan, two pages typed on an AIM letterhead. We said with that $2 million, Hearst should rent trucks, fill them with food, and take them to designated places. We provided maps and suggested distribution points—then in an orderly manner, as the Salvation Army and everyone else does it, just hand it out. We also said they would need plenty of security to keep control of the crowds. That was the plan Hearst chose. In implementing it, however, he canceled the security. The results were predictable—riots and near riots at every giveaway point, and wholesale ripoffs that discredited Hearst and his daughter's abductors.

During that period, Dennis established a national AIM office in Saint Paul and set about distributing copies of the "Twenty Points" and the AIM credo, raising money and recruiting members. I had even more urgent matters on my hands. I had to do something to end Dick Wilson's reign of terror on Pine Ridge. By that time, he had illegally transferred an eighth of our reservation—Sheep Mountain Gunnery Range—to the U.S. Department of the Interior and organized his goons into crews of ten or twelve men to keep each community under control. One of his victims was my dear friend Pedro Bissonette, who was gunned down in October 1973.

Pedro was merely one among many. While Wilson reigned, Pine Ridge became the world's homicide capital. People were murdered at the rate of 170 per 100,000 population—about nine times that of Detroit and nearly the same as in Chile during Augusto Pinochet Ugarte's brutal regime. That figure does *not* include those who "disappeared"—people who have yet to be accounted for. Sixty-nine AIM people were killed and more than 350 others were shot, stabbed, stomped, burned by arson fires, beaten with tire irons or baseball bats, or seriously injured when their cars were run off the road. Those acts are covered by the Indian Major Crimes Act, which gives the FBI exclusive jurisdiction over felonies on Indian reservations. The feds refused to investigate *any* of those incidents, claiming a lack of manpower. In fact, in 1973, 1974, and 1975, more than twenty-five hundred agents were assigned for some significant period to the Rapid City office. In that time, there were never fewer than two hundred agents and other FBI personnel there. In one six-month period, there were more than 350—far more than in San Francisco, Seattle, Cleveland, or Atlanta. Yet the FBI never solved *any* murder of an AIM member or supporter, or even an alleged supporter.

Wilson was coming up for reelection in February of 1974. I was drafted by the Lakota people to run against him. During jury selection, I went home nearly every weekend to campaign. Except for an enclave around Pine Ridge Village and the White Clay district in the southwestern part of the reservation, I was fairly safe from goons as long as I was with armed escorts. Wilson's bullies usually attacked only people who couldn't defend themselves. Nevertheless, I took precautions.

Severt Young Bear was sort of my campaign manager and took me around to each of the communities. My rallies were always packed, even in the most remote parts of the reservation. Although there were often rumors of goon activity, these thugs laid low, wherever we went to speak, so I was able to cover virtually every district without hindrance. On weekends when I couldn't get home, Severt and some of the most prominent people on the reservation campaigned for me, including Ed McGaw from the White Clay District, who spoke there in my stead.

Twelve people entered the January 22 primary. I got the most votes— 534—and Wilson was second with 457. He controlled the election machinery and we knew he would do anything to steal the February 7 runoff, so we asked the BIA and the Department of Justice to send poll watchers. That is entirely within the government's responsibilities as "trustees" of the Indian people. Under U.S. law, we are all wards of the nation. But the same government that had sent observers to Mississippi, Alabama, and Georgia—and to Vietnam, Nicaragua, the Philippines, and other countries around the world—refused to send them to South Dakota on the ground that it had no right to interfere in the internal workings of a sovereign entity. Of course, the United States invokes the facade of Indian self-determination only when it serves its own purposes.

Nor could we have our own poll watchers. BIA cops kept everyone except voters and election officials at least fifty yards away from each ballot box. We couldn't see what was going on inside the polling places. I spent election night in Porcupine, and stayed awake until dawn waiting for the returns. I got 1,714 votes. Wilson got 1,514. But *he* won. The system imposed by the BIA is winner-take-all by district—the candidate who wins the most *districts* is elected. Taking a page from Chicago Mayor Richard Daley's book, Wilson's goons voted early and often, stuffing ballot boxes with votes from ghosts, drunks, hospital patients, recent corpses, and relocated people who hadn't set foot on Pine Ridge in years. Big-city machine politics was successful on an Indian reservation.

The networks covered the election, and CBS had its own chartered jet to bring out film. Dennis and I hitched a ride to Denver on that plane and went to the Federal Office of Civil Rights to file a complaint about the election. Tim Coulter, a Potawatomi lawyer from the Great Lakes area, headed an investigation that soon uncovered evidence of massive illegalities and fraud. I sued the United States, demanding a new election. I won that case, but too late. By the time the suit worked its way to the U.S. Supreme Court in 1976, Wilson had been defeated by Al Trimble in an honest election supervised by independent and government poll watchers.

Back in Saint Paul, it took more than a month to pick twelve jurors and three alternates. The evidence phase of the trial began on February 12. My mother came to court for that first day. There I was, in the worst trouble of my life, with the government calling me every vile name and newspapers filled with the worst that rednecks and reactionaries could dream up about me—and she finally thought that through all of my activities I was doing something right. It was strange, but it felt good.

When Judge Nichol strolled in that morning, he was startled to see fifty or sixty Pine Ridge elders, including five of our chiefs, sitting in spectator seats. They were dressed in traditional finery—men in buckskins and feathered warbonnets, women in beaded dresses with colorful designs across shoulders and down sleeves. He couldn't have failed to notice that when those important visitors had arrived in their chartered bus, they were honored outside the courthouse with appropriate ceremonies, including a sacred drum, singing, and dancing.

Judge Nichol surveyed the courtroom and said, "I want to see all the lawyers and the defendants in chambers." He turned on his heel and left. There he said, "This is all off the record, but I'm not going to allow my courtroom to be turned into a circus. I want all the Indians in those costumes out of here. If they want back in, they're going to have to wear regular clothes." Dennis and I, wearing our usual ribbon shirts, silently studied Nichol. We had been looking at him daily for more than a month, trying to figure out this wiry little Methodist. As prosecutors smirked in their chairs, Mark Lane and Bill Kunstler tried to explain that the elders, by wearing traditional regalia, were paying homage to the judge, that the "costumes" were our Indian equivalent of white ties and tuxedos—the best clothing they had.

Nichol was grimly adamant. "No way," he said.

It got very quiet. Breaking the strained silence, Severt Young Bear, our interpreter, rose to speak. He looked at Nichol and in broken but serviceable English said, "Judge, I wouldn't talk like that if I wore a black dress to work."

Dennis and I laughed. Our lawyers looked away and struggled to contain themselves. Nichol sat thinking. After a long moment, he split a little grin. Then he chuckled. Finally he let it all out—laughing from deep in his belly. When he could speak again, he said, "Okay, let's start the trial."

Before the government could begin its case, Dennis and I stood up and asked Nichol to reconsider his previous ruling against our appointment as cocounsels. "Same ruling," he said. Sitting at the defendants' table, Dennis and I had a quick whispered conference. We got up again and said, "Your honor, we've just fired our lawyers." We hadn't talked it over with anyone, so our attorneys were just as amazed as the judge. He ordered them to talk some sense into us, but when we huddled, I told them, "Every time a prosecutor opens his mouth, we're going to object. We're not going to let them finish a sentence during this entire trial."

"You can't do that," said Lane.

"Yes, we can, we're defending ourselves. It's our lives, not yours," I said.

"Fellows, wait—" begged Kunstler.

"Look, we're not lawyers, we just know what's right," I said. Tilsen and Lane tried to tell us we didn't know how to act as lawyers. Dennis cut them off. "We can act any way we want because we know what's right for us," he said. "If the judge doesn't like our lawyering, he can disbar us."

We got back up and said again, "We fire our lawyers." Nichol had a short fuse, but was just as quick to calm himself and never lost his temper. Red-cheeked and obviously exasperated, he rolled his eyes and pulled a "what next?" face as he ordered us back into chambers.

What bothered the judge more than the notion of reversing himself was that to ensure a fair trial, *he* would be responsible for teaching us some of the rudiments of courtroom protocol if we insisted on representing ourselves. Attorneys being what they are, the prosecutors would always seek to bend rules, so *he* would have to jump in with objections because we wouldn't know what to do. He would have to do double duty as defense lawyer and judge, and that would extend the trial for months. It would also color the daily proceedings, while laying significant grounds for an appeal if we were convicted. When we refused to back down, Nichol reluctantly appointed us cocounsels. Then, of course, we rehired our legal team. Discussing his reversal with a reporter, Nichol quoted Emerson—"Foolish consistency is the hobgoblin of small minds."

From our first meeting, I neither liked nor trusted Nichol. He had gone to a South Dakota law school, served as Washington secretary to that state's Senator Herbert Hitchcock, then briefly as his law partner in Mitchell, South Dakota. Nichol had been a county prosecutor and then a state prosecutor in Minnesota, and had served a few terms in the legislature. As an assistant U.S. attorney in Saint Paul, he had become very buddy-buddy with the FBI and other federal agencies. Nichol got himself elected circuit judge in 1959. Six years later, Lyndon Johnson appointed him to the federal bench. He seemed like the enemy to me.

Fortunately, I was dead wrong about him.

The political character of the trial was not lost on the government. According to legal documents that later emerged, FBI agents visited the publishers' offices of the *St. Paul Dispatch* and the *Pioneer Press*, and leaned on them to reassign reporters then covering the trial and to replace them with people the FBI thought were more suitable. Both papers complied. So much for the First Amendment! We also suspected, but could never prove, that to discourage Indian political protest, the FBI, the BIA, the U.S. Attorney's office, and the National Tribal Chairman's Association had pressured the two main wire services, Associated Press and United Press International, to suppress the truths coming out at our trial. Everybody denied it, of course.

As our trial started in Saint Paul, the defense table was on the right of the courtroom, facing the judge, with a three-man team of prosecutors and, usually, the assistant U.S. attorney, Richard D. Hurd, on the left. The jury box was to their left. Dennis and I sat side by side, with our five attorneys around us. Larry Leventhal sat on the far left of the table amid huge piles of papers, the contents of two enormous square briefcases plus whatever he could tuck under an arm. He was tall, thin, gawky, almost thirty, but looking as though he might still be an undergraduate, filled with nervous energy, very Jewish in appearance, with thick, curly black hair. At the time, I thought he was eccentric, and maybe he is—but the truth is that Larry is a genius. It was months before we realized that besides all the pro bono research and courtroom work he was doing on our case, he also was paying his bills by working for other clients, burning his candle at both ends to help us and to keep himself afloat. After court adjourned every day, he went to his office and worked until all hours of the night. Every once in a while he would appear to nod off in court, his head actually clunking on the table. Then everything would stop until someone shook him. Much more often, Larry's head would go way down, almost to the desk, then he would catch himself and jerk back up. More than once as I watched him bobbing up and down, just at the right moment his eyes would open, his back would straighten, and he would say, "Objection," and cite the right rule or case. How the hell he could sleep and listen to the trial at the same time I'll never know.

Mark Lane sat on Dennis's left. He had started out as my lawyer, but Ramon Roubideaux withdrew because he needed time with his family. He returned to South Dakota to represent Sarah Bad Heart Bull and David Hill in their trials for the Custer courthouse fracas so I let Dennis have Mark. That suited everyone. Bill Kunstler was my lead attorney, and Mark's outsized ego wouldn't subordinate itself to him. Mark was six feet tall, slim and fit, with spectacles framing a pug nose over what I called a raccoon beard—like a Vandyke but running all the way up to his sideburns, with gray hair on either side of his chin. He was very quick on his feet, both literally and when it came to humor and fast thinking. Mark had represented Lee Harvey Oswald, the accused assassin of President Kennedy, until Oswald was murdered. Then Mark went to New Orleans as one of District Attorney Jim Garrison's investigators. By the time he came to Saint Paul, he had written a best-seller, *Rush to Judgment*, and had championed the case of James Earl Ray, convicted killer of the Reverend Martin Luther King Jr.

Dennis's third attorney was Doug Hall, who played the role of elder statesman of the combined defense team. A balding, bespectacled, professorial pipe smoker with a long, aquiline nose and a ponytail, he was an exceptionally honorable man, very knowledgeable about criminal law and quite well regarded in the Twin Cities area. He, too, had a very healthy ego.

Bill Kunstler sat on my right. Then in his early fifties, he was a little more than six feet tall, with long waves of unruly graying hair above a lantern-jawed face. His trademark was his reading glasses, usually worn atop his high forehead like a set of aviator's goggles. He had been hassled by sheriffs while representing Freedom Riders in Mississippi in the early 1960s, and was inside Attica during the violent prison revolt there. Bill got involved with Indians after some Six Nations steelworkers in Philadelphia were framed in the death of Leon Shenandoah, the Onondaga who had represented the entire U.S. Army in John Kennedy's funeral cortege. Bill got them all off. When Wounded Knee started, Oren Lyons, the Onondaga leader, suggested that Pedro Bissonnette call Bill. He responded immediately and was often inside the Knee, offering very good advice. Very wise and, unlike many high-powered lawyers, willing to listen to anyone, Bill had a deep, sonorous bass voice and was a master of courtroom theater.

My other attorney was Ken Tilsen. I called him a banty rooster. He was short and stocky and balding, a fiery Jewish intellectual in eyeglasses. A brilliant defense attorney, Ken was a bulldog who fought tenaciously for what he thought was right. He grew up in a racially mixed Saint Paul neighborhood and became active in leftist politics in high school. He represented black University of Minnesota students who took over Morell Hall. Among them was a young Mississippi woman, a Congress of Racial Equality organizer whom Ken and his wife had practically adopted. They were targeted by COINTEL and repeatedly arrested. During the Vietnam War, he probably handled more draft-board cases than anyone between the coasts. Ken and I didn't meet until Wounded Knee, but he had represented Clyde often during the period when Minneapolis cops arrested him every week.

After the jury had been seated, the government began its case. In the 1880s, Congress passed the Indian Major Crimes Act to give itself jurisdiction on reservations. From it came a body of case law applying only to Indians. The charges against us alleged violations of those laws, so the government's first task was to prove that we actually were Indians. That required the government to trot out the blood-quantum test, an often conflicting list of criteria that boils down to judging a pedigree. I was shocked to learn that the BIA had listed me as 15/32 Indian. That, I learned, was because it had ignored my great-grandmother, a full-blooded Crow. Thus I discovered another BIA wrinkle. On certain reservations, ancestors from other Indian nations don't count. If a Cheyenne and a Sioux have children, the BIA counts them as half-bloods. It dismisses half of someone's heritage with a stroke of the pen. When the BIA "experts" testified about Dennis's ancestry, they even got his birth-date wrong. According to the BIA, he was born five years after his mother had brought him into this world.

The trial was shocking to me in another way. I wasn't prepared to see and hear handsome, clean-cut, all-American white men in short haircuts and IBM-blue suits get up on a witness stand, swear to their One True God on the holiest document of their faith—the Christian Bible—"to tell the truth, the whole truth, and nothing but the truth," and then lie. They didn't try to shade things. They didn't try to keep their testimony *near* the truth. They flat out lied. They put words in my mouth and in Dennis's that we never said. They denied doing things that had been done. They withheld evidence supporting our innocence, and claimed it didn't exist. They spoke in perfectly correct English and answered every question so smoothly it was obvious that they had been rehearsed. They lied in front of the media of the world and in front of a packed courtroom. Even when defense lawyers *caught* them in a lie, they lied again and denied that they had ever lied.

And they didn't even seem ashamed.

I was thirty-four years old and had been through what I thought was a whole lot—but what came out of the mouths of FBI agents and U.S. attorneys during the months of testimony simply blew me away. Even today, I find it hard to believe. I still thought the government could be forced to live up to its own laws. As far back as I could remember, it had been hammered into my head—the white man has the civilized society. But it's impossible for an honorable culture to continue when its people are willing to lie to their god. After a while, I didn't even listen to the testimony. I just looked at the liars and thought about what I was watching. It began to register in my mind why the United States of America doesn't keep its treaties. I had always believed that those who were running things really wanted to follow them. Now I was seeing that they had never intended to. I realized that Watergate was unusual only because so many high-ranking officials *got caught*. America was a society built on lies and deceit.

3 2
▼▼▼▼▼▼▼▼▼

Political Theater

I f you choose to protest the actions of the federal government, the best
time to do so is during a Republican administration. Democrats, in my
experience, appoint competent people as U.S. attorneys. Republicans
appoint political flunkies who may not be bright, but who are loyal and
will follow orders, no matter how absurd. The federal lawyers introducing
what they called "evidence" against us were Earl Kaplan, a Justice Department lawyer from D.C.; William F. Clayton, U.S. Attorney for South Dakota; and his prosecutors, Assistant U.S. Attorneys David R. Gienapp and
Richard Hurd.

Our strategy was never to allow the squeaky-clean, perfectly dressed G-
men to tell their lies without constantly challenging them. We had to show
the jury that although those guys could afford decent tailors, they were still
liars. In addition to what our lawyers did, Dennis and I jumped up to object
or protest at every opportunity. Usually those interruptions came at the
wrong time, legally speaking, but it was guerrilla theater. We were trying to
raise issues that the formal legal system wouldn't allow.

As always, the Great Mystery—some people might call it luck—played a
big part in our defense. On February 18, 1974, Mark Lane was in Deadwood,
South Dakota, a tiny Black Hills town. While waiting to testify to a grand

jury about the murder of Pedro Bissonnette, Mark had a chance conversation with Joseph Pourier, manager of Bison State Telephone Company at Pine Ridge. Pourier himself had installed telephones at the government roadblock and the trading post at Wounded Knee. He said that by FBI order, both phones shared one line, so anyone calling the trading post would be heard at the roadblock. He also said U.S. Marshal Tommy Hudson had demanded a key to the telephone exchange. After giving it to him, Pourier noticed that new wiring had been installed. Later, while putting phones into the BIA headquarters, where the FBI had set up shop, he saw equipment that was used only to monitor telephone lines. The implications of an illegal wiretap at Wounded Knee were staggering. Our attorneys had called to or from that phone during the siege to talk to us and to dozens of other clients around the country—and the FBI had heard every word. So much for attorney-client privilege. So much for the U.S. Constitution!

While cross-examining an FBI agent, we learned of a letter written by W. Mark Felt, the FBI's second-ranking official during the siege. The letter was not in the FBI files, which we had subpoenaed and were legally entitled to see. The handwritten note was to Henry Petersen, head of the Justice Department's Criminal Division. It expressed Felt's dismay after a judge had ruled that the "wiretap application in the Wounded Knee case was based on information from an illegal wiretap." When we subpoenaed Felt and asked him about the letter, he said he had written it only to dispel doubts that the FBI might do something as terrible as unauthorized wiretapping. Felt admitted to writing it on personal stationery instead of FBI letterhead, but denied that his intention was to keep the damning document out of official files. Felt was indicted later for authorizing illegal break-ins during the Watergate era, but was pardoned.

Joseph Trimbach, who had been the FBI supervisor for the Dakotas and Minnesota, testified under oath that there were no wiretaps at Wounded Knee, but later said he had forgotten about them. He also said he had neither seen nor signed a request for a court order to authorize the wiretaps. When that very document was produced, he calmly denied that the signature on it was his. That was so unbelievable that a senior agent was called by the government. He testified that the affidavit submitted over Trimbach's signature wasn't really signed by him—in the FBI, he said, simply because a man's name appears as a signature doesn't mean he actually signed it. Judge Nichol was stunned. He said, "You mean that you submit a document here, an affidavit under oath, signed by Trimbach, and he may not have actually signed it?"

The agent said, "That's why he testified that he knew nothing about it."

"Before I became a judge," replied Nichol, his voice dripping contempt, "I was an assistant U.S. attorney for the Eastern District of South Dakota when Mr. Trimbach was agent in charge here. We became friends, and ever since, on my birthdays, I got a card from him. I'm now shocked to realize that the card I got last week and maybe the ones for years before that were never really sent by him at all."

FBI special agent Gerald J. Bertinot Jr. testified about FBI wiretapping at Wounded Knee. He admitted listening to our conversations. He thought it was necessary even though there was no court order. He tried to persuade the jury that since he and his fellow agents never got a court order and didn't follow their own strict legal procedures, there hadn't really been any wiretapping. In technique and in scope, he was the biggest, boldest liar we had seen yet, leagues ahead of his peers. Then he outdid himself, testifying on several crucial issues relating directly to the charges against us. He claimed to have taken four Molotov cocktails from the trunk of a car at a roadblock. The car was under a flag of truce and was leaving the Knee with Bobby Burnett, son of the Rosebud tribal chairman, dazed and bleeding from a gunshot wound, in the backseat. Under cross-examination, Bertinot said he had seen no flag on the car, hadn't bothered to report the incident or forward the "evidence" until the next day, and hadn't called in to get permission to search. He said the incendiaries had been placed in the trunk by Dennis and me. All that was contradicted by other government evidence.

Late in the day, while Bertinot was still on the stand, Dennis and I both rose and said, almost in unison, "Your honor, we're putting this man under citizen's arrest for illegal wiretapping." That took everyone by surprise. Judge Nichol said, "You're going to have to let him finish his testimony—I won't allow you to arrest him in my courtroom." Dennis and I turned around and, in loud voices, told our WKLD/OC legal assistant to alert AIM security. "Get downstairs and make sure this criminal doesn't leave this building without getting arrested," we said. When the judge had quieted everyone down, Bertinot finished his testimony. Nichol said, "Court is adjourned for the day," and headed for his private exit. As soon as he had gone, bedlam erupted. Dennis and I rushed the witness stand, but several marshals jumped in to hold us off while others got Bertinot out the judge's door.

A few years earlier, Saint Paul had built an innovative system of enclosed second-story bridges and walkways to connect downtown buildings so people could get around during the bitterly cold winters. Knowing that Indians were waiting and watching on every floor, marshals hustled Bertinot through the skywalk to an office building across the street. Dennis and I, backed by a couple of other AIM guys, were right behind. For more than fifteen minutes, we chased those feds all over downtown Saint Paul, through department stores, offices, and little shopping centers. It was like a scene out of *The French Connection*. Bertinot and his escorts ran and dodged and stumbled, knocking things out of the way—people, store displays, news racks, tables. We were on their heels, leaping and dodging and bumping into walls and the debris in our path, while slowly gaining on them. Finally, they rushed through a store and into a parking lot and dove into a waiting car. Bertinot was on the floorboard when it peeled out, burning rubber. He flew to Detroit that afternoon, but our attempted arrest was a public-relations coup that made all the newspapers—and the jury got our message.

Felt's letter and all the other wiretap documents were only a few of what would eventually prove to be hundreds that the FBI had withheld from us, despite the court's repeated orders to turn over *all* such evidence. Among them was a report, prepared by Senator Henry "Scoop" Jackson's subcommittee on Indian affairs, that discussed the involvement of the military at Wounded Knee. We knew everything from Phantom jets and APCs to radio gear and hundreds of support troops had been deployed, and that Colonel Volney Warner, chief of staff of the Eighty-second Airborne, had served as an FBI adviser. All that was illegal without a presidential proclamation. The posse comitatus statute prohibits use of troops in civil matters. Since charges against us included "interference with law enforcement officials lawfully engaged in the performance of their duties," those charges should be dismissed if we could prove illegal military involvement. For months, the feds refused to give us the Jackson report. When finally they were forced to, they withheld the pages proving illicit military participation.

But the spirits continued to guide our defense in strange ways. A few days later, Richard Hurd, the chief prosecutor, accidentally gave a copy of the report *with* the missing text to a newspaper reporter. By chance, our attorney Ken Tilsen later discussed the report with the journalist. It became obvious that they were talking about two different documents. Comparing them, we learned that once again, the government had withheld key evidence. Hurd had the gall to say the omission was "accidental." Judge Nichol was also very skeptical.

Listening to months of testimony, much of it tedious and repetitious, Dennis and I sometimes amused ourselves by drafting tongue-in-cheek press releases. The media became our unwitting collaborators. One such release, reported almost verbatim by the Associated Press, was printed solemnly as page-one news by newspapers throughout the Great Plains. The *Pierre* (South Dakota) *Daily Capital Journal* said:

AIM DECLARES SOUTH DAKOTA A "WAR ZONE"

ST. PAUL, Minn. (AP)—The American Indian Movement today declared South Dakota a "war zone" and called for a national boycott to discourage tourism in the state.

The statement said in part . . . "The Central Committee of AIM warns all tourists that if they travel to South Dakota, Indian people will assume that they are either there to kill Indians or to help Indians."

It advised those going to South Dakota to kill Indians to notify U.S.

Senator George McGovern, Lt. Gov. William Dougherty or U.S. Atty. William Clayton "for further assistance."

AIM said such South Dakota visitors would "be there at their own risk."

Those going to help Indians could fill such roles as doctors, nurses, clerks, teachers, X-ray technicians or ambulance drivers, the statement said. Purpose of the boycott, said AIM, was to discourage tourism, non-Indian travel and vehicles on Indian reservations.

AIM also said all-out-of-state vehicles traveling on Indian reservations and without Indian permits would be stopped and impounded and "cars would not be returned."

Indian patrols will begin "constant surveillance" against non-Indians suspected of being enemies and assassins, AIM said.

It was twenty years before I learned about that newspaper story. When I finally read it, I laughed until I cried.

In late April, Nichol recessed court for a week and went off to a conference, and I went to a sacred pipe ceremony on the Cheyenne River Reservation. It involved the Lakota Nation's most revered object—the sacred white buffalo calf pipe, which was brought to us, according to my ancestors, long ago by Calf Pipe Woman to give us spiritual direction. She appeared to two hunters in search of buffalo, looking very beautiful in a white dress, red leggings, red shawl, and red porcupine quills on her moccasins. On her back she carried a large bundle wrapped in buffalo hide. When one of the hunters expressed carnal desire for the woman, the other one told him to shut up. Calf Pipe Woman came within speaking distance and said, "Why don't you do what you feel like doing?" Approaching her, the aroused hunter took off his clothes. Suddenly the woman and this eager hunter were covered by a glowing white cloud. The other man ran for his life. When he turned around to see what had happened, the cloud rose. Calf Pipe Woman was as before, but the first hunter had become a pile of bones. The woman told the man not to be afraid—such things happened only to people with evil thoughts or who did bad things.

Calf Pipe Woman told the hunter to go to his camp and tell the leader to prepare a lodge in a certain way and to invite the best people in the camp to a ceremony. She then appeared in the camp to say that the sacred pipe in her bundle came from *Wakan Tanka*, the Great Mystery. It was his gift to the Lakota. Through it, *Wakan Tanka* would hear their voices. Calf Pipe Woman instructed my ancestors in the way of the sacred pipe—how to use its powerful medicine for good and never for evil. She taught them the keeping of the spirit, which honors those who leave this world for the next—a ceremony of death, grieving, and letting go—and the releasing of the spirit, the end of mourning. She taught the *inipi* purification ritual. Before leaving, she told the Lakota people, "I may not return as you see me now, but I will come back to tell you about the other sacred ceremonies." Then she walked away, changing into a white buffalo calf and trotting across the prairie to disappear.

Eventually, we Lakota received more holy ceremonies from the Great Mystery. There was the *wiwongwaci*, or sun dance; the *unblecayapi*, or crying for a vision, which is used to seek the spiritual direction that governs all actions in life; the throwing of the ball, which keeps the community well by reminding us of collective responsibilities; the making-of-relatives ceremony, a citizenship rite which brings outsiders into one's family, clan, community, and nation; the entering of womanhood, *hunkayapi*, acknowledging a girl's passage through puberty; and in the late nineteenth century, our most recent ceremony, the *yuwipi*, for curing.

Today, that sacred pipe—the very one brought by Calf Pipe Woman— is kept at Green Grass, South Dakota, on the Cheyenne River Reservation. I had been there first in 1972, when Crow Dog took several people to meet the pipe's keeper after our takeover of Gordon, Nebraska. The sacred pipe was kept in its original buffalo-skin bundle in a little corrugated tin shack that was painted red. At that time, it was not unusual for drunks, usually cow-boys—breeds, not white men—to come out there to raise hell, by driving around and shooting at the tin shack.

For centuries, the sacred white buffalo calf pipe had been kept by gen-erations of women in a single family, but because of BIA-caused dysfunction in that one family, the last female keeper passed it on to her grandson, Orval Looking Horse. The sacred pipe, which less than half a century before had been considered so powerful that the BIA wouldn't even allow it on other reservations, was by the early 1970s all but forgotten. No one came to see it. Only the most traditional full-bloods seemed to care that it still existed, and they kept their reverence as a family secret. I'm amazed that we still have the pipe, that it is not in a museum. What are the chances that some Jewish family had kept the stone tablets Moses brought down from Sinai for all this time? It blows me away to think about it.

That night in April 1974, Orval Looking Horse brought out the big bundle with the sacred pipe inside. We carried it and prayed with it and had a ceremony with it. None of us felt worthy of actually *seeing* the pipe—it was enough to handle the bundle. I knew right then that the Lakota Nation still had a chance, that we could still survive as a people as long as we possess the sacred pipe. I also knew that we couldn't keep it hidden any longer. It belongs to the Lakota people and must be brought to them. Only the pipe can restore *cangleska wakan*, the sacred hoop representing the unity that binds our nation together with shared values and a clan system. The hoop reminds us that everything that is holy and good lies in a circle, that the universe reenergizes itself. Most Eurocentric-male linear thinkers, however, believe that all matter decays and disappears. They know nothing of regeneration or reincarnation— or anything about life itself.

Within the hoop, which encloses the entire universe created by the Great Mystery, is the sacred tree of life, which symbolizes the spiritual strength of the Lakota Nation. For centuries, the tree has been dying. The great medicine man Black Elk said that perhaps only one small root of the sacred tree of life is still alive, and we must nourish it and bring it back to health.

After the sacred pipe ceremony that April, we drove directly from Green Grass to Sioux Falls, arriving on a Friday. We watched the trial of Sarah Bad Heart Bull, David Hill, Robert High Eagle, Dlala Beane, and Kenneth Dahl for several alleged felonies during the Custer courthouse police riot of February 1973. Dahl was a white guy from Hot Springs, the only non-Indian charged in this event. Their attorneys were Ramon Roubideaux and three white men from California, John Pratt, Reber Boult, and David Allen. The prosecutor was Bill Janklow, who was running for state Attorney General. The judge was Joseph Bottum, seventy years old, a rock-ribbed, racist, reactionary Republican party hack. He had lost elections for the U.S. House of Representatives and for governor of South Dakota, but managed to get elected to a job nobody cared about—lieutenant governor. His party cronies helped get him elected to the Seventh Circuit bench in 1969, but he was up for reelection in 1974 and faced a stiff primary challenge.

The defense lawyers had introduced several motions before I arrived. They had asked Bottum to dismiss charges or change the venue because of South Dakota's rampant racism and excessive pretrial publicity. They also asked him to suppress so-called evidence that had been obtained illegally, and to increase the number of peremptory challenges each side could use during jury selection. When Bottum denied those motions, they appealed to the state supreme court and demanded a delay in the trial until there were rulings on those appeals. Bottum responded by suspending for a day the rights of the white lawyers to practice in South Dakota—but he cited Roubideaux, the only Indian, for contempt and threw him in jail.

When the judge entered the courtroom the next day, Indian spectators responded to his racism by refusing to rise to show respect. Bottum blew his top, and had over seventy people dragged out of the courtroom. He then threatened to have anyone arrested who refused to stand when he came into the room. When I met with the defendants' support group we all agreed we would remain seated and get arrested. We expected the cops to get rough, so we decided that only men would go. About twenty Lakota volunteered.

A Lutheran clerical conference was being held in town. When we asked them to send court observers, they responded with sixteen ministers, including four bishops. We also invited the League of Women Voters and alerted the media. When it was time for court to convene, spectators lined up to pass through a metal detector. Only fifteen Lakota people were allowed inside before the marshals closed the courtroom. I was turned away, along with everyone in line behind me. Standing around the third-floor corridor, I thought I had been spared jail. That was okay, for I was due back in Saint Paul for my own trial the next day. Then Minnehaha County Sheriff Les Hawkey came up and said, "Russell Means, the judge would like to see you in his chambers."

"Why?" I replied.

"Your people won't stand when he enters the courtroom, and he wants to see if you can help."

"I don't think I can get them to do that, but I'll meet with him."

Bottum asked me to convince the Lakota that he meant business. I agreed to speak with them, and on my way out of chambers Bottum wished me good luck. In the courtroom, I told the Lakota what Bottum had said, but they didn't change their minds, so I sat down with them. Moments later, the judge entered. The defendants, their lawyers, and most spectators rose, including the ministers and the League of Women Voters' observers. We Indian spectators sat quietly.

Suddenly the hallway and chambers doors burst open and a phalanx of twenty-five policemen poured in, dressed for a riot, in helmets, shields, face guards, and batons. They attacked the first Indians they saw, Roubideaux and David Hill, who were *standing* at the defendants' table. As Hill went down under a hail of blows to his head, two white lawyers pulled Roubideaux under a table and rolled on top of him protectively. A heartbeat later, a cop came at me with a raised club. Rather than get hit, I smashed his face mask and watched his nose twist and flatten against the plastic. Then I took that pig's helmet off and took his club away. The other Lakota were doing much the same. We beat the cops back, they regrouped, then charged again. We repulsed them as before. Once again, they charged, and again we fought them off. Each time they fell back, we had snatched more helmets and more clubs.

The courtroom went wild, with women screaming and ministers scrambling to get out of the way. The cops knocked down three of our guys, including my brother Ted, and dragged them out. Chairs flew through windows. When our people outside saw the broken glass, they started a demonstration, smashing windows and shattering glass doors. In the courtroom, the cops must have realized they couldn't beat us, so they backed off, lined up, and let everyone leave. David Hill's eye was hanging out of his head, so we took him to a hospital. He lost some of his vision.

Early the next morning, Dennis and I went to the airport to catch a plane back to Minnesota. The cops pounced, arresting me for "riot to obstruct justice and injury to a public building" for allegedly kicking in a window as I went downstairs. As usual, they found cops to lie about it.

In a struggle, any news is good news, as Bill Kunstler has often said.

When a television news crew turned up at the jail for a live report, I did an interview condemning South Dakota racism. When Judge Nichol learned of my arrest, he was livid. He called the state's attorney and ranted at him. They knew I was on trial in Saint Paul, he said, and that I had to report back—so they could have worked out any arrest with him. Instead, they held up our trial. Still fuming, Nichol ordered them to put me on the next plane to Minneapolis. I refused to change out of my Minnehaha County jail coveralls and wore them back to Saint Paul and into the courthouse. I wanted the world to see that I was a political prisoner. I got to remind the jurors of South Dakota's racial bigotry by making a speech to Nichol explaining my tardiness.

We made the same point another way. When the trial continued, several witnesses testified about the wounding of FBI agent Curtis Fitzgerald. On about March 11, while chasing a panel truck near Wounded Knee, he got shot in the hand and was taken to an Indian Health Service hospital in Pine Ridge. A couple of doctors testified as to the extent of his wounds and the government introduced evidence of Fitzgerald's treatment. Dennis noticed that the emergency-room admissions sheet had been annotated "VIP." That also appeared on all of Fitzgerald's other hospital records.

Dennis and I insisted on cross-examining the doctors. Judge Nichol warned that a person who represents himself has a fool for a client, and that even very experienced lawyers have difficulty cross-examining expert witnesses such as doctors. "As long as you say on the record that you understand that you could hurt yourself, I'll allow it," he said. We didn't question the doctor about wounds or treatment. Dennis asked, "What does *VIP* mean?" and the doctor hemmed and hawed and finally said, "Very important person."

"Have you ever put *VIP* on the records of any Indian person admitted to the hospital?"

"Not that I can remember."

"Didn't that mean that this white FBI agent was to get special treatment?"

"Not at all."

"Then why did you put *VIP* on his records, since it means 'very important person'? Why distinguish him?"

We went on in that vein for half an hour, until the doctor was a limp rag and everyone in the jury box understood that Indians are treated a hell of a lot differently than white FBI agents in that hospital. By then, the jurors didn't care about Fitzgerald's wounds—they had become irrelevant.

We continued to jump up to do and say things that no lawyer would. We knew we could get away with giving speeches while pretending to cross-examine. The government always objected, and the judge always told the jury to disregard what they had heard—but you can't unring a bell. After the umpteenth time, Nichol told us he knew we were doing it just to influence the jury. By that time, we had accomplished our purpose.

As the trial continued, Hurd and other assistant U.S. attorneys continued to withhold crucial evidence, including a set of photos that Hurd claimed was "missing" before Agnes Gildersleeve's cross-examination. After she was excused and she left the state, Hurd suddenly "discovered" the photos in his briefcase. Nichol got so pissed off at those stunts that he took the FBI's files away and had marshals guard them.

In late June, Judge Bottum concluded the trial of Sarah Bad Heart Bull, Kenneth Dahl, and Robert High Eagle in Sioux Falls. His jury instructions amounted to: "If you're present at a riot, then you're responsible for it." The jury took fifteen hours to come back with guilty verdicts for all three.

A few days later, during another trial recess, I went to Valentine, Nebraska, to party. On a Saturday afternoon I headed up Highway 83 for Mission, South Dakota, with two or three carloads of AIMsters. We stopped outside town at Mission Golf Course, a country club. It was supposedly a private club, but the policy on nonmembers was to serve whites and turn away dark-skinned Indians. We were hungry, so we decided to find out if that was true.

We sat down and ordered soft drinks and cheeseburgers, but the manager came over to tell us to leave, or he would call the cops. We said, "Go ahead." He called the Mission police, even though the property was outside town, on an Indian reservation, and only BIA police had jurisdiction. When the cops arrived—Tom Rhoads, Mission's redheaded chief of police, and Ron Haukaas, a light-skinned breed—Rhoads immediately drew his gun, put it to my head, and said I was under arrest. I slapped his arm away and punched him out. Haukaas went for his gun, but my friend Kenny Kane laid him out. We chased the cops and the other whites out of the building, and some of our guys went to the basement and repossessed money in illegal slot machines. Outside, several AIM brothers trashed the police car. Harvey Kills In Water was kicking the red light off when he was accidentally shot in the head by a gun taken from the car. The guy who pulled the trigger, we later discovered, was an FBI informer. We rushed Harvey to a hospital.

Assured that he was out of danger, I went with Curtis Bald Eagle and Kenny Kane to party on the Rosebud at the Saint Francis home of Theresa Kills In Water and Bernadine Broken Leg, young women with small children. A BIA police supervisor lived directly across the street. That evening, he didn't come home from work. We asked around and learned that the FBI had told the BIA to arrest me and that their cops had been given shoot-to-kill orders. We knew that often when cops want to get people without leaving evidence of illegal tactics, they just firebomb them. We had seen it on Pine Ridge many times. Only a few weeks earlier, the papers had been full of the Symbionese Liberation Army shoot-out in which several people burned to death after police and the FBI surrounded their Los Angeles house and set it ablaze. The Saint Francis home we were visiting was so-called transitional housing—a temporary, substandard structure. Small and flimsy, it afforded no shelter against gunfire. If such a house catches fire, it burns to the ground in less than twelve minutes.

I was tired of getting arrested. I was tired of racism, tired of the BIA punks, tired of the continuing genocide against my people. I decided to make a stand right there. Kenny and Curtis said, "We're with you." We didn't want the cops to hurt Bernadine, Theresa, or their kids, so we sent them all away. We did not intend to die like the SLA people had. Friends brought ammo and grenades. We went outside to dig earthen mounds and fortifications, and set up a T-shaped ambush among the trees around the house and the road leading to it. We then mapped out an escape route and arranged to borrow a car from an AIM brother named Richard Young. He was a well-known auto mechanic and stock-car racer who had the fastest wheels in that part of the country—a far more powerful vehicle than any police cruiser or jeep. We were going to shoot it out with the BIA sellouts, then take off. If they wasted us instead, we were determined to take a few of them with us and make the rest remember they had been in a fight.

When we were ready, we had someone go to the police station to tell them where we were and that we were expecting them to come for us. As we had at Wounded Knee, we held a spiritual ceremony to say good-bye to this world. Just as our ancestors had on similar occasions, we sang, "It Is a Good Day To Die." Then we crouched in the dark, moonless night under a brilliant canopy of stars, and waited.

A Government of, by, and for the Liars

A row of trees lined the house in Saint Francis. Nearby were several junk car bodies—the reservation Indian's auto-parts store—that would make good cover. We sat in darkness, worrying only a little about BIA cops with night-vision devices sneaking up to snipe us down. Shooting without showing their faces was just their style, but it would have taken courage and skill for one or two to approach us on foot, and they were gutless, stupid, hang-around-the-fort types. We passed the time joking around, staying loose. It was a warm night. After a while, Kenny Kane went to a neighboring house and returned with a six-pack. As we drank beer and waited, we talked about our beliefs and reviewed the entire state of Indian affairs. We agreed that we weren't going to submit to the white man or his BIA proxies. Never again would we get down on our knees, we said. There was an air of bravado to our talk. We were bucking up one another's spirits, but the threat was real. It hung over us, invisible but almost palpable in the quiet darkness.

Hundreds of miles away, WKLD/OC lawyers were in a frenzy. A day earlier, after Judge Andrew Bogue had ordered Mario Gonzales, who had become a judge of the Rosebud tribal court, to stop interfering with the arrest of Kenny and myself for the country-club incident, my attorneys had begun to negotiate with the FBI about our surrender. I had declared publicly that

I wouldn't surrender this time, and almost everybody on the reservation knew it. One of our Rosebud friends had called Rapid City to explain the situation, and someone there had called Saint Paul. As worry and panic set in, our lawyers and supporters called one another and the feds. WKLD/OC people began to drive through the night. At about 3:00 A.M., a car without lights turned into the road leading to our ambush. Curtis Bald Eagle, Kenny, and I slipped into our firing positions, checked our weapons, and watched as the car stopped. We could hear other cars nearby, but we couldn't see them. As the car doors opened, we raised our weapons at two dark figures that came toward our house. I popped off the safety. At the last instant, I realized they were Theresa and Bernadine, the women whose home we had borrowed. With them were Ken Tilsen, Mark Lane, and his girlfriend, WKLD/OC investigator Caroline Mugar. In the other cars, they said, were U.S. marshals.

Still fearing that BIA police might come at any moment, I sent Mark's car to the end of the road, as far away as we could still see it, so we could wave it in or send it away if we were attacked. Then we listened to our lawyers. Tilsen did most of the talking. Confirming the BIA's shoot-to-kill order, he said he had arranged with the marshals to guarantee all three of us safe passage. The marshals were scared to death. They knew the BIA cops were trigger-happy and couldn't be trusted, so they had lined up an escape route and local guides to sneak us off the reservation via back roads. Caroline and Mark said they would ride with us in the same car.

"They can go to hell," I said. "We're not giving up. We've had it with oppression. If those BIA cops are so committed to killing us, we want them to try it."

Mark and Caroline pleaded with me, but I wouldn't listen. I said we were going to fight, although I knew full well that even if we got out alive, we would be on the run for the rest of our lives. Then I realized that wasn't fair to Kenny and Curtis. I was the one the BIA wanted dead, and yet those guys were ready to give up their lives for me. I begged them both to leave, but they refused. I even drew down on them. "Leave with the marshals, or I'll shoot your kneecaps. Right here. Right now." They said, "Russ, we're staying for you—we're just as tired of this bullshit as you are. We don't want to live either if we have to submit. We have the right to die if we want to. We have the right to be with you if we want to."

I blinked away tears. After months together in Saint Paul, Curtis and I were very close. Kenny and I always had been like that. For years, I had considered him a younger brother. Even so, I couldn't believe they were willing to die for me.

When Ken Tilsen and Mark saw that they couldn't get through to us by talking about my safety, they raised political issues. Mark finally struck the right chord when he mentioned the trial in Saint Paul. If I died or went on the run, it would create a mistrial, he said. The government would start over and try Dennis alone. It would have the opportunity to introduce all the evidence to a new jury, and the witnesses wouldn't be nearly as clumsy about their lies. Without my presence, nothing about the 1868 treaty would ever get into the official record. If I shot it out or ran away, I would look like a common criminal. It would hurt Dennis, hurt the movement, and jeopardize everything we had worked so long and so hard to accomplish.

I was much more receptive when Ken told me that once safely off the reservation, we would be taken to Pierre to be arraigned and immediately bonded without spending any time in jail. Although I felt responsible for Kenny and Curtis, what made me finally agree was the political argument. I *had* to get the Fort Laramie Treaty issues before the courts. Mark signaled the marshals. When they rolled up, we got into their cars and drove off the reservation on unpaved back roads, mostly without lights. Everything happened exactly as promised. Later that day, I drove to Sioux Falls for my arraignment on the Minnehaha County courthouse charges. Archie Madsen, a Lutheran bishop from Denver, testified that police had attacked the Indians who were peacefully sitting or standing in the courtroom, but the judge seemed not to care. I was bound over for trial.

A few weeks later, I went to a *wacipi* near the Crow Creek Reservation, home of the Crow Creek Sioux, on the east bank of the Missouri River, in South Dakota. It rained, ruining the dancing, so I took off for Sisseton, South Dakota, with Curtis and a carload of young women. We were all half-drunk, reeking of booze, and about to run out of gas when we stopped in a tiny farm town. It was the middle of the night and everything was closed. We went to the police station and said we were the scout car for an AIM caravan en route to Sisseton. We said, "We're going to need fuel, so could you open up the gas station?" Whites believe Indians have scouts, and by that time, AIM's reputation scared hell out of most who had bought into the racial stereotypes created by their grandparents. The cops woke up the whole town—every light in every house was blazing. Every Winchester-toting vigilante for miles around came out in his pickup to surround the gas station and watch us. Of course we had to pay for our gas, but after pooling our money, we could come up with only $3.12—not enough for half a tank. When we had pumped it, we said, "The tank's full. We have to go on to the next town, but the caravan will be along soon and they'll all need gas." We took off and left them waiting. I suppose they went home eventually.

Later that summer, I persuaded the chairman of the Standing Rock Sioux, a Hunkpapa named Pat McLaughlin, to host the First International Indian Treaty Conference, at Wakpala, South Dakota, on his reservation. It attracted more than five thousand Indian people from all over the United States and Canada—the largest intertribal gathering of Indian people ever. That did not please the feds. They sent a Public Health Service doctor to establish a clinic there. On the first day of the conference, after one person became ill, the doctor told the media he had discovered a case of hepatitis. The story and pictures went everywhere. Many people en route to the conference—including United Nations observers and other prestigious international figures—got worried and went back home. At Wakpala, people lined up to get gamma-globulin shots, but after twelve hundred injections, the supply ran out.

The doctor threatened a quarantine, which would have ruined the event, of course. When we demanded a sample of the hepatitis culture from the doctor so we could verify his diagnosis with independent authorities, he said, "Oops! I made a mistake. This isn't hepatitis at all. Sorry."

Despite that and other distractions, representatives from ninety-seven Indian nations showed up. Except for those too ill or infirm to travel, almost every traditional Sioux leader—men and women, Lakota, Dakota, and even Nakota—from all fourteen U.S. Sioux reservations and from Canada showed up. They held workshops among themselves and seemed to have a terrific time, renewing old friendships and speaking in their own language.

To underscore the seriousness of our purpose, we allowed neither drugs nor alcohol at our conference. We searched all vehicles. One of many people who got busted was Vernon Bellecourt, who came with a bunch of white people and a load of booze hidden in his motor home. When we poured the liquor on the ground in front of them, they almost cried. We did the same with the media people, many of whom tried to bring stuff in by stashing it in their motor homes. We're human and we didn't have perfect security, so I imagine a few things slipped through, but I never saw evidence of that.

I went to Wakpala on the weekend, but I knew Judge Nichol wouldn't recess our trial for a week so I could stay. Then I met a young small-town doctor, a white guy who was very pro-Indian. I told him I had to find some way to get sick enough to stay. He proclaimed that I had a bleeding ulcer and couldn't travel, so I sat in a wheelchair and was pushed around camp. Papers around the country ran that photo. Nichol called a recess until I "recovered," but barred me from political activity while I was sick. He said, "If I see you on television out of your wheelchair, there's going to be trouble." The next thing he saw about the conference was a photo of me being pushed in the wheelchair to the conference. He got very mad and said if I could be wheeled to a convention, I could be wheeled to court. By that time, it was too late to schedule trial for that week.

I spent a good bit of time with Bob Yellowbird Steele, a Lakota from Wounded Knee; Jimmy Durham, of Cherokee heritage; and a young Indian woman whose name I no longer remember. Together, we drafted the "International Indian Treaty Council's Declaration of Continuing Independence." Jimmy lived in New York, where the United Nations has headquarters, so I asked him to establish an office for us there. With the blessings of the elders, he agreed. The Lakota, Nakota, and Dakota elders also selected a representative to the International Indian Treaty Council to the United Nations—an ambassador, in effect. They chose to honor me with that task, and I couldn't refuse.

When the conference broke up, Dennis and I returned to Saint Paul in a private plane piloted by Doug Durham. He was a big, dark-haired, light-complected part-Chippewa who had become Dennis' flunky at about the time the trial started. Doug seemed nice enough, but we noticed he wouldn't participate in purification lodge or other spiritual ceremonies. Most AIM people laughed at Doug because it was apparent to us all that he was a chicken-shit. Any streetwise or reservation-raised guy could have creamed him without raising a sweat.

Later, we learned that Doug was no Indian. He was an FBI informant. But I never saw Dennis treat him other than as a servant. He was never allowed into leadership meetings longer than it took to take our orders for food or get instructions on some errand. He was never privy to anything important. Whatever the FBI paid him during the year he hung around Dennis was money poured down a toilet as far as information was concerned. He fed the FBI lies, including things about weapons movements that AIM was supposedly involved in but never was. Even if he never provided the FBI with anything useful, however, the fact that an FBI informer was in a position to overhear conversations between lawyers and clients was an outrage. It was among the worst things the government did to us during our trial.

The feds rested their case on July 24, 1974. Our lawyers brought motions for dismissal of all charges. While we were waiting on Nichol's ruling, Curtis and I headed down to the Rosebud to party for a few days before the sun dance. One night we went with friends to Valentine, a little Nebraska town near the reservation. We wound up at about midnight in a restaurant bar on the narrow main street, shooting pool and drinking beer. Among the other customers were John Fuller, an off-duty cop, and John Iron Shell. I was hunched over a pool table when a woman came running in to say that Fuller and Iron Shell were outside beating Curtis Bald Eagle with cue sticks. I ran to help; the last thing I remember is going out the door. Two days later, I woke up in a Rapid City hospital. My skull had been fractured, my nose broken, and a few ribs cracked. Curtis was in the next bed with a shattered jaw, nose, and cheekbone and busted ribs.

The Indian people with us told me Fuller and Iron Shell had beaten us with cue sticks, and the Valentine cops had watched from a squad car across the street. The police had radioed for an ambulance after the punks left. Our friends didn't trust Nebraska doctors, so they took us to the IHS clinic on the Rosebud. From there, the doctors sent us by ambulance to Rapid City. I'm convinced the attack was a premeditated attempt on my life. Although my face was swollen beyond belief, a few days later we were back in Saint Paul. On August 7, responding to our petition to dismiss all charges, Judge

Nichol threw out those relating to burglary, auto theft, and possession of Molotov cocktails. Another charge had been dismissed before the jury was seated. That left three counts of assault, one of interfering with federal law-enforcement officials in the performance of their duties, and one count each of larceny and conspiracy. Two days later, because of the military's illegal involvement, Nichol dismissed the count of interfering with law enforcement.

Now it was our turn to put on a case. We started on the morning of August 13, called only six witnesses, and rested at about midday on August 16. Our defense was simple. We had every right to be at Wounded Knee because the Fort Laramie Treaty of 1868 had confirmed the Lakota as a sovereign nation whose territorial borders included not only Wounded Knee and the Pine Ridge Reservation, but also millions of acres in Nebraska and the Dakotas, including our sacred *Paha Sapa*, the Black Hills. We had tried to refer to the treaty throughout the trial, starting with one of the first government witnesses, a Pine Ridge BIA employee who had come only to bring a map to show where things had happened during the siege. Larry Leventhal asked him if he was familiar with the treaty, and he said, "Somewhat, but not really." Larry read the description of our territory from the treaty, and said, "I want you to point out on the map where all this is," beginning from the banks of the North Platte River and going up the western side of what is now South Dakota, and then into North Dakota, and so forth. Most of that, of course, wasn't on his map. The BIA guy said, "Well, it would have been down here," and, "It would have been over there." The government objected, but Nichol let it in as evidence. As Larry went through the treaty's description of our land, the BIA guy, a Lakota, interrupted him. "Can I ask you a question?" he said. "What ever happened to all our land?"

In a movie, that would be the end of the trial. In real life, Larry said, "You've asked the right question. I'm going to try to answer that for you. No more questions. Thank you." Throughout the trial, the government had stubbornly resisted all efforts to introduce the treaty itself. Its position was that it was merely a document that the court could look at regarding legal issues, but it wasn't evidence before a jury. During the trial, however, a government witness who had manned a barricade testified about people going back and forth into the Knee. Tilsen asked him about who got in or out. He said, "That would depend on who had the proper credentials."

"What were they? Some type of government document?"

"No, we didn't care about that—that isn't what I mean."

"Then what was the credential?"

"Those who had the 1868 treaty," he replied. "That was their credential." Tilsen showed him a copy of the Independent Oglala Nation's official passport, which had the treaty on one side, and said, "Is this what you mean?"

"Yes, that's what could get people in, the 1868 treaty."

When it was our turn to introduce evidence, we offered the treaty. Hurd and the other government attorneys screamed objections on grounds of relevance. Mark Lane said, "Their witness identified these as being the credentials. How can it not get entered as evidence?" It got in.

Once the treaty was in, we could refer to its provisions. One was that "bad men among the whites" would be punished by the federal government and "bad men among the Indians" would be punished by the Indians. That being so, the FBI and marshals had no business coming on Pine Ridge, and the feds had no jurisdiction over Dennis and me. Another provision said the feds would handle our complaints in a fair and bona fide manner. Our lawyers argued that many complaints had been made to the government, but none was handled. Nichol, who had begun the trial hostile to the treaty, instructed the jury that since it requires the United States to pay attention to grievances and to deal with them in a good-faith manner, jurors could consider whether the United States did or did not honor that in connection with any of our alleged offenses.

Neither Dennis nor I testified. Our witnesses included Gladys Bissonnette and Ellen Moves Camp, OSCRO founders and among the wisest heads and staunchest hearts during and before the siege. Another witness was Agnes Lamont, Buddy's mother, who spoke about the intrusion of federal marshals on the reservation. Frank Kills Enemy testified about events on Pine Ridge after the Reorganization Act of 1934 took away most of what remained of the Lakota people's treaty rights. Our other two witnesses were Vine Deloria Jr., a lawyer with a divinity degree, and historian and author Dee Brown.

Then it was the government's turn to bring in rebuttal witnesses. The first was Louis Moves Camp, Ellen's twenty-two-year-old son. I can only imagine how disappointed she must have been when he walked into the courtroom. Louis had been expelled from AIM on July 4. Dennis had put Louis's belongings on the sidewalk in front of a house we had rented for support staff. Louis couldn't stay away from drugs or booze, and he was always brawling, mouthing off, and disrupting things. We should have ejected him long before then, but we had cut him a lot of slack out of respect for his mother.

Louis was facing about twenty years for robbery and assault with a deadly weapon. I don't know about his guilt or innocence on those charges, but apparently he had decided to make a deal with the FBI and his charges were dropped. Most recently, he had been at the Wakpala treaty conference, and he had been involved with AIM from the time of our meetings at the Mother Butler Center in Rapid City through the early part of the siege of Wounded Knee. It was obvious that the feds saw this as a chance to fill in the gaping holes in their case against Dennis and me.

It was soon apparent that what Louis had to sell the FBI didn't have much to do with anything he actually knew. Societies based on oral tradition such as the Lakota can't function when members pervert the truth; lying is the worst kind of antisocial behavior. Before Louis had testified for ten minutes, his mother got out of her seat in the back of the courtroom and shouted, "Liar!" Nichol ordered marshals to remove Ellen, which led to a tremendous fistfight.

On Monday, Louis got back on the witness stand and continued his litany of lies. He claimed, among many other things, that Dennis and I had planned acts of violence in meetings at the Mother Butler Center, and that we had fifteen to twenty rifles in the basement of the Calico meeting hall. He also said Crow Dog had been in the first car in the caravan to Wounded Knee and I in the second; that I had told people to rip off everything in the trading post; and that along with Carter, Dennis, and Pedro, I had told the Gildersleeves they were hostages and had threatened to kill them. I haven't the stomach to repeat here all of Louis's lies, but some were so outrageous that I almost laughed aloud. I was not amused, however, when he said he had seen Dennis and me firing the shots that paralyzed Marshal Lloyd Grim, or that I had tried to organize a suicide squad to kill Senators McGovern and Abourezk during their visit. Louis said AIM had gotten support from Russia, East and West Germany, Italy, Czechoslovakia, and China, brought by agents who entered Wounded Knee disguised as newsmen; and that Communist operatives had attended the Wakpala conference to offer weapons and ammo and to give me money.

Most of what Louis had to say under oath sounded like some sick FBI fantasy. Although no other government witness had given a credible firsthand account linking Dennis or me to any charge, Louis's testimony connected us to *every* alleged felony. It was devastating to our defense—if the jurors believed him.

But our attorneys established that Louis was nowhere near Wounded Knee when most of the events he described had allegedly occurred. The FBI might have taken time out to confirm Louis's location. They might have given him a polygraph test before putting him on the stand, but Trimbach, the regional FBI boss, sent a personal directive forbidding his people to test Louis. To make sure we didn't know until the last minute that he was a rebuttal witness, Louis had been packed off to a River Falls, Wisconsin, dude ranch with two agents as baby-sitters.

Even with special agents David Price and Ronald Williams to watch him, however, Louis managed to get into trouble. When Mark Lane raised questions about his behavior at the dude ranch, Hurd, the chief prosecutor, assured Nichol it was a case of "public intoxication" and that Louis hadn't even been arrested. While Mark cross-examined an FBI witness about that, Caroline Mugar, Mark's girlfriend, handed Kunstler a note: "The door behind the judge is opening and closing. . . ." Bill went to the bench, handed up the note, and said, "Judge, don't be fearful, but there's a door opening and closing behind you and I want you to be conscious of it." Nichol whirled around to yank open the door leading to his chambers—and into the court-room tumbled an FBI agent. He had been scheduled to testify. Like all such witnesses, he was excluded from the courtroom until called to the stand. Furious, Nichol ordered the door to be locked.

He got even angrier a few days later when Mark Lane brought govern-ment documents into court to reveal what had really happened in Wisconsin. Agents Price and Williams had taken Louis drinking. The agents themselves consumed about fourteen scotch and waters between them, nine of them by Williams, and when the bars closed, they left Louis in the company of a high-school girl he had just met. In the morning, Price was awakened by local cops who said that Louis had been arrested for rape. After Price told the police and a Wisconsin prosecutor that Louis was an important witness in our trial, the local authorities decided it would serve the interests of "justice" if they dropped the matter. Stunned and outraged, the teenage victim wanted to sue not only the police and the FBI, but also her own parents for going along with the cover-up.

During a closed hearing in chambers, prosecutor Hurd had assured Judge Nichol twice that he knew nothing about the rape. Caught in the lie, he wept crocodile tears, lamely mumbling that he had been asked whether Louis had been *charged* with rape and, since he hadn't been charged, correctly answered no. "Mr. Hurd deceived the Court . . . " said Nichol. "It hurts me deeply. It's going to take me a long time to forget it."

On September 12, the three alternates were dismissed and the remaining twelve jurors retired to deliberate. One of them, Therese Cherrier, had sat throughout the trial in the front row, the nearest person to the judge, her face a perpetual frown. Dennis and our lawyers and I were convinced she was angry at us because she had to sit there. Within hours of beginning deliber-ations, the jurors voted unanimously for acquittal on conspiracy charges, then started through the remaining counts. Only one or two jurors voted guilty on the other charges. As we eventually learned, Cherrier was indeed furious at having spent eight months sitting in a courtroom—but she was more pissed at the government. She wanted acquittal on all counts. She said to her fellow jurors, "Are you going to make us sit here and argue when it's obvious they're not guilty of anything except being Indians?" She was so angry that later that day, she had a stroke.

The fact that it was a stroke was not immediately apparent to the doctors who hospitalized Cherrier. During the three days that elapsed until the nature of the illness was determined, our lawyers again petitioned for dismissal of all remaining charges, this time on grounds of government misconduct—all the outrageous things I've mentioned here, as well as many, many more. While Nichol was considering that, the news broke about Cherrier's stroke. Federal rules allow for a jury of fewer than twelve to render a verdict, but only if defendants and prosecutors agree. Dennis and I discussed it with our lawyers and agreed that rather than have a mistrial and go through another trial, we would accept a verdict by eleven jurors. When Nichol asked Hurd, the chief prosecutor, he bucked the decision to Washington. The Department of Justice insisted on a mistrial. Later that day, Hurd went on television to explain that he was convinced the remaining jurors would acquit us, but if there was a new trial, the government wouldn't make the same mistakes, and he might be able to get a conviction on at least one charge.

That was the final straw for Judge Nichol. Less than an hour after Hurd's televised statement, Nichol convened the court. After explaining the events leading to the government's decision to insist on a new trial, he stared angrily at the prosecutors' table. Then he quoted the late U.S. Supreme Court Justice George Sutherland:

The United States Attorney is the representative not of an ordinary part to a controversy, but of a sovereignty whose obligation to govern impartially is as compelling as its obligation to govern at all; and whose interest, therefore, in a criminal prosecution is not that it shall win the case, but that justice shall be done. . . . He is in a peculiar and very definite sense a servant of the law, the twofold aim of which is that guilty not escape nor innocent suffer. . . . But, while he may strike hard blows, he is not at liberty to strike foul ones. It is as much his duty to refrain from improper methods calculated to produce a wrongful conviction as it is to use every legitimate means to bring about a just one.

By that time, I had come to have a lot of respect for Nichol. He was a fair man who had grown up believing that in America, the government didn't do wrong—and he was terribly shocked by what he had seen in the last months. For nearly an hour, he cited case law, referring to the "Pentagon Papers" trial of Daniel Ellsworth, in which Judge Matthew Byrne had dismissed charges because of government misconduct. Nichol castigated Hurd, the government, and the FBI for what they had done during the trial. "[The prosecutor] should not exploit the power and prestige of the government for personal aggrandizement. . . . I didn't realize that the FBI was stooping so low," he added, detailing the thousands of dollars it had paid to Louis Moves Camp, the liquor it had provided him, the FBI's involvement in the dropping of the rape charge, Trimbach's order not to give Louis a lie-detector test, and the bureau's failure to even attempt to corroborate his story. "Misconduct can be of two kinds," Nichol continued. "It can be deliberate . . . or it can rise to such a high degree of negligence that it would be unfair to continue with the trial. . . . " Nichol dismissed all charges against Dennis and me.

I was stunned. The immediate threat of prison was over, and a heavy burden was lifted from my shoulders. Perhaps, like Dennis and our attorneys, I should have been ecstatic. I was grateful to the spirits for their help—I don't try to understand the Great Mystery's strange ways—but I was also devastated. I had gone to Wounded Knee and stayed there to resist because I wanted to show the U.S. government that it had to live up to the Fort Laramie Treaty. All our efforts, all the risks we had gladly taken—and the sacrifices of Buddy Lamont and Frank Clearwater—had been for our treaty. Now, without a jury verdict, there would be no resolution. Nothing would change for my people until the government acknowledged that it *must* live up to that treaty. I was so drained and emotionally deflated that minutes after the trial ended, when Dennis and I appeared on the courthouse steps in triumph, he had to take my hand and wave it in the air.

34

▼▼▼▼▼▼▼▼

Ordeals by Trials

Two days after Judge Nichol had dismissed the remaining Wounded Knee charges against Dennis and me in October 1974, the U.S. Attorney General awarded the Justice Department's Medal of Commendation to prosecutor Richard Hurd and his cocounsel. It was a signal to all federal prosecutors that even those caught violating their oaths of office would be backed all the way to the top, as long as they kept bringing Indians into court or putting them in jail to await trial.

Two weeks later, the Oglala people sponsored a three-day victory party at Porcupine, and about one thousand Indians came from all over South Dakota to celebrate. That frightened Dick Wilson. With his usual sensitivity, he declared martial law on Pine Ridge, citing a mysterious, and fictional, 1972 tribal council resolution permitting him to take any action necessary to quell "an AIM uprising." Backed by goons, he marched on the BIA jail and freed twenty prisoners, mostly other goons awaiting trial on alcohol-related offenses. He told the *Rapid City Journal* that AIM had been bringing guns into Pine Ridge for ten days, but the BIA police refused to do anything until we broke a law. Wilson also publicly accused BIA Superintendent Al Trimble, an Oglala, of vigilantism. By then, Wilson had finalized the illegal transfer of the Sheep Mountain Gunnery Range to the Department of the Interior, so I took Trimble's public rebuke as a sign that the feds no longer needed to kiss Wilson's butt.

After the party, we returned to Saint Paul, where Dennis and I paid a courtesy call on Therese Cherrier, the juror who had suffered a stroke. She was well enough to talk, and after insisting on having photos taken with us, she said she considered Dennis and me heroes. She told us she would never serve on another jury, for she thought the system was ridiculous. Two or three jurors on her panel were so stupid they couldn't follow the facts of our case or apply logic to evaluating evidence, she said. All their decisions had been dictated by their emotions.

The secrets of the jury chamber were especially fascinating to me because of the charges I still faced. Those included yet another indictment that had come down during the Saint Paul trial. It stemmed from my brief visit to a Rapid City motel room the day I came out of Wounded Knee. A white guy from Arizona had offered us guns and explosives. Figuring him for a fed, I had walked out. Along with four others in AIM, I was falsely charged with conspiracy to transport firearms and explosives across state lines. A preliminary hearing was set for early October in Phoenix. A legal defense team headed by attorney Leonard Weinglass—another alumnus of the Chicago Seven— had opened an office there to prepare for trial.

Because Curtis Bald Eagle had totaled my Buick on a highway near Bismarck, North Dakota, I borrowed a white Oldsmobile from a trusting German immigrant lady. With Curtis, I towed a U-Haul trailer to Porcupine with my belongings. I promised to return the car soon afterward. Instead, after dropping off my stuff, I headed for the fall *wacipi* at the University of South Dakota in Vermillion, in the southeastern corner of the state. There I ran into Peggy Phelps, a student at South Dakota State. She was one of a Sisseton family of thirteen children living in Rapid City. While she was in high school, I had found excuses to go visit her family just to be around her. Strong supporters of AIM, the family had participated in many demonstrations, including one at the Rosebud's BIA jail, when I first really noticed how pretty, slender, and long-legged Peggy was. Later in the autumn of 1974, I bumped into her at what we skins called a "white dance" at the Antelope Fair on the Rosebud. I was with another girl, but when I started to dance with Peggy, I forgot all about the first one. After a few drinks, I was feeling quite good. As we were moving around the floor, people stopped dancing and formed a circle, clapping for us. At that wonderful moment, I fell in love with Peggy. After the dance, we went out to an old boarding-school dam and talked until she had to go back to her family. For a while we were almost inseparable, but then she started college. Peggy was preparing for a career in teaching, and planned to attend the National Indian Education Association conference in Phoenix. I was to be in Phoenix for trial, so we agreed to meet.

In Phoenix I learned that the feds knew the only thing linking us to gunrunning was the allegation of one white man. He was a racist fruitcake out to bust Indian balls, and his tales were wildly inconsistent. But instead of dropping charges, the U.S. Attorney's office offered us a deal. If we would plead guilty to lesser offenses, we would get short sentences. When we said we looked forward to proving our innocence in court, he dropped all charges.

With that out of the way, Curtis and I went to the NIEA convention. It was quite a change from the first one I had attended, in 1970. In the years since then, AIM and others had built enough self-pride to turn Indian country upside down. The 1975 convention drew nearly five thousand people, damn near every one of them proud of their heritage. People brought drums and took over hotel parking lots to dance and sing. The convention became one enormous party. I looked up Peggy and we partied, too.

I stuck around Phoenix to earn a little money. Through Chicano and Indian friends, I hustled a few hundred bucks from speaking engagements at Arizona State, my alma mater, and at Scottsdale Community College. In a few weeks, the trials of several other Wounded Knee defendants would begin in Lincoln, Nebraska. I decided to go there via Texas and Oklahoma, stopping to visit Ramon Roubideaux's oldest daughter in Austin and an Oklahoma AIM friend named Mary Ann Anquoe. Curtis had other plans, so he took off. I paired up with an AIM brother, Dick LaGarde. He had somebody's Gulf Oil credit card—one of many that AIMsters had acquired somehow. In those days before computers were everywhere, it took weeks for notice of stolen cards to circulate nationally, so we decided to use that one.

After two weeks of partying, we arrived in Lincoln in December 1974 for the trials of most of the Wounded Knee "non-leadership" cases. Hundreds of people from around the country had been charged with an assortment of felonies that allegedly happened during the siege. About two hundred trials were scheduled. Most of the charges were preposterous. For example, one supply caravan had been stopped at the Nevada border and everyone in it had been busted for interstate transportation of weapons and other nonsensical charges. Sammy Davis Jr. put up the money to get them out of jail. Other defendants had been arrested at the Canadian or Mexican borders or at various state lines, mostly for the "crime" of heading for Wounded Knee to support our cause.

I bunked with the WKLD/OC support staff in a rented house, but Dick got greedy and used his hot Gulf card to rent a Holiday Inn suite. He threw a party, and many AIMsters went over to join him in a good time. Those festivities were cut short when he finally got busted for using the stolen card. Eventually, it cost him six months in jail.

I was in Lincoln on AIM business, so instead partying I sobered up and got to work. One of the more interesting people I met there was Jim

Thorpe's granddaughter, Dagmar, a WKLD/OC volunteer. Among those on trial were my sister Madonna and Lorelei De Cora, who was about to marry my brother Ted.

The lead lawyer for the defendants was Al Krieger, who had made his reputation in New York defending mafiosi. The federal attorneys were talented and energetic enough, but they had no real evidence to work with. Judges dismissed case after case, including those of Clyde Bellecourt, Stan Holder, Madonna, and Lorelei, when they realized the police could produce no evidence. Of the few people who went to trial, none was convicted of any charge made during the Wounded Knee siege. The best the feds could do was get one "guilty" verdict on a Topeka woman. She had stored in her garage a typewriter that had been liberated from the BIA's Washington headquarters when we took it over in November 1972. Crow Dog and Carter Camp were later convicted of being responsible as leaders of the occupation and for "interfering" with postal inspectors who, posing as hippies, had sneaked into Wounded Knee. A white Albuquerque man named Allen Cooper—known in the Knee as "Honky Killer"—pleaded no contest and got ten years for assaulting a federal officer with a firearm. Those charges were brought later, after all the original Wounded Knee felony counts had been dismissed or the defendants acquitted.

In late December I received some good news. A new district attorney had been elected in Scotts Bluff County, Nebraska. After reviewing the evidence and charges against me—resisting arrest, assaulting police officers, illegal possession of a firearm, etc.—he realized they were bogus. In the interest of justice, he decided to dismiss them all. Charges against my brother Ted were dropped as well.

A few days later, on New Year's Eve, the Menominee Warriors Society took over an abandoned Jesuit novitiate in northern Wisconsin. More than a hundred years earlier, Jesuits had taken land from the Indians to build an abbey where they trained new priests. In 1974, they had closed it, but instead of returning the land to the Indians, they planned to sell it to whites. The Menominee armed themselves and took over the property. In response, the governor of Wisconsin called out the National Guard to surround the grounds. An armed standoff resulted, with a lot of tension in the air—shooting could have started with the slightest provocation. AIM came through one of those awful Wisconsin blizzards to offer support. Dennis, with his flunky, Doug Durham, was coordinating things, including dealing with the press. Durham had a brand-new van. I told him, "While we're here, I'm going to use your van." "Yes, sir," he said, ever the wimp. I used the vehicle to haul supplies during the standoff. Then at a leadership meeting, Vernon Bellecourt, of all people, said he had learned that Durham was an FBI informant, and planned to expose him two days later.

Since Dennis was the chief negotiator between Wisconsin authorities and the Menominee people and Marlon Brando was scheduled to come in and take the media spotlight, I saw no point in sticking around. I wrote a memo to Durham, with copies to Dennis and the rest of the leadership, in regard to the van. I said that because several AIM people from South Dakota were there, I was taking them home in it. Any time Durham wanted to retrieve his wheels he could come to Pine Ridge and get it, I added.

On February 26, 1975, a week or two after I got home, AIM brother Dicky Marshall had to appear in tribal court in Pine Ridge Village—goon headquarters. Those courts were run by judges appointed by Dick Wilson, and there were no jury trials. Arming ourselves, we took two cars and Durham's van and drove to the Pine Ridge courthouse. Tom Poor Bear was driving the van, Dicky and several other guys were in the back, and I was in the right front passenger seat. Our presence in Pine Ridge Village was radioed to the goons and to the BIA cops. Duane Brewer, a BIA police lieutenant, and Delmar Eastman, special investigator for the BIA, met us at the courthouse. Brewer reached through the open window and, without a word, punched me. As I started to get out of the van, Eastman and other cops wrapped Brewer in a bear hug.

I was pissed, but the others in our van could see it was a setup to lure us into doing something the cops could shoot us for. The others pulled me back into the seat and told Tom to drive. I calmed down as we took off. The tribal planning center at the airport, about a mile and a half east of Pine Ridge, was a goon hangout. As we went toward it, we saw goons all around the airport and a private plane sitting alone next to the runway. Suddenly a red car pulled ahead of us to block the highway. The van's front passenger seat could swivel 360 degrees, so I turned around to face the rear, put on my seat belt, and told Tom to floor it—"Let's ram that sucker!" I said. When they saw us speed up, the goons moved the red car. As we went by, we pulled back the sliding door on the passenger side and poured rifle fire at them. There were so many guys shooting that it sounded like a bunch of machine guns. Goons jumped in their cars to follow us, so down the road we pulled to the side and stopped. Everybody jumped out. When our pursuers appeared, we opened up on them again. They screeched to a halt, backed up, turned around, and hightailed it. That message got through. No more goons were going to chase us. We took our time heading back to Porcupine.

Passing through Wounded Knee, we had to stop to fix a flat. One of our tires had been nicked by a bullet. While we were changing it, BIA cops and FBI agents drove up to question us about the firefight. Just then a convertible stopped. Out came WKLD/OC lawyers Roger Finzell and William Rossmore, their assistants Eda Gordon, Kathi James, and Martha Copleman, and Bernard Escamilla, a Chicano who had been a defender during the Wounded Knee siege. He was due to be tried in Council Bluffs, Iowa, on Wounded Knee charges, and the attorneys were interviewing witnesses in his case. Finzell advised us not to answer any of the FBI's questions. The feds said they were investigating the shooting at the airport. We said, "Fine, charge us or leave us alone." A G-man came up to me and said, "We've got a report that your van is a stolen vehicle." He followed me back to the van, where I pulled out a copy of my memo to Durham. As I handed it to him, I winked and said, "Doug's a longtime member of the American Indian Movement. He's having some difficulties now, but he knows that once he's cleared of our charges he can come and get his van any time."

That memo seemed to satisfy the FBI agent. When we finished changing our tire, we told the feds we were going to the ranch of my relative, Ted Pourier. We wanted anybody following us after the shoot-out to come there, so we laid an ambush for them—but they never came.

That was because they were busy attacking Roger Finzell and the others in his car. Rossmore, a Connecticut attorney, had flown his own plane into Pine Ridge, the one we had seen parked next to the runway. When Roger drove him back to the airport, they found the plane riddled with bullets and buckshot. Fifteen carloads of goons with rifles and shotguns drove up, surrounded the convertible, broke the windshield, slashed the canvas top, and dragged everybody out. One grabbed Roger's ponytail, and when Dick Wilson said, "Stomp him!" they beat him without mercy. As they were about to cut his throat, Eda Gordon, all of five feet tall and ninety-five pounds, threw herself on top of Roger. Her hand took the blade intended for him. Both lawyers, Escamilla, and the women were hospitalized. Roger signed a criminal complaint naming Wilson, and eventually he and the goons were tried in Rapid City before an all-white jury. For what must have been the only time in the history of South Dakota, Indians were found "not guilty" of an attack on whites.

Those kinds of incidents didn't deter me from living at Pine Ridge. It is my home, and no hang-around-the-fort like Dick Wilson could make me leave. With my brother Dace for a roommate, I lived near Raymond Yellow Thunder's grave in Porcupine. One Saturday night in March, a bunch of AIM brothers came over to party. They ran out of booze and decided to drive to Scenic, a tiny place just north of the reservation, at the edge of Badlands National Park. I wanted to go to bed, so I turned a deaf ear to their pleas to accompany them. They went outside and got in their cars, and then sent my cousin Dusty Lebeau back in to talk me into coming along. Reluctantly, I agreed.

Scenic, an arid, dusty crossroads, consists of perhaps two dozen buildings—a few houses; several ramshackle sheds, barns, and chicken coops; a church; a secondhand store of corrugated steel that looks like a cross between a Quonset hut and half a giant pipe; and the Longhorn Saloon with its Old West–style facade and a weathered wooden porch. With his daughter Twila, Halley Merrill ran the place then and still does. He must be close to ninety now, a big, crusty white guy with a long gray beard and the look of a mountain man from the last century. In her younger days, Twila was quite beautiful, and she is tougher than most men.

We were going to buy some booze and take it back to my place. First I had to use the rest room, a tiny space with a toilet and a urinal, barely big enough to hold two people at the same time. Dicky Marshall, an AIM brother, used the toilet while I was at a urinal next to the door. As I zipped up, a short Lakota I didn't know walked in. He looked up and playfully slapped my cheek as though he had just recognized me. It was crowded, so I said nothing, just scooted out the door. Behind me, I heard Dicky say, "What the hell did you do that for?" As I headed toward the bar, I heard a sudden *pop* from the bathroom. It wasn't much more than the noise a cap gun makes, but it was unmistakably a shot from a .22 pistol.

That wasn't the first time there had been gunplay in the saloon, so people scattered. AIM guys rushed to the bathroom, came back with Dicky, and we all piled into two cars. I was one of eight people jammed into the lead vehicle, a white Olds or Pontiac. Except for me, all the guys in both cars were packing a rifle, shotgun, or revolver. We were off the reservation, in the jurisdiction of the Pennington County sheriff, so we decided the best thing to do was head for Rapid City. As we drove, I asked Dicky why he had shot the guy. He said, "I don't know, the gun just went off." I thought, oh, man—why didn't I stay home and sleep?

Soon we passed a whole line of sheriff's cars with flashing red lights, heading toward Scenic. They were followed by two or three more. After passing us, the cars turned around and chased us. But our car had carburetor trouble and the engine coughed whenever Dave Clifford, the driver, stepped on the gas. We drove that way for miles and miles through the darkness, trailed by a growing string of squad cars with lights and sirens going at speeds that ranged between sixty-five and seventy miles per hour. On the outskirts of Rapid City, Dave turned off the highway into a mobile home complex. It wasn't one of his better moves. We took down some clotheslines before returning to the road, but the cops were waiting. Dave steered through a deep ditch, but crossing some railroad tracks we got high-centered, our wheels off the ground so we could go neither forward nor back.

I was in the back on the passenger side when a deputy with a rifle opened the door. He recognized me and poked the barrel hard at my right eye. I started to bleed profusely, and he swung his gun butt at the side of my head. He missed and smashed the window. I stood there with a handkerchief to my face as cops pulled weapons from our cars. The sheriff came up to me and asked, "Please, can you calm these guys down before we take them to jail, so they'll all go peacefully?"

I said, "Wait a minute, not everyone's involved. Some just happened to catch a ride with us."

"That whole carload of guys is involved—they've all got weapons."

"They have guns, but they had nothing to do with the shooting."

"Well, we're not going to charge them with anything other than having weapons, but we've got to take you all in."

I went over and explained the deal. Everyone agreed to come along. Dicky and I were arrested for attempted murder. The Lakota who had been in the men's room at the Longhorn was Martin Montileaux. The bullet had struck him in the neck, hit a bone or something, and gone up into his head. Dave was charged with felony firearms possession and reckless driving.

I was at the jail for more than three-and-a-half hours before Roger Finzell, our attorney, made deputies take me to a hospital. It took twelve stitches to close my wound. I still have a nasty scar just below the eye socket. We were scheduled for arraignment in the morning, so that night, Dave, Dicky, and I talked in our cell. Dicky said he would admit to the shooting and tell exactly what had happened: While showing his gun to Montileaux in an effort to intimidate him, it accidentally went off. I would plead not guilty.

But when we got to the court, we were immediately met by attorneys from the public defender's office. When we told them our intentions, they said, "Don't plead guilty." They explained that there were extenuating circumstances: Montileaux had struck me without provocation, and that might be enough for self-defense. We all pleaded not guilty. My bond was set at thirty thousand dollars, Dicky's at twenty thousand, and Dave's at much less.

When Montileaux died a few days later, we were charged with murder, which meant possible sentences of life without parole. Because of all that had happened before, prosecutors—from Bill Janklow, South Dakota's new attorney general, down to the most junior assistant state's attorney—were almost desperate to nail me. They poked around trying to find somebody who could say I had been in the bathroom with the gun in my hand when Montileaux was shot. The sheriff's deputies and state's attorneys offered Dicky a plea bargain to get him to roll over and testify against me. Dicky was AIM, Lakota, and Oglala, a fine man then only twenty-four years old, who wouldn't lie to save himself if it meant hurting me.

Because I was still facing several other court proceedings, our lawyers forced prosecutors in the Montileaux case to sever my case from Dicky's and try us separately. We always tried to do that. Trials are expensive for governments, so if they want to come after us, we're going to make them pay. I had been charged with serious crimes all over the Great Plains, but had always showed up for court appearances, so I had acquired a reputation as a good risk for bail. Marlon Brando offered to post my bond on the murder charge. When my lawyers told me that, I said, "What about the other guys?" They said they were on their own. I said, "No deal. All of us get out or nobody gets out." They went back to Brando, who stalled, saying neither yes nor no. My brothers Ted and Bill and my friend John Thomas went to Brando's

Mulholland Drive mansion in the Hollywood Hills and camped there until he promised to bail us all out. Years later, I learned that Brando had called Hugh Hefner, publisher of *Playboy* magazine, and asked him to have the Playboy Foundation, which works to further human and civil rights, put up bond for Dicky and Dave. That came out when Brando agreed to cooperate for a *Playboy* interview, and it increased my respect for Hefner.

I still faced charges for the Custer courthouse police riot, but I caught a break. When Bill Janklow became South Dakota's governor, Mark Meirhenry was elected Attorney General. He had served in the Legal Aid office with Janklow in the 1960s, when we were all on the Rosebud. I believe that Mark, who knew me as a human being and not merely as the focus of racist hysteria, was behind what happened next. The state offered a plea bargain on the eight felony counts from Custer. I had the feeling, and my lawyers agreed, that if I had gone to trial, I almost certainly would have drawn a conviction on at least one count. On the other hand, the state would have had to face tremendous costs to put on that trial because I was backed by WKLD/OC, and the prosecutors knew we would have a strong defense. Instead, they dropped the felonies and I pleaded guilty to simple assault—a misdemeanor.

My sentencing was in Kennebec, South Dakota, a white town just south of the Lower Brulé Indian Reservation. David Hill, who had been with me in the Custer courthouse police riot, was also to be sentenced that day. The man on the bench, Judge John B. Jones, was out of the same mold as Joe Bottum—a hard-bitten old hanging judge. He had been in Kennebec for ages and he loved "his" Indians, but there was no way I was going to be one of them. David was called first. Because of the vicious abuse he had suffered— he had lost much of the vision in one eye after having been clubbed in the Sioux Falls courthouse police riot—trying him again would have been a public-relations nightmare for the state. His lawyers brokered a guilty plea for simple assault, in exchange for unsupervised probation.

That was the only time I ever pleaded guilty, and I had the hardest time getting that word out of my mouth. When the judge said, "How do you plead?" my reply literally stuck in my throat. I had to force it out, and even then I stuttered, "G-g-g-guilty." I had done some reading and expected to get thirty days. That was the maximum penalty when I had been arrested. When the judge said, "I wish I could give you more time, but all the law allows is ninety days," it shocked me. I looked over at my lawyer, but he said nothing. "Wait a minute," I said. "It was only thirty days when I committed the crime. Did it go up?"

"Well, the legislature recently saw fit to pass a new law," said the judge.

I demanded to see the statute, so the clerk brought the South Dakota criminal-code book to the bench. After reading for a few moments, the judge apologized, corrected himself, and gave me thirty days.

Then David Hill stood up. He said, "Your honor, could I do fifteen days and Mr. Means do fifteen days?" It was a nice gesture; I loved Dave for that. The judge chuckled and said, "I know you come from Oklahoma and maybe they do that down there, but we don't. Mr. Means will have to serve his own time." I still had upcoming trials, for the Sioux Falls riot and for the Montileaux murder, so the judge suspended imposition of sentence until my legal affairs were in order.

3 5
▼▼▼▼▼▼▼▼

The Sioux Falls
Massacre

In the spring of 1975, along with my brother Dace, Tom Poor Bear, and Al White Lightning, I attended a community meeting of elders in Mc-Laughlin, just south of the North Dakota line on the Standing Rock Reservation. On the way home, we stopped at a bar to shoot pool, and got into a brawl with an off-duty cop. When he came at me with a beer bottle, I hit him with my cue stick, and down he went.

After we left, he pressed charges against me. I was arrested and arraigned for assault with a deadly weapon, assault to do great bodily harm, assault with intent to maim, and unlawful flight to avoid prosecution—all felonies. After a hearing in Aberdeen, South Dakota, at which I served as my own lawyer, Judge Alfred Nichol, who had tried the Wounded Knee case in Saint Paul, dismissed all charges.

On June 7, with three carloads of AIM brothers, I headed to Fort Yates, North Dakota, where the BIA agency on the Standing Rock was located. At about noon, we stopped in Fort Rice, North Dakota, a little white town, and a couple of guys went into a bar to buy beer. They got into a scuffle with some rednecks, so we rushed in to help. We kicked a few butts, bought our beer, and continued on our way. Minutes later, after our little caravan had crossed the bridge marking the reservation boundary, we saw a BIA police car coming toward us. Whenever I see an Indian cop on *that* reservation, I'm reminded that it was the place where Sitting Bull was murdered. In December 1890, forty-three Indian policemen, acting on orders from General Nelson Miles and BIA agent James McLaughlin—the town in South Dakota is named after him—surrounded the cabin where Sitting Bull slept, and shot him to death.

The cop behind the wheel of this squad car, a hang-around-the-fort named Pat Kelly, was from Cannon Ball, North Dakota, a community settled by survivors of several decimated Sioux bands after the Standing Rock Lakota gave them refuge and part of their reservation. As he approached our caravan, Kelly turned on his flashing lights and stopped. Tom Poor Bear was driving our car, and he braked to a halt, got out, and crossed the highway to see what was going on. Kelly was a husky six-footer in uniform. With him was a young guy in civilian clothes. We didn't know it then, but he was Kelly's son. Suddenly Kelly grabbed Tom by the hair and started to swing him around. AIMsters began to pile out of cars. By the time I got across the highway, Tom was on the pavement. I said to Kelly, "What the fuck do you think you're doing?" and turned to help Tom.

Out of the corner of my eye, I saw the younger Kelly kneeling behind the passenger door and pointing a rifle at me through the V-shaped gap formed by the door and the side panel. Just as I bent down to help Tom up, I heard a gunshot. Something incredibly hot stung my back just above my left kidney, and I went down. I thought it was the kid with the rifle, but it was his father who had shot me, with a .357. I felt no pain. As Tom and I helped each other up, the Kellys ordered everyone else to remain on the other side of the road.

Kelly got on his radio, crowing, "I got Russell Means! I shot Russell Means! I got him!"—as if I were the great prize of an Indian bounty hunt. Within minutes, several BIA cars came racing down the road from Fort Yates. Tom and I were cuffed with our arms behind our backs and thrown into the backseat of Kelly's car. Soon, my left hand and arm were soaked with blood. I still felt no pain, but Tom leaned over to tell me I was seriously wounded.

Instead of being booked at the jail or taken to a hospital, we were all thrown into a big empty cell—the drunk tank. Al White Lightning tore up his T-shirt and Tom's and stuffed them against my wound. My AIM brothers kept shouting, "He's bleeding to death! He needs help!" The jailers ignored them. I lay on a bunk, silent. After a while, my friends yelled, "If you won't take him to the hospital, at least get us a medicine man." More than two hours went by. I became progressively weaker from loss of blood and was starting to gray out when I was finally taken to a hospital. I was hooked to an IV and cleaned up, and then the FBI showed up to question me. I hadn't been booked at the jail, and I figured it was because I was purely a victim.

I've never been a snitch, so I said, "I'm not going to press charges against that young guy. Just forget it."

The bullet had struck exactly where, three years earlier, Alfonso Good Shield had sucked something dark from my body, spit it on the ground, and told me that was where I would be shot, but that I would be all right. His medicine had been very strong indeed. The bullet, which had enough force to shatter an engine block, had entered my body, made a U-turn, and exited without touching any internal organ. The Standing Rock clinic couldn't handle gunshot wounds, so I was taken to a Bismarck hospital and given general anesthesia before surgery. The doctors decided against sewing the huge incision shut because it would invite infection. To this day, I have the four-inch scar from a large hole in my lower back.

While I was in surgery, the BIA issued a news release from Washington, saying that I had been shot in the "abdomen." When I awoke the next morning, a U.S. marshal came into my room and put me under arrest. The charge was interference with a federal officer engaged in official duties. To cover up his shooting me in the back without provocation, Kelly had reported that I had tried to help a "suspect"—Tom—"escape." The rap carried a maximum sentence of ten years. Guards were posted outside my room. A few days later, Bill Kunstler flew in from New York to represent me at an arraignment in my hospital room. A judge came with a court reporter and set my bond at thirty thousand dollars.

When I was strong enough, I went back to the Bismarck house that Dace, Tom, and I shared and, a few days later, drove down to Mission with them. Betty and our kids were staying with Dace's former wife, Karen, and I was going to take Michele and Scott back to Bismarck to spend the summer with me. When I was cruising around the Rosebud just after dark one night with Dace and Tom, a car with three off-duty cops in it pulled alongside us. One of them was John Fuller, the Mission policeman who had almost beaten Curtis Bald Eagle and me to death in Valentine, Nebraska, the previous summer. Suddenly a beer bottle came flying out of the policemen's car and shattered on Dace's window. One of them opened fire, and a bullet grazed my forehead. I started to bleed like a stuck pig. Dace, behind the wheel, reached under the seat for his automatic. Left-handed, he let off several rounds. He left a few holes in sheet metal, but none in flesh.

As luck would have it, we were headed right for the Rosebud hospital. Within a few minutes, I was in the emergency room getting twelve more stitches and a big patch over this latest indignity. The next day, while I lay on a living-room sofa at Karen's house, the FBI questioned me about the shooting. I gave them the names of the cops and described the incident. That was where it ended—no investigation or arrests.

A few days after the shooting, we headed back to Bismarck with Michele and Scott. About a week later, when California schools let out, Sherry and Hank came from Santa Ana, California, with their half sister, Veronica. She is Scott's age; her late biological father was Loren Renville, who had been married to Twila. He was a descendant of the great Santee patriot chief, Gabriel Renville. Twila's ancestor was Chief Gall, the master strategist responsible for Custer's last surprise, so Veronica has quite a pedigree. Later that summer, during the sun dance at Green Grass, we held a making-of-relatives ceremony and Veronica became my daughter. I explained to everyone that I was adopting her because after she came to live with me, I had grown to love her. I still do, as much as I love any of my other children.

I had much to learn about parenthood, however. Since Dace, Tom, and I were more interested in drinking than eating, we sometimes neglected to buy food. My kids were so often hungry that they went shoplifting in grocery stores. When I learned about that many years later, I was deeply ashamed by my thoughtlessness. I also didn't understand then how harmful it was to let my children see me as a drinking father and in casual relationships with a series of women. Added to all the years I was an absentee father, I am responsible for enormous damage to my children. I often beat myself up today with guilt over such behavior. Not only was I a very poor example to my kids, I was such a dummy that I never realized it was happening.

In 1975, however, it was wonderful getting to know my kids after being so long without them. All I asked of them was to tell me the truth. I would do anything for fifteen-year-old Sherry, especially, because I knew she was always straight with me. In contrast, Hank, then a skinny little thirteen-year-old with a wide-eyed air of innocence, had learned to use his appearance to his own detriment, for he often lied. Michele, then nine, went through a particularly tough adjustment. She had been shocked to discover the existence of older siblings, and had to learn to think of herself in a new way. She was no longer my oldest child. As we worked that out, we became close again.

All my kids needed love, but Scott, at seven, needed it most of all. That was one of the most important periods of his life, a time when we should have established a close, loving bond. I had much love inside me, but I didn't know how to be a loving, communicative father. Even when I was almost overcome with the desire to pick up my children, to kiss them and hug them, I didn't. Instead, I was always macho, behaving toward my kids as my own father had treated me. That, too, never occurred to me then.

Since I needed money to support my children, I thought of my Shawnee friends in Oklahoma. They owned land and grew *peji*—literally, "green things"—a general term for grass. We decided to drive down there and get a few pounds of marijuana, bring it back, and start dealing—only to white people, of course. Then we would have money enough to travel around the Dakotas during the summer dancing season. We had all had enough of AIM for a while—we wanted to enter the American economy. *Peji* was a good way to do it. To this day, recreational drugs are among the few commodities still subject to the laws of free-market economics.

Tom and Dace brought their girlfriends and I took my kids. Ten of us piled into Dace's green Pontiac. There was a hole in the muffler and we had no spare tire and no air conditioning, but the car ran fine. In Oklahoma, we stayed with our Shawnee friends for several days. Sherry enjoyed the experience so much that she asked to stay longer. Our friends were planning to come up north soon, so they promised to bring her back. They grew acres of weed and were glad to give us a couple of pounds. When we got back to Bismarck to start our summer of dealing, we found the stuff was as good as anything from Hawaii or Colombia, if not better. Dace came up with the idea of mixing it with dried parsley, four parts herb to one part weed. Consumers never knew it was cut. They would smoke one joint and stay high all day. I didn't so much as touch weed or even a plastic bag that held it. My only link to it was my Shawnee connection and the fact that we lived communally and pooled our money and expenses. I was so out of touch with parenting responsibilities, however, that it never occurred to me that I was sending the wrong message to my kids by involving them, even indirectly, with drugs.

I spent that summer of 1975 partying and working to prepare for my trials. Since May 1973, most of my time had been consumed going to court or getting ready for it. My next case was for getting shot in the back. That proceeding was held in Bismarck, and Larry Leventhal defended me pro bono. Sidney Harring, a lawyer from Buffalo, New York, surveyed potential jurors and found that 68 percent of them felt that "Indians lack ambition," 47 percent believed Indians "carry a chip on their shoulders," and 57.5 percent said "radicals and militants should be sent to prison for the good of society." When it came to me personally, the survey showed that almost 44 percent felt they couldn't give me a fair trial, and almost that many claimed that I should be forced to prove myself innocent! We tried for a change of venue, but the judge, Bruce Van Sickle, refused. It came as no surprise that after several weeks of voir dire, we couldn't seat a jury. I waived my right to a jury trial and let the judge make the decision.

We called about a dozen witnesses, all of them riders in the AIM caravan on the day I was shot. All agreed on the beginning of the incident. Tom went across the highway, Pat Kelly grabbed his hair and threw him around, I went to help him up, and I got shot. Oddly, however, from that point on, everyone remembered something different. Before the trial, when Larry finished taking depositions, he told me that not one story was like another. I started to get worried. I thought, what's going on here? Then Larry explained it to me. The beauty of my witnesses was the consistency of their inconsistency. "The judge, who has a lot of experience in this sort of thing, will know that the nature of eyewitness testimony is that each person sees things in his own way," Larry said. "Precisely because we don't have a dozen stories that are exactly alike, he'll know they're telling the truth."

Pat Kelly and his son testified that we had stopped their car and assaulted them, and they had defended themselves. The prosecution rested, and the judge heard everyone say that Kelly had tried to assassinate me. The point was made that Kelly's son was unlawfully present as a passenger in that car, which undermined the already dubious legality of my arrest. Although Van Sickle was yet another reactionary Republican law-and-order type, he barely bothered to deliberate before pronouncing me not guilty.

At about the time I was exonerated, Dennis Banks was convicted of riot and assault for the Custer courthouse police riot. Earlier in his life, he had served two years in a Minnesota prison, and he thought going back into confinement was pointless. More important, Attorney General Bill Janklow had been quoted as saying every AIM leader should be shot in the head, a comment that was reported over the wire services. Before being sentenced for Custer, Dennis went underground, exiling himself from injustice and becoming a symbol of our people's need for freedom.

After my trial victory in Bismarck, I sent Hank and Sherry back to California and moved to Rapid City with Michele and Scott to prepare for my police-riot trial in Sioux Falls. WKLD/OC's office in Rapid City did some preliminary work in Sioux Falls, but no one there really wanted to get involved in the case. Instead, they recruited a couple of young San Francisco Bay Area lawyers, Alex Reisman and Marvin Rouse, to help Sidney Strange, my court-appointed attorney from Sioux Falls. The California lawyers weren't licensed in South Dakota and could argue in court only behind the legal fig leaf of being under Sid's supervision. In all WKLD/OC's previous cases, the out-of-state guys had been the lead attorneys in all but name, but this time, Sid insisted on running things himself. He had a successful, well-regarded criminal-law practice, so we went along with him.

The summer of 1975 was the time when anti-Indian hysteria in the Dakotas climaxed. On June 26 there was a shoot-out near the home of the Jumping Bull family near Oglala, west of Pine Ridge Village. One Indian and two FBI agents were killed. An enormous manhunt followed, as hundreds of feds swarmed over the reservation. Soon after that, bombs exploded at six or seven BIA offices across the nation, including those on Pine Ridge and in Alameda, California. No one was injured. Of course, the media and police blamed AIM. Then the FBI reportedly accused Charles Abourezk, son of the U.S. senator, of running guns for two thousand AIM "Dog Soldiers"—a Cheyenne warrior society—at training camps in Oklahoma. The FBI leaked the "suspicions" to the media, which convicted Charlie in print because he wore his blond hair in braids and was married to an Indian woman.

Charlie was a dedicated AIMster in those days, but we found the FBI's absurd accusations quite amusing. AIM couldn't afford to buy even one gun, let alone ship thousands or get two thousand "warriors" together. We thanked the FBI for its good PR. By dining on the same propaganda they relentlessly dished out, the feds had built AIM into a vast subversive organization with outlaws and renegades lurking behind every tree. The white man's fear of Indians had increased dramatically as a result. South Dakotans were just as worried about Indians as their great-grandfathers had been. The ghost of Wounded Knee hovered closely over the Dakotas. When prosecutors failed to obtain convictions against the Wounded Knee defendants, indignant editorials proliferated again in newspapers statewide. Their basic message was the same: If so many people had been arrested, something must be dreadfully wrong with a system that couldn't convict them. Surely, said several editorials, "someone must be guilty of something."

Before voir dire began in October 1975 for my own trial, Vernon Bellecourt, Bobby Joe Tiger, and several other people appeared for trial for their roles in the same riot. After interviewing 108 possible jurors, Judge Richard Braithwaite ruled that it was impossible to convene a fair jury, and dismissed all charges. Newspaper editorials around the state trumpeted that Braithwaite had "subverted justice," increasing the pressure on him to obtain a conviction against me.

In all my previous trials, the lead attorneys had been from another state or, like Larry Leventhal and Ken Tilsen, had been so committed to AIM that they didn't care if they permanently pissed off a judge. Sid Strange was a good lawyer, but he was local. He would bring more cases before that judge. If Strange expected to win any of them, he would have been a fool to do the sorts of things Kunstler, Lane, and Tilsen had done in Saint Paul. Instead of sitting quietly and trying to read the judge's mind or hoping he had gotten up on the right side of the bed that morning, they had attacked the court system. Sid counseled me to work with the judge, and he never took the offensive. I have only myself to blame for not insisting that, like Bill Kunstler and Mark Lane, he be willing to risk contempt, or even disbarment if necessary, to force the court to administer justice.

My lawyers, in support of a change-of-venue motion, introduced National Jury Project research proving again that in South Dakota, AIM leaders or even ordinary members couldn't get a fair trial—any more than Indian people in general could. Nevertheless, our motion was denied. After interviewing more than two hundred prospective jurors, none of whom was Indian, and seating only eight or ten, we ran out of peremptory challenges. We knew some people already in the jury box believed strongly that I *deserved* to go to prison simply because I was Russell Means of the American Indian Movement. We knew we could never change their minds, and we couldn't keep any such others off the panel. Sid moved to dismiss charges on the grounds that we couldn't find a fair jury, but Braithwaite ruled against us.

I was astonished. Among the evidence against me was a videotape by local television stations that showed Vernon outside the building, breaking glass on the front of the courthouse. While he did that, I was in a third-floor courtroom. The very judge who had dismissed charges against Vernon—the self-proclaimed AIM leader and among those most hated by law enforcement from coast to coast—wouldn't dismiss mine. My appearance on videotape was limited to helping the injured David Hill.

It was idiocy to go to trial with those rednecks sitting in judgment. Although jury verdicts are rarely overturned on appeal, judges' decisions and law rulings are frequently reversed by appellate courts. After talking the situation over with Strange and my other lawyers, I felt I would be convicted but had a good chance to win on appeal. Accepting the lesser of two evils, I waived my right to a jury and let Judge Braithwaite, son of a founder of the Sioux Falls Ku Klux Klan chapter, decide my guilt or innocence.

Meanwhile, however, after the two agents were killed in a now famous shoot-out on the Jumping Bulls' land near Oglala, the FBI set out to teach the Lakota a lesson that we were a defeated nation and the government could do as it pleased with us. Dozens of Indians were rounded up during reservation sweeps and charged with a variety of offenses. The sheer volume of the cases overwhelmed South Dakota's two federal judges. Since the Constitution guarantees the right to a speedy trial, federal judges William Mehrtens from Miami, Robert J. Kelleher from Los Angeles, and Robert Merhige from Richmond, Virginia, were flown in for periods ranging from two weeks to a month to try everyone. Along with two other out-of-state judges, they presided over the trials of eighty-eight Indians in Pierre and sixty-six in Rapid City.

Those were often grotesque parodies of justice, among the most authoritarian, dictatorial kangaroo courts ever convened. In three months, all those people, most charged with multiple felonies, were run through courtrooms. Defendants and witnesses for several cases stood around in hallways, conversing among themselves without supervision. Anybody could invent any story and get someone to swear it was true. Some trials lasted minutes, and none more than a few days. That meant picking juries, reading charges, hearing witness testimony, all objections overruled, no conferences in chambers, no attempt to learn the truth—boom, boom, boom. Guilty, guilty, guilty. Prison, prison, prison. It was a travesty, the sort of thing few Americans would believe unless they had seen it with their own eyes.

Kenny Kane and I were among those tried in Pierre—for the Mission Golf Club fight—during a one-day Thanksgiving-week recess in the Sioux Falls proceedings. Appearing before Judge Merhige, I represented myself. Kenny had counsel. Like the other trials on that assembly line of injustice, ours was very quick. At least our judge was a fair man, although he indulged in little contemplation. I argued that the Mission cops had no jurisdiction on the reservation and therefore were not acting under color of authority. Merhige said, "I consider this nothing more than a barroom brawl." He threw out eight felony charges and found us each guilty of simple assault. I was sentenced to thirty days in jail.

Kenny, however, was on probation for another recent conviction. A white Rapid City liquor-store owner had beaten two old Indians with a bicycle chain, cutting them badly and breaking their ribs. Nothing was done to the liquor-store owner. To make sure that for the rest of his life he would remember not to treat Indian people that way, Kenny shot him with a .22. That had gotten him five years' probation. Merhige voided the parole and gave him twenty-five months on the assault charge. Then Merhige suspended twenty months and sentenced Kenny to serve the remaining five concurrently. But going to prison cost Kenny his military disability pension.

Since I was still involved in the Minnehaha County courthouse police riot trial, the judge suspended imposition of my sentence until that proceeding ended. The best part was that I reacquainted myself with Peggy Phelps, then in her senior year at South Dakota State. There were lots of girls around, but Peggy stood out. She was slender, with hair down to her waist, very dark, and with a beautiful Indian face.

When I was shot on the Standing Rock, Peggy had tried to visit me in the hospital, but my mother and aunts had turned her away. Now, during the Sioux Falls trial, we renewed our romance. Bursting with enthusiasm, she was naive about so many things, including AIM and her own heritage. Each day's little discovery thrilled and amazed her. It was a beautiful thing to watch—a lovely young woman who was electrified and delighted at being an Indian. She soaked up everything she saw and heard and felt about our culture and history. Being with her recharged me. She gloried in my participation with AIM, and helped motivate me to stay with the movement. We quickly became soul mates, then lovers.

Of the two charges against me in Sioux Falls, "injury to a public building" was so ludicrous that we joked about it. The white man's society prizes property so highly that it believes people should be punished for causing injury to an inanimate object! To get that charge through a grand jury, cops had testified that after we filed out of the courtroom and descended through the stairwell, I had taken a step from the foot of a landing and kicked out a window. The cops had gotten their stories in sync. They each said I had taken *one* step and then let fly. Those windows are ten to twelve feet from the stairs, so my stride would have had to be at least ten feet long. To prove that had never happened, the judge took his court into the stairwell and had me attempt to kick the window. It was so obviously impossible that Braithwaite dismissed that count on the spot.

But those of us charged in the courthouse riot were the first in state history to be indicted under a statute for "riot to obstruct justice." My lawyers argued that the law was unconstitutionally vague. If more than two people met on a street corner and questioned a cop about the legality of what he was doing, they could be arrested. Braithwaite refused to dismiss the charge. I sat in complete awe as the government unfolded an absurd scenario to explain how I had planned the riot in Judge Bottum's courtroom. As the feds had done for my trial after Wounded Knee, the state went looking for evidence to support the charges only after the arrests. According to the prosecuting attorney's arguments, I had come up with a diabolically ingenious plan. According to the prosecution, I had instructed the spectators to refuse to stand. Somehow, I had learned that the Sioux Falls SWAT team would be waiting in the courthouse, and would be called when they refused to stand. When the police swarmed in, I had given a prearranged signal to people outside, telling them to smash courthouse windows and glass doors.

It is still amazing to me.

If those police and prosecutors were to be believed, I was not only a genius, but obviously the most powerful man in the whole country. Looking at the white men who came up with that story, I realized they had to be supremely evil. Not only had they conceived that incredible nonsense, they had accused me of it in a court of law and put it on paper for the world to read. I thought they had to be insane. I could conceive of no other explanation for their actions. Today, I realize that those men had not been raised as I was. They believed in evil, they contemplated it, and it inspired the improbable fantasies they put forth.

When the prosecution rested, we called dozens of witnesses—practically everyone in the courtroom, including four Lutheran bishops, several ministers, and representatives of the League of Women Voters. Every one of them was white, and every one of them described how the police had burst in and started to beat people. We had testimony from David Hill and Ramon Roubideaux, the first to be attacked even though they had had no role in the sit-down demonstration. Bottum was a prosecution witness. On cross-examination, Strange got him to testify that he had invited me into the courtroom to bring peace and that I had asked the people to stand up for him.

Despite all the credible evidence, Braithwaite, on the first Monday of 1976, following on the heels of his frontier forebears, got his Indian. In a travesty of justice, he found me guilty and sentenced me to four years in prison. I looked out the window at the dirty snow covering Sioux Falls and felt worse than I had as a teenager when, overcome with despair, I had contemplated suicide.

On Trial for Murder

After my conviction in Sioux Falls, I went home. The people of Porcupine and some of our Lakota chiefs, holy men, and other elders came to a community honoring ceremony that recognized my courage in standing up for my beliefs. It made my heart feel good. For a while, I felt such an honor might was almost worth being convicted—almost.

I felt even better after my lawyers persuaded Judge Braithwaite to continue my bond while my appeal worked its way through the courts. If the South Dakota Supreme Court turned it down, I would have two more shots. I could petition any U.S. Supreme Court justice for a stay of execution of sentence while we appealed to the full court, which would accept my case for review or not. If it were accepted, they could reverse my conviction and order a new trial. The court could uphold Judge Braithwaite, or refuse to consider my case. Then I would go to prison. But a four-year sentence didn't necessarily mean four years behind bars. As a first felony offender in South Dakota—my previous convictions for the Mission Golf Club incident and my plea in the Custer courthouse police riot had been misdemeanors—I would be eligible for parole in a year, minus "good time," credit for good behavior. I could be free in as little as nine months' time.

As bad as that might be in a racist prison system like South Dakota's, it was nothing compared to what I would face if I were convicted of the murder of Martin Montileaux in Scenic. By that time, the state had dropped charges against Dave Clifford. His only sin was driving a car with Dicky Marshall, several other people, and me in it. In March 1976, despite abundant evidence that no Pennington County jury could be expected to give him a fair hearing, Dicky went on trial in Rapid City. Halley Merrill, owner of the Longhorn Saloon, testified that he had heard a noise like a bump and then a *pop* sound. Then Dicky had left the bathroom. Montileaux, interviewed on his deathbed by a deputy sheriff named Don Phillips, had described the man who had shot him as having shaggy hair. I wore my hair in braids, and Dicky wore a neat ponytail. Montileaux also had said he didn't know Dicky and couldn't identify the gunman. Phillips had a photo of Dicky with him, but after hearing that, he didn't show it to the dying man. Police were unable to match the .22 bullet that doctors dug out of Montileaux with the .22 pistol found in Clifford's car. There were no eyewitnesses who saw Dicky shoot anyone.

It looked as if the state's case was very weak. Then at the last moment— too late for Dicky's lawyers to do a serious investigation—the state produced Myrtle Poor Bear, sister of Montileaux's girlfriend, Marion. Myrtle was a plump, plain woman, several years older than Dicky. Dicky was a fit, handsome, happily married guy who could have had any number of pretty girls but would never have bothered with Myrtle. Nonetheless, for reasons I will never know, she testified that she was his girlfriend and that while drinking together, he had boasted about killing Montileaux. She even supplied a "motive" to allow prosecutors to "prove" that the "murder" was premeditated. She said Montileaux had once beaten up Dicky in a Gordon, Nebraska, bar.

Those were lies. The police and the FBI knew it. The G-men sat on Myrtle's testimony for at least three months before prosecutors "suddenly" located a "new" witness. Just as the FBI had found Louis Moves Camp to fill huge gaps in its case against Dennis and me, Myrtle suddenly appeared to supply what was missing to show that Dicky was the killer. Indian people to this day believe she was mentally unbalanced. Later, when the feds needed someone to say Leonard Peltier had bragged about killing two FBI agents near the Jumping Bulls' home, Myrtle was trotted out again. As implausible a witness as she made, in front of a white jury, the result was the same: Both men were convicted and sentenced to life in prison.

My trial for the Montileaux "murder" was scheduled for summer. After Dicky's conviction, I went to a party at my cousin Greg Zephier's home in a housing project south of Wagner, on the Yankton Sioux Reservation. Drinking beer with my friend—officially, my bodyguard—John Thomas, I met a couple of Indian guys named Weston and Jimmy Weddell. Greg was head of the local AIM chapter. Those hoodlums, barely out of their teens, opposed his leadership. We got into a silly argument about it, politics compounded by macho posturing and alcohol. Suddenly they were pointing weapons at us. They told us to go outside, then ordered me across the street. Weston had a .222, a high-velocity varmint rifle. Weddell carried a .357 revolver in his left hand and a .22 in his right. I crossed the street and turned around. When Weddell said, "Shoot him! Shoot him!" Weston aimed his rifle and pulled the trigger. The bullet struck just below my left nipple; the impact spun me around and I fell down. Weddell slugged John, knocking him to the street. As John started to get up, Weddell shot him from about six inches with his .22. It's a good thing he was right-handed—if he had fired the .357, it would have blown John's head off. Instead, the slug slammed into the bony ridge under John's eye and was deflected downward through his neck.

As the two punks took off, I crawled over to Greg's house. The last thing I remember clearly before the ambulance ride was knocking at the door. The slug had nicked my lung, detoured around my spine, and exited through my back. When I pulled my shirt off in the emergency room, the bullet fell out. When the press reported that the bullet had missed all my vital organs, as in both of my previous shootings, people back home started to say that I didn't *have* any vital organs!

The Indian Health Service staff wanted nothing to do with me, so I was taken about fifty miles to Saint Mary's, the best hospital in Yankton. AIM promptly took over. John and I were given a private room. Because of his wound, he had to have a tracheotomy and was fed through a hole just below his Adam's apple. Always witty, John would finish a can of the chalky liquid food—he was able to eat—and then use a napkin to dab at the hole with mock fastidiousness while smacking his lips. It always cracked me up.

My recovery was delayed when I caught pneumonia, probably as a response to my damaged lung. I was amazed that people from all over the country came to see me. Peggy Phelps tried. I didn't know it until later, but my mother, aunts, and sisters turned her and her mom away. I guess that was because Betty and I were trying to reconcile and she was in town with Michele and Scott. Even with my family running that kind of well-intentioned interference, I had too many visitors—sometimes four or five a day, all of them anxious to do something personal for me. I was soon exhausted trying to give each some tangible sign that the visit had made me feel better. The wire-service story about our having been shot generated newspaper stories all over the country, and people sent them to us. The headlines all said, "Russell Means and Sidekick Shot." I felt badly for John, because those reports never mentioned his name, but I showed my affection by teasing him about it.

Lying in that hospital bed in 1976, I got to thinking: My God, first Curtis Bald Eagle was beaten into a coma and now John was shot in the head—two guys I really love had been nearly killed just for hanging out with me. I decided then that I didn't want to be responsible for more injuries. I knew I would never forgive myself if somebody died defending me or, worse, merely for being with me. I wanted no more special treatment. In AIM, we had always looked out for one another and watched one another's backs; so from then on, I had bodyguards only when traveling and then only if my hosts assigned them. I thought it better to accept them than to embarrass them by refusing.

I had survived four attempts on my life. At the time, I didn't reflect on that beyond giving thanks to the Great Mystery, to the spirits, and to Alfonso Good Shield, whose amazing medicine was still protecting me. Now I recognize that each attempt on my life, along with all my other trials and troubles, contained some important lesson for me. As my dad had taught me, I couldn't blame anyone else for what had happened to me—it was my own damn fault. He also had said that if I could learn from a bad experience, it was actually a good thing. Now I look at my life as a series of teachings designed to put me on a spiritual path. The Great Mystery has designs for me which I don't understand, and over which I have no control. In the 1970s, I expected to be assassinated, but if that had happened, I knew my death would have served some greater purpose. I wasn't going to live in fear or act out of paranoia. My dad also had taught me that when it's my time to go, it's my time to go.

When I was well enough to travel, I went to Rapid City, where Jim Leach and Bruce Ellison of WKLD/OC were working to find good lawyers for my murder trial, scheduled to start in early summer. I also resumed my romance with Peggy. One day I got a call from a Vancouver art dealer named Doug Chrismas who told me that Andy Warhol wanted to do a portrait of me—if I was interested. Chrismas began to make arrangements for me to meet Warhol in New York.

I was also preparing for the second International Indian Treaty Conference at Greenwood in late June 1976. Jimmy Durham, who ran the treaty council's office, had managed to get us an eleventh-floor corner-view suite at 777 United Nations Plaza, directly across the street from the UN building. We had to pay rent, but initially it was donated by the United Methodist Women, who owned the building. Thanks to Jimmy and that office, prestigious representatives of the United Nations, and African nations and organizations came to our conference at Greenwood, my mother's home on the Missouri River.

Unfortunately, the Yankton Dakota were nothing like the Dakota and Lakota of Standing Rock. Only about a half-dozen local families attended. There were a few elders and young people, but most of the Indians who came were from Canada, from other states, or from other Sioux reservations. In contrast to the five thousand who had attended in 1974, only about two hundred Indian people came to Greenwood in 1976. That was a tremendous disappointment. Nevertheless, the conference was significant because Australian aborigines came to tell us about their oppression. That helped to shape the treaty council's worldwide focus on aiding indigenous peoples.

I was responsible for scheduling the conference, which was to occur just before the U.S. Bicentennial on July 4, for which most Indian organizations had made other plans. For example, people from Washington State who had been part of the fishing-rights struggle and had joined the Trail of Broken Treaties remembered the promise we had made at the BIA. If the White House and Congress hadn't adequately addressed the "Twenty Points" within four years, we would come back. Four years had gone by, and nothing had changed, so the group organized a caravan to go to D.C. on Independence Day. It stopped at Greenwood, and the organizers asked us to join them after our conference.

But AIM had also made other plans. After the treaty council, we were going to Montana to celebrate the centennial of the defense of the Greasy Grass, commonly called the Battle of the Little Bighorn, on June 25. The battle was by no means exclusively a Lakota or even a Sioux victory. The Crow and Ree scouts who had led Custer to his fate had added to his humiliation. Among those camped along the Greasy Grass in 1876 was a band of the Northern Cheyenne people, including Chief Two Moon. His great-great-grandson, Austin Two Moon, had invited us to camp on his ranch on the Northern Cheyenne Reservation in Montana.

The afternoon after our arrival, a car from the adjacent Crow Reservation pulled in, packed with passengers. One was a very old woman who came looking for me. When I was a boy, my dad had told me his grandmother was a full-blooded Crow. This woman was a niece of my great-grandmother, as much my grandma as the beloved Twinkle Star of my childhood. I felt overwhelmed with love as she hugged and kissed me and told me how proud she was of me. It was a beautiful surprise. It made me understand how an adopted child must feel when he finally meets his true family.

We arrived in Montana June 22, 1976. The Custer centennial was set for June 25. On June 23, we participated in Cheyenne ceremonies, which also included about five hundred visiting Indians. Then Crow people who were employed at the battlefield came to say that the Park Service had moved ceremonies up a day, hoping to trick us. The next morning, we left early in a caravan of about seventy-five cars. Entering the Crow agency from the east, we found cops waiting—tribal and BIA police, county sheriffs, highway patrolmen, Park Service rangers, the FBI, and three other kinds of law enforcers.

When we paused at the Custer Battlefield turnoff to regroup, a white guy came jogging up to our car, breathless. He was from Ministers for Peace, an ecumenical group that volunteered to act as liaison between whites and Indians. It was an extraordinary group, white clergymen from all over South Dakota—but very naive. This one gasped, "Oh, my God! There's eight police agencies here! It's going to be a massacre! Don't go in—they've got dogs and everything!"

"Calm down," we said. "Don't worry."

"Oh, please don't go. Let us negotiate this."

There was nothing to negotiate, but as we drove on, the same thought struck John Thomas and me. We looked at each other and then he said, "You see how scared that guy was?" I said, "Yeah—but we're so conditioned to racism and violence that we think it's *normal* to be confronted by hundreds of police with dogs!"

We parked along the road, got everybody together, and walked in. We had expected the police dogs, so as we marched in and the cops moved forward to face off against us, we turned loose two of our own German shepherd bitches, both in heat. Instantly, it was like a Mack Sennett movie. Every son of a bitch in the K-9 Corps forgot everything he had been trained for. Many jerked the leashes out of their handlers' hands and ran after the bitches. Our dogs were AIM all the way—they weren't about to let any pig dogs mount them, so they took off, too. Cops whistled and called their dogs. Handlers with animals still on leashes were dragged to and fro. It was total chaos. AIMsters surrounded the crowd of whites, standing shoulder to shoulder with hands inside their coats as though reaching for a gun in a shoulder holster. We knew how to play the game. The Park Service people got scared. They saw that we had planned and organized this, and that we were disciplined.

We went on into the park with Oscar Bear Runner—the World War II veteran who had walked forty miles a night to carry food and supplies into Wounded Knee—carrying the sacred pipe. Our arrival was heralded with a burst of thunderclaps and a light shower; maybe the thunder spirits were putting on their own demonstration. The ceremony was held in the main parking lot. The audience was filled with cavalry buffs, including a descendant of Custer, dressed in dark blue with gold trim. When I went up to the stage and headed for a seat, the Park Service superintendent nervously took out his handkerchief and swabbed it dry. As I sat down, I saw the media people in a frenzy, snapping pictures and rushing around like crazy.

When we had stopped at the Greasy Grass in 1972 on the Trail of Broken Treaties, a different park superintendent had begged us not to erect our memorial to the Indians who had died teaching Custer a few manners. He had promised to get a monument put up for us. That had never happened. In 1976, I got up and said, "You continue to invade our territory and to disrupt our families. Still we come with the sacred pipe, still we come in peace, as we always have. If you don't want peace, if you want to fight, we're here to fight, too." I demanded another meeting with the Park Service. At the ranger station, surrounded by media people, the superintendent promised to put up a monument to honor the Indian dead of Greasy Grass.

The next day at the Cheyenne Reservation, we participated in an honoring ceremony. Descendants of those who had fought against Custer received beautiful warrior medals crafted by a gifted silversmith named Ben

Nighthorse Campbell. As an infant, he had been adopted into a white family. As an adult, he had overcome enormous legal barriers to discover his ancestry, then had found his way back to his people. Today, he represents the citizens of Colorado in the U.S. Senate. Another huge honor was bestowed on me when Austin Two Moon and Ben Campbell presented me with a medal. I was the only non-Cheyenne to receive one.

After the ceremony, I returned to Rapid City. During the previous year, I had been quoted several times in the media as saying that on July 4, AIM was going to blow out the candles on America's birthday cake. That fueled the rumor that AIM would attack the South Dakota State Penitentiary, in Sioux Falls, on July 4 and free Dicky Marshall. By that time, almost every AIM gathering in South Dakota had become an occasion to call out the National Guard. The Bicentennial was no different. Hundreds of guardsmen were deployed to protect the prison. Others surrounded Mount Rushmore.

If AIM had any such plans, I didn't know about them. I didn't really need an alibi, but I decided the July 4 weekend was an excellent time to go fishing. I took Peggy, Sherry, and Hank, and we joined my cousin Janice Means and her husband, a Denver cop, for trout fishing in the headwaters of the Laramie River. After our return to Rapid City, Peggy and I got into a major disagreement and we split up. We loved each other, but when we argued I became too physical. Sometimes I pulled her hair. She wouldn't stand for that. I tried then to minimize my actions, but I recognize now that I had no right to assault her in any way.

My murder trial began in late July of 1976. I was represented initially by Ken Tilsen; a local attorney named Homer Kandaras; and John Ackerman, a well-regarded Texan who helped found the National Association of Criminal Defense Attorneys. Millard Farmer came to help with pretrial motions, including issues related to finding an impartial jury. Farmer, associated with the Southern Poverty Law Center in Alabama, was known for his grasp of constitutional and death-penalty issues. He was in his forties, with a silver mane, a Georgia drawl, a fondness for white linen suits, and a courtly manner that seemed to conjure up Atticus Finch, the Southern lawyer played by Gregory Peck in the film adaptation of Harper Lee's *To Kill a Mockingbird*. Farmer moved into a motel and worked night and day.

I stayed with John Thomas in a housing project where he lived with his wife and kids. It was only a half block from Peggy's home, which made my split with her even more painful. I was on trial for murder, and until Betty arrived with Michele and Scott, I was acutely lonely and felt that I had no one to support me in my struggle.

The night before jury selection began, Phillip Deere, the Muscogee medicine man from Oklahoma who had helped at my Wounded Knee trial, arrived with his family. In John Thomas's backyard, we held a tobacco ceremony.

Afterward, as Deere began to pack up to leave, I said, "The trial's about to start. I need you." "You have nothing to worry about," he said. "It's all been said and done. We've got to go now." He had come all the way from Oklahoma for one ceremony, then turned around and went back. Watching him drive off, I felt very lonely.

The Jury Project people told us that in South Dakota, most people embrace authority. They believe cops don't lie, government is good, and all the other myths of American society. Those people obey every law and blindly follow rules and regulations. They make the worst kind of jury to face, people who can't think for themselves. When Ackerman examined the potential jurors, he became a boot-camp drill sergeant. "I'm going to ask you questions that you answer yes or no," he barked. "Do you understand that?" They always said, "Yes, sir!" The more rigid the potential juror, the more authoritarian Ackerman became. It was amazing. They answered his questions truthfully almost every time. Only when we had finished did Ackerman admit that it was the first time he had ever conducted a voir dire examination. I was astonished—and glad that I hadn't known that before.

One of the first prospective jurors was Jim Czywczynski, the son-in-law of the Gildersleeves who had abandoned his wife and kids when we first occupied Wounded Knee. He said, "No way—I can't give this guy a fair trial," so he was excused. Later that day, another venireman took the stand. When asked his profession, he pointed at me and said, "Because of that guy and all his followers, I can't keep a job. I belong to the National Guard. Every time AIM farts in South Dakota, I have to put on my uniform and chase him. Then I lose my job. I hate him and I'm not going to give him a fair trial." He was excused. I liked his honesty.

As the jury box slowly filled, we started to run out of peremptory challenges. I became very edgy as we got down to the last few prospective jurors. I held my breath when a young University of Minnesota graduate said, in reply to a prosecutor's questions, that he had once met Vernon Bellecourt and had great admiration for AIM. When Jack Klauck, the deputy state's attorney, left the young man on the jury, I marveled at my luck—until I remembered that Deere had said after the tobacco ceremony that I had nothing to worry about. When we had exhausted our peremptories and the state was down to its last, there were two candidates left, an elderly lady and a young junior-high-school teacher. The teacher said that in the last four or five years, since the advent of AIM, she had seen a rebirth of self-dignity and self-pride in her Indian students. "AIM has had nothing but a good effect on these kids," she added.

The older woman, like most of her generation in South Dakota, was a dyed-in-the-wool racist. She still blamed the Sioux for wagon-train attacks, even though there was only one recorded instance of such a skirmish, and it occurred because the settlers had refused pay the toll—two oxen. On that occasion, my ancestors took *all* their oxen as a penalty for refusing to go to our traffic court. When Klauck used his last peremptory, it was to strike the old lady, leaving the young teacher on the jury. I barely made it back to the defense antechamber and shut the door before letting out an *akisa*, as we call our joyful cry. Klauck, the dumb cluck, should have excused the teacher, just as he should have struck the young Minnesota graduate. There was no reason for Klauck to accept two people who said they admired AIM. I had just witnessed a miracle—Deere's medicine at work.

I started the trial in a hopeful mood. We had learned that just before Montilcaux lost consciousness and died, Deputy Don Phillips had recorded his statement that I had nothing to do with shooting him. In any state, a deathbed declaration is considered equal to testimony under oath, yet authorities still had chosen to try me for murder. And our motion for dismissal was denied. Phillips, an early prosecution witness, testified about many things, but not about the victim's statement. On cross-examination, we turned him upside down, stripped him bare, and made a fool of him. Jurors eyed one another with raised eyebrows as Phillips grudgingly repeated Montileaux's last words. Another miracle was that the cops had not only tape-recorded Montileaux's statement but had *kept* the tape.

Other prosecution witnesses included Halley Merrill, the Longhorn Saloon's crusty old barkeep, and his daughter, Twila. They were tough people who had scratched out a living from the Badlands with their hands, their hearts, and their wits. Merrill and his daughter had adopted Indian children; they had lived with us, worked with us, hired us, fired us, sold to us and bought from us and traded with us. They had the kind of regard for Indians that missionaries and do-gooders never feel, the trust and understanding that come only from living with people and respecting them as individuals. Forty years earlier, Halley had played baseball with my father, but he had been unable to pick Dicky or me out of a lineup. At my trial, he still couldn't identify me. The Merrills didn't know a thing except what they had "read in the papers." I owe them a thank-you.

We called one witness. As cocounsel, I examined that witness—my mother, who testified to my character, which is more than she had ever done at home. Although the case against me was laughably weak, there were so many racists in the jury box that my attorney felt it necessary to show them I was a human being with a loving mother. She was a great witness who came across as a strong and caring woman.

For weeks, I had been dickering with Doug Chrismas and Andy Warhol about when to do my portrait. Just before testimony began in this trial, I told them, "By next week, I might be put away for the rest of my life, or I might be dead. Better do it now." The weekend before final arguments, they flew me to New York City and Warhol took more than one hundred Polaroids of me. Then I went out on the town with Warhol—a great host—and several of his friends. I knew it might be the last free weekend of my life, so I resolved to make the best of it. I took Warhol to a Puerto Rican place for some Latin dancing; then he took us all to a ritzy night-club. I got to strut my stuff with Doug's girlfriend, an excellent dancer. We made quite a pair, she in designer clothes and I in braids, boots, Levis, and a ribbon shirt, dancing up a storm.

I returned to the trial and final arguments, which concluded on a Wednesday. I sweated it out. If the jury brought back a guilty verdict, I would be doomed to at least six or seven years—perhaps many more—in a maximum-security prison. By Thursday, it seemed obvious that few jurors had bought our argument that the state never came close to proving any connection between me and the killing. We believed there would be a verdict on Friday because jurors would want to get home for the weekend. We were right. I was with Betty and the kids when the call came that the jury was back.

By that time, I had decided I would be convicted. I could not trust the white man, so I decided to forget about appeals. I wasn't going to spend the rest of my life in prison. With two AIMsters, I made a plan. We each hid a gun in one of our boots. To foil courtroom metal detectors, we wrapped them in plastic, covered that with rubber, and then swaddled them in duct tape. When the verdict was announced, they would shoot the jury and I would kill the prosecutors and the judge. Then we would take white women as hostages, tape guns to their throats, and make a run for it.

We made it through tight courtroom security without incident. Out of sight in the defense antechamber, we hurriedly peeled the wrapping from our guns. When the jury filed in, I was surprised to see that the foreman was the young teacher. When she stood up to hand the bailiff the verdict on a slip of paper that he carried to the judge, I was calm. My first shot was going to hit the prosecutor in his lying face.

"Not guilty," said the foreman. Suddenly weak, I collapsed on the table, then roused myself to give one of the biggest hugs of my life to Ackerman and another to cocounsel Jim Leach. I looked over at my AIM brothers. Their smiles went ear to ear.

Eyewitnesses reported later that the courtroom was pandemonium, that some of my supporters cried and others shrieked with joy. I was in a daze, numbly moving around to exchange bear hugs and handshakes, stunned by the verdict. I had expected to launch a gunfight, and my nervous system was primed and ready. I felt suddenly buoyant, almost weightless. I hadn't realized how much of a load I had been carrying until I set it down. I went into the defense antechamber to collect my thoughts, to let the miracle sink in. I slapped hands with my AIM pals and we hugged.

Looking back, I feel guilty for not having had more faith. When we planned to kill the judge, jury, and prosecutors, we knew exactly what we were doing—our plan was not the result of temporary insanity. White South Dakota felt unadulterated hatred for us, a racism so virulent and pervasive that it could put anybody in a state of mind to martyr himself to fight it. Even so, I never believed that every person on that jury deserved to die. I felt that South Dakota's *racism* deserved to die. Those jurors wallowed ignorantly in racism. The hateful prosecutors were dumb functionaries just following orders. I saw the judge as a dyed-in-the-wool racist. To me they were all symbols of oppression. Killing them would have been a strike at injustice, a calculated expression of frustration and rage that could no longer be contained. In my anger, I didn't see them as individuals or even as human beings.

All these years later, I can still feel my mind-numbing anger, but now I understand it and can control it. I don't react as I once did because I know that the system of injustice is the enemy; racism is the enemy. I'm grateful that my path was guided by the Great Mystery's plan, glad that I didn't have to turn that courtroom into a bloody monument to South Dakota's refusal to dispense justice to Indian people.

When I was calmer, I left the courthouse to meet a throng of reporters. The local media asked the usual dumb questions, but I also spoke with a young woman correspondent from ABC News, one of the best interviewers I've ever met. She asked all the right things: how the verdict affected AIM, how it advanced the Indians' struggle, and what it meant for my family, especially my children. She treated me as a person—not as an ogre, as most white people did. That conversation helped bring me back to reality; as I answered, the numbness receded. When we finished, I drove into the Black Hills to pray.

Then I headed to a victory party at John Thomas's house, where my lawyers told me what they had learned from jurors about their deliberations. The schoolteacher who miraculously had gotten on the jury to become its foreman was one of the town liberals, a leader in progressive causes, especially women's rights. The first vote was ten-to-two for conviction, with the teacher and the young University of Minnesota graduate the only holdouts. That man later told me, "The man [who shot Montileaux] had already been convicted! No way in hell was I going to convict you—I'd have held out until the day I died!" Everybody on that jury had heard and read about me for years. Except for those two honest people, all of them felt I had done *something* to merit prison, whether I was guilty of murder or not. It took two days of dogged discussion for the two to convince the ten that I was on trial only for a killing that it was plain I didn't do.

37

▼▼▼▼▼▼▼▼▼

Sobriety

A fter my trial, I began to prepare for the sun dance at Green Grass. I wanted to make it very special, a *wopila* ceremony of gratitude and thanksgiving. Just before I left, word came that prosecutors in Sioux Falls had asked Judge Braithwaite to revoke my bond, and he was considering it. As a kid learning about Christianity, I had been taught to pray for myself, but Indian teachings are the opposite. We pray for everyone else. Nevertheless, I was so worried about Braithwaite's ruling that I made a vow: If the Great Mystery would keep me out of prison, I would never pray for myself again.

For four days, faithfully fasting and dancing, I prayed for my freedom. Then, for the only time in my life, my chest was pierced on each side, and chokecherry slivers were attached to four buffalo skulls that I dragged around the sacred circle. They represented the four winds, the four directions, the four points of the universe, the four corners of the earth, the four ages each person goes through, and the four epochs of the earth. Those epochs are the times when human beings have walked the planet between cataclysmic changes—after the earth was formed in fire, after the ice age, after the flood, and after an age yet to come, when I believe the earth will become a desert. I pulled the skulls also for the sacred colors—black, red, yellow, and white—

the pigments of the human races that mix together to become brown, the color of our Grandmother and of the fifth race. Most of all, I pulled the skulls to honor my children, the sacred pipe, and the rebirth of my people.

While I danced out the east gate of the sacred circle, I saw Bruce Ellison, one of my lawyers. As the ceremony ended and people shook hands and offered thanks, he told me that Judge Braithwaite had denied the prosecutor's motion. I would remain free until all my appeals were exhausted. Another of my multitude of prayers had been answered. In gratitude, I renewed my vow to the Great Mystery. To this day, I have never again prayed for myself.

A few weeks after the sun dance, in September 1976, I surrendered myself to Custer County authorities and served the thirty days I had received after having pleaded guilty to assault the previous year. It wasn't terribly unpleasant. I pretty much had the place to myself except for a couple of guys who came and went after a few days. I spent hours doing sit-ups and push-ups. For spiritual reasons, I fasted for four days, taking only water.

When they turned me loose, I headed for New York to help Jimmy Durham. We were about the only ones still actively working for the International Indian Treaty Council. It was then the only nongovernmental organization recognized by the United Nations that was dealing with the rights of indigenous peoples. Jimmy had been trying to get the United Nations to sponsor a worldwide conference on the treatment of Indian people in the Western Hemisphere. He had a hard time finding folks to travel outside the United States, so he usually went himself. That was a problem. He is a slender, light-skinned, blue-eyed Cherokee from a band that the United States refuses to recognize. He also insisted on wearing a long, shaggy beard that, with his other physical characteristics, gave him a bizarre resemblance to Abe Lincoln.

Although UN officials seemed very receptive to our plan for a conference, it was unprecedented because the international community had never paid any attention to Indians. We soon learned that dealing with UN bureaucrats was even more difficult than dealing with the BIA. It was easier to work with the UN missions of individual countries and with groups such as the Organization for African Unity and the Non-Aligned Movement.

The Soviets were especially sympathetic because they wanted anyone who dissented against the United States in their camp. Every country in the Western Hemisphere opposed our conference because its purpose was to focus world attention on the oppression, suppression, and repression of American Indians—the silent holocaust that had been going on for nearly five hundred years. We wanted a prestigious site, so we chose Geneva, where the United Nations has a headquarters. We decided on the autumn of 1977, when most General Assembly missions are in session. After we had lined up support from many nations, the United Nations agreed to be a cosponsor. The conference would be one way of telling the world how Indians were treated in America.

Indians in South Dakota, and especially on Pine Ridge, had been the subjects of unrelenting terror sponsored or tolerated by the federal government.

In 1976, Al Trimble, former BIA superintendent, resigned and ran against Dick Wilson, who was seeking a third term as Lakota chairman. Donations from white and breed ranchers whom he had showered with political favors poured in to Wilson, so he had one hell of a campaign chest. He even put out slick political literature—all bullshit—describing his plans for his next term. Because of my lawsuit after Wilson's theft of the 1974 election, Trimble got government-appointed election monitors and easily won the office. That ended goon terror on Pine Ridge, but not government oppression.

Trimble's election did bring federal funds into Pine Ridge, which temporarily improved the lives of many people. One of the few long-term successes was in education, although it took nearly a generation to see results. As people became active in their communities and became empowered, they began to take contracts away from the BIA and the Department of Health, Education, and Welfare. They returned control of Indian education to the community by establishing local school boards. In time, communities on Pine Ridge took charge of their own schooling; in most districts, the schools were contracted out to local control.

The other success was community-based policing. The Oglala Sioux tribe won the BIA police contract and installed a tribal force, a system still used today. Gerald Clifford, Gerald One Feather, and others put together the finest example of community control of law enforcement. Each district hires and fires its own police. Once the annual budget is set, each controls its own share. That structure strengthens the community, and therefore the family. Rather than seeking to arrest people, it works to resolve conflicts without removing them from the community. It was so efficient that the FBI's crime statistics, which use arrests and convictions as indicators of "productivity," declined, according to wire-service reports. The Justice Department began to worry—despite the huge federal law-enforcement presence, not enough Indians were being sentenced to prison.

I don't think this new funding was a master stroke on the part of the government, a switch in tactics from terror to pacification. It was more likely an accidental product of Trimble's ability to shake the money tree. Whatever the reason, as federal funds poured into Pine Ridge to create mostly make-work jobs, many AIMsters were hired as police, property and supply clerks, civic planners, and for other new positions in tribal government. As unemployment fell from 87 percent to a mere 60 percent, desperately poor people who had had nothing to lose became slaves to their new paychecks. Busy with new jobs and families and oblivious to their own continuing oppression, younger people began to feel "empowered."

One of the issues we wanted to take before the international community was the government-sponsored terrorism that had gripped Pine Ridge for years. Before Wilson left office, his death squads and white vigilantes had been responsible for the murders of more than sixty AIM members and more than 250 other Indian people in and around Pine Ridge. Those killings have yet to be investigated, and the effects of those horrific years are still seen and felt around the reservation. People were so terrified that instead of recognizing the source of their calamity—the federal government, personified by the BIA and rubber-stamp tribal government—they blamed AIM.

When I returned to Pine Ridge in the autumn of 1976, the terror had just ended and federal money had begun to flow in. For most, that period on the reservation was a time of happy tranquility. With my trials behind me, I was no longer preoccupied with legal matters. Dace had been chosen as Wanbli district leader and had somehow arranged for a rent-free three-bedroom house. Tom Poor Bear and I had no place to live, so Dace invited us to live with him. Then Peggy and I got back together, and Hank and Sherry moved in with me. Dace and I traded philosophies and feelings. Once again we became close, and I realized how lucky I was to be his brother.

The white man's racist term for Indians is *redskins*, so when referring to ourselves, people of my generation often call one another "skins." Although I had virtually no income and lived practically from hand to mouth during most of the winter of 1976–1977, I hung around with the skins—having fun, joking around, shooting pool. Every once in a while, I would test a cowboy bar or two to see how tough everybody was that day. My drinking increased again. Peggy didn't like it, but she never badgered me about it, mainly because I was so much fun when I was a little gassed. I wasn't blacking out or getting so drunk that I seemed out of control. I sobered up whenever I had AIM business. I told myself that because AIM took so much of my attention, the only time I could relax was when I drank. I really wanted to believe that.

When the dancing season arrived in 1977, I fasted occasionally and enjoyed going to ceremonies. Throughout the Dakotas, at least, our culture enjoyed a spiritual rebirth that is still evident today. Greg Zephier's family restored the sun dance to the Yankton Reservation, another group returned it to Standing Rock, and even Sisseton began to organize one. Soon every Sioux reservation except Crow Creek and Lower Brulé had at least one sun dance. Amid that renaissance of self-dignity and self-pride, Pine Ridge people began to organize. Indian ranchers started to get loans, some to expand their herds and others to resume ranching. It was a heady time. Although most of AIM's newly employed members began to drift away, the nucleus remained strong. Along with other AIMsters, I led civil-rights demonstrations all around the Dakotas during much of 1976 and 1977.

In the spring of 1977, there was a racial disturbance against Indian people on the Sisseton-Wahpeton Reservation, which is Peggy's home. We decided to caravan to Sisseton and confront white city officials. I was on bond while my appeal for the Sioux Falls conviction worked its way through the courts, so I couldn't break the law for any reason. Therefore, I didn't take part in the actual march on the town of Sisseton. The march ended at the courthouse, and I walked in with the local protest leaders to meet white officials. They agreed to everything we asked. When my presence in Sisseton made the news, prosecutors in Sioux Falls asked Judge Braithwaite to revoke my bail on the ground that I had violated his restrictions on civil disobedience. I wasn't notified about that, nor was my attorney—it wasn't legally required. It would be several weeks before the judge ruled. Meanwhile, I was blissfully unaware that my freedom was threatened.

By that time, the mid-1970s, I had noticed how much my drinking was affecting my personal life. When I finally stopped kidding myself that Betty and I were ever going to reconcile, something snapped inside Michele. Her face, wracked by disappointment and anger, is burned into my memory. The special relationship we had always enjoyed was over. Weeks later, after yet another night of Rapid City partying, Michele told me off, in the wonderfully direct manner of all children, explaining how much my boozing hurt her and Scott. Bursting into tears, she said she was ashamed and embarrassed and never wanted to see me drinking again. That cut me deeply.

Nonetheless, plans for the Geneva conference moved ahead, and I began to visit New York more frequently. One night Jimmy Durham and I met with a Soviet reporter at his apartment in the East Fifties. The feds were following us; looking out the window, we saw them fiddling with the reporter's car. He made a call, and some Soviets came down to remove the bugs. To celebrate, we got into a drinking contest—straight shots of vodka. When I left, the reporter asked to be excused because he didn't think he could make it to the front door. I passed out in the taxi. Jimmy and the driver had to carry me upstairs.

I gradually realized how much alcohol was affecting my work. In July 1977, Jimmy asked me to meet him in Geneva for some preliminary work on the September conference and to stop in London to talk with African journalists. My flight left from Washington, D.C. I flew there a day early and spent the evening in a saloon. When a white guy insulted an Indian woman, I got into a fight and tore a ligament in my knee. I ended up with my leg in a cast from crotch to toes. The next morning I flew off in a British Airways 747. Undeterred, I drank gin and played poker with a couple of Brits in the first-class lounge. I got drunk and lost about two hundred dollars. All I had left was a few coins and the phone number of the journalist I was to stay with. He was kind enough to come and get me.

He was the editor of *Africa*, then considered the *Time* magazine of Africa, and he lived in Mayfair, one of London's most exclusive neighborhoods. He took me to his favorite pub, where except for him and a few of his pals, I saw no blacks. When he threw a party, these blacks all brought blonde women. In their magazines, those same men wrote inflammatory articles about Africa's struggle against colonialism, but I could see they were sellouts. I was drinking, and when the conversation turned political, I condemned them for living in an expensive neighborhood, for hanging out with whites, and for consorting with white women. We nearly got into a fistfight. The next day I left for Geneva, but the editor refused to take me to the airport. I called Jimmy collect, and he wired me enough money to pay for a cab.

Everyone I met in Geneva treated me very well, including many wonderful white people from all over Europe. They were very critical of the United States, but comfortable about airing their views in front of me. I realized they didn't consider me an "American." I saw whites in a new light. I had never known any like these friendly, sophisticated people with their good senses of humor. They were interested in my views of the world, especially about the U.S. government. After meeting them, I made it my mission when talking with anyone not from my hemisphere to solicit their opinions about Americans. It was usually enlightening, but not so surprising to me now since the Vietnam War had only ended two years before.

When I returned to the States, I went to the sun dance at Green Grass, where my prayers were for the Geneva conference scheduled for September and, of course, for my people. Afterward, I returned to my summer lifestyle of dancing and partying. By then, I was aware that drinking had begun to cloud my judgment. For the first time, I was drinking on the reservation, even in my own community—I was still living with Dace at Wanbli. I had begun to have blackouts, hours that I couldn't remember afterward. During one of those episodes in late July, I got into a fight with my cousin Warren Means, a man I had held in awe and admiration since childhood. All I remember is regaining consciousness while on my way to borrow a shotgun to try to kill him. Once again, I began to think about quitting booze.

When I woke up at about noon on August 9, after having partied the weekend away during a sun dance, people were passed out all over our house. Ramone Bear Runner and I wanted to keep partying, so we got into his car and headed out. We stopped to see Ted. He had been sober since the previous New Year's Day. When he saw that I had been drinking, he was a little annoyed with me, so I stayed just long enough to thank him for his prayers. We went by the Longhorn in Scenic for a six-pack, then headed toward Rapid City looking for a party.

When we passed Peggy, driving her car, I signaled her to pull over. We talked on the roadside and I told her how much I loved her. I even proposed to her. She said, "I won't marry you as long as you drink." I thought, if Ted could quit drinking, so could I. I said, "Okay, I quit." I opened our remaining two cans of beer and poured their contents into the gutter. To my astonishment, Peggy believed me and agreed to marry me.

She was a woman who had faith in my word. I fell even more deeply in love with her on the spot.

Peggy and I were married in mid-August in the traditional manner by Rick Two Dogs, at his *inipi* in Porcupine. In September, I took Peggy and my daughter Sherry, who was about to enter the twelfth grade, to Geneva for the conference. Others in the AIM contingent included Clyde Bellecourt and Phillip Deere.

One of the first issues to be resolved was what we would call ourselves. The Canadians and the Six Nations people did not want to be known as Indians. The Canadians, who represented Indians and Inuits, preferred *natives*—the term the Canadian government uses. The original inhabitants of northern and western Alaska, the Yupik and Inupiat peoples, are commonly called Eskimos. They also refer to themselves as natives. The debate went on for two days. The Canadians were adamant, but AIM sided with the Central and South Americans, who preferred *Indians*.

The convincing argument came from a short, wiry Panamanian, a fiery speaker. Even those who spoke no Spanish could feel his energy. He said, "Columbus did not set out to find India but a country known to Europeans as Hindustan. Look at the maps he had in 1492 and it's obvious! He wrote of the people he encountered in the New World as *'una gente en dio,'* literally, 'a people in with God' . . . who were 'so peace-loving and generous as if to a fault. Therefore, they would make excellent slaves.' We were enslaved as 'Indians,' we'll gain our freedom as Indians, and then we can call ourselves any damn thing we please!" When he had finished, everyone agreed that all indigenous peoples of our hemisphere would be known as Indians until we could regain our freedom.

Later we met in the hotel basement to agree on an agenda for the opening meeting. In all North America, there are fewer than two million Indians, but there are more than one hundred million in South and Central America, which to us includes Mexico. Naturally, the South Americans wanted to speak first at the historic conference. The Central Americans argued that they should go first. They cited the depredations of Hernán Cortés, the murder of Montezuma. They mentioned their ancestors' rich body of astronomic knowledge, their advanced engineering principles demonstrated by the construction of pyramids, their understanding of mathematics that included use of the zero—and all the rest of their heritage.

The Six Nations delegates didn't see things that way. In the 1920s, the Six Nations had sent a delegate to the League of Nations in Geneva to ask for international recognition of their sovereignty. They have endured for more than eight centuries as their own league of nations; the U.S. Constitution was patterned after the code of their confederacy. They wanted to have the first speaker at our conference. It seemed to me and the other AIMsters that it was arrogant for any North American to want to go first, but we were an organization, not a nation, so we kept that to ourselves and didn't take sides. The discussion became very heated. Finally, Leon Shenandoah, dressed like the other "Sixers" in a traditional Iroquois outfit, issued a threat. If a Six Nations person wasn't the first speaker, they would all boycott the conference. After that was translated into Spanish for the Central and South Americans, the room fell silent. Anxiety and bad feelings seemed to ooze from the walls.

Phillip Deere hadn't said a thing during two hours of arguing and shouting. He got to his feet then and said, "Down home, whenever we're going to have a ceremony or a meeting, we light a fire. It's a sacred fire, and we have to light it in the traditional way. We gather a little brush and twigs and begin to strike the flints together. Sometimes the first spark lights the fire. Other times, it takes a lot of sparks. Finally one will catch and the fire will be lit. We've come here to light another kind of fire. There will be many sparks tomorrow, but we don't know which will ignite the flame."

He sat down, and we all looked at one another. When Phillip's words were translated, all of the Spanish speakers agreed that since the "Sixers" wanted the first spot so badly, their spokesperson, Oren Lyons, could go first. The Canadians would be next. I would speak sometime after the middle of the program. When it came time to select the last speaker, Phillip Deere, who had never asked for the honor, was the unanimous choice.

Clyde suggested that we start the conference with a bang. "We're not just going to wander into that hall," he said. "We're going to march on that building, all as one, singing our sacred songs. We're going up there proud of who we are." We started from across town, our elders leading the way— Phillip, carrying the pipe, Leon and Audrey Shenandoah from the Six Nations, David Monongye, a Hopi who had seen more than one hundred winters, and several elders from South and Central America. Right behind them came the drum. We sang the AIM song. As they always did, Indian people flocked to it, filled with pride and spirituality, infused with courage and the feeling of sovereignty, 120 marchers representing the aspirations of a hundred million oppressed but resolute souls.

Geneva has never seen anything like it, before or since. When we approached the Palace of Nations, every window was filled with people. Those who worked in nearby buildings deserted their offices and ran into the streets to see us. UN security people opened the double doors, and we marched up the stairs with the drum, singing all the way to a second-floor conference room where world leaders have met for more than a century. The world press—except for Western Hemisphere media, which boycotted the entire event—had never seen anything like us Indians, and they played it up.

Our conference lasted four days and was attended by representatives of more than 130 international organizations and nations, including about thirty-five member states of the UN General Assembly. The central issue, of course, was the land, and after that, the treaties, mostly in North America.

Beyond the fact that Indians from throughout the Americas got together to talk for the first time, the most significant achievement of our conference was recognition by the international community that from then on, we had to be dealt with. From that meeting came plans for a conference to include representatives of every indigenous people in the world, and out of that, the UN's Working Group on Indigenous Peoples was created. And all of that was the fruit of the first meeting of the International Indian Treaty Council at Mobridge, South Dakota, in 1974.

Our presence in Geneva was reported in front-page stories throughout Europe. Several governments clamored for our presence, and tours were arranged for the delegates to visit other countries. With my family, I took a few days to enjoy an abbreviated tour sponsored by the governments of Eastern European socialist nations, including official visits to Bulgaria, Hungary, and East Germany.

Before we left Geneva, concern was expressed about what might happen to the Indian delegates from Central and South America when they returned to their homes. There was a very real possibility that they or their families would be jailed, killed, or simply disappear, especially in Guatemala, Panama, Bolivia, and Colombia, where governments don't think twice about killing Indians. Delegates from nations that were UN members persuaded the General Assembly to pass a resolution in New York to monitor South and Central American delegates and their families for at least two years, so that if anything happened to them, the whole world would know.

As it turned out, only one Indian was sent to jail after the conference— me. I got word that because I had been present at the Sisseton civil-rights demonstration earlier in the year, Judge Richard Braithwaite had voided my bond. I had about fifteen days to report to the South Dakota State Penitentiary, at Sioux Falls, to begin serving my four-year sentence.

When I returned via New York, I flew straight to Sioux Falls. With my new wife, daughter, and lawyers, I went immediately to the South Dakota State Penitentiary on the bluffs overlooking the falls and the city named for them. Surrendering myself outside the massive brownstone walls, I was immediately handcuffed, then led inside to what guards call "orientation" and cons call the "fish tank"—a place to hold new prisoners until they adjust to confinement.

A Colombian Indian friend had promised in Geneva that if I went to prison, he would have all the missionaries in his homeland killed. I sent him no message about my imprisonment, so I suppose many a missionary down there in 1977 owes me his or her life. The morning after I went behind the walls, my lawyers got me back out on a writ of habeas corpus. I went to the federal court and appeared before Judge Nichol. The State of South Dakota argued that I had broken restrictions on my bond by participating in civil disobedience, but my lawyers pointed out that all I had done was attend a meeting with the Sisseton city fathers and law-enforcement officials. Nichol said, "What's wrong with that judge? You can't throw a man in prison for exercising his right of free speech. This is lunacy!" My bond was continued pending my appeal, and I returned to prison just long enough to collect a few belongings. Indian convicts—there are many in that pen—shouted as I was released, "Nobody can get Russell Means! You'll never get him in here! You'll never kill him!" They were still shouting when I drove away.

3 8
▼▼▼▼▼▼▼▼▼

The Longest Walk

D ennis Banks was still on the run. California Governor Jerry Brown had refused to honor an extradition request. He knew it would have amounted to a death sentence if Dennis went into a South Dakota prison, so he was free as long as he stayed in California. Nevertheless, he occasionally disguised himself to truck around the country for a while, including occasional excursions to Pine Ridge and Minnesota, before sneaking back into California. Dennis was chancellor of D-Q University near Davis, California, a Chicano and Indian school established by local Indians at an abandoned Nike missile site they had taken over. *D-Q* stands for Deganawidah, an honored Six Nations prophet, and Quetzalcoatl, the ancient Toltec deity.

In February 1978, Dennis started the Longest Walk, setting out on foot from Alcatraz with Lee Brightman. The purpose was to protest a new tide of anti-Indian legislation—an average of about thirty anti-Indian bills a year, many of them blatant attacks on our treaties and on issues of Indian sovereignty—that was being considered by Congress.

Chief among Brightman's concerns was an insidious new form of genocide—the forced sterilization of Indian women, which had become commonplace. By 1969, despite an infant-mortality rate worse than in any country in the Western Hemisphere—about one death for every three live births—

Indians had become the fastest-growing ethnic minority in America. That apparently was unacceptable to the U.S. government. If we didn't follow the buffalo into near extinction, it would be harder to seize the rest of our land. Between 1972 and 1976, the Indian Health Service sterilized 42 percent of all Indian women of childbearing age. The sterilization program affected practically every fertile Indian woman who walked or was carried into an IHS hospital. Pregnant women who came to deliver their babies were tricked or forced into signing release forms. When they came out of anesthesia, they had had tubal ligations. Even women who went in for appendectomies or sore throats were told that if they did not submit to sterilization, their chil dren would be taken away or their families would lose welfare benefits.

Nobody knew about the sterilization program until some strong-willed Indian women, led by Dr. Connie Uri, dug the facts out of the government's own reports. They tried to obtain publicity about it but got nowhere. They then asked Brightman and me to try for national exposure. I had many friends in the media, including the producer of a network news program, but even he couldn't get the story aired. We hoped the Longest Walk would get us on live television and radio, where we could disseminate the story to the American public.

The plan was to walk all the way across the country, picking up marchers along the way and finishing with a rally in Washington, D.C. The marchers went as far as they could each day, then were shuttled to a campsite to rest overnight. In the morning, they were driven back to where they had stopped the night before, and the walk continued. Although the walk generated a lot of initial fanfare, it faded off the national news radarscope once it reached Nevada. The walkers trudged on through Utah and Colorado. By the time they got to Kansas, things were falling apart. Fewer than forty people were still involved. Dennis called Minneapolis and asked for help. Clyde Bellecourt and my brother Bill went down with an AIM contingent and reorganized. They instilled discipline and, to the chagrin of some of Dennis' supporters, took over the money. They got cities to open parks for overnight camping and to contribute meals from food banks. They sent advance parties to round up donations, both cash and goods such as tennis shoes or gasoline for support vehicles. They got publicity by arranging for the walkers to be presented with keys to cities or by getting mayors to proclaim "Indian Day" or anything else that would get the community involved and attract the media. By the time it got to Kansas City, Missouri, the march was once again generating national publicity that attracted hundreds of walkers from everywhere in the country.

Since Clyde and Bill had turned things around and I was preoccupied with several projects around Pine Ridge, including treaty issues, I stayed away from the walk. Then the South Dakota Supreme Court ruled on my case, upholding the trial judge's decision. Suddenly the possibility of prison loomed again. I decided it was time to go on my first *umblecayapi*—crying for a vision. With Richard Moves Camp, a powerful young medicine man—Ellen's nephew—I built an altar of red cloth on Eagle Nest Butte, southwest of Wanbli on Pine Ridge. My son Scott came along to help with the ceremony. Richard selected a place for me among towering ponderosa pines on the west face of the butte. Nearby was an eagle's nest. For a time, I could see its occupants soaring above me in the distance. I was naked, because we seek to meet the Great Mystery just as we came into the world, covering ourselves at night only with a buffalo robe. I didn't have one, so I brought a star quilt, a light layer of filling in a coverlet with tiny diamond-shaped patches of cotton sewed into a star design. Scott and Richard left, and I began to pray in the bright sun.

Gradually, the sky filled with dark clouds, and sheets of water fell. Soon my quilt was sopping wet. Well after nightfall, the rain broke and I dozed off but was awakened by a shadow swooshing by my face, and then another—a pair of nighthawks buzzing the red altar cloth. It was a moonless night, and they came plummeting silently out of the darkness to dive-bomb the cloth at a point a few feet from where I sat. They went on for a long time, two tiny but fierce fliers, wings fluttering as they clawed and beaked the altar.

Then I heard an owl very close-by. Indigenous peoples in every corner of the world believe that the owl is a messenger of death. If one visits your home, it means someone close to you will die soon. That night, however, I got a different message. I felt the owl was trying to tell me it would make sure nothing would bother me.

Before dawn, I was awake to pray. It rained again, but by midmorning the sun reappeared and everything but my quilt was soon dry. I sat praying all day and on into the evening. Summer twilight often lingers until nearly ten in the northern Plains, and when darkness finally approached, I looked up. To the northwest, on the usual weather track for the Plains, was an enormous storm front, miles high and wide and tens of miles long. The cloud tops were gorgeous shades of pink from the last rays of the setting sun; the bottoms were dark and menacing. I was sure they held hail—one mean storm, heading right for me. Shivering and fed up with rain and cold, I spoke plainly to the thunder spirits. I said, "Give me a break here! Enough! I can't pray while I'm being pelted with hail and rain! Please—no more."

The air became very still. As the storm approached, I heard the distant rumbling of thunder and the crackle of lightning, saw the sudden flickering of bolts deep within the clouds. Around me, birds and insects sought cover and the butte grew silent. The wind that always announces such storms blew in my face, cold and strong. Dark and angry, as irresistible as anything in nature, the clouds bore down upon me.

I prayed harder.

Suddenly I could smell the storm on the breeze—the ozone, perhaps—

a special sweet taste. I knew that in half a minute or less I would be drenched. My prayers became almost frantic.

The wind shifted, then died.

Before my eyes, the entire mass of roiling clouds altered its course from south-southeast to due south, skirting the butte by perhaps a mile. As I prayed my thanks, the huge storm sailed majestically past me, drenching most of Pine Ridge, and then resumed its original course. As darkness fell, the air atop Eagle Nest Butte warmed and a canopy of stars appeared.

White men may scoff, but I know the thunder spirits heard my prayers and took pity on me. I *saw* what happened.

I spent the rest of the night in prayer. Every now and then, the owl issued a reminder that it was still watching. The nighthawks came again, dark shapes against the starlight, hurling themselves at my altar. When I prayed through the second dawn of my crying for a vision, it was plain to me that the owl and the nighthawk had joined me in a spiritual alliance. From that time on, their medicine has helped to safeguard me. Later, I would realize that thunder and lightning had also become my friends and protectors.

I was to report to Sioux Falls on July 27, 1978, to begin serving my four years. My options were accepting that sentence or petitioning a U.S. Supreme Court justice for a stay of execution of sentence. If I got one, I could then ask the full court to hear my case. If nothing else, that probably would delay my entry to prison for at least a year. Since I didn't know if that strategy would succeed, I made sure to get in another sun dance before going to prison, one that was run by my uncle and cousins, the Zephiers, on the Yankton Reservation.

Afterward, I got a call from the Reverend John Adams, who had been so helpful to us at Wounded Knee. He was with the United Methodist Church's national office in Washington. Adams said there was trouble on the Longest Walk and he needed help, especially since it was approaching D.C. and he had to devote his time to fund-raising for the walk. I agreed to come if I could bring Peggy and Sherry. Because I was going to Washington, I decided to try to get a petition for a stay of execution of sentence before Supreme Court Justice Thurgood Marshall.

I joined the Longest Walk in Pennsylvania. Among the celebrities who came to stroll at least a few miles were Muhammad Ali, accompanied by squadrons of media types, and an elderly bonze who was spiritual leader of Japan's Buddhists. The walk's leaders, who included people from Pine Ridge, said to me, "We need more publicity, and your name can generate it, so can we use you?"

"Of course," I said. "That's what AIM and I have always been about, and that's how Indian people should use AIM." Adams had lined up hotel rooms for us, but I preferred to stay with the walkers, now almost three thousand strong. I camped out with the Lakota people. In that way, I met people from all over the country. but the California bunch, Dennis's people, were resentful of what AIM and my brother Bill had accomplished, and an undercurrent of dissension ran through the walk.

I spent my evenings with the walkers, but drove into Washington almost every day to work on my Supreme Court case and to help Adams line up some events in the capital. One day in the United Methodist Church's offices, I got a call from Senator Jim Abourezk's assistant. She said, "It's an emergency—a confrontation between the Longest Walk and the Maryland National Guard." She came over and picked me up, and we drove out to learn what the problem was. As it happened, the guardsmen had come to set up a field kitchen and a mobile dispensary to feed the marchers and take care of minor medical problems such as blistered feet. The Californians and some others among the walkers had said, "Hell, no! We don't want the U.S. Army here!" When we had calmed everyone down, Clyde stood up and said, "Five years ago, when I was inside Wounded Knee, if anybody had told me that the U.S. Army would want to feed me and all my people for free—and put up a hospital tent for us—I'd have called them stark, raving mad. I'm not going to pass this up! We're going to let them put up their tents, and we're going to eat their food. Think about it." That was the end of the rebellion.

When the media blitz began, I appeared on ABC's *Good Morning, America*, where I finally got the sterilization story out, as well as on NBC's *Today*, the *CBS Morning News*, several local television talk shows, and in D.C. papers. After those shows aired, some of the walkers, especially those who had trekked all the way from California, demanded a secret meeting with me. I took John Thomas along to watch my back. Those guys were pissed off because I was in the news. They said I didn't deserve the attention because I hadn't been on the walk from the beginning. I guess they had been putting one foot in front of the other for so long that they had forgotten why they had come— to focus national publicity on Indian causes. They were so consumed by petty jealousies that they had lost sight of the message we were trying to get out.

An Indian man who had helped found D-Q University made a big speech about how disappointed he was in me. He said I had the potential to be a great leader, but I had to watch my ego. Other Californians jumped on John Thomas with accusations that he had ripped off the money, and with it was eating in good restaurants and staying in a fancy motel. It was all a sick fantasy. John lived no better than anyone else on the walk. I noticed one big, well-built guy who looked as though he had just gotten out of prison, with tattoos covering his arms and neck. He paced back and forth, occasionally shouting, "It's a good day to die!"

John and I each had a piece tucked into our boot, but we said nothing. As the torrent of abuse went on, we just stood, eyeing each other and the seething mass of hysteria. Finally it was quiet, except for the guy who kept saying, "It's a good day to die!" I wanted to tell them that I had joined the walk only as a favor to Adams and had allowed my name and image to be used only to help our struggle. I wanted to say that I was a few days from going to prison for the crime of standing up for my people. I knew John was close to taking out his piece and giving Mr. Tattoo an opportunity to find out if it were indeed a good day to die, but I was so disgusted with those shortsighted, ego-consumed guys that I could barely speak. I said, "Are you all through now? Why don't you get the entire leadership in here and ask *them* why I'm the one on the news. Do that. Ask them."

Then we left. They never said another word to me, but they left a lasting impression. It was a sad day when I realized that despite all AIM had achieved, many Indians still didn't recognize the enemy. Instead, they were so twisted by a bitter legacy of colonialism that they would fight their brothers and sisters for a few moments on the white man's television, for the mention of their names in the white man's newspaper, for a few crumbs of what they imagined was dignity. I decided right then not to petition for a stay of execution of sentence. It was a very long shot, anyway, and I was tired of messing with guys such as the Californians.

That decision left me only a few days of freedom. When the walk reached D.C. on July 17, Marlon Brando joined those at the head of the procession, thus ensuring more media coverage. I knew every hang-around-the-fort Indian in the world would crawl out of his hole to march alongside Brando for a share of the glory, and I didn't want to be with those sellouts. I didn't join the march.

So many people were trying to get into D.C. to support us that the Beltway became a vast parking lot. At least eighty thousand marchers—the biggest crowd since the Poor People's March, and far more than an Equal Rights Amendment demonstration the previous week—entered Washington through the black ghetto, stopping at Malcolm X Park. With Sherry and Peggy, I waited at the Washington Monument and watched the walkers arrive. The scene was awesome. When everyone had gathered around the monument, there were a couple of speeches and an announcement that we would reassemble and march on Capitol Hill the next day to show our displeasure to Congress.

When we convened in the morning to march to Capitol Hill, Senator Edward Kennedy showed up uninvited. By then, America had become aware of his sponsorship of Senate Bill 1, an omnibus crime bill which included unconscionable mandatory sentences and other provisions that robbed people of their rights under the Fourth, Fifth, and Sixth Amendments. Although white people would suffer under the bill, I was most concerned because it sought to increase the provisions of the Indian Major Crimes Act from fourteen felonies to about twenty-six. Among the proposed provisions were sentences of as much as ten years in federal prison for such infractions as breaking a window or spitting on a government building. The bill would have stripped Indians of protection against illegal search and seizure, the right to an attorney while being questioned at length, and the loss of other civil liberties.

Kennedy mingled with the walk's leaders, but also with all the D.C. bureaucrat Indians in the top layer, who make very good livings exploiting the misery of their own people. Traditional Indians don't believe in voting in the white man's world, but nearly all the sellouts were Democrats brainwashed into believing that the Kennedy family was God's gift to the Indians. When Kennedy mounted the steps to deliver a speech about how his crime bill would do wonders for everyone and how we should support it, nearly everybody paid attention. Even AIM's lawyers, reclining on the grass, lay back on their elbows to listen. I had read the bill, however, and knew what it really meant, so I ran up to Clyde and said, "We've got to do something!" He handed me his bullhorn. "You do it," he said. I didn't want to be out front, so I ran over to some skins, including my brother Bill. None would confront Kennedy. When I went to our lawyers, they said, "It's an Indian thing. You guys have got to do it." I was surprised to hear that, but of course they were right. It was up to Indians to stand up for their own rights.

I took Clyde's bullhorn, and when the senator finished speaking, I said, "Wait a minute! Not only is your bill bad for white people, it's ten times worse for Indians." As I went down the list of reasons, Kennedy grabbed the bullhorn and interrupted. He lost all control. His necktie got too tight, his face swelled up, and he turned purple—he looked as if he were choking. I just let him sputter.

The next day, Senator Jim Abourezk's staff and the Indian lawyers arranged to get together with Kennedy's people and talk about the crime bill. That was the first Indian input. The proposed legislation had been written by Kennedy's staff, so he didn't even know what provisions in it pertained to Indians. We had appointed Larry Leventhal to head our team, but when Kennedy sent word that he refused to attend the meeting unless I did, I went along. I was flattered, but as soon as we both showed up and agreed that our lawyers and his would hassle things out, Kennedy and I left. The omnibus crime bill never got through Congress, but since then, a steady stream of more narrow bills have been enacted. Today, most of the key provisions of Kennedy's original bill have become law. The major exceptions are the revisions to the Indian Major Crimes Act, which have not changed much since 1978. Strangely, there is now far more crime everywhere in America except Indian reservations.

When President Jimmy Carter agreed to meet with people from the Walk, each group chose representatives, mostly elders. When the one hundred or so Lakota met, several elders were chosen, but only one person was selected unanimously, and I felt deeply honored. As with Wounded Knee, when I was sent to meet with White House officials, it was a humbling experience to be chosen by my people. There is no way I can ever repay what I owe them, because everything I am or want to be is because of them. Of course I declined the honor. After all, the job of the President of the United States is to oppress me, my children, and my people. Meeting somebody like that is an insult to my ancestors' integrity. When the delegation, minus me, went to the White House to demand that Congress and the government end their policy of terrorizing Indians and destroying our heritage, Carter and Vice President Walter Mondale were kept waiting for more than an hour—not intentionally, but because we live on Indian time. To the white man, we're always late, but to us, as a free people, there *is* no time. Things take as long as they take, and therefore we're never in a hurry.

When we announced that we would be filing a $300 million damage suit on behalf of Indian women who had been tricked or coerced into sterilization by the IHS, Senator Abourezk forced the government into a moratorium on that program. Two years later, however, the genocide resumed with a new name—"family planning." Although it consumes more reams of paper and includes a supposedly mandatory waiting period, the government is still stealthily sterilizing Indian women.

The week after the Longest Walk concluded in the spring of 1978, the U.S. House of Representatives passed a resolution saying that national policy was to protect the rights of Indians "to believe, express and exercise their traditional religions, including but not limited to access to sites, use and possession of sacred objects, and the freedom to worship through ceremonials and traditional rites." Naturally, it was a nonbinding resolution that changed nothing, but it allowed white politicians to claim they had voted to support Indians' rights. Nothing changes in that town—it's still a brick wall.

39

▼▼▼▼▼▼▼▼▼

Prison

I've experienced everything white "civilization" offers—jails and skid-row gutters, nightclubs and penthouses, airplanes, cars and trains, schools and universities—and there is nothing about the white man or his society that intimidates me. His clubs and guns and dogs and threats don't scare me. I've faced them all. His religion doesn't frighten me. I don't fear his god any more than I dread the Great Mystery. In 1978, the only thing I hadn't experienced was prison—but many people better than me had already gone there, so I never even considered going underground or into exile.

As soon as I went behind the walls, Sid Strange, my lawyer, requested another writ of habeas corpus from Judge Alfred Nichol. In his oral argument, Strange said the few Indians convicted for their roles in the Sioux Falls courthouse police riot were the only ones ever convicted under that South Dakota statute, and therefore it was arbitrary and malicious prosecution. Nichol denied the writ, then lectured from the bench. He said that had I raised this issue to the South Dakota courts, "my decision probably would have gone the other way." I wanted to hit Sid upside the head. The son of a bitch! He's a lawyer—he should have known that was what he was supposed to do! Two years later, the South Dakota legislature repealed the law I had been convicted of breaking, but refused to apply the change retroactively.

I entered prison at a time when an Irish patriot named Bobby Sands had starved himself to death in Belfast's notorious Long Kesh Prison to protest England's colonization of Northern Ireland. I felt the same kind of love for my own land and people. When I went to prison, I made up my mind to show my people exactly how I felt by beginning a spiritual fast that could end with my death.

My incarceration was big news around the Great Plains. The whites finally had gotten me. Like all prison newcomers, I was allowed out of my cell only for meals. I lay on my bunk in a cell six feet by eight, feeling the thick walls around me. I was in "Granite City"—the South Dakota State Penitentiary. I wasn't going to go over those walls, under them, through them. The only way out, I knew, was to walk through the same door I had come in. As I lay there, I acknowledged the walls and their power. I thought, since I'm imprisoned, I'm going to act as if I'm in prison. I won't do anything that will offend anyone. I'm going to do my time and not complain.

The Indian inmates treated me like a Mafia don. A steady stream of trusties came by my cell, each bringing me gifts. Where men are locked behind bars and denied all contact with women, there is little available to them that they consider more precious than such magazines as *Playboy*, *Hustler*, and *Penthouse*. The Indian residents of that penitentiary honored me with many pristine copies of the latest issues of those and other magazines. I also received cigarettes, which are like currency behind the walls. They arrived like offerings by the handful, by the pack, by the carton. Other trusties smuggled cookies and candy into my cell. I knew they were giving me what they valued most, and it made me feel indebted and very humble.

When I entered the dining hall for the first time, I saw Dicky Marshall, who was serving life for having killed Martin Montileaux, sharing a corner table with three other Indians. He had one of them leave and invited me to join him. I didn't eat, but spent a few minutes catching up with Dicky. After the first ten days, I was assigned to a permanent cell, the last on Cellblock D, the fifth and topmost tier. It was in a corner, with a walkway on two sides used only by guards and trusty messengers. I thought it was the ideal place, the farthest from everything else in the joint.

At the next meal, I went to my regular seat. When the hall was full, I stood up. "I'd like to have your attention," I said. "My name is Russell Means, I'm an Oglala Lakota patriot and a leader of the American Indian Movement. I'm in here for riot to obstruct justice. AIM has a lot of lawyers and we're willing to work with any and all of you about prisoners' rights." As soon as I opened my mouth, doors clanged shut to seal off the room. The guards scrambled into gas masks and broke out shotguns. I kept talking. I said, "That's what AIM is here for, and we're going to shake up this—"

I was interrupted by a standing ovation. The entire prison population cheered and clapped. When I sat down, a guard wrote me up for "inciting to riot." When I went to the kangaroo court that purports to dispense justice to inmates, a prison official said, "What do you have to say for yourself?" I said, "Even though we're paying our debts to society, we still have First Amendment rights. What I said in there was that I'm willing, through AIM, to help anyone who needs a lawyer to pursue a case involving prisoners' rights. If you want to deny any of us, including those in AIM, the right to legal counsel, then I'm guilty." They let me off with a warning never to do that kind of thing again.

A few days later, South Dakota Governor Harvey Wollman came to see me. Governor Richard Kneip had just resigned to become U.S. ambassador to Singapore, and Wollman had become governor. Ignoring what anyone else might think, he came just to meet me and shake my hand. He said, "I admire you and I'm proud of what you stand for—except I don't like your methods." Ah yes, my methods—I had heard that before. I guess that meant he was against self-defense.

In acknowledging the prison walls, I had also determined that I would be courteous to the guards. So, "Yes, sir," "No, sir," "Please," "Thank you," "Excuse me," "You're welcome," and all the other polite phrases were in constant use whenever I spoke. That astonished the guards, who represent the bottom 7 percent of the human race, people with little intelligence who make their living using force and fear to warehouse human beings and violence to purvey a point of view. The screws must have thought that an AIM leader demonized by the media as a tough, militant diehard would act in prison like a juvenile delinquent, pouting and throwing tantrums. When I presented myself as a polite and considerate person, it blew them away. They went on their best behavior and began to call me "Mr. Means" instead of "Hey, Means." Soon those guards, so eager for the slightest excuse to bash a prisoner's head open or throw him into solitary, lost their fear of me. Many came to the walkway outside my cell to ask questions about AIM and why I had done—or hadn't done—things they had read about in a newspaper. They wanted the truth, and I told it.

I put in for a job as the chaplain's runner, as messengers are called. The chaplain had an opening for only half a day, so I worked mornings. We got along very well. He never asked me to carry a message or fetch something from another part of the prison. I think he respected me and didn't want to demean me with petty errands among the general population, but he had no qualms about keeping his afternoon runner hopping around Granite City. I wouldn't have minded roaming around, but I admired him for not making me a messenger boy. Instead, although he occasionally asked me to do some typing, I mostly used his typewriter for my own correspondence.

Following my dad's advice, I sought to turn a bad thing into a good thing by learning what made the white man tick. I spent most afternoons in the prison law library reading, mostly about criminal, Indian, and prisoners' rights cases. I also read Kim Il Sung's book on revolution. It had been smuggled in long before and stashed among the statutes; someone told me where to find it. When I decided to study the Eurocentric male's worldview, friends outside sent me books by European philosophers. I read Engels, Marx, Descartes, Locke, Rousseau, Plato, and Aristotle—not everything, of course, but enough. Only Aristotle had a clue about liberty, but look how far back that was! Rousseau had some worthwhile views, but that was because of what he had learned from Indians about individual freedom through representative government. I found it amazing. After reading those alleged philosophers who knew nothing about human liberation, I made up my mind that I was no longer a militant but a born-again "primitive." I would rely on the wisdom of my ancestors.

Among the other prisoners were many AIMsters, including Kenny Kane, who was serving time for having violated his parole during the Mission Golf Club incident. He served nearly five years—about four of them in solitary confinement because he wouldn't take shit from anyone, especially guards. He wasn't allowed reading material in solitary, so he passed the time taking care of his hair by biting off the split ends one by one. Each time he got out of the hole, he would do something to get written up. Then back he would go. Maybe he shouldn't have done some of the things he did, but he was determined to show that he couldn't be broken. Another AIM brother who was constantly in solitary was Vincent Bad Heart Bull, serving seven years for burglary. It was his brother Wesley who had been stabbed to death by Darld Schmitz. Because of Vincent's name, the guards picked on him and wrote him up for the slightest infraction. He, too, never broke.

The warden was Herman Solem, a retired Air Force lieutenant colonel. The cons called him "Herm the Sperm." We had some good talks and eventually developed a grudging respect for each other. When I arrived, he let the press in to talk to me because he knew they would interview him too. He was no fame-seeking fool. The prison needed certain things, and he used his time on the tube to lobby for them.

The biggest story in Granite City, of course, was my fast. Herm became far less cooperative with the media after word got out that I wasn't eating. Once I began to look gaunt, he wouldn't let me be interviewed anymore. I imagine he was under pressure from his superiors in Pierre. Whatever the reason, he did what he could to foster the impression that I was eating secretly. He had some reporters interview Major Rist, head of the guard force, who said, "We can't say for sure that he's eating, but we see him in the mess hall and we see him go into the commissary." Of course I was in those places—I was fasting, but that didn't mean I didn't use soap, shaving cream, toothpaste, and other essentials, or that I had given up my opportunity for mess-hall camaraderie.

By suggesting that I wasn't fasting, Herm created a "controversy" that helped me get even more publicity. The prison doctor, who knew that I had suffered from a bleeding ulcer since my trial in Sioux Falls, began calling me in daily to check my urine, because starvation first affects the liver and bowels. That was fine with me. I had been a hustler for so long that I knew how to manipulate the system; so to relieve the boredom and break up the routine, every morning I told the doctor that my hemorrhoids were bothering me. They weren't, but once I said that, I got to soak every day in a hot tub for about an hour, relaxing and reading before I went to "work" in the chaplain's office and then to the law library. All that time, of course, prison authorities were trying to find a way to make me eat. They got a few people to try to start conversations with me about eating, but it was no use.

Even during my fast, my mother never visited. She said she didn't want to see me in prison. Ted and Bill came once each. Peggy was there every two weeks, braving blizzards or ice storms or tornadoes to drive clear across the state. Sometimes she brought my kids, especially Scott. When I needed someone at the worst time in my life, Peggy was there. I'll always love her for that.

Eventually, starvation began to take a toll on my strength. I could no longer make it around the ball field during exercise period. I had to stop halfway. Then, walking up and down five tiers to my cell got to be a mighty labor. I had to rest several times en route. Finally, when I could barely stand, a prison doctor ordered me into a Sioux Falls hospital.

Almost immediately, Herm came to see me. He pulled a chair next to my bed and in a low voice said, "We know how weak you are. We know you're not foolish enough to try to make a break. That's why we trust you and we're going to leave your room unguarded. If anybody wants to visit you, it's up to the hospital to grant permission." I just looked at him, thinking, yeah, right—the state's most hated Indian, a maximum-security prisoner, and they're not going to watch me? I'm sure the place was crawling with plainclothes cops. If I had tried to walk out, they would have shot me. It was so obviously a setup that I lost all respect for Herm. At about one in the morning, he was back to say, "Well, the press got wind that I'd left you unguarded, so we had to put men around the hospital."

Right!

What I didn't know when I started my fast was that in the United States, unlike England, prison authorities, and therefore the state, are responsible for the well-being of prisoners in their charge. Families of injured prisoners can sue for damages. The next morning, the thirty-fifth day of my water-only fast, court was convened by telephone. South Dakota Circuit Judge Wayne Christensen, attending a conference in Spearfish, a resort town northwest of Rapid City, got on a conference call with state Attorney General Mark Meirhenry and me. Mark said he wanted to have me force-fed. I said, "No way!" The judge asked, "What will you do if I order them to feed you?"

If they were going to strap me down and jam tubes into me, I would have been too weak to resist physically. I could have argued that the First Amendment, which guarantees freedom of religion, gave me the right to a spiritual fast, but judging by Christensen's tone of voice, I didn't think he cared about anything I told him. I said, "I'll follow the court's ruling." The next day, he ruled that I was to be force-fed if necessary. Nurses gave me my first nourishment intravenously.

Soon after that, I was astonished by a visitor. The man whom I had publicly called George "Custer" McGovern came in and chatted with me. The senator gave me a copy of his memoirs, *Grass Roots*. When he autographed it, he wrote, "To a man I do not understand, and probably never will." I loved him for being honest. That remains one of my favorite inscriptions. Although I was impressed with McGovern and came to admire him, I'll never forgive him for his actions during Wounded Knee, when he encouraged the feds to wipe us out.

When McGovern left, the press came in. They could see then that authorities had lied about my fast, and that rumors planted by the sellouts and others who had condemned me as a fake were lies. I had lost almost seventy pounds—I was down to 135—and looked as if I were straight from a Nazi concentration camp. Doctors told the media I had come dangerously close to damaging my liver. My fast actually cured my bleeding ulcer—it just disappeared. After I recovered my strength, I began a program of jogging and running, a regimen that continues to this day. Before that, I had thought regular exercise was silly and that youth lasted forever.

About two weeks after I had begun to eat again, AIM planned a two-day rally for Dicky and me outside the prison walls. On the morning of that day, I walked, with a Sisseton Sioux named Sidney Kitto, into the yard for morning exercise. Something was strange. There were no guards in sight. I don't remember another time when that had happened.

Suddenly a kid came running up with a big pipe wrench and whacked the back of Kitto's head. As Kitto doubled over in pain, I turned around to watch the kid run away. When I turned back again, there was a guy I had never seen before. He stabbed me just below my left nipple with a shank—a made-in-prison knife. I said, "You motherfucker!" and he came at me again. I tried to kick him in the balls, but I missed. A skin named Rich—a weight lifter who worked in the kitchen—was on the mess-hall loading dock. Before I could be stabbed again, Rich grabbed a garbage can and bounced it off my assailant, yelling for him to drop the shank. The man with the shank snarled, "You fucking snitch," then turned and ran.

I chased him back around the kitchen and into the cellblock. A wall of guards standing almost shoulder to shoulder parted to admit him, then closed ranks. When not one guard tried to disarm him, I shouted, "What are you doing? Why are you protecting that punk?"

"We're not protecting anyone!" said a supervisor.

"Bullshit!" I said as skins came running from everywhere. The man who had attacked me held his shank until Vincent Bad Heart Bull broke through the line of guards to kick him in the face and then in the groin. Guards surged forward. In the heartbeat before the brawl blossomed into a full-scale riot, Dicky jumped in front, yelling, "Wait! Stop! It's a setup!"

He was so obviously right that we stopped. Somebody with a lot of power in that prison was willing to risk the lives of many guards to stop me. Those skins were really pissed—I've never seen them like that before or since. If Dicky hadn't saved the day, we would have seized that prison and done serious damage, and probably killed several of the most notorious racists and sadists among the guards.

Instead, we dispersed peacefully. I was sewed up and brought back shirtless to meet the press. Although the blade had penetrated deeply, it was deflected by a rib and once again had missed my vital organs. I met then with Marlon Brando, Harry Belafonte, and Bill Kunstler, who had flown in for the planned rally. I felt very honored, and surprised that Harry was there. During the Wounded Knee trial, I had embarrassed myself by getting drunk in his New York apartment and being disrespectful to him, so he had plenty of reason to ignore me. That is not Harry's way, however. The rally lasted two days. Accompanied by the media, Brando, Clyde Bellecourt, and Kunstler were allowed into the prison to speak to Indian prisoners.

A Sioux Falls grand jury investigated the incident. I was subpoenaed to testify, and said all I knew was that I had turned around and been stabbed. The assailant, a man named Schillinger, also testified, along with several others. An all-white grand jury decided that I was at fault—in effect, that my chest had attacked his knife. Bad Heart Bull was sent to solitary for having thumped Schillinger. In contrast, although he admitted to having a deadly weapon, my attacker wasn't even punished. He was transferred from maximum-security Sioux Falls to Oxford, a medium-security federal pen in Wisconsin. The man who had attacked Kitto, Schillinger's constant companion, became a trusty and was moved to a cottage outside the walls.

After the rally, Milo Goings, the AIMster who had been wounded in the knee at Wounded Knee, assigned himself as my bodyguard. In the ensuing week, I learned quite a bit about the pig who had stabbed me. He belonged to the Aryan Brotherhood, a white-supremacist prison group, and a few years earlier had allegedly knifed other inmates in other federal prisons. The most curious thing about Schillinger was that he was a federal prisoner serving time in a state prison. He wasn't the only such in Granite City. The United States reimburses the states for those convicted of federal offenses who request transfers to be close to their families. Schillinger, however, had never been in South Dakota before and had no kin there. There was no legitimate reason for his transfer to Sioux Falls just before I began to serve my time. Although he was a recent arrival who had killed or injured three other dark-skinned prisoners, authorities immediately made him a trusty. It seems that with Schillinger's history, there could have been only one reason for him to be in the South Dakota State Penitentiary—to kill me. If he had succeeded, I'm sure he would have been freed or otherwise rewarded.

Indians constituted a third of the prison population, but with a few exceptions, they behaved like a beaten people, oppressed by inmates and warders. Even before ending my fast, I worked to form an AIM chapter in the prison. There were other behind-the-walls groups such as the all-white Granite City Jaycees, with officers, bylaws, and monthly meetings with refreshments and speakers from outside. Every morning, AIM held a meeting in the yard, and almost 90 percent of the Indian inmates attended. Many white bikers, attracted by AIM's views on individual liberty, also joined us. I gave speeches about freedom and independence and what I had learned in the law library about prisoners' rights. We petitioned for recognition as an official group, but of course the warden refused.

The most effective civil-rights action in prison is a meal boycott, because it's dramatic and it costs the state money for spoilage and garbage. The bosses start to listen when you refuse to eat in their mess hall. AIM organized two such food strikes. The first made the media sit up and pay attention to what was going on behind the walls. When we planned a second one, we invited the Jaycees to join us. Their president lived two cells from me. He said, "We ain't joining." When I told the AIM guys, they said, "Let's play football." At that time in that prison, major disagreements between groups of inmates were settled by playing flag football. Shanks, shivs, and other weapons weren't allowed on the field, but even so, our brand of ball was about ten times as violent as an NFL game. Players wore no padding but were allowed to use teeth, fingernails, elbows, knees, feet—any part of the body. The team that was still standing at the end of the game won the debate. The Jaycees were in charge of recreation equipment—basketballs, volleyballs, golf clubs, barbells, whatever. Milo and I walked up to their rec shack and I said, "Tomorrow night, the field, football, AIM against the Jaycees. Got that?" They nodded their heads. Once the challenge was made, it's either ball play or knife play. That evening as I stood in the shower line, the Jaycee president slipped in behind me and said, "Russ, we're going to join your boycott."

Between AIM meetings and boycotts, Herm knew what I was doing behind the walls. I think it worried him. After three months in prison with an impeccable disciplinary record, I was eligible for trusty. I went before a board and gave them my yes-sir, no-sir, thank-you-sir routine. After stalling for a week, they notified me that I would become a trusty. Then I put in for a transfer to the trusty cottage, outside the walls.

Trusties get a few hours of unsupervised release every month. At first I got four hours, then eight, and finally twelve hours a month, the maximum. I could go downtown and do nearly anything I wanted as long as I was back for the evening count. When I was made a trusty, I applied for work release. Some white community activists volunteered to find me a job, but no business in Sioux Falls would take me. The activists got in touch with Jim Abourezk, who had a local office, and he hired me. I was the only convict ever to work for a U.S. senator while doing time. Prison officials were really pissed. They had been sure I would never get a job. My wages, $3.54 an hour, were paid directly to the prison to offset the cost of my incarceration.

At work, I studied everything in the office files about Indian water rights. Soon I knew about nearly everything of consequence in that field that had happened within the United States. That knowledge would be useful to me during the years in trying to understand incidents that had occurred on Indian reservations. In that way, prison became a kind of graduate school for me. In a manner of speaking, I got my Ph.D. in white studies. My job ended in January 1979, when Jim decided not to run for reelection.

While looking for another job, I heard from Wayne Duchaneaux, a young man I had met at the Green Grass sun dance a few years earlier. His brother ran the Rapid City Indian Service Council, a social-service center based in the Mother Butler Catholic mission. He hired me, and I got a room in the Alcoholics Anonymous halfway house, located in the same building that had housed the old Butler Center five years earlier. I was back where AIM had planned its protests and demonstrations before Wounded Knee.

Living there, I had to go to an AA meeting every Wednesday night. It always started with people introducing themselves—"I'm Michael and I'm an alcoholic." Despite years of binge drinking and the blackouts and lapses in judgment I had suffered before I quit drinking, I didn't consider myself or most Indian people of my generation to be alcoholics. I still feel that with some exceptions, most of us have drinking problems only because of what the white man has done to our lives. Whenever I had to introduce myself at AA meetings, I always said, "My name is Russell Means. I'm a *convict*."

Rapid City didn't have many good restaurants, but I made it a point to visit as many as I could and to make sure I was seen by the rednecks. I knew it would ruin their meal. Sure enough, every time I was seen enjoying myself, the place would be full of people mumbling and grumbling, "That goddamn guy's supposed to be in prison! What's this world coming to?" They gulped down their food or left it uneaten. I'm sure some people wrote to complain about me. I loved it that my movements were reported in the press, often in breathless front-page stories that mentioned where I had been sighted and what I was doing.

I was the Indian Service Council's second-in-command, and we were doing a good job in the community; I could see things slowly improving. But I had been working in Rapid City for only about two or three weeks when Duchaneaux didn't show up at the council office. All that week, he didn't come to work. To this day, I don't know where he went or why. He just vanished without a word of explanation. One morning as I got ready for work, prison guards came and said, "You've got to go back."

I said, "Wait a minute while I call the warden." On the phone, Herm said, "I'm sorry, I can't let you stay there. You've got no supervision."

I replied that the board of directors supervised me. "No," he said, "got to have it on the job."

I said, "You can tell everyone in America how successful your work-release program is. You put Russell Means out on a job and in weeks he shot right to the top. That's successful work release."

"Nice try, Russell," said Herm. "Get your ass back to Sioux Falls."

I returned to that damn cottage. It had rooms instead of cells, so living there was better than being inside the walls, but it was still an impersonal institution with a long list of arbitrary rules to deny personal freedom. One of the things I've noticed among white people is that the ultrarich and the ultrapoor have similar lifestyles. If you dress them alike and don't allow them to speak—their diction is noticeably different—they would get along perfectly, because both are trashy. Rich whites are brought up with nannies and governesses and servants, so they never have to take care of themselves. Poor whites in that cottage lived just that way. Their rooms looked as if they had been bombed. I was infuriated to learn that they smoked in the shower and threw cigarette butts in the drain and in toilet bowls. When I bathed in the trusty cottage and guys came in with cigarettes dangling from their lips, I made them leave.

"When you're around me, here's what you've got to do. Smoke out there, finish your cigarette, put the damn thing out in an ashtray, and *then* take your shower," I told them. It pissed them off, but I didn't care.

Once I understood that the opposite extremes of white society are really one and the same, I was no longer astonished by a U.S. space program that leaves trash on the moon and everywhere else it goes—or by strip-mining, clear-cutting of timber, and everything the industrial society does to despoil our Grandmother, the earth.

The next guy who hired me was the president of the local NAACP chapter, a black man who owned a small business. I became his marketing director, and did so well for him that he gave me 10 percent of the business. We called a big press conference to announce it. I loved shoving that down the throats of South Dakota rednecks. When I heard that South Dakota's judges were having a convention in Sioux Falls's most prestigious hotel, the downtown Holiday Inn, my boss and I made sure we got a good table there. When Attorney General Meirhenry and all those judges broke for their noon meal, they entered the restaurant to see a black man and me dining in style. That room was pretty quiet for a while. When Herm heard about it, he called and said, "Russ, lay off. Give us a break." It got so that he hated seeing or hearing my name in the media because the story usually mentioned him, too.

At one of my prison press conferences, I said, "It's time for the cowboys and Indians to get together." Not long after that, Ken Tilsen's son Mark and some other guys came to visit me at the wholesaler's. They told me they wanted to unite the white ranchers and Indian peoples of the Great Plains to fight the multinational corporations who planned to strip-mine in the Black Hills. Among others, Union Carbide and Kerr-McGee, which became notorious through the Silkwood case, had located deposits of gold, taconite iron ore, and high-grade uranium. I was honored that they had come all the way to Sioux Falls to share their plans. Although the alliance couldn't be my first priority until I was out of prison and had rebuilt AIM, I thought it was a good idea. Soon after that, Mark, Bruce Ellison, my sister Madonna, and several white ranchers formed the Black Hills Alliance.

I wrote a proposal, and through contacts with national church groups, my boss/partner got a grant—several thousand dollars—to expand the business. He promptly emptied the till and left town. His creditors were left holding empty bags, and I was out of a job again.

My colleagues in the trusty cottage included a black man who had worked during his sentence with a white inmate to invent a pick-proof lock. When the white guy got out of prison, he gave his partner all rights to the invention. I became friends with the black guy—I've forgotten his name. We agreed that after our releases, we would go into business together to manufacture locks. About two weeks before his scheduled release date, a white biker reported him for taking some extra bread from the mess hall. The black guy couldn't ignore that. The inflexible macho code of the streets and jails demanded that he nail that biker for snitching on him. I was there when it happened. The biker was sitting in an easy chair when my friend, cursing him as a snitch, poked about fifteen holes in him. The biker didn't die, but the black guy had to go back behind the walls for a few more years. We still planned to go into business together, but I couldn't until he got out of prison.

My last work-release job was for Legal Aid. After a few days in that office, I was eligible for parole. When I went before the parole board, it could have set me free that very day or forced me to wait up to 120 days. The board members made me wait, no doubt hoping I would get into some kind of trouble so they could keep me longer. When I was finally released in August 1979, I had served a year, three days, and 22.5 hours.

Most cons leaving prison give away their possessions. I kept only a few clothes and some treasured gifts, including a leather briefcase and belt that Dicky Marshall had made for me. My last stop in Granite City was to clear my personal account with Major Rist. Before turning over my money, he insisted on deducting twenty dollars for the denim coat I was wearing, a gift from an inmate who had altered it into a stylish, beaded, waist-length jacket. I stacked my things on the sidewalk. Then Peggy came with my kids. After we had kissed a while, I was so excited that I jumped behind the wheel of her car and took off with them, leaving all my stuff on the sidewalk. Until officials mailed it to me, I didn't even miss it, because I was a free man.

Part IV
▼▼▼▼▼▼▼▼

REBIRTH

1978–1992

▼▼▼▼▼▼▼▼

40
▼▼▼▼▼▼▼▼

Black Hills Alliance

I returned to Pine Ridge to find AIM in disarray and everything I valued in peril. Al Trimble had lost his bid for reelection as tribal president the preceding February. Funding promptly dried up for most of the programs he had launched. The reservation became chaotic as unemployment rose again to more than 85 percent and the only source of income was government handouts and make-work programs. In my absence, nearly every incident of alcohol-related lawlessness had been blamed on AIM. As far as most people were concerned, we flattened tires and busted windows, shot up houses, ripped off old people, beat up men and women. So the moment I got home, I called an AIM meeting. I said, "We're going to clean ourselves up—no more drinking." Everybody agreed, including my brothers and all the hard-core AIMsters with whom I had partied for so many years. I knew some would probably slide inevitably into marijuana, so we emphasized alcohol— that's where all the trouble comes from.

With funding from some churches, we caravanned around the Dakotas to put out word about the new AIM. I had to go to New York for some International Indian Treaty Council business, so midway through the reservation tour, I turned the caravan over to my brother Bill. When I returned a few weeks later, AIM's image had been magically cleansed. People were no longer claiming that AIMsters raised hell. Since Pine Ridge was still plagued by gunfights, vandalism, and thuggery, that told me the earlier accusations against AIM had been baseless.

I wanted to bring employment opportunities to my people, so I pressed ahead with my plan to build a factory in Kyle to manufacture pick-proof padlocks. Initially, I planned to employ sixteen people. With a clever name for the locks, I was hopeful that I could market them in the United States and overseas, especially in Europe, where I felt a lot of people would buy a good Indian-made product. I had a long-range business plan. After five years of building the product and the company, I would sell out to Yale Locks and retire. For help in getting started, I contacted South Dakota State University, an institute in Butte, Montana, and an alternative-energy center in Washington state. All were initially very receptive to my plans, and I had no trouble finding investors to pledge start-up capital.

There was, however, one wrinkle. I insisted on tapping the geothermal water under Pine Ridge, to heat the factory building and to confirm the Lakota right to that resource. My work in Senator Jim Abourezk's office had taught me that under the law, claiming title in perpetuity required nothing more than drilling a hole in the ground, then using the warm water for anything—even heating an outhouse. But as soon as I mentioned geothermal rights, all the goodwill shown by my supporters dried up and my investors pulled back. It seemed as if nobody wanted Indian people to claim their rights. The factory plan fizzled.

By that time, the traditional elders of the Pine Ridge Treaty Council and the Landowner's Association, who had kept everything together for seven decades, were almost all gone. The few still alive were mostly ill or enfeebled. The next generation, men and women in their fifties and sixties, were a different breed, having been raised in boarding schools and taught to hate themselves and their culture. The council and the association splintered into factions that could accomplish nothing.

That left AIM as the only effective organization on Pine Ridge. As we reorganized, people from all over the reservation came to our Wednesday-night meetings in Porcupine. Many Lakota men, jealous of our accomplishments, didn't want to be identified with AIM. It takes discipline and courage to be in the American Indian Movement. You must love your people and believe in who you are. We're subjected to name-calling by our own people, by white racists, by the press, by government, by the police. Remaining in AIM requires faith and commitment.

As we refashioned AIM into an organization that would bring a better quality of life to our people, we pursued new ventures. My brother Ted and his wife, Lorelei, backed by AIM, founded a health center in Porcupine—the first such facility in Indian country with no connection to the Indian Health Service. My personal contribution was to get a shovel and help dig the foundation. The center has prospered even to this day, largely through the love, dedication, and perseverance of Ted and Lorelei. Dace became assistant director of the Crisis Center, an independent facility in Pine Ridge village run by AIM's Roberta Arkeketa, which provided help or referrals for every kind of crisis imaginable. The center was always busy.

Mark Tilsen came to see me with a couple of guys who said they would help AIM build a radio station. Dave Little, who had lost the use of an arm in Vietnam, got started on the project. I thought up the call letters—KILI, which in Lakota slang means strong or tough or cool or boss or bad. To get money to build the station, I wrote the first grant proposal, which then was funded by the Corporation for Public Broadcasting. We couldn't afford a lightning rod, so when KILI went on the air, we held a ceremony and put an eagle feather on top of the antenna. Because we get so many thunderstorms on Pine Ridge, white people just shook their heads, but that tower has yet to be struck by lightning. KILI Radio, a station with repeaters on other reservations to beam its signal all over the Plains, remains one of my proudest achievements.

In 1979 revolution came to Iran. Because of our Geneva conference and our friendly ties to the Palestine Liberation Organization, AIM had some credibility in that part of the world. Like the PLO, we are vitally interested in regaining our country and our sovereignty. John Thomas, known as John T., a witty, lovable guy who gets along with everybody, served as our roving ambassador, visiting Lebanon, Iran, and Egypt. When the Revolutionary Guards took as hostages everyone in the U.S. embassy in Tehran, we sent John T. there to see what he could do. We didn't trust the phones—I'm sure the CIA and the Iranians listened to every call—so he flew back to New York to confer with Bill and me. John T. had incredible news. "They'll allow the hostages to send letters and packages home through us," he said. "But we must deliver each one ourselves—we can't just drop them in a mailbox."

We went again to the Reverend John Adams for funding. Adams, the miracle worker, *borrowed* money for us from individual churches. Later, he had to raise funds from wealthy Christians to repay them. He went with John T. to Tehran. Since he was white and it wasn't safe for him to be on the street, he stayed in a hotel room while John T. called and made contacts. They returned to JFK Airport with two duffel bags full of letters from the hostages to their families. From the start, the hostages were daily front-page news in every U.S. newspaper. Each network aired four or five hostage stories a week, and ABC even created a special late-night news program to update and explore that ongoing story—"Nightline." Legions of men and women from dozens of nations had offered to bring letters from the hostages, but the Iranians allowed only us Indians to carry them. Expecting a lot of media attention, we called a press conference in an airport VIP room.

Except for a reporter from one rinky-dink Brooklyn radio station, nobody showed up. Carl Stokes, who'd been mayor of Cleveland when I ran the Indian Center there, was a WNBC-TV reporter. I called him and he sent a WNBC film crew to follow John T. and Adams as they delivered hostage mail in Manhattan, Brooklyn, and Queens. Then other local stations and newspapers jumped on the story. The networks ignored us. We contacted them all, as well as *Time* and *Newsweek*, calling each several times. I'm sure the State Department, which has less clout at the local level, must have pressed the national media to spike the story because it was bad PR to call attention to the government's inability to deal with the crisis.

Adams was able to raise enough money for us to charter private planes to deliver the mail nationwide. He got some United Methodist people and some Indian people, and we spread out around the country. Adams and AIM received stacks of heartrending thank-you letters from relatives of hostages. We filled four huge duffel bags with letters and gifts and delivered them to the hostages in Tehran. When Adams and John T. returned from Iran with another load of hostage mail, absolutely no one covered the story—so we just delivered it and didn't even try for media attention.

My sister Madonna had helped found Women of All Red Nations (WARN), which conducted a thorough scientific study of Pine Ridge water and found uranium and other toxic contamination in every community. The worst area was around Oglala, in the western end of the reservation. It was an important discovery, but instead of announcing it immediately, WARN continued to gather supporting data for months. In the autumn of 1980, WARN held a press conference to announce the findings and to ask the tribal council to deal with this problem. As newspapers reported, the feds repudiated the study and tried to make it seem as if WARN was lying or hadn't done a thorough job. That wasn't the case, but that's how the media played it.

That made me angry. I suggested that AIM take over the IHS hospital. A few other AIMsters said, "Let's demonstrate in front of it." Almost everyone else said they didn't want to do anything—this was WARN's thing. I said, "It's no longer only WARN's concern. They've done their study, and now it's being tossed into the dustbin of history. It will disappear forever unless we do something to call attention to it." When virtually every Dakota AIM leader nixed my plan, I took the hint and resigned. I wrote a letter explaining my reasons—my leadership had been questioned, so my credibility had suffered to the point that I felt I could no longer be effective. I gave a copy to the press. I was disappointed, but not heartbroken. The struggle would continue, and I would participate in it, but I would no longer have a home base and I wouldn't be calling any more meetings.

With diminished AIM responsibilities, I turned my attention to the Black Hills Alliance, which was doing well. Even Posse Comitatus, a white-supremacist group, was cooperating with the alliance. So were many white ranchers, an entire generation of feisty, independent-minded people who didn't want to see multinationals come in and pillage the Black Hills. I realized that all people of the land eventually find a common denominator in their love for their Grandmother, the earth. I loved shaking the callused hands of those old ranchers. We looked each other in the eye and knew that even if we weren't always in agreement, even if we didn't like each other, we respected each other. I knew those crusty old-timers believed in the U.S. Constitution, just as I do.

Still, many whites refused to join the alliance because they considered it too radical to associate with "Indian lovers." They formed their own groups and began to lobby the legislature in Pierre for more regulation. I don't believe in government overseeing anything; it can't even manage itself. At least we had gotten people to understand the problem and try to do something about it.

A year earlier, the alliance had networked with peace-movement activists—old hippies and Yippies throughout the United States—to sponsor a walk into the Black Hills. It was a success, so in 1980 they sponsored the International Gathering for Survival, an outdoor convention to discuss ways of protecting the earth from industrial and government rapists and exploiters. We met on a sheep ranch seven miles south of Rapid City. Thousands of people from all over the world attended, and there were many innovative alternative-energy exhibits. The gathering took place in lovely rolling pastures with the beautiful Black Hills as a backdrop. Anyone could feel the power of the thunder spirits who gather above the hills.

It was there that I gave my most famous speech,* "For America to live, Europe must die." I come from an oral society and am an extemporaneous speaker. That was my only speech written in advance. It has been fiercely praised, and talked about ever since. It became a chapter in Ward Churchill's book on Marxism and was reprinted in *Mother Jones* as the December 1980 cover story. The magazine described it as a "searing cry of protest against the desecration of American Indian lands, an affirmation of the native cultures whose survival is threatened, and—unexpectedly—a strong attack on the leftists of the world. . . ."

I said there is no difference between Europe's supposed intellectual development—the product of a few thousand years of genocidal, reactionary thinking—and the theories of Marx and Hegel and their fellow anarchists and leftists. They all sing the same old song. As far as their effects on indigenous people and our sacred Grandmother are concerned, both capitalism and Marxism worship "efficiency" and rationalism, and thus are dedicated to the death of spirituality. Because *being* is a spiritual proposition but *gaining* is a

*See Appendix.

material act, Eurocentric thinkers see, for example, not a lovely mountain lake to be enjoyed for the sense of beauty and wonder it evokes, but a resource to be developed into a product to be consumed or applied or exploited. When the mountain has been pulverized to gravel spread on roads and the lake has been turned into a cesspool of industrial contaminants, the Eurocentric thinker is happy just long enough to consider his quarterly profit statement— an abstraction. Reality—the lake and the mountain—and the joy of its existence are gone forever.

Half of all U.S. uranium reserves and a third of the West's coal, are under reservation land, I said. Pine Ridge, with enormous uranium deposits, had been designated as part of a "National Sacrifice Area." In other words, white men decided they needed cheap energy and nuclear bombs more than we Indians needed our homes. The most efficient way to extract and process ore is to dump the radioactive waste near the mine, making the region uninhabitable forever. Those who sought the uranium also wanted to pump out the water beneath our territory, thus ensuring that *no* living thing could survive on our land.

"We are resisting being turned into a National Sacrifice Area," I said. "We are resisting being turned into a national-sacrifice people. The costs of this industrial process are not acceptable to us. It's genocide to dig uranium here and drain the water table."

I concluded by explaining that despite five centuries of repression and genocide, the American Indian was still in touch with traditions and prophecies; that we learn from nature, from our elders, and from the spirit powers. As long as European thinkers continued to molest the earth, an environmental catastrophe was inevitable. When it was over, we Indians would still be here to inhabit our hemisphere, even if we were reduced to a few people living high in the Andes.

Mother Jones compared my remarks to Martin Luther King's "I have a dream!" speech and to Mario Savio's call for Berkeley students to bring the university's machinery to a halt. For several years, Julius Nyerere, of Tanzania, repeated my words all over Africa. My talk made national and international headlines. Except for noting the arrests of people suspected of smoking dope, however, the Rapid City media ignored not only my speech but the whole event, which included a concert that drew such noted singers as Bonnie Raitt and David Soul. The alliance did force the South Dakota legislature to place a moratorium on strip-mining in the Black Hills. Later, we chased out Union Carbide and Kerr-McGee and all the other corporate motherfuckers who literally and figuratively tried to rape our sacred Grandmother.

41

▼▼▼▼▼▼▼▼▼

Tatuye Topa Najinwin

While I was in prison, Peggy had moved from our house in Wanbli to a trailer in Kyle, near the center of Pine Ridge. I was so much in love with her and so grateful for her support during my imprisonment that when she said she was ready to start a family, I was eager. She's a spiritual person, very tradition-minded, and knew that the moon watches over women and controls their time of purification—what whites call the menstrual cycle. Hers coincides with the full moon; she is so attuned to the rhythms of the universe that she could feel when each egg was released inside her. We were able to determine the exact moment of conception.

In March 1980, it was time for our first child to be born. I had to borrow a car from a white woman, a teacher, to take Peggy a hundred miles to a Rapid City hospital. When my older children had been born, fathers weren't allowed to participate. They had to stay in the waiting room until the child was born, then settle for looking at it through a glass. This time, I shared the whole experience of birth with my wife. It was so phenomenal, such a miracle, that I thought, how could we ever break up? I told that to Peggy and we both believed it. The spirits first named our daughter Hé Ḣaka Luta, Red Elk Woman.

My daughter's birth began one cycle, just as another was ending.

For years, my mother had suffered from high blood pressure—or so she was told by the IHS doctors. Periodically, she was induced to enter the hospital for rest to bring it down. Although doctors tried many different drugs on her, they never tried to learn what caused her problem. Nothing, in fact, worked. Early in 1980, when I was in Cleveland for a speaking engagement, I got word that my mother, who had been visiting her brother in Tucson, was hospitalized and not expected to live. Just as Mom had refused to visit me in prison because she didn't want to see me caged, I wanted to remember her as she had been in my life. I didn't go to Tucson. When she died that night, I headed for Porcupine. I felt cold and empty.

In my culture, when someone close to you dies, you cut your hair. My brothers and I did it in the traditional way—with a knife. We gathered up Mother's possessions and, in the Lakota manner, burned her clothes, then gave away everything else except a few family pictures. We held a wake in Porcupine. Mom had asked to be buried in the front yard of Grandma Aggie's place in Greenwood, so we took her home and held a second wake in the tribal hall. I was amazed. Despite the fierce South Dakota winter, people came from Minnesota, Wisconsin, Nebraska, Kansas, and all over the country to show their respect. Her mourners included several important Indian educators whom I had not suspected she knew. One was Lionel Bordeaux, president of Sinte Gleska College, in Rosebud. He had started a movement to encourage Indians to establish colleges on their own reservations. My mother had fostered his early efforts.

When I got up at the wake to speak, I said, "While I was in prison, feeling very low, I wrote my mother a letter condemning her and blaming her for all my troubles. When I rose the next morning and reread it, I felt ashamed. I tore it up, then wrote another in which I thanked her for all the good things she had given me." When we went through her personal effects, I was surprised to learn that she had made photocopies of that letter and sent them to people she knew all over the country. I drew some comfort from the fact that she had gone to the spirit world knowing I appreciated her lifetime of sacrifice.

In our tradition, we bury the dead after four days of mourning. When the time came, a blizzard was howling across the prairie, so as quickly as decency allowed, we put Mother's casket in the ground and shoveled earth on it. Then everybody retreated to the shelter of cars. I remained, kneeling at the foot of the grave in the bitter cold with wind-driven snow stinging my face. Thinking I was alone, I finally let it all out, wailing and crying, tears freezing on my cheeks. When I got up and turned around, there was Joe Bat Richards, an AIM brother, waiting for me. It was a wonderful thing for him to do, and from that moment I've felt very close to him.

Of all her sons, Ted took our mother's death the hardest, so I asked him to keep her spirit. For us, hair holds memory. In our tradition, some of the loved one's hair is used to make what white men would call an altar—a special place of remembrance. The keeper of the spirit does not participate in social events for four seasons, and during that period of bereavement, stays at home, making offerings to the altar. The community also honors the person who has moved on to the spirit world, bringing remembrance gifts to put at the holy place. In that way, we keep our loved one's spirit within us. At the end of a year, we have a ceremony to observe the releasing of the spirit from the community to make its passage to the next world. We then have a give-away. We distribute all the gifts brought and buy even more to give away.

During the first part of 1980, while my mother's presence remained strong, we held a ceremony at the home of Rick Two Dogs, a medicine man. There my mother's spirit gave her name, Tatuye Topa Najinwin, to my infant daughter. It means "Woman Who Stands Strong in the Four Winds." That described my mother perfectly. As she turned out, it was also most appropriate for my daughter.

I continued to commune with the spirits as a frequent participant in Rick Two Dog's *yuwipi* ceremonies. At one of them, the spirits said a period of chaos and confusion was coming and the *Iktomi*—a being personified by the spider, who imparts wisdom through trickery—would soon return. Every indigenous people in the world has such a teacher to show them that life is tricky. The white man, unfortunately, thinks it is the devil and refuses to consider his wisdom.

Not long after that *yuwipi*, the *Iktomi* paid me a visit. About forty miles south of Rapid City, in the southeastern corner of the Black Hills, lies Wind Cave. Relying on our oral tradition, some Lakota elders say our ancestors first emerged from the underground world there to live on the earth. Late in the spring of 1980, I helped to organize a temporary return of my people to our Paha Sapa, and my brother Bill handled most of the negotiations with officials at Wind Cave National Park. Although we circulated posters throughout Indian country and made provision for hundreds of Indian people to attend, only about fifty or sixty Pine Ridge AIMsters came to camp out.

I hadn't yet been to the Black Hills to cry for a vision, so I decided to do it then. Rick Two Dogs put my son Scott, Kenny Kane, and me on the mountain above the cave. Scott pledged to stay two days and nights, and Kenny and I would stay four. Kenny came down the first night, but Scott fulfilled his vow. Naked and alone, with only a buffalo robe to sit on inside an altar bound with colored tobacco ties, I faced the east. While crying for a vision, we neither eat nor drink. Hunger never bothers me much, but by the time Scott left, I was mighty thirsty.

Sitting and praying, I noticed legions of crawling and flying insects. I saw a tremendous variety of flies—different kinds, sizes, and colors. I must have nodded off, because suddenly I was staring at the iridescent green head of a colossal fly. It was so big I felt as if I were in the first row of a movie theater, looking up at the screen. The fly said, "*I* am your medicine. From now on, flies will protect you." It added that since I had had my vision, I could go back down the mountain and break my fast.

Then I woke up. I was happy—only two days and I was finished! I cleaned the site, gathered up the robe—and suddenly stopped. I thought, wait a minute—that's too easy. And I thought some more. *I'm Russell Means, big-time tough guy—and I'm going to go down and tell my people that my medicine is the fly? The fly eats shit!* I said, no way. I put everything back and returned to my prayers. I knew the *Iktomi* had tried to trick and shame me. It was a close call. I still get the shudders when I think about it. If I had told everybody my medicine was the fly, it would be so to this day. All the traditional people would snicker whenever my name was mentioned.

As I stood praying on the fourth day, I looked abruptly to my left, to the north, to see a huge pronghorn antelope with a white rump. It was far larger than any antelope I had ever seen or heard about—at least the size of a mule deer. It ran away and vanished in the trees. I sat down, and as I meditated, my head drooped. Then I looked up again. To the northeast, a little more than a hundred yards away across the clearing, was a big old black buffalo bull, pawing the ground, snorting and staring at me through red-rimmed eyes. For the first time in my life, I was almost petrified. I grabbed my pipe from the robe by the altar and started to pray.

Within minutes, the bull calmed down and walked slowly to the west. I watched him for quite a while. Periodically, he stopped to gaze at me for what seemed like a long time, then resumed his progress down the slope and into the trees. I prayed a little more, then decided to check on the bull's progress. That side of the mountain, above the AIM camp, was very steep, so there was no way a buffalo could descend quickly. I moved to the edge of the cliff and peered down. The bull had disappeared! There was no way he could have gotten down the mountain that quickly. Although I saw people moving around in the camp below, none seemed to have noticed him. Later, when I asked, none said they had seen him.

Doubters and rationalists will say the huge antelope and the buffalo were figments of my imagination, that after nearly four days without food or water, I was hallucinating—or that they were mere passersby, dumb beasts with nothing on their minds. But I have no doubt they were real, and they were sent in answer to my prayers. By recognizing one another's spiritual powers, we were joined together. The antelope and the buffalo will be my medicine as long as I live in this world. In my prayers, I thanked the Great Mystery for sending them, and for helping me to recognize the *Iktomi*.

Yellow Thunder Camp

O n New Year's Eve, I attended another of Two Dogs's *yuwipis*. The spirits said that in the next year, 1981, something would have to be done about the Black Hills—and that we Lakota would have to do it. After that, during my daily exercise run, I added to my dawn thank-you prayers a request for some sign to guide me. What exactly did we have to do? Then one day I struck up a conversation with a white lawyer who worked for the Black Hills Alliance. I don't remember much about it except that he said, "There's no law against camping in the Black Hills." The proverbial lightbulb went on. Suddenly I knew what to do—just set up a camp and reclaim the Black Hills. Possession is nine-tenths of the white man's law.

I suddenly got very excited, and started to tell everybody I knew in Rapid City, Pine Ridge, and in AIM about this idea. I said we wouldn't have to worry about what Governor Bill Janklow might do; if we camped on federal land, it would be out of his hands. I explained, "We'll go in unarmed with the sacred pipe so everyone will know that we're peaceful," and other Indians would join us.

My ideas were met with great skepticism. Most Lakota people, having survived four years of Pine Ridge terror, did not want to risk their lives for the Black Hills, which seemed far from their homes. Even Rick Two Dogs counseled against going in. But my brother Bill and I were determined to tap the power of the sacred pipe. We would return with it to our holy land with whatever supporters we could muster.

I was still on parole and couldn't participate in anything that might involve lawbreaking, so Bill took over. Because four is our most sacred number—and Martin Luther King Jr., a champion of spirituality and nonviolence, had been assassinated on the fourth day of the fourth month—we chose the anniversary of his death, April 4, to return to the Black Hills. We made announcements on KILI Radio and put up posters around the reservation saying that in the morning, we would form a caravan to Victoria Lake, a few miles outside Rapid City. It is one of only two federally owned sites in the Black Hills with year-round water, a lake about the size of a beaver pond, surrounded by eight hundred acres of U.S. Forest Service land. Its adjacent parcels are owned by the state or by individuals.

Some fifty-one people, about half of them Indians, showed up for the caravan. The whites were led by a great guy, a peace-loving Quaker named Nick Meinhart. When they arrived at about 10:00 A.M., some friendly Forest Service rangers stopped by to advise them to get a fire permit. Bill immediately drove to their station and submitted the paperwork; once signed, it was good for six months. I bet the rangers who suggested it were fired or transferred to some remote corner of Alaska, because once we had that permit, we couldn't be forced to leave.

Meanwhile, I was driving around Rapid City with Peggy, periodically calling the Black Hills Alliance office to see if everything was peaceful in the hills. When I learned that there were no problems, I called my parole officer and asked to move to the campsite. He said, "Sure, as long as no laws have been broken." As I drove into the hills at about 4:00 P.M., I told Peggy, "We ought to name this place in honor of the Yellow Thunder family, because after Raymond Yellow Thunder was murdered in Gordon, the Lakota stood up as a people for the first time in this century."

Just as we arrived, it started to snow. Bill and the others came running to greet us and to say that they had set up an *inipi* lodge and held a purification ceremony, during which they had chosen a name for the site—Yellow Thunder Camp. It was an uncanny moment. My brother also mentioned that since that morning, the campers had experienced the gentle rain of spring, the baking heat of summer, the sleet of autumn, and now the wind and snow of winter—all four seasons in a single day. Everyone in camp was sure that was a sign that our return to our sacred Paha Sapa was a holy act.

It also proved to be the beginning of the finest and most important time of my life. I suddenly felt a sense of love for the land, and I lived there for the next two years, leaving only to conduct BHA or AIM or treaty council business. For more than eight consecutive months, I spent every night in camp, commuting daily to the BHA offices in Rapid City. We set up tents and a communal kitchen. After a few days, when they saw it was safe, Indian people started to trickle in. Some left after only a short while but others stayed for years, so it is hard to say exactly how many were in camp at any one time. This return to our holy land was major news, reported around the world. With visitors arriving from everywhere, we planned to make our settlement permanent, which meant defining its nature and purpose. After much talk, we decided that Yellow Thunder Camp would become a spiritual youth camp, a live-in school where orphans and so-called troublemakers could learn to live as free people. Instead of teachers and classrooms—a sixth-century Roman Catholic invention that rips people from their families and community to isolate them by age group and turn them into robots—we agreed that the whole community would participate in teaching. Our classroom would be the breast of our sacred Grandmother.

Some hippies from Washington state offered to make us canvas Lakota-style tipis with linings at cut-rate prices—they even sent them on credit. The problem was, we had no one who knew how to put them up. A bearded mountain man I knew was a tipi maker who, with his Japanese wife, lived year-round in one at eleven thousand feet in the Colorado Rockies. He donated a tipi in exchange for enough gasoline money to haul it to us. When he showed us how to erect it, we joked about our ancestors spinning in their graves at the notion of Indians having to learn from a white man how to put up their tipis.

Tipi is a Lakota word that means a safe, secure home. It represents a woman's womb; she comforts you, keeps you warm, and protects you from the dangers outside. The lodge poles represent men—look at how many it takes to support a woman in the right way! Those men come together at their apex and are joined to form an intricate circle. When they are tied together in unity, only the wind that travels in a circle can dislodge them. The door is round, low to the ground, and small. White anthros and histos have opined that that is to make it difficult for enemies to get in, but the real reason is that it symbolizes the entrance to a woman. The location also ensures that all who enter come in a humble way.

Other poles go up outside to what white men call flaps. Those represent the woman's arms. At night, they are crossed outside to let them enfold us, keeping us warm and comfortable. In the morning, we open her arms and the door at the bottom, and clean air comes in while old, stale air goes out— just like a woman in her time of purification. Thus a tipi-dwelling family gets an education about women and men standing in unity, a constant reminder to all about how to conduct themselves in life. All Indians dwellings face east, for spiritual reasons and out of common sense. Especially in summer, the heat of the day comes in the afternoon, when shade is at the front door.

As modern architects confirm, the tipi, by design, is the finest mobile home ever invented. Structurally, it is an inverted cone. When heat rises, it has no place to go except back down, so a tipi is easy to keep warm. The outer skin sits about two inches off the earth; the inside lining reaches to the ground. Air enters from the outside, serving as insulation as it is drawn up between lining and skin. It also carries smoke and stale air out the top. Moving the flaps controls the volume of air drawn in—they act like stove dampers.

We learned all that and more from a truly special man named Shorty Blacksmith. A smallish breed who suffered from a very bad self-image, like most skins of our generation, Shorty was dirt-poor and drank too much, but he had a wealth of information. His knowledge of the Lakota language alone ought to have brought him a doctorate in linguistics at any university. People in Yellow Thunder Camp listened to him. For one of the few times in his life, he became an important man, full of ancient stories and remembrances, but nevertheless cursing himself because he hadn't paid what he felt was enough attention to his elders when he was growing up. Compared with everyone else in camp, however, he was an inexhaustible fund of traditional wisdom.

Since we had no telephone in camp, people from the Black Hills Alliance came out on the morning of June 2 to tell me some bad news. A couple of days earlier, Father James O'Connor, a Jesuit at Saint Isaac Jogues in Rapid City, had died of a heart attack. His fellow priest, Father Richard Pates, had been shot in the buttocks by robbers who had made off with the priests' wallets and the parish television set. My nineteen-year-old son, Hank, and his pal Freeman Mesteth had just been arrested for the crimes.

By the time I had rushed into Rapid City, the press was hot on the story and the Black Hills Alliance phones were ringing off the hook. When I finally got to see Hank, he said he had confessed to police. He, Freeman, and Brian Phelps, Peggy's fifteen-year-old brother, after having drunk steadily for two days, had gone to the rectory to rob it. Brian, fortunately, had passed out in the backseat of the car and played no part in the incident. Freeman, who carried and used a .22 pistol, had confessed also.

Because the victim was a Catholic priest, I had a tough time finding anyone local to represent Hank. Although he was assigned a lawyer from the Public Defender's office, I called around the country to get help. Bill Kunstler volunteered his services pro bono, and the National Jury Project sent people from New York City to help during jury selection. As his confession detailed, Hank had been unarmed and so drunk that he had no clear idea what he was doing during the robbery—an obvious case of diminished capacity. At his arraignment, he pleaded not guilty.

By that time, Yellow Thunder Camp was a hot issue in the region, and anything connected to AIM was usually good for a few headlines. I knew that in such a superheated atmosphere my son would be the target of all the hatred the courts, prosecutors, media, and public had long hoarded for me.

That is exactly what happened. Of course Hank and Freeman deserved punishment; if someone dies during a robbery, it's a serious matter. Aside from a few juvenile arrests, however, it was Hank's first offense. Nevertheless, the media vilified my son. The state attorney's office, after threatening both young men with the death penalty, allowed each to plead guilty to a list of lesser charges—first-degree manslaughter, armed robbery, and two counts of aggravated assault. Before Hank was sentenced, Father Pates told the court that he had forgiven Hank for all that had happened, and hoped he would have the chance to change his life for the better.

I, too, forgave Hank. It's much harder to forgive myself for all the years I wasn't around for him, for the other years when I could find no way to show him how much I loved him, and for all the times when my drinking provided him with the wrong example to follow. When he went to prison, it felt like a piece of my heart had been chewed off. Judge Merton Tice Jr. slapped Hank and Freeman with maximum sentences that ran to three figures. Hank eventually made parole and straightened himself out, but Ken Tilsen is still trying to get Freeman out of Minnesota's Stillwater Prison, where he was transferred several years ago.

Despite the personal tragedy, I had made a commitment to Yellow Thunder Camp. I couldn't let Hank's troubles distract me. At a meeting with the Black Hills Alliance board of directors, those of us from the camp said, "Now that we've gotten a moratorium on strip-mining and chased out the big corporations, the ranchers have what they wanted. We feel the focal point of this organization, the priority for all funding, should now become Yellow Thunder Camp." In an insulting and condescending manner, the white directors replied, "Maybe we'll consider taking you on as a program."

I blew up. I said, "You think repossession of our holy land is a fucking *program*? You will *consider* it?" All the Indians returned to camp. The yearly election of the board was coming up, so my brother Bill said, "Let's organize ourselves as the Buffalo Party and go in there and take over." That's what we did. On election day, we left a couple of people to watch the camp while everyone else went down to vote all but one of the incumbents off the board. We reelected Marv Kammer, a white rancher who had supported us and Madonna's group, Women of All Red Nations. All four new board members were Indians.

When the new board began to reorganize the alliance office, the whites we had worked with for two years departed en masse. It really surprised me. I had learned another lesson in the white man's language to whites, *alliance* meant they would work with Indians when they were in control, but if we asserted any semblance of independence, there was no more cooperation. Looking back, I realized that in my language, *Black Hills Alliance* translates as "*Lakota Khe Sapa*," literally, a relationship, like the traditional Lakota Nation itself, of blood and common interests devoted to one issue—our sacred Black Hills. Our feeling was always that the organization was ultimately about Indian people returning to our holy land—a message that the whites had missed. Two days after the election, whites abandoned the alliance office. My priority was Yellow Thunder Camp, so we turned over day-to-day management of the alliance to an Ojibwa guy.

I spent much of the summer of 1981 raising money. Willie Nelson gave a benefit concert and also donated $10,000 from his own pocket. Because the International Treaty Council had worked with the Baath Socialist Party of Iraq, my brother and I knew a great guy, an Iraqi living in New Jersey. Through his efforts, the Baath donated $10,000 to Yellow Thunder Camp. With that, the concert money, and Nelson's donation, we bought a geodesic dome to use as our cookhouse and community meeting hall. A white architect from Boulder, Colorado, designed it for us. An older fellow named Vern agreed to build it. He was a gruff, bearded, hippielike engineer who had given up on white civilization to become a mountain-dwelling hermit and experiment with alternative-energy devices. At about that time, a team from the Farm, a Tennessee hippie commune established in the early 1960s, arrived to help us with communications. They put up a tower for a radio antenna, built a radio shack, and installed a two-way link with the alliance office.

I've never told anyone this, but when as a young man I learned that Crazy Horse had said he would return from the spirit world as thunder, I knew *I* was coming back as lightning. While I was part of Yellow Thunder Camp, lightning started to follow me around. The first time was at a treaty gathering. A storm began to build over the mountains during the meeting. As we left, we could see it coming, angry flashes muffled by black clouds— one hell of a hailstorm. As we drove away, we watched it roll through camp, and we barely made the ten miles to the blacktop before it hit us. Since that day, whenever I go someplace where a significant message is required, the thunder spirits deliver it. It's always good—the *wakinyan* are good spirits who brings the cleansing and refreshing rain.

My parole term ended in August and I was again a free man. As late summer gave way to fall and the dome rose amid the tipis in our leafy U-shaped valley, the camp was a peaceful, happy place. We built a solar-heated shower on the big rocks that had dammed the creek and created the lake. We started Lakota language lessons, and, with George Tall, I taught political classes under the trees or on the meadow. We were "cash poor," but there was always plenty to eat. Our goats gave milk and our chickens provided eggs. Our creek and pond offered excellent fishing, and our gardens produced so many vegetables that we began to sun-dry them for winter. George was a master hunter who stealthily staked out watering points and waited patiently with a .22 rifle. He never used more than one bullet to bring down a deer.

He and our other hunters were so successful that after a time many people, tired of venison, clamored for hamburgers.

That summer, I discovered an unhurried life that all indigenous people once shared. Without telephones or clocks, we learned that when you are free, there is no time. I sat endlessly among the trees, watching and contemplating, trying to understand the messages of life by observing it. I began to grasp the beauty and grace of being in the present, of living in harmony with everything in the natural world. The white man calls this the idyllic lifestyle of "primitives," but I discovered that I had enrolled in the university of the universe. Our relatives, the wild creatures who share this earth with us, never stop teaching if we are prepared to learn from them. At night, I watched the fireflies playing, rolling themselves into little balls of pulsing fire that cascaded down the mountainside, then exploding into a million tiny lights as the swarm dispersed.

In those early months before we kept dogs in camp, deer strolled among our tipis unafraid. Wild turkeys fluttered in to check us out, and raccoons boldly explored our dwellings. Even eagles swooped into the lower branches of trees to study us. I was amazed to find that our two-legged kin, the birds, would talk to me. That is true of all creatures, but birds, such as the hawks and owl that had visited during my vision quest, are the friendliest. If I sat quietly, they came, at first just to look me over. Soon they abruptly departed, returning to watch some more. Then they left again, only to come back a little later. Usually, on their third visit, I spoke to them and they answer.

When an Indian says that animals talk to him, he means it—but not in the sense of "Hey, Russ, what do you know?" Birds and insects and other animals speak in many ways. In nature, everything that lives communicates with everything else. Some make noises that tell others of their approach. Others use colors to announce who they are. At first, I didn't know those things. Through day after day of observation, I realized that the birds were going through a routine with me, giving me opportunities to respond. Once I began to communicate, I acknowledged them as they had acknowledged me, and I announced myself as they did. I became a mockingbird, mimicking their songs. After establishing communication, they began to show me things in various ways, but always simply so I could understand. They told me when the wind was about to rise or when the weather was ready to change, when someone or something was coming. They showed me easily overlooked miracles such as how to play and have fun with my own kind—how to enjoy life.

There among the birds and trees, it came to me that except for other people, the only living things that the white man takes the time to try to communicate with are his dog or cat. Unfortunately, he doesn't watch or listen to them. He never tries to draw understanding from them. True communication is an exchange of information, but the white man doesn't understand how to commune with nature.

As we went back to being full-time Indians at Yellow Thunder Camp, we taught ourselves the three Ls—listen, look, and learn. We realized that the three Rs of the white man's education have nothing to do with life. You can write the best book in creation or come up with elegant equations to solve some mathematical mystery, but that is mere knowledge. It doesn't teach you how to get along with anything or anyone. Indigenous people around the world teach only the three Ls. Instead of believing that the universe depends on what we think, we teach that we must use our hearts to achieve harmony with our fellow creatures.

The white man looks upon the world as being filled with predators and prey and thinks that is the reason for the colors and sounds peculiar to different animals. I once debated that in a Pierre saloon with a Methodist preacher, the father of David Soul. We got into a discussion about the character of a square foot of earth. Considering the variety of insects and microscopic life forms, he said, "It's a vicious world. It's all about death and violence." I said, "I look upon that same world as sharing and sacrificing. Some sacrifice that others may live. Watching the hunter and the hunted, you will discover that nature has a way of compensating those whose fate is to become food. At the moment when it's no longer possible for them to escape, they go into shock and no longer feel fear or pain." Since continuous sacrificing and sharing are the natural processes of life, all life is positive—insight learned by communicating with all our relatives in nature. At Yellow Thunder Camp I began to realize that there are two cultures on earth, one industrial and the other indigenous: One is about death, the other about life.

The wonder-filled quality of my life caused me to consider what Black Elk had said, that maybe one root of the sacred tree of life still lives, and if we nurture it, perhaps the tree will bloom again. As I recognized that Yellow Thunder Camp was that struggling root, I became more determined than ever to nurture it.

When we established Yellow Thunder Camp, we were often visited by rattlesnakes. Once, after returning from the alliance office in Rapid City, one of the younger men came running up to say he had found a rattlesnake by the cliff. I said, "What did you do with it?"

"I didn't kill it. I took it over the ridge and let it go."

"Don't do that anymore," I said. "*We* are the invaders. This is their home. Next time you see a rattlesnake, apologize to it, walk around it, leave it alone." We all started to do that, and soon the rattlesnakes left—not in twos and threes, but all at once. Little miracles like that happened all the time, glad reminders of why we had chosen to live there.

Peggy, however, was not as eager to settle in Yellow Thunder Camp. She had a teaching job on Pine Ridge that would have required a daily round-trip commute of about 250 miles. She could have quit her job, of course, but she preferred to live in Kyle and bring our daughter, Tatuye Topa Na-jinwin, to see me on weekends. As the months went by, I could feel Peggy pulling away from me. Our love, which had seemed invulnerable, began to disintegrate as she came to regard Yellow Thunder Camp as a rival for my affections. It was soon obvious that she saw my devotion to that holy land and my preference for traditional living as a threat to my commitment to her. She never liked living there, and complained that I neglected her and Tatuye. It made me very sad, because I had been down that path before. Twila had felt threatened by my involvement with the social scene at the Irish Pup, and Betty by my dedication to the Cleveland American Indian Center. I wished I had married a woman who truly loved whatever I did, who understood that although some men merely have jobs, I have a calling. Since I had joined AIM to serve my people, my work is much more than a vocation—it not only consumes my time and energy, it defines my identity.

Among the activist liberal causes of white America in the early 1980s, Yellow Thunder Camp became a cause célèbre that attracted all sorts of Indian and white visitors, especially Europeans. The whites ranged from hippies and well-meaning supporters to searchers and scholars. Some sought to view our culture without taking even a moment to learn what we are truly about. A visiting San Francisco anthropologist said, "I see you have division of labor by sex and age—and the entire camp is ruled by the male." When she started to go on, I told her, "You don't understand a thing. In four hours, you've determined what we are and how we are and why we are. Get the hell out of here." Once again, I was reminded why I can't stand anthros and archies and socios—they make snap judgments based on superficial observations.

We also had many Buddhist visitors. One Japanese monk came to live with us. He neither spoke nor understood English, and we never knew his name. He was always called "the Buddhist monk." We gave him a tiny, one-person house trailer down by the creek, the best accommodations we had, although I always felt that he really wanted to stay in a tipi. Like true Indians, Buddhists rise very early to pray with the morning star. As he climbed the hill each morning to pray, he banged a drum in rhythm with alternate steps. Without quite realizing it, all the Indian men got into a little contest with him. We would all try to be standing outside our tipis saying our prayers before we heard the first beat of his drum.

I pulled the early security shift, so my partner and I were always up before anyone else. I liked to stroll through the encampment. One morning as I went by the cookshack, I saw the monk in his saffron robe inside. A couple bags of rice and beans had broken open to spill on the dirt floor. As I watched, silent and invisible, the monk picked up one grain of rice at a time and dropped it into his little cup. Then he filled a second cup with spilled beans. I watched him do that four or five days in a row, each time taking from the floor just enough for his meal. It came to me that he was showing us how we ought to live as Indians, in a humble way without wasting anything. Embarrassed, I called the camp together, all but the monk. I told them that we should pick up the spilled food, each grain and each bean, to show respect for what Grandmother Earth has given us. I told them what I had seen the monk do, and the lesson I had taken from it.

Although we attracted legions of liberal supporters from around the world, the continued presence of eighty or so Indians living peacefully in the Black Hills also reawakened the frontier mentality and inflamed white racism. The *Rapid City Journal* quoted one elderly woman who warned that property values in the western half of the state had plummeted because the Indians were "restless." She also said her mother had come to South Dakota in a covered wagon and was attacked by Indians—and now she was in the same danger! Even after it became obvious that we had no intention of leaving our little camp, white people reacted as though the entire Sioux Nation, dispersed through five states and two Canadian provinces, was poised to attack.

Since the previous April, a few days after we set up camp, the Forest Service, which controls the issue of permits for use of public land in forests, had fought to drive us out of Yellow Thunder Camp. Equipped with enough rule books and regulations to choke a nation, the officials began to demand more and more paperwork before they would grant a renewal. After years of costly, taxpayer-supported public-relations campaigns, the average urban American views the Forest Service as an agency of conservationists and environmentalists. The truth is exactly the opposite. The Forest Service is probably the largest road-building corporation in America, and its primary concern is economic exploitation of taxpayer-owned lands for the benefit of a few large corporations. Whether the issue is water rights, endangered species, timber-cutting policies, or something else, it always advocates whatever enriches the loggers, paper companies, and mining corporations.

Once we understood that we were in a paper war, we went on the offensive. With Ward Churchill and a Boulder-based architect, we developed a proposal to establish Yellow Thunder Camp as a spiritual youth camp. Vine Deloria Jr. wrote the government in support of our proposal, calling it one of the finest ideas ever conceived for the use of public land in the Black Hills.

There was ample precedent for our kind of usage. Since the 1920s, Christian churches had maintained schools and camps in the Black Hills. There were Boy Scout camps in the national forest, as well as ski resorts, golf courses, and retreats for corporate executives. Every South Dakota college and university with a forestry program was using federal land. According to uncontroverted testimony in our subsequent federal lawsuit, every Indian application to the Forest Service to use Black Hills land had been turned down—and every non-Indian one approved. We really wanted to help our youths, so we decided to try the white man's paper route. The local rangers, who had welcomed us initially, recommended approval and sent it to Forest Supervisor James Mathers. He lived in Custer, which carefully nurtured the legacy of its namesake and hadn't forgotten or forgiven AIM's demonstrations at its courthouse. In contravention of Forest Service rules and congressional guidance, he arrogantly decided that our six-month fire permit would expire after five months. He told us that if we didn't leave by then, we would be removed. He said he would *consider* our proposal only after we had left.

That pleased Governor Bill Janklow, who told reporters, "It's about time the Forest Service showed some balls." He also told the press, "The Sioux are not going to invade our Black Hills and get away with it. If that was state land, I'd have them off of there in hours. I'd call in the National Guard."

I called a press conference at Yellow Thunder Camp, at which I challenged Janklow and Attorney General Mark Meirhenry personally to lead the force they wanted to eject us from our holy land. I would lead the defenders. I said, "Let's do this mano-a-mano. I'll take you both on—one at a time or together, however you want it, and if I win, we stay in the Black Hills. If you win, we'll leave." Janklow replied, "That kind of challenge does not deserve a response."

In August, we received an ultimatum—leave, or take our chances with the National Guard. We set up a system to monitor the guard's headquarters and its logistical center near the Sioux San, as Rapid City's IHS hospital is called. AIMsters from Pine Ridge came up to reinforce Yellow Thunder Camp, and we called a meeting to discuss our options. I went around the circle to ask each person what he or she felt we ought to do. Mark, a white ally, said, "We can't respond to violence with violence—we came up here because this is a spiritual camp." He went on with a long, rambling, circuitous talk about nonviolence being the way to go. I sat there thinking about what Malcolm X had said—"If you want us to be nonviolent, why do you kill us?" or words to that effect. One by one, the Indians spoke. They made no flowery speeches, but they all said, "Let's fight."

I spoke last, explaining to the white people that *we* were not the ones committing violence, but we believe in self-defense. This is our home, where our ancestors are buried. This is our future. This is our holy land, and we had had enough and were going to fight—again.

Preparing for an assault, we built a variety of booby traps. There was only one possible helicopter landing zone nearby. We planted tipi poles to slice off rotor blades. We prepared forest foot trails, fitting them with spikes in pits camouflaged by leaves and grass. Infantrymen would take many foot injuries on their way in. We had some good weapons and a lot of walkie-talkies. We knew the guardsmen could monitor our radios, so we made sure they knew they were dealing with veteran fighters. We wanted them to know that even if they wiped us out, they would pay a heavy price. We were prepared to fight to the death, so we sent our women and children and the pacifists out. Mark, the nonviolence advocate, stayed, to his credit.

Expecting an attack at night or at dawn, we sent patrols out after sundown. We anxiously awaited battle. Since we weren't burdened with women or children, we looked forward to luring the white soldiers into the forest for a running fight that would allow us to use our intimate knowledge of the terrain. The guardsmen never came. We had called Janklow's bluff. Instead of sending tanks, choppers, APCs, and troops, he sent a cop of some kind to the alliance office and served us with a federal lawsuit. I really had wanted to crack a few racist heads, so it was a disappointment, but we comforted ourselves with the thought that it was a spiritual victory.

43

▼▼▼▼▼▼▼▼

Catch The Bear

Our presence at Yellow Thunder Camp brought into focus the Fort Laramie Treaty of 1868, signed by Lieutenant General William Tecumseh Sherman on behalf of the United States and by the leaders of the Lakota and Cheyenne Nations for their people. It confirmed that my ancestors' territory extended from the north branch of the Platte River in present-day Nebraska, eastward through Iowa to the Missouri River, and north through the Dakotas, Wyoming, and Montana to Canada. In the center were the Black Hills. Our rights to the *Paha Sapa* were confirmed in a document written in English that clearly stated the treaty could be amended only by the vote of three-fourths of all adult male Lakota.

The United States desperately had sought that treaty after it had been defeated in battle after battle. Sadly, all that fighting would have been unnecessary if the United States had kept the terms of the 1851 Fort Laramie Treaty that granted a right-of-way through Indian country to the West Coast. When white soldiers began to establish forts along the Bozeman Trail to Montana's goldfields, my ancestors demanded that they be removed. Our people waited until 1866, when the Civil War had exhausted the white men economically, militarily, and spiritually. Then the Lakota defended their land, attacking the white armies and driving them away.

Just as we believed Nixon and his henchmen in the early 1970s, our ancestors had signed the treaty in 1868 believing the words of President Andrew Johnson and Generals Sherman, John B. Sanborn, William S. Harney, and Philip Sheridan, known for the statement, "The only good Indian is a dead Indian." Four years later, without Lakota permission, Sheridan sent George Armstrong Custer to seek gold in the Black Hills. My forefathers allowed him to meander unmolested through our holy land with a big expeditionary force. When Custer found what he was looking for, the Grant administration quickly leaked the news, and within months, our holy land was invaded by an army of miners and prospectors. Our people journeyed through our holy land, the *Khe Sapa*, and visited it for spiritual strength and renewal, but we had no permanent settlements there. Unlike the California goldfields, where miners butchered whatever Indians they encountered, there were no confrontations, no massacre of innocents. My people, however, warned U.S. military leaders and civilian agents that if the miners remained, we were going back to war, but they left those early fortune hunters alone. My ancestors believed that when the white leaders in Washington learned what was going on, they would behave like human beings, honoring their word by forcing the miners to leave.

Instead, in June 1876, Sheridan sent Custer and the Seventh Cavalry to solve the "Indian problem," in what would become one of the most famous Indian-white confrontations of the nineteenth century. Instead of encountering defenseless women and children—their usual victims—the marauders ran into adult males along the banks of the Greasy Grass. They paid a big price for that mistake. Embarrassed and humiliated, the United States began to look for other ways to repudiate the treaty. Whites couldn't get three-fourths of adult Lakota males to renounce the Fort Laramie Treaty, so they liquored up a few hang-around-the-forts—altogether, less than a ninth of the Lakota Nation—and, after many threats, got them to put their marks on an agreement they couldn't read. This new document surrendered the Black Hills to the U.S. government. The larceny was called the "1876 Agreement."

When the vast majority of my ancestors still refused to give up the *Paha Sapa*, the whites threatened to ship them to Indian Territory, in what is now Oklahoma. The Lakota replied, in effect, "We whipped you once, we'll whip you again—so come on." The U.S. officials said, in substance, "Sell us the Black Hills or starve." White agents refused to deliver treaty goods, including food and hunting ammunition. Still, our people refused to sell. The whites took our holy land anyway in 1876, murdering Crazy Horse the next year and Sitting Bull in 1890 and anyone else who seemed a possible threat to their lust for gold. Because of enforced starvation and dozens of other acts of genocide, my ancestors soon became too weak to resist militarily. White miners plundered the Black Hills of more than $1 billion in gold, and far more in other minerals, with no attempt at compensation.

In the 1930s, the government formed the Indian Claims Commission. The BIA told my grandfathers and grandmothers that attorney Ralph Case had been appointed to represent them. By 1957, Case had incompetently surrendered more than twenty-five million acres of our Powder River hunting grounds, and had waived claim to more than fifty-seven million dollars that the government said it had given the Lakota in goods and services to pay for the Black Hills. However, the white man's records show that the sum was not to buy what we would not sell; rather, it was reparation for years of treaty violations. Case was finally replaced in 1957, when lawyers from Strasser, Spiegelberg, Fried and Frank, a well-connected law firm which represented several other Indian nations, took over our claim in return for a third of the settlement. We never wanted money! We wanted our land. We wanted the U.S. government to keep its promise. Ignoring that, the white lawyers pursued, on the Sioux Nation's behalf, $17 million plus interest from 1868—a total of $105 million for our holy land.

Would anyone dare suggest that Muslims might take *money* in exchange for Mecca? Who is foolish enough to offer to buy Jerusalem from Israel? Which real estate developer would offer the pope a great deal for the Vatican? Yet in 1979, the Court of Indian Claims, which no longer exists, said it was ready to pay the Lakota for *our* holy land. The lawyers pocketed their ten million dollars and washed their hands of us. The entire Lakota Nation lives in four of the seven poorest counties in America; the most impoverished people in America are the Lakota of Pine Ridge. Yet we refused to accept payment for the Black Hills. With interest, the "settlement" is now worth well over $300 million, but still we refuse to take money that means nothing for a holy land that means everything.

For most of this century, such men as Fools Crow, Frank Kills The Enemy, and Weasel Bear dedicated their lives to the treaty councils. Carefully stored in their basements or in attic trunks are documents dating from the 1880s, before the allotment acts began to carve up what was left of our reservations. Dirt-poor, dismissed as ignorant, can't-even-speak-English "blanket asses" by many of their own people and especially by those who ran tribal councils on behalf of the BIA, those staunch Lakota people nevertheless continued to fight for our treaty. Until AIM came to Pine Ridge in 1970, nobody listened to them.

The primary goal of the American Indian Movement has always been to force the United States to live up to its own laws by meeting the obligations it took on when it signed our treaties. AIM failed to do that, but we did help restore respect to our traditional elders. After our many protest demonstrations, after Wounded Knee, after hundreds of AIMsters died or were imprisoned, people around the world began to invite Lakota elders to speak at universities. Many, such as Fools Crow and Matthew King, were interviewed for documentary films. The world wanted to hear the truth that only they could testify to from personal experience. By 1981, when we returned to the *Paha Sapa* to establish Yellow Thunder Camp, many of those old treaty defenders had gone on to the spirit world.

The few who remained—elderly medicine men living at Pine Ridge, Rosebud, and Standing Rock, men who possessed a mysterious communication system among themselves—often came to Yellow Thunder, arriving nearly simultaneously, to sit under the trees and revel in being in the Black Hills again. One thing that had always mystified me was their deep and abiding reverence for the *Khe Sapa*. After all, they rarely visited those hills except to pray at Bear Butte. To get there, they had to pass through the ugly sprawl of cheap tourist attractions that white men had erected along the roads leading to the abomination of Mount Rushmore. Then one day, sitting in Yellow Thunder Camp, I realized that after only a few days, the soil, the air, and the spirit of the holy land had become part of my body, and would be so forever. When I had to leave the Black Hills, my body cried out to return; each time I did, I felt instantly in harmony. That's what living in the *Khe Sapa* means to a Lakota.

Living peacefully and honorably in Yellow Thunder Camp, we worked hard to accommodate the Forest Service's ceaseless demands for paperwork, complying with myriad mindless rules and regulations and dealing with the lies and innuendoes published by white bureaucrats in the press. We hoped and believed that we could continue to *use*—not own—a mere eight hundred acres of our holy land unmolested. When in the summer of 1982 the Forest Service filed a lawsuit to eject us, we responded with our own suit filed by Bruce Ellison and Larry Leventhal. It said that since we had followed all their requirements in submitting our proposal, and since there were many precedents for using public land in the way we had requested, Forest Supervisor James Mathers had acted arbitrarily and had discriminated against Indians when he refused to allow us to have a spiritual youth camp.

Our suit also documented how in so doing, Mathers had violated Forest Service regulations and the American Indian Religious Freedom Act of 1978, which gave us the right to pray in our holy land. When that act had become law, Indians around the country had rejoiced. We thought it meant that no longer would we have to hide in remote reservation gullies to hold our sacred ceremonies, that we wouldn't have to mute our drums to avoid discovery by vigilantes, or beg permission from the Indian Health Service to hold a sun dance. The law was on our side, and we expected to win.

Soon after we filed, attorney Bruce Ellison had a conversation with the chief deputy U.S. marshal in Rapid City. He said that before the decision was made to avoid armed confrontation, the government had planned to deal "decisively" with Yellow Thunder Camp. "He told me this wasn't going to be any seventy-one-day Wounded Knee thing," Ellison said. "He said something like, 'This was going to be over in a half hour or forty-five minutes.' They had brought in the special operations group, and it would have been incredibly bloody."

At that time, all three federal judges in South Dakota owned land in the Black Hills, so each recused himself from our case. In November 1982, Donald E. O'Brien, a federal judge in Sioux City, Iowa, began hearing the case. In December, while Larry Leventhal and our other attorneys were due to present our evidence, the U.S. Marshal's Service refused to serve our witnesses with subpoenas or to pay token witness fees required by law. We were astounded. The marshals had performed those routine matters, ordered by Judge O'Brien, all during pretrial proceedings. Now, without offering any reason, they refused.

All nine judges of the Eighth Circuit Court of Appeals ordered the marshals to comply. In time, they did, but it was May 1985 before the trial reconvened in Deadwood, South Dakota. After hearing the evidence, O'Brien ruled in our favor. The Forest Service immediately appealed, and the reason for the strange actions of the Marshal's Service became clear. The government was trying to delay the trial. It had used the time well. In the three years since we filed our suit, Roger Wollman, brother of the governor and the same South Dakota Supreme Court justice who had denied habeas corpus to Dicky Marshall after his murder conviction, was appointed to the Eighth U.S. Circuit Court of Appeals. With two other Republican rednecks, he reviewed the appeal. Ignoring the facts, they ruled that any agency of the federal government has an arbitrary right to refuse to issue a permit to anyone. We appealed, first for a hearing by the entire nine-judge panel, and when that was refused, the U.S. Supreme Court.

While our case worked its way through the system, the Forest Service and white vigilantes continually harassed us. We were bound by a court order that said we could stay in the Black Hills but everything had to remain as it was until the appellate decision came down, so we couldn't improve or build anything. Early in our stay, we were bothered by white motorists who came roaring into the middle of camp on motorcycles, pickup trucks, or four-wheelers. Since we had small children roaming around, we had to put a stop to that. Before the court ruling, we built a gate, and that handled the problem.

It also created another. White racists couldn't stand the idea that Indians wanted a little privacy. Our camp was alongside a creek. To the northeast, a bluff ran along the stream. A Forest Service road followed the watercourse and made a right turn through ninety degrees before heading south to the dam. Most of the road was outside the eight hundred acres we used, but some, including an L-shaped area atop the bluff, was inside it. White motorists would stop there to call us "prairie niggers," among other names, and to yell such brilliant remarks as, "Fuck Yellow Thunder Camp! Fuck Crazy Horse! Fuck Sitting Bull!" Sometimes they fired guns at us, trying to terrorize the camp, but fortunately, no one was hit. We reported the shootings to the sheriff, but nothing was ever done. Eventually, it got so bad that we put a guy named Ron Two Bulls and a couple of other defenders on the ridge near the road for security.

Even before we finished building the geodesic dome that became the center of our community, we started a school. Many Indian parents from Rapid City jerked their kids out of white public schools and brought them to our camp. We covered the three Rs with a little classroom instruction and lectures, but mostly our students were outside, learning about their culture and traditions, usually in their own language. It wasn't quite total immersion, but almost. The kids loved it.

Not long after our January new-moon feast, the Forest Service said our horses were present illegally and we had to buy permits for them. We tried, but after a big runaround, the white officials said our camp wasn't established for horses, so they would have to go. One day when most of the men were away, the camp women saw Forest Service rangers steal our herd of saddle horses. We never got them back.

As cold settled over the Black Hills at the end of 1981, most of the white people who had been with us through summer and fall departed. Only about seventy people stayed in camp. That's when I realized why I had never read anything about how Indians lived in winter, about how my ancestors used those months to make moccasins and clothing and to observe spiritual rituals. Fearing the weather, the white archies and anthros who "studied" Indians left when it got cold. That is a clue to the mind-set of the Eurocentric male world—weather is always in the way of industrial societies. I remembered my childhood, when I loved playing football in the mud or swiping plums when I knew neighbors would never come out in the rain to chase me away. I also loved even the heat and dust of summers that seemed to last forever. In camp, we appreciated all kinds of weather. We welcomed the snow. Although most nights were well below freezing, we quickly acclimated. In fact, because our tipis were so efficient with heat and we had only pitch pine instead of slower-burning hardwoods, we were often *too* warm at night. In late winter, when it was 50 degrees at midday, we rolled up the tipi linings and sides, and many of us went around in T-shirts.

Traditionally, Indian people have believed that when any human being comes to visit, it's an opportunity to show hospitality and generosity, so we never turn anyone away. As we struggled against hatred and racism, Yellow Thunder Camp became a big hit internationally. That winter when more than one hundred thousand English people—mostly women—held a massive demonstration against the storing of U.S. nuclear weapons on their soil, some carried banners that said "Yellow Thunder Camp." When the snow thawed in the spring, many Europeans began to arrive, along with even more Indian people, including several who had found living in Rapid City a struggle. We became a huge extended family.

Every morning after the *inipi*, I joined the communal breakfast, where we always made offerings to the spirits. I dug a hole in the earth with a hunting knife, placed some food in it, and said a prayer. One morning, a German woman who had come a week earlier to help plant our gardens saw me doing that and went crazy. She screamed, "I can't take it! No more! I'm leaving!" The women tried to calm her down, but she yelled, "That macho pig—his knife represents his penis, and every morning he symbolically rapes Mother Earth, then kills her."

That was so silly that the Indian women laughed aloud. Some of the white women took her seriously, but men of every race, including me, were astonished beyond laughter. We couldn't believe she had thought that up without ever asking us about the ceremony. She got her backpack and left camp.

She was the only European nut who came to camp, but we had many such Americans. They included two men, one in his twenties and the other somewhat older, who came walking up wearing only boxer shorts with lipstick painting their faces and bodies. Tiny chicken feathers protruded from bandannas tied around their foreheads. As they approached our gate, both threw up their right hands and said, "How! We come in peace. Take us to your chief." Not knowing whether to laugh or cry, I yelled for everyone to come see the spectacle. These guys said, "We want to live with you. We want to live the Indian way." I stared at them and said, "You ain't staying here. Find out how to be a human being, then come back. Now get out of here."

Other new residents of camp included a skin who said he had broken his parole, and two others who said they were on the run from police. Following the principles of our culture, we couldn't turn them away. We felt that by letting them stay, our spirituality and dedication to ancestral ways might have a good effect on them. Instead, they were nothing more than dyed-in-the-wool crooks. They recruited a couple of misguided women from the camp and pulled a string of strong-arm robberies in Rapid City. When we finally heard what they were doing, I spoke with them and they agreed to leave. Within a few hours of their departure, however, one got into a shootout and killed a dope dealer. When he was arrested and authorities learned where he had been living, we got some bad press.

Another pair of newcomers said they had just been released from the federal penitentiary at Englewood, Colorado. One was Collins Catch The Bear, a Lakota of about twenty-one. The other was a black man several years older who called himself Wanbli No Heart and claimed to be part Lakota. There was something peculiar about No Heart. He seemed obsessed with security, and kept trying to get people to help him dig bunkers and foxholes. Whenever he left camp, he festooned his camouflage fatigues with big sheath knives and a belt ax. Most important, he would not or could not last through all four rounds of the *inipi*. In time, we learned that our purification lodge was a kind of character barometer. Anybody who couldn't complete the ritual was questionable politically and/or morally. The spirits exposed them; eventually they were revealed as snitches sent to infiltrate the camp.

A paralegal named Jan Hamil, who was working for Bruce Ellison on the Yellow Thunder case, was contacted by a man claiming to be in the Justice Department's Community Relations Service. He falsely told her that he was an old pal of Bruce's. The guy set up a clandestine meeting with Hamil, and Bruce went along. The fed said he had learned that vigilante landowners who lived nearby were planning a violent confrontation to force us to respond in kind so we would be blamed for the incident.

About three weeks later, I was in the Black Hills Alliance office when Rondi, a lovely young Norwegian woman who lived in camp, came to say that a man had been shot. I drove out, then ran up to the bluff overlooking camp. Catch The Bear, No Heart, and a couple of skins were standing around. On the ground, dressed in camouflage fatigues, was a big white guy in his late fifties, a gun nut named Clarence Tollefson. He liked to fish and hunt in the area, and when we arrived he felt we had invaded his territory. Everyone in camp had seen him on the ridge brandishing guns, threatening and cursing us. We had reported his license-plate number to the sheriff, but nothing came of it. Tollefson traveled in a four-wheel-drive pickup with a small arsenal, including a .357 Magnum pistol and a scoped, heavy-caliber rifle.

One glance, and I knew he was dead. Blood and gray brain matter had trickled out of a small hole in the back of his head. I sat down under a tree thinking, oh man, what now? I said a little prayer. Finally I said, "We're going with the truth. Somebody call the sheriff right now." While we waited, I listened to Catch The Bear tell what had happened: Tollefson had returned to the bluff and was sitting in his truck, haranguing the camp. On duty as security guards, Catch The Bear and No Heart went up and told him to leave. Strangely, No Heart picked a fight with Tollefson and punched him in the face a few times. The older man reached for a .357. As he started to point it toward No Heart, Catch The Bear shot him with a .22 rifle.

The only witnesses were No Heart and Catch The Bear. It seemed like an obvious case of self-defense, but as the truth emerged layer by layer, the situation became more complex. I told Catch The Bear that we would get him the best lawyers and he probably would get off—but after he was arrested, we learned that he hadn't completed his term at Englewood. Instead, he had been finishing his sentence in a Rapid City halfway house when No Heart, whom he had known from prison, persuaded him to walk away and join Yellow Thunder Camp. No matter what happened with the shooting rap, Catch The Bear would have to serve five years for escape.

We soon learned that Wanbli No Heart was really James Jones, a convicted first-degree murderer working undercover for the U.S. Marshal's Service. A transvestite drawn to Indians, he had kept one Indian as his kid while he was in Englewood serving a life term. Despite that, Jones was allowed to go outside the gates of the maximum-security prison without guards. Ten days later he turned up in Rapid City, armed and cashy. While living in camp, Jones had often wandered around Rapid City with skins who were stopped and searched by deputy sheriffs, but for some reason he was never questioned, much less arrested.

Jones became the prosecution's star witness when he told police that he had never hit Tollefson and that Catch The Bear had fired without provocation. Jones left camp and we never saw him again. I think he went into the witness protection program. Right after the shooting, FBI officials unilaterally went to Judge Donald O'Brien, who was hearing the Yellow Thunder Camp case, and cited Tollefson's death as reason to close the camp immediately. To his credit, O'Brien refused. Catch The Bear was represented by Jim Leach, a Rapid City attorney, and Gerry Spence, a flamboyant Wyoming man widely regarded as America's best trial lawyer. With Jones exposed as a government agent-provocateur, the case against Catch The Bear was weak. Even a felon is allowed to act in self-defense, and the government's agent had provoked the shooting. But a white man was dead by the hand of an Indian and no prosecutor would chance political suicide, so Catch The Bear had to be tried. Despite the judge's ruling that it was irrelevant and would prejudice the jury, prosecutors began by making an inflammatory opening statement. Because of that egregious misconduct, the judge dismissed the case, but when the state appealed, the all-star white racists of the South Dakota Supreme Court reversed him and remanded the case for trial.

Gerry Spence was the first lawyer I had ever met who didn't seem like one. A colorful talker, a larger-than-life swashbuckler, I liked him instantly. Gerry asked me to find another eyewitness, one who could testify that Tollefson had drawn his gun before Catch The Bear shot him. Unfortunately, I had satisfied myself that there were no other eyewitnesses.

As it happened, Catch The Bear was offered a deal. Instead of facing life imprisonment without parole, he could plead guilty to manslaughter and get a reduced sentence, seven or eight years, to be served concurrently with what he owed for escape. He knew he had to do five years anyway and wasn't looking forward to another long, ugly trial. He might have thought, "What's two or three more?" Without consulting anyone, he took the deal. I was saddened. With a viable defense and the best attorney in the country, he had had a good chance at getting off with time served. Instead, he went to prison for a crime he didn't commit.

44

▼▼▼▼▼▼▼▼

Paha Sapa Sun Dance

We held our first sun dance at Yellow Thunder Camp in the summer of 1982. Because of everything our *Khe Sapa* meant to us, we were determined to make it as traditional as possible. Fools Crow, who came to Yellow Thunder often, was so old, honored, and respected that we didn't ask him to run the ceremony; we merely invited him to join us. In late spring, we took the Yellow Thunder Camp pipe around to eight holy men on the Pine Ridge, Rosebud, Cheyenne River, and Standing Rock Reservations. Such men cannot refuse the pipe, and having accepted it, they must honor their commitments or the spirits will be offended, and it will come back on them. Despite that, all eight failed to come to our sun dance. But Leonard Crow Dog—to whom we hadn't even taken the pipe, because of his relative youth—came to run it for us. Down on the plains, most of the medicine men we had invited to Yellow Thunder Camp held their own sun dances instead. Those had become status events that supposedly reflected the medicine man's reputation in how many dancers attended and how large the "arena" was. Just as with white men, bigger was considered better.

In early summer, we cut saplings and skinned their bark to provide a framework for the sacred hoop that surrounds the sun dancers. There were twenty-eight poles—exactly as many as the days in a woman's purification cycle, and exactly as many ribs as in a buffalo. When the hoop is complete, the sides are closed off from view. Those assisting the dancers enter the hoop at gates represented by flags in each of the four sacred colors—black for west, red for north, yellow for east, white for south. There is one break in the holy hoop, the east door where the dancers and all good things enter, and all bad things leave. The singers sit on the south end, shaded by pine boughs leaned against the saplings. In building our sacred hoop in the orthodox way, we learned another lesson from our ancestors. In contrast to modern sun dances, which drew hundreds of people, traditional rites were small events. With only twenty-eight poles, the hoop can't be very much more than thirty or thirty-five feet across. There isn't room for very many dancers.

By that time, I had participated in more than a dozen sun dances. Before each one, we ceremonially cut a cottonwood tree to symbolize the tree of life, just as our forebears had. Although I'm not fluent in my language, I know that the Lakota name for the tree our ancestors had chosen translates to "the tree with the whistling leaves." There were no cottonwoods near Yellow Thunder Camp, however. On a windy day weeks before the sun dance, the eldest of the Thunder Shield brothers came up and said very quietly, "Come, let's go among the trees. I want to show you something." He took me to a mixed grove of conifers and deciduous trees, where we sat down. Suddenly I noticed a peculiar whistling noise—the wind surging through the leaves of an aspen. I love aspens. They are beautiful, unruly anarchists, the Indians of the forest, rooting themselves anywhere and everywhere. Aspens seem to have a mind of their own. They will share space with other trees, but the Forest Service hates them because they can't be controlled. Planted in one place, they may die out or flourish, but their seedlings will spring up far away in following years. We sat there enjoying the wind as it sighed through the green bower, until I figured it out. The tree with the whispering leaves was the aspen, not the cottonwood, and it grew only in the hills. I said, "We never sun danced on the plains, did we?"

Thunder Shield shook his head. "Not before the white man came." Once again, I was struck by how enjoyable it was to be around traditional Indians, wise people who allow others to experience each discovery firsthand instead of delivering lectures. That year, for the first time in more than a century, Lakota sun dancers used an aspen. After it was chopped down, a girl who had yet to become a woman was chosen to mark it, since only a pure person may first touch the tree that sacrificed itself for our dance. With traditional ceremony, a hole was dug in the center of the sacred hoop and filled with the four sacred foods—*wasná*, a mixture of buffalo meat sweetened with chokecherry juice; *wasín*, buffalo marrow; *chanté*, buffalo heart; and *çikau*, fat from the buffalo's hump.

The tree was then carried in and placed upright. In the aspen's fork, we put a chokecherry bundle and hung cloth in each of the sacred colors, along with tobacco ties—akin to prayer bundles—representing personal prayers from those who tied them on. The man and the buffalo skull were tied to the branches. Then ropes, later attached to dancers who pierced themselves, were tied to the tree. The tree would remain for four days, to be taken down after the feast and giveaways.

Sun dances are rarely held next to water, but the only place at Yellow Thunder with a suitable clearing was near the creek. That made it doubly hard for the fasting dancers, who could hear small children splashing in the water. In subsequent years, we held the dance later in summer, after the creek had dried up.

We built a bonfire to heat rocks for our *inipi*. While I was sun dancing, Forest Service rangers came to say that we couldn't have a fire like that. It was too windy, and the blaze could get out of control. While the dance continued, people wouldn't allow the rangers in. We knocked away unburned wood and didn't put in rocks to be heated, but the fire still burned. By the time the dancers were headed back to the *inipi*, the rangers, accompanied by deputy sheriffs, had drawn their guns and were making threats. A few AIMsters began to slip away to their cars, where they kept their weapons.

Still wearing my dance outfit, I invited the rangers in. They said, "We-'ve got a court order that if there's a fire danger—and there is—we have to contain your fire." They brought in metal pipe and heavy-gauge mesh and started to build an enclosure around our fire. As their work continued, I took part in a judicial hearing by radiophone. I told the judge, "This sacred fire will not harm the forest. Don't you Christians have faith in anything?" The judge said, "No, no, sparks can fly in the wind and set off a forest fire."

Nellie Red Owl, from Batesland, South Dakota, and several other old women—especially those who had kept the rangers and police out while the sun dance was going on—were willing to go to jail. They angrily cussed out the intruders. While the rangers dripped sweat and built the restraining screen as fast as they could, the old women were on them. Some people were as angry at me for letting the rangers in as they were at the white men for defiling our ceremony. I explained, "The sun dance is for peace. Once it begins, we can't have a confrontation. We must act in respectful ways." It was obvious that the white men didn't like what they had to do. I felt a little sorry for them because they had to carry out orders or lose their jobs.

When the screen was completed, we stoked up the fire with fast-burning pitch pine. Suddenly the wind blew hard and the fire blossomed with a mighty roar. Despite the heavy mesh cage, big burning flakes soared into the air. Turning to my cousin Greg Zephier, I said, "Look! The spirits won't let the fire stay in jail." Then the metal mesh began to burn. The rangers looked on

When AIM first rolled into Wounded Knee, I took several defenders and seized this church. Until someone burned it down, it remained the center of our resistance during the siege. *(UPI/Bettmann Archive)*

TOP: Leonard Crow Dog, an amazing medicine man, was our spiritual leader during the siege of Wounded Knee. Those prepared to die for their beliefs were daubed with Crow Dog's special paint. *(UPI/Bettmann Archive)*

RIGHT: When the White House sent Assistant U.S. Attorney General Harlington Wood *(third row center, hatless)* to "negotiate" with us at Wounded Knee, we escorted him to our conference tipi in style. On horseback are Robert Free *(left)* and Sid Mills. *(AP/Wide World)*

OPPOSITE: Dick Wilson showed the press a partial list of the patriots who held Wounded Knee to call attention to his murderous activities as president of the Oglala Sioux tribe.
(UPI/Bettmann Archive)

ABOVE: The Reverend Ralph Abernathy *(left)* came to Wounded Knee to show support for our struggle. Dennis Banks is pictured with us. *(UPI/Bettmann Archive)*

RIGHT: Clyde Bellecourt *(left)* and Ramon Roubideaux went to Kyle, South Dakota, to meet White House emissaries a few weeks after the siege of Wounded Knee ended. The government sent low-ranking men with no authority to discuss our 1868 treaty. *(AP/Wide World)*

Gladys Bissonnette was one of
the wise, strong Lakota women
who taught me so much during
the siege of Wounded Knee.
(UPI/Bettmann Archive)

Pete Catches was my sundance
mentor and hero, and as brave a
man as ever walked. He joined
in the occupation of Wounded
Knee even though he had just
had major surgery and had to
change his bandages twice daily.
(UPI/Bettmann Archive)

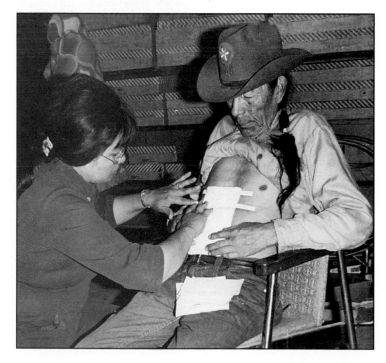

Grandpa Frank Fools Crow welcomed me back to Saint Paul for the resumption of my Wounded Knee trial in February 1974. *(UPI/Bettmann Archive)*

Judge Alfred Nichol waved to me as we left the Saint Paul federal building on the second day of my Wounded Knee trial. (*UPI/Bettmann Archive*)

When Judge Alfred Nichol, citing government misconduct, threw out all remaining Wounded Knee charges, Dennis Banks grabbed my hand and celebrated the moment on the steps of the federal courthouse in Saint Paul. (*UPI/Bettmann Archive*)

TOP: In September 1977, I visited Geneva, Switzerland, to attend the first international forum on American Indians of the Western Hemisphere. *(Courtesy Peggy Phelps Means)*

RIGHT: The Longest Walk, a national demonstration to shame Congress into rescinding hundreds of anti-Indian laws, started in California and Seattle and ended in Washington, D.C., on July 15, 1978. *(AP/Wide World)*

OPPOSITE: Senator Edward Kennedy, red-faced and flustered, yells into the mike because I challenged his pending Omnibus Crime Bill, the infamous Senate Bill 1, during the Longest Walk, in Washington, D.C., in 1978. *(Courtesy G. E. Rust)*

A couple of hours after I was stabbed in prison, Marlon Brando joined my press conference at the South Dakota penitentiary. Behind us are my daughters, Sherry *(left)* and Michele *(kneeling)*. *(Courtesy Peggy Phelps Means)*

When Iranian students seized the U.S. embassy in 1979, they allowed the Reverend John P. Adams and John Thomas, representing AIM and the International Indian Treaty Council, to bring mail from the hostages to their families. *(UPI/Bettmann Archive)*

At Yellow Thunder Camp in 1982, Shorty Blacksmith taught us much about our ancestors' way of life. *(Author's collection)*

I celebrated my forty-fourth birthday in Las Vegas with Larry Flynt, who wore a T-shirt announcing our political partnership in seeking the Republican nomination for president. *(Author's collection)*

Brooklyn Rivera, shown here with his mother, is to me a great man, as smart and strong a leader of his Miskito people in Nicaragua as Red Cloud was of my ancestors in the last century. *(UPI/Bettmann Archive)*

Peter MacDonald led his Dineh people toward economic independence and sovereignty, which was too much for the BIA to allow. *(AP/Wide World)*

This is how I looked
when I checked myself
in for treatment on
December 2, 1991.
*(Courtesy Cottonwood
de Tucson)*

This is how I looked when
I completed treatment.
(Courtesy Cottonwood de Tucson)

On July 3, 1994, I was among ten elders honored by the Standing Rock Sioux tribe for our work on behalf of the 1868 Fort Laramie Treaty. For our honors dance, shown here, we received the traditional song last performed for Chief Gall after the Seventh Cavalry's defeat along the Greasy Grass River in 1876. To my left, in sunglasses, is Auntie Faith, who was among those honored. *(Photo by Marvin J. Wolf)*

Kenny Kane and I got together in May 1993
for a speech at Ohio State, in Columbus.
(Courtesy Kenneth Kane)

This is how I appeared in makeup for *The Last of the Mohicans,* in 1991.
(Courtesy Scott Means)

in shock and disbelief. "They ain't going to believe this back at district," said one. The mesh melted, leaving only the frame. Shaking their heads, the Forest Service workers dismantled what was left and took off.

In Yellow Thunder Camp, we all smiled at one another. No one had to speak. Everyone had seen and understood the power of the spirits. Gathering our hot rocks, we entered the *inipi* to give thanks to the Great Mystery.

45
▼▼▼▼▼▼▼▼▼

Fighting among Ourselves

T he same summer that we were participating in the sun dance at the Yellow Thunder Camp, Dennis Banks organized a summit in San Francisco. His goal was to put AIM back together as a national organization. Most of the old-time AIM leaders, with the notable exception of Carter Camp, came together in an old elementary school off Army Street. We ironed out past differences and agreed never again to criticize one another in public. Instead, we would keep our disagreements within AIM, as we had at the beginning. For that and other reasons, it was a good meeting. One thing we didn't act on was a suggestion from Janet McCloud, a leader from Washington state, that we find ways to get Indian men to lead the fight against the physical abuse of women in their own communities. We never took it up as an issue, and I still regret that we didn't.

Maybe I failed to press that subject as hard as I could have because by then my split with Peggy was virtually complete. Our estrangement went deeper than two people growing in different directions. It was mostly because of our own dysfunction as a couple, but also as a people. After a century of colonization, we Indian people have learned to excel at fighting among ourselves. We have, regrettably, learned to mirror white society. Peggy and I made Yellow Thunder Camp our do-or-die issue. I wouldn't put my personal life in front of its survival, and she couldn't accept that it was even more important to me than our marriage. She wouldn't come up to camp and I wouldn't go down to see her at Kyle. We considered ourselves divorced.

In the autumn of 1982, after the AIM meeting, Dennis decided to hold the first International Tribunal on Illegal Acts and Violations of Human Rights by the United States. It wasn't just an Indian Nuremberg; we would address everything the United States had done around the globe. Elders, highly educated academics, and laypeople from all over the world, including participants from South Africa, Palestine, and India, came to D-Q University, near Davis, California, to testify. In the middle of the meeting, President Ronald Reagan signed into law a statute that ended federal recognition of original Hawaiian sovereignty. Within hours, Kilauea erupted, its lava chasing hundreds of *haoles*—nonnatives—out of homes and businesses. Many Hawaiians attending the tribunal rejoiced at the sign, and so did we Indians.

On the last day of the conference, people who had remained behind at Yellow Thunder Camp called to say that state police had set a deadline after which no one would be allowed in or out. I invited everyone at the tribunal to visit the camp. When Dennis said something like, "I'll be there if I have to," it made the wire services, because he was still a fugitive from white man's justice in South Dakota. With his usual flair for the flamboyant gesture, Dennis then announced that he was organizing an airlift to Yellow Thunder Camp, to arrive on the day police had threatened to cut us off.

I telephoned the press to announce that I was returning to Rapid City for two days of marches against racism. That scared the rednecks so much that they closed and locked a BIA park near the city's Sioux Museum. For a couple of days, almost everyone driving a car with out-of-state plates got stopped by the police. Among them was a rich, elderly white lady from San Francisco. Along with other women in her car, she was forced to spread-eagle herself on a highway. South Dakota cops have no respect for anyone they consider an Indian lover.

The threat to isolate Yellow Thunder Camp evaporated when Judge O'Brien issued a restraining order, but Dennis's airlift, a fine piece of theater, continued as planned. It began the day before the march. One plane got lost for several hours, but the other found Yellow Thunder Camp and dropped food, clothing, and tools. Media people assembled for the event because of a rumor that Dennis was going to parachute in. He was, of course, still in California, enjoying the idea that every cop in South Dakota was busy stopping cars and spread-eagling tourists to look for him. When Charlie Abourezk came into town for the march, he passed out hundreds of little white-and-red buttons that said, "I am *not* Dennis Banks."

We invited people from all over the country to join us on the Walk for Religious Freedom. About 250 marched, including about fifty whites. I was amazed at the number of white people in offices and storefronts who waved, gave us the clenched-fist power sign, or circled a thumb and forefinger to make an "OK" signal. It was an encouraging sign that perhaps things were beginning to change. Among the marchers were Kwame Touré (formerly known as Stokely Carmichael) and Louis Farrakhan, a quiet black man in a sharp-looking topcoat. At first, I didn't know who he was. He said very little and had a soft voice and humble manner. When I learned that he was head of the Nation of Islam, I asked him to speak. He inspired Indians and whites alike with a dynamic speech condemning racism.

After two days of marches and speeches, Rapid City was once again on the national map. The one thing that annoyed me was that only about two hundred Indians participated in the march; half were from Pine Ridge and nearly all the rest from out of state. Few Rapid City skins came out, and most waited until the march's peaceful conclusion before slipping into the park to hear the speeches. Practically all of them were homeless people. They were obviously scared—with good cause—but I can excuse only so many. Living in the most racist city in the nation, Rapid City Indians weren't afraid to go to jail for being drunk, but they wouldn't stand up for themselves.

Among the marchers were Steve Pipkin and his wife, Mary, who had heard me speak at the international tribunal. Steve later told me that he had said to himself, "This is the guy I want to relate to in terms of Indian people; his philosophy and religious beliefs are just what I believe." At the march, he came up and introduced me to his wife and kids. A nice-looking man a few years younger than me, he lived in California and was independently wealthy from a publishing business he had founded. He said he wanted to be with Indians and help them. Many whites have said that kind of thing to me, but when I asked him to donate to Yellow Thunder Camp, he wrote out a check for one thousand dollars.

As I got to know Steve, I was even more amazed. His father was a fundamentalist Christian preacher, and Steve had been raised to follow in his footsteps. Breaking with that tradition, he had dropped out of a Bible school, served in Air Force missile silos, then gone into business. He had sold part of it to a good manager, then took his kids out of school to travel around the country for a few years. Other Indian people, learning that he had been in the air force, suspected that he was a fed. Nevertheless, I felt his sincerity and believed in him. Meanwhile, he amazed me by making quarterly donations of two thousand dollars to Yellow Thunder Camp. When he came to visit, we almost instantly bonded. He was one of very few white men with a Christian and a military background with whom I felt comfortable. He further proved his sincerity in the *inipi*. Through our friendship, I developed more respect for Christianity and for white people in general. I began to realize that they are not all hatemongers and that some are very decent. It was nice having a white family in my life. It hadn't happened since I was a little kid.

After a few years, Steve saw that my interests weren't limited to Yellow

Thunder Camp. He wanted me to be successful in spreading my message of Indian independence, dignity, and self-determination, so he made me a partner in his business. To this day, I receive royalties, now about twenty-four hundred dollars a quarter, money that goes to help my family.

While the Yellow Thunder Camp lawsuit worked its way through the courts, we tried to outflank the Forest Service by getting Congress to pass a bill setting aside those eight hundred acres for a spiritual youth center. We knew that if Congress compelled the Forest Service to issue a usage permit to Indian people, the bureaucrats couldn't claim it was against rules and regulations, or take refuge in precedents that fostered racism.

We sent Nick Meinhart, leader of the whites at Yellow Thunder Camp, to Capitol Hill to lobby for us. His only preparation for the task was that he had raised money for Quaker organizations. He arrived in D.C. knowing nothing about how the legislative process works. After a few weeks, he called to say he had gone around to see the most important Senate and committee staff people and had spoken with Reagan administration officials. All had advised him to try for a nonbinding congressional resolution. That wasn't why we had sent him to Washington. We wanted a bill passed, so he got Representative Shirley Chisholm, of New York City, to sponsor a Yellow Thunder Camp bill and to enlist fifty cosponsors. We wanted hearings in South Dakota or, failing that, in D.C. However, South Dakota's congressional delegation—up for reelection—fought us and delayed a hearing until it was time to start their campaigns, then canceled it. Our bill died when Congress adjourned for the year so its members could campaign for reelection.

As summer faded into fall and the weather turned chilly, most of the whites left camp again. By the end of 1982, most of my time was spent trying to keep the Black Hills Alliance going. At about that time, I got a call from Jerome War Cloud, director of the Cleveland American Indian Center, who said the Cleveland baseball team had offered to settle the lawsuit I had brought against it in 1970. Because it was the longest-pending suit in the history of Cuyahoga County, Ohio, and all plaintiffs had moved out of state, Jerome's lawyers had advised him to settle. Otherwise, the judge might throw the case out. In return for keeping the odious mascot Chief Wahoo, the team had offered thirty-five thousand dollars. After checking with his board of directors, Jerome gave me half. I turned the money over to the alliance, which was almost broke.

As our community dwindled to a small core bunch, I became aware of an ugly truth. Some Indian people made important contributions to our camp and obviously enjoyed the spiritual dimensions of living there, but many others just couldn't remain sober. Every so often, they went out and got drunk, and sometimes got thrown in jail. Then they came back, looking sheepish.

Sadly, the guys I counted on most to help run the camp were still drinking. My biggest disappointment was George Tall. The full-bloods, people more comfortable speaking Lakota than English, looked up to him. He has a rare touch with people; to this day, I envy his quiet, peaceful ways, a leadership quality I've seen otherwise only in elders. George, however, still had to have his drinking binges. As many times as I got him to the door, he always refused to go through it into freedom and self-sufficiency. Most Indians are like that: Their self-esteem is so low that they can't permit themselves to grow into the beautiful human beings that they might become.

I wasn't so dazzling myself, but after five-and-a-half years of sobriety, I had learned that I didn't need booze to relax or laugh, and I didn't have to force myself to have fun. I had discovered that when I began to assume responsibility for my own actions, there was no longer a need for the brawling I had so often indulged in while drinking, except for rare incidents of self-defense. I still had addictions, including cigarettes and coffee, but my behavior was more principled. Being sober also made me realize why I enjoyed fighting for my people. It's the right thing to do. When you fight for your people, you also fight for yourself.

Gradually I began to realize that the type of residents we were attracting had changed. Our community had become little more than a safer alternative to living on the streets or mooching from relatives—a place to sleep, eat, and detoxify. We had lost our school, most of our children, and our spiritual commitment. Many of our staunchest people left in early 1983. I realized then that I was the only one keeping Yellow Thunder Camp alive. After much thought, I decided it would have to stand or fall on its own. As I told reporters, I was tired of baby-sitting. If the people didn't have the commitment to nourish the root of the tree of life that once had lived at Yellow Thunder Camp, I wasn't going to do it for them.

The next Pine Ridge election was scheduled for January 1984. I decided I might run again for president of my nation, as I had in 1974. I conferred with Ward Churchill, my brother Bill, Shorty Blacksmith, and Nellie Red Owl. I also sought the advice of my Uncle Matthew King and of Grandpa Fools Crow. When everyone counseled me to go for it, I consulted with several other Indians, including male and female elders, an educated woman, a teenage girl, and a male scholar. Each helped to draw up a postelection plan of action. My principal contribution to it was the concept of immediate independence. If I was elected, I would give the BIA and every federal agency from that day until the end of their fiscal year—about six months—to leave Pine Ridge. That included the Indian Health Service and state welfare representatives. Every government bureaucrat or official, Indian or not, would have to leave the reservation. We would also terminate all land leases to non-Indians, totally disconnect from the white man's legal strictures. That was within our rights. Every law passed without our consent since the 1868 treaty remains illegal, since for us there is no white man's law except treaty law. We called my election platform "True Revolution for the Elders, Ancestors, Treaties and Youth"—TREATY.

Nonetheless, I had too much respect for spirituality to eject the white missionaries. Instead, the day I took office I planned to say to them, "You've had over a century to try to convert us to your faith. If you've failed, admit it and leave. If you've succeeded, then your church on our reservation must now become self-sufficient—just like non-Indian churches in Beverly Hills or New York. If you can take care of your own needs, then you're welcome to stay." That would mean, of course, that everyone would leave.

I hoped to create new opportunities on the Pine Ridge Reservation. We are people of the land who know that as long as we take care of our Grandmother, she will take care of us. I wanted to let people settle on the land, build on the land, farm or ranch or garden on the land. I wanted to open the door to using alternative energy in pollution-free manufacturing or anything else people cared to try. We would return to our traditional institutions and again become self-sufficient. Everyone would be free—free to be responsible for themselves. With no more government handouts, people would have to rely on their own brains, their own energy, and their own heritage to put food on their tables and roofs over their heads. As a nation and a community, we would have to make sure that the sick and the infirm were cared for.

I knew that many Indians, conditioned to accepting the white man's dole, would be frightened of freedom. I had no qualms about seeing that kind of person leave. People were leaving almost daily, hundreds of economic refugees departing Pine Ridge every year, most of them young, energetic, and ambitious. With a chance to work and to live decently, most of those people would stay. The parasites, addicted to welfare payments or make-work jobs, surplus food commodities, and other handouts, would leave. We would all be better off.

TREATY's plan was reproduced in newspaper form and, on February 27, distributed at the commemoration ceremonies marking the tenth anniversary of the siege of Wounded Knee and the rebirth of the Independent Oglala Nation. To some of us—more than a dozen men and women—the ION still lives. We remain part of it and continue to act and conduct business as a government in exile. During the ceremonies, I announced my candidacy for tribal president and said that, if elected, I would accept no salary at all.

To run for president, I had to live on the reservation, so I got a post-office box in Porcupine. I kept my tipi at Yellow Thunder Camp and stayed with various friends and relatives around Pine Ridge. One day I got a call from an old friend, a woman who had read my TREATY platform. She knew someone who knew Bill Zimmerman, the gutsy pilot who had flown into Wounded Knee during the siege and then had written a book about it, *Airlift to Wounded Knee.* He had his own public-relations firm in Santa Monica, California. Hoping that he might be willing to do some pro bono work for me, I called him.

I was confident of enough support at Pine Ridge to get through the primary with enough votes to qualify for the runoff. I wanted to use broadcasting to reach my constituents. Even though Reagan's Federal Communications Commission had done away with the "equal-time" requirement, KILI Radio had instituted its own policy of offering airtime to all candidates. That meant I would get little support from the station I had helped to found. About two dozen people were running for tribal president, so every time I said something on KILI, every one of them would get on the air, too. Even more disappointing, KILI wouldn't support me editorially, even though it was AIM's station. Under the influence of Mark Tilsen's leftist, do-gooder philosophy, the station was trying to be everything to everybody—and therefore was nothing to anyone.

Because KILI had virtually shut me out, I intended to send my message over white-owned radio stations in surrounding communities, including Rapid City. I was also going to get on television. I went to Santa Monica and met with Zimmerman. He told his partner and everyone in his office, "I knew one day we'd be doing PR for a presidential race," and ecstatically announced that I was his *first* presidential candidate. Bill was willing to donate his time and expertise, as well as his staff's, but he couldn't pay the expenses. He estimated that I needed more than twenty thousand dollars.

One of Bill's people was a very sharp, hardworking young man who knew how to run direct-mail fund-raising. He helped write a letter. The key sentence said, "Now I understand what it's really all about—this time it's ballots, not bullets." Using the Black Hills Alliance's mailing list, I got an incredible response to that letter—nearly 100 percent—and raised more than thirty-five thousand dollars. Zimmerman and the guy who wrote the letter still have trouble believing how much I took in.

As we got closer to election time, I went around the reservation to speak. When people heard my platform and realized we were going to sever the federal umbilical cord that had kept us as dependent children for more than a century, some of the breeds, especially a rancher named Hunter, in Kyle, said things such as, "You're going to start a war." Like many in Indian country, he didn't understand the meaning of being free. Nations with treaties, like the Lakota, have international law on their side. We are supported by every relevant precedent in U.S. constitutional law and by everything in natural law. With all that on our side, we don't need armed struggle. Especially in those times before the demise of the Soviet Union, the United States couldn't afford the worldwide embarrassment of using its military to stomp on our legal rights. Five years later, the Lithuanians did exactly what I was proposing—citing their treaties, they forced a Soviet pull out.

The political ignoramuses of Pine Ridge didn't know that people around the world already loved us. The moment we became independent, everybody would want to help us in every way we could possibly need. I tried to explain all that as I went around to presidential forums in each community, but the TREATY platform scared the hell out of many people. Sellouts refused to listen to any new options. In that, they seem to me like Democrats who think the government way is the *only* way to solve problems. Because independence and freedom were so scary, few Indians, including my brothers, got involved with my campaign. Even AIM supporters and some of the traditional people were honestly frightened by my ideas. But even though the Lakota had been colonized for more than a century, and even though they feared freedom and were intimidated by responsibility, they were still willing to support my plan because they knew it was better than what they had. Only the old guys, the few elders who had grown up free without learning hatred of their own culture, had no doubts at all. They said, "We'll go back to the way it was at the beginning of the century. We stayed away from the loafer camp," as they call Pine Ridge Village, "and they left us alone out here. In those days, there were no reservation land leases and you could ride horseback from Pine Ridge to Wanbli and never hit a fence." Those were things I wanted to see reinstated.

It was senseless to run a media campaign until after the primary, and the campaign funds I had raised represented a small fortune to any Pine Ridge resident. When people came to me for assistance, I couldn't turn them all down. I gave money only to those without heat in their homes. I visited them to make sure I wasn't being conned. The poverty I saw was enough to make anyone cry. I don't know how those people made it through any winter. With the price of propane being what it was, I had given away more than ten thousand dollars before spring.

The primary election was scheduled for a Tuesday in the latter part of January 1984. Late on the afternoon of the Friday before it, the executive committee of the Oglala Sioux tribe met—the vice president, secretary, treasurer, and a tribal councilman. President Joe American Horse was away on business, so Vice President Paul Iron Cloud chaired the meeting. A relative, and a close friend of my brother Ted's, Paul was among those running for president. The committee met in closed session and voted me off the ballot on the ground that I had a felony conviction from the state of South Dakota. As on most Indian reservations, everything shuts down at 4:30 P.M. Friday. When, at a little after 4:00, I learned I was off the ballot, there wasn't a damn thing I could do about it. The tribal judges were gone for the weekend. On Sunday, I got on the phone to Larry Leventhal in Minneapolis and we put together a motion for a temporary restraining order. I showed up at 8:00 A.M. Monday in the Pierre courtroom of Judge Donald J. Porter, fairest of the state's federal judges, with my handwritten paperwork. He was pissed off—he had only about half an hour to catch a plane. He didn't even read my motion. Glancing at the first page of the complaint, he said, "Denied, lack of jurisdiction," and off to the airport he went.

I got back to the Pine Ridge tribal court by midday for two days of standing-room-only hearings on the election. The chief judge was a white lawyer, an incompetent who, after having failed in the white world, accepted the tiny salary of a tribal judge. I argued that because of the 1868 treaty, South Dakota has no jurisdiction over Pine Ridge or over Indian people living there, and therefore my conviction had no relevance on the reservation. I also described the circumstances that led to my arrest, including the fact that I had been acting on behalf of my people, at Judge Joseph Bottum's request, when the riot occurred.

Although I was confident of winning on my own, I also brought in Frank Kills The Enemy to testify about the treaty. Very humbly dressed, that crusty old traditional got into the witness box but refused to sit. Traditional Indians address matters of importance while standing. He also refused to take an oath on a Bible. He said, "Everyone in this courtroom and on this reservation knows me and knows my word is good. That's all you need to know." He turned to the judge and, in broken English, lectured him as though he were a little kid. The judge turned bright red, but sat there and listened as Kills The Enemy told him he was a guest who had been given a very important job. He must show his gratitude to the people by allowing them to make their own choices in the election. Kills The Enemy went on to remind the judge at length that the United States made the laws we lived under. If he respected U.S. law, then he must respect the treaty. Otherwise, he would dishonor himself; if he couldn't follow the law, he should leave the reservation.

The judge proceeded to render one of the most atrocious legal opinions I have ever read. Poorly written, it said the "Sioux nation"—the judge's words—had the inherent right to determine who would represent it with elections, and ought to choose responsible, honest, God-fearing individuals. I said, "That's right! I totally agree with that. Put my name on the ballot." Instead, he ruled against me.

I wanted to take my case to the tribal supreme court, comprised of three traditional elders, but Iron Cloud, as acting president, had laid them off the previous week. I'm not certain it was entirely his idea to ban me from the ballot, but he had convened the meeting and participated in the voting despite his obvious conflict of interest as a candidate. I think he and his fellow councilmen acted at the behest of the BIA, which feared me as much as I hated it—and Iron Cloud saw an easy way to get rid of a serious rival.

Many people around Pine Ridge were dismayed with the results of the election and called mass meetings in Oglala and Porcupine. Hundreds of people came from all over the reservation to express their dissatisfaction. I got up at Porcupine and said, "If you're going to participate in an electoral system, then you must get together like this *before* the election—not after! It's too late now—there's nothing you can do about this one. If you're dissatisfied with the results, you'd better start working now for the next vote." I added that people who embraced a political system like the white man's should form a party and run candidates in every district, but that kind of electoral system was never meant to change anything. It's just a tool for the majority. "That's why Indian people always rule by consensus," I said, throwing our culture back at them.

They all agreed—but that was the last such meeting held at Porcupine. Life goes on at Pine Ridge just as it has since the BIA took control. Relocation and/or extermination is still the policy, and Indians do their part in helping to carry it out.

46

▼▼▼▼▼▼▼▼▼

Larry Flynt

Sometimes we don't get to choose our political allies. So it happened in 1983, when one of the world's most notorious pornographers asked for my support. My campaign manager, Roger Iron Cloud—Paul's cousin—received two campaign contributions of one thousand dollars each, one from Larry Flynt, the publisher of *Hustler*, and one from his wife, Althea, along with an invitation to a party at his Bel Air home. Since Flynt also offered to pay for first-class airfare, hotel rooms, and a rental car, we accepted. I needed something more formal to wear. As much as AIM detested used clothing, we had put that kind of donation to good use at Yellow Thunder Camp. Rummaging through piles of garments and shoes, I picked out a pair of pretty good cowboy boots and a corduroy sport coat with leather elbow patches to wear to Flynt's mansion.

I had seen *Hustler*, Flynt's magazine which left nothing to the imagination, and I had read about his trials for alleged violation of pornography laws. I knew that after he had been shot by a never-apprehended sniper in the South, he had been paralyzed from the waist down. Roger and I stood around the Flynts' swimming pool until Larry appeared in his wheelchair to shake our hands. His wife was a slender, very pretty woman with jet black hair who had been featured in his magazine. The love between her and Flynt was mutual and very deep—I saw it. She stayed with him even though he was dead, sexually speaking. I could tell he was in great, constant pain from his wound. Later when the pain became unbearable, he had his spinal cord severed.

After chatting with the Flynts for a few minutes, I went to get some fruit juice, and I met former child evangelist-turned-Hollywood-actor Marjoe Gortner. "Hello there," he said. "That's a *nice* sport coat. It that Manuel's?" I said, "No, it's "Room-ahge," as my dad had always called old clothes he got from places like the Salvation Army. Gortner said, "Oh, I haven't heard of that designer. Where's he located?"

"South Dakota," I said, straight-faced.

"Oh," he said as I walked off.

A few weeks later, Roger and I were invited back to Flynt's home for a private dinner party. That time, he sent his Lear jet to Rapid City to bring us to California. Over appetizers, Flynt startled me with an announcement. He was about to mount an effort to become the Republican nominee for president of the United States. He went around the table to introduce several big-time advisers, experts, men who had previously run national political campaigns. Then Flynt dropped the other shoe. "I really wanted Jesse Jackson as my running mate," he said. "But Jesse's a Democrat and he turned me down. Now I'm asking you—will you join my ticket to run for vice president?"

I couldn't have been more surprised. I managed to say, "What?"

Flynt explained that he had $20 million in cash, his own money, that he was prepared to spend on this effort. I said, "Before I give you my answer, let me call AIM." Roger and I talked briefly about the pros and cons of associating myself with a notorious pornographer, wondering what this was really all about and if Flynt was serious. Then I dialed Clyde Bellecourt, who advised me not to get involved with Flynt. Dennis Banks, Larry Leventhal, and my brother Bill, however, all thought the publicity was worth the risk. They said yes—and that was good enough for me.

The next day, Flynt called a press conference to announce our candidacy. Afterward, he gave Roger and me each one thousand dollars in cash for "walking-around money." We hadn't played in that league before, so I asked Flynt, "How much are you supposed to tip at restaurants?" He said, "Tip the valets and doormen five bucks. If you go to a real nice upscale restaurant, slip the maître d' a hundred dollars. At a middle-of-the-road restaurant, twenty dollars is enough. If you go to a greasy spoon, give him five dollars." I looked at Roger and he looked at me. I said, "Do we know any greasy spoons that have a maître d'?" When I could speak without laughing, I said, "If that's the way we're going, I guess we'll need some tip money." Flynt gave us each another thousand dollars.

A little later, I went into Flynt's private office and asked him, "What's really going on here?" He called in his security chief, campaign manager, and a couple of other people. I recall his saying, "I'm a pornographer. I have a right to be one, and I want to be the best pornographer there is. I'm really concerned about the First Amendment—but Reagan has proven that *he's* obscene. Now I want to remove that threat from this country." As we talked over the next two days, we got down to the nitty-gritty. Twenty states whose total delegates were the minimum number required to win inclusion in the national primary would be targeted. One of those was Wisconsin, which has many Indian people. I knew some skins there who could plausibly present themselves as Republicans and who would become delegates. When we got to the convention, they would place Flynt's name in nomination.

Realistically, we knew we'd never get that far. Flynt's political advisers believed that rather than allow an infamous pornographer's name to be placed in nomination for the highest office in the country under the gaze of the world media, the party bosses would sit down with us in a back room and work out a deal. In return for Flynt's withdrawal, the party would get the religious right off his back. My deal point was Article VI, Paragraph 2 of the U.S. Constitution, which says treaties are the supreme law of the land and judges in every state are bound by them. I wanted that enforced, especially when it came to Indian treaties, so in exchange for Flynt's and my bowing out, the party would have to make public commitments about Article VI.

I had to admire a guy who would spend twenty million of his own money to back his political beliefs, but we both knew it was a very dangerous move. Many people in this country have been killed for far less. Accordingly, Flynt agreed to hire a bodyguard for me. He also hired John Thomas. After having gotten shot with me on the Rosebud, he had done excellent service for AIM and the International Treaty Council on the Longest Walk and during the Iranian hostage crisis.

On the third day of my visit, Roger and I went into Flynt's office. He was behind his desk in a wheelchair, and I noticed a briefcase on the floor next to the desk. He pushed it toward me and said, "Open it." It was full of money. I remember Flynt told me, "Go ahead, take a bundle." I looked at him for several seconds, then reached down and took out a packet. "You want to count it?" he said. "There are a hundred hundred-dollar bills in there." That was ten thousand dollars. I looked at Roger and he looked at me. Wow!

Roger and I flew home the next day. I gave some of Flynt's money to KILI Radio, some to the International Indian Treaty Council, and the rest to Yellow Thunder Camp to buy new tools and a used pickup to haul firewood. In the next several months, Flynt was in the news because of contempt-of-court charges he faced in Los Angeles. He also had several other cases being argued in the appellate courts. I began to fly around the country with him in his private jet. I got the best of everything, including limousines and magnificent hotel suites.

Flynt gave me another ten-thousand-dollar bundle before I flew with him to D.C., where his bodyguards got busted for carrying weapons. Before he went to the U.S. Supreme Court, he warned me that he was going to do something outrageous. I didn't trust him, so I didn't go along. Instead of taking part in his circus, I met with Kwame Touré and the All-African People's Revolutionary Party, trying to get black voters to listen to Larry Flynt. After the chief justice adjourned court for the day, I was told that Flynt had unbuttoned his coat and shirt to reveal a T-shirt with a picture of an ejaculating penis. As news photographers snapped away, U.S. marshals hustled him out of the building. They couldn't arrest him for contempt because court had adjourned, but he got what he was after—massive publicity.

Despite the repellant, exploitive nature of some photos and cartoons that appear regularly in *Hustler* and other Flynt magazines, I believe Flynt is a sincere man. He gave other Indians and me almost thirty five thousand dollars, money that went to good causes. Once the word got out in Hollywood that he had twenty million dollars to spend, his Bel Air mansion was deluged by all kinds of people, most with their hands out. Many, many Christian missionaries asked him for a few bundles of hundreds. Flynt constantly dipped into that briefcase to dish out cash. He was also a supporter of Madalyn Murray O'Hair, the noted atheist. I met her when she came to his mansion to get money.

One afternoon I walked into Flynt's living room to find comedian and activist Dick Gregory getting measured for a tailor-made suit. He seemed a little embarrassed. A little later, Flynt said, "I'm giving $100,000 to Dick and he's going to take it to Coretta Scott King." I said, "Wait just a minute. There are needful organizations in Washington, East Saint Louis, Atlanta, Los Angeles, San Francisco, Cleveland, and other cities. You can have Dick deliver it, but why not pick out ten community organizations and Dick can take ten thousand dollars to each?" "Great idea," said Flynt. "Right on," said Dick.

When Flynt expressed a hankering to get into the recording industry during this period, I had him bring in Floyd Westerman—Red Crow—now a well-known Hollywood actor and recording artist, to help out. Flynt also wanted to start some new publications, among them a rock-and-roll magazine for Althea to run, and a magazine called *Rebel*. For *Rebel*'s first issue, I wrote an opinion piece about the Israeli invasion of Lebanon in 1983. Flynt was also thinking about starting an Indian magazine. At my urging, he hired John T. to help bring in Indian writers to do columns for *Hustler* and his other magazines and to develop, staff, and operate a magazine by and for Indians.

Flynt got John T. a suite at the Ramada Inn so he could bring his wife and children to town. On the night he arrived, he went to a party announcing *Rebel* magazine, got drunk, and made a fool of himself. I was disappointed but not alarmed. I knew him as a fun-loving but responsible guy. Something, however, had changed. I didn't know it until later, but John T. stayed in that suite for weeks, drinking steadily, hosting big parties for Indian people from around southern California, even inviting some of his brothers to come from Oklahoma to party with him. Soon he was having problems with the hotel management, the sorts of things that come up when you're drunk all the time.

Meanwhile, Flynt was defending dozens of lawsuits alleging violation of obscenity statutes, and trying to get into the Republican Party. As his distasteful stunt at the U.S. Supreme Court showed, however, he was going too far overboard. While appearing for a federal trial concerning First Amendment rights in Los Angeles, he came to court one day wearing the American flag as a diaper. He had a voracious hunger to be in the news, and he thought bizarre behavior was the key to media attention. When the diaper stunt brought him a fine of twenty thousand dollars for contempt of court, he hauled in a truckload of loose pennies. The judge said, "OK, Mr. Flynt. You will now count every one of those pennies to make sure it's the right amount. You have until eight tomorrow morning. Court's adjourned." The judge walked out, and Larry called in everyone on his magazine staff to count pennies. They were there all night.

That, of course, made the newspapers and television news, but I could see that he wasn't paying much attention to his campaign for the Republican nomination. The next time he went to court, it was for trial on a First Amendment issue. He had top-notch lawyers who told him all he had to do was testify truthfully, to stick to subjects that were relevant, and he would win. The government's case was very weak. In the middle of the trial, Flynt threw up his hands and said, "Judge, forget it. I admit everything. I'm wrong." I was shocked. He was in a position to strike a blow for what was right, but instead he just wanted attention.

I walked out of the courthouse and strolled around downtown LA to my old haunts on Main and Spring streets and along Broadway. Mostly I just wanted to think. Finally I caught a cab back to my cottage at the Beverly Hills Hotel, where I called Flynt and told him I was through.

"You're not serious?" he said.

"Yes, I am. You had a chance to strike a blow for the struggle for what's right, and you blew it."

He tried to jolly me into coming back, but I had made up my mind. Before I could finish packing, Flynt's entourage arrived in two limos and parked next to my cottage. Someone came in to ask me to come outside, where his people said he wanted me to come back to Bel Air and discuss my decision with him. I said, "No, I've had it."

All the way back to South Dakota, I thought about Flynt. He was a buffoon, a clown, obsessed with publicity. He was certainly rich, but he would never be more than that. But John Thomas was my brother, and his failure hurt me deeply. He had had a shot at something few people—especially Indians—would ever get. He had paid no attention to his responsibilities. He had partied for more than a month, wasted almost thirty thousand dollars on rental cars, hotel rooms, and booze—and had accomplished nothing. He could have ended up as a magazine publisher, set for life, and he could have made a big impact for his people. None of our plans came to fruition because he didn't do what he had said he would. As much as I love him and his family, I can never forgive him for that.

47

▼▼▼▼▼▼▼▼▼

Gloria

The life expectancy of a male American Indian was 44.5 years in 1984. As May 10, 1984, approached, I became increasingly aware that by that measure, my life would soon be over. Instead of brooding, I joined some AIM leaders at a conference on the Navajo reservation in Arizona.

The subject I spoke on there was the way we had schooled our children in their culture at Yellow Thunder Camp. Afterward, an older man I had known for years—an Omaha (pronounced U-*mah*-hah) from Nebraska named Leon Grant—brought his Navajo wife and two adult daughters to the stage to meet me. One of them was tall, slim, graceful, and she radiated class. Her name was Gloria. I thought, I've got to find some way to meet this woman again.

The next day there was a powwow at the high school. I went with Glenn Morris, a Shawnee and a University of Colorado professor, as well as a Harvard lawyer and codirector of Colorado AIM. After a while, he came up, very excited, to say, "You've got to see this beautiful woman." We went into the gym, where he pointed her out. It was Gloria. I said, "Yeah, nice," thinking maybe I was going to have some competition.

The dance at the powwow was about to begin just as I saw her. Plains Indian dances include one for the Soldier Society, an ancient brotherhood of defenders, called the gourd dance. As it began, Gloria and her sister politely took me to the circle and stood me next to their father, who was being honored in celebration of his birthday. To show respect for Leon, people came up to put money at my feet. Afterward, I gave it to the singers on his behalf. When the dance ended, I had a moment to talk to Gloria and her sister. I wanted to thank them for the respect they had shown by putting me next to their father. My opening line was original, if not brilliant. I said, "Hi, how are you doing? Are you married?"

"Yes," said Gloria. She started to blink rapidly. "To a white man. He's not here, but he's a good man." It looked as though she was trying hard to stand up for her absent husband. I wondered about that as I said, "Do you have kids?"

"No."

If she had been happily married and had a child, I would have walked away. The instant she said she was childless, I knew her husband must be merely a carpetbagger. I had a lot more in common with her than he or any other white man could. I had no idea how or when, but as far as I was concerned, it was all over except the formalities. She would be mine. Wildly excited but trying not to show it, I said, "We'll talk later, OK?"

"OK," she said with a little smile. A thrill shot through me from my scalp down to my toes, yet I was not mentally undressing that elegant and beautiful woman. I had no thought about taking her to bed. It was more of a spiritual feeling, that we were complementary halves of a single soul that were soon to become one.

I immediately told Glenn that Gloria was married, since I knew his values wouldn't permit him to go after another man's wife. I would like to think that if Gloria had been married to an Indian, I wouldn't have pursued her, but from the moment I looked into her eyes, I was thinking only with my heart. For the rest of the evening, I sat with a Pine Ridge guy named Poor Thunder. He had a drum and had taught his Navajo friends some Lakota songs. I helped them sing, but the real reason I chose that spot was so I could stare at Gloria while racking my brain for words that would attract her. She knew I was looking at her; I could see it made her nervous. Finally I hit on an angle. There was an upcoming meeting of the National Indian Education Association in Phoenix. Maybe I could parlay that into an excuse to see her again. During a break in the dancing, I went over to her and said, "I want to speak at the National Indian Youth Council. Do you know anyone on that board?"

"Oh, I'm with the NIEA—I can help. Do you have a résumé I can give them?"

"I don't do résumés. I'll give you a copy of one of my speeches"—the one in *Mother Jones*—"and if you want me to speak, you can take it from there. . . . What are you doing tomorrow?" I added.

"We're going to Chinle to celebrate my dad's birthday."

"My son Scott is dancing at First Mesa on the Hopi, so I'll be over that way. Could we meet Monday?"

"No, I'm working. I teach school."

"What do you teach?"

"Art."

We traded small talk for a while, then made a date to meet on Monday for breakfast at the Navajo Inn, where I was staying. When I arrived late, Gloria, nervous and shy, stuttered with her eyes, blinking rapidly and looking down. I found that endearing. It told me she had attached importance to our meeting. We talked about her life. She told me how much she wanted kids, but her husband didn't.

The words leaped out before I could think. I said, "I love kids—I want to have more. Will you marry me?"

"You already have children. Why do you want more?"

"Because I love them. I could give you a big line and all that, but I want to marry you. I just know it's right."

"I'm already married!"

"I don't care—he's only a white man, and from his actions, it's clear that he thinks you and your people aren't good enough to bear his children." Gloria seemed to agree without saying so.

We talked until she was late for work, but we never mentioned my speech. Just before we parted, I asked for her phone number and she wrote it down for me. Then she realized what she was doing and gave me her work number. I checked out of the motel, happy and whistling, and drove toward home. As I hit the Colorado line, I suddenly thought, why the hell did I *propose*? Why couldn't I be like other guys and have a nice safe affair? Why did I have to go whole-hog and let my feelings all hang out? Why did I just blurt out, "Will you marry me?"

I decided I could live with it, but as I drove on, I thought of the words of my Uncle Matthew King—"It's all in the blood." I remembered what Betty's Hopi parents had worried over when I had come to marry their daughter twenty years earlier—and all their fears had been realized in Michele and Scott, who will never be quite sure whether they are Lakota or Hopi. I reflected on what I had learned again at Yellow Thunder Camp: Golden eagles do not mate with bald eagles; our relatives follow the original instructions given them by the Great Mystery. If we have respect for life, we must make sure future generations will enter a world at least as strong as ours was when we came into it. I thought, what the hell has gotten into me? I realized that the old love bug had bitten me in the ass again. I didn't care about anything except being with Gloria.

It was evening when I got home, but I couldn't wait until morning, when she would be at work—I just had to hear her voice. I had my daughter

Veronica call her—and, of course, her husband, Gary Davis, answered. Gloria came to the phone wondering who Veronica was, and was startled to hear my voice. She asked me not to call her at home again, so I telephoned her at school, sometimes twice a day. Soon she was pouring out her heart to me, and I was sharing my dreams with her.

As I had suspected, Gloria was very unhappy in her marriage. Things were so strained that there was no physical contact between her and Davis. We arranged a meeting during the last week of May, in Albuquerque, where we planned an extended rendezvous in San Francisco. I was so afraid she wouldn't come that when her plane landed, I made my way to the door of the aircraft—something I had never done before—or since. When she appeared at last, I was filled with joy. We went to a Fisherman's Wharf restaurant with a panoramic view of the harbor and the bay and I sat next to her rather than across the table, because I wanted to be as close as possible. After eating, we walked along the pier among the boats. Then, in full view of the diners peering through the huge windows, I eased my body against hers and we held each other. After a while, I kissed her very tenderly. That was the kiss that sealed our commitment to each other. I was hopelessly and totally in love, and happier than I could ever remember.

We stayed in Berkeley in the home of an absent friend, honeymooning for four days, scarcely leaving the apartment except for a sacred pipe ceremony on Alcatraz. When we parted, every bone in my body cried out to be with her again. I had never met a woman who fulfilled me so completely. When she returned to Phoenix, Gloria told her husband that their eight-year marriage was over. They had been married in the traditional manner; and in the Navajo way, when a man removes his clothing and personal items from a woman's home, they are divorced. Davis took his possessions and moved out.

After he left, Gloria and I were on the phone constantly. We agreed to meet in Denver, and from there I took her to an International Indian Treaty Council conference in Sisseton, South Dakota. One of the speakers was a Palestinian. His English wasn't good, and I was very familiar with the issues— I had heard the same rap about conditions in the refugee camps and the Occupied Zone countless times before—so I was soon bored. I wanted to be alone with Gloria. Impatient to leave, I started to tug at her. "Come on, let's get out of here," I whispered. "No, this is interesting," she replied. "I've never heard any of these things before, and I had no idea what the Palestinians have endured." Then it dawned on me. What was I thinking? How could I show so little respect? No matter how often I had heard their message, I wouldn't walk out on my own elders—so why would I do that to people from other cultures? It woke me up and embarrassed me. That kind of thing hasn't happened again—an insight I owe to Gloria.

After the conference she went home, and I went to Albuquerque with Glenn to meet Phillip Anaya, his classmate at Harvard Law School. Anaya worked for Tom Lubban, who represented the Western Shoshone. Their research had confirmed what the Shoshone had been saying for generations—because their only treaty cession in 1851 to the United States was a right-of-way to the California goldfields, the tribe still possessed aboriginal title to all land in Nevada. Although the few remaining Shoshone raise horses and cattle, the U.S. Bureau of Land Management had illegally claimed jurisdiction over all their land.

Many Shoshone ranchers refuse to pay grazing and usage fees for their own land, so the BLM periodically raids their ranches and confiscates their livestock. When that happened to two elderly women, the Dan sisters, they sued for the return of their herds and for punitive damages. While their case worked its way through the courts, the BIA, without the tribe's knowledge, hired attorneys who went before the Indian Claims Commission with a claim for wrongful appropriation of their Nevada land. The commission awarded the tribe $27 million dollars—a few cents an acre. Very surprised to learn about the settlement, the Shoshone said, "We didn't ask for this money and we don't want it, because we never agreed to sell our land."

When the Dan sisters' lawsuit reached the U.S. Supreme Court, the government twisted the law, ducking the larger issue of land ownership and turning the case into a personal claim. The high court refused to hear their appeal, thus upholding lower-court rulings, which held that the Dan sisters must pay grazing fees and penalties—and would never get their cattle and horses back. In yet another example of the white man's justice, the BLM was given a license to steal Indian livestock. The final irony of the case is that Shoshone lands are not being used by non-Indians—so it was a clear-cut case of theft, among the most blatant by the federal government in this century.

When I heard about all that from Anaya and Lubban, I concluded that the U.S. government wanted to force all Indians to become welfare recipients. There are very few Western Shoshone. They have no tourist attractions and live in remote corners of the state, so they are largely out of sight and out of mind. Why not leave them alone? Because the U.S. government's policy is to impoverish all Indian people, including those who for centuries have been self-sufficient and productive, even by the standards of white society.

Lubban asked me to do something to help the Shoshone and the Dan sisters. "As much as I want to, as much as this is a terrible injustice and these women deserve every bit of support, I follow AIM's policy," I replied. "I don't go anywhere unless I'm invited."

"Well, I'm inviting you," said Lubban.

"You might be from the lost tribe of Israel, but you're not an Indian and don't live among the Shoshone," I said. "Unless they ask me to get involved, I can't." The Shoshone never did ask for my help, but the lesson of the Dan sisters has remained on my mind. I knew the white man couldn't let those Indians have their rights because then other Indians would demand the same. It galled me that there was no national outcry over the case, that the media and ordinary Americans didn't know or care what happened to Indians. If I couldn't go charging around championing the Dan sisters without an invitation, I could take another look at the history of Indian policy in this country and publicize my observations, at least by speaking at universities and in Indian country.

I learned that after 1891, most Indians were confined to America's concentration camps—the so-called reservations. The practice of religion and other forms of Indian expression went underground. Within about fifteen years after we were "pacified," Indians had made the socioeconomic adjustment to farming and ranching and were running horses and cattle on our reservations and becoming successful, outperforming their white counterparts in farming and ranching. When the United States saw this, they passed new laws and illegally opened up more Indian land to white homesteading.

The myth of pioneer America is that people swarmed out to the frontier because they were tough and independent. In reality, few white men wanted to leave the safety and comfort of "civilization." The government had to bribe immigrants to get them out of the eastern cities. Besides land—Indian land—the government had to offer free farm implements, livestock, and even cash before homesteaders would come.

In that way, white immigrants became mercenaries to settle our land. Still we survived, even prospered, while white farmers, unaccustomed to living on Grandmother Earth, struggled and even failed. Some returned to the East. That wouldn't do, so after the turn of the century we had federal "stock reduction" programs. They came and shot our horses, cows, and sheep right in front of us so whites could get higher prices for their own stock. That set us back, but we made still another adjustment. In about ten years, we were again making it economically. There were no fences on reservations, so herds were run communally, whole communities pitching in for branding, calving, and roundups. We had little cash, but it didn't matter. We bartered with one another, Oglalas from Pine Ridge swapping for produce or Missouri River fish with Yanktons. They also traded with local whites.

When World War I came along and many Indian farmers went off to fight, the government came in with another stock reduction plan. Unwilling to believe that a people who had lived in harmony with nature for millennia and who knew all there was to know about their environment could care for their land, the government introduced "land management" and white "experts." They installed "boss farmers" in each community. Indians couldn't do anything without their permission—and they acted only on orders from the bureaucracy. This was accompanied by yet another stock reduction—but this time, instead of shooting the animals, they hauled them away.

Still, it took only another dozen years to recover from this third assault. About the time prosperity returned to the reservations, the Depression hit.

The industrial world shuddered to a halt and white workers relearned the lessons of misery. Ironically, it was the best of times for reservation Indians, especially on the Plains. Whole families lived in cast-off military tents, even through those bitter winters—but institutions like the extended family survived and prospered because people still had control of their economic lives. When Civilian Conservation Corps camps were established to give people jobs building roads and other public works, many Indians were employed. Their wages and those of the whites became an enormous boon to the local economy. By 1934, Indians once again prospered.

So that year the Congress passed the Wheeler-Howard Act, also known as the Indian Reorganization Act, which was supposed to give tribes self-rule and eventually end their dependency on the federal government. Thirty years later, the South African government decreed the Bantu Development Act, which institutionalized apartheid in Africa. Except for slight differences, those two documents are almost identical. The Indian Reorganization Act created red apartheid in America. It imposed tribal constitutions that forced us into the evils of elective government.

The act provided that each reservation could accept the BIA's constitution or reject it by a *majority* of the popular vote. This in itself was illegal. The Fort Laramie Treaty specified that changes can't be made unless three-fourths of adult males agree to them. While virtually no Indians favored the act, voting isn't part of our tradition—we believe in consensus and avoid participating in such divisive rituals. Among thousands of eligible Hopis, for example, only nine voted in the Indian Reorganization Act election. So it was throughout Indian country. Hardly anyone voted except a handful of hang-around-the-forts. Nevertheless the BIA announced—after the election, of course—that because travel on reservations was so "difficult," everyone who didn't vote *against* the act would be counted as a "yes" vote. Thus the Wheeler-Howard Act was passed by an "overwhelming majority." Once "accepted," the act could not be rescinded by tribal councils, even though it made economic opportunity virtually impossible by putting tribal affairs into the hands of people who couldn't assemble a consensus, thus assuring that continuing political instability would discourage all outside investment. That left all important matters in the hands of BIA agents who bucked all decisions to Washington. The boss farmer, who had at least lived on the land, now gave way to faceless bureaucrats thousands of miles away.

A few years later World War II began and great numbers of young Indians, convinced by U.S. propaganda that if Germany and Japan won, their people would be even worse off, enlisted for military service. For most, it was the first time they had seen the outside world; they returned to their homes much changed. Within a few years, relocation began, and with no way to support themselves on reservations, tens of thousands left for the cities.

Despite the devastating effects of U.S. Indian policy, still there were aboriginal people prospering in dignity and preserving their traditions. The United States stole two billion acres of our land—but we still had almost fifty million acres. Under it was 40 percent of all mineral reserves remaining in this country, including vast quantities of low-sulphur coal and uranium. By all the rules of capitalism, American Indians should be the wealthiest people on earth, richer per capita than the Saudis or Japanese. The federal government, however, holds all our land in trust and allows America's wealthiest corporations to exploit our oil, gas, coal and other minerals in return for token royalties. As of this writing, less than 500,000 Indians live on reservations, yet we and our lands contribute more than six billion dollars to America's gross national product. The American taxpayer pays two billion dollars to the government's Indian Affairs offices, of which more than 80 percent is taken by administrative costs. We give six billion dollars and are repaid two hundred million? Hardly a fair deal.

When I called Gloria on August 22, 1984, she said, "Guess what? I'm pregnant!" Overjoyed, I said, "I'll drive down to Albuquerque to see you tomorrow." We headed back to Yellow Thunder Camp, where we were joined spiritually through a Lakota marriage ceremony. Eventually we would also participate in traditional rites in Porcupine and at Chinle. To please Gloria and her family, devout Christians all, we were also blessed at the Presbyterian Church. To ensure that our children would be enrolled as members of the Oglala Sioux tribe, I bit my tongue and participated in a civil marriage ceremony recognized by the BIA. A few days after the first of the ceremonies, Gloria and I went on our honeymoon—to Tripoli, to attend a conference, which included Louis Farrakhan and the Nation of Islam.

In 1984, when Jesse Jackson ran for president, Farrakhan held a rally for him at a Chicago National Guard armory and invited me to speak. I issued a challenge to Jesse, his Rainbow Coalition, and the Nation of Islam to get involved in the Indians' land struggle and to study U.S. government Indian policies and how they were being applied around the world. It was a night of political hoopla, and people had come to lionize Jesse. Few were interested in a dose of reality, so my words were not well received.

Listening carefully to the other speakers, I was amazed to hear Farrakhan scolding his own people, yet also pumping them up. I had never heard a black man speak to his own that way, using all the hateful racist words and phrases such as *spade, coon,* and *nigger* that are so offensive to people of color. Farrakhan spoke also about Islam and Zionism, throwing blame around and condemning Jewish people for certain acts. But as hard as he was on Jews, he got on his own people many times worse. It was a masterful speech, starting slowly and thoughtfully, his voice becoming louder as he picked up the pace to condemn blacks while simultaneously reminding them of their untapped potential. He castigated blacks for continuing down a road toward exploitative misery when they could change themselves. He reached a crescendo of enthusiasm as he told them how to use the beauty of their souls, and then abruptly concluded with wisdom, thoughtfulness, and hope.

Every time I've been with Farrakhan I have admired his personal kindness and gentle ways. He is a humble person who always gives credit to others—first to Islam, then to his people. Always very polite, he compliments those around them. He's not afraid to take heat for his words. When he speaks in public, whether at New York's Madison Square Garden, the Los Angeles Forum, the Chicago Armory, or anywhere else, tapes of his speeches are available for anyone to dissect or criticize. I admire that in any person.

From the moment we met, Farrakhan showed great respect for Indian people. Of all the non-Indian leaders who say they are allied with Indian people, only he brought his whole family into the *inipi*. Only he and his wife and sons camped out with us and stayed to help us pray at our 1984 sun dance—actions we have never before seen from non-Indian leaders. Even today, when New Age wanna-bes and hippies come to our sun dances, they do it in search of selfish goals, hoping that by appropriating our religious ceremonies for their own use, they will find a path to personal liberation. Farrakhan had no agenda except being there to participate, to share spirituality with Indian people. I'll respect him for that as long as I live.

My married life with Gloria began when we returned from a honeymoon in Libya in September to live in my hillside log cabin at Porcupine. At Yellow Thunder Camp, Shorty Blacksmith and other elders had taught me many new things, including my responsibilities as a father in an extended family. In the clan system of the traditional closed Lakota community, everyone has a role in raising children. To us, life begins at conception. The first twelve months of a baby's life are broken into four quadmesters, and in each we have a different responsibility. Gloria's pregnancy was a very beautiful time for me. Fascinated by the life growing inside her, I was reawakened to the knowledge and the stories that my grandparents had filled me with when I was young. For the first three months, I sang to the child in Gloria's womb. For the next quadmester, I continued to sing, but I also began to talk to our baby, which we both felt sure was a girl. In the third quadmester, I divided my time almost equally between song and storytelling.

Early in her pregnancy, Gloria went for a sonogram, but when we saw the little fetus squirming in pain, trying in vain to get away from the waves of intense sound blasting into the womb, I made the technician turn the machine off immediately. How can we scream at our children that way? I realized again that the brutality and violence of Western medicine is yet another indicator of how primitive it can be.

That was a tough time for Gloria. Her parents had ostracized her for her abrupt divorce and for marrying outside her Navajo heritage and refused to visit us at Pine Ridge. Despite her increasingly obvious pregnancy, she threw herself into AIM, taking an active role in a series of demonstrations. Gloria carried signs at Bismarck jails and courthouses to show support for Leonard Peltier, the AIMster who had been convicted wrongly of having killed two FBI agents at the Jumping Bull ranch in 1975. She also joined a demonstration against the brutal incarceration of a young Pine Ridge woman who had fasted to protest being jailed and beaten after she refused to testify before a grand jury.

During Gloria's third quadmester, an Indian woman named Margaret Yankton came to us and said she had had a dream. Our child, despite what we believed, would be a boy, she said, and we should consider naming him *Tatanka*—male buffalo. A few weeks later, in January—the eighth month of Gloria's pregnancy—we drove back from Rapid City through the Badlands, north of Pine Ridge. It was a dark, moonless night, about twenty degrees below zero. Suddenly an enormous black bull buffalo appeared in front of my headlights. He was standing astride the highway on the first part of a gentle S curve near the reservation boundary. As I slammed on the brakes, he ambled to the shoulder and walked past us on Gloria's side. Pulling up as quickly as I could, I turned the van around and started to look for him. Both sides of the road were lined with high barbed-wire fences. As I drove along, searching with high-beam headlights, I realized it was impossible for an animal that size to leap the fence, and there were no breaks in it. We never saw him again—the bull had apparently vanished into thin air! Gloria and I knew then that our child *was* a boy, and we would name him Tatanka.

Gloria's father is an Omaha, a nation that follows a patrilineal line, so our son belongs to the Deer Clan. We were honored to name him, according to the clan's wishes, Xila Sábe, Black Eagle. Few Indian nations allow two animals in a single name, but we Lakota are among the exceptions. *Sapa* means "black" and *Wanbli* means "eagle" in Lakota, so our son would be named Tatanka Wanbli Sapa Xila Sábe—Black Buffalo Eagle.

I was so emotionally involved with the developing baby that I experienced a sympathetic pregnancy, including swollen ankles, tender nipples, morning sickness, and everything else. When Gloria's water broke on February 18, 1985, I was so excited that I gathered up all the stuff we had packed for the hospital, loaded them in the van—and drove off without her! I was about two miles down the road before I realized what I had done.

Only weeks before, Gloria and I had demonstrated at Pine Ridge Hospital over the death of a dehydrated infant, whom IHS doctors had misdiagnosed and given a drug that had caused its agonizing death. Before that, no Indian had successfully sued the IHS, but after our demonstration, the Young Bear family filed suit and the hospital paid off. If they had insisted on a trial, they might have won ten times or more what they settled for, but at least a precedent had been established. For the first time, Indians could hold accountable those who practiced medicine on them. Because of that, Pine

Ridge Hospital officials wanted nothing to do with Gloria. They sent her to Rapid City Regional Hospital in an ambulance. I followed.

With Peggy, I had witnessed the miracle of Tatuye Topa Najinwin's birth. Just thinking about what women go through to create life fills me with a sense of wonder each time I witness a child's entrance into this world. As I had believed when Peggy gave birth, it seemed impossible to break the bond forged by sharing the beauty of that experience. Even today, I don't think a couple can ever really break apart after sharing the birth of their child.

Gloria's water had broken, but she wasn't dilating. I stayed up all night in the labor room until Sherry came to help. After twenty-five hours of labor, Tatanka's heartbeat became very erratic, so we decided on a Caesarean—a good thing, since his umbilical cord was wrapped around his neck. Gloria recalls that as soon as Tatanka emerged, I cried, "He's a darkie!" I was very proud of his coloring and his thick black hair. Like most brown babies, he had a blue birthmark that would disappear before he was two.

I wiped the blood from his face, ears, and eyes and held him close. I wouldn't let the nurses have Tatanka back. I began to sing to him. One of the white women in the delivery room, perhaps an anesthesiologist or the head nurse, said something like, "I suppose we'll have to listen to these savage chants now." Gloria heard her, but fortunately I didn't. I held Tatanka for four hours, walking through the corridors singing and talking to him in Lakota. It was a beautiful time. According to South Dakota law, every newborn must have a solution of silver-nitrate drops placed in its eyes to prevent the transmission of venereal disease from mother to child. To me, it is the ultimate insult, the most offensive thing I can think of. I wanted to scream and punch the doctors every time I think of that assault on motherhood that demeans and dehumanizes the birthing canal and the wonder of life itself. When I finally took my son to where doctors put drops in his eyes, I said, "You're not going to do this in my presence. I won't be part of allowing it." I took my son to Gloria and left the room.

For the next three months, I never left Tatanka's side. He must have thought I was his mother and Gloria was just a feeding bag. When he awoke in the middle of the night, I got up and walked with him. Only I could get him to quiet down; I sang the *Inkpata*, a little boy's song. I didn't mind losing sleep—I loved caring for him so much that it never seemed a burden. As I fulfilled my fatherly responsibilities, I came to understand a bit about motherhood. That was so soul-satisfying, so inherently good, that it was beyond description. At the same time, I was sad—because my people were colonized by the white man, at forty-five I was just beginning to comprehend and enjoy the life I should have known at twenty. If my ancestors had remained a free people, I could have raised *all* my children that way.

4 8
▼▼▼▼▼▼▼▼▼

Nicaragua

B efore Tatanka's birth and after returning from my honeymoon in Libya,
I had gone to Washington in the fall of 1984 to see Francisco Campbell,
the Nicaraguan ambassador to the United States. AIM and the International Indian Treaty Council wanted to take the 1868 Fort Laramie Treaty
issue to the International Court of Justice, but we needed a member nation
to sponsor us. Nicaragua had been among the court's founders and AIM had
ties to the Sandinistas that predated the revolution, so I felt they should and
would help us. I therefore attended a reception at the Nicaraguan embassy
at which the press attaché tried to drum up media interest in a forthcoming
visit by Jaime Wheelock, the Nicaraguan minister of agriculture and one of
President Daniel Ortega's closest confidants.

That was at the height of the Reagan administration's anti-Sandinista
hysteria. No reporters covered Wheelock's arrival at Dulles Airport. I was
there with an AIM delegation and a sacred drum. Because Indians were the
original inhabitants of this hemisphere, I thought it was highly appropriate
that Indians should greet an international visitor. We brought symbolic gifts
of welcome—an expensive piece of Indian beadwork, a bit of tobacco, and
an eagle feather. A short, slender, Irish-looking man in his late twenties,
Wheelock was from a wealthy family that had long been prominent in the

Nicaraguan oligarchy. As he descended the stairway from the plane, we welcomed him with the AIM song. He swept past without a word, not even
glancing at us, motioning vaguely with his hands as if to say, "Give that stuff
you brought to one of my underlings." I've been around the world, and no
one else except Americans had ever snubbed me or other Indians so blatantly.

I had an appointment to see Wheelock. Later that day, I went to his
suite at the Madison Hotel. I waited for about four hours; then his aides said
he had to leave for a reception, but I could have fifteen minutes with him.
Wheelock acted as if he didn't want to dirty himself by touching me, and
wouldn't shake my hand. I told him the United States had breached international law when it unilaterally violated our treaty, and we wanted to sue
for damages in the world court. I remember him saying, "The Nicaraguan
government is afraid of the U.S. government and what it can do to us economically, so we don't want to do anything that could antagonize Washington or jeopardize our position in the international community."

"What happened to the Sandinistas' revolutionary fervor?" I asked.
"What did all your slogans mean? What about the justice that the revolution
was supposed to bring? Isn't that why we fought alongside you?"

"Well, now reality has set in and we must deal with it," he replied. Speaking
as though I were a third-grader, he explained that he hadn't come there to take
risks, and that his government would never drag the United States to the world
court on our behalf. That seemed to smash to smithereens AIM's new treaty
strategy, but I couldn't believe that Wheelock's statements accurately reflected
his government's position. I tried not to take his obvious distaste personally. I
knew that despite the departure of Somoza, Latin America's economic system—
a creature of feudal oligarchies established to exploit the land and the indigenous
people—had never changed. Its way of life rests on the most vile racism known
on earth. The conquistadores and their descendants tortured and murdered Indians in ways even the Nazis couldn't have stomached. Most whites in Latin
America still treat dogs and farm animals better than they treat Indian people.
Even their churches collaborate in indoctrinating people to look on us as primitive subhumans. Racism is institutionalized in every aspect of their society.

I knew a cultural attaché whom we had affectionately nicknamed Low
Rider. A dedicated revolutionary who had worked for the struggle with leaf-
lets and demonstrations in the streets of San Francisco and by fighting in the
Nicaraguan mountains, he had become the Sandinistas' informal liaison to
AIM. When *he* spoke about solidarity, I believed him, so we could talk
straight up. After leaving Wheelock, I found Low Rider and said, "Your revolution hasn't changed the oligarchy a bit."

He emphatically disagreed. "Oh, no, these guys are different. Wheelock
comes from one of the established families, but look how young he is! He's
in there for change." He promised to try to find someone else among the

Sandinista leadership who would be more receptive to our request. That night at an embassy reception for Wheelock, I cornered Ambassador Francisco Campbell and put it to him directly. "What about Wheelock's snubbing us? What kind of bullshit is this?" I said.

"You misunderstand," he replied soothingly. "At this time in Nicaragua, we're forging new relationships with the U.S." He went on in that vein until I realized it was a different recording of the same old tune.

Several AIMsters witnessed that insult and the one at the airport, but when I mentioned it to my brother Bill, he said I had been offended because I wasn't treated with the usual degree of respect that Russell Means had become used to. But that wasn't it. Unfortunately, I now know Bill doesn't understand that it isn't a matter of people choosing their favorite Indian. When one Indian anywhere in the world is treated with racial hatred, all Indians are victims. Bill has yet to fully understand the depth and scope of the hatred that the Western Hemisphere focuses on Indians.

A few weeks later, in November of 1985, a Chicano/Indio lawyer named Jim Anaya, a law-school classmate of Glenn Morris's, asked if I wanted to investigate how Nicaragua's Miskito Indians were faring. The Sandinistas were negotiating with MISURASATA, a coalition of Nicaraguan Indians formed during the honeymoon year after the revolution and led by Brooklyn Rivera. In 1981, many Nicaraguan Indian leaders had been arrested. The Miskito people had charged that their rights were being systematically violated. Indians had hoped that the Sandinistas would keep their revolutionary promises and allow self-determination and autonomy within their territories. The new regime kept saying that was what they wanted; but more and more, it looked as if they were out to incorporate Indian lands and people within a Marxist, state-controlled economy—and were willing to use military force to do it if necessary. When the Sandinistas began forced relocation, the Indians declared war. In May, MISURASATA met with the Sandinistas to resolve differences, but the talks broke down.

A second round of talks was coming up at the presidential palace in Bogotá, Colombia, and Anaya invited me to go as an observer. I said, "I'll check with Bill and with the AIM leadership, but you know our position. We're pro-Sandinista. We don't support the Contras." Anaya reassured me that the Miskitos were not "Contra Indians." I called Bill and asked him what he thought about my going. He had visited Nicaragua's Atlantic coast as a guest of the Sandinistas, and had been told that Moravian priests controlled the Miskito communities, and villagers did whatever they were told to do. Bill said the Sandinistas had proof that the Miskito people were not truly indigenous—not really Indians—because in the sixteenth century, they had separated from the dominant mixed-blood Spanish-speaking culture. Somehow, in the last hundred years, they had made up their own language!

I said, "When did the Sandinistas make you an anthropologist?" and he laughed it off.

Finally, he said, "Go on down there—I'm confident you'll see Brooklyn Rivera for what he is."

I called Larry Leventhal, and he said, "You should go and find out." Finally, I called Clyde Bellecourt, who said he didn't want me to go—it wasn't AIM's business. Nevertheless, I charged my tickets and left.

At the presidential palace in Bogotá, I met Lumberto Campbell, military commandant of Nicaragua's Atlantic coast region, which includes the Miskito homeland. After a friendly handshake and some small talk, I said, "Tell me one thing—are Brooklyn Rivera and MISURASATA Contras?" He told me, "We wouldn't be here if they were." That was good enough for me.

Among the observers at the peace talks were Indians from Central and South America, representing tens of millions of Indian people in Panamá, Costa Rica, Peru, Ecuador, Bolivia, Colombia, and Mexico. Every one of them had come to support MISURASATA. No matter what my brother Bill believed, how could I insist that they and Lumberto Campbell were wrong?

Brooklyn Rivera was in his early thirties, a wiry, good-looking man of average height. His wavy black hair was cropped short and he sported a thin mustache. Fluent in four or five languages, he had a graduate degree in math. He sat for long periods listening to a barrage of "expert" advice from groups that included the American Indian Law Resource Center. The center had hired Armstrong Wiggins, a MISURASATA lawyer and a refugee from Nicaragua, as its liaison with the struggle inside Nicaragua. The rest of those guys, however, acted just like white men, telling Brooklyn in detail what he should do and how he should do it. My respect and admiration for him grew as I watched him listen to hours of conflicting advice and, with the interests of his people paramount, make one wise decision after another.

The U.S. State Department was telling the American public that Rivera was the leader of no more than a dozen people living in refugee camps in Costa Rica. I didn't believe that, but I had no inkling that MISURASATA was anything but an organization in exile. Within a few days of my arrival in Colombia, however, I began to hear that the group also had fighters inside Nicaragua.

I became more and more disgusted with the insults the Sandinistas laid on MISURASATA. They were much like the offensive remarks I had heard from BIA staff members in the 1950s and 1960s, expressions of a mentality that assumed Indians were so stupid that everything had to be explained as though we were little children. Every time they talked that way, the MISURASATA delegates would reply so wisely and simply that the Sandinistas should have been embarrassed—but like the fat BIA woman who "taught" me how to dial a telephone, they apparently had no shame. Even in public, Tomás Borgé Martinez, representing the Sandinistas at the Bogotá peace conference, called the Miskito people "monkeys hanging around in trees." I wanted to know how those "monkeys" got him to an international peace conference.

The Sandinistas insisted that actual negotiations be held behind closed doors, so none of the observers could watch. Even so, we met with Rivera every day. When the Sandinistas abruptly walked out of the talks, I called Bill and told him I was attending a press conference to support MISURASATA and Brooklyn Rivera. My brother went nuts. He didn't ask how I had arrived at that decision; he just screamed at me. He called me a sellout and a goon and cursed me with every obscenity he could think of. When he paused for breath, I said, "Wait, you don't know what you're saying! Brooklyn is like Red Cloud, a great leader." That only set him off again. When he quieted down, I asked Bill not to condemn Brooklyn until he had seen him in action. "Never! I only want to see him at the other end of a gun—and I'll pull the trigger!" he shouted. His anger mystified me. Bill had never met Brooklyn, but he certainly knew me well enough to know I had some idea of what I was doing.

Just about every organization attending the peace talks was at the press conference. I said, "I do not support the racist policies of the United States of America and I do not support the racist policies of Nicaragua. . . . I have a record of fighting against the imperialists. . . . I'm going to go home, get a hundred AIM warriors, return to Nicaragua with a shovel in one hand, a rifle in the other, and the sacred pipe of peace in my heart. It will depend on the Sandinistas which hand we use."

Bill went bananas over that. Worse, he wouldn't talk to me or return my calls. I was confident in my decision, and believed my integrity was beyond reproach. I had been jailed countless times for my beliefs, gone to prison for those beliefs, survived five assassination attempts for them. I was sure that as soon as I got home and laid out the facts, people in AIM would share my support for the Miskito people. Instead, I returned to a maelstrom of hatred—the most intense I had encountered since I sued the Cleveland Indians baseball team. The entire Left rose up to condemn me.

For years, the International Indian Treaty Council had been building up a status of most favored organization with the Sandinistas. Council leaders got free plane trips to Managua, where they were feted at receptions and treated like heads of state. By publicly announcing support for MISURASATA, I had undermined what they had built up. To guys such as Vernon Bellecourt, AIM was always supposed to be on the far left of whatever white man's movement was most popular. Supporting Brooklyn Rivera and Indians who were fighting for their lives, their people, and their culture against the "darlings" of the Left—the Sandinistas—wasn't part of that plan.

So firmly does the Left control higher education in America that all my scheduled lectures at state universities and community colleges around the country were immediately canceled. Everyone from Ted Kennedy to the hippies condemned me as a traitor to AIM. Clyde and Vernon issued press releases. Clyde claimed he had kicked me out of AIM, which was absurd. AIM hadn't had a national office since Dennis had gone underground almost ten years earlier. Every chapter is autonomous, and I never belonged to Clyde's.

In short, they treated me like an Indian. As far as the Left is concerned, no Indian has integrity unless he goes along with their programs. For that alone, I despise the Left. What hurt me most was not that my own brother and the Bellecourts, especially Clyde, had publicly vilified me and sided with a government against Indian people. I knew then that if I maintained even informal involvement with AIM's leadership, I would have to turn away from my search for Indian freedom and independence to address their attacks—in short, I would have to join the fight among ourselves.

A few weeks after my return from Colombia, I was invited in early fall to go into Nicaragua on a fact-finding mission with representatives of other North American Indian groups. Brooklyn said if I could get myself to Costa Rica, his people would take us into Miskito country along the Atlantic coast. I recruited a small contingent to come along, including Glenn Morris and Long Soldier, an Oglala Lakota College student who came as a reporter for his school newspaper. The others were Hank Adams, director of the Survival of American Indians Association; Chauncy Whitworth, a Dakota from the Fort Peck Reservation; and another guy representing Washington state Indians involved in the fishing-rights struggle. Tagging along were Bob Martin, a free-lance television reporter from Albuquerque; and a correspondent from a Tokyo magazine.

In early October of 1985, we flew to San José, Costa Rica, where MISURASATA leaders took us to Miskito refugee camps on the way to Puerto Limón, on the Atlantic coast. Because Costa Rica's land border with Nicaragua is mostly impassable rain forest, MISURASATA used motorized canoes to bring supplies into and people out of their homeland. We helped the Miskito people fell a giant tree and turn its trunk into a huge dugout canoe. We left the first week in November—the start of the Caribbean gale season. After staying overnight in a little village north of Limón, we loaded our gear and supplies aboard our canoe. More than thirty feet long and six feet wide, it had powerful twin outboards.

Early the next night, two Sandinista patrol boats appeared and chased us out to sea. As we headed for some low-lying keys, the wind came up. The seas began to grow, and soon we were battling waves as high as twelve feet. I sat in the bow; as we topped one wave, I glanced back. The stern of our boat was *below* me—almost straight down. Gray-green waves broke over our canoe, and we were bailing constantly. The seas were so rough that we had little choice but to head back to Costa Rica, but the furious waves had smashed our compass. The captain of our boat, a Miskito named Eustice, was as familiar with the coastal currents as a New Yorker is with the subway system. I'm not sure how he did it, but he didn't seem to need a compass or even the stars to navigate.

Seated on top of the supplies and wearing a life vest, I was so seasick that I didn't care if I was washed overboard. I would have welcomed anything to end the dizzying rock and roll of the angry ocean. The others kept encouraging me, "Hang on, make sure you're secure!" but I didn't give a shit. "Help us bail!" they shouted, but I still didn't give a shit. I felt worse than I ever imagined a man could feel. Eustice shouted above the wind's roar to tell us that if the seas got much bigger, our canoe might break apart. If that happened, we should each try to grab a piece of anything that floated and hang onto it, he said.

At dawn the wind slackened and the seas subsided to rolling six-foot whitecaps. I looked around at a panorama that seemed right out of a Turner seascape. Even our twin fifty-five-horsepower engines couldn't keep us heading into the swells. Time after time, we struggled sideways through wave troughs, with water pouring in over the gunwales. Somehow, Eustice and his boatmen steered us through the storm—a miracle I'll never forget. Finally we neared the mouth of a big river where warmer, lighter fresh water mixed with the cooler, heavier salt seas to create vicious riptides. Even laden with all our supplies, our craft rode like a surfboard. It looked as if the swirling water would toss us around until we broke into pieces. Eustice said, "If you're in the canoe when it gets busted up, you'll probably get slammed around and killed—so we'll tell you when to jump and swim for it."

Suddenly we were in a bay with a beach on each side. Brooklyn and the other Miskito people yelled for us to jump, then took their own advice. Glenn and Eustice and I looked at one another and stayed put. For some reason, I wasn't scared. I watched wide-eyed as we sped headlong toward the beach, driven by the current and what was left of the storm. We were alone as the shoreline rushed up at us. Suddenly we were past all the turmoil, floating slowly on calm waters. In a few minutes, our dugout gently nudged the bottom as the bow ran up on a beach of white crystalline sand.

Everyone was safe. Paddling up the estuary to a little cay with a house, we unloaded the boat, then headed into Limón with our camouflage raincoats turned inside out to show bright yellow linings—we didn't want to look like soldiers making a clandestine entry. It would be months before we could return to Nicaragua. We were eager to get home and tell America's leftist organizations, which so often had professed support for Indian rights, that Brooklyn and his followers were willing to make peace with the Sandinistas, but only as full partners. We hoped that once they had the facts, those groups would work to persuade the Sandinistas to forge an agreement with MISURASATA to guarantee Indian autonomy. There was at least one good reason why the Left should want that. As allies, the Sandinistas and MISURASATA would be far more effective against the CIA-backed Contras.

Despite all I had heard in the refugee camps, when I returned from Costa Rica I still had faith in the purity of the Nicaraguan revolution. I still believed it was *the* revolution, the turning point for this hemisphere. Everyone in AIM believed it would be the dawn of a new era for Indians, that the Sandinistas would be the first government to deal with us as human beings. When I reflect on how naive and stupid I was, I'm almost ashamed to talk about it.

Shortly after my return to the United States, Colorado AIM called for a leadership meeting to straighten out our disagreement over the Sandinistas. Neither my brother Bill nor the Bellecourts showed up. Dennis Banks gave what was effectively his retirement speech. He said it was time for younger people to take the helm and that he was stepping down. He wished everyone well and concluded by saying he would always be identified with the American Indian Movement. Nothing about AIM's position on Nicaragua was resolved.

Elsewhere around the country, instead of showing a constructive interest in our eyewitness account of what was happening in Miskito country, everyone from liberal Democrats to full-blown Marxist ideologues joined in vilifying us. The lefties all but lined up to challenge everything we told them. They demanded concrete evidence of the Sandinista atrocities we had heard about from Miskito people. Our integrity, never questioned when we spoke out about U.S. Indian policy, was suddenly suspect. Not even reporter Bob Martin's photos and videotaped interviews with refugees were acceptable proof. The Left was behaving like the John Birch Society, demanding evidence of a standard usually reserved for murder trials.

I had conversations with Hank Adams and with Brooklyn Rivera, who was then working out of a Washington, D.C., office provided by the Indian Law Resource Center. We decided that if the Left wanted proof, we would travel through Miskito country long enough to get that proof. The day after Christmas, I appeared on the *Larry King Show* to explain why I was returning to Miskito territory, and then I headed back to Costa Rica. Besides Brooklyn, our group included Bob Martin, Hank Adams, and Clem Chartier, a Métis from Saskatoon, who was president of the World Council of Indigenous People. We assembled in Puerto Limón in the first week of January 1986 and loaded our canoe with food, supplies, and gasoline. Our plan was to spend two weeks or so touring coastal villages, taking photos and videos and tape-recording depositions as we went.

We left Costa Rica in the afternoon, and at dark put in at a low-lying island several miles offshore in Nicaraguan waters. I had expected to have to sneak into the country, but at noon the next day, Eustice and two other boatmen began to reload our canoe. Brooklyn flashed a grin and said, "Get ready, I'm going home." As we headed in, I thought, this is great. We're going into an Indian nation that's so secure we can arrive safely in broad daylight. When we went ashore, I was astonished. Lined up in ranks on the beach were about a hundred MISURASATA warriors waiting to welcome us. It made me proud to be an Indian.

I noticed that some of the warriors seemed to be Creoles or ladinos. When I asked about that, I learned that many Nicaraguan Creoles had joined MISURASATA because it was the most effective way of resisting Sandinista policies. Ladinos, people of mixed Indian and European blood, had rallied to the MISURASATA cause from as far away as the Pacific coast because the Indians were by far the best-organized group fighting the Managua regime.

We spent two days as honored guests in the village of Kwamwatla, where just about everyone came to greet us, and nearly every family offered to feed us. We also spoke with elders' councils and leaders from nearby communities who came to tell us about conditions in their areas.

On the first day, Bob Martin, a trained medic, was asked to patch up a wounded warrior. Few doctors or nurses venture into Miskito country, so he was asked to treat sick and wounded people of all ages throughout our journey. In Kwamwatla, he went from house to house, bandaging wounds, treating minor ailments, and making extensive notes on every disease he encountered. People, especially children, were dying of white man's ailments, such as malaria, measles, and whooping cough, that could easily have been cured with inexpensive drugs—if any had been available.

From Kwamwatla, our canoe took us north to Ariswatla, where we took more depositions. Our next destination was farther north, near Puerto Cabezas, Sandinista military headquarters for the Atlantic coast. To get there, we had to go back to the coast, passing through Prinsapolca, a town occupied by about 250 Sandinista troops. We moved by night in our seagoing canoe and several smaller ones over the Miskito's amazingly efficient transportation system of lagoons, jungle marshes, rivers, and canals. As we neared Prinsapolca, the engines were shut down and the boatmen began to paddle. There was a ragged chorus of metallic clicks as rifles were loaded and rounds were chambered. Then it was quiet. I was told to lie down in the boat, but I raised my head to look around a few times. The river was lined with houses on stilts. From beneath them, I saw, from time to time, flashlights blinking coded messages. Feeling naked and exposed, I whispered to Brooklyn, "Give me a gun!" He said, "They're all in use."

Prinsapolca is strung out along a meandering river. We paddled for several minutes at a time in nearly total silence until a few blinks from a flashlight halted us and we waited for a signal that it was safe to continue. We went deeper and deeper into a town that was crawling with Sandinistas. It was so quiet that my own heartbeat sounded like a drum. Then faintly, I heard the sound of waves breaking on a beach ahead. We were approaching the sea, and the time of greatest danger. The Sandinistas had surely posted a heavy guard at the river's mouth. The tension became almost unbearable as we eased along, stopping and waiting and moving ahead, with the ocean's roar growing louder by the minute. Suddenly we were paddling into breakers. After a few minutes, we started the engines and headed northward out to sea. We were safe—at least for the moment.

At Wounta and later, inland, at Layasiksa, we walked through savanna country for hours before reaching the jungle. Then we climbed to the mountain village of Sukupin on our way to Yulu, where we completed our observation of Indian life in the region. The Miskito, as well as the Sumu and Rama peoples, maintain a traditional balance with the natural world. We saw a prosperous region that offers a peaceful, comfortable lifestyle in which to cultivate Indian values. We found no evidence that the Miskito people had traded their heritage for pie-in-the-sky promises from the Moravian Church. Instead, we saw that even those who professed belief in Christianity had adapted that European doctrine to their own traditional values. The church had been "Indianized" far more than the people had been Christianized.

Under the Somoza regime, Managua's dictators didn't try to do much for the Indians, but they didn't try to do much *to* them, either. Indian regions were self-sufficient and largely self-governing. All that had changed when the Marxists came to power. The Sandinistas were trying to force the Indians to integrate with the rest of the country by using all the tools of traditional colonialism. We were amused to learn that MISURASATA was actually a Sandinista creation. The acronym means "Miskito, Sumu, and Rama Indians *with* the Sandinistas," and the coalition was supposed to convince Indians to join the revolutionary government. When Managua, with typical Eurocentric arrogance toward Indians, chose MISURASATA's leader themselves, their true purpose was exposed. Their hand-picked Miskito, Steadman Faggoth, was a CIA-backed opportunist who was accused of having worked with Somoza's dreaded National Guard. One of his first acts was to denounce several genuine Miskito leaders, including Brooklyn Rivera and Armstrong Wiggins, as tools of the CIA. After arresting them, the Sandinistas discovered their mistake, but by then their credibility with the Indians was nil.

Confusing matters still more, when Faggoth was exposed, he led a small group to Honduras, where they called themselves MISURA and allied themselves with the CIA-backed contras. When MISURA collapsed, Faggoth took off for Miami. The remaining handful of his followers formed yet another splinter group that obeyed the Contras in return for salaries and supplies. When it became obvious to Foggy Bottom that MISURASATA wanted nothing from the CIA and would instead defend Indian interests, the CIA started another "Indian" organization, operationally a Nicaraguan equivalent of the BIA. So although Managua and Washington continued to loathe each other, they did have one thing in common. The last thing either wanted was for Indians to exercise autonomy and self-determination.

In the village of Layasiksa, we took several depositions from people who described how Sandinistas had rounded up about twelve thousand Miskito and Sumo people who lived along the Río Coco, and had relocated them to concentration camps farther south. Everywhere we went, I noticed that there were few teenage boys. When I asked about that, I learned that the Sandinistas were trying to keep the Indians from raising an army by systematically murdering young men. In Ariswatla, Sandinista helicopters had landed troops who rounded up all boys between the ages of twelve and sixteen, herded them into a local schoolhouse, and set it afire, burning them alive. As I continued to ask about the absence of young men, I heard the same story, with minor variations, in almost every village. In Wounta, soldiers had clubbed the youngsters to death. In a village near Sukupin, children had been buried alive. In several other communities, they had been machine-gunned.

We collected depositions from many other teenagers who had been abducted and forced to serve in the army. Dozens of Miskito women said they had been raped by Sandinista soldiers. I was only a little relieved to learn that although those atrocities still occurred, they were increasingly rare since MISURASATA forces had taken control of the countryside and forced the Sandinistas to change tactics. Denied control of roads and waterways, in recent months the Sandinistas had taken to bombing and strafing Indian communities. They had also begun to use airmobile operations, landing infantry to seize certain villages. Surrounded by hostile territory, however, the Sandinistas were trapped in those enclaves; they had to resupply and reinforce by air. Managua's bully boys had managed to create their own little Vietnam.

Arriving in each Miskito hamlet or town, our small party was greeted like heroic liberators. The outpouring of warmth and friendship was even greater than I had experienced during the siege of Wounded Knee or in Yellow Thunder Camp.

The Sandinistas must have realized eventually that the information our tiny group was accumulating might cause them international grief, so they set out to kill us before we could tell the world what their revolution was really about. Long before we reached Layasiksa, the moccasin telegraph had brought us word that troops were hunting for Brooklyn Rivera in his hometown, Big Sandy Bay. Later, our radios monitored Sandinista military traffic from Puerto Cabezas that made it apparent we had become the objects of a massive manhunt.

Nicaragua's Atlantic coast road system begins near the edge of a village called Lapan. There we left our canoe. Brooklyn and a few men calmly commandeered a military truck—the driver and guard surrendered without protest—and we drove north to Yulu, a town less than thirty kilometers from the Sandinista headquarters at Puerto Cabezas. Virtually under the guns of the Sandinistas, we wandered around for two days. If anybody had snitched on us, we would have been dead meat. But Brooklyn showed no concern for that possibility: The people feared and loathed the Managua regime.

When we finished interviewing in Yulu, we headed home by way of Layasiksa. Although the Sandinistas had recently destroyed almost everything the villagers owned, including their priceless traditional clothing, jewelry, and art, the villagers prepared a feast. The Miskito people put together outfits from leaves and grass and danced for us in celebration of our visit. They serenaded us with an old guitar and instruments made from hollow sticks, and we danced the night away. Resting there on that Sunday morning, January 21, 1986, we noticed that some villagers were packing their belongings and leaving. We had heard by MISURASATA radio that an American wire-service story had just confirmed our identities, our presence, and our mission on the Atlantic coast. I figured that had spooked the Miskito people.

At about one that afternoon, a C-1 Bird Dog spotter plane swooped low over the village. Knowing all too well what was coming, the Miskito women began to whimper and wail, round up their children, and look for places to hide. Within minutes, two push-pull tank busters—two-seater attack planes with propellers in front and back—appeared low on the horizon. Not wanting to provoke the Sandinistas or to provide any excuse for attack, Brooklyn ordered his warriors not to fire at the planes. Hank, Bob, and Clem, all wearing civilian clothes, were ordered to join the civilians heading for an open area near the lagoon. I was wearing camouflage gear, so I remained with the warriors in the village.

The Sandinista planes came roaring in to drop five hundred-pound bombs. The ground shook as shrapnel and splintered trees flew everywhere. Beneath the forest canopy, we could hear but not see the aircraft. We ran from tree to tree, trying to anticipate where the next bombs would fall.

I guessed wrong.

A jagged sliver of shrapnel dug a furrow in my belly. There was a bit of blood, but again, no vital organs were hit. I could tell it wasn't going to kill me—at least not right away. Crouching by a tree, I looked up and saw Condor, a MISURASATA veteran, nonchalantly leaning against the trunk. When our eyes met, he winked and gave a little smile.

When the planes had dropped their last bombs and buzzed off, Brooklyn's warriors huddled. They estimated that it would take about an hour and a half for the push-pulls to return to their base, refuel, rearm, and return. By then, it would be late afternoon. We decided to disperse, wait out the second attack, and try to escape when it was over. It would be dark before the Sandinista planes could return for a third strike.

Two hours came and went with no sign of the Sandinistas. Just to make sure, we waited another thirty minutes before loading our canoe and motoring onto a lagoon that widened into a large lake. Suddenly I heard the familiar snarl of a spotter plane. Our canoe was a sitting duck. Eustice cracked the throttle wide open, but as we sped for shore, the push-pulls began to circle to attack. The nearest cover was a swampy tangle of mangrove with a floating field of giant lily pads at one end, but even traveling flat out, we were never going to outrun those planes. Orange flame blossomed under their wings as they began a strafing run. Two youngsters in the bow of my canoe stood up and emptied their AK–47s at the planes, tossing their rifles into the center of the boat before diving overboard. I looked back. Eustice had disappeared. I grabbed my fatigue jacket—my passport was in a pocket—and jumped in after them. When I surfaced, I saw everyone dive each time the planes made a run. The water was chest deep to me, but everyone else had to tiptoe or swim. I thought, this is bullshit, I'm not going to go underwater and wait to die— I'm going to stand up and watch those Marxist motherfuckers! Brooklyn and Hank were trying to cover their heads and arms with lily pads and rubbery green leaves. As the planes returned for strafing runs, they ducked under-water. I watched while the push-pulls came yet again. Four rockets swooshed downward, bracketing the spot where Eustice's head had ducked beneath the waves moments before. Fountains of water soared skyward. I figured he had been blown to pieces.

Suddenly, swimming for shore seemed like a good idea.

As the planes came around for another pass, I decided to see how fast a Plains Indian could do the Australian crawl. I beat Clem Chartier to the mangroves, but not by much. Among the slippery roots, we discovered David Rodríguez, a MISURASATA *comandante*, writhing in pain. His knees were shattered and his chest was a mass of shrapnel wounds. I tried to carry him closer to shore, but he screamed in pain. He asked me to break a trail for him so he could pull himself along. I was awed by his courage and toughness. Clem helped me bend mangrove roots and the stems of water plants out of the way so David could float through. It was slow going. Then we heard someone moaning, "Mama! Mama!" I helped David as Clem went back into the lagoon for a warrior perhaps fourteen years old. His name was Péko. When Clem got him in, we saw that his left shoulder, upper arm, hip, and thigh were shredded by shrapnel. The boy stared at me in shock and agony.

Traveling through the swamp required great effort. The wounded, much as Clem and I, were covered with mud. Then the marsh opened into what looked like a little canal. I towed David across so he could hang onto some branches, let the water cleanse his wounds, and give him relief from the pain. He said he could hang on, so I left him to help Clem with Péko. Ahead, we saw dry land, but we had to cross what looked like a small pond to get there. The water was only about three-and-a-half feet deep, so I waded in. Suddenly I sank into the bottom. The mud had taken hold of my legs and was sucking me in. The more I struggled to free myself, the deeper I sank. I yelled, "It's quicksand! Go back!" The water was at my chin; in a terrifying moment, I realized I was trapped.

Clem said, "Relax, Russell, give it up to God."

I murmured a quick prayer, *"Tunkasila Wakan Tanka"*—Revered Great Mystery—and relaxed.

Then I said, *"Unci Maka, unsimala,"* Grandmother Earth, pity me.

She let go of my legs and, relaxed, I floated to the surface and paddled across the water to safety. I called to Clem to swim across, and he brought Péko halfway. I grabbed him and lifted him as gingerly as possible onto the little spit of dry land. My thrashing had muddied the water, and his wounds were covered with it. We washed them with clear water from the lagoon.

As we stood on our dry spot, we saw Bob Martin swimming back to our canoe; he was only 40 to 50 yards away through the mangroves. He climbed in and tried to start an engine, pulling on the starter cord over and over. Bob was Clem's best buddy, so he started waving and yelling, "Bob! Over here! We've got two wounded!" Bob turned to look in our direction, then returned to starting the engine. He got it started, then inexplicably took off in the other direction. That was the end of what had been a very close friendship between Bob and Clem.

I couldn't bear to look at Péko's wounds—pounds of human flesh turned into raw meat. I had a tough time helping to wash them. Fortunately, Clem did a great job. My respect for him increased as I saw that he knew what to do. While we were waiting, Hank Adams showed up. After what seemed like hours, we heard an engine—a MISURASATA canoe with warriors found the inlet where David was clinging to branches. They took the wounded and sent another canoe back to bring us to a spot in the jungle where Brooklyn, many of the local villagers, and the rest of our group had gathered.

In addition to Péko and David, three MISURASATA warriors had been wounded and three others killed. Miraculously, I found Eustice wrapped in a blanket, sitting under the trees at a small, smokeless fire and eating fruit and fish. I asked him, "How did you survive those rockets?" He said, "Only God knows!" Péko died the next day. I'll never forget his big dark eyes. They remind me of my son Scott's.

As we sat around the fires eating and drinking the best coffee I've ever tasted, Bob realized he had lost his journal, cameras, and film—everything in his knapsack. He and an older man went back to search and returned with the cameras, lenses, and a little film. The journal, however, was gone.

It was too dangerous to travel by water during daylight, so at dawn, we went ashore to walk through the jungle. One of our young warriors climbed a tree to hoist a length of wire that served as a radio antenna, and we made contact with MISURASATA headquarters. We were directed to a night rendezvous with our canoes. Another canoe came alongside and a medicine man came aboard to tend the wounded. After singing songs and applying herbal medicines, he slipped back into the night and vanished as silently as he had appeared. For days, I slept only an hour or two a night in the canoe and ate little except wild fruit and what fish we could catch.

By radio, we learned that the Sandinistas had found Bob's journal, which listed all the villages we had visited and all the people he had interviewed. One by one, all the villages we had toured were bombed. People were arrested. Few of them ever came back to their homes. Meanwhile, MISURASATA told us the Sandinistas were moving their forces toward us from three sides. Our choices were to continue farther into the interior or to head for the coast. If they had been alone, Brooklyn and his men might have opted for the interior, where they could elude the Sandinistas easily. But because we *norteamericanos* could tell the outside world what was really happening in Nicaragua, we headed for the coast, where we had the best chance of getting out of the country.

As we headed east, Sandinista aircraft were overhead constantly. Every time I heard them, I felt a stab of panic—a reflex that would continue for months afterward. Cut off from the outside world, we were unaware that when reports of the Layasiksa bombing had reached the American media, Nicaraguan Ambassador Francisco Campbell had baldly denied it. "We do not bomb Indian villages," he said. "Not for any reason." A few days later, when pictures of the bomb craters appeared in U.S. newspapers, he backtracked. The Sandinista air force had bombed "Contra positions near Layasiksa," he said. The Sandinistas also cited my statement from Bogotá about bringing a hundred AIM warriors to Nicaragua as proof that I was trying to overthrow their government. Sure. Hank, Bob, Clem, and I were going to drive the Marxists out of Managua.

The army couldn't find us, but Indians from villages we passed on our trek seemed to have no trouble. Every night, they came through the jungle to warn us about Sandinistas in the vicinity. When I offered to give myself up if it would stop the bombing and hunting, Brooklyn's men asked if I knew how the Sandinistas treated prisoners. Then they said, "We came in together, we'll go out together."

It took more than two weeks of travel through very rugged country before we approached the coast. We made camp, and as we waited for darkness, two elders and a younger man came to speak with Brooklyn. After a time, he came over to Hank, Clem, and me and said, "These elders want to talk to you." They were men who appeared to be in their eighties. Brooklyn translated verbatim. They said, "We apologize to you. We want to ask your forgiveness." Knowing what was coming, my eyes filled. I didn't want them to see, so I bowed my head very low, but the tears rolling down my cheeks gave me away.

They continued, "We don't normally treat visitors this way. When guests come, we open our homes to them and offer them feasts. We give them gifts and try to show our best hospitality." That is pure Indian, and it made me feel very proud and humble. I knew many North American Indians who would have said, "We have to live here after you leave, and if you hadn't come, none of this would have happened and our people wouldn't be killed and maimed." But those Miskito elders knew who the enemy was.

Afterward, Brooklyn asked why I had cried. I told him, "It was the beauty of the moment. I finally met Indians who know what it's all about." When we left, they returned to their village to put their lives on the line againso we could escape.

I never knew the name of the small village where we emerged from the jungle, but it squatted along the west bank of a small lagoon that emptied into a cove. The Sandinistas had an outpost on the north side of a sand spit that extended partly across the mouth of the cove. While we waited in the jungle for darkness, I performed a special tobacco ceremony that Dennis and I had learned from Sam Drywater, a Cherokee holy man. I gave each man in the boat a little tobacco to hold in his left hand until we were at sea. I asked that all of them go along with the ceremony, even if they didn't believe in the spiritual power I was invoking. After nightfall, we paddled along the north bank. The new moon was a tiny sliver and the jungle was pitch black. As we drifted closer and closer to the garrison on the sand spit, our paddles hissing as they bit carefully into the dark water, our friends in the village cranked up a diesel generator to power their church's lights. The villagers began a prayer meeting with a loud and enthusiastic hymn. Their kids and dogs joined in the general clamor. Just as we passed the Sandinista compound, red tracers arced over our heads, followed by the stuttering roar of assault rifles. I almost swallowed my heart. Suddenly it was quiet again. Perhaps bored with their duties, the soldiers had relieved the tedium by making a little noise. I'll never know for sure.

We moved almost silently through the cove and out to sea. When we were out of small-arms range, we rested, hugging one another and the two villagers who had risked their lives to guide us to safety. When they had slipped over the side and were swimming strongly for shore, we got ready to start our outboards. We had only a few minutes before the tide would push us back to the village; once we tried to crank, everyone for miles around would know we were there. Both motors started at once. We released our tobacco to the wind with a prayer. Bob Martin, his eyes big as saucers, said, "I believe! I believe!"

We had used almost eight drums of gasoline coming from Costa Rica, but gas was scarce among the Miskito people. All we could get for our escape was two full drums and one about a third full. We decided to head north toward Honduras, which was closer than Costa Rica. Our canoe rode so low in the water that it was invisible to shore-based radar, so we decided to try to slip past Puerto Cabezas.

As we passed it well out to sea, the running lights of two gunboats appeared low on the horizon. Within minutes we saw that they were converging on us. Eustice opened the throttles and we ran away with the current to the southeast. Our Johnson 55s drove us so fast that we skipped from wave top to wave top, landing with a crash that was hellish torture for our wounded. My own injury had begun to heal, but the pitching and tossing made me seasick. As the lights faded behind us, we knew we couldn't go north to Honduras—we would never get past the patrols. We had only one chance—San Andres, a speck in the Caribbean about 140 miles southeast of Puerto Cabezas. The island belonged to Colombia, so we would be safe there.

First, however, we had to cross more than a hundred miles of open sea without even a compass to guide us. Within minutes, we noticed a more immediate problem. Near the bow, a long crack had opened in the bottom of our boat; it had probably split after hitting waves at high speed. We shut off one engine and ran the other at barely more than an idle, to conserve gasoline and to keep the hull from splitting open. We stuffed clothing in the crack and used plastic milk jugs to bail.

As daylight approached, we began to worry about Nicaraguan planes and fishing boats, which are radio-equipped and double as a network of coastal sentries. But we saw only one other vessel, which appeared briefly on the eastern horizon, then faded away. As the day went on, the sun seemed to crawl across the sky. We were in the middle of an endless ocean, and it seemed as if we were going nowhere. The sun burned down on us. When I wasn't bailing, I studied the waves, looking for some pattern, some indication of the current—a hopeless task. There was nothing else to do but think, and I didn't want to get my mind wrapped around our possibilities. We would run out of gas before we reached the island; we would miss it entirely and lose ourselves at sea; our canoe would split open and we would be at the mercy of the sharks. The day crawled along monotonously, the *putt-putt-putt* of our motor a hypnotic lullaby that all of us expected would stop at any moment.

Just as the sun began to go down, we pumped the last of our gasoline into the outboard tank. A few minutes later, Bob Martin, standing in the bow, yelled the sweetest words I've ever heard: "I see it! Land! I see land!"

Everyone cheered, and a rush of excitement flooded over me. As the faint smudge on the horizon became a firm line and then a panorama of jungled hills and red-roofed homes, it was apparent that Eustice had guided us to the precise center of San Andres—an unimaginable feat of navigation. As the sun dropped over the horizon, we used the last of our gasoline to drive our canoe up on the white sands of a beach. Tourists in skimpy bathing gear gawked at our stained camouflage fatigues, ragged beards, and my braids.

The police didn't know what to make of us. They sent for ambulances to take our wounded to the hospital. Immigration officials came, gruff bureaucrats who herded us into a dumpy waiting room until Brooklyn could make a phone call to his friend, the governor of San Andres. In minutes, we went from being mysterious strangers to welcome guests. I called Gloria from our hotel, and she cried when I told her I was safe.

While the Sandinistas were chasing us, my brother Bill, concerned for my safety, had tried to stop them from hunting us down and killing us. Their response was, "He knew the risks and he's in our country illegally—so he'll just have to take his chances like anyone else." So much for personal rapport and solidarity between the Sandinistas, AIM, and the International Indian Treaty Council. When it came to killing Bill Means's brother, the Marxists said essentially what the U.S. government had said at Wounded Knee—"You broke the law and we're coming to kill you."

Brooklyn was on good terms with the president of Colombia, who was so interested in peace in Nicaragua that he had hosted several meetings between the Sandinistas and MISURASATA. He had even tried to broker a peace agreement between the United States and the Sandinistas. During our four days on San Andres, we got first-class treatment. The Colombians picked up our hotel tabs until arrangements were made through the U.S. embassy in San José to fly us back to Costa Rica. There we met with State Department representatives who told us that Brooklyn was unimportant, that he led only a few dozen men, and that MISURASATA was nothing of consequence. Hank and I jumped all over them, but those guys knew only what they had been told.

It was unfortunate that most of the depositions, the video, and the film we had taken were lost in Bob Martin's knapsack. He had salvaged enough, however, to put together a thirty-minute documentary that was aired by the ABC affiliate in Albuquerque. I didn't need the film or notes to remind me of what I had seen and heard. I will never forget the young Miskito mother who, after giving birth beside a river, was forced to watch while a Sandinista officer decapitated her baby and tossed its tiny body into the water—or the young Miskito man whose genitals were severed and shin bones smashed because his brother was in MISURASATA. Those Indians were struggling to survive the same kind of genocide my own ancestors had faced. I could not turn away and let them fight alone.

Moonies and
Libertarians

M ISURASATA didn't want or need AIM warriors to help it fight for
freedom. But these freedom fighters *could* have used international recognition and some money for medical supplies and military equipment.
When I returned to the United States, however, hoping to rally public support by telling their story on the university lecture circuit, the same people
who had welcomed me for years wouldn't even take my calls.

On February 27, 1986, at the annual memorial for the liberation of
Wounded Knee in 1973, AIM held another summit conference in Oglala,
South Dakota. Dennis Banks and all the other leaders came except Vernon
Bellecourt, but when my brother Bill and Clyde Bellecourt turned up hours
late, they appeared to me so high that Clyde sat with his mouth agape, a
pathetic sight. Bill delivered a scathing denunciation of everyone who opposed him, the Bellecourts, and the Sandinistas. Trying to smooth things
over, I salvaged an agreement. As we had promised four years earlier in San
Francisco, the AIM leaders, including Clyde and Bill, would not use the media to air our differences. We didn't know that at that very moment, Vernon
was in Denver holding a press conference to denounce Hank Adams, the
Colorado AIM leaders, and me as CIA agents and Contras.

A few weeks after that fiasco, I heard from Steve Eagle, who had been born on the Rosebud but adopted by a white family. As a young man, he had found his way into Sun Myung Moon's Unification Church, the so-called Moonies. Long before I had gone to Nicaragua, Steve visited me in Porcupine. I learned that his church had much to offer to Indian people, including the use of trucks, buses, vans, and other equipment. But there was a price. As with all other missionaries, those who wanted to use the Moonies' machinery were subjected to proselytizing. All I knew about the Moonies was what I had read in the press. They were reportedly a mind-control cult, and their leader, Moon, had been nailed by the Internal Revenue Service. Whenever the government uses an agency like the IRS to go after someone, it is a sure sign that it is afraid of him. I usually admire anybody who attracts that much official venom, but I knew hardly anything about Moon or what had gotten him in trouble.

Steve Eagle is a very sincere young man who wanted to help his people. He never tried to convert me, but he wanted me to work with his church. I said I would be willing to do that as long as they respected my own spiritual views and didn't attempt to alter them. On behalf of the Moonies, he invited me to a convention at the Omni Hotel in Washington, D.C. It was a meeting of a political arm of the Unification Church, which was rabidly pro-Contra. I found myself sitting among hundreds of right-wing conservatives, the same John Birchers and reactionaries who AIM had struggled against in the 1970s. When I saw what I had gotten myself into, I was flabbergasted.

Some guys approached to ask if I would be willing to speak about my experiences in Nicaragua. Since my usual avenues of expression had been blocked by the Left, I agreed. I spoke at length about Sandinista atrocities we had documented and about MISURASATA, alone and outnumbered but still taking on the Sandinistas daily. I described how Managua dominated the skies, but the Indians controlled their roadless territory in classic guerrilla fashion. There were many retired generals and colonels present, and I hoped they would see the wisdom of backing the indigenous people instead of a bunch of outlaws living in a neighboring country and making raids across the border. That was my first experience with right-wing Republicans; as I mingled with them, I learned that they admired what I had done in Nicaragua and what MISURASATA represented.

My speech went over so well that the Moonies sponsored me on a speaking tour. They booked me into many of the same left-wing universities where right-wingers had turned out to picket and demonstrate against AIM in the 1970s and early 1980s. Wherever I spoke, of course, the Moonies had their literature available. They didn't shy away from who they were. Each program included introductory remarks, my speech, and a documentary movie put together by a guy who had gone into Miskitia to film the Indian war, including some of the Sandinistas' atrocities.

Only a few audiences, including Colorado AIM and Chicano communities in Seattle and Los Angeles, were polite. They supported the Sandinistas but listened respectfully to what I had to say. My experience at the University of Vermont was more typical. Although I had had a warm reception there only two years earlier, some of the thirty-something hippies who hang around universities draped a banner across the chapel where I spoke: "Means + Moonies = Meanies."

In the film that was shown at my speaking engagement, a Miskito elder is shown talking to his wife after the Sandinistas had destroyed everything in their village.

"Why? Why?" he says, tears rolling down his face. At that, a guy in the audience got up and yelled, "Lies! Bullshit! CIA lies!"

I waited for the university's security force to silence him, but he continued to rant and rave. If I had been on the speaker's platform at the time, I would have dealt with the interruption verbally, but he was showing disrespect for an elder who was not there to defend himself. I rose from my pew to walk around to the other side where the guy was yelling. Without a word, I dropped him with one punch. The movie continued as he was carried away; no one disrupted it again.

When I was introduced, the right-wingers gave me a standing ovation. After my talk, I took questions. The left-wingers used the opportunity to make statements. One guy went down a list of what he claimed were my lies. He said he had firsthand information from Hank Adams that I hadn't been wounded. I pulled up my shirt and showed everyone the scar.

Many people, including Hank Adams, condemned me for hanging around with the Moonies. I was disgusted. The Left knew nothing about the Unification Church except what they read in the white man's newspapers. The Left denounced the bought-off, corporate-owned news media of America as a tool of the multinationals and the government—and then quoted it to vilify the Moonies! During my speeches, I said, "Catholics are the most vicious killers in this hemisphere—not only historically but to this very day. The atrocities in Guatemala are the work of Catholics with the participation of the Church. Priests point out Indian leaders in their villages and death squads take them away. Yet no one criticizes me for hanging around with Catholics! Instead, you denounce me for hanging around with Moonies when all they're doing is helping me use the First Amendment rights that the institutions of the Left refuse to me." I might have added that President Efrain Rios Mont's Pentecostal Christians wiped out hundreds of Mayan villages that in 1983 and 1984, and killed at least fifteen thousand Indians and created a million refugees in Guatemala.

My speaking engagements spanned several months, during which I learned many things about the Right. One was that no matter who you are or where you come from, if you share their views they'll give respect to anyone who deserves it. They respected me because I'm anti-Communist and approved of my view that no government anywhere is good. As George Washington put it, "Government is force." I also learned that the Right will listen to good arguments. I don't agree with their intolerant views on many issues, including the death penalty and prison sentences, but their view of economics in our present world is on the right path: free markets, but not the kind of unbridled free enterprise that leads inevitably to corporate socialism.

Maybe I was being used by the Moonies—but I was using them in return. I got the word out about the Miskito, Sumo, and Rama peoples, and I got to know several good conservatives in Congress, including Barry Goldwater. Over the years, he had opposed almost everything I stood for, but when we met in his Senate office, we looked each other in the eye. Although he said nothing, his handshake was firm, and I could tell he respected me as a fighter. I respected him in the same way.

While I lobbied the Republican side of Capitol Hill, the Indian Law Resource Center worked on the clique led by Ted Kennedy. At the same time he was championing Indians who had been removed from their land by the Sandinistas, he was trying to displace other Indians from their homes in his own state. The late Jacqueline Kennedy Onassis had bought some property on Gay Head, Massachusetts, on the west coast of Martha's Vineyard, where the few remaining Wampanoag people had been pushed. The Wampanoag had heard that she apparently didn't want Indian neighbors, so Ted was going to sponsor a bill to relocate them. Fortunately, it was never introduced and the Indians remained just where they were.

In that same year, 1986, Congress allocated about $100 million for the Contras. In early spring, Ward Churchill and I met with Elliot Abrams, undersecretary of state for Central America—the government's point man for Nicaragua. Immaculately groomed but evil in appearance—all he lacked was horns and a tail—he was perfectly suited for his job. Abrams toed the party line, insisting that Brooklyn Rivera represented only twenty or thirty people in Costa Rica. After listening to Abrams's patronizing bullshit, I called him on each of his errors, describing my experiences in Nicaragua.

I said, "Nobody pays attention to MISURASATA because they're Indians. They get no funding from any government. What little weaponry they have has been liberated from the Sandinistas. Yet these people control the northeastern Atlantic coast of Nicaragua—one third of the country!" I pointed out that Miskitia could be a foothold for freedom fighters to take over the whole country—but only if MISURASATA was in charge of operations in its territory. A remarkably closed-minded man, Abrams wouldn't listen, so we walked out.

Lobbying on the Hill did have some effect. Congress stripped $10 million from the Contra appropriation and earmarked it for MISURASATA. I was asked to attend a meeting in the White House with Caspar Weinberger, Reagan's national security adviser—the same guy Nixon had sent as CREEP's bagman to pay our way home after the Trail of Broken Treaties in 1972. As usual, I refused to set foot in the White House, and Weinberger wouldn't leave his office. He sent a guy named Hernandez, the National Security Council's Latin American honcho, to meet me in a bar across from the Executive Office Building.

Hernandez said, "What does MISURASATA want?"

I said, "First of all, military training for their officers." He wrote it down on a pad. "That can be arranged," he said.

"They don't want the CIA to disburse the money," I added.

He said, "MISURASATA had peace talks with the Sandinistas. Now they're talking with us. How do we know which side they're on?"

"They've been fighting the Sandinistas longer than the U.S. has," I replied.

"We just can't trust Indians—we don't know which side you're on."

"This meeting's over. You're not sincere. You're just like Elliot Abrams!" I said. As I walked out, I wondered, where do they find guys like that? Throughout government, from the State Department to the Office of Expendable Indoor Plumbing Supplies, clones of the same mindless, gutless bureaucrats are in charge.

The State Department insisted that only the CIA could dole out MISURASATA's grant. Apparently nobody in the government knew that in Latin America, almost everyone from the lowest peasant to the wealthiest oligarch, from the most wretched political prisoner to the most distinguished head of state, reviled the CIA. When U.S. aid comes with CIA strings, they know they will be jerked around by those seeking to increase their power and wealth at the expense of people they are pretending to help.

MISURASATA effectively told the CIA to take its money and shove it. That ten million dollars was never restored to the Contras, and the next Congress ended all funding. The Left, led by Vernon Bellecourt and my brother Bill, spent months condemning Ward Churchill, Glenn Morris, Jim Anaya, the Indian Law Resource Center, and me for working on behalf of our Indian brothers. By shaving the Contras' money, we did far more to stop them than the leftists did with their pro-Sandinista rhetoric.

When I completed my lecture circuit in late spring, the Unification Church invited me to an international conference in Korea. I was impressed with it and them because they did something I'd never seen another Western religion do: They invited anyone—lay members or clergy—from any of the twenty-eight Christian denominations attending the meeting to challenge their teachings in a public forum. Every night after supper, a couple of young Moonies mounted the ballroom stage and took Bible questions from the Christians. The challengers lined up, Russian and Greek Orthodox and Catholic priests and preachers representing the Methodists, Presbyterians, Pentecostals, Church of Christ, Baptists—every denomination I'd ever heard of and some I hadn't—most with verses marked in open Bibles. The Moonies said, "Okay, give us your best shot." The Christians acted with anger and hatred, citing the scripture and attacking Moonie theology. They shouted each other down and yelled out questions. The Moonies calmly refuted each accusation and condemnation by citing a Bible verse—and each answer came with wisdom and generosity. The angrier the Christians got, the nicer the Moonies behaved. I was astonished.

Sun Myung Moon's followers call themselves the Unification Church because they want to bring all Christians together. To me, their theology boils down to this: Once there was heaven on earth, and it's possible again if all Christians will unify to work toward that objective. Moon, cornered by reporters from the Christian media, was asked, "Are you really the reincarnation of Jesus Christ—the Second Coming?" He replied, "Yes—but isn't *everyone* part of Christ?" I loved his answer.

I was asked to speak at a banquet on the last night of the conference. I said I was a born-again primitive and I hoped and prayed that Moon *is* Jesus Christ. Then I scolded the Christians. I said, "What's wrong with you people? Why are you worried about whether he is or is not the Messiah? Who cares? Listen to what he's saying. Listen to what his church is *doing*. Why haven't any of you ever shown that you were so committed to your faith that you could say to those of other beliefs, 'Take your best shot,' night after night?" I got a standing ovation and several Moonies hugged me. Churchmen from around the United States came up to say, "We want you to speak at our church. . . ." I never heard from any of them.

After I got back to Porcupine, Steve Eagle and I put together a business proposal to use Unification Church resources to help Indian people, but of course the Moonies never responded. In fact, I never heard from them again, which I attribute to their racist perception that Indian people are primitive and incapable of handling their own affairs.

After returning from South Korea in 1986, I got a phone call from Honey Lanham, a woman with a drawl who sounded somewhat like Dolly Parton. When we first met in Denver a few years earlier, she had introduced me to the founder and national officers of the Libertarian Party. What the party stood for—free-market economics and no government interference in people's lives—sounded just right to me. Libertarian thinking closely parallels that of my culture. Libertarians are limited by their linear, Eurocentric male mind set, and they are 99 percent middle-class whites, but taken as a whole, they are the best political group of people in the United States. I was thrilled to learn that it is a party of principle; the platform does not change from year to year. Libertarians do not compromise. They do not sell out. In contrast, Demopublicans insist that politics is the art of compromise. I believe politics should be the art of principles. Then it wouldn't be filled with the likes of Bill Clinton, Newt Gingrich, and Bob Dole and others in Congress. We would have few problems as a nation if our principled politicians never compromised on the principles of liberty and justice for all.

Not long after I met the Libertarians, Congressman Thomas Daschle ran for the U.S. Senate from South Dakota. I told the Libertarians I had a candidate I wanted to run against him. I knew Daschle from the time he had been an aide to Senator Jim Abourezk. I didn't want him to get George McGovern's seat because I knew him to be a less-than-honorable man who held strong racist views toward Indian people. I was getting sick and tired of people such as Daschle. I wanted to send a message to all South Dakota politicians that Indians *do* count, and that they ignore us at their peril. I also wanted to show the power of the swing vote, mostly to Indian people themselves, who still don't know how to use it. Since Indians always support Democrats, state Republican political strategy never includes them. I called Roland Ryan, a good friend and AIM supporter from Sisseton. His wife, Barbara, is a poised, articulate, intelligent Dakota who had a successful career as a paralegal. I believed that if my name were kept out of it and she ran against Daschle as a Libertarian, she would get enough of the Indian vote to ensure a Republican victory. After that, no South Dakota politician would ever neglect his Indian constituents.

A few weeks after speaking to Ryan, I drove through a blizzard to meet the Ryans for lunch in Watertown, South Dakota. When I told them about the Libertarian Party and laid out my strategy, Barbara was very receptive. I also explained in detail why we wanted to defeat Tom Daschle: He had consistently opposed bills related to every issue important to South Dakota Indians, including the Black Hills, water, and treaty rights. He had supported bills favoring the state's robber-baron mining interests and corporate agribusiness. Barbara seemed willing, even eager, to run, but at the last minute her husband, for reasons never clear to me, squelched her intention. I had no one else to take her place on such short notice, so my plans to defeat Daschle came to nothing. Today, he's a power in the Senate—and still, judging by his voting record, a racist.

I was totally surprised, however, when Honey Lanham called after I returned from Korea in 1986. At first I thought some crackpot or drunk was trying to imitate her voice.

She said, "Hi, y'all. Would you consider running for the presidency of the U.S.?"

I said, "Wait a minute. Who is this?"

She said, "I'm serious, child." I put my hand over the mouthpiece and turned to Gloria. "You aren't going to believe this, but I've just been asked to run for president! What do you think?"

Gloria said, "That decision will rest entirely with you." I told Honey I needed a little time to consider it. When I called her back, I said I hadn't made up my mind, but was inclined to give it a shot.

Honey reached Larry Dodge, a Montana Libertarian, on a conference call. We talked about how I might make a run for the party's nomination. They explained that although actual selection would be done at a convention, the Libertarian hierarchy had anointed former Republican Congressman Ron Paul, a gynecologist and gold investor from the Houston area, as the standard-bearer. Honey and Larry were unhappy with him. They felt that Paul was a Republican masquerading as a Libertarian, and was generally intolerant of women's rights. That was why they wanted me to run against him. They suggested that I come down and speak to Texas Libertarians to see if I could attract any serious support in Paul's own backyard.

I asked myself, why me? If the idea was to broaden the party's appeal with a minority candidate, there were a few black Libertarians who would undoubtedly bring in more support from America's thirty million blacks than I could from a mere million Indians. Then I learned that one of Honey's associates in Dallas had explored my past, including my TREATY election platform at Pine Ridge. This person had examined my principles to see where I stood on individual liberty and self-determination. He could find nothing to show I had ever been anything except an unannounced Libertarian. He concluded that I came closer to the party's ideal than anyone else they knew, so they wanted me for who I was and what I stood for.

I flew to Texas. Honey, Larry, and I toured the state in Honey's car, visiting Libertarian strongholds, sometimes making two speeches a day to gatherings ranging from a few dozen to more than a hundred. At each, I discussed my principles. I said I believed in individual liberty and free-market economics. I stated that I favored the decriminalization of drugs and prostitution because I believed people should be free to do anything as long as they don't harm others. Talk-show hosts like to ridicule that point, but we believe people should have total freedom of choice. On the same ground, I opposed mandatory use of auto seat belts and motorcycle helmets. That, of course, would be tempered by laws enforcing unlimited liability. If someone injured another person, the offending party would not be able to hide behind anything or anyone. He would be held personally responsible for all damage.

Ron Paul's supporters were in every audience, easy to spot because they were the buttoned-down, suit-and-tie crowd. They fired some hard questions, such as the economic theories of Ludwig von Mises, or Milton Friedman's latest proposal about free-market economics. I was a political novice. When I was asked about things such as how to improve productivity in America, all I could do was rely on the teachings of my ancestors. What I said always seemed to make sense to most people in my audience, who were, with few exceptions, highly educated. They responded so positively to my talks that by the time we reached San Antonio, on about our third stop, I had made up my mind to run. A militant American Indian running for president! The story made all the wires.

When I returned to Porcupine, Gloria and I got ready to kick off my campaign at the party's San Francisco convention, in February 1987. Ron Paul still had the party elite in his corner, so I knew it would be an uphill battle. I figured that once word got around that the majority of his own state was against him, it would send a message to the rank and file.

Besides having a lot of money behind him, Paul had been chosen largely because of a letter of resignation he wrote after losing his seat in Congress through reapportionment. Repudiating and condemning the Republican Party, he said Reagan wasn't really a conservative and didn't represent conservative Republicans. That happens to be true. Reagan has been anything but an FDR Democrat. Just look at how he expanded the size of the federal government, tripled the national debt, and raised taxes on the middle class. By sounding like a Mussolini Fascist, he persuaded many conservatives to delude themselves. Paul's letter had convinced many important Libertarians that he was the embodiment of their politics.

After my campaign started, I spent only twelve days of the next six months in Porcupine. My campaign managers, Honey and Larry, encouraged me to use my credit cards for travel expenses and promised that the campaign would raise the money to pay me back. I traveled across America, concentrating on state conventions. The fact that I visited every one of them impressed many Libertarians. I took all but one delegate in Michigan and a majority in most of the smaller states. I visited forty-six states, including a few where groups from neighboring states joined together. In Hawaii, I introduced the Libertarian Party to the American Indian community and to the real Hawaiians. Until then, those people had known nothing about Libertarians or their political philosophy. Many found that the party offered ideas they could embrace. My only bad experience was in Massachusetts, where the Libertarians were as cold as the fish in their bay. Perhaps that was because of my striking resemblance to Chief Massasoit—or because I had demonstrated at Plymouth Rock against the Pilgrim Fathers.

Ron Paul, who hadn't planned to campaign much, got scared because the press followed me everywhere I went. He began to hit almost every spot I had visited. He was mostly ignored by the media, who seemed quite interested not just in me but in the Libertarian platform. I'm sure that the ability to generate headlines was one of the reasons I had been asked to run. Another was that I could open doors that Paul couldn't. In Atlanta, Coretta Scott King held my hand during a ceremony to commemorate her late husband's birthday. That led to an invitation to speak at a welfare-rights convention, where I explained why Libertarians are against welfare and public schools— anything that destroys the family or undermines personal responsibility. My message was different from Paul's because it was sincere, delivered in plain English and without resorting to the euphemisms and false facades of white man's politics, or the dull, dry rhetoric of economics.

I really wanted the party's nomination. I was blown away when I realized that those backing me did so out of respect for the beliefs I had defended as a member of the American Indian Movement and as an Oglala Lakota. They saw through the media hype surrounding my public persona as a violence-prone Indian desperado, and chose instead someone who lived by his principles. In selecting me as their candidate, they honored my culture as a tested value system that they felt was their country's best hope for the future.

Even if I won the Libertarian nomination, I would, of course, still have to run against the Republican and Democratic candidates. I knew the odds against winning were infinitesimally small but even in losing, I could count on the press to report what I said about Libertarian concepts. We believe that the U.S. Constitution can and should evolve to keep pace with the times, but what it says at any given time is inviolate. We believe in self-defense, but we're the most peace-loving people in America. Our country doesn't need an enormous, costly military establishment, because most of our "foes" would be friends if we stopped treating them like enemies. The National Guard should return to its original mission—militias assembled in time of need to protect states against incursions by the federal government. If we honored the Second Amendment, which guarantees us the right to bear arms, we the citizens would be better armed than our government. It could never *force* us to do anything.

A Libertarian administration would be a minimalist one. We wouldn't have an FDA, an FCC, an IRS, an INS, or any of the other regulatory agencies. Instead, everyone and every entity who wronged another person would be personally liable, because only people free to be responsible can build a responsible society. Our present society reflects everything that is antithetical to these views and the situation is getting worse every day. Generations of children have never been taught to take responsibility for their lives. The result is a country speeding toward right-wing socialism, its corporations in collusion with government to dictate economic policy and protect their own interests by eliminating opportunity. Few Americans believe that, and they won't until they are destitute or imprisoned—but Congress is spending billions to build new prisons. Soon there will be enough cells for everyone who refuses to obey new laws that restrict individual liberties. Just one example— owning property on which a few wild marijuana plants grow can cost you the land and everything on it, and bring as much as a decade in prison.

By the time that I got to the national convention in Seattle, I thought we had waged a successful campaign. It had perked up the party; many inactive members and people who had drifted away rejoined because of my candidacy. I went to the assembly with a majority of the delegate votes and confident of winning. Unfortunately, the party has a few rules I didn't know about. Not every delegate selected by state conventions was able to come to Seattle, and those who couldn't were replaced according to each state's party rules. Since the party is committed to individual liberty, those replacements could vote for any candidate. That cost me many delegates. In Michigan, where I had won all but one, there were so many alternates that I wound up with only three votes. Despite all I had done for Libertarians in Hawaii, I didn't get a single Hawaiian vote, because all the Hawaiian delegates I had won were replaced. South Dakota was allocated three delegates, but none came to Seattle, so Paul got the national party leaders to appoint three Texans: his wife and two sons. When the first ballot was counted, he won by three votes.

Ironically, while his national campaign was under way, somebody absconded with a big chunk of Paul's campaign funds. Things went downhill from there. He failed to mount a national television advertising campaign and ignored most of his convention promises. Paul and the other national and state Libertarian candidates went down to ignoble defeat. I had spent nearly fifteen thousand dollars of my own money in pursuit of the nomination—an enormous sum to me. Larry and Honey, who had promised to raise money to pay me back, didn't mention that it would take years. Eventually, Honey kept her promise. In the meantime, I was unable to pay my credit-card bills, and ruined my credit rating forever.

I would, however, do it all over again. By becoming the first Indian ever to run for president of the United States on the principles of my culture and in trying to get justice for my people, I had enlarged the Libertarians' scope and sphere. In running for president, I came to realize that for Indian people to be free, *all* Americans must be free. Using policies perfected in the colonization of my people, the government is now trying to turn the whole country into one huge Indian reservation. Land policies mirroring those developed by the BIA have been applied to family farmers and ranchers to squeeze them out. With people no longer needed on the land, food production has been taken over by corporate agribusiness, the beneficiary of enormous government subsidies that place them among America's biggest welfare recipients. In education, colonial policies developed for Indians have proven so effective in creating a generation of docile automatons that federal funding has systematically eliminated local control in most school districts. Nearly all Americans are now educated in government schools, with curricula and schedules dictated by bureaucrats in state capitals and in Washington, D.C. Just as the BIA did with reservation Indians, government policies polarize communities and races across America—a way of controlling nearly every aspect of people's lives. Indian economic policy, proven again as an agent of subjugation and exploitation in the Third World, has been returned to the United States through laws enabling state and regional direction of what used to be private enterprise.

When the government chose the military option to eliminate a dissident religious group in Waco in 1993, death squads such as those first developed on Pine Ridge Reservation were used.

Now the government wants to turn all Americans into welfare recipients by taking control of health care because, as demonstrated with my people, long-term welfare destroys families and creates a pliant, easily manipulated society. As an Indian and a Libertarian, I saw that unless something was done to awaken the people, as William Shirer wrote in the 1950s, America will be the first country to become fascist democratically—a process that has begun.

5 0
▼▼▼▼▼▼▼▼

Indian Banana Republics

The lawsuit we had filed to keep the Forest Service from closing Yellow Thunder Camp finally reached the U.S. Supreme Court in 1987. The Court refused to hear our appeal, so that was the end of it. The U.S. Forest Service, the whore of corporate agribusiness, had won another round. Even if appeals courts still overturned trial judges to interpret laws to suit their political agendas, however, we had proved that we could confront racism head-on in federal court. Yellow Thunder Camp had served as an exercise in freedom and a reawakening to the wisdom of our ancestors. It had enriched many lives. By lobbying Congress, we had also helped to renew hope around the country. Some of the finest things that have happened for Indian people in recent years came about because we showed our people it was possible for grass-roots organizations to protect their interests. Even though the Black Hills bill, sponsored by Senator Bill Bradley of New Jersey, which would have returned control of our *Paha Sapa* to Indians, was not passed into law, it helped to forge an enduring partnership among Indian peoples.

Sometimes, however, direct action of the kind AIM had perfected in the early 1970s was still required. By 1988, I had been to the so-called Custer Battlefield three times, demanding and getting promises from the Park Service superintendent that the service would put up a memorial to the Indian men, women, and children whom Custer had attacked. Nothing had happened. The Cheyenne people asked me to do something once and for all. Because the lies told by Park Service guides about what really happened at the Greasy Grass offend me, I made it a personal crusade.

The white man has always claimed that Custer fought three thousand Indian warriors who were armed with repeating rifles—even though the cavalry had no weapons of that kind. As for the number of warriors, that outrageous assertion is backed by a mountain of alleged studies, archaeological digs and anthropological analyses. It is all a lie. If there were three thousand warriors in the village attacked by the Seventh Cavalry, then there would also have to be about three thousand women, at least six thousand children, and another three thousand elders—the parents and grandparents of the warriors and their wives. That would be fifteen thousand people altogether. It would have made the encampment on the Greasy Grass one of the biggest population centers on the Great Plains! Anyone who has ever been to the Little Bighorn River, as the white man calls the stream, will see that fifteen thousand people, even "primitives" who ate only two meals a day, couldn't live there. Even if they could have found enough food, there were few trees for firewood—surely not enough for fifteen hundred cooking fires, assuming that ten people used each one.

There might have been enough water in the river for fifteen thousand people—assuming they rarely bathed—but what about their horses? At that time in my people's history, men from sixteen years and up accumulated horses, which were the only measure of wealth in a hunting society. Most men in their twenties and thirties kept herds. For the sake of argument, if each of three thousand warriors had only a horse for himself, one for his parents, and one to drag the travois, which included his tipi and household possessions, there would have been nine thousand horses blanketing the prairie. Each needed more than forty pounds of grass or hay per day—360,000 pounds of fodder and therefore 180 tons of manure daily. Custer would have smelled those Indian horses fifty miles away and known he was headed for the mother of all Indian camps. He never would have attacked with only 276 men.

He did attack probably not more than three hundred Indian fighting men, because he knew that most had no firearms. There was no munitions factory stashed behind the hill to produce repeating rifles and ammunition. But if the cavalry men were better armed, if they had the element of surprise, they failed to realize they were attacking men whose families were also in danger. Everyone knew Custer's reputation—that he would kill every Indian he could find and burn the belongings they needed for survival. So the Indians fought.

The Park Service rangers still say my ancestors were so afraid of retribution that after the battle, they disbanded the camp and fled. If there had been three thousand warriors, they would have feared nothing. The actual size of the camp was about fifteen hundred people—still very big in a society in which thirty to forty lodges was a typical village. Aside from a few Arapaho and a village of Northern Cheyenne people, these were Lakota, the same people who had defeated the bluecoats and forced them to beg for a treaty of peace at Fort Laramie only eight years earlier. Only eight days before the encounter on the Greasy Grass, they had defeated General George Crook's expeditionary force, an army equipped with cannon, on Rosebud Creek. The Lakota had never known defeat in battle against white men—why would they *flee* after a victory?

When I returned to the Custer Battlefield in 1987, Park Service docents were still telling the same old lies. For the fourth time, a superintendent promised that he would get the government to put up a memorial to the Indians who had been killed defending their way of life. He said, "I'll personally put it through the system and make sure it happens." I said, "Not good enough. We gave you three chances; you struck out." We marched to the monument area atop a low hill. A granite obelisk honoring Custer's killers stands at the highest point. While I gave a speech about Custer, several AIMsters began to dig near it. Others began to mix cement. In a few minutes, they erected a new monument, an innocuous slab of iron with an inscription, on the south side of the hilltop. I said we would return for each of the next three years and place more memorial plaques on each side of the white man's monument—one for the Lakota, one for the Cheyenne, one for the Arapaho, and one for the Crow. We would surround the white man's phallic symbol just as Custer was surrounded by Crazy Horse's defenders—unless the United States built its own monument to the Indian dead.

The Park Service later dug up our plaque. Then the officials made a slick move. They appointed as battlefield superintendent an Indian named Barbara Booher, a career bureaucrat who had served for years in Alaska. She formed a commission to get a bill through Congress to fund our monument. Ben Nighthorse Campbell, then a congressman, ramrodded the bill; we got it passed after two tries. The commission includes several whites but no reservation Indians or elders. Booher used the pretext that I was a former convict to keep me off it. Enos Poor Bear, who attended the first commission meeting, got the Oglala Sioux tribe to present me with an eagle feather for my efforts in getting the monument started. My people have given me many other feathers, but that was the first from a BIA-oriented tribal council.

When Yellow Thunder Camp closed, I became even more resolute in my determination to gain freedom for my people. After returning from the Libertarian convention in Seattle in September 1987, Gloria and I agreed that we would start a new life together among her Navajo people in Arizona, as I had promised her before we married. It was a bittersweet moment when we left our little log cabin in Porcupine. In the Indian way, Gloria went from room to room calling to our spirits that we were going. Then together we told the house where we had shared so much laughter and loving that we were leaving.

Navajo is a Spanish word used by the conquistadores for a people who have always called themselves Dineh. Despite that, in the early 1980s, the Navajo tribal council—which included no traditional people and few elders—voted to keep *Navajo* as its official name. Their reservation, about the size of West Virginia, includes parts of New Mexico, Arizona, and Utah. Chinle, precisely in the middle of the Dineh Nation at the entrance to Canyon de Chelly, about ninety-five miles from Gallup, New Mexico, became our new home. At first, we lived with Gloria's parents. During her previous marriage, she had bought a tiny trailer to live in while her husband built a new house. Within a short time, we moved into it.

I have always felt that there is enough money in the world for everyone, so whatever came my way was fine. When I didn't make much money, I never worried about it. Until I met Gloria, I rarely bought anything for myself except underclothes and socks. Everything else was given to me by friends or supporters of AIM. After Gloria and I started a family, however, I felt the need to make things easier for them. For the first time since joining AIM, I began to look for ways to make money.

Thinking about money reminded me how the American Indian Movement had never been much interested in financial matters. When we began to champion our rights, we engendered a lot of hope among Indian people. But now the times had changed, and our movement had run out of steam. The leaders were older, and most had turned to looking after their families. The younger generation, which had played no personal role in the struggle of the 1970s, saw their hopes crushed by colonization because reservation politics remained under federal domination. I realized that for the spiritual renaissance to continue, there had to be an economic revolution based on Indian sovereignty. I believe establishing economic links between Indian nations and countries around the world will provide a base from which to develop independence and restore sovereignty. With few assets but a telephone and my contacts around Indian country, I began to pursue ideas that I hoped would lead to opportunities for Indian nations. In the process, I also hoped to earn a little money for my family.

I got to know the Hopi tribal chairman, Ivan Sydney, when he asked me to help with a Hopi-Navajo land dispute that had been going on since 1976. Although the Dineh had been relatively ineffective in lobbying Congress and had launched few initiatives with its public-relations firm in Washington, D.C., the Hopi were being portrayed in the white man's media as villains who had forced the Dineh from their homes. The Hopi wanted to counter that impression. I was promised a consulting fee to create a proposal for developing a PR agency owned and operated by the Hopi people.

Through Ward Churchill, I met a successful Colorado-based public-relations consultant. We drafted a plan for the Hopi to establish a privately owned, for-profit agency that would be separate from tribal government and could take advantage of a favorable business climate in that part of the country for Indian-owned businesses. The consultant, a white woman, would run the day-to-day operation, and I would be adviser on Indian issues. As we built the business, we would train Hopi people to take over. By the fourth year, the agency would be an all Hopi one and we would bow out. We brought the tribal council a sophisticated multimedia presentation that included video, charts, graphs, and printed summaries. I spent about one thousand dollars of my own money, and I was very proud of the package. But to this day, I've never had a response of any kind from the Hopi tribal council. Eventually, word filtered back that the Hopi had elected a new council that knew nothing about our proposal and didn't want to talk about it.

Shortly after that, I got a call from Robert Hodge, a Wall Street financier who had read about me. He was doing business with China. The Chinese needed wool and wheat, and were willing to work through his brokerage with Indian nations to establish trade. He had also lined up investors interested in starting an independent bank on a reservation—the first. Great Western Bank of Arizona had four branch offices on the Dineh reservation. CitiBank, a New York company, had just bought it out and announced plans to close two of those branches. I went to see the local manager and asked if those two were for sale. They were.

As a possible buyer, Hodge requested information from CitiBank about the branch banks. What they gave him revealed just how racist that institution's policies were; most successful banks lend about 40 percent of deposits to their community. Great Western, however, had lent only 2 percent—and claimed it was losing money. The data showed the bank refused to make loans to the most dependable, responsible people on the reservation—the traditionals—because they don't speak English! When we opened negotiations, CitiBank asked about five million dollars for its two branches. Hodge thought it would probably accept half of that. "The way they're doing business, they should pay *us* to take over," he said.

The Dineh tribal chairman was Peter MacDonald, who insulated himself with layers of bureaucracy to keep the public away. The only official I was allowed to see was a blond Mormon kid fresh out of college, who didn't have enough management experience to run a pizza parlor. I said, "We're not asking the Dineh Nation to buy anything or put up any money. All I need is permission to buy these bank branches in association with individual Dineh or other Indians." The guy would not hear me out. He insisted instead on trying to impress me with everything he had learned in school about banking. I left.

The bank was federally chartered, so I didn't need the tribe's permission to buy it. On the other hand, I had been promoting Indian sovereignty for many years, so I wasn't going to try to ram anything down the throats of the Dineh people. Hodge's investors wanted to put up 49 percent of the purchase price. I tried to find local people to become majority partners, but few were willing to invest in their own development.

Hodge and I then decided to approach other Indian reservations. My first thought, of course, was Pine Ridge, but I couldn't get to the tribal chairman, Malvin Cummings. Robert Fast Horse, his executive officer, said the reservation was too poor to support a bank. Then I called Sam Coson of the White Mountain Apache, in Arizona, whom I had helped to defeat the incumbent chairman, Ronnie Lupe. Coson said he was interested in an independent bank for his reservation, so I put his people in touch with Hodge's office. They negotiated for more than six months. Finally Hodge threw up his hands; his investors were fed up with the Apache people. Disgusted, he called to ask, "What is it with you Indians? You don't *want* to succeed, is that it?" When he calmed down, he explained that each time he had gotten the Apache officials to the brink of an agreement to form a partnership to buy the bank, they had backed down or failed to keep appointments or even return his phone calls. I still don't understand it.

While working on the bank deal, I also pursued trade with China for the Dineh. Peter MacDonald had started an accelerated economic-growth program. When I tried to talk to its managers, they were all too busy to see me. I met with underlings to explain that the Chinese wanted to buy Dineh wool, and were willing to pay a better price than they could get locally through their co-ops. A trade deal with China would also enhance the sovereign powers of the Dineh Nation, I added. Unfortunately, I was speaking with young Dineh who had meaningless titles that caused them to believe they were among the elite. They couldn't listen to just anybody, especially a notorious militant such as Russell Means. Like all bureaucrats, they instinctively dodged any issue they didn't understand—and since they were working for the federal government, they understood almost nothing. I might have been able to arrange a series of smaller deals between the individual wool co-ops and the Chinese, but with MacDonald in power, there was only one place to go on the reservation, and that was his economic program. His bureaucrats muttered soothingly and did nothing.

China also wanted wheat, so I headed to the Fort Peck Reservation in northeastern Montana, home of the Dakota and the Nakota-speaking Assiniboin. Income from oil royalties had contributed to their development; they also grow wheat. I went before their oil and gas committee, the most politically powerful entity on the reservation, and made my pitch. They could get a better price for wheat from China than by selling locally or to Russia under Reagan's grain deal. I wanted them to think about more than just Indian wheat. If Fort Peck led the way, any Plains Indian who leased land to white wheat growers could sell his lessee's wheat for the same price—high enough above local market rates for both to profit. Such cooperation between cowboys and Indians would demonstrate the sovereign power of the Fort Peck Reservation as it helped to break down racial barriers.

The committee unanimously supported my proposal, which meant the tribal council's approval was pro forma—it never opposed the oil and gas committee. I went back home—and someone called to tell me that the committee had reversed itself. The reason was simple: The BIA had told the Fort Peck leaders—off the record, naturally—that according to BIA lawyers, my proposition was illegal. If they went ahead with it, federal funding for reservation programs could be cut. That was nonsense; the deal was perfectly legal, and the BIA knew it. Anything that makes Indians less dependent on the government, however, threatens the bureaucratic empire because it leads to fewer BIA jobs. The BIA invoked the golden rule—if you have the gold, you make the rules. The tribal council members, without seeking outside legal opinions, rolled over and waved their backsides in the air.

After that disaster, I went to New York to renew my friendship with Gines Serran-Pagan, a Spanish anthropologist who had lived at Yellow Thunder Camp. While visiting his East Village apartment, I met a guy I'll call Jack, who had years of experience in international transportation. He introduced me to people in the carting industry, including those in a company that wanted to get into hauling goods for the government. Because Indian-owned companies get first preference on BIA and Indian Health Service contracts, we talked about forming a trucking subsidiary with me as majority partner. The more we considered that, the more promising it appeared.

Jack also knew high-level people in a Polish-American joint venture called AmeriPole that had a forty-ship fishing fleet in the Pacific and needed a harbor with a dry dock. There was just one place in the Puget Sound area where such a port could be built—the Lummi Reservation on the northwest side of Bellingham Bay. The Lummi not only had the waterfront, they also had the only permit to build a port and were actively seeking investors. I have always had tremendous respect for the Lummi. They have kept IRS agents off their reservation at gunpoint, demonstrating their sovereignty. They are among the most economically progressive Indians in North America, winning important court cases against the IRS and establishing their right to fish in any way they see fit. Individual Lummi aren't liable for taxes on their catches. I thought a port deal would be ideal for them.

After forming a Delaware corporation called Tipi Enterprises, Jack and I met with AmeriPole's president, chief executive officer, and chairman. Then

I called the Lummi. My main contact was a young man in charge of economic development. I said, "These people want to build a port for you. They'll finance 100 percent of it and give 51 percent to the tribe." I further explained that the Lummi wouldn't have to go to the BIA for even a dollar. He sounded very interested.

I went back to Chinle. By phone, I arranged for AmeriPole officers to visit the Lummi, tour the reservation, and look over the site of the proposed port. AmeriPole's three top men would come from Poland, another would come from New York, and their fishing-fleet manager would fly down from Anchorage. When I called the Lummi to set up the visit, the tribal chairman was out fishing for salmon—that's how most of his people make their living— so I spoke to the young economic-development guy I had talked to earlier. I told him the AmeriPole executives wanted to take the Lummi leaders to dinner the night of their arrival. The following day, they wanted to meet with the tribal council. Jack sent a fax to the vice chairman, confirming the times and flight numbers of their arrivals in Bellingham and the hotel where they planned to stay. I phoned the same information to my contact.

Jack lived in New Jersey. Early one morning, he called me at Chinle, very upset. Nobody had met the AmeriPole people at the airport. No one had called or come to their hotel. They had traveled halfway around the world and were wondering if they had made a mistake. It was 9:10 A.M. in Bellingham. I said, "They run on Indian time. Give them a chance." Then I called the Lummi tribal offices, but no one was around except a secretary. I told her in no uncertain terms to get somebody, anybody, over to Bellingham to pick up those people and take them to the reservation.

Jack was going bananas. His fees on an initial investment of thirty-five million dollars were at stake, and that was his first big venture. Some clerk finally got to the hotel and took the AmeriPole guys across Puget Sound to the reservation, then left them to roam around by themselves. Eventually, someone took them to a meeting. They told the Lummi why they had come, but after about ninety minutes, the Indians hadn't replied to AmeriPole's questions. They just sat there and said nothing at all. The Poles discovered they were talking with people who had no authority; except for the vice chairman, they were all low-level tribal government employees. The vice chairman, afraid to say anything without the chairman's okay, just clammed up. The Lummi could have had a port and an entire fishing fleet coming in and out. They could have had enough decent jobs and economic growth to ensure that they, their children, and their children's children would have had no financial worries. The AmeriPole people knew incompetence when they saw it. They left, never to return.

Disgusted, Jack called to read me the riot act. "I'm not working with you or any Indians. You guys don't want success, and you're lazy!" I remember him saying. He was right, and I don't blame him for feeling that way.

All he had to sell was his credibility, and that went down the toilet with the Lummi deal—along with any chance I had of getting into the trucking business. I felt especially bad for Jack because he had worked so hard. I often wonder what has become of him.

Around this time I heard from a white woman in Arlington, Texas, who had served as Liberia's counsel-general in New Orleans. She was into channeling and out-of-body experiences; her spiritual guide, she said, was an Indian who had directed her to get in touch with me. Out of our telephone friendship came a business proposition: Because of the AIDS scare, latex condoms were in great demand and prices were rising. The best latex rubber comes from West Africa, especially Liberia. My channeling pal and her husband had access to Liberian rubber and wanted to build a latex manufacturing plant as a joint venture with an Indian nation, where since there was no state jurisdiction, there were overhead and tax savings. They were willing to give 51 percent ownership to the Indians. The plant would employ about two hundred people. I knew that the Crow reservation was ideal. It had, among other things, a big river with enough water for manufacturing latex products.

Richard Realbird was then chairman of the Crow. I didn't know it then, but he was in deep trouble with the government. Officials were auditing reservation records, looking for fraud and finding, instead, mismanagement and poor record-keeping. What I did know was that in the previous six years, he had lifted his nation from a $10 million annual dependence on BIA welfare to only about $600,000 a year. The key to that transition was winning a lawsuit against one of the energy companies over royalties owed from coal mining. Instead of letting the Crow collect their judgment, however, the BIA had found a legal pretext to impound the money, leaving them so broke they couldn't pay their electric bill. When I called Realbird, he mentioned that he was involved in a political dispute with the BIA, but he also said he was very interested in talking about the latex plant. I set up a meeting in Denver between the investors, which included the Liberian ambassador, my channeling friend from Texas, and the Crow economic-development team.

The Crow never sent anyone to Denver. The investors, however, remained enthusiastic about what they felt could be a highly profitable venture, so they agreed to drive twelve hours from Denver to the reservation when I arranged a meeting. But before they arrived, BIA police raided Richard Realbird's offices, confiscated his files, and, in effect, took over the Crow tribe. When the investors arrived, there was no one to meet them and everything was in obvious disarray. Few things are less attractive to investors than political instability, so that was the end of that deal. They didn't even want to discuss going to another reservation.

At about that same time, I was in touch with some Frenchmen who wanted to buy the Hart Ranch, a big dude ranch in the Black Hills, southwest of Rapid City. If the Oglala Sioux at Pine Ridge became majority partner and put the property in federal trust, the Frenchmen were willing to put up all of the purchase price in return for 49 percent ownership. That arrangement would have been required because the government says we Indians are incompetent to handle our own legal affairs, and therefore it holds all Indian land in trust. Trust property is exempt from state and local taxes and regulation. I thought it was perfect. The tribe would own hundreds of acres in the Black Hills and the French would get a tourist attraction, a giant western theme park with "cowboy" attractions and those based on Indian cultures.

Paul Iron Cloud, who four years earlier had made sure my name was off the tribal presidential ballot, had become president of the Oglala Sioux. Randy Plume was his executive officer. I put my French contact's representative in touch with Randy, who seemed enthusiastic. A few weeks later, however, my contact, a retired doctor from Scottsdale, Arizona, called to say the tribe didn't want anything to do with the Hart Ranch. A friend at Pine Ridge told me what had happened: When Iron Cloud realized what a tremendous deal it was, he became afraid that I would take credit for it, come back to Pine Ridge, and run against him for president. He nixed it.

I was disappointed but not surprised. That incident, like the inexplicable behavior of the Lummi, the Fort Peck fiasco, the Hopi disaster, and all the others, is typical of Indian tribal governments. There is little political continuity—few top leaders serve consecutive terms. Council members generally care about nothing but keeping their jobs, collecting their paychecks, and spending government funds.

The kind of treatment my proposals received throughout Indian country is also typical of people who don't respect themselves. They think they don't *deserve* success, so each time, they create the circumstances to fail. That tragedy of Indian society is another legacy of the Indian Reorganization Act of 1934, which institutionalized a relationship in which the client—in this case, tribal government—must please the patron, the federal government. Never mind that the U.S. Constitution mandates that government is the servant of the people. The act re-created a feudal system in which serfs must satisfy their lords. Although BIA-created tribal councils and presidents or chairmen ostensibly have control over their reservations, they are dependent on congressional appropriations managed by federal agencies. If they displease the bureaucrats, the money dries up. Instead of exercising their sovereignty, each reservation is a banana republic with a small class of elites, which can perpetuate itself as an oligarchy only as long as Washington approves. The BIA has total control—but councils take the blame for failures.

The "Outlaw"
Navajo Government

Before the BIA raided the Crow Indian Reservation in 1988 and sent Richard Real Bird to prison for what amounted to sloppy bookkeeping, they began investigating Peter MacDonald, chairman of the Navajo tribal council. Clever with his use of public relations, a man who liked being in the news, MacDonald was an early proponent of sovereignty. During his first twelve years in office, he was the architect of big change. When I rodeoed on that reservation in the 1960s, it was common to see drunks lying on highways, staggering around the streets of border towns like Gallup, or passed out in parks or alleys. On weekends, when the jails weren't big enough to hold all the drunken Indians, some towns threw fences around parking lots and pitched hundreds of Navajo people inside to sleep it off. I found it embarrassing to be an American Indian around that reservation.

MacDonald ended all that. Chairman for all but four of the years between 1970 and 1990, he presided over an amazing transformation. Members of an entire nation lifted themselves up to stand with pride and dignity as human beings. Although alcoholism is on the rise again, the Navajo are still widely regarded as a responsible, progressive, and advanced nation. Even more important, Pete MacDonald is the only elected Indian official I know who publicly identified the BIA as the enemy of his people. He wasn't afraid to say it in the media, even at the National Press Club in Washington, D.C.

Pete stood up for his people. When some were being relocated from Hopi lands, he went out with hammer and nails to fix houses in which the BIA had refused to allow any repairs for twenty years. Of course, he took care to invite the press, so the BIA would be embarrassed. Many people find Pete autocratic, but he is very tradition-minded and can speak the beautiful Dineh language in all its full richness. He worked to instill pride by celebrating and enhancing the old values—something I've seen little of elsewhere in Indian country.

After leading his people through a cultural renaissance, MacDonald pursued economic independence. The Navajo Reservation is the Saudi Arabia of coal. It has brought thousands of jobs and a steady flow of royalties that have gone, in part, to improve reservation life. Some people say the Dineh are raping their own land by strip-mining, or wasting their water by tapping underground sources to use in the production of coal. Pete, however, forced the mining companies to reclaim mined-out areas, replanting trees and trying to make things the way they used to be, as much as possible. It's impossible to put things back the way the Great Mystery made them, but the Dineh do try.

Pete's economic plans were well under way by 1989, but he made a few major blunders. One was the expansion of the reservation's land base and water resources by buying Big Boquillas Ranch for thirty-five million dollars. When it was discovered that the whites who arranged the sale went away with a profit of six million, some people on the reservation got angry. The feds were also pissed off because MacDonald had bought a huge and successful operation, added to the reservation's land base while diversifying its holdings, and never asked BIA permission. Next, he put together big-time investors to finance construction of tourist facilities in and around the reservation. Then Pete announced that he was going to float a $100 million bond issue through a Japanese bank to finance economic development. The collateral was a small fraction of the Navajo coal reserves. Not only did he fail again to consult the BIA, but such a clear expression of sovereignty could lead to total economic independence! With $100 million in venture capital, the Navajo wouldn't have to line up, caps in hand, to beg money from the BIA. They could handle their own affairs.

That was a no-no to the BIA. If the Navajo could manage, maybe the Apache could, too. Maybe the Lakota or the Western Shoshone or the Hopi could become self-sufficient. Pretty soon, *all* Indians would behave as if they were human beings, free to run their own lives. If that happened, why would they need a Bureau of Indian Affairs except to protect white-owned corporations that exploit Indian land? What would all those bureaucrats do? Go out and look for real jobs? The BIA began to look for ways to stop Mac-

Donald before he could demonstrate to the whole world how useless and unnecessary and evil and corrupt the BIA is.

In January 1988, the U.S. Senate Select Committee on Indian Affairs contacted me. The staff had begun an investigation of BIA corruption, and wanted me to testify about tribal governments. Because my many attempts to spark private enterprise had been foiled by tribal-government incompetence and BIA pressure to stymie anything smacking of autonomy, I said yes. I said I would also testify about other areas of the investigation, including natural resources, health, and education.

Among those who went to Washington to testify were former President Richard Nixon and the chairmen or presidents of several tribes, including Twila Martin, head of the Turtle Mountain Reservation in North Dakota. I knew her as a member of AIM. Others came as well. Wilma Mankiller, a major AIM supporter during the occupation of Alcatraz, was by then principal chief of the Cherokee Nation of Oklahoma. The Senate subcommittee included Tom Daschle of South Dakota, and John McCain and Dennis DeConcini from Arizona. Its chairman, Daniel Inouye of Hawaii, made an opening speech, then left. As the first to testify, I reminded the senators that I was the only witness who wasn't being paid by the federal government.

AIM had been demanding an end to the BIA since 1968. I called once again for the abolition of the genocidal bureau. It confused the senators. They said things such as, "Do you think that's realistic?" When they asked Twila about it, her reply startled me. She said something such as, "I don't think it's feasible, but we need to study it." Nor could I believe Wilma, who said, "No, don't eliminate the BIA. It should be reduced and there should be more consultation with tribal governments"—or words to that effect. I knew then that they, too, had compromised. It made me very sad.

Most people who run for tribal-government posts try to convince people they are the best beggars on the reservation. "You elect me, and I'll beg Washington, D.C., better than the others," they effectively say during campaigns. If they don't get lots of money from the government, they don't get reelected. Phillip Martin, chief of the Mississippi Choctaw, who called my suggestion "totally ridiculous," is an excellent example. He has been reelected regularly for nearly thirty years.

I wasn't really disappointed with the hearings; they were about what I had expected. Indian leaders had visited Washington, D.C., for close to two centuries. Red Cloud, Cornplanter, Seneca, Red Jacket, Tecumseh, and, more recently, Fools Crow and Matthew King had spoken for their people, knowing that they represented sovereign entities. They treated the representatives of the United States as their equals and spoke their minds. I tried to give my own testimony with the same dignity.

I saw clearly where the so-called investigation of BIA corruption was going. The senators were primarily interested in blaming the victims—

Indians. They were after MacDonald, leader of the largest and richest Indian nation—the main one making a serious effort for economic independence. DeConcini, one of the five senators who let Charles Keating get away with bilking thousands of people out of billions until after his own reelection campaign, asked if I had evidence of mismanagement or tribal corruption. He expected and wanted me to jump on Pete. Instead, with C-Span and CNN taping me, I told him about my experience with the Lummi. DeConcini pointing his finger at MacDonald seemed ludicrous. Long before anyone had ever heard of Charles Keating, the DeConcini family had made a fortune ripping off Arizona Indians' water rights. Someday all the details of that story will become public. When they do, the DeConcini family wheeling and dealing will make the Los Angeles scandal that inspired the film *Chinatown* seem like a rain puddle.

The next morning, DeConcini and I were on NBC's *Today Show*. True to form, blathering about "corrupt tribal governments," he said more than $2 billion a year went to Indian governments, and Congress wanted to find out where it was going. I said, "What the Senator fails to mention is that we Indians have 40 percent of the natural-resource reserves of the U.S. We contribute $6 billion annually to the gross national product. We get $2 billion back—but 80 percent of that goes to bureaucratic costs and government overhead. That's not a fair trade." Bryant Gumbel changed the subject, but I had nailed DeConcini.

After I appeared on television, I got a call from MacDonald. He said, "When you get home, can I see you?" We met at Window Rock, Arizona, where some people were sniping at him because, while renovating his offices, he had put in an expensive mahogany door. That door became a big issue in Navajo politics and was used against him for a long time. Years earlier, grand juries had investigated Pete and one panel had dutifully delivered an indictment, but the trial jury acquitted him. The investigation about Big Boquillas Ranch had revealed that the white man who made $6 million off the deal did so through fraud. He was granted immunity to testify against MacDonald. He stole the money and then, because he was white, he got to keep it.

Pete asked for my advice about Big Boquillas Ranch and about his other troubles. I said, "Here's what you've got to do. Announce to the news media that you're chartering a jet and going to Washington to appear before Congress. Make sure they know your arrival time and when you intend to testify. You're the leader of the Navajo Nation, so travel like a head of state. Bring enough of an entourage to fill two or three stretch limousines. Take your wife and maybe a son or daughter and a grandchild. Drive up to Capitol Hill and have your office arrange security so that when your limos pull up, they can hold the press and everyone else back. If they refuse to allow you to testify, hold your press conference right on the Capitol steps. Tell the media what you had intended to talk about; say that you can't understand why they won't let you speak—then leave and go home."

Pete said, "What if they let me testify?" I said, "In your speech, say you're not going to participate in a kangaroo court where you can't cross-examine your accusers. Say that you're shocked and offended that the white man who illegally made six million dollars from the sale of the ranch was granted immunity to testify against you. Then explain that if Big Boquillas Ranch was a good deal for the white seller, it was a better deal for the Navajo. When you've finished, don't answer any questions. Just get up and leave. Go directly to the airport."

Pete astounded me with his next question. He said, "What if they cite me for contempt of Congress?" I said, "You *have* contempt for Congress! It's not a fair hearing! *Pray* they hold you in contempt—it's the best thing they could do! If they cite you, condemn them for using their almost infinite power to try to crush the leader of a small nation. It'll be the mouse against the eagle. You'll have world public opinion on your side." In other words, change the rules, I continued. Make the issue not yourself, but the United States trying illegally to crush Navajo aspirations.

I swear before the Great Mystery, I wish Pete had taken my advice. Instead, he did nothing and wound up dealing with the feds from a position of weakness. While he was making up his mind, however, his supporters asked me to speak out against the BIA. I organized a march in Gallup and announced that I would investigate the BIA area director, Fred Stevens. If I found evidence of misconduct, I would place him under citizen's arrest for crimes against the U.S. Constitution. After the march, I went with four Navajo council members—MacDonald's supporters—to meet with the area director at Window Rock. Stevens was a wiry, one-sixteenth San Carlos Apache about three inches shorter than me and about my age. He looked and acted like a white man. He said, "Russell Means can only come into this office if he keeps his mouth shut—and I'll only talk with you councilmen." We agreed, and went into his spacious office. A squad of plainclothes BIA goons came in and stood around in the back of the room. The councilmen were responsible people with long service to the Dineh people as elected representatives, but Stevens spoke to them in such a patronizing way that it made my blood boil. After about twenty minutes I was so insulted that I said, "I can't take this anymore! You're ridiculous! I'm placing you under citizen's arrest. Are you going to come peacefully or not?"

"No," he said.

I grabbed him in a headlock and he reached up to jerk one of my braids. I wore leather braid wraps, an old street trick, and they slid right off. While I was trying to subdue him for resisting arrest, uniformed cops and the BIA goons jumped me. I wouldn't let go of Stevens, so each time they yanked my arms, I jerked his head around like a rag doll. A television crew and still photographers took pictures of the brawl, and they were sent all over the country. Before I was bailed out, I had become a hero to many people in Navajo land.

The BIA officials decided it was too dangerous for them to put me in the Window Rock jail, so they shipped me to their eastern Navajo agency at Crownpoint, New Mexico. When I appeared in court, I wasn't charged with assault on a federal officer in the performance of his duties, a felony that carries a maximum sentence of ten years. The feds knew that was exactly what I wanted. My defense at trial would have exposed to the international media the whole range of illegal activities practiced by the BIA. Instead, the feds sacrificed Stevens, and I was taken to tribal court.

At a preliminary hearing I argued that the Navajo Nation had no jurisdiction, an assertion based on two previous cases. In the Oliphant decision, the U.S. Supreme Court held that white people are not under the criminal jurisdiction of tribal courts. In other words, a white man living on a reservation can rob, steal, rape, or commit murder and Indians can't do a damn thing about it except ask the feds to find and try him. At that time, another case that would expand Oliphant was moving through the appellate courts. A Lakota charged by Pima tribal authorities claimed that they lacked jurisdiction because he wasn't a Pima. So far, every court had agreed.

Navajo courts being what they are, the judge disagreed with me, but he knew the Pima case would end up in the Supreme Court, so he delayed my trial until that ruling. Many months later, when the high court affirmed Pima, the charges against me were dismissed. That caused a big stink in Indian country because tribal councils, like all governments, are obsessed with control. Feeling threatened because they couldn't arrest or put visiting Indians in jail, they got Congress to pass a new law that gave them jurisdiction over any U.S. Indian on their reservations. They still have no authority to try whites, blacks, Asians, Chicanos, or Indians from Canada.

While the Navajo charges were still hanging over me, I found myself on the sidelines of another court battle. When Gloria had married her first husband, Gary Davis, it was recognized in the traditional manner by the Navajo Nation and its tribal court system. We supposed they would also recognize the traditional Dineh divorce. When a man moves out of the home he has shared with his wife, taking everything he owns, that is the end of their marriage. In June 1984, Davis had taken his belongings and moved to Phoenix. As far as Gloria and I were concerned, they were divorced.

I've never felt that I needed any white man's paper to justify my life, so the Great Mystery was all I needed to sanctify my marriage to Gloria. I find ridiculous the whole idea of a government licensing marriage. It's equally idiotic that when two people can't get along and decide to break up, they have to go to the white man for yet another piece of paper. The white man's religion is even more absurd—churches sanctifying marriage—but it's not a marriage until the sex act has been performed. There are exceptions. Catholics can get married and have children and then annul the whole thing as if they never were married. Then what do priests tell the kids—that they never had a father? So insulting to my intelligence and integrity is the white man's way that I don't look to him for permission to do anything.

More than two months after Gloria and I were married, Davis filed for divorce in Navajo tribal court. When he later learned that Gloria was with me, he amended his complaint to claim paternity of our son, Tatanka. Davis couldn't have believed he was the father. I'm quite sure he did that only to punish Gloria and to reap temporary celebrity by attempting to shame me. When she and Davis got into court, his best friend testified under oath that Davis, a counselor for Navajo high-school students in Fort Defiance, Arizona, not only smoked marijuana but bought and sold it too. Gloria also testified that while they were married, Davis had smoked dope. Davis had had a vasectomy shortly after he and Gloria were married. He underwent an operation to reverse it a few months before Gloria told him to leave. He swore that he had had sex with Gloria nine months before Tatanka's birth. Gloria, however, testified that she and Davis had quit sleeping together months before they split up. The judge, an older Navajo with many years on the bench, ruled that Davis was not Tatanka's father.

Davis appealed to the Navajo supreme court. I had supposed that tribal courts were created for the benefit of the Navajo people, but I would soon learn that when whites challenge custody of half-Navajo, half-white children, the courts consistently give them to whites. In Gloria's case, the court expressed self-hatred by ruling that the issue of paternity had not been determined to its satisfaction, and remanded the case back to district court.

By that time, the original judge had been replaced by a younger man hated my guts. By denouncing the BIA, I had become embroiled in tribal politics. Although I found much to admire about MacDonald, my support for him was not intended to ally myself with any reservation faction. I was merely saying that the U.S. government had no legal or moral right to go after the elected leader of a sovereign nation. Nevertheless, the hyenas and jackals who hoped to gain something from Pete's downfall began to perceive me as his political ally, and therefore as their enemy. The judiciary committee of the tribal council, controlled by his opponents, appointed judges who loathed MacDonald. Among them was young Robert Yazzi, who detested me for my attacks on the BIA, and hated AIM. It came as no surprise that he was chosen to hear Davis' paternity suit.

I got an inkling of how things would go on the first day, We wanted our white attorney to try to get the court to accept that the case was about a traditional Navajo divorce and therefore the judge had nothing to decide. Our lawyer, however, ignoring our suggestions, called no witnesses except

Gloria, and refused to discuss his reasons for not listening to us. Before this trial, records of the original court proceedings had been "lost." Yazzi refused to consider the lost record as relevant and he also forbade us to reintroduce evidence from the divorce trial or to allow any evidence about Davis's character. He said, "The only issue before this court is paternity."

In all courts I'm familiar with or have researched, case law gives credence to the mother. It is the mother who knows the father of her child. Although the Navajo judge was obviously angry at *me*, his ruling nevertheless came as a shock, especially after Davis withdrew his motion for blood testing after I had agreed to it. Regarding Gloria, he said, "She is not to be believed." He decreed that Tatanka was the son of Gary Davis. We wanted to appeal, but our lawyer withdrew from the case, saying only that he wanted nothing further to do with us. We found another white lawyer who practiced in Navajo courts, but he was soon appointed to the bench in a neighboring county. Our fourth attorney was a Navajo, Albert Hale. He failed to show up for our hearing, and the judge threatened to cite Gloria for contempt because she had appeared without counsel. We found yet another Navajo lawyer, Richie Nez, to pursue our appeal. He filed a day late, and the Navajo supreme court refused to accept our pleading.

While all this was going on, I submitted Tatanka's name to the standing enrollment committee of the Oglala Sioux tribe. They are some of the very few people in tribal government who take their jobs seriously. They examine questions of ancestry and determine if someone is an Oglala or not—a rigorous inquiry. After Tatanka Wanbli Sapa passed the tests and was enrolled, I got the Oglala Sioux tribal court to issue a temporary restraining order against the Window Rock district court, the Navajo supreme court, and the Navajo government from proceeding further in the case. Under federal law, they had ten days to respond before a hearing for a preliminary injunction.

The Navajo court failed to answer, in part because by then the Navajo Nation was operating under an interim government. In defiance of the law, the BIA had frozen the Navajo Nation's bank accounts, fired all pro-MacDonald officers on the tribal police force, replaced them with BIA cops, and forcibly evicted MacDonald—a military coup d'état. To add a veneer of legality, Stevens, the BIA area director, dubbed thirty-odd anti-MacDonald council members "the Forty-Niners"—implying that they were a majority of the seventy-seven-person council—ruled that they constituted a legal quorum, and got them to validate MacDonald's ouster. The rump government next waived its sovereignty by granting several western states jurisdiction over Navajo people living on the reservation. They spent about three million dollars of tribal funds to hire a white law firm in Albuquerque to prosecute Pete for a long list of offenses. After two trials, he was convicted only of a questionable expenditure—and misappropriation of a rental car.

Just as the feds had used perjured testimony to try to imprison Dennis

Banks and me after Wounded Knee, they went after MacDonald just as ag-
gressively. For two years, they spoon-fed lies and half-truths about Pete to
the Arizona media. They transferred his trial from Phoenix to Prescott, Arizona, where there are far more Indian haters per capita. Among the charges
he faced was a conspiracy rap. After Pete was forced out of office, some people
held a peaceful protest at Window Rock. Tribal police opened fire, killing
two of Pete's supporters. The feds prosecuted the demonstrators and sent
about a dozen to prison. Pete, who wasn't even there, was convicted of conspiracy for allegedly having masterminded the protest. He was also convicted
on several other charges.

The Dineh will reap the benefits of MacDonald's vision and courage for
generations to come. Yet the man who did far more for his people than
anyone else in this century is rotting in jail because it suited the political
agenda of a U.S. senator—and because colonized Navajos, led around by the
BIA, found it expedient to crucify their own best hope for dignity through
independence.

While Pete was going through his ordeal, I continued to fight for Gloria
and Tatanka. When the Navajo court refused to reply to the Oglala Sioux
court's preliminary injunction, it was made permanent. That prohibited the
Navajo courts from moving forward on the paternity case, because Tatanka
is enrolled with the Oglala Sioux tribe. In the United States, courts of similar
jurisdiction operate on a principle called comity. That means courts of one
state recognize the jurisdiction and validity of others. Indian courts on different reservations are bound likewise. Nevertheless, the new Navajo government and judiciary refused to recognize the ruling by the Oglala Sioux
court—an unprecedented breach of comity. They ruled that since Gloria is a
Navajo, they alone have jurisdiction. The Navajo courts washed their hands
of the matter and turned it over to Navajo Social Services for enforcement.
Fortunately, the social workers in Chinle understood the situation. They are
people who grew up in the community and are in touch with traditional
Navajo beliefs; many are also members of Gloria's Bitterwater Clan. They
sent a letter to Gloria saying she had to let Davis visit Tatanka. She ignored
it, and they never came to our house. But I couldn't be sure that Davis
wouldn't try to kidnap my son. One of the most difficult things I ever had
to do was tell him that a white man was trying to take him. I keep reassuring
him that I'll never let that happen, but I can't imagine what trauma that
might have inflicted on his five-year-old mind.

By early 1989, amid all the court hassles, I was angrier than I can ever
remember. I was pissed off at almost everything and everyone. I took some
of that rage out on my family. Gloria and I got into an argument over
something so trivial that I can no longer remember what it was. In my rage,
I lost control and yanked her hair. I knew it was wrong, but I didn't realize
that it was as bad as a punch or a kick. Gloria asked tribal police to escort

her while she got her clothes. When she returned to our house, she said she wouldn't come back until I left, and that she would get a court order to force me out. "Don't bother, I'll go," I said.

"By the way," said Gloria, "when I went to the police, I signed two blank complaint forms."

"Blank?"

"Yes."

I knew I was in trouble. The cops could fill in those forms and allege anything about me at all. After all the confrontations I had had in the 1970s, I knew they would do so. Expecting the police, I decided I wasn't going to jail. I borrowed guns and ammunition and fortified my home office with mattresses and furniture piled against windows and walls. I was ready to shoot it out. Cops like to come at night, so I stayed awake until daylight. When Gloria called to ask when I would leave, I said, "I'm expecting the cops to arrest me—but I'm not going." When Gloria called the station, however, they said no warrant had been issued. I took my things and drove to Albuquerque, where I found an apartment.

That day or the next, the police filled out both blank forms Gloria had signed and issued a warrant for my arrest on two counts of assault and battery. Gloria and I learned about this when an Associated Press story, fueled by a police press release, went nationwide. Newspapers across the country ran the story. Suddenly a slew of my university speaking engagements were canceled. The schools weren't about to have wife abusers addressing their students. Although Gloria and I were still living apart, she wanted to help clear this up. We called a joint press conference, where she made a beautiful statement explaining our situation and condemning the police for tricking her into signing blank documents and then issuing an arrest warrant. We sent it to the wire services and to every newspaper that had carried the earlier story, but only the *Navajo Times* carried it.

After six weeks in Albuquerque, Gloria and I patched things up and I returned to my family. The separation had forced me finally to examine my inner rage. It was overwhelming me. I was constantly seething—I couldn't keep it down, and I had no way to vent it. After the Window Rock protest killings, few Indians were willing to participate in demonstrations. AIM was no longer in the vanguard for Indian rights. After I tried to arrest Stevens, Vernon Bellecourt publicly condemned me as being "out of step with the times." I found myself brooding about the setbacks and frustrations of previous years: the racism in the federal judiciary that strangled Yellow Thunder Camp; the incompetence and selfishness and downright stupidity of tribal governments that rejected and defeated attempts to put them on the path to independent economic development; the downfall of a hero such as Peter MacDonald, who ought to be a role model for Indian children for all time to come. Things seemed more and more hopeless. If there was any revolutionary zeal among my people, I couldn't see it, even in college students. I saw them sliding back to the "powwow" way, becoming part-time Indians, caricatures of what we once had been.

As my rage fed on thoughts of the injustices Indians still faced, I confronted the reality that despite everything I had done, despite all the efforts of the American Indian Movement, genocide against my people continued— and I began to wonder if my life had meant anything at all. I began to wonder if my death might mean more. I began to edge across the hazy line between reason and madness.

After AIM had taken over BIA Headquarters in 1972, we were denounced by dozens of tribal executives and BIA officials. At the time, I had advocated an assassination program to kill key Indian sellouts; I thought it would send a message to our people. Fortunately for me and the sellouts, AIM's leadership rejected my idea.

Now, I thought, I'll do it myself.

52

▼▼▼▼▼▼▼▼▼

The Movies

I could feel the rage boiling from my every pore. I seethed and brooded and plotted for weeks—a mass of conflicting emotions. I began to compile an "enemies list," à la Nixon. I sorted through a roster of selected sell-outs—presidents and chairmen of tribal governments who had collaborated in the BIA's dirty work. I added others to the list—tribal judges and BIA police. I planned to kill a few rednecks at random, too, just the way they have butchered South Dakota Indians for generations. Most of the whites I wanted dead were U.S. congressmen, senators, federal and state appellate judges— the most visible proponents of the institutionalized racism that underlies government. I even developed scenarios for each killing.

I believed I could succeed in carrying out many assassinations, but I also knew the law of averages was against me. Eventually, I would be caught. I planned to die in a gunfight, a martyr to my people. I told no one of my plan, not even Gloria. I added names to my list until I felt I probably couldn't kill many more before I was stopped. I was, of course, quite insane.

The only thing that kept me from putting my deranged plan into action was the values of my ancestors. I admired the elders who personified my cultural heritage, and I wanted to become like them—wise and patient. I also wanted to be free. I wanted to see just one Indian nation liberate itself, to be accepted as an equal among the family of nations. I knew that once I began to assassinate sellouts and oppressors, I would never live to see that. Two powerful forces were thrashing around inside me, my frustrations against my good intentions. I've never believed in evil, but my madness was twisting mass murder into an act of redemption. My inner struggle was not over goals; it was over means. Should I follow the dead-end assassination trail or the freedom-through-liberation path that might allow me someday to take my place as a respected elder? Both were equally possible. As time went on, a disturbing notion flitted beneath the surface of my awareness. *Maybe uncontrollable rage was my problem.* So fixed was I on my agenda of death, however, that I refused to let that idea become a conscious thought.

One day in 1991 in Chinle, the phone rang. A beautiful human being named Bonnie Timmermann, a highly respected casting director, called to ask if I would be interested in auditioning for an important role in a major motion picture. I don't get many calls like that! She explained that director Michael Mann was going to make *The Last of the Mohicans,* based on James Fenimore Cooper's 1826 novel. She had me in mind for the title role of Chingachgook, adoptive father of Hawkeye, the film's principal hero. Mann would be in Los Angeles for a couple of days that week, Bonnie said. If she sent me a script overnight, could I go to LA in three days' time to audition?

"That's the day before I'm scheduled to speak at a Libertarian convention in Monterey," I replied. "I'm flying out of Gallup late that afternoon. I could leave here in the morning, do the audition, and go up to Monterey afterward—if you'll buy me a ticket and get me to and from the airport." Bonnie agreed, and put me on the phone with an assistant, a young woman, to take down the details. I told her that I only fly first class.

When I hung up, images swarmed through my mind. I dimly remembered *The Last of the Mohicans* from junior high. Its plot and language were so difficult to follow that I had never finished it. When I gave a class report about it, I had made up my own story. As a kid, I loved the movies, and our elaborate cowboys-and-Indians games were very much like filmmaking. I rounded up the neighborhood kids, cast myself as the star, and choreographed scenes with crude costumes and lots of stunts. My sister Madonna recalls that I usually pulled everyone into a semicircle, assigned roles, and drew plans in the dirt with a stick. In one of my scenarios, my three-year-old sister Mabel Anne was captured by "Blackfeet" and tied to a telephone pole over an anthill. Sometimes those productions went on for days, pausing only for meals and sleep. Madonna recalls that I once said, "When I'm big, I'm going to be a movie star and make movies where the Indians win!"

Now here I was, in my fifties, with a chance at a starring role. I knew nothing about the entertainment business, so I had no idea that actors customarily pay their own way to auditions, or that I couldn't learn all I needed about my part by skimming the script en route to Hollywood. When I went to the airport to pick up my ticket, it was coach class. I thought, there goes my movie career, and left to handle some business around Gallup. After lunch, I flew to Monterey on my original ticket. First class, of course. The next day, Bonnie got on the phone and tracked me down at the convention. "What happened?" she said. "We sent a limo to the airport to bring you to the studio. Michael Mann was waiting for you."

"You sent me a coach ticket; I made it clear to your assistant that I only fly first class." Bonnie was very apologetic. She knew I wasn't an actor by profession and so I was ignorant of the movie business. Probably she and Mann were aware that I was involved in many different projects and also trying to make a living for my family. They showed me great courtesy by paying my expenses and rescheduling my audition. I got to Hollywood a couple of weeks later. I mounted a stool and sat in front of a video camera to read from the script. Knowing nothing of screenwriting, I said, "I ain't gonna read this shit! Indians don't talk this way!"

The look on Bonnie's face told me she was about to die of embarrassment. She had taken a liking to me, however, so she tried to salvage what was rapidly turning into a fiasco. She said, "OK, then improvise." I spoke to the camera in what I felt was more appropriate language. Later, she said, "You'll have to come back tomorrow to read for Michael Mann." Since I hadn't planned on staying in Los Angeles overnight, I had no clothes—not even a toothbrush. An assistant casting director said, "Buy what you need, give us the receipts, and we'll reimburse you."

When I finally got to read for Michael, I began by paraphrasing the script. Turning to Bonnie, he said, "What is this?" Obviously embarrassed, she said, "Oh . . . I . . . uh . . . I told him it was OK to improvise." Michael turned to me and said, "Could you just read the lines as they're written?"

"But Indians don't talk this way!"

"Would you just do me a favor and read the lines the way they're written?" He sounded a little edgy.

"OK, the way you want it is the way you'll get it."

I read the script. In my own mind, both it and my performance were crap. I would later learn that Michael wrote it, and that he's a genius in his own right. But he must have seen something in me that he wanted to explore further. He asked me to come to New York for a second reading with Daniel Day-Lewis, who was to play Hawkeye.

Before that, Bonnie arranged a private session with Sondra Lee, a drama coach. She is a fantastic teacher who has worked with such talents as Robert De Niro, Donald Sutherland, and Marlon Brando. A tiny, very lovely person, Sondra blew me away by gushing about how much she admired my work on behalf of Indian people. She even asked for my autograph. Taking out the script, she showed me a scene near the end, and said, "Here are the lines that are going to win or lose you the part."

I had only two hours with Sondra to prepare for my reading. The most important thing I learned was about screenwriting. It was the key that unlocked the whole acting mystery and gave me immense respect and admiration for writers. With a phrase, a word, or even emphasis on a single syllable, writers can alter the whole meaning of a scene. Actors owe them everything or nothing. The other wonderful thing I got from Sondra was the advice to forget about acting. "Just *become* the part," she said. At the audition, much to my astonishment, I really got into it. Michael had me go through several pages leading to what was—for me, at least—a very heavy scene. By the time I got to the few lines Sondra had said were critical, I *was* Chingachgook. In the story, I had just lost my son Uncas, so I cried. When I finished that scene, I threw the script down and sat back on the couch to look at Michael and Daniel. I said, "I cried!" The look on their faces told me they were surprised by my reaction to my own performance.

I related to Chingachgook because, like him, I had lost a son—Hank, to prison. Also, I was still fighting to keep Gary Davis from stealing Tatanka. But it was more than that, of course, something I couldn't explain at the time. Perhaps it's because being an Indian means not thinking about doing, but simply *being*. In slipping into Chingachgook's character, I could share our common heritage and our way of living in the present moment. I'm forever grateful to Sondra for unlocking the latent acting talent within me.

I did get the part, a sizable chunk of money, and a new career. In mid-May 1991, along with the other principal male actors, I went to Columbus, Georgia. Every morning for two weeks, we crossed the Chattahoochee River into Alabama to attend a training camp for mercenaries. I knew how to shoot, of course, but I had never before handled eighteenth-century muskets or flintlock pistols. We also practiced stunt fighting with tomahawks and war clubs, woodland lore, and other skills, such as making fire, which everyone on the frontier knew in 1754. We then went to make the movie in the Blue Ridge Mountains of North Carolina, the only place in America that resembles upstate New York as it was in the 1700s, and a very beautiful area.

I had always hated the way Indians were depicted in Hollywood. Except for a few movies with Chief Dan George, I can't recall a single film in which even one Indian character was developed as a human being. Instead, they were two-dimensional stereotypes, cardboard figures of marauding savages circling the wagons, or red Step'n Fetchits like Tonto playing second banana to white Lone Rangers. Most white people probably felt that *Dances with Wolves* was the first movie to show Indians in a sympathetic, three-dimensional way. But I thought of it as a *Lawrence of the Plains*, an overblown saga that merely substituted a new cliché for the old, the reverse side of the same racist coin. Most of its Indians were good guys, but they remained simple savages who needed a "civilized" white messiah, played by Kevin Costner, to become their savior. The producers wouldn't chance a backlash by allowing the white hero to take an Indian wife, so his romance was with a white woman whom the Indians had raised from childhood. Once again, Indians were reduced to subhumans.

Knowing that an enormous international television audience would be watching the Academy Awards ceremony in 1991, I had planned to bring Indian people from around the country to the show for a big demonstration against *Dances with Wolves*. After weighing the pros and cons, however, I decided the sympathy for Indians the movie had engendered outweighed its continued reliance on stereotypes. I also know, however, that the same "noble savage" sentiment had served as midwife to the birth of the Bureau of Indian Affairs. Indian people are dying of sympathy. What we want is *respect*.

The Last of the Mohicans was an entirely different kind of film. Michael's screenplay appealed to me because all its major Indian characters, including villains, were developed into realistic human beings with substance. For perhaps the first time in cinema history, the bad Indian—in this case, Magua—has a good reason for being that way. His family has been slaughtered by English soldiers who raided his village. Magua, played brilliantly by Wes Studi, an Oklahoma Cherokee, was also intellectually superior to his white counterparts—French and English generals. Wow! It also made me happy to see that Michael insisted on historical accuracy. The story was set in 1757, when Indians and whites on the frontier were economic and social equals who shared the same fashions in clothing and visited one another's homes. That equality probably had arisen because in that era, Indians were militarily and economically superior to Europeans. I don't care *why* it happened, but I felt it was good to remind white America about a facet of history that it has forgotten or never learned. Politically, the movie is about individual rights and responsibilities. Relentlessly antigovernment, whether English or French, it is an anarchist statement that reflects my own culture and my own views.

In Cooper's book, Chingachgook has a son, and the family wants to head west to Kentucky because the East has become overcrowded and government has begun to restrict individual liberty. The book describes Hawkeye, a white man, as Chingachgook's contemporary, but in Michael's screenplay he became my adopted son. Uncas, played by Eric Schweig, is Chingachgook's natural son. When he dies at the end, I become the last Mohican—a symbolic reminder of what has happened to Indian civilization.

There was only one scene in *Mohicans* that I took exception to. I call it the "African village scene" because it looked like something out of a 1950s film about the Congo. The tribal chief sat on his primitive throne while his people clamored for the blood of the white princess. Then the white prince came in and saved her. We had a white princess, and sure enough, she was saved by two white princes. Despite my objections, Michael insisted that the scene was necessary. Gone are those kinds of portrayals in movies about Africa, since white colonialism has been driven off the continent and Africans have become more influential in the world. Maybe that's why some people in Hollywood have tried to transfer the stereotype to Indians.

The business of filmmaking was new to me, and I soaked in every detail. The day I realized that Michael was a genius was when we worked for three-and-a-half hours and did sixty-five takes with four camera angles to get two or three seconds on the screen. He wanted a certain facial expression, and we just kept at it until he got it. He is so focused and such a perfectionist that some people find him difficult to work for, but I came to comprehend that he is dedicated to putting the best performance on the screen and nothing else matters as much. That is all to an actor's ultimate benefit, so I find nothing wrong with working to accomplish the most I'm capable of. As for myself, Michael told the *Los Angeles Weekly* I had "delivered in spades" for him.

I had a wonderful experience with Eric Schweig, a Canadian Inuit who had been adopted by a white family as an infant. According to Eric, his adoptive parents abused him physically and treated him like a slave, so he ran away at age sixteen. We shared a trailer during filming. As we got to know each other, we developed a deep affection. About midway through the shooting schedule, I held an Indian adoption ceremony. In front of some of the cast and crew—and the Great Mystery—I said I wanted to be Eric's father because I loved him. In his whole life, no one had ever publicly told him that. Eric broke down and cried—and I did, too, when I found out why.

The other guy I came to greatly respect and admire was Daniel Day-Lewis. While we were in training in Alabama, he told me, "We're going to be a family in this movie, so we should talk about family." We talked more than a bit during the production. He told me about his relationship with his father, the English poet Cecil Day-Lewis, who had died when Daniel was young. I told him about my own dad. As we became closer, we began to go running together. The producers didn't like that because although he was constantly eating, running made him lose weight. There was no way Daniel was going to stop running. I love to watch him. He moves with the deceptive speed and effortless grace of a gazelle. If he had trained through his twenties, he might have been the best runner in the world at a mile or longer.

As we began to share our feelings and our outlooks on life, we became very close. To this day, I consider Daniel a good friend. On the set, he is every director's dream, the consummate professional, never complaining about anything. He is also every actor's best friend, sticking around off camera to remain in the line of vision, thus making it easier for the other actors to perform. But most of all, he *becomes* his character. Off the set, he was never without his flintlock, even when it was hours before he was scheduled to be on camera. One evening as I sat around the Hilton Hotel in Columbus, Georgia, talking with other members of the cast, Daniel came by for a moment and introduced his lady friend. Steven Waddington, the beefy blond

Englishman who played Hawkeye's rival in the movie, said, "He's in his *American* mode. He's already in the part—has to be an American throughout this whole film." And so he was, for months, using the speech that was characteristic of a British colonial American.

Despite Michael's enlightened attitudes about Indians, I nevertheless experienced Hollywood bigotry during the production. Some crew people and even actors casually called me and other Indians "chief" and "redskin" to our faces! When the weather turned wet, I was laughingly accused of having done a "rain dance"—a joke, but insensitive nonetheless. When I wore my traditional choker, some people referred to it as a dog collar.

I lived quite comfortably on location and had the use of a car, but hundreds of Indian extras were quartered in an abandoned Boy Scout camp. It was little better than a concentration camp—cinder-block buildings with six to eight people crammed into hellhole rooms designed for two. It was a hot, humid summer, and there was little ventilation indoors. They were thirty miles from the nearest town, and the only way to get there was to walk. Most of the Indian extras' scenes were shot at night, but since they had no transportation, they had to stay in camp during the hottest part of the day. They couldn't even see a doctor, and because of the many battlefield stunt scenes, they always had lots of bruises and strains and cuts.

Since union rules don't apply in North Carolina—it's a right-to-work state—the producers cut every labor corner they could. The technicians soon went on strike for better conditions and a union contract. They got both. Later, in the middle of filming, hundreds of Indian extras went on strike. Of the cast, only Eric, Daniel, and I joined them on the picket line. I was asked to carry their demands to producer Hunt Lowry; because of that, the media reported that I had organized the walkout. It was over in four hours and the strikers got everything they demanded, but a few days later, the real leaders of the strike were quietly laid off.

Some of the most obvious racism during the production came from a director's assistant, who liked to verbally abuse and exploit Indians. Eric and I had several encounters with him. He went out of his way to see to it that production workers fouled our temporary home. When we were away on the set, the assistant told these people to use the toilet in our trailer instead of their own outdoor "porta-potties." When it rained, we returned to find our place filled with muddy tracks. Even when the weather was good, our toilet waste tank was always full. We were mystified about this until a female worker finally told us what was going on. I was outraged; there were many other trailers near ours, but the assistant never told people to use the john in Daniel Day-Lewis's trailer or in Madeleine Stowe's—or in Hunt Lowry's.

The assistant also filed incorrect time sheets that, in defiance of Screen Actor's Guild rules, denied extras and actors overtime wages—including me. I kept careful records of his abuses and wrote memos to Hunt Lowry and made an official complaint to the Director's Guild. When I confronted the assistant about these matters, he was with a bunch of cops and I came very close to getting busted for assault. Since Hollywood isn't that big a place, I knew that sooner or later, I would run into him again and when I did, I would hit him so hard and fast with my left that he'd be crying for my right.

The rage that had been smoldering deep in my heart and mind had not vanished simply because I was involved in making a movie. It had merely been masked as I dealt with acting and with the day-to-day necessities of life on location. I took note of all the racist incidents that I saw and heard about, and the harassment some of the stuntmen directed at makeup artists and hairdressers. I listed them in almost daily memos to Lowry. It was a way to vent my anger, but it wasn't enough.

As angry as all those things made me, I never forgot I was there to do a job. During *Mohicans*, I fell in love with acting. I hadn't realized I was an artist until I became an actor. In Western civilization, actors, poets, painters, sculptors, musicians, singers, and other artists are always the first to recognize the need for social change. After them come intellectuals who grab hold of their ideas and put them in a form educated people can understand. Finally, when the people who live and work on the land join in, a revolution has a chance of succeeding. I love being an artist—it fits in with being a revolutionary.

The movies offered me something else, too—a better way to get messages about my people to the world. Ours is a celebrity-driven society. If Marlon Brando has something to say, he can always get on television—not because he's smarter than everyone else, but because he's famous. After my decades of devotion to my people, the Great Mystery had led me to a place where what I had to say would have more credibility than ever before. Just as important, the motion-picture industry has been instrumental in creating and reinforcing institutional racism about Indians. Working from within that tremendous venue of expression, I could become an agent for change.

5 3
▼▼▼▼▼▼▼▼▼

Good-bye, Columbus Day

When I had finished making *Mohicans,* I still had done nothing to curb
my anger. My assassination plots were still very much alive. In fact, my
list had lengthened by one.

Mohicans wrapped on October 11, 1991—not a day too soon. Colorado
AIM had asked to be its executive director, and I had to be in Denver the
next day. That was, of course, Columbus Day. To indigenous people of this
hemisphere, the celebration is the ultimate affirmation that since 1492, Western society has regarded us as expendable. Columbus was a murdering heathen who "discovered" the heaven on earth that was home for my ancestors
and immediately set about turning it into a living hell for them. Denver was
where Columbus Day was first celebrated in 1907. It was also in Denver, that
the territorial government decided that fighting Confederates was too dangerous, so the whites murdered red people in their villages and reported "Indian unrest" to be such a threat that they could spare no troops to fight for
the Union. Heading the genocidal Colorado Volunteers was an ordained
Methodist minister, Colonel John Chivington, who became famous for his
massacre of Cheyenne women and children at Sand Creek in 1864—and for
saying afterward, "I believe it is right and honorable to use any means under
God's heaven to kill Indians."

For years, Colorado AIM had been trying to get the Denver populace to stop celebrating Columbus Day and to understand that by honoring the first transatlantic slave trader, the city was affirming and supporting genocide. It was Columbus who sowed the seeds of Manifest Destiny. In the Europe of his time, it was against church law to enslave or murder human beings, although such canon rarely prevented wholesale murder. To enslave Indians for his own enrichment, he had to convince the Church that indigenous people were subhuman, and therefore could be slaughtered or enslaved with impunity. To persuade the church that they were subhuman, Columbus accused the Indians of such unnatural acts as cannibalism—a lie. Later, Cortez accused the Aztecs of human sacrifice—another lie, but my own recent conversations and experiences with Aztec medicine men convinced me that their ancestors, aided by a masterful understanding of plants which temporarily slow the body's functions to near-paralysis, performed open-heart surgery. This has been partly confirmed by recent archaeological and pharmacological research. In order to conceal this truth and sell the lie of human sacrifice, the Franciscans who accompanied Cortez burned every Aztec book. The church policy of genocide was the basis for European colonization of two continents—and as the 1994 revolt in Chiapas illustrated, nothing has changed.

For years, I had been telling AIMsters that we had to start planning to do something about the five-hundredth anniversary of Columbus' arrival, in 1992. I thought it should be something very dramatic that would make international news, but only Colorado AIM shared my enthusiasm. Glenn Morris began a four-year program to educate Coloradans about Columbus and his legacy of oppressive laws and policies against Indians. We also held a rally around the statue *Discovery of America*, near the state capitol in Denver's Civic Center Park. I threw a can of water-soluble red paint on it to symbolize the centuries of bloodshed Columbus was responsible for inciting. I was arrested, but the charge was dismissed.

There hadn't been a Denver Columbus Day parade in more than thirty years, but in 1990, the Federation of Italian-American Organizations, which claimed to represent about sixty thousand people in metropolitan Denver, decided to have one. Glenn and Colorado AIM tried to establish a dialogue with FIAO to explain why we were offended by the idea of honoring a murderer. We suggested that they change the theme. We said, "We'll join your parade if you don't have it on Columbus Day. Have it the day before or the day after and celebrate Leonardo da Vinci or Sophia Loren or Joe Di-Maggio—anyone except Columbus." An arrogant FIAO leader said, "The police are with us." We said that if they went ahead as planned, we would stop the parade—and they broke off communications. A few days before the event, however, we went to see the FIAO officials again and worked out an agreement whereby AIM would lead the parade. Afterward, we would set up an intercommunity group to discuss the elimination of future Columbus Day parades. As soon as the parade was over, however, FIAO canceled negotiations and refused to talk with us. AIM then asked Denver Mayor Federico Peña—one of the lawyers who had defended me in Scottsbluff in 1972—to remove the Columbus statue from Civic Center Park. When he refused, we offered to contribute new statues to complement Columbus's, including one honoring Hitler. In hindsight, we should have offered one of Mussolini, too.

Another Columbus Day parade was scheduled for 1991. That's why I hurried from North Carolina to Denver after finishing *Mohicans*. Early on the morning of October 12, I joined an AIM rally that drew about 450 people. I'm embarrassed to say that only about 150 of the ten thousand Indians in greater Denver came to the rally. After the governor and grand marshal passed the reviewing stand, about two hundred of us moved into the street and blocked the parade. We waited to be arrested. We wanted to flood Denver's courtrooms, cost the city some money and effort. The police assembled their tactical squad and brought in buses to haul us away. After about forty-five minutes, the cops arrested the four principal leaders—Margaret Martinez, Glenn Morris, Ward Churchill, and me. They took us to a bus and said, "Get your people out of the way and we'll just cite everybody—we won't take them to jail." We had stopped the march and the media people had swarmed around taking pictures, so we agreed. As soon as everybody was out of the way, the parade resumed and the cops didn't issue any more citations. It was a trick. I've got to hand it to the police for pulling a good one on us.

The four of us were charged with serious misdemeanors that carried a total of two years' jail time. We went to court in June 1992, and the trial lasted two days. We defended our actions in stopping the parade by citing an international treaty on the prevention of genocide signed by President Reagan and ratified by the U.S. Senate. According to the treaty, "hate speech" is not acceptable because it promotes genocide. We offered documentation proving that acts of genocide by the United States are continuing, including the forced relocation of the Navajo, Department of Agriculture programs that compel Indians to eat substandard and unhealthy food, and medical experiments on unwitting Indian subjects in Alaska and Minnesota. We argued that by promoting stereotypical racist images of Indians, the parade encouraged genocidal practices. The jury, comprised of people reflecting the multiethnic nature of Denver, found us not guilty.

The verdict stirred up the press, especially the *Rocky Mountain News*, historically a newspaper for Indian haters. In the last century, its editorials had advocated annihilation of all Indians in Colorado and had lauded Chivington for the Sand Creek Massacre. After our acquittal, there was an outpouring of anti-AIM editorials. Colorado AIM wasn't among the groups labeled as "fringe organizations" of troublemakers, ex-convicts, and malcontents. Its principal leaders, Ward Churchill and Glenn Morris, are professors. Glenn is also a lawyer whose views are published frequently in local editorial pages. Many other AIM members are professionals, prestigious and accomplished people who cannot be refuted, dismissed, minimized, or trivialized. So well regarded is AIM that many Colorado community organizations—black, white, and Asian—have called on our security force to help protect their demonstrations, especially on Martin Luther King Day. In the wake of our acquittal, however, the infuriated Denver media focused editorial hatred on Glenn, excoriating him as a "brownshirt"—a Nazi—for his desire to end the parade. More hatred poured out on radio talk shows.

Meanwhile, AIM was organizing and mobilizing for the next year and the five-hundredth anniversary of Columbus's "discovery" of America. Fifty local and statewide organizations—including the Colorado Council of Churches, the NAACP, the Urban League, the Nation of Islam, the New Jewish Agenda, Making Waves, MeCHA, a national Chicano student organization, and the conservative Hispanics of Colorado—agreed to march with us on Columbus Day. We said repeatedly that although we were adamant about stopping the parade, we would do so peacefully. The media people acted as if they had never heard us utter the word. Broadcast and print reporting continuously ballyhooed our "threats," hysterically reiterating that we were planning violence. Raising the specter of a conspiracy, they attempted to whip up public opinion against us.

Seven times, FIAO and AIM met to try to resolve the crisis peacefully, with negotiations facilitated by Ben Nighthorse Campbell, a city of Denver representative named Steve Newman, and the U.S. Department of Justice's Community Relations Service. The FIAO "negotiator" summed up his organization's position—he told me something like, "You Indians had better understand, this isn't your country anymore, it's our country now, and you had better get with the program." That was the end of the dialogue. How could AIM reply except by showing those racist rednecks that this is still our country and always will be?

When AIM spokesmen were invited on a few radio shows, they calmly said their piece, backed by history and facts and law. Glenn, Ward, and I met often with the police. We told them we preferred to follow the methods of Mahatma Gandhi and Martin Luther King, but we had also learned from Malcolm X. We said, "Touch our women or children, and we will defend ourselves by any means necessary."

I gave talks to support groups and at strategy sessions. About three weeks before the 1992 parade, we had held a meeting with non-Indian support groups in the basement of an Indian church. There were many people, black and white, who hadn't been in demonstrations since the 1960s. Some expected a police riot, so we told them how to prepare—bring a first-aid kit. Bring a handkerchief that can be soaked with vinegar in case the police throw tear gas. Don't wear contact lenses, because if you're gassed, you'll go blind. Don't wear earrings or anything the police can grab.

I said, "We want to stop this parade, but we don't want to break the law. Don't spread out along the parade route and attack individual floats. Please don't bring marbles and roll them on the streets, because many police will be riding horses and they will fall down—we don't want that." I also said, "Please don't bring any female dogs that are in heat. The police K-9 corps will smell them and get all excited and run away and cause confusion. Someone could get hurt."

After saying all that, half kidding, I added, "Wait! This is going to be a *peaceful* demonstration, and I'm so sure of that I'm bringing my seven-year-old son! I know we're going to win because we have spiritual power behind us." I arrived on the day of the parade to find the cops obviously worried. The chief of police had gone on television to announce that vacations had been canceled, and all Denver officers had reported for duty. Mounted police and dogs were assembled, fire trucks hooked to hydrants, and hoses manned. The SWAT team was out in force. FIAO had lined up a policemen's auxiliary organization, and had drawn the tentative support of some press organization. The FIAO had also gotten slick. It got police permits for the parade route and for a gathering on the capitol steps, where we had held rallies since 1989.

We set up our audio system and people started to flood in. A crowd of more than fifteen hundred, including about 250 Indians, came to march with us. We had many Chicanos, a few black leaders, and lots of Italians, more than were scheduled to march in the parade. But there was no parade! The floats never came. Only after the cancellation was announced did a few Italians wander in. Within five minutes of that announcement, another thousand AIM supporters, people who had been hanging back to see if something bad was going to happen, came rushing in—twenty-five hundred people dedicated to peace and an end to racism. It was the grandest feeling. I was filled with elation and pride. Nonviolence had succeeded, and self-determination was alive.

On the day we stopped the parade, Indian people throughout the Americas held a variety of anti-Columbus demonstrations. Ours was the only event that yielded a tangible victory. I believe that was because we alone had prepared for day by organizing for four years. We enlisted the support of all the responsible people in Colorado, and we educated the community so well that the media, despite a mighty effort, could not stir up anti-Indian hysteria.

There wasn't even any talk of a 1993 Columbus Day parade. Instead, AIM held a little ceremony in the park and planted four donated aspens. When the Denver city officials heard we were offering them, one said, "Could you please make it some other kind of tree? We like to keep the park neat and clean, and aspens proliferate—they grow anywhere." That's why we chose them! There was no 1994 Columbus Day Parade in Denver—but today there are quite a few young aspens growing in Civic Center Park.

54
▼▼▼▼▼▼▼▼▼

Treatment

Our second son had been conceived in the spring of 1990. Gloria's Bitterwater Clan had already named him Nataanii Nez, Dineh for "tall, statesmanlike leader." I was pleased to have another child on the way, but relations with my wife, strained since when we had separated in 1988, continued to deteriorate. We bickered constantly throughout her pregnancy, and I found reasons to leave home for days at a time. For that reason and others, I didn't fulfill as many of the responsibilities of fatherhood as I should have during that important time. However, when I was home I sang and talked to him, as I had with Tatanka. Gloria had vowed to have this baby by the natural method, but after twenty-six hours in labor, she was exhausted but hadn't dilated. When the baby's heartbeat became erratic, she agreed to have a Caesarean. Our son was born on January 8, 1991.

To the consternation of the Navajo nurses at that Catholic hospital, I carried my newborn son for two hours, singing and talking and praying. When he began to turn yellow, often a sign of liver trouble, the doctor insisted that I relinquish him to nurses who would stick him with needles to reverse the jaundice. They even enlisted Gloria to get me to do so, but I refused. Instead, my son Tatanka joined me in a tobacco ceremony. Holding

Nataanii Nez high in the air, we sent our prayers to the Great Mystery. Later, I gave him to the doctor and he immediately found no jaundice!

As I had done with Tatanka, for the next three months I fulfilled my parental obligations. I stayed home and got to know my new son. I played with him and spoke to him until he knew my voice and smell and we had "bonded," as they say in the white magazines.

Gloria and I, however, continued to drift apart. While I was in North Carolina making *Mohicans*, I had written her a letter in which I shared many thoughts about our relationship. I meant to say how much I loved and admired her, how good we were together when our lives were in sync, but somehow she understood my words to mean exactly the opposite of what I had intended. Because of that and our past troubles, she refused to visit me on location. Our marriage seemed headed for disaster. I stayed married mostly because I wanted to raise my sons. I had cheated all my other children, and I felt this was my last chance to be a real father.

Looking for help, Gloria began to see a marriage counselor. When I returned to Chinle after *Mohicans*, she persuaded me to join her. After two sessions, Sister Adelaide, a Catholic nun, convinced me to enter a thirty-day residence program for treatment of my anger. She was very emphatic that I couldn't go merely to save my marriage. I must go to save *myself*. Suddenly, that made a lot of sense to me.

I wanted to start the new year off right and Christmas has never been a good time for me—I like nothing about it—so I decided to go in December 1991. I wouldn't commit myself until I went home to Pine Ridge and spoke to my Oglala people, including a spiritual leader and several others whose opinions I respected. Everyone said, "Don't go," suggesting instead that I enter the *inipi* purification lodge, go *unblecayapi*, cry for a vision, or wait for summer and *wiwongwaci*, the sun dance. I had performed all those ceremonies, but they hadn't made me less angry. I reasoned that since I had a white man's kind of problem, maybe I should try a white man's kind of solution. I headed down to Cottonwood de Tucson, then considered one of America's finest treatment centers.

The Cottonwood people sent a guy with a van to pick me up at the airport. One of the things shown in its brochure was a gym with free weights. Before checking in, I asked about them and was told that the weights had been given away. It was as good an excuse as any, so I said, "I ain't going. One of the main reasons I came down was because you had free weights."

"That's up to you," said the intake counselor. I put my suitcases back in the van. Then I thought, maybe I'd better try this. I returned to the reception area, but in a few minutes, I found something else I didn't like and blew my stack, shouting that I wasn't coming in. I marched outside again.

It was very hard, committing myself—about the hardest thing I had ever had to do. But finally, I signed myself in. Fortunately, Gloria's employer, the

Arizona school system, provided insurance that covered the fee of thirteen thousand dollars. No visitors were allowed for the first two weeks. After that, I was allowed one visit weekly until "graduation." Gloria brought our sons down to see me.

The place was filled with wealthy patients—millionaires and top executives from major corporations, even a lawyer who owned his own mental-health hospital. Everyone, including me, was anonymous. I was assigned a bed in a room shared with three other guys, two of them alcoholics. A sponsor, another patient who served as a big-brother type, took me around and introduced me to everybody. I was pissed off because, except for two Chicanos and a Navajo woman, I had seen only white people. I became even more angry at learning that what the Cottonwood staff called "family of origin" psychotherapy seemed like nothing more than a twelve-step program like Alcoholics Anonymous. Although they claim otherwise, it is based on Christian precepts. They might refer to their god as a "Higher Power," but they use the word "Him" and act as if there were only one. How can a supreme being, acting as giver of life, be masculine? I was steaming.

The first morning one of my roommates, an oil-company vice president, rose early to shower. The light and noise woke me. I took that as thoughtless and rude. Very loudly, I let him know I was displeased that he had to wake up everybody in the goddamn compound. The next day he and the other alcoholic moved into another room. I thought sure I scared them away, but the real reason, I learned, was because Cottonwood's management wanted to separate chemical dependents from those with other problems.

Because of the need to handle administrative details and meet my doctors, on my first day of treatment I left some group sessions early or arrived after they had started. Thus I was a few minutes late to the "large group," where about fifteen or twenty people were taking therapy. After everyone said hello, I was asked to give my name, why I was there, and three feelings describing how I felt. I told them I was in for my anger and I could think of only two feelings—anger and sadness. Try as I could, I couldn't come up with any more feelings. I was so out of touch with myself that I had become a prisoner of my rage.

Later, I went to an anger workshop. Late again, I missed the orientation and entered the room to find a guy holding a baseball bat and eyeing a huge cube of sponge rubber.

"What's going on?" I whispered to the guy next to me. He said, "He's about to beat his mother." I thought to myself, give me a break. Sure enough, the man began to beat the rubber cube with a plastic bat. He really got into it, cussing his mom, really whipping her. I thought, this guy's nuts! What did I get myself into here? I told myself I could walk out any time— but I resolved to give it two more days.

The next morning, I attended "small group"—two other guys, a shrink, and me. An hour passed before I learned the shrink was a sex therapist. One patient, a blond guy I'll call Gabe, began by telling about being fucked in the ass by his father, beginning at age four and continuing throughout his boyhood. For nearly two hours, I listened to him describe how that had affected him as a teenager and an adult. Gabe told about the perverted things he had done in sleazy porno joints. He described depraved sex acts he had performed. He had grown up to become an enforcer for the mob, and he recounted in detail some things he had done on the job. I told myself that my life and problems were nothing compared to Gabe's. If he could tell the truth about himself, so could I. He became my role model for honesty. I made up my mind to stay in the program and to be completely truthful about myself and my feelings.

During my first few days, I noticed a certain white woman in my large group. She was very conscientious about completing the written assignments we were expected to work on each evening. I chose her as a role model also, deciding that even though I hate to write, I would be just as thorough with my own homework.

I noticed several guys crying in group therapy sessions. At first I thought, what a bunch of fucking wimps! I was raised in Western society and brought up with the Eurocentric male worldview that said, "Tough guys don't cry. Men are always in control." I rarely allowed myself to cry.

As I began to meet more people, I learned that my AIM look, a perpetual scowl, made everyone scared of me. As the week unrolled, I began to realize I was in a safe, completely sincere environment. A few people might have been faking, but everyone seemed as honest as possible. I began to feel my own honesty coming out. Then I noticed a guy with a cross on his back. He carried it while walking around the grounds, when he came to therapy, even when he ate. It made me think, here's a guy who believes he's Jesus Christ. What kind of loony bin is this? Eventually, I made friends with him and learned that he was a car salesman, a great guy, so accommodating to others that that was a cross he had chosen to bear. Carrying an actual wooden cross was a way of getting that point across to him. The therapists assigned certain people to do things like that. A woman who tried to mother everyone had to carry around a bunch of dolls. A guy who talked a lot had to remain silent for seventy-two hours. Because I was always throwing tantrums, I was told to act like an eight-year-old throughout the three-day Christmas holiday.

After a few days, much of my skepticism boiled away and I started to see that there was a rationale to treatment. It's a formulized approach, a way of teaching us about ourselves. Once you catch on to how it works, you can make great inner changes. Besides group therapy, there were different exercises and experiential workshops in which mood music was used to help us take inner trips. With eyes shut, I imagined what it was like to fly or jump off cliffs. I learned how to relax. To allow the therapy to work, I had to make many spiritual compromises. I had to resurrect my parents' spirits, which Indians traditionally avoid. Once we've gone through grieving for loved ones and let them go on to the next world, it's disrespectful to bring them back, especially for negative reasons. But I had to do it. The therapists also put a lot of emphasis on eye contact, which Indians find discourteous, but I decided to go along with that, too.

Through it all, I maintained my Indian spirituality. Just before dawn, when the crickets, owls, coyotes, and other night people have gone to rest and the birds and day people haven't gotten up yet, everything is quiet. Even the wind dies down. That is the time when the entire world waits for our prayers, the time when the Indian male must say thank-you prayers. Then the east wind brings the morning star, which gives us the dawn of a new day and a chance to avoid repeating the mistakes of yesterday. Each morning, I rose in darkness, went outside, and greeted the morning star. I recited my thanks as I watched for the thin band of light that appears along the horizon to announce dawn's arrival.

After a couple of days, I was joined by another patient, who stood behind me and watched me pray. The next dawn, he was accompanied by a woman, and on the following morning four people were observing me. That grew to seven or eight and then about a dozen. Then my therapist called me in and told me that Cottonwood didn't need or want a guru. He told me to tell the others that they couldn't pray with me anymore.

"Wait a minute," I said. "What about the First Amendment? Don't we have the right to pray in our own way?" The doctor convinced me that there were good reasons for each patient to find their own path to spirituality. I suddenly realized the immensity of white Americans' spiritual void. It made me sad but prideful that those people, without understanding a word that came from my mouth in prayer, were drawn to my ancestors' ways and could feel the blessed connection with all that is sacred and holy and good.

Spirituality alone, however, would not cool the rage simmering within me. That required therapy. My turn to spill my guts came during the third week in the small group. First the therapist asked me to recall all my mother's bad behaviors. He wrote them on one side of a chalkboard—a litany that included anger, abusiveness, impatience, perfectionism, and disciplinarianism.

"Now list the good ones," he said. That inventory, which included strength, dependability, conscientiousness, ambition, energy, and generosity, was about half the length of the first list. I thought, wow, what a bad mom I had! The doctor said, "Now do the same for your dad." I recalled his alcoholism, that he never stood up for me, that he was irresponsible, untrustworthy, and undependable. On his better side were wit and a sense of humor, likability, an easygoing attitude, wisdom, patience, and the graceful way he moved. Even so, Pop's good list was only half as long as his bad. I thought, what lousy parents! No wonder I'm having problems—it's all *their* fault. As

if he had just read my mind, the therapist said, "Now give us the bad behaviors you have from both parents." When I had finished, he said, "Now
all your good behaviors from them." I saw that my ratio of good to bad was
about one to eight. I had all my parents' bad qualities, but few of their good
ones. With more therapy I came to understand that I had many other good
behaviors—but in that moment of confronting reality, I was stunned. I was
ill-tempered, impatient, filled with rage, a demanding perfectionist who always sought control. I was a liar, a fake. I was undependable. Looking at my
behavior through my own children's eyes, I couldn't feel sorry for myself.

In many workshops, therapists spoke about discovering one's "inner
child." Most people are forced to become premature adults. Their parents,
or whoever raised them, put adult responsibilities on them at an early age.
I realized that my grown-up duties had begun soon after my brother Dace
was born. Even when I was only three years old, if *he* did something
wrong, *I* was punished, as my mother often said, "Because you're the oldest—you should know better." I hated that phrase. I grew up knowing that
whenever I heard it, I was going to get a beating. Once I got a diary for
my birthday, and after a week of making entries, I read it. On six of those
seven days, I had gotten a strapping. Who wants to keep track of that? I
threw the diary away. Sometimes I wanted to scream at Mom that I was
only a child. That would have brought on another beating, so instead I
asked my dog, Sox, "How come it's always *me* that has to know better?
Why can't I just be a kid?"

In large group, we explored our genealogies, going back generations to
examine the behaviors of our parents and how they got them. We did the
same with grandparents and great-grandparents. I was surprised to see that
some of those rich people and executives could remember meeting their
grandparents only once or twice. Others didn't know their great-grandparents' names.

Seeking the source of all those behaviors, I recalled that my mom and
dad had gone to boarding school but my grandparents hadn't—at least, not
for long. So I knew where most of my parents' behaviors had come from—
a BIA whip, the club and the hose and the stick, and the bag of beans or
marbles they were forced to kneel on. My dad's alcoholism came from his
low self-esteem. He didn't think he was much of a man, and he spent his
whole life trying to prove it. Only his wit and quiet grace allowed him to
survive. To avoid being crushed, my mother got by on strength and an iron
will. Those were revelations to me.

Life at Cottonwood wasn't all workshops and exercises. As my inhibitions
diminished, I felt free to hug white men and women and to sit down with
anyone and talk about my feelings. I spoke often with a lawyer who had had
several heart attacks and almost worked himself to death. He was from a well-
to-do home; his dad had owned a business. I thought of him as having grown

up rich. To me, anybody who didn't have to mow his lawn, anyone who could hire people to clean his home, was rich. I listened to the problems of the wealthy and thought that compared with what I had faced, they were as insignificant as my difficulties were to Gabe's, the mob enforcer.

In the second week, I joined a large-group experiential workshop for anger, in which we took turns role-playing. The therapist, a woman, asked me to select individuals from the group to represent everyone who was important in my life, including Sox. Sox was an unresolved issue with me. I had left him behind when I went to live in Winnebago at fifteen. For eight months, my mother's letters told me that his spirit had gone—he moped around, acting as though I had died. When I returned, he was deliriously happy, wagging his tail in a circle and jumping on me. For an hour, we ran and hugged and had fun. When I moved to Los Angeles, I left him with Mom. She took care of him until he became deaf; then she had him put to sleep. In the role-playing, I apologized to my best and most faithful friend for the way I had ignored him at the end of his life. I acknowledged the shame I felt for having abandoned him in his old age.

Other people stood in for my sisters Madonna and Mabel Ann, and for Marilyn, who had died recently. I thanked them for their contributions to a beautiful part of my life, and I shared many wonderful memories. Then I spoke to each of my brothers—Dace, Bill, and Ted. I apologized to them. Not only did they have to grow up with the same parents I had had, they also had to grow up with *me*. I said I was sorry for not having known what I was doing when I hurt them. I had thought I was doing right and, just as our mother had, I had beaten them into obedience. I said I would visit each brother in real life and try to make things right between us. That day hasn't come yet, but I'm still working on it.

To represent my dad, I picked a big, burly Chicano I had become friendly with. My previous surrogates had taken a couple of steps forward when I chose them. When my friend started forward, I said, "No, stay there, you fucking wimp!" It was the first time I had ever talked to my dad that way. I don't know where it came from—it just popped out of my mouth. I went over and stood in front of him. "Hang down your head," I said. "You're nothing." Suddenly I realized that while I was growing up, I had built a false image of a father of strength and athletic prowess. Despite all his boyhood sports trophies, he had never displayed any of those qualities to me or my brothers. He had never stood up for us. He had failed to support us emotionally and financially.

I knew those were among my own behaviors and I would have to deal with that, but the biggest issue was my mother. I told the therapist, "I don't know if I can do this—and I ain't touching that baseball bat." She said, "Picture your mother when she was a little girl." Mom was the oldest child in her family. She had told me that her parents often compared her looks with her sisters' and taunted her. They called her ugly. I recalled a picture taken when she was three or four. She wore a white dress and white shoes and she smiled. She had never looked ugly to me. The therapist said, "Remember, she didn't grow up thinking, I can hardly wait to become a mother so I can fuck up my oldest son's life." That hit me hard. I thought, that's right, she *didn't* grow up thinking that. But she was beaten regularly in the BIA boarding schools. She was taught that that was the way to raise children. So when she beat me, it was really those sadistic school matrons beating me. It was the U.S. government beating me. Then the therapist said, "It's okay to hate your mother's behaviors and still love *her*." As I realized what those beatings were really about, all the details of my childhood of pain and humiliation came cascading out. I shared my innermost secrets, even the fact that as a toddler I had been beaten into being toilet trained, and these emotional scars remain to this very day.

Next, the therapist got me to share some positive aspects of my mother. I spoke about her strength and courage, and her determination to raise four sons with little help from my father. As she had given me freedom to roam our neighborhood, she had taught me responsibility. When it came time for the role-playing exercise, I chose to represent my mother, a very skeptical lady who had expressed great doubts about the whole treatment program and kept insisting that it was phony. The therapist asked me to share with her some of the names Mom had called me when she was angry. Standing next to the foam cube, "Mom" started yelling at me: "Greaser! You're irresponsible! You're no good! You liar! I wish you were never born! You're dirty! You dirty, no-good, irresponsible liar!" I took the plastic bat and started to hit the cushion—and lost all control. I went crazy. I whacked that cushion to punish my mother for all the times she had strapped me. I hit as hard as I could, striking back at last for all the pain and humiliation and shame she had beaten into me. I beat her and beat her and beat her until I could hardly raise my arms—and then I broke down and bawled like a baby in front of all those people, and I didn't care. They understood, and suddenly I felt great. All at once, I understood—anger was my way of covering up a lack of self-esteem. My mother had told me I was no good—and because children worship their mothers, I had believed her.

After I understood where my anger came from and what I used it for, I was able to participate more fully in the workshops and therapy sessions. Letting all my secrets go felt great. I was free to acknowledge and identify and enjoy dozens and dozens of different feelings. It was so wonderful and liberating that I can't fully explain it to anyone who hasn't been through treatment.

With the ability to open myself up, I developed close friendships with several people at Cottonwood, men and women. As treatment continued, I discovered tools that would enhance my good behaviors and allow me to get control over negative ones. I learned that because anger is an honest emotion, it's OK to be angry in appropriate ways. Since then, I've never again experienced that sick feeling of seething rage. My anger has been the healthy kind that I can recognize and put in proper perspective. Treatment has allowed me to finally free myself. I have no more pain inside. I can now accept life. I can deal with my impatience and with my imperfections. I'm no longer afraid to cry.

In thirty days of intensive work, I had completed the first five steps of the twelve required. As this is being written, I'm working on step eight, recognizing the people I've hurt in my life. My next step is making amends. Of all the people for whom I've caused pain, my children have suffered the most. The oldest four have now gone through treatment themselves. I've been there for each of them during their family week.

At Cottonwood, I came to understand that life is not about race or culture or pigmentation or bone structure—it's about *feelings*. That's what makes us human beings. We all feel joy and happiness and laughter. We all feel sadness and ugliness and shame and hurt. Life is not an "ouch!" contest. Nobody cares who has the best reason to suffer. If you're rich and hurting, you feel no different than someone who is poor and hurting. Then I realized that if the human family has all the same feelings, all any of us should worry about is how to deal with them. Forget about "saving the environment." Never mind "race relations." Don't worry about "justice." Deal with feelings and relationships. The cultures of every indigenous society in the world are based on improving relationships—the individual's connection with a dolphin, a wolf, an eagle, a tree, a rock, a spider or snake or lizard, with other human beings, with the clouds and with the wind.

I had often wondered how best to decolonize my people. Treatment made me realize that there is no need for all of them to get into the whys and wherefores of colonization that have led them down the path to self-destruction. It must be done one human being at a time. Without that kind of help, Western society does not allow people to come to terms with their feelings. With honesty and with therapy, my people can be made whole again.

Epilogue
▼▼▼▼▼▼▼▼▼

Return with me now to Greenwood, South Dakota, where my mother sleeps forever beneath what was once Grandma Aggie's front yard. Just below the house is the Missouri River. A couple of years ago, when the *wakinyan*—thunder spirits—wept for months over centuries of abuse suffered by Grandmother Earth, the Missouri and every other stream for a thousand miles around escaped from its banks, turning middle America into a vast inland sea. Perhaps a few white men now understand where the real power on our planet lies.

From Greenwood, take the blacktop county road a few miles north to Marty, the tiny town serving as the seat of the Yankton tribal government. Just beyond is South Dakota 18. Each evening, as dusk slowly gathers above the plains, a stream of cars and tour buses rushes westward through smooth, rolling hills toward the garish beacons of Fort Randall Casino, an ugly cluster of oversized mobile homes and hastily erected buildings.

There are many Indian faces behind the hotel desk and in the restaurant kitchen and among the roulette wheels, green felt tables, and slot machines. Dark-skinned security guards in leather-belted, cop-clone uniforms, with guns hanging heavily from their hips, lean against counters, stroll aimlessly among the gamblers, pour their nights and days down a neon-lit sinkhole. Middle-aged boozers with purple-veined faces gulp cheap liquor served by Indian bartenders. Tourists from Des Moines, Chicago, and Denver—and from Stockholm, Frankfurt, Budapest, and Tokyo—fork through cheap breakfasts prepared by aging Yankton cooks. Some of the dealers, croupiers, and waitresses are Indians. Like their white coworkers, their lives are filled with the mindless cries of hopeful gamblers, the whir of slot machines, the dull clink of chips, the clatter of tumbling roulette balls. There are no clocks in those rooms, and few windows. No one prays for the beauty of the sunrise. No one tastes the approaching rain or smells tomorrow on the east wind. No one does anything except pursue the white man's money.

The casino and hotel generate income for the Yankton Sioux tribe and for white investors and contractors. They provide monotonous dead-end jobs that permit a few dozen families to live a little better than their welfare-addicted cousins. In the veins of those casino workers run the blood of War Eagle, Padaniapapi, Medicine Cow, White Swan, Iron Bear, Feather Necklace, Crazy Bull, Jumping Thunder, Big Tobacco, Mazzahetun, Numkalipa, Walking Elk, Getanwokapi, Hinhanwicasa, Eagle Woman, Lies Down All A-Jingle, Blazing Star, Laughs at Iron Woman, and the other Ihanktonwan mothers and fathers. When they and their brethren gave up the hunt for the plow in 1858, they reserved 430,000 acres for themselves and their descendants. By this century, two-thirds of it belonged to white men. Today, of the little land remaining in Indian hands, most is leased to whites. A few Ihanktonwan families stubbornly cling to their farms and countryside homes, but my mother's nation, like so many others, is no longer a people of the land.

About two hundred miles west of Fort Randall is the Bennett County town of Martin, where my father slumbers through eternity in an out-of-the-way family cemetery. To the west of that hamlet is Pine Ridge. There, in 1989, Grandpa Fools Crow, after a life that spanned about a hundred winters, finally passed on. He was the last of the Lakota leaders born in the previous century, the last living link to the men who had humbled the bluecoat armies, the last raised by people born in freedom, the last whose mind was not contaminated by a white man's school. Now he is in the rear guard of his generation, following the path to the spirit world.

People came to Pine Ridge from all over the world to honor Fools Crow's memory. At his wake, we brought in the sacred drum and sang the AIM song that Severt Young Bear gave us during the Gordon demonstrations. Several people gave talks. When it was my turn, I reminded everyone that Fools Crow was always a beacon to his people. Never a Christian, he maintained the honorable traditions of our ancestors by living as an example of their beauty. I recalled that in 1975, while I was on trial for the Minnehaha County Courthouse police riot, he had brought a busload of elders by my place in Sioux Falls. All these wonderful old men and women got off and shook my hand. They were on their way to Washington, D.C., where Fools Crow became the only Indian ever to open a joint session of Congress with a prayer.

Indians come to funerals bringing gifts for the family so they can give them away, honoring our tradition of redistributing wealth. We brought many fine things for Fools Crow, and his family thanked us warmly, but I was amazed that his grandchildren, fervent Episcopalians, wanted none of the customary Lakota ceremonies. In fact, they wouldn't even allow medicine men or traditional people to attend. Along with everybody in AIM, I was outraged. People with little or no money had made personal sacrifices and endured hardships in traveling to Pine Ridge from other reservations. To them, burying Fools Crow with the trappings of Christianity was blasphemous, but they were too respectful to say anything. Rather than disrupt things, I left. The funeral was a media event. Hang-around-the-fort Indians put on headdresses and carried the coffin and got their pictures in newspapers and on television. Those who had fought against everything Fools Crow stood for elbowed aside everyone who valued his integrity and perseverance. It turned my stomach.

After that absurd and demeaning travesty, I made up my mind that no sellout would ever weep crocodile tears over my grave for the white man's cameras. I instructed my family, when my time comes, not to allow some bloodsucking mortician to drain my veins down a sewer to further foul the water. Let no one pump me full of chemicals to pollute the soil as my flesh decays. Wrap my body in a blanket, take it to any mountain, and return it to our sacred Grandmother Earth. Let me repay her for all the beauty she has given me. Let my body nourish her and her children as she has nourished me and my children. Don't mark the spot. I want no archaeologists or anthropologists poking at my bones.

I hope to be remembered as a fighter and as a patriot who never feared controversy—and not just for Indians. When I fight for my people's rights, when I stand up for our treaties, when I protest government lies and illegal seizures and unlawful acts, I defend all Americans, even the bigoted and misguided.

The achievements of my people unroll behind me from the misty dawn of time. Measured against them and against the lives of all who came before me, my own span on this earth is no more than the arc of a single arrow. I don't know how long or how high the Archer intends me to soar, but so far it has been a thrilling, awesome, magnificent flight.

Before I was six, my grandparents gave me a sense of my heritage, of my duties to my people and to my culture. My mother gave me her strength of will. My dad, the gentlest man I've ever known, taught me to laugh at life's obstacles and at my own failings. My brothers gave me pride and love.

Because of my extended family—especially Grandpa John Feather—there has always been a spiritual dimension to my life. Not until after Wounded Knee, however, did I begin to realize that the Great Mystery was guiding my path, speaking to me in many ways and saving me from the negative consequences of my actions. Each time I left the path I was born to walk, someone or something came along to save me. I ought to have died on Carquinez Heights when my soapbox racer was smashed by the big sedan one Easter Sunday. I should have drowned in the Missouri at the Cheyenne River Reservation when bigger kids held my head under the water. Battered senseless, I was supposed to freeze to death in a Sioux City snowbank. I was ready to drop out of high school when Miss Fridhandler appeared and began to motivate me. Who but the Great Mystery could have planted the irresistible urge to join my mother and brother on the sudden trip to Los Angeles that saved me from a long prison sentence or an ignoble death as a junkie?

I've been shot three times, stabbed and beaten unconscious, strafed and bombed, sucked down by quicksand, and chased across the ocean in a leaky canoe. When I went to prison, the Great Mystery turned it into a positive experience. When I was out of my mind with frustration and rage, ready to commit mass murder, Michael Mann suddenly transformed my life with a new career. I was ready to explode when the counselors at Cottonwood de

Tucson saved me from myself. Somehow, the twists and turns of my life have kept me on a straight path and have brought me into contact with many good and beautiful people representing all the sacred colors of the human race.

Why?

Some of my people say it is because I am the flesh-and-blood spirit of a long-dead Lakota leader. In 1972, my cousin Barbara Means told a literary agent that I was the reincarnation of Crazy Horse. After Wounded Knee, an old Indian told me the same thing in the Los Angeles County jail. In the winter of 1977, Guy Dull Knife, a respected Lakota elder who taught Indian studies at Wanbli College Center, told Peggy and me the same thing. I wish it were true, but I've never felt that in my heart.

Then what does the Great Mystery want with me?

I feel it has to do with saving the indigenous worldview—the last and only hope for the earth's future. We all share a spiritual commonality—American Indians and the Samme of Lapland and the Ainu of Hokkaido, the Inuit of Alaska, Canada, and Siberia, the Maori, the real Hawaiians, the Samoans and the rest of the Polynesians, the Arunta, Murngin, Kariera, and all the other aboriginal peoples of Australia, the Miao, Rhade, and Hmong and all their cousins who live above the clouds in the mountains of Southeast Asia, the San of the Kalahari Desert, and dozens of other African tribes. We have similar origin stories. We settle our disputes through consensus and with little bloodshed. Because we understand that the proper balance between female and male must be maintained, the vast majority of us maintain matrilineal societies that preserve harmony with all the life that surrounds us. Once, everyone on this earth was indigenous. Once, we all lived among our kin in communities of people that raised their own children and set their own standards of conduct. We knew everyone and everyone knew us, so we behaved with respect toward one another. We lived on the land, were part of it, felt we could not live without it—so we respected the earth and everything on it.

In time, however, some people allowed material surpluses to enrich a few beyond others. Thus began the breakdown of societies that maintained respect for all life. Today, the dominant society in America and around the industrialized world is male and Eurocentric. It is based on *believing* things— a linear mathematical concept which comes from the head. Indigenous peoples have beliefs, but our actions toward everything in the universe are governed by our *feelings*, which come from our hearts. Societies that live in accordance with their beliefs remove themselves from the necessity to feel. When you take yourself away from the trees, you have no feelings for trees. When you take yourself away from the insects, you have no feelings for insects. When you take yourself away from the birds, you have no feelings for birds. When you take yourself away from the buffalo or the deer or the wolf or the bear, you have no feelings for your four-legged relatives. When you take yourself away from feelings for human beings, it becomes easy to dehumanize them, easy to kill them, easy to make war on them.

Long before the first satellite circled the globe, the great Oglala holy man Black Elk had a vision. He said he was taken out into space to look down on the earth, and in so doing, he knew that it was holy. Today, that same vision is on television every day. Millions of pictures of the earth have been taken by astronauts and cosmonauts and unmanned cameras. When you look at the earth from space, you know Black Elk was right, that the whole universe is our tabernacle. Indigenous people *feel* that the earth is our Grandmother. She lives. Those who can't sense that special bond of love have no problem in raping the earth—or raping women. To end violence against women, you have got to stop rape against the planet. That's how you build civilizations that endure.

Since the rise of the followers of Jesus Christ, the world's power center has shifted from the Middle East to Europe. The Eurocentric male sees himself in the image of his god, and has gone about conquering the world to make everybody believe as he does, killing millions to save their souls. Conquest brings power, control, and wealth, but in his quest to be godlike, the Eurocentric male has forgotten that he can't coerce life to obey his wishes.

Thus, in the last century, Eurocentric male-oriented nations, the United States foremost among them, have tried to force the rest of the world to become just like them—the most wasteful people on earth. America wastes its energy, its water, its land, its food, its forests, and its people. The U.S. government and the Demopublican corporate socialists who control it want China, with well over a billion people, to industrialize, to raise its "standard of living" so people there can buy American products. Where will the Chinese find the natural resources necessary to sustain lifestyles like the materially wealthy nations of the West? Soon, a billion people will live on the Indian subcontinent. Where will *they* find resources to waste on the American scale? Eurocentric male society, the only living thing that eats its own environment, does not understand the logic of inevitable self-destruction.

Sadly, the white man equates happiness with the pleasing of his senses. My Uncle Matthew King used to shake his head and say, "The white man is like a little child; you have to be patient with him." But Grandmother Earth is running out of patience. What Eurocentric societies have done to indigenous peoples all over the world they are now doing to themselves—poisoning the land and air and water, abusing one another as they abuse our sacred Grandmother. We are approaching the abyss of species suicide.

In their arrogance, science addicts who call themselves environmentalists blather about those who are destroying the earth. They miss the point. They are destroying *themselves*, not the earth. No matter what industrialized societies do to themselves and to the human race, the earth has eons to heal itself.

Indigenous people feel that time is only the white man's linear mathematical construct. We understand *immortality*. Time is not a line stretching from one point to another, but a cycle of eternal renewal. Compared with how long it takes the wind and water to turn a rock into sand, our lifetimes on this earth amount to less than the blink of an eye. In eternity, there is no death. Your body is returned to Grandmother Earth, but your spirit survives. Your blood survives in your children—procreation is immortality. Anybody who doesn't believe in reincarnation has never seen a leaf fall from a tree, never seen a bud emerge from a barren branch, never looked at the heavens and marked the death of worlds and suns and galaxies and the births of new ones. Indigenous people know that there is no beginning and no end. If the rest of the human race would accept that, feel that, live that, they would no longer fear the unknown, they would no longer fear the darkness called death. They would accept that the darkness is part of them; it is their friend.

Our Grandmother will restore herself and all her children. The winds will be there, the mountains and the plains will be there, and the thunder spirits and the cleansing rain clouds. All our relatives will be there, the green things and the wingeds and the four-leggeds, those that swim in the seas and crawl through the soil, those that live in both water and air, those which inch along on their bellies, and those which hop or leap or jump or soar. Every living being that follows the instructions laid down by the Great Mystery will be there. Human beings are the only creatures *not* following those mandates, so the question is, will we be part of Grandmother Earth's restoration?

There are a few hopeful signs, among them the breakup of the Soviet Union. That should help end the senseless arms race that has impoverished America's spirit, even as the breakup frees whole nations to pursue independence and spiritual freedom. Even more promising, the end of white domination in South Africa has begun to bring about the return of lands to their aboriginal owners. A government has decided to ignore deeds and titles in favor of human values, in favor of what is just and right. The whites whose forefathers stole the land will receive compensation, but they can't live there anymore. Looking at what happened in South Africa, I am encouraged. Maybe someday we can convince the United States to live up to its own laws and return what its government has stolen to its rightful owners.

When Fools Crow died, the Lakota became a nation without a rudder. My people are in trouble, just as the spirits had said at Rick Two Dog's 1981 New Year's Eve *yuwipi*. The *Iktomi*, Trickster, has returned, and there is confusion among us. A great sickness is coming; the signs are clear. Just look at our powwows, those mockeries of our culture that shame us by fostering "weekend Indians" with no knowledge of their grandparents' language, no appreciation for traditional Indian values, no links to the land. The powwow is the lazy way to be an Indian. Now the Navajo are doing it, the Hopi and

Zuñi and all the other Pueblo nations are doing it, Indians from the Northwest Coast and people from the Great Lakes, from the Northeast, from Texas, Louisiana, and Florida. Wherever Indian people live, they have ripped off Plains Indian songs and have corrupted our traditional dances and ceremonial attire. They have stolen and adulterated my culture and have turned themselves into living parodies of my ancestors. Powwow Indians are Plains Indian wanna-bes, no different from New Agers who appropriate what is comfortable for them but won't live the lifestyle that created the trappings. They don't understand that a slice of a pie isn't the whole pie—but they wonder why they are always hungry.

Look, too, at tribal politics. Sovereignty remains an elusive dream because only sellouts ever get involved in tribal government. Look what happened to a man such as Peter McDonald. It's shameful to see us quarreling and acting like everyone else in the industrialized world. Look, too, at the more than thirty brands of missionaries and evangelists who swarm around the reservations. Now even the Baha'is are trying to find converts among Indian peoples.

I've traveled widely among Indian people in the United States. Except for people in a few isolated pockets in remote parts of the country, specifically some Hopi and some Dineh and some Miccosukee in the Everglades, I see that the colonial policies of the U.S. government have succeeded at least 99 percent. We are losing our roots. Nowadays, when I meet so-called traditional Indians and they share their culture, they always say their grandmothers or grandfathers told them this or that. Only a few years ago, the elders I met never felt the need to justify themselves by citing experts who were no longer around. They said, "*This* is the way it is. *This* is the way things are." They knew who they were and what they were.

We Indians need allies, yet too often we reject non-Indians who support our right to follow traditional ways and who want to join us. Some of those wanna-bes claim Indian ancestry but look as if they could answer a central-casting call for a Mississippi redneck sheriff. If we were as self-assured as our grandpas, we would say, "What a compliment! They want to be part of us. Welcome!" If we were confident in ourselves, we would know that our forebears were attuned to the universe, that our ways are righteous and superior to Eurocentrism. Instead, most Indian people condemn and rebuff those who reject the white man's path and embrace our values.

Industrial society creates alienation. More and more people of every color can no longer bear the strain of living in artificial surroundings. They have worked and fought their way up through the ranks of automatons, they have accumulated wealth and position, they have sacrificed their souls to their corporate masters' bottom lines—but materialism did not bring inner satisfaction. They have a few ties to the land. Their families are scattered across the country—grandparents in Sun Belt retirement towns, parents in Chicago or

New York or Denver, children in Seattle or Cincinnati or Philadelphia. They don't know where they came from or where they are going. They are drift-wood.

With the passing of Fools Crow's generation, my people became like those rootless ones. In some urban areas, a third generation of Indian people has reached maturity without ever feeling a connection to the land their fore-bears revered. That is not an accident. After relocation became a political liability, the BIA became more subtle. For example, when I lived in Albu-querque in the mid-1960s, few Indians were there, and practically none from the twenty-one Pueblo nations along the Rio Grande. In the 1970s, the BIA established a finance center in Albuquerque and gave job preference to In-dians. People from Santo Domingo, Zia, San Felipe, Cochiti, and Jemez—all the Pueblo nations from Acoma to Zuñi—flocked from their reservations to live in the city. Urban assimilation over the last three decades threatens to accomplish the destruction of Indian culture as efficiently as cavalry raids and massacres.

It is not too late to restore Indian values to the generations growing up far from their land. Unfortunately, the more "educated" we Indians get, the more embarrassed we are about our origins. We lose confidence in our her-itage and its institutions. Instead of respecting our elders, who were raised in wisdom and whose traditional role was to teach succeeding generations, we pay them only lip service. If they can't speak English, we rarely ask their advice on decisions of any importance. Even when we do, it is because something has gone wrong in our lives and we want the old guys to give us an immediate fix. We want redemption—just like Christians who pray to Jesus. When our elders offer insight and thoughtful questions instead of absolution or cook-book-style instructions, people go away disappointed and disillusioned.

The white man schools his children for only a few hours a day while segregating them by age group. They are isolated from their parents, grand-parents, uncles, aunts, brothers, and sisters—isolated from the entire com-munity for twelve years. That can lead only to adults with a very narrow understanding of what community life is all about. Indigenous peoples around the world know a better way—immerse the child in the community, let the community be the teacher. That is what we did at Yellow Thunder Camp. When I visited the Maori in what whites call New Zealand, I saw that that is precisely how they teach their children. From preschool through third grade, they experience total immersion in Maori culture, language, and com-munity life. Children are taught the three Ls—look, listen, and learn. When they enter the fourth grade of racially integrated government schools, they are at the top of their classes athletically and academically.

My wife Gloria borrowed from that idea to create the most revolutionary approach to Indian education since we were forced into the white man's schools. A Dineh medicine man contributes his knowledge of plants, rocks, and the sky. As director of the Chinle Center for Curriculum Development, Gloria incorporates his wisdom, in book form, into the daily lessons of every child in the school system. She is assisted periodically by three university professors—an astronomer, a biologist, and a geologist. The Dineh healer can't speak good English and has never been to a white man's school, but his insight into plants native to the area is based on centuries of use for healing and other purposes. The white man doesn't understand and has never bothered to find out about those purposes. The medicine man respects the spirits who live in the soil and in the rocks—as in everything—so he knows more about the land than any geologist could. Every traditional Indian village had people who tracked our constellations and told us what the stars foretold about our lives.

Whether you get your food at A & P or Safeway raise it yourself, whether you wear clothes from Neiman-Marcus or from Kmart or sew them at home, the stars and planets and everything in the heavens have an effect on everything you do daily. The Dineh healer lives that tradition and notices things that university astronomers don't even look for. The students of Chinle will come to understand that their medicine man is more valuable than all three professors. Most important, they will learn what industrialized society doesn't allow—to know their universe, to know their community, to know themselves.

Our great-grandfathers knew all about sovereignty and self-determination, but our parents were forced to forget those things. There isn't much to brag about on the reservations and on the urban Indian ghettos, but just about every admirable quality that remains in today's Indian people is the result of the American Indian Movement's flint striking the white man's steel. In the 1970s and 1980s, we lit a fire across Indian country. We fought for changes in school curricula to eliminate racist lies, and we are winning. We fought for community control of police, and on a few reservations it's now a reality. We fought to instill pride in our songs and in our language, in our cultural wisdom, inspiring a small renaissance in the teaching of our languages. We fought for our dignity. Today, at least on most reservations, elders, headmen, and other leaders are treated with respect. A few urban Indian communities have finally begun to recognize the need to address the cultural education of their youths. Thanks to AIM, for the first time in this century, Indian people stand at the threshold of freedom and responsibility.

In Central and South America and in much of Canada and parts of Alaska, millions of Indian people have managed to maintain their traditions. The Miskito, Sumu, and Rama of Nicaragua, and many Indian nations in parts of Costa Rica, Panama, Mexico, Brazil, and other countries, which have up to now been insulated from industrial society, still nurture their indigenous roots. I see hope among the Indians of northern Canada and Alaska, but also danger. As investors continue to seek minerals and timber, they relentlessly destroy the people who live on the land.

If we are to survive as a people our future must be our past—rejoining the family circle. Return to our traditional clan system. Because it resolves conflict peacefully, the clan system also ensures individual liberty. The extended family and the core-family unit—my term for what whites call the "nuclear" family—are essential in building community self-determination, and it is the community that provides the only means for us to preserve the institutions that traditionally guided every aspect of our lives as human beings. The white man could learn this from us.

We must become independent nations to show non-Indians how to perceive us as men and women and children with our own view of the world, people with good reasons for being who we are. When we become as real to other races as they are to themselves, when they get to know us as human beings instead of two-dimensional symbols, they will no longer be able to demonize and dehumanize us. Then the Bureau of Indian Affairs will be disbanded and the government's genocidal policies will be abolished forever. The rest of the hemisphere will follow suit.

None of that will be possible without freedom. By inventing, without constitutional foundation, the concept of "plenary power," Congress took for itself absolute control over every dimension of American Indians' lives. The Supreme Court, moreover, has consistently denied us our spiritual rights. Those decisions have served to enforce state jurisdiction over all kinds of Indian economic endeavors. As long as my people are not allowed to make mistakes, to succeed or fail on our own merits, we can never attain sovereignty and independence.

How does one attain freedom? How can we fight city hall? The BIA? The federal government? How can we succeed in reestablishing our individual rights as guaranteed by the Constitution? It's as simple as this—people of every color must stand up on their hind feet and begin to act like human beings. Start with yourself! Understand that freedom is responsibility. Before you can champion individual rights, you must recognize that you cannot be free and accept government handouts, whether they are federal farm subsidies, corporate subsidization, aid for dependent children, or state-paid medical care. The next step, in the words of Kwame Touré (formerly Stokely Carmichael), is to organize, organize, organize. Take your message to the streets—but even though government is not going to give away anything, force begets only brutality and injustice. I have swallowed my share of official violence, and I now feel that real change cannot come except through non-violence.

My goal is to return to Pine Ridge and rebuild my own extended family on land that once belonged to my father. I will build a treatment center with therapy based on traditional values, where Indian people will learn to improve their relationships without confrontation. I will establish a total-immersion school to teach Lakota children the beauty and superiority of their people's sciences, knowledge, and wisdom. In that way, I will begin to rebuild the Independent Oglala Nation. I have sworn on the sacred pipe that in my lifetime, I will see a free and independent Indian nation, responsible for its own economic destiny, beholden to no government, and recognized by the world community. I hope it will be the Lakota, but if not, then the Dene or Miskito or Cree or Hawaiian or Inuit.

In the first half of this century, Black Elk was led down the path blazed by Red Cloud, Crow Dog, Crazy Horse, Sitting Bull, and others of their generation. I feel that Black Elk's purpose was to preserve our nation's sacred tree of life. He was partly successful. Despite the efforts of the U.S. government, I believe the last root of our tree still lives—just enough to regenerate the tree, and with it, our people's spiritual survival.

I believe Yellow Thunder Camp was a living manifestation of that root. Although the campsite in our holy land is now abandoned, the flame of spirituality it symbolized continues to burn among some of my people. It is my duty to nourish that sacred root. That's why I was led to the American Indian Movement, which allowed me to use my anger in constructive ways. That's why I was led across the seas to visit other indigenous cultures—to acquire experience that would help me nurture the root. That's why I was led into the motion-picture business—to provide a platform to tell Indians and people everywhere the truths they have long ignored. The sacred tree of life is their last hope.

I believe my life should serve as an example for those who will follow Black Elk's path after I depart for the spirit world. I want Indian youths to take heart, to have faith. I want them to know that although the white man insists that they are wasting their miserable lives by living with few material goods on reservations or in ghettos, their lives can be good if they live as true Indians, faithful to the principles of their ancestors. I want them to know that the Great Mystery is there for everyone and has a path for them. It is not strict and narrow. It winds and twists and branches off in every direction, but as long as they follow it freely and respectfully, it will take them where they are meant to go.

One of the white man's enduring myths is about a great leader called Moses, who lived long ago when my ancestors were still a free people and his tribes were captives in Egypt. Moses went to the pharaoh and begged, "Let my people go." Greedy and stubborn, the pharaoh did not listen, so the god of Israel sent plagues to punish and frighten the Egyptians. Today, my people's tribes are captives of the white man's greed and stubbornness. His plagues punish us all—with choking clouds of unbreathable air, poisoned water, soil desecrated with chemicals and radioactivity, violence stalking every community, homeless people crowding streets and parks, parents abusing children, legions of addicts sniffing or eating or smoking or injecting drugs, hospitals filled with people dying of cancer or heart disease or AIDS. And even worse may be yet to come, for the white man shows no sign of changing his ways. Just as the pharaoh ignored Moses, the U.S. government did not hear my forebears. I say to my nation and to all indigenous peoples: To hell with the pharaoh! Let us embrace the ideals of our ancestors. Let us show the white man how to find peace of mind by living in harmony with the universe. Let us show him how to honor and protect our Grandmother. Let *us* go.

Appendix:
"For America to Live, Europe Must Die"
▼▼▼▼▼▼▼▼▼

The following speech was given by Russell Means in July 1980, before several thousand people who had assembled from all over the world for the Black Hills International Survival Gathering, in the Black Hills of South Dakota. It is Russell Means's most famous speech.

The only possible opening for a statement of this kind is that I detest writing. The process itself epitomizes the European concept of "legitimate" thinking; what is written has an importance that is denied the spoken. My culture, the Lakota culture, has an oral tradition, so I ordinarily reject writing. It is one of the white world's ways of destroying the cultures of non-European peoples, the imposing of an abstraction over the spoken relationship of a people.

So what you read here is not what I've written. It's what I've said and someone else has written down. I will allow this because it seems that the only way to communicate with the white world is through the dead, dry leaves of a book. I don't really care whether my words reach whites or not. They have already demonstrated through their history that they cannot hear, cannot see; they can only read (of course, there are exceptions, but the exceptions only prove the rule). I'm more concerned with American Indian people, students and others, who have begun to be absorbed into the white world through universities and other institutions. But even then it's a marginal sort of concern. It's very possible to grow into a red face with a white mind; and if that's a person's individual choice, so be it, but I have no use for them. This is part of the process of cultural genocide being waged by Europeans against American Indian peoples' today. My concern is with those American Indians who choose to resist this genocide, but who may be confused as to how to proceed.

(You notice I use the term *American Indian* rather than *Native American* or *Native indigenous people* or *Amerindian* when referring to my people. There has been some controversy about such terms, and frankly, at this point, I find it absurd. Primarily it seems that *American Indian* is being rejected as European in origin—which is true. But *all* the above terms are European in origin; the only non-European way is to speak of Lakota—or, more precisely, of Oglala, Brulé, etc.—and of the Dineh, the Miccousukee, and all the rest of the several hundred correct tribal names.

(There is also some confusion about the word *Indian*, a mistaken belief that it refers somehow to the country, India. When Columbus washed up on the beach in the Caribbean, he was not looking for a country called India. Europeans were calling that country Hindustan in 1492. Look it up on the old maps. Columbus called the tribal people he met "Indio," from the Italian *in dio*, meaning "in God.")

It takes a strong effort on the part of each American Indian *not* to become Europeanized. The strength for this effort can only come from the traditional ways, the traditional values that our elders retain. It must come from the hoop, the four directions, the relations: it cannot come from the pages of a book or a thousand books. No European can ever teach a Lakota to be Lakota, a Hopi to be Hopi. A master's degree in "Indian Studies" or in "education" or in anything else cannot make a person into a human being or provide knowledge into the traditional ways. It can only make you into a mental European, an outsider.

I should be clear about something here, because there seems to be some confusion about it. When I speak of Europeans or mental Europeans, I'm not allowing for false distinctions. I'm not saying that on the one hand there are the by-products of a few thousand years of genocidal, reactionary. European intellectual development which is bad; and on the other hand there is some new revolutionary intellectual development which is good. I'm referring here to the so-called theories of Marxism and anarchism and "leftism" in general. I don't believe these theories can be separated from the rest of the European intellectual tradition. It's really just the same old song.

The process began much earlier. Newton, for example, "revolutionized" physics and the so-called natural sciences by reducing the physical universe to a linear mathematical equation. Descartes did the same thing with culture. John Locke did it with politics, and Adam Smith did it with economics. Each one of these "thinkers" took a piece of the spirituality of human existence and converted it into a code, an abstraction. They picked up where Christianity ended: they "secularized" Christian religion, as the "scholars" like to say—and in doing so they made Europe more able and ready to act as an expansionist culture. Each of these intellectual revolutions served to abstract the European mentality even further, to remove the wonderful complexity and spirituality from the universe and replace it with a logical sequence: one, two, three. Answer!

This is what has come to be termed "efficiency" in the European mind. Whatever is mechanical is perfect; whatever seems to work at the moment—that is, proves the mechanical model to be the right one—is considered correct, even when it is clearly untrue. This is why "truth" changes so fast in the European mind; the answers which result from such a process are only stopgaps, only temporary, and must be continuously discarded in favor of new stopgaps which support the mechanical models and keep them (the models) alive.

Hegel and Marx were heirs to the thinking of Newton, Descartes, Locke and Smith. Hegel finished the process of secularizing theology—and that is put in his own terms—he secularized the religious thinking through which Europe understood the universe. Then Marx put Hegel's philosophy in terms of "materialism," which is to say that Marx despiritualized Hegel's work altogether. Again, this is in Marx' own terms. And this is now seen as the future revolutionary potential of Europe. Europeans may see this as revolutionary, but American Indians see it simply as still more of that same old European conflict between *being* and *gaining*. The intellectual roots of a new Marxist form of European imperialism lie in Marx'—and his followers' —links to the tradition of Newton, Hegel and the others.

Being is a spiritual proposition. *Gaining* is a material act. Traditionally, American Indians have always attempted to *be* the best people they could. Part of that spiritual process was and is to give away wealth, to discard wealth in order *not* to gain. Material gain is an indicator of false status among traditional people, while it is "proof that the system works" to Europeans. Clearly, there are two completely opposing views at issue here, and Marxism is very far over to the other side from the American Indian view. But let's look at a major implication of this; it is not merely an intellectual debate.

The European materialist tradition of despiritualizing the universe is very similar to the mental process which goes into dehumanizing another person. And who seems most expert at dehumanizing other people? And why? Soldiers who have seen a lot of combat learn to do this to the enemy before going back into combat. Murderers do it before going out to commit murder. Nazi SS guards did it to concentration camp inmates. Cops do it. Corporation leaders do it to the workers they send into uranium mines and steel mills. Politicians do it to everyone in sight. And what the process has in common for each group doing the dehumanizing is that it makes it all right to kill and otherwise destroy other people. One of the Christian commandments says, "Thou shalt not kill," at least not humans, so the trick is to mentally convert the victims into nonhumans. Then you can proclaim violation of your own commandment as a virtue.

In terms of the despiritualization of the universe, the mental process works so that it becomes virtuous to destroy the planet. Terms like *progress* and *development* are used as cover words here, the way *victory* and *freedom* are used to justify butchery in the dehumanization process. For example, a real-estate speculator may refer to "developing" a parcel of ground by opening a gravel quarry; *development* here means total, permanent destruction, with the earth itself removed. But European logic has *gained* a few tons of gravel with which more land can be "developed" through the construction of road beds. Ultimately, the whole universe is open—in the European view— to this sort of insanity.

Most important here, perhaps, is the fact that Europeans feel no sense of loss in all this. After all, their philosophers have despiritualized reality, so there is no satisfaction (for them) to be gained in simply observing the wonder of a mountain or a lake or a people *in being*. No, satisfaction is measured in terms of gaining material. So the mountain becomes gravel, and the lake becomes coolant for a factory, and the people are rounded up for processing through the indoctrination mills Europeans like to call schools.

But each new piece of that "progress" ups the ante out in the real world. Take fuel for the industrial machine as an example. Little more than two centuries ago, nearly everyone used wood—a replenishable, natural item—as fuel for the very human needs of cooking and staying warm. Along came the Industrial Revolution and coal became the dominant fuel, as production became the social imperative for Europe. Pollution began to become a problem in the cities, and the earth was ripped open to provide coal whereas wood had always simply been gathered or harvested at no great expense to the environment. Later, oil became the major fuel, as the technology of production was perfected through a series of scientific "revolutions." Pollution increased dramatically, and nobody yet knows what the environmental costs of pumping all that oil out of the ground will really be in the long run. Now there's an "energy crisis," and uranium is becoming the dominant fuel.

Capitalists, at least, can be relied upon to develop uranium as fuel only at the rate at which they can show a good profit. That's their ethic, and maybe that will buy some time. Marxists, on the other hand, can be relied upon to develop uranium fuel as rapidly as possible simply because it's the most "efficient" production fuel available. That's *their* ethic, and I fail to see where it's preferable. Like I said, Marxism is right smack in the middle of the European tradition. It's the same old song.

There's a rule of thumb which can be applied here. You cannot judge the real nature of a European revolutionary doctrine on the basis of the changes it proposes to make within the European power structure and society. You can only judge it by the effects it will have on non-European peoples. This is because every revolution in European history has served to reinforce Europe's tendencies and abilities to export destruction to other peoples, other cultures and the environment itself. I defy anyone to point out an example where this is not true.

So now we, as American Indian people, are asked to believe that a "new" European revolutionary doctrine such as Marxism will reverse the negative effects of European history on us. European power relations are to be adjusted once again, and that's supposed to make things better for all of us. But what does this really mean?

Right now, today, we who live on the Pine Ridge Reservation are living in what white society has designated a "National Sacrifice Area." What this means is that we have a lot of uranium deposits here, and white culture (not us) needs this uranium as energy production material. The cheapest, most efficient way for industry to extract and deal with the processing of this uranium is to dump the waste by-products right here at the digging sites. Right here where we live. This waste is radioactive and will make the entire region uninhabitable forever. This is considered by industry, and by the white society that created this industry, to be an "acceptable" price to pay for energy resource development. Along the way they also plan to drain the water table under this part of South Dakota as part of the industrial process, so the region becomes doubly uninhabitable. The same sort of thing is happening down in the land of the Navajo and Hopi, up in the land of the Northern Cheyenne and Crow, and elsewhere. Thirty percent of the coal in the West and half of the uranium deposits in the United States have been found to lie under reservation land, so there is no way this can be called a minor issue.

We are resisting being turned into a National Sacrifice Area. We are resisting being turned into a national sacrifice people. The costs of this industrial process are not acceptable to us. It is genocide to dig uranium here and drain the water table—no more, no less.

Now let's suppose that in our resistance to extermination we begin to seek allies (we have). Let's suppose further that we were to take revolutionary Marxism at its word: that it intends nothing less than the complete overthrow of the European capitalist order which has presented this threat to our very existence. This would seem to be a natural alliance for American Indian people to enter into. After all, as the Marxists say, it is the capitalists who set us up to be a national sacrifice. This is true as far as it goes.

But, as I've tried to point out, this "truth" is very deceptive. Revolutionary Marxism is committed to even further perpetuation and perfection of the very industrial process which is destroying us all. It offers only to "redistribute" the results—the money, maybe—of this industrialization to a wider section of the population. It offers to take wealth from the capitalists and pass it around; but in order to do so, Marxism must maintain the industrial system. Once again, the power relations within European society will have to be altered, but once again the effects upon American Indian peoples here and non-Europeans elsewhere will remain the same. This is much the same as when power was redistributed from the church to private business during the so-called bourgeois revolution. European society changed a bit, at least superficially, but its conduct toward non-Europeans continued as before. You can see what the American Revolution of 1776 did for American Indians. It's the same old song.

Revolutionary Marxism, like industrial society in other forms, seeks to "rationalize" all people in relation to industry—maximum industry, maximum production. It is a materialist doctrine that despises the American Indian spiritual tradition, our cultures, our lifeways. Marx himself called us "precapitalists" and "primitive." *Precapitalist* simply means that, in his view, we would eventually discover capitalism and become capitalists; we have always been economically retarded in Marxist terms. The only manner in which American Indian people could participate in a Marxist revolution would be to join the industrial system, to become factory workers, or "proletarians," as Marx called them. The man was very clear about the fact that his revolution could occur only through the struggle of the proletariat, that the existence of a massive industrial system is a precondition of a successful Marxist society.

I think there's a problem with language here. Christians, capitalists, Marxists. All of them have been revolutionary in their own minds, but none of them really means revolution. What they really mean is a continuation. They do what they do in order that European culture can continue to exist and develop according to its needs.

So, in order for us to *really* join forces with Marxism, we American Indians would have to accept the national sacrifice of our homeland; we would have to commit cultural suicide and become industrialized and Europeanized.

At this point, I've got to stop and ask myself whether I'm being too harsh. Marxism has something of a history. Does this history bear out my observations? I look to the process of industrialization in the Soviet Union since 1920 and I see that these Marxists have done what it took the English Industrial Revolution 300 years to do; and the Marxists did it in 60 years. I see that the territory of the USSR used to contain a number of tribal peoples and that they have been crushed to make way for the factories. The Soviets refer to this as "the National Question." the question of whether the tribal peoples had the right to exist as peoples; and they decided the tribal peoples were an acceptable sacrifice to industrial needs. I look to China and I see the same thing. I look to Vietnam and I see Marxists imposing an industrial order and rooting out the indigenous tribal mountain people.

I hear a leading Soviet scientist saying that when uranium is exhausted, *then* alternatives will be found. I see the Vietnamese taking over a nuclear power plant abandoned by the U.S. military. Have they dismantled and destroyed it? No, they are using it. I see China exploding nuclear bombs, developing uranium reactors, and preparing a space program in order to colonize and exploit the planets the same as the Europeans colonized and exploited this hemisphere. It's the same old song, but maybe with a faster tempo this time.

The statement of the Soviet scientist is very interesting. Does he know what this alternative energy source will be? No, he simply has faith. Science will find a way. I hear revolutionary Marxists saying that the destruction of the environment, pollution, and radiation will all be controlled. And I see them act upon their words. Do they know *how* these things will be controlled? No, they simply have faith. Science will find a way. Industrialization is fine and necessary. How do they know this? Faith. Science will find a way. Faith of this sort has always been known in Europe as religion. Science has become the new European religion for both capitalists and Marxists; they are truly inseparable; they are part and parcel of the same culture. So, in both theory and practice, Marxism demands that non-European peoples give up their values, their traditions, their cultural existence altogether. We will all be industrialized science addicts in a Marxist society.

I do not believe that capitalism itself is really responsible for the situation in which American Indians have been declared a national sacrifice. No, it is the European tradition; European culture itself is responsible. Marxism is just the latest continuation of this tradition, not a solution to it. To ally with Marxism is to ally with the very same forces that declare us an acceptable cost.

There is another way. There is the traditional Lakota way and the ways of the other American Indian peoples. It is the way that knows that humans do not have the right to degrade Mother Earth, that there are forces beyond anything the European mind has conceived, that humans must be in harmony with *all* relations or the relations will eventually eliminate the disharmony. A lopsided emphasis on humans by humans—the Europeans' arrogance of acting as though they were beyond the nature of all related things—can only result in a total disharmony and a readjustment which cuts arrogant humans down to size, gives them a taste of that reality beyond their grasp or control and restores the harmony. There is no need for a revolutionary theory to bring this about; it's beyond human control. The nature peoples of this planet know this and so they do not theorize about it. Theory is an abstract; our knowledge is real.

Distilled to its basic terms, European faith—including the new faith in science—equals a belief that man is God. Europe has always sought a Messiah, whether that be the man Jesus Christ or the man Karl Marx or the man Albert Einstein. American Indians know this to be totally absurd. Humans are the weakest of all creatures, so weak that other creatures are willing to give up their flesh that we may live. Humans are able to survive only through the exercise of rationality since they lack the abilities of other creatures to gain food through the use of fang and claw.

But rationality is a curse since it can cause humans to forget the natural order of things in ways other creatures do not. A wolf never forgets his or her place in the natural order. American Indians can. Europeans almost always do. We pray our thanks to the deer, our relations, for allowing us their flesh to eat; Europeans simply take the flesh for granted and consider the deer inferior. After all, Europeans consider themselves godlike in their rationalism and science. God is the Supreme Being; all else *must* be inferior.

All European tradition, Marxism included, has conspired to defy the natural order of all things. Mother Earth has been abused, the powers have been abused, and this cannot go on forever. No theory can alter that simple fact. Mother Earth will retaliate, the whole environment will retaliate, and the abusers will be eliminated. Things come full circle, back to where they started.

That's revolution. And that's a prophecy of my people, of the Hopi people and of other correct peoples.

American Indians have been trying to explain this to Europeans for centuries. But, as I said earlier, Europeans have proven themselves unable to hear. The natural order will win out, and the offenders will die out, the way deer die when they offend the harmony by over-populating a given region. It's only a matter of time until what Europeans call "a major catastrophe of global proportions" will occur. It is the role of American Indian peoples, the role of all natural beings, to survive. A part of our survival is to resist. We resist not to overthrow a government or to take political power, but because it is natural to resist extermination, to survive. We don't want power over white institutions; we want white institutions to disappear. *That's* revolution.

American Indians are still in touch with these realities—the prophecies, the traditions of our ancestors. We learn from the elders, from nature, from the powers. And when the catastrophe is over, we American Indian peoples will still be here to inhabit the hemisphere. I don't care if it's only a handful living high in the Andes. American Indian people will survive; harmony will be reestablished. *That's* revolution.

At this point, perhaps I should be very clear about another matter, one which should already be clear as a result of what I've said. But confusion breeds easily these days, so I want to hammer home this point. When I use the term *European*, I'm not referring to a skin color or a particular genetic structure. What I'm referring to is a mind-set, a worldview that is a product of the development of European culture. People are not genetically encoded to hold this outlook; they are *acculturated* to hold it. The same is true for American Indians or for the members of any other culture.

It is possible for an American Indian to share European values, a European worldview. We have a term for these people; we call them "apples"—red on the outside (genetics) and white on the inside (their values). Other groups have similar terms: Blacks have their "oreos"; Hispanos have "coconuts" and so on. And, as I said before, there *are* exceptions to the white norm: people who are white on the outside, but not white inside. I'm not sure what term should be applied to them other than "human beings."

What I'm putting out here is not a racial proposition but a cultural proposition. Those who ultimately advocate and defend the realities of European culture and its industrialism are my enemies. Those who resist it, who struggle against it, are my allies, the allies of American Indian people. And I don't give a damn what their skin color happens to be. *Caucasian* is the white term for the white race: *European* is an outlook I oppose.

The Vietnamese Communists are not exactly what you might consider genetic Caucasians, but they are now functioning as mental Europeans. The same holds true for Chinese Communists, for Japanese capitalists or Bantu

Catholics or Peter "MacDollar" down at the Navajo Reservation or Dickie Wilson up here at Pine Ridge. There is no racism involved in this, just an acknowledgment of the mind and spirit that make up culture.

In Marxist terms I suppose I'm a "cultural nationalist." I work first with my people, the traditional Lakota people, because we hold a common worldview and share an immediate struggle. Beyond this, I work with other traditional American Indian peoples, again because of a certain commonality in worldview and form of struggle. Beyond that, I work with anyone who has experienced the colonial oppression of Europe and who resists its cultural and industrial totality. Obviously, this includes genetic Caucasians who struggle to resist the dominant norms of European culture. The Irish and the Basques come immediately to mind, but there are many others.

I work primarily with my own people, with my own community. Other people who hold non-European perspectives should do the same. I believe in the slogan, "Trust your brother's vision," although I'd like to add sisters into the bargain. I trust the community and the culturally based vision of all the races that naturally resist industrialization and human extinction. Clearly, individual whites can share in this, given only that they have reached the awareness that continuation of the industrial imperatives of Europe is not a vision, but species suicide. White is one of the sacred colors of the Lakota people—red, yellow, white and black. The four directions. The four seasons. The four periods of life and aging. The four races of humanity. Mix red, yellow, white and black together and you get brown, the color of the fifth race. This is a natural ordering of things. It therefore seems natural to me to work with all races, each with its own special meaning, identity and message.

But there is a peculiar behavior among most Caucasians. As soon as I become critical of Europe and its impact on other cultures, they become defensive. They begin to defend themselves. But I'm not attacking them personally; I'm attacking Europe. In personalizing my observations on Europe they are personalizing European culture, identifying themselves with it. By defending themselves in *this* context, they are ultimately defending the death culture. This is a confusion which must be overcome, and it must be overcome in a hurry. None of us has energy to waste in such false struggles.

Caucasians have a more positive vision to offer humanity than European culture. I believe this. But in order to attain this vision it is necessary for Caucasians to step outside European culture—alongside the rest of humanity—to see Europe for what it is and what it does.

To cling to capitalism and Marxism and all the other "isms" is simply to remain within European culture. There is no avoiding this basic fact. As a fact, this constitutes a choice. Understand that the choice is based on culture, not race. Understand that to choose European culture and industrialism is to choose to be my enemy. And understand that the choice is yours, not mine.

*   *   *

This leads me back to address those American Indians who are drifting through the universities, the city slums, and other European institutions. If you are there to learn to resist the oppressor in accordance with your traditional ways, so be it. I don't know how you manage to combine the two, but perhaps you will succeed. But retain your sense of reality. Beware of coming to believe the white world now offers solutions to the problems it confronts us with. Beware, too, of allowing the words of native people to be twisted to the advantage of our enemies. Europe invented the practice of turning words around on themselves. You need only look to the treaties between American Indian peoples and various European governments to know that this is true. Draw your strength from who you are.

A culture which regularly confuses revolution with continuation, which confuses science and religion, which confuses revolt with resistance, has nothing helpful to teach you and nothing to offer you as a way of life. Europeans have long since lost all touch with reality, if ever they were in touch with it. Feel sorry for them if you need to, but be comfortable with who you are as American Indians.

So, I suppose to conclude this, I should state clearly that leading anyone toward Marxism is the last thing on my mind. Marxism is as alien to my culture as capitalism and Christianity are. In fact, I can say I don't think I'm trying to lead anyone toward anything. To some extent I tried to be a "leader," in the sense that the white media like to use that term, when the American Indian Movement was a young organization. This was a result of a confusion I no longer have. You cannot be everything to everyone. I do not propose to be used in such a fashion by my enemies. I am not a leader. I *am* an Oglala Lakota patriot. That is all I want and all I need to be. And I am very comfortable with who I am.

Index
▼▼▼▼▼▼▼▼▼

ABC, 268, 363, 378
Abernathy, Rev. Ralph, 269
Abourezk, Charles, 348–49, 378, 433
Abourezk, Jim, 115, 137, 139, 166, 266–67, 381, 390, 483
Abrams, Elliot, 480
Ackerman, John, 359, 360
Adams, Hank, 224, 227–28, 233, 236, 466, 477, 479
   and the twenty points, 228–30
Adams, Rev. John, 269, 281, 377, 399–400, 464, 470, 472, 473
Adelaide, Sister, 524
Adelstein, Stan, 287
Agnew, Spiro, 165, 277
Airlift (Zimmerman), 437–38
Alcatraz Island action, 105–6
alcoholism and Indians, 21–22, 29, 43, 45–46, 180, 325, 397–98, 477
Ali, Muhammad, 377
Allen, David, 317

Allies (Seven Council Fires)
   See Lakota Nation; Seven Council Fires
America's Concentration Camps, 122–23
American Horse, Joe, 439
American Indian Movement (AIM), 148, 155, 432–33
AIM Patrol, 163
alcohol and drug use, 180, 325, 397–98, 477
Bad Heart Bull murder and trial, 243–44, 248
Banks/Bellecourt schism, 208–12, 214, 215–16
BIA building (Washington, D.C.) occupation, 230–35
BIA sit-ins, 158, 192
COINTEL and, 250
Colorado AIM, 519–22
credo, *xiii*
Custer Battlefield Monument, 226, 357–59

American Indian Movement (*continued*)
Custer courthouse police riot, 243–46, 317–18, 341–42, 348
and dissident groups, 217–18, 250
FBI and, 348–49
Forest Service, suit against, 422–23, 489
Gordon (Nebraska) takeover, 194–201, 213–15
KILI (AIM radio station), 399, 408, 438, 444
Longest Walk, 374, 377–81
A Man Called Horse demonstrations, 158
Mayflower II, 177–78
media and, 158, 160, 161, 165, 170, 209–10, 399–400, 410–11, 416
Menominee Warriors Society action, 336–37
Mexicans, relations with, 239–40
Mount Rushmore protests, 167–70, 182–86
National Council of Churches confrontation, 149–53
NIEA conference, 173
Ojibwa Reservation protest, 160–61
Plimoth (Plymouth) Plantation demonstration, 175–78
police brutality, 162–63, 206, 239–41
as pro–Sandinista, 459–61, 466
Rapid City flood, 216
Red Ribbon Grand Jury Hearings, 202–7
Russell Means conflict, 463–64, 466, 481
Scottsbluff conference, 239–41
Sturgis (South Dakota) action, 247–48
Trail of Broken Treaties, 222–35, 236–38
twenty points, 228–30, 235, 303
UN Geneva conference, 365–66, 368–72
Walk for Religious Freedom, 433–34
women's involvement, 247, 251, 265–66, 400
Yellow Thunder Camp, 407–10, 411–18, 422–27
American Indian Press Association, 194
American Indian Religious Freedom Act, 422

Americans for Indian Opportunity, 231
Anaya, Jim, 461, 481
Anaya, Phillip, 451–52
Anderson, Jack, 236
Anquoe, Mary Ann, 335
Antell, Will, 173
Arconge, Mabel. *See* Feather, Mabel Arconge
Arconge, Theodore (Russell's great-grandfather), 26
Arconge, Walter (Mabel's grandfather), 26
Arizona State University (Tempe), 126, 130
Arkeketa, Roberta, 399
Attack Him, John, 222
Avery, Eleanor, 57
Avery, Patty, 57

Bad Cob, Tom, 287
Bad Heart Bull, Sarah, 243, 244, 308, 317, 320
Bad Heart Bull, Vincent, 385, 388
Bad Heart Bull, Wesley, murder and trial, 243–44, 248
Bad Voice Elk, 6
Bald Eagle, Curtis, 320, 321, 323, 326, 334, 355
Banai, Eddie Benton, 175, 180
Banks, Dennis, 148, 157, 173, 180, 181, 219, 253, 443
and AIM, 163, 198, 336–37, 432–33, 466, 477
and alcohol, 166–67
arrest and trial (Wounded Knee), 294, 299–303, 305–10, 311–15, 319–21, 326–32
Banks/Bellecourt schism, 208–12, 214, 215–16, 223
Custer courthouse police riot, 243–46, 348
D–Q University, 374, 378, 433
Legal Justice Center, 181
Longest Walk, 374, 377–81
Mayflower II, 177–78
NCAI confrontation, 164–66
NCC confrontation, 149–53
Ojibwa Reservation protest, 160–61
Red Ribbon Grand Jury Hearings, 202–7

Siege of Wounded Knee, 259, 269, 273

Trail of Broken Treaties, 223, 227, 236

underground, 348, 374

Banks, Kamook, 292

Battle of the Little Bighorn, 15–16, 225–26

Bayliss, Robert, 195

Beane, Dlala, 317

Bear Runner, Edgar, 239, 251, 252, 260, 275, 369

Bear Runner, Oscar, 264–65, 358

Belafonte, Harry, 236, 388

Bellecourt, Charlie (Clyde's brother), 184

Bellecourt, Clyde, 148, 157, 173, 174–75, 181, 210, 370, 371, 477
and AIM, 163, 198, 225, 230–35, 348, 375, 443
arrest and trial (Wounded Knee), 294
Banks/Bellecourt schism, 208–12, 214, 215–16, 223
Bellecourt/Camp feud and shooting, 295–96, 300–301, 388
National Council of Churches confrontation, 149–53
NCAI confrontation, 164–66
Ojibwa Reservation pageant protest, 160–61
and the police, 163–64, 185
Russell Means conflict, 463–64, 466
Siege of Wounded Knee, 272, 336

Bellecourt, George (Clyde's brother), 184

Bellecourt, Peggy (Clyde's wife), 184

Bellecourt, Vernon (Clyde's brother), 157, 282, 360
and AIM, 180–81, 210, 233, 234, 236, 336, 349, 350, 477
and alcohol and drugs, 180, 325
arrest and trial (Wounded Knee), 294
Bellecourt/Camp feud, 295–96, 301
Russell Means conflict, 463–64, 466, 481, 508

Benevidez, Leroy, 46

Bernie, Oscar, 27

Bernie, "Skin," 27

Bertinot, Gerald J., Jr., 313–14

Big Foot, 253, 285–86

Big Ruby, 80

Birch, Randi, 281

Bishop Hare Episcopal School (Rosebud Reservation), 77

Bissonnette, Gladys, 251, 252, 265, 270, 279, 328

Bissonnette, Pedro, 78–79, 249, 251, 252, 258, 261, 270, 275, 294, 308
murder of, 304, 312

Black Bear (Ihanktonwan chief), 6

Black Elk (Oglala holy man), 537, 543

Black Elk, Wallace, 270

Black Hills. See Paha Sapa

Black Hills Alliance, 392, 400–402
Yellow Thunder Camp, 407–10, 411–18, 422–27

Black Horse, 272–73

Blacksmith, Mabel Arconge. See Feather, Mabel Arconge "Twinkle Star"

Blacksmith, Raymond (step grandfather), 24

Blacksmith, Shorty, 410, 436, 456

Blue Arm, Uris, 119, 120

Bogue, Judge Andrew, 186, 282, 287, 322

Bordeaux, Lionel, 404

Borgé Martinez, Tomás, 462–63

Borglum, Gutzon, 167

Bottum, Joseph, 317–18, 320, 352

Boult, Reber, 317

Bowen, Dennis, 175, 192–93

Boyajian, Aram, 281

Bradley, Bill, 489

Brainard Indian School (Hot Springs, South Dakota), 43–44

Braithwaite, Judge Richard, 349, 350, 352, 364, 365

Brando, Marlon, 224, 302, 337, 340–41, 378, 388

Brave Eagle. See Means, Russell

Brewer, Duane, 337–38

Brewer, Gabby, 78

Briggs, Fred, 281

Brightman, Lehman "Lee," 167, 170, 173, 374

Broken Leg, Bernadine, 320, 323

Brown, Dee, 285, 328

Brown, Jerry, 274

Bruce, Louis, 191–92, 231

Buchanan, Johnny, 34

Bureau of Indian Affairs (BIA), 4, 10, 18, 78

Burean of Indian Affairs (*continued*)
  and AIM, 161, 182, 191
  AIM sit-ins, 158, 192
  BIA building (Washington, D.C.),
    AIM occupation of, 230–35
  BIA building, vandalism and looting,
    233–34
  corruption, 236, 501–2
  and cultural genocide, 10–11, 19, 21
  and land scams, 205
  propaganda of, 159
  relocation, 68, 72, 77–82, 140, 141–
    48, 194
  and single surnames, 8
  termination, 96
  See also Indian schools
Burleigh, Dr. Walter, 7
Burnett, Robert, 223, 313
Bury My Heart at Wounded Knee
  (Brown), 285
Byrne, Matthew, 331

Caesar, Manuel, 97
Cahn, Edward S., 203
Camp, Carter, 211, 279, 294, 336
  Bellecourt shooting, 295–96, 300–
    301
Camp, Craig, 295
Campbell, Francisco, 459, 461, 473
Campbell, Lumberto, 462
Carter, Jimmy, 380–81
Case, Ralph, 421
Case, Robert, 198
Catch The Bear, Collins, 425–27
Catches, Pete, 146, 186–88, 252, 265,
  271
Catholic Church, 227
  AIM protest against, 160–61
  and reservation land, 160, 336–37
CBS, 378
Chapman, Irv, 281
Chartier, Clem, 466, 470, 471–72,
  473
Cherrier, Therese, 302, 330, 334
Cheyenne Nation
  history, 419–22
  sacred white buffalo calf pipe, 315–17
Cheyenne River Reservation, 40–41, 72
Chicago Indian Center, 144
Chief Eagle, Dallas, 237–38
Chillicothe Indian School, 19

Chinle Center for Curriculum
  Development, 540–41
Chino, Wendell, 165
Chippewa (Ojibwa), 9
Chips, Godfrey, 210–12
Chips, Wallace, 210–12, 221
Chisholm, Shirley, 435
Chrismas, Doug, 356, 361
Christensen, Judge Wayne, 386
Churchill, Ward, 416, 436, 481, 493,
  520
Claremont, Jimmy, 206
Clark, Carol, 290–91
Clark, William, 5
Clay, Chris, 131–32, 133
Clayton, William F., 311
Clearwater, Frank, 292
Cleaveland, Moses, 192
Cleveland AIM (CLAIM), 155
Cleveland American Indian Center, 145,
  147–48, 153–61, 191, 192–93,
  218, 435
Cleveland Fund, 147
Cleveland Indians suit, 155, 435
Cleveland Public Library, 157
Cleveland Public Schools, 156–57
Clifford, Dave, 339–41, 354
Clifford, Gerald, 366
Colburn, Wayne, 251, 268
Colorado AIM, 519–22
Columbus Day protests, 518–22
Community Action Program (CAP),
  136–40
Cook, Lee, 216, 219, 231, 234
Cooper, Allen "Honky Killer," 336
Copleman, Martha, 337
Coson, Sam, 494
Cottier, Belva, 93
Cottier, Chalk, 93, 102, 105–6
Cottonwood de Tucson treatment
  center, 524–31, 535–36
Coulter, Tim, 305
Cowles, Ronald, 37
Crazy Bull (Ihanktonwan chief), 6
Crazy Horse, 290, 412, 543
Crook, General George, 491
Crow, John O., 192, 216
Crow Dog (Brulé Lakota), 175, 543
Crow Dog, Henry, 182, 284
Crow Dog, Leonard, 174–75, 182, 204,
  241, 296–97, 428

arrest and trial (Wounded Knee), 294, 336
Custer courthouse police riot, 243–46
ghost dance, 285–86
as *Heyoka,* 210, 211
Siege of Wounded Knee, 263, 264, 269, 270, 274, 279, 287
Crow Dog's Paradise, 175, 182, 282, 284–85
Crow Indian Reservation, 225–26, 499–500, 501–2, 506–7
Crow people, 147
Crusade for Justice, 268
Cummings, Malvin, 494
Curley (Custer's scout), 226
Custer, George Armstrong, 247, 420, 489–90
  Battle of the Little Bighorn, 225–26
  Crow scouts, 226
  death of, 15–16
Custer Battlefield Monument, 226, 357–59, 489–91
Custer courthouse police riot, 243–46
  trials, 317–18, 341–42, 348
Czywczynski, Jim, 202, 260, 360

Dahl, Kenneth, 317, 320
Dakota Indians. *See* Seven Council Fires
Daschle, Thomas, 483, 501
Davis, Gary, 451, 504–8
Davis, Gloria. *See* Means, Gloria Grant Davis
Davis, Sammy, Jr., 335
Dawes Act, 10
Day–Lewis, Daniel, 512, 515
DeConcini, Dennis, 501, 502
De Cora, Conrad, 52–53, 114, 115
De Cora, Dawn, 114
De Cora, Lorelei. *See* Means, Lorelei De Cora
Deere, Phillip, 301–2, 359–60, 370, 371
DeLoria, Frank (Ihanktonwan chief), 6, 17
Deloria, Vine, Jr., 17, 328, 416
Department of Interior. *See also* Bureau of Indian Affairs
Department of Justice
  and AIM, 250
  and COINTELPRO

(Counterintelligence Program), 250
  and the Red Ribbon affidavits, 205, 223
DeSersa, Aaron, 269
Dineh Nation, 493–94
Dodge, Larry, 484, 485
Dorion, Pierre, 5
D-Q University, 374, 378, 433
Duchaneaux, 390–91
Dull Knife, Guy, 536
Durham, Doug (FBI informant), 326, 336
Durham, Jimmy, 325, 356, 365

Eagle, Steve, 477–78
Eagle Butte (Cheyenne River Reservation), 79, 119–20
Eagle Elk, George, 188, 189
Eagle Woman (Padaniapapi's niece), 5
Eastman, Delmar, 337
Echohawk, John, 199
Elbert, Ted, 281
Ellison, Bruce, 356, 365, 392, 422
Ellsworth, Daniel, 331
Emerson, Ralph Waldo, 307
Erickson, Ralph, 268, 270
Escamilla, Bernard, 272, 337–38
Eustice (Nicaraguan boat captain), 464–65, 466–67, 470–71
Exon, J. J., 198

Faggoth, Steadman, 468
Farmer, Millard, 359
Farrakhan, Louis, 455–56
Fast Horse, Lizzie, 115, 167, 186
Fast Horse, Robert, 494
Fast Thunder, Steve, 158
Feather, Buddy (Russell's great uncle), 17
Feather, Evelyn (Russell's aunt), 120
Feather, John (Russell's great grandfather), 8
Feather, John, II (Russell's grandfather), 8, 11–12, 17, 535
  stories of, 13–15
Feather, Mabel Arconge "Twinkle Star" (Russell's grandmother), 10, 11, 12, 24, 43
  and Christianity, 15, 39
  on the death of Custer, 15–16

Feather, Theodora Louise (Russell's mother). *See* Means, Theodora Louise Feather

Feather In The Ear. *See* Feather Necklace

Feather Necklace (Ihanktonwan chief)
and Christian missionaries, 7–8
and the Ihanktonwan treaty, 6–7
and theft of treaty goods, 7

Fein, Judith, 112

Felker, Barbara, 57

Felt, W. Mark, 312, 314

Fills The Pipe, Ed, 222

Finzell, Roger, 337–38

Fire Lame Deer, John, 296

First Mesa, 108, 109

Fitzgerald, Curtis, 319

Flying Hawk, Dave, 283

Flynt, Althea, 442–43, 445

Flynt, Larry, 442–48

Fools Crow, Frank (Lakota holy man), 112, 189–90, 252, 253, 285, 296, 421, 538

Fools Crow, Grandpa, 189, 205, 271, 292–93, 534

Fort Laramie Treaty (1868), 105, 167–68, 182, 183, 261, 276, 327–28, 419–20, 454

Fort Lawton (Washington), Indian seizure of, 173

Fort Peck Reservation, 494–95

Fox, Mrs. (school teacher), 36, 45

Frank's Landing confrontation, 224

Frederick, "Grandma Aggie" Agnes (Russell's great–aunt), 15, 26, 39

Frederick, Henry, 26

Free, Robert, 227, 235

Fridhandler, Adele, 60–61, 535. *See* Mrs. Levine

Frizell, Kent, 278–79, 286

Fryer, Don (dance instructor), 99

Fulbright, J. William, 261

Fuller, John, 326, 345

Funmaker, Wally, 81

Gall, Chief, 346

Garagiola, Joe, 155

Garment, Leonard, 235, 293

George, Chief Dan, 513

Getanwokapi (Ihanktonwan treaty delegate), 6

Ghost Dance, true story of, 285–86

Gienapp, David R., 311

Gildersleeve, Agnes, 267, 320

Gildersleeve, Clive, 202–3

Goes Ahead (Custer's scout), 226

Goings, Milo, 272, 388, 389

Gonzales, Corky, 268

Gonzalez, Mario, 219, 220, 322

Good Shield, Alfonso, 221, 345, 356

Gordon (Nebraska), AIM takeover (Yellow Thunder murder), 194–201

Gordon, Eda, 337–38

Gordon Journal, 195, 200

Gortner, Marjoe, 443

Grant, Leon, 131, 448–49

Grass Roots (McGovern), 387

Gray Fox, Lucille, 155

Great Mystery *(Wakan Tanka)*, 4, 8, 297–98, 356
anthropologists and, 16–17
ceremonies, privacy of, 17
cultural genocide and, 10–11, 19
sacred white buffalo calf pipe, 315–17
See also Paha Sapa

Greene, Bruce, 199

Greenwood, South Dakota, 3–5, 533

Gregory, Dick, 269, 445

Grim, Lloyd, 282

Hairy Moccasin (Custer's scout), 226

Hale, Albert, 506

Hale, Timmy, 110, 119, 120

Half Yellow Face (Custer's scout), 226

Hall, Doug, 282, 308

Hamil, Jan, 426

Haney, Michael, 301

Harden, Fred "Bosco," 52, 53, 54, 66, 67, 68, 72, 76, 81, 83, 92

Harden, Marilyn Travesie (Russell's cousin), 25, 40–41, 52, 65, 68, 72

Hare, Dean, 195

Hare, Leslie D., 195, 199, 213–15

Hare, Melvin P., 195, 199, 213–15

Harring, Sidney, 347

Harris, Junior, 35

Harris, LaDonna, 231

Harris, Richard, 158

Harrod, Larry, 37

Hart, William S., 420

Hart Ranch, 497–98

Hat, Sally, 265–66
Haukaas, Ron, 320
High Eagle, Robert, 317, 320
Hill, David, 244–46, 308, 317–18, 341–42, 350, 352
Hinhanwicasa (Ihanktonwan treaty delegate), 6
Hitchcock, Herbert, 307
Hodge, Robert, 493–94
Hog Farm commune, 236
Holden, Aaron, 281
Holder, Stan, 259, 264, 294, 336
Hope, Bob, 192, 193
Hopi people, 108–9, 125–26, 492–93
Howe, Reynold, 81, 83
Hudson, Tommy, 312
Hunter, Billy, 53, 54
Hunter, Dave, 54
Hurd, Richard D., 307, 311, 314, 320, 327–31, 333

I–CARE, 300
Ihanktonwan
    Christian missionaries and, 7–8
    and the Santee rebellion, 7
    treaty monument, 4–5
    U.S. treaty with (1858), 4–7
    See also Seven Council Fires
Ihanktonwan treaty delegation, 5–7
Indian Center (San Francisco), 95–96, 100–101, 105
Indian Claims Commission, 421, 452
Indian culture, 533–44
    destruction of, 10–11, 19, 21
    dress, 69
    graves, desecration of, 196
    pipe ceremony, 204, 238, 264, 315–17
    powwows, 69, 448–49, 538–39
    songs, 69, 112, 115–16, 117, 118–19
    tipis, 409–10
    tobacco and, 182–83, 359–60
    as tourist attractions, 110–12, 115–16
Indian culture (dancing), 42, 69
    and the American flag, 116–17
    champion dancers, 119
    circuit, 110–20
    contests, 144
    dance outfits, 105, 112
    face paint, 117–18
    gourd dance, 448–49

ghost dance, 285–86
    Hopi, 108–9
    payment, 119
    sun dance, 146, 182, 186–90, 296–97, 364–65, 369, 377, 428–31
    "wanna-bes," 144
    whistles, 118
Indian Family Services, 300
Indian Health Service, 22, 206, 355
Indian identity, 69, 156–57
Indian Law Resource Center, 481
Indian Major Crimes Act, 304, 308, 379–80
Indian people
    alcoholism, 21–22
    anthropologists and, 16–17
    "apples," 164
    and constitutional freedoms, 21
    diet, 21–22
    fishing rights, 223–24, 357
    "Indian" as a term, 370
    and land claims, 205, 452–55
    life expectancy, 159, 448
    media trivialization of, 107
    police brutality, 162–63, 206
    and prison, 389
    self-hatred, 160
    sterilization, 374–75, 381
    tribal courts and jails, 206
    unemployment, 21, 98–99, 161, 398
    See also Great Mystery; murder; rape; reservations; smallpox; treaties
Indian Reorganization Act, 454, 498
Indian schools, 43–44, 51–52, 77, 227
    brutality of, 18–20, 28
    Carlisle, Pennsylvania, 18, 113–14
    murder at, 20
    sexual abuse, 19–20
    as tourist attractions, 113–14
Inouye, Daniel, 501
Intermountain (Mormon) School, (Provo, Utah), abuse at, 20
International Indian Treaty Conferences, 324–26, 356–57, 365
International Indian Treaty Council, 459, 463
International Tribunal on Illegal Acts and Violations of Human Rights by the United States, 433
Iowa Technical College (Ottumwa), 116, 120, 121–24

Iron Cloud, Bill, 110
Iron Cloud, Paul, 439, 498
Iron Cloud, Roger, 442
Iron Moccasin, Melvin, 41
Iron Shell, John, 326
Iroquois Confederation (Six Nations), 279, 370–71

Jackson, Jesse, 443, 445
James, Kathi, 337
Janklow, Bill, 115, 137–39, 317, 341, 348, 407, 417
Janklow, Mary, 138
Janklow, Russell, 138
Jefferson, Thomas, 168
Jim, Robert, 165–66
Johnson, Andrew, 420
Johnson, Herb, 156
Jones, Judge John B., 341
Jordain, Roger, 165
Joseph, Chief (Nez Percé), 150
Jumping Thunder (Ihanktonwan treaty delegate), 6

Kammer, Marv, 411
Kandaras, Homer, 359
Kane, Kenny, 320–321, 323, 350–51, 385, 405, 463
Kaplan, Earl, 311
Kaplow, Herbert, 281
Keating, Charles, 502
Keith, Hobart, 251
Kelleher, Robert J., 350
Kelly, Pat, 347–48
Kelly brothers, 107
Kennedy, Edward, 261, 379–80, 463, 480
Kerr–McGee, 392
Kicking Bear, 285
KILI (AIM radio station), 399, 408, 438, 444
Kills In Water, Harvey, 320
Kills In Water, Theresa, 320, 323
Kills Straight, Birgil, 194–95, 222, 251
Kills The Enemy, Frank, 205–6, 328, 421, 440
Kinder, Ellis, 36–37
King, Coretta Scott, 485
King, Martin Luther, Jr., 408
King, Matthew (Russell's great–uncle), 189, 252, 450, 527

Kirby Cats, 70–72
Kitto, Sidney, 387, 388
kiva, prayer and meditation in, 109
Klamath Nation and termination, 96
Klauck, Jack, 360–61
Kneip, Richard, 383
Kowalski, Mr. (school teacher), 61
Krieger, Al, 336
Kunstler, William, 274, 282, 297, 303, 306, 308, 318, 345, 349, 388, 410

Lakota Nation
   Alcatraz Island action, 105–6
   history, 419–22
   Mexicans, relations with, 239–40
   Mount Rushmore protests, 167–70, 182–86
   sacred white buffalo calf pipe, 315–17
   sun dance, 146, 182, 186–90, 296–97, 428–31
   See also Paha Sapa; Pine Ridge; Rosebud Sioux Reservation; Seven Council Fires; Wilson, Dick, Wounded Knee
Lakota treaty (1868), 105, 167
Lamont, Agnes, 252, 292, 328
Lamont, Buddy, 292
Lane, Mark, 282, 296, 297, 302, 306, 308, 311–12, 323, 328–330, 349
Lanham, Honey, 482, 483, 485
LaPlante (Mabel Arconge's first husband), 11
Larvie, Sonny, 115, 119
Last of the Mohicans, The (Mann film), 511–17
Law Enforcement Assistance Administration, 237
Leach, Jim, 356, 427
Lee, Sondra, 512
Legal Justice Center, 181
LeGarde, Dick, 335
Leventhal, Larry, 164, 282, 297, 302, 307–8, 327, 347–48, 349, 422, 423, 439, 443
Levine, Mrs. Adele Fridhandler (school teacher), 62, 74
Lewis, Meriwether, 5
Lewis and Clark expedition, 5
Libertarian Party, 482–88
Lincoln, Abraham, 167
Lincoln, Mary Todd, 6

Little Big Man, 290
Little Hawk, Lilliam, 300
Loesch, Harrison, 231
Lone Wolf, Don, 84
Long, Vernon, 237, 251, 252, 259, 261
Long Soldier, 464
Looking Horse, Orval, 316
Looks Twice (John Feather's story), 13–14
Loop, Bobby, 35
Lowry, Hunt, 516
Lubban, Tom, 452
Lummi Reservation, 495–96, 502
Lupe, Ronnie, 494
Lutter, Bernard, 195, 199
Lyman, Stanley, 251
Lyons, Oren, 279, 308, 371

McCain, John, 501
McCaw, Wallace, 167
McCloud, Janet, 432
MacDonald, Peter, 493, 494, 499–500, 501–2, 506–7, 539
McDonald, Mrs. (school teacher), 36
McGaw, Ed, 188, 189, 304
McGovern, George, 159–60, 232, 266–67, 276, 387
McLaughlin, James, 344
McLaughlin, Pat, 324
McNab, Sandy, 216, 219, 231
Madrid, Rocky, 269, 272, 275–76
Madsen, Archie, 324
Malcolm X, 417
Man Called Horse, A, AIM demonstrations against, 158
Manhart, Father Paul, 259, 266
Manifest Destiny, 168
Mankiller, Wilma, 501
Mann, Michael, 511, 512, 515, 535
Marshall, Dicky, 337, 339, 354, 359, 383, 387–88, 392
Martin, Bob, 464, 466, 467, 470, 472–75
Martin, George, 223
Martin, Phillip, 501
Martin, Twila, 501
Martinez, Francisco "Kiko," 241
Martinez, Louis, 269
Martinez, Margaret, 520
Massasoit (Wampanoag chief), 176, 178
Mathers, James, 417, 422

Mayflower II, 177–78
Mazeroski, Bill, 80
Mazzahetun (Ihanktonwan treaty delegate), 6
Means, Austin "Murph," Jr. (Russell's uncle), 17, 43
Means, Barbara (Russell's cousin), 536
Means, Bertha (Russell's cousin), 51
Means, Betty Sinquah (Russell's 2nd wife), 94–95, 100, 107, 108–10, 112, 113, 114, 120, 140, 141–48, 154, 161, 174, 238, 279, 284, 345, 355, 359
Means, Bill (Russell's brother), 27, 77, 115, 135, 188, 259, 296, 340–41, 375, 380, 386
  activism, 408, 436, 443, 477
  Russell Means, conflict with, 463, 466, 476, 481
Means, Dace (Russell's brother), 21, 26–27, 43–44, 95, 127–28, 135, 218, 338, 344
  activism, 241
  childhood and education, 30, 32, 35–36, 38, 41, 66
  drug and alcohol use, 57, 346–47
  of
  girlfriends, 94, 96–97
  playing cowboys and Indians, 34–35
  Russell and, 74, 93–94, 345, 367
Means, David (Russell's cousin), 51
Means, Dennis (Russell's cousin), 223
Means, Eugene (Russell's grandfather), 17
Means, Eugene (Russell's cousin), 51
Means, Gloria Grant Davis (Russell's 4th wife), 448–51, 455–58, 491–92, 523–25
  activism, 457, 540–41
  divorce and custody battle, 504–8
Means, Gus (Russell's great uncle), 17
Means, Hobart (Russell's uncle), 17
Means, Johnny (Walter's twin brother), 17, 77, 128–29
Means, Laureen (Russell's aunt), 17
Means, Lorelei De Cora (Ted's wife), 336, 398–99
Means, Karen (Dace's 3rd wife), 345
Means, Michael (Russell's cousin), 51
Means, Michele Bridget (Russell and Betty's daughter), 102, 107, 110,

Means, Michele Bridget (*continued*)
120, 127, 142, 156, 174, 238,
284–85, 345–46, 348, 355, 359
health and Indian cure, 121–22, 123–
24
Means, Nataanii Nez (Gloria and
Russell's son), 523–24
Means, Paula (Dace's 2nd wife), 218
Means, Peggy Phelps (Russell's 3rd
wife), 334, 351, 355, 356, 359,
367, 369–70, 377, 378, 393, 403,
408, 414–15, 432–33
Means, Phoebe (Quentin's wife,
Russell's aunt), 51, 53
Means, Quentin (Russell's uncle), 17,
51, 53, 128–29
Means, Robert "Casey" (Russell's
uncle), 17, 128–29
Means, Russell (childhood)
ancestors, 4, 6–7, 8, 17–18
and Blackfoot (bike), 33–34
at Brainard Indian School, 43–44
on the Cheyenne River Agency, 40–
41
delinquency of, 33–34, 51, 52–53,
54–55
discipline of, 28–29, 30–31
extended family, 9–10, 11, 24–25
friends, 34–35, 36–37, 46–48, 51, 54
Greenwood (South Dakota), 11–12,
24, 26–27
and horses, 27, 41–42
household chores, 38–39
Indian names, 13, 120, 221
playing cowboys and Indians, 34–35
and Sox (Russell's dog), 32–33
and sports, 37, 53–54, 123, 130
and the twins, 26–27
Vallejo (California), 23–24
Winnebago Reservation, 51–52
See also Blacksmith, Raymond;
Feather, Mabel Arconge; Travesie,
Faith
Means, Russell (adulthood)
alcoholism and sobriety, 52, 53, 67–
68, 70, 73–74, 78, 86, 89–90, 130,
140, 179–80, 215–16, 223, 289,
335, 346, 367, 368–70, 390
BIA relocation, 77–82, 140, 141–48
burglaries, 59
cafeteria scam, 90–91

Dace, depending on, 74, 93–94, 338,
345, 367
deafness, 134–35
drug dealing, 346–47
drug use, 57–62, 63, 64, 74–75
and fighting, 35, 36–37, 53–54, 84–
85, 114, 326, 343–44, 354–55,
369, 503–4
4-F status, 64–65, 85
homelessness, 89
hustling, 133–34
and the "Irish Pup," 67–68, 70, 73–
74
Kirby Cats, 70–72
Los Angeles stay, 66–75
pickpocket scam, 87
police, dealings with, 64, 75
San Francisco, 93–102
selling blood, 73–74, 133
shortchange scam, 90
Means, Russell (education)
Arizona State University (Tempe),
126
conventional schools, 25, 36–38, 43–
44, 45–50, 51–52, 56–57, 62–63
Indian, 12–15, 15–16, 35–36, 60–61,
62–63
Iowa Technical College, 116, 120,
121–24
Oakland City College, 62–63
Sawyer School of Business, 80, 84,
87–88
Means, Russell (employment), 47, 53,
54–55, 63
Carte Blanche (data–processing), 83–
84
CEO, 144, 153
computer operator, 126
construction, 107–8
dance instructor, 99–100
employment agency, 143
General Petroleum (Los Angeles), 67
janitor (Cow Palace), 101–102
in Los Angeles, 66–67, 76–92
Pine Ridge, 219–21
rodeo riding 130–31, 133, 139–40
in San Francisco, 97–98, 99
See also Means, Russell (Indian
identity): dancing
Means, Russell (family life), 69
child support, 91

children, 79, 81, 86, 102, 107, 110, 120, 121–22, 123–24, 238, 239, 279, 284–85, 345–46, 346–47, 348, 355, 359, 377, 378, 393, 403–4, 405, 411, 415, 523–24
divorce and custody battle, 504–8
girlfriends, 37, 57, 70–71, 78, 94–95, 170–73
and 1st wife (Twila), 71–72, 81, 83, 239, 279
and 2nd wife (Betty), 107, 108–10, 112, 113, 114, 120, 140, 141–48, 154, 161, 174, 238, 279, 355, 359
and 3rd wife (Peggy), 334, 351, 355, 356, 359, 367, 369–70, 377, 378, 386, 393, 403, 408, 414–15, 432–33
and 4th wife (Gloria), 448–51, 455–58, 491–92, 504–6, 507–8, 523–25
women, attitude toward, 96–97, 113, 265–66, 400
Means, Russell (Indian identity), 12–15, 15–16, 35–36, 60–61, 62–63, 69
Alcatraz Island claim, 105–6
and braids, 155
Chicago Indian Center, 144
Cleveland American Indian Center, 145, 147–48, 153–61, 191, 218
Cleveland anniversary protest, 192–93
Cleveland Indians, suit over mascot, 155, 435
dance outfits, 105, 112
dancing, 42, 54, 69, 110–20, 144–45, 182, 186–90, 296–97, 364–65, 448–49
face paint, 117–18
headman, confirmation of, 222–23
and Hopi cultivation, 124–25
Indian Center (San Francisco), 95–96, 100–101, 105
Indian names, 13, 120, 221
Intertribal Car, 130–35, 136–37
Jim Abourezk campaign, 166
National Conference of Welfare Workers, NAC protest at, 158–60
and racism, 23, 25–26, 51–52, 56–57, 63, 107–8, 143
Means, Russell (Indian identity/AIM involvement), 218
Bad Heart Bull murder and trial, 243–44, 248

Banks/Bellecourt schism, 208–12, 214, 215–16
BIA building (Washington, D.C.) occupation, 230–35
BIA sit-ins, 158, 192
Cleveland AIM (CLAIM), 155
Custer centennial, 357–59
Custer courthouse police riot, 243–46
Fort Lawton seizure, 173
Gordon (Nebraska) takeover (Yellow Thunder murder and trial), 194–201, 213–15
honors and awards, 358–59
image, 175
International Indian Treaty Conference, 324–26
Longest Walk, 374, 377–81
A Man Called Horse demonstration, 158
Mayflower II, 177–78
media and, 155, 160, 165, 193, 215, 288–89, 378
Menominee Warriors Society action, 336–37
Mount Rushmore protests, 167–70, 182–86
as national coordinator, 181–82
National Council of Churches confrontation, 149–53
NCAI confrontation, 164–66
NIEA conference, workshop panel at, 173
Ojibwa Reservation pageant protest, 160–61
Pine Ridge elections, 209, 304–5, 366, 436–41
Plimoth (Plymouth) Plantation demonstration, 175–78
Rapid City flood, 216
Red Ribbon Grand Jury Hearings, 202–7
resignation from, 301
Scottsbluff conference, 239–41
Sturgis (South Dakota) action, 247–48
Trail of Broken Treaties, 222–35, 236–38
UN Geneva conference, 365–66, 368–72
Means, Russell (siege of Wounded Knee)

Means, Russell (*continued*)
  Crow Dog's Paradise, trip to, 282–83,
    284–85
  firefights, 271–73, 280–81, 282–83
  list of demands, 259, 261, 271
  media and, 262, 264, 266–67, 268,
    270, 276–77, 281, 282, 288–89,
    293
  negotiations, 268, 269, 269–70, 275–
    76, 278–79, 286–87
  White House delegation, 286–88
  See also Wounded Knee (siege of)
Means, Russell (Indian identity/AIM
    post–Wounded Knee)
  AIM/Bill Means conflict, 463–64,
    466, 476, 481
  anger treatment, 534–31, 535–36
  assassination plans, 509, 510–11, 518
  campaign for president (Libertarian
    Party), 482–88
  campaign for vice president (with
    Larry Flynt), 443–47
  Columbus Day protests, 518–22
  consulting, 492–98
  and the Dan sisters, 452–53
  "For American to live" speech, 401,
    545–54
  Forest Service, suit against, 422–23
  fund raising, 412, 442, 444
  Independent Oglala Nation, 271,
    274–75, 279, 437, 543
  Iran hostages, 399–400
  KILI (AIM radio station), 399, 408,
    438, 444
  media, 399–400, 416–17, 466–67,
    502, 369, 503–4
  MISURASATA (Nicaraguan Indian
    coalition), support of, 461–76,
    480–81
  and the Moonies, 478–80, 481–82
  movie career, 511–17
  Walk for Religious Freedom, 433–34
  Yellow Thunder Camp, 407–10, 411–
    18, 422–27, 489, 491
Means, Russell (Indian identity/
    religion)
  chest piercing, 364–65
  Christianity, 14–15, 39–40, 78, 109,
    122
  and the Great Mystery, 297–98, 382
  Iktomi visit, 405–6

  kiva, prayer and meditation in, 109
  pipe ceremonies, 204, 238, 315–17
  sun dances, 182, 186–90, 296–97,
    364–65, 367, 369, 377, 428–31
  tobacco ceremonies, 359–60
  umblecayapi (crying for a vision),
    376–77
  yuwipi ceremonies, 405, 407, 538
Means, Russell (trials and jail)
  acquittals and dismissals, 336, 344,
    520
  acquittals and dismissals (Wounded
    Knee trial), 326–27, 330, 331–32
  arrests, 287, 289–91, 294, 295–96,
    369, 503–4, 520
  conspiracy to transport firearms, 334–
    35
  convictions and pleas, 352, 353
  Custer courthouse police riot, 341–42
  FBI and, 307, 312–14, 319, 326
  fast in prison, 385–87
  illegal wiretap (Wounded Knee trial),
    312–14
  imprisonment, 372–73, 377, 382–93
  Indian dress, 305–6
  jury selection (Wounded Knee trial),
    301–2
  legal defense, 164, 274, 282, 296,
    297, 302, 303, 306, 307–9, 311–
    12, 327–28, 330, 334, 347–48,
    349, 356, 359
  media and, 307, 314–15, 392
  Mission Golf Course fight, 320–21,
    322–24, 350–51, 353
  Montileaux murder and trial, 339–40,
    354, 356, 359–63
  police brutality and, 239–41, 318–19
  shootings and knifing of, 344–46,
    347–48, 355–56, 387–88
  Sioux Falls courthouse police riot,
    318–19, 351–52
  WKLD/OC, 282, 300–301, 302,
    323, 356
  work–release, 390–93
  Wounded Knee trial, 299–303, 305–
    10, 311–15, 319–21, 326–32
Means, Sandy (Dace's 1st wife), 94, 218
Means, Scott Sinquah (Russell and
    Betty's son), 124, 125, 160, 238,
    284–85, 345–46, 348, 355, 359,
    405

Means, Sherry, (Russell and Twila's
daughter), 79, 81, 91, 239, 346,
359, 370, 377, 378
Means, Tatanka Wanbli Sapa Xila Sábe
(Gloria and Russell's son), 457–58,
504–8
Means, Tatuye Topa Najinwin (Peggy
and Russell's daughter), 403–4,
405, 415
Means, Ted (Russell's brother), 27, 34,
46, 77, 127–28, 135, 386, 404–5
activism, 166, 175, 183, 191, 241,
318, 336, 340–41, 398–99
alcoholism and sobriety, 191, 369
and Indian dancing, 115, 117, 119
rodeo riding, 130–31
Means, Theodora Louise Feather
(Russell's mother), 4, 15, 18–19,
28, 31, 46, 62, 66, 114, 361
children, 28–29, 35–36
and Christianity, 38–39
death of, 404–5
employment, 29, 107
and Russell, 48–49, 62, 386
and Russell's marijuana plants, 59
Walter (husband), relationship with,
48–49, 102, 127
Means, Twila Smith (Russell's 1st wife),
71–72, 81, 83, 85–86, 91, 239,
279
Means, Veronica (Russell's cousin), 51,
451
Means, Walter "Hank" (Russell's
father), 17–18, 20, 31, 43, 114,
124
Alcatraz Island claim, 105–6
and alcoholism, 29–30, 43, 45–46,
127, 131–35
children, 30–31
employment, 20–21, 22, 27
marital problems, 46, 48–49, 102
and religion, 39–40
Means, Walter Dale "Hank" (Russell
and Twila's son), 86, 91, 239,
346, 359
robbery conviction, 410–11
Means, Warren (Russell's cousin),
369
Means, Wesley (Russell's uncle), 17
Means, Wesley "Tody," Jr. (Russell's
cousin), 42–43, 48

media
and AIM, 158, 160, 161, 165, 399–
400, 410–11
Alcatraz Island action, 106
American Indian Press Association,
194
BIA buildings bombings, 348
BIA corruption, 502
and the BIA files, 236
Cleveland anniversary protest, 193
Custer courthouse police riot, 246
Indian people, trivialization of, 107,
520–21
Longest Walk, 375, 378
and the MISURASATA, 466–67
Mount Rushmore protest, 170
on police brutality, 162–63
and Russell Means, 155, 160, 392,
466–67, 502, 369, 503–4
Sioux Falls courthouse police riot,
318–19
UN Geneva conference, 372
Wounded Knee, Siege of, 262, 264,
268, 270, 276–77, 281, 282, 288–
89, 293
Wounded Knee "hostages," 266–67
Wounded Knee trial, 307, 314–15
Yellow Thunder Camp, 416–17
Yellow Thunder murder and trial,
195, 197, 199–200, 214–15
Medicine Cow (Ihanktonwan chief), 6
Mehrtens, William, 350
Meinhart, Nick, 408, 435
Meirhenry, Mark, 341, 386, 417
Menard, Mary, 187
Menominee Warriors Society, 336–37
Merhige, Robert, 350–51
Merrill, Halley, 338–39, 354, 361
Merrill, Twila, 338–39, 361
Mesteth, Freeman, 410–11
Metacomet (Wampanoag chief), 176
Mexican-American Legal Defense and
Education Fund, 241
Miles, General Nelson, 344
Milkie, Bobby, 37
Milkie, Donny, 37
Milkie, Ronnie, 37
Milkie, Timmy, 37
Miller, Joanne, 37
Mills, Sid, 224–25
Milo, Harriet, rape and murder of, 247

Ministers for Peace, 357
Miskito people (Nicaragua), 461–76
MISURASATA (Nicaraguan Indian
   coalition), 461–76, 480–81
Mitchell, George, 151, 164
Monatachee, Muggy, 113
Mondale, Walter, 381
Monongye, David, 371
Monongye, Preston, 112
Montileaux, Martin, murder and trial,
   339–40, 354, 356, 359–63
Moonies, 478–80, 481–82
Moore, Bruce, 198
Morris, Glenn, 448–49, 451, 464–65,
   481, 519, 520
Mother Jones, 401–2
Mount Rushmore protests, 167–70,
   182–86
Moves Camp, Ellen, 251, 252, 265,
   270, 279, 328
Moves Camp, Louis, 328–30, 354
Moves Camp, Richard, 376
Mugar, Caroline, 323, 329
murder, 268–69, 304
   of Indians, 20, 194–201, 213–15,
      243–44, 248, 304, 312, 348
   Indians accused of, 247, 308, 339–
      40, 426–27
*My Brother's Keeper—The Indian in
   White America* (Cahn), 203
Myer, Dillon S., 96

Nadewisou, 9. *See also* Seven Council
   Fires
Nakota. *See* Seven Council Fires
National Association for Indian Nurses,
   194
National Conference of Welfare
   Workers, 158–60
National Congress of American Indians,
   181
   AIM confrontation, 164–66
National Council of Churches, 151–52
   AIM confrontation, 149–53
National Indian Association of Students,
   194
National Indian Conference of
   Alcoholism and Drug Abuse, 157–
   58
National Indian Education Association
   (NIEA), 173, 181, 334–35, 449

National Indian Youth Council, 449
National Jury Project, 300, 301–2, 349,
   360, 410
National Urban Indian Council, 147–
   48, 194
National Urban Indian Organization
   (NUIO), 147–48
Native American Church, 147
Native American Committee (NAC),
   158–60
Native American Committee Red Berets,
   164
Native American Rights Fund, 199
Navajo people, 448–49, 491–92, 506–7
NBC, 378, 502
Nelson, Willie, 412
New Congress for Community
   Development, 239–40
Newman, Steve, 521
Nichol, Judge Alfred, 344, 372–73, 382
   Wounded Knee trial, 300–303, 305–
      10, 311–15, 319–21, 326–32
Nighthorse Campbell, Ben, 358–59
Nisqually Indians, 224
Nixon, Richard, 191, 216, 232, 269
No Heart, Wanbli (James Jones), 425–
   26
Northern Cheyenne Reservation, 227
Numkalipa (Ihanktonwan treaty
   delegate), 6
Nyerere, Julius, 402

Oakland City College, 62–63
O'Brien, Judge Donald E., 423, 427
O'Conner, Phil, 281
O'Connor, Father James, 410
Oeningai (Dave Summers), 41
Office of Economic Opportunity
   (OEO), 136–40, 144
   corruption, 140
Office of Indian Affairs, 8
   See also Bureau of Indian Affairs
Oglala shoot–out, 348, 350
Oglala Sioux and community-based
   policing, 366
Oglala Sioux Civil Rights Organization
   (OSCRO), 237, 249, 250–51
   Independent Oglala Nation, 271,
      274–75, 279, 437, 543
   See also Wounded Knee
Ogura, Dr. George I., 199

O'Hair, Madalyn Murray, 445
Ojibwa (Chippewa) people, 9
  damn, protest at, 179–80
  Leech Lake Reservation, 209–12
  pageant, AIM protest at, 160–61
  yuwipi ceremony, 210–12, 538
Old Horn, Sarge, 145, 146, 147, 156,
  193, 297
Onassis, Jacqueline Kennedy, 480
One Feather, Gerald, 196, 366
Oregon State and Indian fishing rights,
  223–24
Ortiz, Dr. Alfonso, 173

Padaniapapi (Ihanktonwan chief), 5–7
Padilla, Ken, 241
Paha Sapu (Black Hills), 182, 407, 420–
  21, 422, 489
  Khe Sapa, living in, 420, 422–22,
    428–31
  Yellow Thunder Camp, 407–10, 411–
    18, 422–27
  See also Great Mystery
Papaneau, 279
Pates, Father Richard, 410
Patterson, Pat, 57
Paul, Ron, 484–85, 487
Péko (MISURASATA warrior), 471–72
Peña, Federico, 241, 520
Perez (dance instructor), 99, 100
Petersen, Henry, 312
Phelps, Brian, 410
Phelps, Peggy. *See* Means, Peggy Phelps
Phillips, Don, 354, 361
Picotte, Charles, 5–6, 6
Picotte, Honoré, 5
Pierre (South Dakota) *Daily Capital
  Journal,* 314–15
Pine Ridge, 11, 17, 77–79, 534
  alcoholism, 21–22
chiefs meeting at Calico, 252–53
  housing, 22, 77, 205–6
  Legal Aid, 219–21
  murder and violence at, 237, 249–51,
    252–53, 269, 283–84, 296, 304,
    337–38, 367
  pipe ceremony, 204
  segregation at, 209
  Sheep Mountain Gunnery Range,
    250, 303–4, 333–34
  tribal court, 337, 440

tribal president elections, 209, 304–5,
  366, 397, 436–41
unemployment, 21, 398
  See also Lakota Nation; Oglala Sioux
    Civil Rights Organization; Rosebud
    Sioux Reservation; Wilson, Dick;
    Wounded Knee
Pine Ridge Landowner's Association,
  398
Pine Ridge Treaty Council, 398
Pioneer Press, 307
Pipkin, Mary, 435
Pipkin, Steve, 434–35
Plume, Randy, 498
Plimoth (Plymouth) Plantation
  demonstration, 175–78
  Mayflower II, 177–78
  Plymouth Rock, painting, 178
police brutality, 206
  and Chicanos, 239–41
  Custer courthouse riot, 243–46
  Minneapolis, 162–63
  rape, 196–97, 206–7
  Scottsbluff conference, 239–41
  Siege of Wounded Knee, 268–69
  Sioux Falls courthouse riot, 318
Poor Bear, Myrtle, 354
Poor Bear, Tom, 337, 344–45, 347,
  367
Poor Bear, Webster, 271–72
Poor Thunder, 449
Porter, Judge Donald J., 439–40
Posse Comitatus (white–supremacist
  group), 400–401
Pourier, Joseph, 312
Pourier, Ted, 338
Powers, Keith "Punch" (Russell's
  cousin), 43–44
Powless, Herb, 287–88
powwows, 69, 448–49, 538–39
Pratt, John, 317
Pretty Boy (Ihanktonwan chief), 6
Price, David, 329–30
Puyallup Indians, 224

racism, 23 239–41, 247 263, 300, 320
  educational, 25–26, 51–52, 56–57, 63
  in employment, 107–8, 143, 242–43
  on reservations, 138, 367–68
  tourism and, 111
  See also murder; rape

Raitt, Bonnie, 402
rape, 469
  of Indians, 196–97, 206–7, 252–53
  Indians accused of, 247, 252, 330
Rapid City, 216, 242–43
Rapid City Indian Service Council, 390–91
Rapid City Journal, 216, 333, 416
Rave, Harold, 54
Ray, Charlie, 281
Reagan, Ronald, 433, 444, 485, 520
Real Bird, Richard, 497, 499
Red Bow, Buddy, 187–88
Red Cloud, Charlie, 205, 252
Red Cloud, Chief, 105, 285, 543
Red Owl, Nellie, 430, 436
Red Ribbon Grand Jury Hearings, 202–7
Reed, Robert, 36–37
Reinhardt, LaVerne, 70, 71
Reisman, Alex, 348
relocation. *See under* Bureau of Indian Affairs
Renville, Gabriel, 346
Renville, Loren, 346
Renville, Veronica, 346
reservations, 10–11, 96, 122–23, 136–40, 453
  alcoholism, 21–22
  community–based policing, 366
  and constitutional freedoms, 21
  diet, 21–22, 138–39, 159
  housing, 22, 138–39, 205–6
  racism on, 138
  relocation, 68, 72, 77–82, 194
  trading post abuses, 202–3
  uranium reserves and, 249–50
  See also Cheyenne River Reservation; Crow Indian Reservation; Fort Peck Reservation; Indians; Lummi Reservation; Northern Cheyenne Reservation; Pine Ridge; Rosebud Sioux Reservation; Sisseton-Wahpeton Reservation; Winnebago Reservation; Wounded Knee; Yankton Sioux Reservation
Rhoads, Tom, 320
Rist, Major, 385, 392–93
Rita (Dace's girlfriend), 96
Rivera, Brooklyn, 462–68, 473–76
Rocky Mountain News, 520

Rodríguez, David, 471
Rosebud Sioux Reservation, 19, 77. *See also* Crow Dog's Paradise; Pine Ridge; Wounded Knee
Rossmore, William, 337, 338
Roubideaux, Ramon, 282, 287, 308, 317–18, 352
Rouse, Marvin, 348
Rubideaux, Sylvester, 119
Running Bull (Ihanktonwan treaty delegate), 6
Rush to Judgement (Lane), 308
Ryan, Barbara, 483
Ryan, Roland, 483

Saint Labra Catholic School, 227
St. Paul Dispatch, 307
Salway, Lucky, 130–31
Samuels, Dr. Jesse, 199
Sanborn, John B., 420
Sanchez, Richard, 46
Schillinger (Russell's assailant), 388
Schmitz, "Mad Dog," 243–44, 248
Schweig, Eric, 515
Scottsbluff conference, 239–41
Seneca people, 164–65
Serran–Pagan, Gines, 495
Seven Council Fires (Allies/Sioux), 4–7, 9–10, 18
  See also Lakota Nation; reservations
Shenandoah, Audrey, 371
Shenandoah, Leon, 308, 371
Sheridan, Philip, 420
Sherman, General William Tecumseh, 420
Shirer, William, 488
Short, Clive, 198
Short Bull, 285
Sinquah, Betty. *See* Means, Betty Sinquah
Sinquah, Dennis, 124
Sinquah family, 108
Sioux Falls courthouse police riot and trials, 318–19, 348, 349
Sioux people (Seven Council Fires)
  Great Sioux Uprising, 169
  Independent Oglala Nation, 271, 274–75, 279, 437, 543
  meaning of name, 209
  Mexicans, relations with, 239–40

smallpox epidemic, 8
  See also Lakota Nation; Oglala Sioux
    Civil Rights; Organization; Pine
    Ridge; Rosebud Sioux Reservation;
    Seven Council Fires; United Sioux
    Tribes; Wilson, Dick; Wounded
    Knee
Sisseton–Wahpeton Reservation, racial
  disturbance at, 367–68
Sitting Bull, 285, 344, 543
Sixkiller, Jess, 147–48, 194
Six Nations (Iroquois Confederation),
  279, 370–71
Skenadone, Rod, 248
smallpox, 8, 10
  infected blankets, 5
Smells, Madonna Travesie (Russell's
  cousin), 25, 40–41, 114, 115
  activism, 184, 191, 336, 392, 400
Smells, Sylvester, 191
Smith, Michael V., 198–99
Smith, Twila. See Means, Twila Smith
Soldier Society, 448
Solem, Herman, 385–86, 389, 391
Soul, David, 402
South Dakotans for Civil Liberties, 282
Sox (Russell's dog), 32–33
Spence, Gerry, 427
Standing Elk (Ihanktonwan treaty
  delegate), 6
Standing Rock Reservation (North
  Dakota), 18
Steinmetz, Father Paul, 252
Stevens, Ernie, 192, 216, 219
Stevens, Fred, 503–4, 508
Stokes, Carl, 146–47, 193, 400
Strange, Sidney, 348, 349
Strasser, Spiegelberg, Fried and Frank,
  421
Sturgis (South Dakota), 247–48
Sully, Thomas, 168
Summers, Dave (Oeningai), 41
Survival of American Indians
  Association, 224
Sutherland, George, 331
Sydney, Ivan, 492

Taken Alive, Mrs., 206
Tall, George, 412, 436
Teal, James, 239
Tecumseh, General William, 419

Tennison, Mrs. (school teacher), 37–38
Thanksgiving, history of, 176–77
Thomas, Gary, 219, 220, 258, 269
Thomas, John (John T.), 340–41, 354–
  55, 359, 378, 399–400, 444, 445
Thompson, Jannette, 195, 199
Thorpe, Dagmar, 336
Thorpe, Jim, 114
Thunder Shield, 429
Tice, Judge Merton, Jr., 411
Tiger, Bobby Joe, 349
Tilsen, Ken, 282, 297, 302, 308–9,
  314, 323, 349, 359
Tilsen, Mark, 392, 411, 438
Time magazine, 162–63
Timmermann, Bonnie, 511
Tipi Enterprises, 495–96
Todd, J. B. S., 6
Todd County High School, 19
Tollefson, Clarence, murder of, 426–27
Tosconi, Mr. (school teacher), 37
Touré, Kwame, 445
Track, Roy, 130
Travesie, Faith (Russell's aunt), 18, 24,
  40–41, 52, 53, 79
Travesie, Louis "Jockey" (Russell's
  uncle), 53, 79
Travesie, Mabel Ann (Russell's cousin),
  25, 40–41
Travesie, Madonna. See Smells,
  Madonna Travesie
Travesie, Marilyn. See Harden, Marilyn
  Travesie
treaties, 4–7, 261
  Dawes Act, 10
  fishing rights, 223–24, 357
  Fort Laramie/Lakota (1868), 105,
    167–68, 182, 183, 261, 276, 327–
    28, 419–20, 454
  International Indian Treaty
    Conferences, 324–26, 356–57, 365
  Trail of Broken Treaties, 222–35,
    236–38
  treaty goods, theft of, 5, 7, 10
  twenty points, 228–30, 235
treaty monument (Greenwood, South
  Dakota), 4–5
Trimbach, Joseph H., 261, 268, 276,
  312–13, 329
Trimble, Al, 305, 333–34, 397
Trudell, John, 167, 173, 175, 178, 236

Tulalip Indians, 224
Tuttle, Sonny, 110, 112, 113, 132
Two Dogs, Rick, 370, 405, 407–8, 538
Two Moon, Austin, 359

UN Geneva conference, 365–66, 368–72
UN's Working Group on Indigenous Peoples, 372
Union Carbide, 392
United Indians of America, 167
United Sioux Tribes, 237–38
United Tribes of Alcatraz, 167
Uri, Dr. Connie, 375
U.S. Army Corps of Engineers and the Seneca people, 164–65
U.S. treaties. See treaties

Van Sickle, Bruce, 347–48
Vietnam Veterans Against the War, 271, 277

wacipi (dancing). See *under* Indian culture
Waddington, Steven, 516–17
Wakan Tanka. See Great Mystery
Walk for Religious Freedom, 433–34
Walking Elk (Ihanktonwan treaty delegate), 6
Waln, Sonny, 136, 140
Wampanoag people
  and Jacqueline Kennedy Onassis, 480
  Plymouth demonstration, 175–78
War Cloud, Jerome, 435
Warhol, Andy, 356, 361–62
Warner, Volney, 314
Washington, George, 167–68
Washington state and Indian fishing rights, 223–24, 357
Waukazo, Muriel, 167
Weasel Bear, 252, 421
Weddell, Jimmy, 354–55
Weddell, Weston, 354–55
Weinberger, Caspar, 235
Weinglass, Leonard, 334
Westerman, Floyd "Red Crow," 176, 445
Wheelock, Jaime, 459–61
White Lighting, Al, 344
White Man Runs Him (Custer's scout), 226

White Shield, Randy, 70, 81, 84, 91
White Swan (Custer's scout), 226
White Swan (Ihanktonwan chief), 6
Whitesell, Sidney, 133, 135
Whitewater, Eddie, 267–68
Whitworth, Chauncy, 464
Wiggins, Armstrong, 468
Williams, Jeff, 281
Williams, Ronald, 329
Williamson, John, 7
Wilson, Dick, 196
  goon squads, 237, 249–51, 252–53, 269, 283–84, 296, 304, 337–38, 366–67
  impeachment proceedings against, 250–51
  and the media, 333
  opposition to, 237, 249, 252–53, 276
  Pine Ridge elections, 209, 304–5, 366, 397, 436–41
  and Russell Means and AIM, 236–37, 242
  Sheep Mountain Gunnery Range deal, 250, 303–4, 333–34
  and the Siege of Wounded Knee, 269, 275, 276–77, 333
  See also Oglala Sioux Civil Rights Organization; Pine Ridge
Winnebago Reservation (Nebraska), 51–52
Withorne, Harold, Jr., 247–48
Wiyaka Napin. See Feather Necklace
Wollman, Harvey, 383
Wollman, Roger, 423
women
  activism of, 247, 251, 265–66, 400
  attitudes toward, 96–97, 113, 265–66, 400
  sterilization of, 374–75, 381
  violence toward, 96–97
Women of All Red Nations (WARN), 400, 411
Wood, Harlington, 275, 277
Woodward, Mrs. (school teacher), 45
Wounded Knee
  Catholic Church of the Sacred Heart, 202, 259
  mass grave of the massacre victims, 202
  as a tourist attraction, 202–3

trading post and museum, 202–3, 261–62

Wounded Knee (siege of), 257–73, 274–83, 284–93
  ammunition and weapons, 258, 270, 280–81
  arrests and trials, 287, 289–91, 294, 295–96, 299–303, 305–10, 311–15, 319–21, 326–32, 335–36
  casualties, 271–72, 291–92
  Crow Dog's Paradise, trip to, 282–83, 284–85
  detainees, 259, 260, 266–68
  FBI and, 261, 268, 307, 312–14, 319, 326
  federal indictments, 275
  firefights, 271–73, 280–81, 282–83
  ghost dance, 285–86
  as the Independent Oglala Nation, 271, 274–75, 279, 437
  jets buzzing, 260–61, 270
  legal support and advice, 274, 282, 287, 297
  list of demands, 259, 261, 271
  living conditions, 277–78
  media and, 262, 264, 266–67, 268, 270, 276–77, 281, 282, 288–89, 293
  medical assistance, 268–69
  negotiations, 268, 269, 269–70, 275–76, 278–79, 286–87
  OSCRO and, 259, 261
  pipe ceremony, 264
  police harassment and murder, 268–69
  provisioning, 264–65, 275, 281
  red paint, 274
  reinforcements, supporters and visitors, 269–70, 271, 279
  resolution, 292–93
  underground railroad out of, 282–83
  U.S. Marshal's and, 260
  vandalism and looting, 261–62, 263
  White House delegation, 286–88
  white-supremacist and, 282
  women's involvement, 265–66, 268, 278
  See also
    Czywczynski, Jim; Manhart, Father Paul; Means, Russell (siege of Wounded Knee); Pine Ridge; Rosebud Sioux Reservation

Wounded Knee Legal Defense/Offense Committee (WKLD/OC), 282, 300–301, 302, 323, 348, 356

Wounded Knee Winona, 278

Wovoka (Paiute medicine man), 285

Yakima Indians, 224

Yankton Dakota (people), 356. See also Ihanktonwan

Yankton Sioux Reservation, 4, 6, 8

Yazie, Judge, 113

Yellow Eagle, Irma, 145

Yellow Thunder, Raymond, murder and trial, 194–201, 213–15, 408

Yellow Thunder Camp, 407–10, 411–18, 422–27, 489, 491

Yellowbird Steele, Bob, 325

Young Bear, Severt, 195, 196, 219, 222, 251, 252, 260, 304, 306

Youth International Party (Yippies), 217–18

Yowytewa, Richard (Hopi medicine man), 123–24

Zephier, Alvin (Russell's relative), 77, 79, 80

Zephier, Greg (Russell's cousin), 354, 430

Zephier, Mitchell (Russell's cousin), 183, 185

Zimmerman, Bill, 269, 437–38

Zotigh, Ralph, 113

<u>Articles of a Treaty</u> made and concluded by and between Lieutenant General William T. Sherman, General William S. Harney, General Alfred H. Terry, General C. C. Augur, J. B. Henderson, Nathaniel G. Taylor, John B. Sanborn and Samuel F. Tappan, duly appointed Commissioners on the part of the <u>United States</u> and the different Bands of the <u>Sioux Nation</u> of Indians by their Chiefs and Head men whose names are hereto subscribed, they being duly authorized to act in the premises.

Article I

From this day forward all war between the parties to this agreement shall forever cease. The Government of the United States desires peace and its honor is hereby pledged to keep it. The Indians desire peace and they now pledge their honor to maintain it.

If bad men among the whites or among other people, subject to the authority of the United States, shall commit any wrong upon the person or property of the Indians, the United States will, upon proof made to the Agent, and forwarded to the Commissioner of Indian Affairs at Washington City, proceed at once to cause the offender to be arrested and punished according to the laws of the United States and also reimburse the injured person for the loss sustained.

If bad men among the Indians shall commit a wrong or depredation upon the person or property of any one, white, black or Indian, subject to the authority of the United States and at peace therewith, the Indians herein named, solemnly agree that they